Library of America, a nonprofit organization,
champions our nation's cultural heritage
by publishing America's greatest writing in
authoritative new editions and providing resources
for readers to explore this rich, living legacy.

GARY SNYDER

GARY SNYDER

COLLECTED POEMS

Jack Shoemaker
Anthony Hunt
editors

THE LIBRARY OF AMERICA

Gary Snyder: Collected Poems
is published with support from

MARGARET & WILLIAM HEARST

BRUCE R. BAILEY, TOKYO

THE POETRY FOUNDATION

Contents

MYTHS & TEXTS

LOGGING

HUNTING

BURNING

THE BACK COUNTRY

REGARDING WAVE

LEFT OUT IN THE RAIN

MOUNTAINS AND RIVERS
WITHOUT END

I

II

DANGER ON PEAKS

THIS PRESENT MOMENT

UNCOLLECTED POEMS, DRAFTS,
FRAGMENTS, AND TRANSLATIONS

RIPRAP
AND
COLD MOUNTAIN POEMS

This book is dedicated to:

SPEED MCINTURFF

ED MCCULLOUGH

BLACKIE BURNS

JIM BAXTER

ROY RAYMONDS

ROY MARCHBANKS

SPUD MURPHY

JACK PERSCHKE

JOE DUPERONT

JACK HAYWOOD

STANLEY PORTER

CRAZY HORSE MASON

In the woods & at sea.

— *Riprap* —

riprap: a cobble of stone laid on steep,
slick rock to make a trail for horses
in the mountains

Mid-August at Sourdough Mountain Lookout

Down valley a smoke haze
Three days heat, after five days rain
Pitch glows on the fir-cones
Across rocks and meadows
Swarms of new flies.

I cannot remember things I once read
A few friends, but they are in cities.
Drinking cold snow-water from a tin cup
Looking down for miles
Through high still air.

The Late Snow & Lumber Strike of the Summer of Fifty-Four

Whole towns shut down
          hitching the Coast road, only gypos
Running their beat trucks, no logs on
Gave me rides. Loggers all gone fishing
Chainsaws in a pool of cold oil
On back porches of ten thousand
Split-shake houses, quiet in summer rain.
Hitched north all of Washington
Crossing and re-crossing the passes
Blown like dust, no place to work.

Climbing the steep ridge below Shuksan
          clumps of pine
          float out the fog
No place to think or work
          drifting.

On Mt. Baker, alone
In a gully of blazing snow:
Cities down the long valleys west
Thinking of work, but here,

Burning in sun-glare
Below a wet cliff, above a frozen lake,
The whole Northwest on strike
Black burners cold,
The green-chain still,
I must turn and go back:
            caught on a snowpeak
            between heaven and earth
And stand in lines in Seattle.
Looking for work.

Praise for Sick Women

I

The female is fertile, and discipline
(contra naturam) only
            confuses her
Who has, head held sideways
Arm out softly, touching,
A difficult dance to do, but not in mind.

Hand on sleeve: she holds leaf turning
            in sunlight on spiderweb;
Makes him flick like trout through shallows
Builds into ducks and cold marshes
Sucks out the quiet: bone rushes in
Behind the cool pupil a knot grows
Sudden roots sod him and solid him
Rain falls from skull-roof mouth is awash
            with small creeks
Hair grows, tongue tenses out—and she

Quick turn of the head: back glancing, one hand
Fingers smoothing the thigh, and he sees.

2

Apples will sour at your sight.
Blossoms fail the bough,
Soil turn bone-white: wet rice,
Dry rice, die on the hillslope.
   All women are wounded
Who gather berries, dibble in mottled light,
Turn white roots from humus, crack nuts on stone
High upland with squinted eye
    or rest in cedar shade.
Are wounded
In yurt or frame or mothers
Shopping at the outskirts in fresh clothes.
Whose sick eye bleeds the land,
Fast it!   thick throat shields from evil,
      you young girls
First caught with the gut-cramp
Gather punk wood and sour leaf
Keep out of our kitchen.
Your garden plots, your bright fabrics,
Clever ways to carry children
Hide
   a beauty like season or tide,
      sea cries
Sick women
Dreaming of long-legged dancing in light
No, our Mother Eve: slung on a shoulder
Lugged off to hell.
    kali/shakti
Where's hell then?
In the moon.
In the change of the moon:
In a bark shack
Crouched from sun, five days,
Blood dripping through crusted thighs.

Piute Creek

One granite ridge
A tree, would be enough
Or even a rock, a small creek,
A bark shred in a pool.
Hill beyond hill, folded and twisted
Tough trees crammed
In thin stone fractures
A huge moon on it all, is too much.
The mind wanders. A million
Summers, night air still and the rocks
Warm.   Sky over endless mountains.
All the junk that goes with being human
Drops away, hard rock wavers
Even the heavy present seems to fail
This bubble of a heart.
Words and books
Like a small creek off a high ledge
Gone in the dry air.

A clear, attentive mind
Has no meaning but that
Which sees is truly seen.
No one loves rock, yet we are here.
Night chills. A flick
In the moonlight
Slips into Juniper shadow:
Back there unseen
Cold proud eyes
Of Cougar or Coyote
Watch me rise and go.

Milton by Firelight
Piute Creek, August 1955

"O hell, what do mine eyes
            with grief behold?"
 Working with an old
 Singlejack miner, who can sense
 The vein and cleavage
 In the very guts of rock, can
 Blast granite, build
 Switchbacks that last for years
 Under the beat of snow, thaw, mule-hooves.
 What use, Milton, a silly story
 Of our lost general parents,
            eaters of fruit?

 The Indian, the chainsaw boy,
 And a string of six mules
 Came riding down to camp
 Hungry for tomatoes and green apples.
 Sleeping in saddle-blankets
 Under a bright night-sky
 Han River slantwise by morning.
 Jays squall
 Coffee boils

 In ten thousand years the Sierras
 Will be dry and dead, home of the scorpion.
 Ice-scratched slabs and bent trees.
 No paradise, no fall,
 Only the weathering land
 The wheeling sky,
 Man, with his Satan
 Scouring the chaos of the mind.
 Oh Hell!

 Fire down
 Too dark to read, miles from a road
 The bell-mare clangs in the meadow
 That packed dirt for a fill-in

Scrambling through loose rocks
On an old trail
All of a summer's day.

Above Pate Valley

We finished clearing the last
Section of trail by noon,
High on the ridge-side
Two thousand feet above the creek
Reached the pass, went on
Beyond the white pine groves,
Granite shoulders, to a small
Green meadow watered by the snow,
Edged with Aspen—sun
Straight high and blazing
But the air was cool.
Ate a cold fried trout in the
Trembling shadows. I spied
A glitter, and found a flake
Black volcanic glass—obsidian—
By a flower. Hands and knees
Pushing the Bear grass, thousands
Of arrowhead leavings over a
Hundred yards. Not one good
Head, just razor flakes
On a hill snowed all but summer,
A land of fat summer deer,
They came to camp. On their
Own trails. I followed my own
Trail here. Picked up the cold-drill,
Pick, singlejack, and sack
Of dynamite
Ten thousand years.

Water

Pressure of sun on the rockslide
Whirled me in a dizzy hop-and-step descent,
Pool of pebbles buzzed in a Juniper shadow,
Tiny tongue of a this-year rattlesnake flicked,
I leaped, laughing for little boulder-color coil—
Pounded by heat raced down the slabs to the creek
Deep tumbling under arching walls and stuck
Whole head and shoulders in the water:
Stretched full on cobble—ears roaring
Eyes open aching from the cold and faced a trout.

For a Far-Out Friend

Because I once beat you up*
Drunk, stung with weeks of torment
And saw you no more,
And you had calm talk for me today
        I now suppose
I was less sane than you,
You hung on dago red,
        me hooked on books.
You once ran naked toward me
Knee deep in cold March surf
On a tricky beach between two
        pounding seastacks—

* The first line of this poem has been criticized with good reason. The circumstance
that gave rise to the poem, as I remember it, happened in the early fifties in Berke-
ley. Coming out of a late party one night with my date who was really smashed,
she started beating on me in some anger and I let her whack me (protesting)
til I got her into the car—my father's old Packard. It says something about the
poem and how things have changed that in writing the poem down I thought
that saying I'd hit her was the more manly, or even gentlemanly, thing to say, an
idea that comes from chivalry, perhaps. I never laid an ungentle hand on her. My
critics, especially my colleague Sandra Gilbert, have said that there is no excuse
for treating violence against women casually, and they are absolutely right. This
note seems the best way to deal with the problem rather than eliminate the poem
or change the line in silence.

I saw you as a Hindu Deva-girl
Light legs dancing in the waves,
Breasts like dream-breasts
Of sea, and child, and astral
       Venus-spurting milk.
And traded our salt lips.

Visions of your body
Kept me high for weeks, I even had
       a sort of trance for you
A day in a dentist's chair.
I found you again, gone stone,
In Zimmer's book of Indian Art:
Dancing in that life with
Grace and love, with rings
And a little golden belt, just above
       your naked snatch
And I thought—more grace and love
In that wild Deva life where you belong
Than in this dress-and-girdle life
You'll ever give
Or get.

Hay for the Horses

He had driven half the night
From far down San Joaquin
Through Mariposa, up the
Dangerous mountain roads,
And pulled in at eight a.m.
With his big truckload of hay
       behind the barn.
With winch and ropes and hooks
We stacked the bales up clean
To splintery redwood rafters
High in the dark, flecks of alfalfa
Whirling through shingle-cracks of light,

Itch of haydust in the
     sweaty shirt and shoes.
At lunchtime under Black oak
Out in the hot corral,
—The old mare nosing lunchpails,
Grasshoppers crackling in the weeds—
"I'm sixty-eight" he said,
"I first bucked hay when I was seventeen.
I thought, that day I started,
I sure would hate to do this all my life.
And dammit, that's just what
I've gone and done."

Thin Ice

Walking in February
A warm day after a long freeze
On an old logging road
Below Sumas Mountain
Cut a walking stick of alder,
Looked down through clouds
On wet fields of the Nooksack—
And stepped on the ice
Of a frozen pool across the road.
It creaked
The white air under
Sprang away, long cracks
Shot out in the black,
My cleated mountain boots
Slipped on the hard slick
—like thin ice—the sudden
Feel of an old phrase made real—
Instant of frozen leaf,
Icewater, and staff in hand.
"Like walking on thin ice—"
I yelled back to a friend,
It broke and I dropped
Eight inches in

Nooksack Valley
February 1956

At the far end of a trip north
In a berry-pickers cabin
At the edge of a wide muddy field
Stretching to the woods and cloudy mountains,
Feeding the stove all afternoon with cedar,
Watching the dark sky darken, a heron flap by,
A huge setter pup nap on the dusty cot.
High rotten stumps in the second-growth woods
Flat scattered farms in the bends of the Nooksack
River. Steelhead run now
                    a week and I go back
Down 99, through towns, to San Francisco
                                    and Japan.

All America south and east,
Twenty-five years in it brought to a trip-stop
Mind-point, where I turn
Caught more on this land—rock tree and man,
Awake, than ever before, yet ready to leave.
                    damned memories,
Whole wasted theories, failures and worse success,
Schools, girls, deals, try to get in
To make this poem a froth, a pity,
A dead fiddle for lost good jobs.
                    the cedar walls
Smell of our farm-house, half built in '35.
Clouds sink down the hills
Coffee is hot again. The dog
Turns and turns about, stops and sleeps.

All Through the Rains

That mare stood in the field—
A big pine tree and a shed,
But she stayed in the open
Ass to the wind, splash wet.
I tried to catch her April
For a bareback ride,
She kicked and bolted
Later grazing fresh shoots
In the shade of the down
Eucalyptus on the hill.

Migration of Birds
April 1956

It started just now with a hummingbird
Hovering over the porch two yards away
                              then gone,
It stopped me studying.
I saw the redwood post
Leaning in clod ground
Tangled in a bush of yellow flowers
Higher than my head, through which we push
Every time we come inside—
The shadow network of the sunshine
Through its vines. White-crowned sparrows
Make tremendous singings in the trees
The rooster down the valley crows and crows.
Jack Kerouac outside, behind my back
Reads the *Diamond Sutra* in the sun.
Yesterday I read *Migration of Birds*,
The Golden Plover and the Arctic Tern.
Today that big abstraction's at our door
For juncoes and the robins all have left,
Broody scrabblers pick up bits of string
And in this hazy day
Of April summer heat

Across the hill the seabirds
Chase Spring north along the coast:
Nesting in Alaska
In six weeks.

Tōji
Shingon temple, Kyoto

Men asleep in their underwear
Newspapers under their heads
Under the eaves of Tōji,
Kobo Daishi solid iron and ten feet tall
Strides through, a pigeon on his hat.

Peering through chickenwire grates
At dusty gold-leaf statues
A cynical curving round-belly
Cool Bodhisattva—maybe Avalokita—
Bisexual and tried it all, weight on
One leg, haloed in snake-hood gold
Shines through the shadow
An ancient hip smile
Tingling of India and Tibet.

Loose-breasted young mother
With her kids in the shade here
Of old Temple tree,
Nobody bothers you in Tōji;
The streetcar clanks by outside.

Higashi Hongwanji
Shinshu temple

In a quiet dusty corner
          on the north porch
Some farmers eating lunch on the steps.
Up high behind a beam: a small
          carved wood panel
Of leaves, twisting tree trunk,
Ivy, and a sleek fine-haired Doe.
          a six-point Buck in front
Head crooked back, watching her.
The great tile roof sweeps up
& floats a grey shale
Mountain over the town.

Kyoto: March

A few light flakes of snow
Fall in the feeble sun;
Birds sing in the cold,
A warbler by the wall. The plum
Buds tight and chill soon bloom.
The moon begins first
Fourth, a faint slice west
At nightfall. Jupiter half-way
High at the end of night-
Meditation. The dove cry
Twangs like a bow.
At dawn Mt. Hiei dusted white
On top; in the clear air
Folds of all the gullied green
Hills around the town are sharp,
Breath stings. Beneath the roofs
Of frosty houses
Lovers part, from tangle warm
Of gentle bodies under quilt
And crack the icy water to the face

And wake and feed the children
And grandchildren that they love.

A Stone Garden

1

Japan a great stone garden in the sea.
Echoes of hoes and weeding,
Centuries of leading hill-creeks down
To ditch and pool in fragile knee-deep fields.
Stone-cutter's chisel and a whanging saw,
Leafy sunshine rustling on a man
Chipping a foot-square rough hinoki beam;
I thought I heard an axe chop in the woods
It broke the dream; and woke up dreaming on a train.
It must have been a thousand years ago
In some old mountain sawmill of Japan.
A horde of excess poets and unwed girls
And I that night prowled Tokyo like a bear
Tracking the human future
Of intelligence and despair.

2

I recollect a girl I thought I knew.
Little black-haired bobcut children
Scatter water on the dusty morning street—
& walked a hundred nights in summer
Seeing in open doors and screens
The thousand postures of all human fond
Touches and gestures, glidings, nude,
The oldest and nakedest women more the sweet,
And saw there first old withered breasts
Without an inward wail of sorrow and dismay
Because impermanence and destructiveness of time
In truth means only, lovely women age—
But with the noble glance of I Am Loved
From children and from crones, time is destroyed.
The cities rise and fall and rise again

From storm and quake and fire and bomb,
The glittering smelly ricefields bloom,
And all that growing up and burning down
Hangs in the void a little knot of sound.

3
Thinking about a poem I'll never write.
With gut on wood and hide, and plucking thumb,
Grope and stutter for the words, invent a tune,
In any tongue, this moment one time true
Be wine or blood or rhythm drives it through—
A leap of words to things and there it stops.
Creating empty caves and tools in shops
And holy domes, and nothing you can name;
The long old chorus blowing underfoot
Makes high wild notes of mountains in the sea.
O Muse, a goddess gone astray
Who warms the cow and makes the wise man sane,
(& even madness gobbles demons down)
Then dance through jewelled trees & lotus crowns
For Narihira's lover, the crying plover,
For babies grown and childhood homes
And moving, moving, on through scenes and towns
Weep for the crowds of men
Like birds gone south forever.
The long-lost hawk of Yakamochi and Thoreau
Flits over yonder hill, the hand is bare,
The noise of living families fills the air.

4
What became of the child we never had—
Delight binds man to birth, to death,
—Let's gather in the home—for soon we part—
(The daughter is in school, the son's at work)
& silver fish-scales coat the hand, the board;
The charcoal glowing underneath the eaves,
Squatting and fanning til the rice is steamed,
All our friends and children come to eat.
This marriage never dies. Delight
Crushes it down and builds it all again

With flesh and wood and stone,
The woman there—she is not old or young.

Allowing such distinctions to the mind:
A formal garden made by fire and time.

Red Sea
December, 1957

The Sappa Creek

Old rusty-belly thing will soon be gone
Scrap and busted while we're still on earth—
But here you cry for care,
We paint your steel shelves red
& store the big brass valves with green
Wheel handles. Dustpan and wastecan
Nestle in the corner—
Contemplating what to throw away.
Rags in bales, the final home for bathrobes,
Little boy bluejeans and housewife dresses
Gay print splash—all wiping oil off floorplates,
Dangling from hip pockets like a scalp.
Chipping paint, packing valves, going nuts,
Eating frozen meat, we wander greasy nurses
Tending sick and nervous old & cranky ship.

At Five a.m. off the North Coast of Sumatra

At five a.m. off the north coast of Sumatra

An alarm bell woke me, I slept on a cot on the
                                    boatdeck,
it was deep in the engine-room ringing,
then the lookout's bell on the bow bonged three times
dead-ahead-danger, the engines whined down,

the ship shuddered and twisted,
Full Astern, I jumped up and saw in the dark
dark land: where we never thought island would be.
the ship swung full right and the engines
went dead-slow-ahead
quiet, like drifting.
first dawn in the east making light behind black
                                        island hills,
the morning star broke from the clouds,
and then the breeze came from ashore:
mud leaf decay and soft life of plant jungle:
I went back to the cot and lay breathing it.
after weeks of sea air machine.
the ship found its course and climbed back to full speed
and went on.

Goofing Again

Goofing again
I shifted weight the wrong way
flipping the plank end-over
dumping me down in the bilge
& splatting a gallon can
of thick sticky dark red
italian deck paint
over the fresh white bulkhead.
such a trifling move
& such spectacular results.
now I have to paint the wall again
& salvage only from it all a poem.

T-2 Tanker Blues

Mind swarming with pictures, cheap magazines, drunk
    brawls, low books and days at sea; hatred of machin-
    ery and money & whoring my hands and back to
    move this military oil—
I sit on the boat-deck finally alone: borrowing the
    oiler's dirty cot, I see the moon, white wake, black
    water & a few bright stars.
All day I read de Sade—I loathe that man—wonder
    on his challenge, seek sodomy & murder in my
    heart—& dig the universe as playful, cool, and
    infinitely blank—
De Sade and Reason and the Christian Love.
Inhuman ocean, black horizon, light blue moon-filled
    sky, the moon, a perfect wisdom pearl—old sym-
    bols, waves, reflections of the moon—those names
    of goddesses, that rabbit on its face, the myths, the
    tides,
Inhuman Altair—that "inhuman" talk; the eye that sees
    all space is socketed in this one human skull. Trans-
    formed. The source of the sun's heat is the mind,
I will not cry Inhuman & think that makes us small and
    nature great, we are, enough, and as we are—
Invisible seabirds track us, saviours come and save us.

Recall a cloud of little minnows about our anchored ship
    in the green lagoon of Midway. Corpse of a frigate-
    bird on the beach, a turtle-shell a foot across flesh
    clinging still—
And out through narrow reefs to sea again, a month to
    go to Persia. All the big wood Buddhas in Japan
    could bob these waves, unnoticed by a bird—
Yesterday was the taste of seawater as I swam; now crack
    my joints, all that I see & miss & never lose floods
    in—
Damn me a fool last night in port drunk on the floor &
    damn this cheap trash we read. Hawaiian workers
    shared us beer in the long wood dredgemen's steel-
    men's girl-less night drunk and gambling hall, called

us strange seamen *blala* and clasped our arms &
    sang real Hawaiian songs,
Bearded and brown and all the blood of Pacific in them
    laughing, tattered shirts and tin hats, three-o-five an
    hour;
Damn me not I make a better fool. And there is nothing
    vaster, more beautiful, remote, unthinking (eternal
    rose-red sunrise on the surf—great rectitude of
    rocks) than man, inhuman man,
At whom I look for a thousand light years from a seat
    near Scorpio, amazed and touched by his concern
    and pity for my plight, a simple star,
Then trading shapes again. My wife is gone, my girl is
    gone, my books are loaned, my clothes are worn,
    I gave away a car; and all that happened years ago.
    Mind & matter, love & space are frail as foam on
    beer. Wallowing on and on,
Fire spins the driveshaft of this ship, full of smooth oil &
    noise—blood of the palms d'antan—sweet oil of the
    gritty earth—embraced in welded plates of perfect
    steel.

Cartagena

Rain and thunder beat down and flooded the streets
We danced with Indian girls in a bar,
        water half-way to our knees,
The youngest one slipped down her dress and danced
        bare to the waist,
The big negro deckhand made out with his girl on his lap
        in a chair her dress over her eyes
Coca-cola and rum, and rainwater all over the floor.
In the glittering light I got drunk and reeled through
        the rooms,
And cried, "Cartagena! swamp of unholy loves!"
And wept for the Indian whores who were younger than me,
        and I was eighteen,
And splashed after the crew down the streets wearing
        sandals bought at a stall

And got back to the ship, dawn came,
        we were far out at sea.

Columbia 1948—Arabia 1958

Riprap

Lay down these words
Before your mind like rocks.
        placed solid, by hands
In choice of place, set
Before the body of the mind
        in space and time:
Solidity of bark, leaf, or wall
        riprap of things:
Cobble of milky way,
        straying planets,
These poems, people,
        lost ponies with
Dragging saddles
        and rocky sure-foot trails.
The worlds like an endless
        four-dimensional
Game of *Go*.
        ants and pebbles
In the thin loam, each rock a word
        a creek-washed stone
Granite: ingrained
        with torment of fire and weight
Crystal and sediment linked hot
        all change, in thoughts,
As well as things.

— Cold Mountain Poems —

HAN-SHAN READING A SCROLL, *attributed to Lo-ch'uang*
(13th century). Hanging scroll; ink on paper. Berkeley Art Museum,
University of California, Berkeley.

Preface to the Poems of Han-shan
by Lu Ch'iu-yin, Governor of T'ai Prefecture

[*Kanzan, or Han-shan, "Cold Mountain" takes his name from where he lived. He is a mountain madman in an old Chinese line of ragged hermits. When he talks about Cold Mountain he means himself, his home, his state of mind. He lived in the T'ang dynasty—traditionally A.D. 627–650, although Hu Shih dates him 700–780. This makes him roughly contemporary with Tu Fu, Li Po, Wang Wei, and Po Chü-i. His poems, of which three hundred survive, are written in T'ang colloquial: rough and fresh. The ideas are Taoist, Buddhist, Zen. He and his sidekick Shih-te (Jittoku in Japanese) became great favorites with Zen painters of later days—the scroll, the broom, the wild hair and laughter. They became Immortals and you sometimes run onto them today in the skidrows, orchards, hobo jungles, and logging camps of America.*]

No one knows just what sort of man Han-shan was. There are old people who knew him: they say he was a poor man, a crazy character. He lived alone seventy li west of the T'ang-hsing district of T'ien-t'ai at a place called Cold Mountain. He often went down to the Kuo-ch'ing Temple. At the temple lived Shih-te, who ran the dining hall. He sometimes saved leftovers for Han-shan, hiding them in a bamboo tube. Han-shan would come and carry it away; walking the long veranda, calling and shouting happily, talking and laughing to himself. Once the monks followed him, caught him, and made fun of him. He stopped, clapped his hands, and laughed greatly—Ha Ha!—for a spell, then left.

He looked like a tramp. His body and face were old and beat. Yet in every word he breathed was a meaning in line with the subtle principles of things, if only you thought of it deeply. Everything he said had a feeling of the Tao in it, profound and arcane secrets. His hat was made of birch bark, his clothes were ragged and worn out, and his shoes were wood. Thus men who have made it hide their tracks: unifying categories and interpenetrating things. On that long veranda calling and singing, in his words of reply Ha Ha!—the three worlds revolve. Sometimes at the villages and farms he laughed and sang with cowherds. Sometimes intractable, sometimes agreeable, his nature was happy of itself. But how could a person without wisdom recognize him?

I once received a position as a petty official at Tan-ch'iu. The day I was to depart, I had a bad headache. I called a doctor, but he couldn't cure me and it turned worse. Then I met a Buddhist Master named Feng-kan, who said he came from the Kuo-ch'ing Temple of T'ien-t'ai especially to visit me. I asked him to rescue me from my illness. He smiled and said, "The four realms are within the body; sickness comes from illusion. If you want to do away with it, you need pure water." Someone brought water to the Master, who spat it on me. In a moment the disease was rooted out. He then said, "There are miasmas in T'ai prefecture, when you get there take care of yourself." I asked him, "Are there any wise men in your area I could look on as Master?" He replied, "When you see him you don't recognize him, when you recognize him you don't see him. If you want to see him, you can't rely on appearances. Then you can see him. Han-shan is a Manjusri hiding at Kuo-ch'ing. Shih-te is a Samantabhadra. They look like poor fellows and act like madmen. Sometimes they go and sometimes they come. They work in the kitchen of the Kuo-ch'ing dining hall, tending the fire." When he was done talking he left.

I proceeded on my journey to my job at T'ai-chou, not forgetting this affair. I arrived three days later, immediately went to a temple, and questioned an old monk. It seemed the Master had been truthful, so I gave orders to see if T'ang-hsing really contained a Han-shan and Shih-te. The District Magistrate reported to me: "In this district, seventy li west, is a mountain. People used to see a poor man heading from the cliffs to stay awhile at Kuo-ch'ing. At the temple dining hall is a similar man named Shih-te." I made a bow, and went to Kuo-ch'ing. I asked some people around the temple, "There used to be a Master named Feng-kan here. Where is his place? And where can Han-shan and Shih-te be seen?" A monk named Tao-ch'iao spoke up: "Feng-kan the Master lived in back of the library. Nowadays nobody lives there; a tiger often comes and roars. Han-shan and Shih-te are in the kitchen." The monk led me to Feng-kan's yard. Then he opened the gate: all we saw was tiger tracks. I asked the monks Tao-ch'iao and Pao-te, "When Feng-kan was here, what was his job?" The monks said, "He pounded and hulled rice. At night he sang songs to amuse himself." Then we went to the kitchen, before the stoves. Two men were facing the fire, laughing loudly. I made a bow. The two shouted HO! at me. They struck their hands together—Ha Ha!—great laughter. They shouted. Then they said, "Feng-kan—loose-tongued, loose-tongued. You don't recognize Amitabha, why be courteous to us?" The monks gathered round, surprise going through them. "Why has a big official bowed to a pair of clowns?" The two men grabbed hands and ran out of the temple. I cried, "Catch them"—but they quickly ran away. Han-shan returned to Cold Mountain. I asked the monks, "Would those two men be willing to settle down at this temple?" I ordered them to find a house, and to ask Han-shan and Shih-te to return and live at the temple.

I returned to my district and had two sets of clean clothes made, got some incense and such, and sent it to the temple—but the two men didn't return. So I had it carried up to Cold Mountain. The packer saw Han-shan, who called in a loud voice, "Thief! Thief!" and retreated into a mountain cave. He shouted, "I tell you man, strive hard!"—entered the cave and was gone. The cave closed of itself and they weren't able to follow. Shih-te's tracks disappeared completely.

I ordered Tao-ch'iao and the other monks to find out how they had lived, to hunt up the poems written on bamboo, wood, stones, and cliffs—and also to collect those written on the walls of people's houses. There were more than three hundred. On the wall of the Earth-shrine Shih-te had written some *gatha*. It was all brought together and made into a book.

I hold to the principle of the Buddha-mind. It is fortunate to meet with men of Tao, so I have made this eulogy.

1

The path to Han-shan's place is laughable,
A path, but no sign of cart or horse.
Converging gorges—hard to trace their twists
Jumbled cliffs—unbelievably rugged.
A thousand grasses bend with dew,
A hill of pines hums in the wind.
And now I've lost the shortcut home,
Body asking shadow, how do you keep up?

2

In a tangle of cliffs I chose a place—
Bird-paths, but no trails for men.
What's beyond the yard?
White clouds clinging to vague rocks.
Now I've lived here—how many years—
Again and again, spring and winter pass.
Go tell families with silverware and cars
"What's the use of all that noise and money?"

3

In the mountains it's cold.
Always been cold, not just this year.
Jagged scarps forever snowed in
Woods in the dark ravines spitting mist.
Grass is still sprouting at the end of June,
Leaves begin to fall in early August.
And here am I, high on mountains,
Peering and peering, but I can't even see the sky.

4

I spur my horse through the wrecked town,
The wrecked town sinks my spirit.
High, low, old parapet-walls
Big, small, the aging tombs.
I waggle my shadow, all alone;
Not even the crack of a shrinking coffin is heard.
I pity all these ordinary bones,
In the books of the Immortals they are nameless.

5

I wanted a good place to settle:
Cold Mountain would be safe.
Light wind in a hidden pine—
Listen close—the sound gets better.
Under it a gray-haired man
Mumbles along reading Huang and Lao.
For ten years I haven't gone back home
I've even forgotten the way by which I came.

6

Men ask the way to Cold Mountain
Cold Mountain: there's no through trail.
In summer, ice doesn't melt
The rising sun blurs in swirling fog.
How did I make it?
My heart's not the same as yours.
If your heart was like mine
You'd get it and be right here.

7

I settled at Cold Mountain long ago,
Already it seems like years and years.
Freely drifting, I prowl the woods and streams
And linger watching things themselves.
Men don't get this far into the mountains,
White clouds gather and billow.
Thin grass does for a mattress,
The blue sky makes a good quilt.
Happy with a stone underhead
Let heaven and earth go about their changes.

8

Clambering up the Cold Mountain path,
The Cold Mountain trail goes on and on:
The long gorge choked with scree and boulders,
The wide creek, the mist-blurred grass.
The moss is slippery, though there's been no rain
The pine sings, but there's no wind.
Who can leap the world's ties
And sit with me among the white clouds?

9

Rough and dark—the Cold Mountain trail,
Sharp cobbles—the icy creek bank.
Yammering, chirping—always birds
Bleak, alone, not even a lone hiker.
Whip, whip—the wind slaps my face
Whirled and tumbled—snow piles on my back.
Morning after morning I don't see the sun
Year after year, not a sign of spring.

10

I have lived at Cold Mountain
These thirty long years.
Yesterday I called on friends and family:
More than half had gone to the Yellow Springs.
Slowly consumed, like fire down a candle;
Forever flowing, like a passing river.
Now, morning, I face my lone shadow:
Suddenly my eyes are bleared with tears.

11

Spring-water in the green creek is clear
Moonlight on Cold Mountain is white
Silent knowledge—the spirit is enlightened of itself
Contemplate the void: this world exceeds stillness.

12

In my first thirty years of life
I roamed hundreds and thousands of miles.
Walked by rivers through deep green grass
Entered cities of boiling red dust.
Tried drugs, but couldn't make Immortal;
Read books and wrote poems on history.
Today I'm back at Cold Mountain:
I'll sleep by the creek and purify my ears.

13

I can't stand these bird-songs
Now I'll go rest in my straw shack.
The cherry flowers out scarlet

The willow shoots up feathery.
Morning sun drives over blue peaks
Bright clouds wash green ponds.
Who knows that I'm out of the dusty world
Climbing the southern slope of Cold Mountain?

14

Cold Mountain has many hidden wonders,
People who climb here are always getting scared.
When the moon shines, water sparkles clear
When wind blows, grass swishes and rattles.
On the bare plum, flowers of snow
On the dead stump, leaves of mist.
At the touch of rain it all turns fresh and live
At the wrong season you can't ford the creeks.

15

There's a naked bug at Cold Mountain
With a white body and a black head.
His hand holds two book-scrolls,
One the Way and one its Power.
His shack's got no pots or oven,
He goes for a walk with his shirt and pants askew.
But he always carries the sword of wisdom:
He means to cut down senseless craving.

16

Cold Mountain is a house
Without beams or walls.
The six doors left and right are open
The hall is blue sky.
The rooms all vacant and vague
The east wall beats on the west wall
At the center nothing.

Borrowers don't bother me
In the cold I build a little fire
When I'm hungry I boil up some greens.
I've got no use for the kulak
With his big barn and pasture—
He just sets up a prison for himself.
Once in he can't get out.
Think it over—
You know it might happen to you.

17

If I hide out at Cold Mountain
Living off mountain plants and berries—
All my lifetime, why worry?
One follows his karma through.
Days and months slip by like water,
Time is like sparks knocked off flint.
Go ahead and let the world change—
I'm happy to sit among these cliffs.

18

Most T'ien-t'ai men
Don't know Han-shan
Don't know his real thought
& call it silly talk.

19

Once at Cold Mountain, troubles cease—
No more tangled, hung-up mind.
I idly scribble poems on the rock cliff,
Taking whatever comes, like a drifting boat.

20

Some critic tried to put me down—
"Your poems lack the Basic Truth of Tao"
And I recall the old-timers
Who were poor and didn't care.
I have to laugh at him,
He misses the point entirely,
Men like that
Ought to stick to making money.

21

I've lived at Cold Mountain—how many autumns.
Alone, I hum a song—utterly without regret.
Hungry, I eat one grain of Immortal-medicine
Mind solid and sharp; leaning on a stone.

22

On top of Cold Mountain the lone round moon
Lights the whole clear cloudless sky.
Honor this priceless natural treasure
Concealed in five shadows, sunk deep in the flesh.

23

My home was at Cold Mountain from the start,
Rambling among the hills, far from trouble.

Gone, and a million things leave no trace
Loosed, and it flows through the galaxies
A fountain of light, into the very mind—
Not a thing, and yet it appears before me:
Now I know the pearl of the Buddha-nature
Know its use: a boundless perfect sphere.

24

When men see Han-shan
They all say he's crazy
And not much to look at
Dressed in rags and hides.
They don't get what I say
& I don't talk their language.
All I can say to those I meet:
"Try and make it to Cold Mountain."

Notes

The preface:
Feng-kan is reckoned in the traditional line of Zen Masters, but in mid-T'ang the Zen people did not yet constitute a separate Buddhist sect. They were rather a "meditation-group" living in the mountains or the monasteries of the T'ien-t'ai (Japanese Tendai) sect, and the Vinaya (discipline) sect.

Manjusri is the Bodhisattva of wisdom, Samantabhadra the Bodhisattva of love, Amitabha the Bodhisattva of boundless compassion.

A *gatha* is a short Buddhist poem.

A doggerel eulogistic poem, also by Lu Ch'iu-yin, follows the biography: I have not translated it.

The poems:
4—a rare example of a poem in the literary manner. Han-shan usually writes in the colloquial, as very few Chinese poets have done.

5—the gray-haired man is Han-shan himself. Huang is "The Book of the Yellow Emperor" and Lao is Lao-tzu, the *Tao Te Ching*.

15—the Way and its Power, i.e., the *Tao Te Ching*.

22, 23—the full moon, the pearl. Symbols of the Buddha-nature inherent in all beings.

Most of Han-shan's poems are written in the "old-song" (*ku-shih*) style, with five or seven characters to a line.

Afterword

I grew up with the poetry of twentieth-century coolness, its hard edges and resilient elitism. Ezra Pound introduced me to Chinese poetry, and I began to study classical Chinese. When it came to writing out of my own experience, most of modernism didn't fit, except for the steer toward Chinese and Japanese.

Although I had written a fair number of poems, by the time I was twenty-four I was ready to put poetry aside. My thinking had turned toward linguistics, the Whorfian hypothesis, North American oral literatures, and Buddhism. My employment skills were largely outdoors.

So in the summer of 1955 after a year of Oriental languages graduate school, I signed on with the Yosemite National Park as a trail crew laborer. They soon had me working in the upper reaches of the Piute Creek drainage, a land of smooth white granite and gnarly juniper and pine. It all carries the visible memory of the ice age. The bedrock is so brilliant that it shines back at the crystal night stars. In a curious mind of renunciation and long day's hard work with shovel, pick, dynamite, and boulder, my language relaxed into itself. I began to be able to meditate, nights, after work, and I found myself writing some poems that surprised me.

This collection registers those moments. It opens with a group of poems written around the transparency of mountains and work, and finishes with some that were written in Japan and at sea. The title *Riprap* celebrates the work of hands, the placing of rock, and my first glimpse of the image of the whole universe as interconnected, interpenetrating, mutually reflecting, and mutually embracing.

There is no doubt that my readings of Chinese poems, with their monosyllabic step-by-step placement, their crispness—and the clatter of mule hooves—all fed this style. I went from the Sierra Nevada to another semester's study at Berkeley and then a year's Zen study in Kyoto, and nine months in the engine room of a tanker in the Pacific and Persian Gulf.

On my second trip to Japan, with the help of Cid Corman and Lawrence Ferlinghetti, the first edition of *Riprap* (500 copies) was printed in a tiny shop a few streets away from the

Daitoku-ji Zen Temple complex. It was folded and bound East Asian style.

The little book moved. After a second Japanese edition of 1,000 was gone, Don Allen's Grey Fox Press picked it up and printed it in America. Don and I decided to add my translations of the T'ang era mountain Chan poet Han-shan. I had started these in a seminar at Berkeley with Chen Shih-hsiang. Chen was a friend and teacher. His knowledge and love of poetry and his taste for life were enormous. He quoted French poetry from memory and wrote virtually any Chinese poem of the T'ang or Sung canon from memory on the blackboard. Chen's translation of Lu Chi's *Wen Fu*, "Prose-poem on Writing," gave me the angle on the "axe handle" proverb "When making an axe handle, the pattern is not far off," as it applies to poetry. (Mind is manifesting mind.)

I would have gone on to do more Chinese poetry translation had I stayed with the academy, but my feet led me toward the zendo.

The idea of a poetry of minimal surface texture, with its complexities hidden at the bottom of the pool, under the bank, a dark old lurking, no fancy flavor, is ancient. It is what is "haunting" in the best of Scottish-English ballads and is at the heart of the Chinese *shi* (lyric) aesthetic. Du Fu said, "The ideas of a poet should be noble and simple." Zen says, "Unformed people delight in the gaudy, and in novelty. Cooked people delight in the ordinary."

There are poets who claim that their poems are made to show the world through the prism of language. Their project is worthy. There is also the work of seeing the world *without* any prism of language, and to bring that seeing *into* language. The latter has been the direction of most Chinese and Japanese poetry.

In some of the riprap poems, then, I did try for surface simplicity set with unsettling depths. It's not the only sort of poem I do. There is a place for passion and gaudiness and promiscuous language. The plain poems that I launched in this book run the risk of invisibility. But the direction they point is perhaps my favorite, and what a marvelous risk!

The poems also made their way back to the Sierra Nevada, where trail crews still place sections of literal riprap. I gather the poems are appreciated as much for their sweat as their art. Veteran trail crew foreman (now historian) Jim Snyder told me how the book is now read by firelight in work camps in the back country.

MYTHS & TEXTS

So that not only this our craft
is in danger to be set at nought;
but also the temple of the great
Goddess Diana should be despised,
and her magnificence should be destroyed,
whom all Asia and the world worshippeth.

—Acts 19:27

— Logging —

The morning star is not a star
Two seedling fir, one died
                    Io, Io,
Girdled in wistaria
Wound with ivy
                    "The May Queen
Is the survival of
A pre-human
Rutting season"

The year spins
Pleiades sing to their rest
                    at San Francisco
                    dream
                    dream
Green comes out of the ground
Birds squabble
Young girls run mad with the pine bough,
                                        Io

2

But ye shall destroy their altars,
    break their images, and cut down their groves.
                                    —*Exodus 34:13*

The ancient forests of China logged
    and the hills slipped into the Yellow Sea.
Squared beams, log dogs,
    on a tamped-earth sill.
San Francisco 2×4s
    were the woods around Seattle:
Someone killed and someone built, a house,
    a forest, wrecked or raised
All America hung on a hook
    & burned by men, in their own praise.

Snow on fresh stumps and brush-piles.
The generator starts and rumbles
                    in the frosty dawn
I wake from bitter dreams,
Rise and build a fire,
Pull on and lace the stiff cold boots
Eat huge flapjacks by a gloomy Swede
In splintery cookhouse light
                    grab my tin pisspot hat
Ride off to the show in a crummy-truck
And start the Cat.

"Pines grasp the clouds with iron claws
like dragons rising from sleep"
250,000 board-feet a day
If both Cats keep working
& nobody gets hurt

                    3

"Lodgepole Pine: the wonderful reproductive
power of this species on areas over which its
stand has been killed by fire is dependent upon
the ability of the closed cones to endure a fire
which kills the tree without injuring its seed.
After fire, the cones open and shed their seeds
on the bared ground and a new growth springs up."

Stood straight
                    holding the choker high
As the Cat swung back the arch
                    piss-firs falling,
Limbs snapping on the tin hat
                    bright D caught on
Swinging butt-hooks
                    ringing against cold steel.

Hsü Fang lived on leeks and pumpkins.
Goosefoot,
   wild herbs,
      fields lying fallow!

But it's hard to farm
Between the stumps:
The cows get thin, the milk tastes funny,
The kids grow up and go to college
They don't come back.
    the little fir-trees do

    Rocks the same blue as sky
Only icefields, a mile up,
       are the mountain
Hovering over ten thousand acres
Of young fir.

4

Pines, under pines,
    Seami Motokiyo
    The Doer stamps his foot.
    A thousand board-feet
Bucked, skidded, loaded—
(Takasago, Ise) float in a mill pond;
A thousand years dancing
Flies in the saw kerf.

Cliff by Tomales Bay
Seal's slick head
  head shoulders breasts
  glowing in night saltwater
Skitter of fish, and above, behind the pines,
Bear grunts, stalking the Pole-star.

Foot-whack on polished boards
Slide and stop; drum-thump.

"Today's wind moves in the pines"
                         falling
And skidding the red-bark pine.
Clouds over Olallie Butte
Scatter rain on the Schoolie flat.
A small bear slips out the wet brush
                      crosses the creek
Seami, Kwanami,
                Gone too.
Through the pines.

5

Again the ancient, meaningless
Abstractions of the educated mind.
                wet feet and the campfire out.
Drop a mouthful of useless words.
—The book's in the crapper
They're up to the part on Ethics now

                skidding logs in pine-flat heat
                long summer sun
                the flax bag sweet
Summer professors
                elsewhere meet
Indiana? Seattle? Ann Arbor?
                bug clack in sage
Sudden rumble of wheels on cattle-guard rails.
                hitching & hiking
                looking for work.

"We rule you" all crownéd or be-Homburged heads
"We fool you" those guys with Ph.D.s
"We eat for you" you
"We work for you" who?
        a big picture of K. Marx with an axe,
"Where I cut off one it will never grow again."

O Karl would it were true
    I'd put my saw to work for you
& the wicked social tree would fall right down.

(The only logging we'll do here is trees
And do it quick, with big trucks and machines)
      "That Cat wobbles like a sick whore"
So we lay on our backs tinkering
                         all afternoon
The trees and the logs stood still
It was so quiet we could hear the birds.

6

"In that year, 1914, we lived on the farm
And the relatives lived with us.
A banner year for wild blackberries
Dad was crazy about wild blackberries
No berries like that now.
You know Kitsap County was logged before
The turn of the century—it was easiest of all,
Close to water, virgin timber,
When I was a kid walking about in the
Stumpland, wherever you'd go a skidroad
Puncheon, all overgrown.
We went up one like that, fighting our way through
To its end near the top of a hill:
For some reason wild blackberries
Grew best there. We took off one morning
Right after milking: rode the horses
To a valley we'd been to once before
Hunting berries, and hitched the horses.
About a quarter mile up the old road
We found the full ripe of berrytime—
And with only two pails—so we
Went back home, got Mother and Ruth,
And filled lots of pails. Mother sent letters
To all the relatives in Seattle:

Effie, Aunt Lucy, Bill Moore,
Forrest, Edna, six or eight, they all came
Out to the farm, and we didn't take pails
Then: we took copper clothes-boilers,
Wash-tubs, buckets, and all went picking.
We were canning for three days."

7

Felix Baran
Hugo Gerlot
Gustav Johnson
John Looney
Abraham Rabinowitz
Shot down on the steamer Verona
For the shingle-weavers of Everett
        the Everett Massacre November 5 1916

Ed McCullough, a logger for thirty-five years
Reduced by the advent of chainsaws
To chopping off knots at the landing:
"I don't have to take this kind of shit,
Another twenty years
        and I'll tell 'em to shove it"
        (he was sixty-five then)
In 1934 they lived in shanties
At Hooverville, Sullivan's Gulch.
When the Portland-bound train came through
The trainmen tossed off coal.

"Thousands of boys shot and beat up
For wanting a good bed, good pay,
        decent food, in the woods—"
No one knew what it meant:
"Soldiers of Discontent."

8

Each dawn is clear
Cold air bites the throat.
Thick frost on the pine bough
Leaps from the tree
        snapped by the diesel

Drifts and glitters in the
        horizontal sun.
In the frozen grass
        smoking boulders
        ground by steel tracks.
In the frozen grass
        wild horses stand
        beyond a row of pines.
The D8 tears through piss-fir,
Scrapes the seed-pine
                        chipmunks flee,
A black ant carries an egg
Aimlessly from the battered ground.
Yellowjackets swarm and circle
Above the crushed dead log, their home.
Pitch oozes from barked
        trees still standing,
Mashed bushes make strange smells.
Lodgepole pines are brittle.
Camprobbers flutter to watch.

A few stumps, drying piles of brush;
Under the thin duff, a toe-scrape down
Black lava of a late flow.
Leaves stripped from thornapple
Taurus by nightfall.

9

Headed home, hitch-hiking
leaving mountains behind
where all Friday in sunlight
fighting flies fixed phone line
high on the lake trail,
dreaming of home,
by night to my girl and a late bath.
she came in naked to the tub
her breasts hung glistening
and she scrubbed my back.
we made love night-long.
she was unhappy alone.
all Sunday softly talked,
I left, two hundred miles
hitching back to work.

10

A ghost logger wanders a shadow
In the early evening, boots squeak
With the cicada, the fleas
Nest warm in his blanket-roll
Berrybrambles catch at the stagged pants
He stumbles up the rotted puncheon road
There is a logging camp
Somewhere in there among the alders
Berries and high rotting stumps
Bindlestiff with a wooden bowl
(The poor bastards at Nemi in the same boat)
What old Seattle skidroad did he walk from
Fifty years too late, and all his
                     money spent?

Dogfish and Shark oil
Greasing the skids.
"Man is the heart of the universe

the upshot of the five elements,
born to enjoy food and color and noise . . ."
Get off my back Confucius
There's enough noise now.
What bothers me is all those stumps:
What did they do with the wood?
Them Xtians out to save souls and grab land
"They'd steal Christ off the cross
                    if he wasn't nailed on"
The last decent carpentry
Ever done by Jews.

II

Ray Wells, a big Nisqually, and I
            each set a choker
On the butt-logs of two big Larch
In a thornapple thicket and a swamp.
            waiting for the Cat to come back,
"Yesterday we gelded some ponies
"My father-in-law cut the skin on the balls
"He's a Wasco and don't speak English
"He grabs a handful of tubes and somehow
            cuts the right ones.
"The ball jumps out, the horse screams
"But he's all tied up.
The Caterpillar clanked back down.
In the shadow of that racket
            diesel and iron tread
I thought of Ray Wells' tipi out on the sage flat
The gelded ponies
Healing and grazing in the dead white heat.

12

A green limb hangs in the crotch
Of a silver snag,
Above the Cats,
            the skidders and thudding brush,
Hundreds of butterflies
Flit through the pines.
"You shall live in square
            gray houses in a barren land
            and beside those square gray
            houses you shall starve."
—Drinkswater. Who saw a vision
At the high and lonely center of the earth:
Where Crazy Horse
            went to watch the Morning Star,
& the four-legged people, the creeping people,
The standing people and the flying people
Know how to talk.
I ought to have eaten
Whale tongue with them.
            they keep saying I used to be a human being
"He-at-whose-voice-the-Ravens-sit-on-the-sea."
Sea-foam washing the limpets and barnacles
Rattling the gravel beach
Salmon up creek, bear on the bank,
Wild ducks over the mountains weaving
In a long south flight, the land of
Sea and fir tree with the pine-dry
Sage-flat country to the east.
Han Shan could have lived here,
            & no scissorbill stooge of the
            Emperor would have come trying to steal
            his last poor shred of sense.

On the wooded coast, eating oysters
Looking off toward China and Japan
"If you're gonna work these woods
Don't want nothing
That can't be left out in the rain—"

13

T 36N   R 16E   S 25
Is burning. Far to the west.
A north creek side,
          flame to the crowns
Sweeping a hillside bare—
          in another district,
On a different drainage.

Smoke higher than clouds
Turning the late sun red.

Cumulus, blowing north
          high cirrus
Drifting east,
          smoke
Filling the west.

The crews have departed,
And I am not concerned.

14

The groves are down
                    cut down
Groves of Ahab, of Cybele
Pine trees, knobbed twigs
     thick cone and seed
     Cybele's tree this, sacred in groves
Pine of Seami, cedar of Haida
Cut down by the prophets of Israel
     the fairies of Athens
     the thugs of Rome
                    both ancient and modern;
Cut down to make room for the suburbs
Bulldozed by Luther and Weyerhaeuser
Crosscut and chainsaw

squareheads and finns
high-lead and cat-skidding
Trees down
Creeks choked, trout killed, roads.

Sawmill temples of Jehovah.
Squat black burners 100 feet high
Sending the smoke of our burnt
Live sap and leaf
To his eager nose.

15

Lodgepole
cone/seed waits for fire
And then thin forests of silver-gray.
in the void
a pine cone falls
Pursued by squirrels
What mad pursuit! What struggle to escape!

Her body a seedpod
Open to the wind
"A seed pod void of seed
We had no meeting together"
so you and I must wait
Until the next blaze
Of the world, the universe,
Millions of worlds, burning
—oh let it lie.

Shiva at the end of the kalpa:
Rock-fat, hill-flesh, gone in a whiff.
Men who hire men to cut groves
Kill snakes, build cities, pave fields,
Believe in god, but can't
Believe their own senses
Let alone Gautama. Let them lie.

Pine sleeps, cedar splits straight
Flowers crack the pavement.
        Pa-ta Shan-jen
(A painter who watched Ming fall)
        lived in a tree:
"The brush
May paint the mountains and streams
Though the territory is lost."

— *Hunting* —

first shaman song

In the village of the dead,
Kicked loose bones
   ate pitch of a drift log
   (whale fat)
Nettles and cottonwood. Grass smokes
      in the sun
Logs turn in the river
   sand scorches the feet.

Two days without food, trucks roll past
   in dust and light, rivers
   are rising.
Thaw in the high meadows. Move west in July.

Soft oysters rot now, between tides
   the flats stink.

I sit without thoughts by the log-road
Hatching a new myth
watching the waterdogs
   the last truck gone.

Atok: creeping
Maupok: waiting
 to hunt seals.
The sea hunter
 watching the whirling seabirds on the rocks
The mountain hunter
 horn-tipped shaft on a snowslope
 edging across cliffs for a shot at goat
"Upon the lower slopes of the mountain,
on the cover, we find the sculptured forms

of animals apparently lying dead in the
wilderness" thus Fenellosa
On the pottery of Shang.

It's a shame I didn't kill you,
    Yang Kuei Fei,
Cut down in the old apartment
Left to bleed between the bookcase and the wall,
I'd hunt you still, trail you from town to town.
But you change shape.
    death's a new shape,
Maybe flayed you'd be true
But it wouldn't be through.

"You who live with your grandmother
I'll trail you with dogs
And crush you in my mouth."
    —not that we're cruel—
But a man's got to eat

3

this poem is for birds

Birds in a whirl, drift to the rooftops
Kite dip, swing to the seabank fogroll
Form: dots in air changing line from line,
    the future defined.

Brush back smoke from the eyes,
    dust from the mind,
With the wing-feather fan of an eagle.
A hawk drifts into the far sky.
A marmot whistles across huge rocks.
Rain on the California hills.
Mussels clamp to sea-boulders
Sucking the Spring tides

Rain soaks the tan stubble
Fields full of ducks

Rain sweeps the Eucalyptus
Strange pines on the coast
          needles two to the bunch
The whole sky whips in the wind
Vaux Swifts
Flying before the storm
Arcing close hear sharp wing-whistle
Sickle-bird
          pale gray
          sheets of rain slowly shifting
          down from the clouds,
Black Swifts.
          —the swifts cry
As they shoot by, See or go blind!

4

The swallow-shell that eases birth
    brought from the south by Hummingbird.
"We pull out the seagrass, the seagrass,
    the seagrass, and it drifts away"
—song of the geese.
"My children
    their father was a log"
—song of the pheasant.
The white gulls south of Victoria
    catch tossed crumbs in midair.
When anyone hears the Catbird
    he gets lonesome.
San Francisco, "Mulberry Harbor"
    eating the speckled sea-bird eggs
    of the Farallones.
Driving sand sends swallows flying,
    warm mud puts the ducks to sleep.

Magical birds: Phoenix, hawk, and crane
    owl and gander, wren,
Bright eyes aglow: Polishing clawfoot
    with talons spread, subtle birds
Wheel and go, leaving air in shreds
    black beaks shine in gray haze.
Brushed by the hawk's wing
    of vision.

—They were arguing about the noise
Made by the Golden-eye Duck.
Some said the whistling sound
Was made by its nose, some said
No, by the wings.
    "Have it your way.
We will leave you forever."
They went upriver:
The Flathead tribe.

    Raven
    on a roost of furs
No bird in a bird-book,
    black as the sun.

5

the making of the horn spoon

The head of the mountain-goat is in the corner
    for the making of the horn spoon,
The black spoon. When fire's heat strikes it
    turn the head
Four days and hair pulls loose
    horn twists free.
Hand-adze, straightknife, notch the horn-base;
    rub with rough sandstone
Shave down smooth. Split two cedar sticks
    when water boils plunge the horn,

Tie mouth between sticks in the spoon shape
    rub with dried dogfish skin.
It will be black and smooth,
    a spoon.

Wa, laEm gwała ts!ololaqe ka · ts!Enaqe laxeq.

6

this poem is for bear

"As for me I am a child of the god of the mountains."

A bear down under the cliff.
She is eating huckleberries.
They are ripe now
Soon it will snow, and she
Or maybe he, will crawl into a hole
And sleep. You can see
Huckleberries in bearshit if you
Look, this time of year
If I sneak up on the bear
It will grunt and run

The others had all gone down
From the blackberry brambles, but one girl
Spilled her basket, and was picking up her
Berries in the dark.
A tall man stood in the shadow, took her arm,
Led her to his home. He was a bear.
In a house under the mountain
She gave birth to slick dark children
With sharp teeth, and lived in the hollow
Mountain many years.
          snare a bear: call him out:
honey-eater
forest apple
light-foot

Old man in the fur coat, Bear! come out!
Die of your own choice!
Grandfather black-food!
                    this girl married a bear
Who rules in the mountains, Bear!
                    you have eaten many berries
                    you have caught many fish
                    you have frightened many people

Twelve species north of Mexico
Sucking their paws in the long winter
Tearing the high-strung caches down
Whining, crying, jacking off
(Odysseus was a bear)

Bear-cubs gnawing the soft tits
Teeth gritted, eyes screwed tight
                    but she let them.

Til her brothers found the place
Chased her husband up the gorge
Cornered him in the rocks.
Song of the snared bear:
          "Give me my belt.
          "I am near death.
          "I came from the mountain caves
          "At the headwaters,
          "The small streams there
          "Are all dried up.

—I think I'll go hunt bears.
                    "hunt bears?
Why shit Snyder,
You couldn't hit a bear in the ass
          with a handful of rice!"

7

All beaded with dew
            dawn grass runway
Open-eyed rabbits hang
            dangle, loose feet in tall grass
From alder snares.
The spider is building a morning-web
From the snared rabbit's ear to the snare

            down trail at sunrise
            wet berry brush
            spiderwebs in the eyes
Gray chunk rocks roll down
Splinter pines,
            bark the firs,
                    rest in maple shade.

I dance
On every swamp
                    sang the rabbit
            once a hungry ghost
            then a beast
            who knows what next?

Salmon, deer, no pottery;
Summer and winter houses
Roots, berries, watertight baskets—
Our girls get layed by Coyote
We get along
                    just fine.
The Shuswap tribe.

8

this poem is for deer

"I dance on all the mountains
On five mountains, I have a dancing place
When they shoot at me I run
To my five mountains"

Missed a last shot
At the Buck, in twilight
So we came back sliding
On dry needles through cold pines.
Scared out a cottontail
Whipped up the winchester
Shot off its head.
The white body rolls and twitches
In the dark ravine
As we run down the hill to the car.
                       deer foot down scree
Picasso's fawn, Issa's fawn,
Deer on the autumn mountain
Howling like a wise man
Stiff springy jumps down the snowfields
Head held back, forefeet out,
Balls tight in a tough hair sack
Keeping the human soul from care
                  on the autumn mountain
Standing in late sun, ear-flick
Tail-flick, gold mist of flies
Whirling from nostril to eyes.

                —

Home by night
           drunken eye
Still picks out Taurus
Low, and growing high:
          four-point buck

Dancing in the headlights
          on the lonely road
A mile past the mill-pond,
With the car stopped, shot
That wild silly blinded creature down.

Pull out the hot guts
          with hard bare hands
While night-frost chills the tongue
          and eye
The cold horn-bones.
The hunter's belt
          just below the sky
Warm blood in the car trunk.
Deer-smell,
          the limp tongue.

———

Deer don't want to die for me.
          I'll drink sea-water
Sleep on beach pebbles in the rain
Until the deer come down to die
          in pity for my pain.

9

Sealion, salmon, offshore—
Salt-fuck desire driving flap fins
North, south, five thousand miles
Coast, and up creek, big seeds
Groping for inland womb.

Geese, ducks, swallows,
                    paths in the air
I am a frozen addled egg on the tundra

My petrel, snow-tongued
          kiss her a brook her mouth

of smooth pebbles her tongue a bed
       icewater flowing in that
Cavern dark, tongue drifts in the creek
          —blind fish

On the rainy boulders
On the bloody sandbar
I ate the spawned-out salmon
I went crazy
Covered with ashes
Gnawing the girls breasts
Marrying women to whales
Or dogs, I'm a priest too
I raped your wife
I'll eat your corpse

10

Flung from demonic wombs
       off to some new birth
A million shapes—just look in any
       biology book.
And the hells below mind
       where ghosts roam, the heavens
Above brain, where gods & angels play
       an age or two
& they'll trade with you,
Who wants heaven?
       rest homes like that
Scattered all through the galaxy.

     "I kill everything
     I fear nothing but wolves
     From the mouth of the Cowlitz
         to its source,
     Only the wolves scare me,
     I have a chief's tail"
—Skunk.

"We carry deer-fawns in our mouths
We carry deer-fawns in our mouths
We have our faces blackened"
—Wolf-song.
"If I were a baby seal

                         every time I came up
I'd head toward shore—"

II

songs for a four-crowned dancing hat

O Prajapati
            You who floated on the sea
            Hatched to godhead in the slime
Heated red and beaten for a bronze ritual bowl
The Boar!
            Dripping boar emerged
            On his tusk his treasure
Prajapati from the sea-depths:
Skewered body of the earth
Each time I carry you this way.

The year I wore my Raven skin
   Dogfish ran. Too many berries on the hill
Grizzly fat and happy in the sun—
   The little women, the fern women,
They have stopped crying now.
   "What will you do with human beings?
Are you going to save the human beings?"
   That was Southeast, they say.

12

Out the Greywolf valley
in late afternoon
after eight days in the high meadows
hungry, and out of food,
the trail broke into a choked
clearing, apples grew gone wild
hung on one low bough by a hornet's nest.
caught the drone in tall clover
lowland smell in the shadows
then picked a hard green one:
watched them swarm.
smell of the mountains still on me.
none stung.

13

Now I'll also tell what food
we lived on then:

Mescal, yucca fruit, pinyon, acorns,
prickly pear, sumac berry, cactus,
spurge, dropseed, lip fern, corn,
mountain plants, wild potatoes, mesquite,
stems of yucca, tree-yucca flowers, chokecherries,
pitahaya cactus, honey of the ground-bee,
honey, honey of the bumblebee,
mulberries, angle-pod, salt, berries,
berries of the one-seeded juniper,
berries of the alligator-bark juniper,
wild cattle, mule deer, antelopes,
white-tailed deer, wild turkeys, doves, quail,
squirrels, robins, slate-colored juncoes,
song sparrows, wood rats, prairie dogs,
rabbits, peccaries, burros, mules, horses,
buffaloes, mountain sheep, and turtles.

14

Buddha fed himself to tigers
& donated mountains of eyes
      (through the years)
To the blind,
          a mountain-lion
Once trailed me four miles
At night and no gun
It was awful, I didn't want to be ate
      maybe we'll change.

Or make a net of your sister's cunt-hair
Catch the sun, and burn the world.

Where are you going now?
Shake hands.
Goodbye, George Bell . . .
      that was a Kwakiutl woman
      singing goodbye to her man,
      Victoria B.C., 1887

The mules are loaded
      packs lashed with a vajra-hitch
      the grass-eaters steam in the dawn
      the workers are still asleep
      light swings on the high cornice
      on the chill side of the mountain, we
      switchback
      drink at the waterfall
      start to climb
"Stalk lotuses
Burst through the rocks
And come up in sevens."

15

First day of the world.
White rock ridges
new born
Jay chatters   the first time
Rolling a smoke by the campfire
New! never before.
bitter coffee, cold
Dawn wind, sun on the cliffs,
You'll find it in *Many old shoes*
High!   high on poetry & mountains.

That silly ascetic Gautama
thought he knew something;
Maudgalyâyana   knew hell
Knew every hell, from the
Cambrian to the Jurassic
He suffered in them all.

16

How rare to be born a human being!
Wash him off with cedar-bark and milkweed
                 send the damned doctors home.
Baby, baby, noble baby
Noble-hearted baby

One hand up, one hand down
"I alone am the honored one"
Birth of the Buddha.
And the whole world-system trembled.
"If that baby really said that,
I'd cut him up and throw him to the dogs!"
said Chao-chou the Zen Master. But
Chipmunks, gray squirrels, and

Golden-mantled ground squirrels
                brought him each a nut.
Truth being the sweetest of flavors.

Girls would have in their arms
A wild gazelle or wild wolf-cubs
And give them their white milk,
                those who had new-born infants home
Breasts still full.
Wearing a spotted fawnskin
           sleeping under trees
           bacchantes, drunk
On wine or truth, what you will,
Meaning: compassion.
Agents: man and beast, beasts
Got the buddha-nature
All but
Coyote.

— Burning —

second shaman song

Squat in swamp shadows.
       mosquitoes sting;
         high light in cedar above.
Crouched in a dry vain frame
     —thirst for cold snow
     —green slime of bone marrow
Seawater fills each eye

Quivering in nerve and muscle
Hung in the pelvic cradle
Bones propped against roots
A blind flicker of nerve

Still hand moves out alone
Flowering and leafing
         turning to quartz
Streaked rock   congestion of karma
The long body of the swamp.
A mud-streaked thigh.

Dying carp biting air
      in the damp grass,
River recedes. No matter.

Limp fish sleep in the weeds
The sun dries me as I dance

One moves continually with the consciousness
Of that other, totally alien, non-human:
Humming inside like a taut drum,
Carefully avoiding any direct thought of it,
Attentive to the real-world flesh and stone.

Intricate layers of emptiness
This only world, juggling forms
                  a hand, a breast, two clasped
Human tenderness scuttles
Down dry endless cycles
Forms within forms falling
                              clinging
Loosely, what's gone away?
                        —love

In Spring the Avocado sheds dead leaves
Soft rattling through the Cherry greens
Bird at this moment
All these books
    wearing a thin sweater
    & no brassiere
    in failing light
One glance, miles below
Bones & flesh knit in the rock
    "have no regret—
chip chip
          (sparrows)
& not a word about the void
To which one hand diddling
Cling

                        3

Maudgalyâyana saw hell

    Under the shuddering eyelid
    Dreams gnawing the nerve-strings,
    The mind grabs and the shut eye sees:
    Down dimensions floating below sunlight,
    Worlds of the dead, Bardo, mind-worlds
    & horror of sunless cave-ritual
    Meeting conscious monk bums
    Blown on winds of karma from hell

To endless changing hell,
Life and death whipped
On this froth of reality (wind & rain
Realms human and full of desire) over the cold
Hanging enormous unknown, below
Art and History and all mankind living thoughts,
Occult & witchcraft evils each all true.
The thin edge of nature rising fragile
And helpless with its love and sentient stone
And flesh, above dark drug-death dreams.

Clouds I cannot lose, we cannot leave.
We learn to love, horror accepted.
Beyond, within, all normal beauties
Of the science-conscious sex and love-receiving
Day-to-day got vision of this sick
Sparkling person at the inturned dreaming
Blooming human mind
Dropping it all, and opening the eyes.

4

Maitreya the future Buddha

He's out stuck in a bird's craw
                last night
Wildcat vomited his pattern on the snow.

Who refused to learn to dance, refused
To kiss you long ago. You fed him berries
But fled, the red stain on his teeth;
And when he cried, finding the world a Wheel—
           you only stole his rice,
Being so small and gray. He will not go,
But wait through fish scale, shale dust, bone
          of hawk and marmot,
          caught leaves in ice,
Til flung on a new net of atoms:

Snagged in flight
Leave you hang and quiver like a gong

Your empty happy body
Swarming in the light

5

jimson weed

Now both
Being persons—alive
We sit here
The wind
Whirls
        "Don't kill it man,
The roach is the best part"
            still an incessant chatter
On Vulture Peak
Crack of dawn/   calor/canor/dulcor   faugh

I hold it
I tell of it, standing
I look here
I look there
Standing
            great limp mouth
            hanging loose in air
            quivers, turns in upon itself,
            gone
            with a diabolical laugh
The night bat
Rising flies, I tell it
I sing it

"Jesus was a great doctor, I guess he was
the best gambler in the United States"
At Hakwinyava

Imagine a dark house
Blue

6

My clutch and your clutch
   batter the same bough
Elliptical, bird-light
   stink of spilled wine.
Whirling hills, lost out of mind.

When Red Hand came to the river he saw
a man sitting on the other side of the river
pointing with his arm. So Red Hand
sat and pointed with his arm until nightfall
when he suddenly realized that it was
only a dead tree with a stretched out limb
and he got up and crossed the river.

March wind
  blows the bright dawn
  apricot blossoms down.
  salty bacon smoking on the stove
  (sitting on Chao-chou's *wu*
     my feet sleep)

Ananda, grieving all night in the square
   gave up & went to bed & just then woke
The big trucks go by in the half-asleep night,
Ah, butterflies
Granite rots and crumbles
Warm seas & simple life slops on the ranges
Mayflies glitter for a day
Like Popes!

    where the sword is kept sharp
    the VOID
    gnashes its teeth

7

Face in the crook of her neck
            felt throb of vein
Smooth skin, her cool breasts
All naked in the dawn

                    "byrdes
sing forth from every bough"
            where are they now
And dreamt I saw the Duke of Chou

The Mother whose body is the Universe
Whose breasts are Sun and Moon,
            the statue of Prajna
From Java: the quiet smile,
The naked breasts.

"Will you still love me when my
    breasts get big?"
the little girl said—

"Earthly Mothers and those who suck
the breasts of earthly mothers are mortal—
but deathless are those who have fed
at the breast of the Mother of the Universe."

8

John Muir on Mt. Ritter:

After scanning its face again and again,
I began to scale it, picking my holds
With intense caution. About half-way
To the top, I was suddenly brought to
A dead stop, with arms outspread
Clinging close to the face of the rock
Unable to move hand or foot

Either up or down. My doom
Appeared fixed. I MUST fall.
There would be a moment of
Bewilderment, and then,
A lifeless rumble down the cliff
To the glacier below.
My mind seemed to fill with a
Stifling smoke. This terrible eclipse
Lasted only a moment, when life blazed
Forth again with preternatural clearness.
I seemed suddenly to become possessed
Of a new sense. My trembling muscles
Became firm again, every rift and flaw in
The rock was seen as through a microscope,
My limbs moved with a positiveness and precision
With which I seemed to have
Nothing at all to do.

9

Night here,   a covert
All spun, webs in one
              how without grabbing hold it?
—Get into the bird-cage
              without starting them singing.

"Forming the New Society
              Within the shell of the Old"
The motto in the Wobbly Hall
Some old Finns and Swedes playing cards
Fourth and Yesler in Seattle.
O you modest, retiring, virtuous young ladies
              pick the watercress, pluck the yarrow
"Kwan kwan" goes the crane in the field,
              I'll meet you tomorrow;
A million workers dressed in black and buried,
We make love in leafy shade.

Bodhidharma sailing the Yangtze on a reed
Lenin in a sealed train through Germany
Hsüan Tsang, crossing the Pamirs
Joseph, Crazy Horse, living the last free
    starving high-country winter of their tribes.
Surrender into freedom, revolt into slavery—
Confucius no better—
      (with Lao-tzu to keep him in check)
"Walking about the countryside
      all one fall
To a heart's content beating on stumps."

10

Amitabha's vow

"If, after obtaining Buddhahood, anyone in my land
    gets tossed in jail on a vagrancy rap, may I
    not attain highest perfect enlightenment.

    wild geese in the orchard
    frost on the new grass

"If, after obtaining Buddhahood, anyone in my land
    loses a finger coupling boxcars, may I
    not attain highest perfect enlightenment.

    mare's eye flutters
    jerked by the lead-rope
    stone-bright shoes flick back
    ankles trembling: down steep rock

"If, after obtaining Buddhahood, anyone in my land
    can't get a ride hitch-hiking all directions, may I
    not attain highest perfect enlightenment.

    wet rocks buzzing
    rain and thunder southwest

hair, beard, tingle
wind whips bare legs
we should go back
we don't

II

        Floating of vapor from brazier
Who hold emptiness
Whose bundle is broken, blank spot in creation
        still gong in a long-empty hall
                perceptions at idle play

    Q. What is the way of non-activity?
    A. It is activity
Ingather limbs, tighten the fingers
Press tongue to the roof
Roll the eyes
        dried & salted in the sun
In the dry, hard chrysalis, a pure bug waits hatching
Sudden flares: rush of water and bone
Netted, fitted
Flicker of action, nerves burnt in patterns
        fields of cabbages
        yet to consume
Imprint of flexible mouth-sounds,
Seared in the mind, on things.

Coyote: "I guess there never was a world anywhere"
Earthmaker: "I think if we find a little world,
        "I can fix it up."

12

I have terrible meditations
On the cells all water
        frail bodies
Moisting in a quiver;
Flares of life that settle
Into stone,
The hollow quaking of the soft parts
Over bone

The city of the Gandharvas,
        not a real city,
Only the memory of a city
Preserved in seed from beginningless time.
        a city crowded with books,
Thick grass on the streets,
        a race of dark people
Wearing thin sandals, reading all morning in alleys
Glazing black pots at night.

        the royal feast—
One man singing
Three join the chorus
        fifty-stringed *seh*
  red strings in the sound-board
     black wine
     raw fish
     plain soup
"Herrick thou art too coorse to love"
Hoarse cry of nighthawk
Circling & swooping in the still, bright dawn.

13

Spikes of new smell driven up nostrils
Expanding & deepening, ear-muscles
Straining and grasping the sounds

Mouth filled with bright fluid coldness
Tongue crushed by the weight of its flavors
        —the Nootka sold out for lemon drops
(What's this talk about not understanding!
        you're just a person who refuses to see.)

Poetry a riprap on the slick rock of metaphysics
"Put a Spanish halter on that whore of a mare
& I'll lead the bitch up any trail"

(how gentle! He should have whipped her first)

        the wind turns.
        a cold rain blows over the shale
        we sleep in the belly of a cloud.
(you think sex art and travel are enough?
                you're a skinful of cowdung)

South of the Yellow River the Emperor Wu
Set the army horses free in the mountain pastures,
Set the Buffalo free on the Plain of the Peach Grove.
Chariots and armor were smeared with blood
        and put away. They locked up
        the Arrows bag.
Smell of crushed spruce and burned snag-wood.
        remains of men,
Bone-chopped foul remains, thick stew
Food for crows—
        (blind, deaf, and dumb!
        shall we give him another chance?)
At Nyahaim-kuvara
Night has gone
Traveling to my land
        —that's a Mohave night
Our night too, you think brotherhood
Humanity & good intentions will stop it?
As long as you hesitate, no place to go.

Bluejay, out at the world's end
        perched, looked, & dashed

Through the crashing: his head is squashed.
          symplegades, the *mumonkwan,*
It's all vagina dentata
          (Jump!)
"Leap through an Eagle's snapping beak"

Actaeon saw Dhyana in the Spring.

          it was nothing special,
     misty rain on Mt. Baker,
     Neah Bay at low tide.

14

A skin-bound bundle of clutchings
          unborn and with no place to go
Balanced on the boundless compassion
Of diatoms, lava, and chipmunks.

Love, let it be,
Is a sacrifice
          knees, the cornered eyes
Tea on a primus stove after a cold swim
Intricate doors and clocks, the clothes
          we stand in—
Gaps between seedings, the right year,
Green shoots in the marshes
Creeks in the proper directions
Hills in proportion,
Astrologers, go-betweens present,
          a marriage has been.

Walked all day through live oak and manzanita,
Scrabbling through dust down Tamalpais—
Thought of high mountains;
Looked out on a sea of fog.
Two of us, carrying packs.

15

Stone-flake and salmon.
The pure, sweet, straight-splitting
                        with a ping
Red cedar of the thick coast valleys
Shake-blanks on the mashed ferns
                        the charred logs
Fireweed and bees
An old burn, by new alder
Creek on smooth stones,
Back there a Tarheel logger farm.
(High country fir still hunched in snow)

From Siwash strawberry-pickers in the Skagit
Down to the boys at Sac,
Living by the river
            riding flatcars to Fresno,
Across the whole country
Steep towns, flat towns, even New York,
And oceans and Europe & libraries & galleries
And the factories they make rubbers in
This whole spinning show
            (among others)
Watched by the Mt. Sumeru L.O.

From the middle of the universe
& them with no radio.
"What is imperfect is best"
            silver scum on the trout's belly
            rubs off on your hand.
It's all falling or burning—
            rattle of boulders
            steady dribbling of rocks down cliffs
            bark chips in creeks
Porcupine chawed here—
                        Smoke
From Tillamook a thousand miles
Soot and hot ashes. Forest fires.
Upper Skagit burned I think 1919

Smoke covered all northern Washington.
      lightning strikes, flares,
Blossoms a fire on the hill.
Smoke like clouds. Blotting the sun
Stinging the eyes.
The hot seeds steam underground
      still alive.

16

"Wash me on home, mama"
        —song of the Kelp.
A chief's wife
Sat with her back to the sun
On the sandy beach, shredding cedar-bark.
Her fingers were slender
She didn't eat much.

"Get foggy
We're going out to dig
Buttercup roots"

Dream, Dream,
Earth! those beings living on your surface
none of them disappearing, will all be transformed.
When I have spoken to them
when they have spoken to me, from that moment on,
their words and their bodies which they
usually use to move about with, will all change.
I will not have heard them. Signed,
          (   )
          Coyote

17

the text

Sourdough mountain called a fire in:
Up Thunder Creek, high on a ridge.
Hiked eighteen hours, finally found
A snag and a hundred feet around on fire:
All afternoon and into night
Digging the fire line
Falling the burning snag
It fanned sparks down like shooting stars
Over the dry woods, starting spot-fires
Flaring in wind up Skagit valley
From the Sound.
Toward morning it rained.
We slept in mud and ashes,
Woke at dawn, the fire was out,
The sky was clear, we saw
The last glimmer of the morning star.

the myth

Fire up Thunder Creek and the mountain—
                    troy's burning!
The cloud mutters
The mountains are your mind.
The woods bristle there,
Dogs barking and children shrieking
Rise from below.

Rain falls for centuries
Soaking the loose rocks in space
Sweet rain, the fire's out
The black snag glistens in the rain
& the last wisp of smoke floats up
Into the absolute cold
Into the spiral whorls of fire
The storms of the Milky Way
"Buddha incense in an empty world"

Black pit cold and light-year
Flame tongue of the dragon
Licks the sun

The sun is but a morning star

Crater Mt. L.O. 1952–Marin-an 1956

end of myths & texts

THE BACK COUNTRY

FOR KENNETH REXROTH

". . . So
—when was it—I, drawn like blown
cloud, couldn't stop dreaming of
roaming, roving the coast up and
down . . ."
—Basho

— *I* —
Far West

A Berry Feast

For Joyce and Homer Matson

I

Fur the color of mud, the smooth loper
Crapulous old man, a drifter,
Praises! of Coyote the Nasty, the fat
Puppy that abused himself, the ugly gambler,
Bringer of goodies.

    In bearshit find it in August,
    Neat pile on the fragrant trail, in late
    August, perhaps by a Larch tree
    Bear has been eating the berries.
          high meadow, late summer, snow gone
    Blackbear
        eating berries, married
    To a woman whose breasts bleed
    From nursing the half-human cubs.

        Somewhere of course there are people
        collecting and junking, gibbering all day,

"Where I shoot my arrows
"There is the sunflower's shade
        —song of the rattlesnake
        coiled in the boulder's groin
"K'ak, k'ak, k'ak!
        sang Coyote. Mating with
        humankind—

        The Chainsaw falls for boards of pine,
        Suburban bedrooms, block on block
        Will waver with this grain and knot,
        The maddening shapes will start and fade
        Each morning when commuters wake—
        Joined boards hung on frames,
                a box to catch the biped in.

and shadow swings around the tree
Shifting on the berrybush
from leaf to leaf across each day
The shadow swings around the tree.

2

Three, down, through windows
Dawn leaping cats, all barred brown, grey
Whiskers aflame
bits of mouse on the tongue

Washing the coffeepot in the river
the baby yelling for breakfast,
Her breasts, black-nippled, blue-veined, heavy,
Hung through the loose shirt
squeezed, with the free hand
white jet in three cups.
Cats at dawn
derry derry down

Creeks wash clean where trout hide
We chew the black plug
Sleep on needles through long afternoons
"you shall be owl
"you shall be sparrow
"you will grow thick and green, people
"will eat you, you berries!
Coyote: shot from the car, two ears,
A tail, bring bounty.

Clanks of tread
oxen of Shang
moving the measured road

Bronze bells at the throat
Bronze balls on the horns, the bright Oxen
Chanting through sunlight and dust
wheeling logs down hills
into heaps,
the yellow

    Fat-snout Caterpillar, tread toppling forward
    Leaf on leaf, roots in gold volcanic dirt.

When
Snow melts back
        from the trees
Bare branches   knobbed pine twigs
        hot sun on wet flowers
Green shoots of huckleberry
Breaking through snow.

3

    Belly stretched taut in a bulge
    Breasts swelling as you guzzle beer, who wants
                Nirvana?
    Here is water, wine, beer
    Enough books for a week
    A mess of afterbirth,
    A smell of hot earth, a warm mist
    Steams from the crotch

"You can't be killers all your life
"The people are coming—
        —and when Magpie
Revived him, limp rag of fur in the river
Drowned and drifting, fish-food in the shallows,
"Fuck you!" sang Coyote
           and ran.

Delicate blue-black, sweeter from meadows
Small and tart in the valleys, with light blue dust
Huckleberries scatter through pine woods
Crowd along gullies, climb dusty cliffs,
Spread through the air by birds;
Find them in droppings of bear.

  "Stopped in the night
  "Ate hot pancakes in a bright room
  "Drank coffee, read the paper
  "In a strange town, drove on,
  singing, as the drunkard swerved the car

"Wake from your dreams, bright ladies!
"Tighten your legs, squeeze demons from
        the crotch with rigid thighs
"Young red-eyed men will come
"With limp erections, snuffling cries
"To dry your stiffening bodies in the sun!

Woke at the beach. Grey dawn,
Drenched with rain. One naked man
Frying his horsemeat on a stone.

4

Coyote yaps, a knife!
Sunrise on yellow rocks.
People gone, death no disaster,
Clear sun in the scrubbed sky
                    empty and bright
Lizards scurry from darkness
We lizards sun on yellow rocks.

See, from the foothills
Shred of river glinting, trailing,
To flatlands, the city:
            glare of haze in the valley horizon
Sun caught on glass gleams and goes.
From cool springs under cedar
On his haunches, white grin,
            long tongue panting, he watches:

Dead city in dry summer,
Where berries grow.

Marin-an

sun breaks over the eucalyptus
grove below the wet pasture,
water's about hot,

I sit in the open window
& roll a smoke.

distant dogs bark, a pair of
cawing crows; the twang
of a pygmy nuthatch high in a pine—
from behind the cypress windrow
the mare moves up, grazing.

a soft continuous roar
comes out of the far valley
of the six-lane highway—thousands
and thousands of cars
driving men to work.

Sixth-Month Song in the Foothills

In the cold shed sharpening saws.
            a swallow's nest hangs by the door
setting rakers in sunlight
falling from meadow through doorframe
            swallows flit under the eaves.

Grinding the falling axe
sharp for the summer
            a swallow shooting out over.
over the river, snow on low hills
sharpening wedges for splitting.

Beyond the low hills, white mountains
and now snow is melting.   sharpening tools;
            pack horses grazing new grass
bright axes—and swallows
            fly in to my shed.

The Spring

Beating asphalt into highway potholes
            pickup truck we'd loaded
road repair stock shed & yard
a day so hot the asphalt went in soft.
            pipe and steel plate tamper
took turns at by hand
then drive the truck rear wheel
a few times back and forth across the fill—
finish it off with bitchmo round the edge.

the foreman said let's get a drink
& drove through woods and flower fields
            shovels clattering in back
into a black grove by a cliff
            a rocked in pool
            feeding a fern ravine
                        tin can to drink
numbing the hand and cramping in the gut
surging through the fingers from below
            & dark here—
let's get back to the truck
get back on the job.

A Walk

Sunday the only day we don't work:
Mules farting around the meadow,
                        Murphy fishing,
The tent flaps in the warm
Early sun: I've eaten breakfast and I'll
                        take a walk
To Benson Lake. Packed a lunch,
Goodbye. Hopping on creekbed boulders
Up the rock throat three miles
                        Piute Creek—

In steep gorge glacier-slick rattlesnake country
Jump, land by a pool, trout skitter,
The clear sky. Deer tracks.
Bad place by a falls, boulders big as houses,
Lunch tied to belt,
I stemmed up a crack and almost fell
But rolled out safe on a ledge
                      and ambled on.
Quail chicks freeze underfoot, color of stone
Then run cheep! away, hen quail fussing.
Craggy west end of Benson Lake—after edging
Past dark creek pools on a long white slope—
Lookt down in the ice-black lake
                    lined with cliff
From far above: deep shimmering trout.
A lone duck in a gunsightpass
                    steep side hill
Through slide-aspen and talus, to the east end,
Down to grass, wading a wide smooth stream
Into camp. At last.
           By the rusty three-year-
Ago left-behind cookstove
Of the old trail crew,
Stoppt and swam and ate my lunch.

Fire in the Hole

Squatting a day in the sun,
      one hand turning the steeldrill,
one, swinging the four pound singlejack hammer
                    down.
three inches an hour
granite bullhump boulder
             square in the trail.
above, the cliffs,
             of Piute Mountain waver.
sweat trickles down my back.

why does this day keep coming into mind.
a job in the rock hills
        aching arms
                        the muletracks
                                arching blinding sky,
        noon sleep under
                snake-scale juniper limbs.

that the mind
        entered the tip of steel.
the arm fell
        like breath.
the valley, reeling,
                on the pivot of that drill—
twelve inches deep we packed the charge
        dynamite on mules
                        like frankincense.
Fire in the hole!
Fire in the hole!
Fire in the hole!

jammed the plunger down.
thru dust
                        and sprinkling stone
strolld back to see:
hands and arms and shoulders
free.

Burning the Small Dead

Burning the small dead
                branches
broke from beneath
        thick spreading
                whitebark pine.

                        a hundred summers
snowmelt   rock   and air

hiss in a twisted bough.

    sierra granite;
                mt. Ritter—
                black rock twice as old.

Deneb, Altair

windy fire

Trail Crew Camp at Bear Valley, 9000 Feet. Northern Sierra—White Bone and Threads of Snowmelt Water

Cut branches back for a day—
trail a thin line through willow
        up buckbrush meadows,
        creekbed for twenty yards
   winding in boulders
       zigzags the hill
into timber, white pine.

gooseberry bush on the turns.
hooves clang on the riprap
        dust, brush, branches.
        a stone
  cairn at the pass—
strippt mountains hundreds of miles.

sundown went back
        the clean switchbacks to camp.
bell on the gelding,
stew in the cook tent,
black coffee in a big tin can.

Home from the Sierra

Woke once in the night, pissed,
checkt the coming winter's stars
built up the fire
still glowing in the chilly dawn.

Washing the mush pot in the lake
frost on the horse turds
a grayjay cased the camp.

All morning walking to the car
load up on granite stone,
seedling sugar pine.

Down to hot plains.
Mexicans on flatcars in the San Joaquin.
cool fog
smell of straw mats
cup of green tea
by the Bay.

Foxtail Pine

bark smells like pineapple: Jeffries
cones prick your hand: Ponderosa

nobody knows what they are, saying
"needles three to a bunch."

    turpentine tin can hangers
    high lead riggers

"the true fir cone stands straight,
the doug fir cone hangs down."

—wild pigs eat acorns in those hills
cascara cutters

tanbark oak bark gatherers
myrtlewood burl bowl-makers
little cedar dolls,
          baby girl born from the split crotch
                    of a plum
               daughter of the moon—

foxtail pine with a
clipped curve-back cluster of tight
          five-needle bunches
     the rough red bark scale
and jigsaw pieces sloughed off
               scattered on the ground.
—what am I doing saying "foxtail pine"?

these conifers whose home was ice
age tundra, taiga, they of the
          naked sperm
do whitebark pine and white pine seem the same?

          a sort of tree
          its leaves are needles
          like a fox's brush
(I call him fox because he looks that way)
          and call this other thing, a
               foxtail pine.

A Heifer Clambers Up

     a heifer clambers up
          nighthawk goes out
                    horses
     trail back to the barn.
          spider gleams in his
                    new web
     dew on the shingles, on the car,
          on the mailbox—
     the mole, the onion, and the beetle
          cease their wars.

                        worlds tip
        into the sunshine, men and women
                get up, babies crying
        children grab their lunches
                                and leave for school.
        the radio announces
                in the milking barn
                                in the car bound for work
        "tonight all the countries
                will get drunk and have a party"
        russia, america, china,
                                singing with their poets,
        pregnant and gracious,
                sending flowers and dancing bears
                                to all the capitals
        fat
                with the baby happy land

August on Sourdough, a Visit from Dick Brewer

You hitched a thousand miles
                        north from San Francisco
Hiked up the mountainside   a mile in the air
The little cabin—one room—
                        walled in glass
Meadows and snowfields,   hundreds of peaks.
We lay in our sleeping bags
                        talking half the night;
Wind in the guy-cables   summer mountain rain.
Next morning I went with you
                        as far as the cliffs,
Loaned you my poncho—   the rain across the shale—
You down the snowfield
                        flapping in the wind
Waving a last goodbye   half hidden in the clouds
To go on hitching
                        clear to New York;
Me back to my mountain   and far, far, west.

Oil

soft rainsqualls on the swells
south of the Bonins, late at night. Light
from the empty mess-hall
throws back bulky shadows
of winch and fairlead
over the slanting fantail where I stand.

but for men on watch in the engine room,
the man at the wheel, the lookout in the bow,
the crew sleeps. in cots on deck
or narrow iron bunks down drumming
passageways below.

the ship burns with a furnace heart
steam veins and copper nerves
quivers and slightly twists and always goes—
easy roll of the hull and deep
vibration of the turbine underfoot.

bearing what all these
crazed, hooked nations need:
steel plates and
long injections of pure oil.

The Wipers Secret

Down in the bilges
or up out of sight on the bulkheads
time after time
year after year
we paint right over the dirt.

The first engineer
he knows.
but what can he say?
the company says
save time.

Once Only

almost at the equator
almost at the equinox
exactly at midnight
from a ship
the full

moon

in the center of the sky.

Sappa Creek near Singapore
March 1958

After Work

The shack and a few trees
float in the blowing fog

I pull out your blouse,
warm my cold hands
        on your breasts.
you laugh and shudder
peeling garlic by the
        hot iron stove.
bring in the axe, the rake,
the wood

we'll lean on the wall
against each other
stew simmering on the fire
as it grows dark
        drinking wine.

Rolling in at Twilight

Rolling in at twilight—Newport Oregon—
    cool of september ocean air, I
saw Phil Whalen with a load of groceries
    walking through a dirt lot full
      of logging trucks, cats
        and skidders

    looking at the ground.

I yelld as the bus wheeld by
    but he kept looking down.
      ten minutes later with my books and pack
        knockt at his door

"Thought you might be on that bus"
      he said, and
    showed me all the food.

Hitch Haiku

They didn't hire him
        so he ate his lunch alone:
the noon whistle

—

Cats shut down
        deer thread through
men all eating lunch

—

Frying hotcakes in a dripping shelter
    Fu Manchu
Queets Indian Reservation in the rain

—

A truck went by
                    three hours ago:
Smoke Creek desert

———

Jackrabbit eyes all night
    breakfast in Elko.

———

Old kanji hid by dirt
on skidroad Jap town walls
            down the hill
to the Wobbly hall

                    Seattle

———

Spray drips from the cargo-booms
a fresh-chipped winch
            spotted with red lead
young fir—
            soaking in summer rain

———

        Over the Mindanao Deep
Scrap brass
dumpt off the fantail
falling six miles

———

[*The following two were written on classical
themes while travelling through Sappho, Washington.
The first is by Thomas L. Hoodlatch.*]

        Moonlight on the burned-out temple—
                wooden horse shit.

Sunday dinner in Ithaca—
　　　　the twang of a bowstring

———

After weeks of watching the roof leak
　　　　I fixed it tonight
by moving a single board

———

A freezing morning in October in the high Sierra
crossing Five Lakes Basin to the Kaweahs with
Bob Greensfelder and Claude Dalenberg

　　　　Stray white mare
　　　　　　　　neck rope dangling
　　　　forty miles from farms.

———

Back from the Kaweahs

　　　　Sundown, Timber Gap
　　　　　　　　—sat down—
　　　　　　　　　　　dark firs.
　　　　dirty;　　　cold;
　　　　too tired to talk

———

Cherry blossoms at Hood river
　　　　　　　　rusty sand near Tucson
mudflats of Willapa Bay

———

Pronghorn country

Steering into the sun
                    glittering jewel-road
        shattered obsidian

———

The mountain walks over the water!
Rain down from the mountain!
                high bleat of a
cow elk
        over blackberries

———

A great freight truck
                    lit like a town
through the dark stony desert

———

Drinking hot saké
                        toasting fish on coals
            the motorcycle
out   parked in the rain.

———

Switchback

    turn, turn,
    and again,   hard-
    scrabble
    steep travel a-
    head.

How to Make Stew in the Pinacate Desert
Recipe for Locke & Drum

A. J. Bayless market bent wire roller basket buy up parsnips,
onion, carrot, rutabaga and potato, bell green pepper,
& nine cuts of dark beef shank.
They run there on their legs, that makes meat tasty.

Seven at night in Tucson, get some bisquick for the dump-
lings. Have some bacon. Go to Hadley's in the kitchen right
beside the frying steak—Diana on the phone—get a little plas-
tic bag from Drum—
Fill it up with tarragon and chili; four bay leaves; black pep-
per corns and basil; powdered oregano, something free, maybe
about two teaspoon worth of salt.

Now down in Sonora, Pinacate country, build a fire of Oco-
tillo, broken twigs and bits of ironwood, in an open ring of
lava: rake some coals aside (and if you're smart) to windward,
keep the other half ablaze for heat and light.
Set Drum's fourteen-inch dutch oven with three legs across
the embers.

Now put in the strips of bacon.
In another pan have all the vegetables cleaned up and peeled
and sliced.
Cut the beef shank meat up small and set the bone aside.
Throw in the beef shank meat,
And stir it while it fries hot,
lots of ash and sizzle—singe your brow—

Like Locke says almost burn it—then add water from the
jeep can—
add the little bag of herbs—cook it all five minutes more—and
then throw in the pan of all the rest.
Cover it up with big hot lid all heavy, sit and wait, or drink
budweiser beer.

And also mix the dumpling mix aside, some water in some
bisquick,

finally drop that off the spoon into the stew.
And let it cook ten minutes more
and lift the black pot off the fire
to set aside another good ten minutes,
Dish it up and eat it with a spoon, sitting on a poncho in the
dark.

13.XII.1964

Sather

old Norwegian by me on the bus,
"travel makes you big"
          night ride through Redding,
Red Bluff, north;
"those forests on Snoqualmie Pass
          just like the streams and woods
          where I grew up—"
an island in the North Atlantic,

Everett at age nineteen
a sailor on a schooner, 1912,

                    those
loftiest mountains.
how things change.
"I used to like this country—
now I think I'll live in France"
all my kids grown up.
               was a fireman on a coaler,
          a logger full of snoose,
     a dried out Scandinavian
          fisherman's son gone off to
               the Northwest.
name is Sather.
          "means 'mountain summer pasture'
          like they have in Norway—it's a
common name—"
                    where we take our cow.

& up Queets Basin country,
    that year, 1964,
        was still in August,
        ten feet under
        snow.

29.X.1964

For the Boy Who Was Dodger Point Lookout
Fifteen Years Ago

[On a backpacking trip with my first wife in the Olympic
mountains, having crossed over from the Dosewallips drain-
age, descended to and forded the Elwha and the Goldie, and
climbed again to the high country. Hiking alone down the
Elwha from Queets basin, these years later, brings it back.]

The thin blue smoke of our campfire
down in the grassy, flowery,
heather meadow
two miles from your perch.
The snowmelt pond, and Alison,
half-stoopt bathing like
Swan Maiden, lovely naked,
ringed with Alpine fir and
gleaming snowy peaks. We
had come miles without trails,
you had been long alone.
We talked for half an hour up
there above the foaming creeks
and forest valleys, in our
world of snow and flowers.

I don't know where she is now;
I never asked your name.
In this burning, muddy, lying,
blood-drenched world
that quiet meeting in the mountains
cool and gentle as the muzzles of
three elk, helps keep me sane.

— II —

Far East

Yase: September

Old Mrs. Kawabata
cuts down the tall spike weeds—
                more in two hours
than I can get done in a day.

out of a mountain
of grass and thistle
she saved five dusty stalks
                of ragged wild blue flower
and put them in my kitchen
                        in a jar.

Pine River
for Tetsu

From the top of
        Matsue castle
miles of flat ricefields
hills, and a long lake.
a schoolboy looks through a
home made telescope
        over the town.
new stores dwarf
this hilltop tower,
diving dolphins on the
        roof like horns—
nobody now quite
knows how they hoisted
        huge cut stone.

the Matsudaira family
owned it all,
sat in this windy
        lookout spire
in winter: all their
little villages
under snow.

Vapor Trails

Twin streaks twice higher than cumulus,
Precise plane icetracks in the vertical blue
Cloud-flaked light-shot shadow-arcing
Field of all future war, edging off to space.

Young expert U.S. pilots waiting
The day of criss-cross rockets
And white blossoming smoke of bomb,
The air world torn and staggered for these
Specks of brushy land and ant-hill towns—

    I stumble on the cobble rockpath,
Passing through temples,
Watching for two-leaf pine
    —spotting that design.

in Daitoku-ji

Mt. Hiei

I thought I would
sit with the screens back
and sing: watching the
half gone   moon rise late
but my hands were too numb
to play the guitar
the song was cold mist
the wine wouldn't warm
so I sat at the border
of dark house and moon
in thick coat—seeing stars rise
back of the ridge.
like once when a lookout
I took Aldebaran
for fire.

Out West

In the cross field
all day a new gas cultivator
cough cough   down each row
frizzing the soil, fine chopper "friable"

before it was cucumber,
    the boy in a straw hat
    clumsily turns at the end of a run
                  shifting levers,

through deodar limbs come the gas fumes
    cucumber vines
    poles and straw ropes
    torn down, two crops a summer,

last year the family
was out there with hoes.
the old woman dead now?

one-eyed chop tongue rotary
bucks and wheezes,

    that straw hat shaped like a stetson
    wearing those tight blue jeans.

Kyoto

Ami   24.XII.62

Hair a wild stroke of black
    on white
          pillow—
knees flexing up playing
      white sheets and gown,
gold-brown grass on the hillside
      clouds over twisted pine

jabs of rain down from Mt. Hiei
"we never thought he'd be a boy"

nobody home at the house
        the father has gone off to teach
        the light at the gate is still on
"he's been printing on broken stone"
                thru the window.

lettuce and onions no matter how cold.
does he know? that he has a new boy?
the dog has stoppt barking
sits shivering
and shivering
            tied to the woodshed door frame.

The Public Bath

the bath-girl

        getting dressed, in the mirror,
            the bath-girl with a pretty mole and a
        red skirt is watching me:
                am I
                    different?

the baby boy

        on his back, dashed with scalding water
        silent, moving eyes
        inscrutably
        pees.

the daughters

        gripping and scrubbing his two little daughters
            they squirm, shriek at
                soap-in-the-eye,

wring out their own hair
      with grave wifely hands,
   peek at me, point, while he
   soaps up and washes their
         plump little tight-lip pussies
   peers in their ears,
            & dunks them in hot tile tub.
            with a brown-burnt farmboy
            a shrivelled old man
            and a student who sings *silent night.*

   —we waver and float like seaweed
   pink flesh in the steamy light.

the old woman

      too fat and too old to care
         she just stands there
               idly knocking dewy water off her
                           bush.

the young woman

      gazing vacant, drying her neck
         faint fuzz of hair
         little points of breasts
               —next year she'll be dressing
                     out of sight.

the men

      squatting soapy and limber
      smooth dense skin, long muscles—

      I see dead men naked
      tumbled on beaches
                  newsreels, the
                     war

A Volcano in Kyushu

Mount Aso   uplands
horses, rimrock

> the sightseeing buses crammed.
> to view bare rock, brown grass,
>   space,
>   sulphury cliffs, streakt snow.
>   —whiffing the fumaroles
> a noseless, shiny,
> mouth-twisted middle aged man.

bluejeans, check shirt, silver buckle,
J. Robert Oppenheimer:
>   twenty years ago
>   watching the bulldozers
>   tearing down pines
>   at Los Alamos.

Eight Sandbars on the Takano River

> Well water
> cool in
> summer

> warm in
> winter

> white radish root
> a foot long
> by its dark
> dirt hole
> green top
> her son.

cherry blossoms

the farmer never looks up
the woman serves sake
the tourists are sick or asleep

gone wild
straw berry vine
each year more small
sour
mulcht by pine.

white peeld logs
toppld in sap
scalpt branch
        spring
             woods

dragonfly
why wet moss
      your black
      stretch-stretch-
wing perch

strawberrytime

walking the tight-rope
high over the streets
with a hoe and two buckets
              of manure.

straight-backt
swaying stride
twelve-foot
     pine pole
      lightly,
on her head.

Asleep on the Train

Briefcase, tight garter
                over the knees
                peep of fat little thighs
roll and lean with the fall of the train

                eyes
shut.   mouth open.   so young women
tire with the rest   tired workers.
jerk with the speedup and slow

go-ahead signals flash by
the Special Express
has only one stop

where they wake from their trance
to themselves.

Four Poems for Robin

Siwashing it out once in Siuslaw Forest

I slept under   rhododendron
All night   blossoms fell
Shivering on   a sheet of cardboard
Feet stuck   in my pack
Hands deep   in my pockets
Barely   able   to   sleep.
I remembered   when we were in school
Sleeping together   in a big warm bed
We were   the youngest lovers
When we broke up   we were still nineteen.
Now our   friends are married
You teach   school back east
I dont mind   living this way
Green hills   the long blue beach
But sometimes   sleeping in the open
I think back   when I had you.

A spring night in Shokoku-ji

Eight years ago this May
We walked under cherry blossoms
At night in an orchard in Oregon.
All that I wanted then
Is forgotten now, but you.
Here in the night
In a garden of the old capital
I feel the trembling ghost of Yugao
I remember your cool body
Naked under a summer cotton dress.

An autumn morning in Shokoku-ji

Last night watching the Pleiades,
Breath smoking in the moonlight,
Bitter memory like vomit
Choked my throat.
I unrolled a sleeping bag
On mats on the porch
Under thick autumn stars.
In dream you appeared
(Three times in nine years)
Wild, cold, and accusing.
I woke shamed and angry:
The pointless wars of the heart.
Almost dawn. Venus and Jupiter.
The first time I have
Ever seen them close.

December at Yase

You said, that October,
In the tall dry grass by the orchard
When you chose to be free,
"Again someday, maybe ten years."

After college I saw you
One time. You were strange.
And I was obsessed with a plan.

Now ten years and more have
Gone by: I've always known
        where you were—
I might have gone to you
Hoping to win your love back.
You still are single.

I didn't.
I thought I must make it alone. I
Have done that.

Only in dream, like this dawn,
Does the grave, awed intensity
Of our young love
Return to my mind, to my flesh.

We had what the others
All crave and seek for;
We left it behind at nineteen.

I feel ancient, as though I had
Lived many lives.

And may never now know
If I am a fool
Or have done what my
       karma demands.

The Levels

   wild cat kittens
   born in the ceiling
       play sky gods
   thundering over the room.

           was it claude in the night?
was it thieves?

           above our northbound steps
the wild cat brood walks west

a hawk sails over the roof
a snake went under the floor

           how can hawks hunt in the rain?

I walk through the hallway:
the soul of a great-bellied cloud.

The Firing
for Les Blakebrough and the memory of John Chappell

Bitter blue fingers
Winter nineteen sixty-three A.D.
           showa thirty-eight
Over a low pine-covered splay of hills in Shiga
West-south-west of the outlet of Lake Biwa
Domura village set on sandy fans of the sweep
           and turn of a river
Draining the rotten-granite hills up Shigaraki
On a nineteen-fifty-seven Honda cycle model C
Rode with some Yamanashi wine "St Neige"
Into the farmyard and the bellowing kiln.
Les & John
In ragged shirts and pants, dried slip
Stuck to with pineneedle, pitch,
           dust, hair, woodchips;
Sending the final slivers of yellowy pine
Through peephole white blast glow
No saggars tilting yet and segers bending
           neatly in a row—
Even their beards caked up with mud & soot
Firing for fourteen hours. How does she go.

Porcelain & stoneware: cheese dish. twenty cups.
Tokuri. vases. black chawan
Crosslegged rest on the dirt eye cockt to smoke—

The hands you layed on clay
Kickwheeld, curling,
              creamd to the lip of nothing,
And coaxt to a white dancing heat that day
Will linger centuries in these towns and loams
And speak to men or beasts
When Japanese and English
Are dead tongues.

Work to Do Toward Town

Venus glows in the east,
              mars hangs in the twins.
Frost on the logs and bare ground
              free of house or tree.
Kites come down from the mountains
And glide quavering over the rooftops;
              frost melts in the sun.
A low haze hangs on the houses
              —firewood smoke and mist—
Slanting far to the Kamo river
              and the distant Uji hills.
Farmwomen lead down carts
              loaded with long white radish;
I pack my bike with books—
              all roads descend toward town.

Nansen

I found you on a rainy morning
After a typhoon
In a bamboo grove at Daitoku-ji.
Tiny wet rag with a

Huge voice, you crawled under the fence
To my hand. Left to die.
I carried you home in my raincoat.
"Nansen, cheese!" you'd shout an answer
And come running.
But you never got big,
Bandy-legged bright little dwarf—
Sometimes not eating, often coughing
Mewing bitterly at inner twinge.

Now, thin and older, you won't eat
But milk and cheese. Sitting on a pole
In the sun. Hardy with resigned
Discontent.
You just weren't made right. I saved you,
And your three-year life has been full
Of mild, steady pain.

Six Years

January
the pine tree is perfect
Walking in the snowhills the trail goes just right
Eat snow off pine needles
            the city's not so big, the
                    hills surround it.
Hieizan wrapped in his own cloud—
Back there no big houses, only a little farm shack
            crows cawing back and forth
            over the valley of grass-bamboo
                    and small pine.

If I had a peaceful heart it would look like this.
            the train down in the city

            was once a snowy hill

February
water taps running, the sun part out
cleaning house   sweeping floor
knocking cobwebs off the shoji   pap pap
wiping the wood and the mats with a wet rag
hands and knees on the veranda
cat-prints—make them a footwiper
                              of newspaper
wash the motorcycle.   fold clothes
start a new fire under the kama.
fill Mrs. Hosaka's kerosene stove tank,
get the cat hairs
out of the kotatsu.
take the sheets in from the bamboo poles
        where they're drying
put away the poles
stand them up below the eaves and
tie them with strings.
scrub out the floor of the bath and move the
                    mirror
            and towel rack
sweep out the genkan footprints
oil the clutch cable of the motorcycle
through the oil nipple under the handle grip
        —take off sweater now because it's
                too hot
            put back on the denim jacket   work
Nansen mews angrily because he feels so sick
all the different animals are persons

what will I do about *Liberation*.
6:30   bath
charcoal.   black.   the fire part red
the ash pure white

March
  Up in dirt alley
            eat korean food

drink white doboroku out of bowls
broil strips of beef & liver over coals
finish off with raw cow's womb
     in sauce, jade-white and oyster smooth
piss against the slab posts of the highways
         overhead,
bar girl girl-friend with a silver trinket cup
  hung on a neck-chain, she, gives us,
     all beer free.

  sift through night streets,
  Kato, Nagasawa, me, Sakaki,
  okinawan awamori bar
  clear glasses full up to the brim
  like flavord gin—must millet—
  with choppt onion.
        whirl taxi by
  glass door opening sharks, their,
     eyeballs to the sky—
     in coffee, tight butt tress;
  to station where the world trains meet
  I south around the loop
  yellow writhing dragon full of drunks
    & hall the windy concrete of
       Zojoji.

April

Firework bangs echo up the valley
  a twelve-foot snake banner
  glides off a bamboo pole at the top of a pine
two hundred people for lunch.
black umbrellas drying in the sun
—wash the red lacquer bowls
  and arrange on trays;
      cherry
  white blooms through the hilly country.

in the back right, lotus root
agé, konyaku, and a mikan.

front center sliced vinegared
    cucumber and udo.
middle, sweet red beans and
    salt yellow pickles.
front right soup
    white floating tofu
front left a tall red bowl with a bowl-like
    lid full of white steaming rice;
back left, low bowl with a round cake
    of special-fried tofu under the lid.

used trays come back
wash in heated water:
a wood tub three feet wide
drain in a five-foot basket
    on bamboo grating,
dry lacquer-ware twice and stow it in boxes
    carry them up to the
    right front corner of the white-plastered
    store house
        joined to the temple by a plank
        over the mud out back where
        corrugated iron sheets tilt
            over stacks of short firewood.

zokin in buckets of water.
wipe the long wood beams
wipe the feet of the Buddha
wipe under bronze incense stands
firecrackers boom from the shrine down the road
    five *go* of vinegar, four *go* of sugar
    five *sho* of rice;

old women half double scuttle to toilets
hoisting kimono   enroute to the door

the PA loudspeaker plays songs, plays the chants
    of the priests in the hall, the
        Dai-Hannya, Perfection
        of Wisdom

at Dragon Cloud Temple.
Five Hundred year Festival over
    they load in the busses
    or walk to their farms.

we wash ricepots, teacups, and bowls
baskets, dippers, buckets, and cauldrons,
take a bath, drink saké, and eat.
sitting on stools in the high-ceilingd kitchen

wind in the fir and the pine—
get under the quilts laid out on the mats
talk in the dark, and sleep.

May

    Sitting and resting on the crest, looking far
out over Yokkawa
to a corner of Ohara—
Sugi and fir and maple on the half-logged hill

    A delicate little hawk floats up
hunting delicate little country mice to eat.   Lute
Lake; the noble Sugi—a tree as great as Redwood, Douglas
Fir, Sequoia, Red Cedar, Sugar Pine.

    (To hell with all these cultures—history
after the Jurassic is a bore.   Sugi like Sequoia;
Hinoki like a cedar)

    Light wind, warm May sun & old woman bundling
brush by the trail—
men planing beams in a cool tin-roof shed
for the new Shaka-dō—fine double-edged saws
hand worn brush-hooks
battered jikatabi, funny breeches, cotton head-things
like the Navajo—
relit cigarette butts, sturdy walkers—hills and trails
of rocks and trees and people.

Quiet grey-wood copper-roofed old temple.   Down
and off into the Ogi village fields, and on along
steep ridges through bamboo brush to Ohara, Jakko-in.
Jizo there with his bug-scare clanker staff

(Night ride America; thin-lipped waitress whores—)

June
    students listen to the tapes—
Miss Nunome in a green dress
  she usually wears something open at the neck a dab.
Yamada-kun who can't look or answer straight
  yet seems not stupid
        "A nap is 'provisional sleep'"

Blue jumper on a white blouse (Miss Yokota)
                  car honks outside
Pink fur sunset
Miss   ?   in a crisp white pleated skirt falling in
        precise planes—her cheeks ruddy with rouge
        "people call her 'Janie'"
        "people collar Janie"

Van Gogh print on the wall: vase of flowers all yellow
          & tawny.
Sun setting on Atago Mountain

    "strength   strap   strand   strut   struck
    strum   strung   strop   street   streak"

    "cord   ford   gorge   dwarf   forthnorth
    course   horse   doors   stores   dorm   form
    warp   sort   short   sport   porch"

 pingpong game in the hall
Motorcycle rumbles in the streets—
horns—dark nights rain up sudden on the tin bar
        roof next door

"try tea   buy ties   weigh Tim   buy type
flat tea   bright ties   greet Tim   met Tess
stout trap   wet trip   right track   light tread
high tree   Joy tries   gay trim   fry tripe"

Why that's old Keith Lampe's voice, deep & clear

"ripples   battles   saddles   doubled   dazzled
wondered   hammered   eastern   western   southern"

Language torn up like a sewer or highway
& layed out on text
Page and tape.

July

kicking through sasa
       bear grass bamboo
            pass into thickets.
       dowse a wand knocking down spider
          net us on all sides
          sticky and strong

chirrr; semi
  hangs under   bamboo leaf

       in the heat
       sweat
   kick through sasa
snaking uphill in thickets

below, taro
  terraces down to the beach.
swim among mild red jellyfish

      a woman pickt shells, stoopt over
               bare breasted
      kneedeep in seaweed rocks
      her two boys

        play in the tall cliff
            shade

cross away.
          from bamboo to pinegrove
          three axes
                someone
          naps under a tree

                  August
night   town of lights
at sea
    unpainted rough prowed squid fishers
boats with their gas mantle lamps
miles off shore.
                counted two hundred.
                wind curls on the salt-
                sticky chest, caked ribs
      sticky sea

day dodging sun
    zigzagging barefoot
    on blistering rocks
    to dive, skim under reefs
            down along ledges
    looking for oysters or snails
            or at fish

night without blanket
sleeping on sand.
          the
    squid-fisher lights.
one-lung four-cycle engines

they sleep all day under the eaves
                headland houses
    half-naked on mats.
the wives gather shells

coarse-tongued, sun black
or working at carrying rocks
for the new coast road

   eating big lunch balls
   of cold rice.

tobacco and grapes on the dunes.
some farmers come down to the beach
in the dark   white lanterns
   sending out rowboats, swinging
a thousand-foot net
   five times down the length of the beach.
we help haul
            tumbling pockets

            glittering eyes and white bellies—
   a full-thighed young woman
   her dress tucked up in her pants
            tugs and curses
   an old man calling
   across the dark water sculling

the last haul a yard-wide ray
   she snaps off his switching
      devil-tail stinger
   & gives us three fish.

they beach their boats
full of nets
their lamps bob over the dunes

we sleep in the sand
and our salt.

September
Rucksack braced on a board, lashed tight on back,
sleeping bags, map case, tied on the gas tank

sunglasses, tennis shoes, your long tan in shorts
north on the west side of Lake Biwa
Fukui highway still being built,
      crankcase bangd on rocks—
          pusht to the very edge by a blinded truck
  I saw the sea below beside my knee:
you hung on and never knew how close.

   In Fukui found a ryokan cheap
washt off each other's dust by the square wood tub
ate dinner   on worn mats
    clean starcht yukata
    warm whisky with warm water,
all the shoji open, second floor,
    told each other
  what we'd never said before, ah,
    dallying on mats
      whispering sweat
    cools our kissing skin—

next morning rode the sunny hills, Eihei-ji,
got the luggage rack arc-welded
back through town and to the shore,
    miles-long spits and dunes of pine

and made love on the sand

October

The Rich have money; Give to the Rich!
   —J.C.: "All suffering is self-willed."
   you CAN take it with you
   [THE OTHERWORLD FORWARDING SERVICE
   leave your money with us;
   we'll get it through]—
Low-order Tantric phenomena.

   "God in cinders; wreck on child."

J.C.'s law—"You can't get out of the same trap
until you get into it."   Hemp
    "retted" with dew or water; then the fibers
    "scutched"
Somehow life has been like . . . every day is Flag Day for me . . .
Cold turkey   with all the tremens

    [File your absence
     with NULL & VOID
        —Gilt-edged Insecurities—
    loose ends bought in vacant lots
        & the
     NOWHERE VACUUM TRUST]

      says the Armpit from Outer Space.

"1000 shares of *mikan* futures" (she's a
    Kshatriya—hell yes,
    let her run things)

Promiscuity: they sell themselves short.
        All
       Dragon-Riders

All,   Dharma Kings.

November
    hoeing the hatake, pull out all the clover bulb—
    long white root stem, deep
       and other long roots.
    "those daikon will rot in December, the frost;
       smoothing the row.
    "this daikon will live through the winter.
    but it don't taste so good as the other

    white lime sprinkld on fresh turnd furrows like snow
    these acid soils.   see that daikon?
       all yellow because the ground sourd.
    tiny gobo seeds, grow into twisty two foot long roots.

          spinach seeds next
soaked over night in warm water
left from the bath.   makes them germinate quick.

dump weeds from the wheelbarrow back in the bamboo grove
peas planted in double rows, making holes
                            four inches apart
with fore finger, stick in two seeds
                      poke it in
    later fertilize all with the dippers
    yoke of wood buckets, that "human" smell
    not near so bad as you think

clean off these heavy heavy boots
when the soil is all tilld and the winter seeds
sowed
                casts of mud
            with the back of a sickle
            stooping in gravel

December

Three a.m.—a far bell
    coming closer:
fling up useless futon on the shelf;
outside, ice-water in the hand & wash the face.
    Ko the bird-head, silent, skinny,
    swiftly cruise the room with
    salt plum tea.

Bell from the hondo chanting sutras.   Gi:
deep bell, small bell, wooden drum.
    sanzen at four
    kneel on icy polisht boards in line:

Shukuza rice and pickles
barrel and bucket
dim watt bulb.
    till daybreak nap upright.
                sweep

garden and hall.
frost outside
               wind through walls

At eight the lecture bell.   high chair.
Ke helps the robe—red, gold,
     black lacquer in the shadow
     sun and cold

Saiza a quarter to ten
soup and rice dab on the bench
feed the hungry ghosts
     back in the hall by noon.
two o clock sanzen
three o clock bellywarmer
     boild up soup-rice mush.
dinging and scuffing.   out back smoke,
               and talk.

At dusk, at five,
black robes draw into the hall.
     stiff joints, sore knees bend
     the jiki pads by with his incense lit,
                    bells,
     wood block crack
& stick slips round the room
on soft straw sandals.

seven, sanzen
tea, and a leaf-shaped candy.
kinhin at eight with folded hands—
     single-file racing in flying robes leaning
               to wake—

nine o clock one more sanzen
ten, hot noodles,
three bowls each.

Sit until midnight.   chant.
     make three bows and pull the futon down.

roll in the bed—
black.

A far bell coming closer

Envoy to Six Years
Down in the engine room again
Touching a silver steam line
　　　　with a tiny brush.
Soogy the oil sump—gloves and rags—
—"how long you say you been Japan?
　　　six years eh you must like the place.
　　　those guys in New York
　　　　　　　bunch of fuckin crooks.
　　　they ain't just selling
　　　little two-bit caps, they making books."

Rinse out the soogy rag in kerosene,
And wipe off sooty oil condenser line
Driving forward geared turbine—
The driveshaft treetrunk thick,
Bearings bathed in flowing oil,

The belly of the ship.

— *III* —
Kālī

On a corpse / dread / laughing /
four arms / a sword / a severed head /
removing fear / giving /
wearing skulls / black / naked

When I went down
to sea-lion town
my wife was dead
the canoes were gone

Alysoun

My mother called you Robin.
I curst your blisters
when we fought brush
hunting the trail
in the forest gorge of the Elwha—
forded creeks and found the path,
climbed three switchback miles
to camp and cook   by dark.
You whimpered all night long
with evil dreams
in a tossing bed by me
under the low limbs of a Silver fir.

To Hell with Your Fertility Cult

To hell with your Fertility Cult, I
never did want to be fertile,
you think this world is just
a goddamn oversize cunt, don't you? Everything
crowding in and out of it like a railway
terminal   and isn't that nice?
all those people going on trips.
well this is what it feels like, she said,
—and knocked the hen off the nest, grabbed
an egg and threw it at him, right in the face,
the half-formed chick half clung, half slid
half-alive, down over his cheekbone, around
the corner of his mouth, part of it thick
yellow and faintly visible bones and it drippt
down his cheek and chin
—he had nothing to say.

For a Stone Girl at Sanchi

half asleep on the cold grass
        night rain flicking the maples
under a black bowl upside-down
on a flat land
        on a wobbling speck
smaller than stars,
                        space,
the size of a seed,
        hollow as bird skulls.
light flies across it
        —never is seen.

a big rock weatherd funny,
old tree trunks turnd stone,
        split rocks and find clams.
                all that time
loving;
two flesh persons changing,
        clung to, doorframes
        notions, spear-hafts
in a rubble of years.
                touching,
this dream pops. it was real:
        and it lasted forever.

Robin

I always miss you—
last fall, back from the mountains
you'd left San Francisco
now I'm going north again
        as you go south.

I sit by a fire at the ocean.
How many times I've
hitchhiked away;
                the same pack on my back.

Rain patters on the rhododendron
cloud sweeps in from the sea over sand dunes
and stoopt lodgepole pine.

Thinking of the years since we parted.
last week I dreamed of you—
buying a bag of groceries
                    for Hatch.

Sutton Lake, Oregon, 16 June 1954

North Beach Alba

waking half-drunk in a strange pad
making it out to the cool gray
        san francisco dawn—
white gulls over white houses,
        fog down the bay,
tamalpais a fresh green hill in the new sun,
driving across the bridge in a beat old car
        to work.

Could She See the Whole Real World with Her Ghost Breast Eyes Shut Under a Blouse Lid?

"A woman smells like fresh-plowed ground"
"A man smells like chewing on a maple twig"
 Rockslides in the creek bed;
        picking ferns in the dark gorge.

Goldwire soft short-haired girl, one bare leg up.
Cursing the morning.
        "it's *me* there's no—"

Yellow corn woman on the way to dead-land
        by day a dead jackrabbit,

by night a woman nursing her live baby.
Bridge of sunflower stalks.
Nursing a live baby.
                         daytime, dead-land, only a hill.
Cursing the morning.
"My grandmother said they stepped single
& the hoof was split"—deer

Yellow corn girl
Blue corn girl
Squawberry flower girl

"Once a bear gets hooked on garbage there's no cure."

Night

All the dark hours everywhere repairs
and rights the hearts & tongues of men
and makes the cheerful dawn—

the safe place in a blanket burrow
hissing in ears and nibbling wet lips
smoothing eyebrows and a stroke up the back of the knee,
licking the nape of the neck and tickling the tense
breast with fluttering eyelid, flitting
light fingers on thin chest skin,
feeling the arteries tangle the hollow groin,
arching the back backward, swinging sidewise,
        bending forward, dangling on all fours.

the bit tongue and trembling ankle,
joined palms and twined legs,
the tilted chin and beat cry,
hunched shoulders and a throb in the belly.
teeth swim in loose tongues, with toes curled.
eyes snapped shut, and quick breath.
hair all tangled together.

the radio that was never turned off.
the record soundlessly spinning.
the half-closed door swinging on its hinges.
the cigarette that burned out.
the melon seeds spit on the floor.
the mixed fluids drying on the body.
the light left on in the other room.
the blankets all thrown on the floor and the birds
       cheeping in the east.
the mouth full of grapes and the bodies like loose leaves.
the quieted hearts, passive caress, a quick exchange
      of glances with eyes then closed again,
the first sunlight hitting the shades.

A Dry Day Just Before the Rainy Season

DRUNK last night
    drunk the night before

talking and shouting and laughing, maybe
I should've been home reading—
"all right *don't* leave me alone—
    do something with me then!"
              the landlady's son
heard through a back wall window.

Sunday morning, november, plenty of birds
a pair of red-shafted flickers
        on the peach tree
     stretch wings
        showing the white-flash back
      linnets crack seeds at the feed tray.

Not too hung over—
I suppose I'll get drunk tonight.
one year: from rain to wistaria,
apricot blossoms, all night singing,
     sleeping on the floor,

off to work in the Sierra
     back in august
    cool fog, dryness,
leaves on the fruit trees fall.

Soon the rain starts again.
smell of burning leaves.
orange berries, red berries a
       sudden jump cat
          —I know him—
bee rattles in a flower
    this warm sober day

I wonder what I said to everybody

Another for the Same

  a cut reed floating
  a sort of Lady Komachi
  wiser than me
  the best of your beauty

  always hidden, yū

  "a glow of red leaves in dark woods"
  in your gray eyes.
  look at me stranger
  I've been hungry, alone, cold,
  but not lonely
  must I be lonely with you?
  Danae to sunlight, starlight,
  wind, snuffing it on every
            high hill
  of the mind.

  you really are going nowhere
  I wish I was going with you.
  to rock, to space

    —I cannot shake this love of mine
which is so much less
than yours.

This Tokyo

Peace, war, religion,
Revolution, will not help.
This horror seeds in the agile
Thumb and greedy little brain
That learned to catch bananas
With a stick.
        The millions of us worthless
To each other or the world
Or selves, the sufferers of the real
Or of the mind—this world
Is but a dream?   Or human life
A nightmare grafted on solidity
Of planet—mental, mental,
Shudder of the sun—praise
Evil submind freedom with de Sade
Or highest Dantean radiance of the God
Or endless Light or Life or Love
Or simple tinsel angel in the
Candy heaven of the poor—
Mental divinity or beauty, all,
Plato, Aquinas, Buddha,
Dionysius of the Cross, all
Pains or pleasures hells or
What in sense or flesh
Logic, eye, music, or
Concoction of all faculties
& thought tend—tend—to this:
        This gaudy apartment of the rich.
The comfort of the U.S. for its own.
The shivering pair of girls
Who dyked each other for a show
A thousand yen before us men

—In an icy room—to buy their relatives
A meal. This scramble spawn of
Wire dirt rails tin board blocks
Babies, students, crookt old men.
          We live
On the meeting of sun and earth.
We live—we live—and all our lives
Have led to this, this city,
Which is soon the world, this
Hopelessness where love of man
Or hate of man could matter
None, love if you will or
Contemplate or write or teach
But know in your human marrow you
Who read, that all you tread
Is earthquake rot and matter mental
Trembling, freedom is a void,
Peace war religion revolution
Will not help.

27 December 1956

Kyoto Footnote

She said she lived in Shanghai as a child
And moved to Kobe, then Kyoto, in the war;
While putting on her one thin white brassiere.
She walked me to the stair and all the girls
Gravely and politely said take care,
     out of the whorehouse into cool night air.

The Manichaeans
for Joanne

Our portion of fire
      at this end of the milky way
(the Tun-huang fragments say, Eternal Light)
Two million years from M 31
      the galaxy in Andromeda—
My eyes sting with these relics.
Fingers mark time.
      semen is everywhere
Two million seeds in a spurt.

Bringing hand close to your belly
      a shade off touching,
Until it feels the radiating warmth.

Your far off laughter
Is an earthquake in your thigh.
Coild like Ourabouros
      we are the Naga King
This bed is Eternal Chaos
            —and wake in a stream of light.

Cable-car cables
Whip over their greast rollers
Two feet underground.
      hemmed in by mysteries
      all moving in order.
A moment at this wide intersection,
Stoplights change, they are
      catastrophes among stars,
A red whorl of minotaurs
            gone out.
The trumpet of doom
      from a steamship at Pier 41.

Your room is cold,
      in the shade-drawn dusk inside
Light the oven, leave it open

Semi transparent jet flames rise
fire,
Together we make eight pounds of
Pure white mineral ash.

Your body is fossil
As you rest with your chin back
—your arms are still flippers
your lidded eyes lift from a swamp
Let us touch—for if two lie together
Then they have warmth.

We shall sink in this heat
of our arms
Blankets like rock-strata fold
dreaming as
Shiva and Shakti
And keep back the cold.

Artemis

Artemis,
Artemis,
so I saw you naked—
well GO and get your goddam'd
virginity back
me, me,
I've got to feed my hounds.

Madly Whirling Downhill

madly whirling downhill
THE WITCH
who can make the electric lights go out
who can, as she sits in her apartment under the street
make you follow.

the two of them lived for years
in an old house in town.
no one ever came to see about bills
no one ever entered or left it
    that house.

he knows what the end will be
calm and he doesn't care,
    there is no one, no way
      to save him.

Xrist

Your hanging face I know, I know your tree.
You can't hide under Hebrew
    & I don't pity you
Burning yourself alive in Athens to impress the mob
Having your last wild fling—in drag—at the altar—
    robed in cornstarch
    and stolen Toltec jewels
        Ziggurat rotgut
Cutting your own balls off—dog priests—kybele
The mincing step—shy glance—Graves thot you lame
Horrified virgin dropping in a pool.
    whipping the bullshit roarer
Your flayed penis flaring
Gold wrought infibula
       —circumcized girls.

New World popcorn, Polynesian spit—
Dropping a log on the couple where they fuck
      the dance, the whips,
Saviour of Man!
  —who put the hell to be harrowed?

The bruisd snake coils in the grass
He is wise;
      there are trees in high places;
Keep your blood off the crotch of our tree.

More Better

Uncle,   Oh uncle
  seventy dogs

O centipede
      bit me in bed
wind in the red leaf berry tree

     whynes

Bull you are
too brown.

The Persimmon
was too fat   the tree its

branches too bent down.

For Plants

The ancient virgin
picking mushrooms
in the damp forest
gloom

    Peyotl
    dream-child bud
glowing in hollow desert
    HO   hands
  gather the holy baby
faceted jewel bush
        child of the
sky is solid rainbow
      squash maiden
      corn girl

hair prongs   root

suck magic from dirt, rains
　　wash down rainbow
and bury him under the floor.

long trumpet of thornapple flower
datura highsmoke
scoopt in blanket
　　james. town. weed.

gum of hashish
passt through the porthole
bumboat to tanker

　　half-glimpst
　　"glow of red lips in dark hair"
　　slave-of-god-dancer

hidden
　　　　in glittering fall.

ear, eye, belly
　　　　cascara　　calamus

cut bark is vapor
of paradise odor—
brick for a pillow
rolld in a blanket,
　　　　to see

Artemis naked:
the soft white
　　　　buried sprout
of the world's first
seed.

What Do They Say

The glimpse of a once-loved face
                    gone into a train.
Lost in a new town, no one knows the name.
          lone man sitting in the park
Chanced on by a friend
                    of thirty years before,
                    what do they say.
Play chess with bottle caps.
          "for sale" sign standing in the field:
                    dearest, dearest,
Soot on the sill,
          a garden full of weeds

The Six Hells of the Engine Room

The Hot Air Hell of the fiddley where rails
are too hot to touch and your shoes burn

The oily cramp Hell of the bilges
painting underside pipes—saltwater and oil
ankledeep slosh in the shoe.

Inside-the-boiler Hell, you go in through a
hot brick hole where it's black
and radiates heat

Back of the boilers-Hell soogying valve-wheels
                    and flanges

Shaft Alley Hell getting rubbed by the rough
spinning shaft

Paint Locker Hell, it smells fumes,
your hands get all sticky.

Maya
for Peter Orlovsky

white clothes—white skin—
white cows—
          the dream of India—
                    and flowers—
teeth stained red,
hair silver
like that old Jain jeweller
wouldn't touch meat

a little *O* now and then

Mother of the Buddhas, Queen of Heaven,
Mother of the Sun; Marici, Goddess of the Dawn
for Bhikku Ghosananda

                old sow in the mud
                bristles caked black
                down her powerful neck

                tiny hooves churn
                squat body slithering
                deep in food dirt

                her warm filth,
                deep-plowing snout,
                dragging teats

                those who keep her
                or eat her
                are cast out

                she turns her small eye
                from earth to
                look up at me.

Nalanda, Bihar

Wandering the Old, Dirty Countries

—in your clean overalls
who's poor?
              Evtushenko or the
              shop foreman won't say.
I'm not speaking for America,
But for poets—
              well yes malnutrition
Bad teeth, shit-stained babies
Flies around the eyes,
And nobody pities them
              but the humanist bourgeoisie
              and the Komsomol kids.

              over the jolting buses
Bustards   loosefeathered
Vultures hunched on hills

That fat baby flesh, *khol* eyes
              feed them well.
Them soviets, them
U.S. men
Helping.

On Our Way to Khajuraho

On our way to
              Khajuraho
the bus stoppt, we ate
              guavas
cheap.
              a toilet
with a picture of a woman and a man,
                            two doors,
              in the square
dusty village somewhere on the way.
       a girl thirteen

gave pice in change
to an old woman bought some sweets;
the men of Bundelkhand
wear elf-tongued
     flowery leather shoes.

she must have been low caste.
the girl stood off
     little coins
crosst from hand to hand

Anuradhapura City of the Pleiades
for Joanne

Anuradhapura city of the Pleiades
    is
      cool and grassy
underfoot.
white monkeys, white
    granite
  posts lie tumbled crisscross
    white
dome stupa with the spire tower gold

network oak like
her black dress on
kneeling thighs
  making a rubbing
       on the foot floor
  moon shape stone;
lion, elephant, geese;
ring below the stairs.

of all the buildings nothing but a plinth.
  us married;
meadows of new grass.

Circumambulating Arunachala

for centuries sadhus live and die
in dolmen rock-slab huts near
        Arunachala

Small girls with gaudy flowers
flash down the bare walk road,
        the weight, the power,
the full warm brilliance of the human mind
        behind their eyes:
                they die or sicken in a year.

Below the hill—
wells, ponds, spiky trees,
carvd fragments of soft bodies,
        female bellies,
                centuries old.

7: VII

I can't look out over cities without thinking of carpenters,
plumbers, hod-carriers, cement-mixer truck drivers, plasterers

how many hours were they paid for to build up Seattle, or
Portland, (which has such dark carpets—such white fir skulls—)
skeleton lathe behind plaster laid on so cool—creamy under the
trowel—dries to a powder, spidery lines. block bricks, shake
roofs

san francisco white stairstep-up rooflines. stucco & tile
houses laid out in rows in the Sunset—photos after the quake
the weird frames of half-broken buildings. lunchpails in unfin-
ished walls—how long since eyes laid on that rafter

in the hills they cast mud & fire it for rooftiles—the gray
waves of Kyoto—highschool kids study their english or math
in cramp ceilinged second floor rooms to the racket of looms

on the ground floor, the shimmering heat of the sun-facing
southward scree roof—

new buildings reinforced concrete strung full of wiring and
piping, Plant in the basement—walls knock in the night—
laundry ghosts chatter on flat modern roofs looking off at the
shrine forest hills

the drainage of streets, hollow mountains in rows, noisy with
alien molecules burning at speeds past belief, how they sift—
how they clutter—

layers of mohenjo-daro, nine cities deep, a kiln at the end of
the age built out in the street

forests are covered with mud and asbestos, the riverbeds
sucked up and cast into plates hung on melted-down oxides

mankind your bowels are as grinding and heavy as those
which forced leaves into coal, burned sand to obsidian; you
draw up and lead along water, your arm rises and falls, you
break through things as they are.

Nanao Knows
for Nanao Sakaki

Mountains, cities, all so
                light, so loose.   blankets
Buckets—throw away—
Work left to do.
                it doesn't last.

Each girl is real
                her nipples harden, each has damp,
                her smell, her hair—
—What am I to be saying.
There they all go
Over the edge, dissolving.

Rivetters bind up
Steel rod bundles
For wet concrete.
In and out of forests, cities, families
        like a fish.

Lying in Bed on a Late Morning

Lying in bed on a late morning
A new girl beside me,
        I hardly know—

Half-awake, dreaming,
I smile the smile,
        you smile, when you sing.

Dreaming and smiling,
    dream of your long smooth legs.

Looking at Pictures to Be Put Away

Who was this girl
In her white night gown
Clutching a pair of jeans

On a foggy redwood deck.
She looks up at me tender,
Calm, surprised,

What will we remember
Bodies thick with food and lovers
After twenty years.

The Truth Like the Belly of a Woman Turning
for Ali Akbar Khan

The truth
like the belly of a woman turning,
      always passes by.
      is always true.

throat and tongue—
     do we all feel the same?
      sticky hair curls

quivering throat
pitch of jaw
         strung pull
      skinnd turn, what will
    be the wrack
         of all the old—

who
cares.
     CRYING
all these passt,
       losst,
           years.

     "It always changes"
       wind child
       wound child

MOTHERS AND DAUGHTERS
    live oak and madrone.

For John Chappell

Over the Arafura sea, the China sea,
   Coral sea, Pacific
chains of volcanoes in the dark—

you in Sydney where it's summer;
I imagine that last ride outward
late at night.
                    stiff new gears—tight new engine
up some highway I have never seen
too fast—too fast—
        like I said at Tango
            when you went down twice on gravel—

Did you have a chance to think
o shit I've fucked it now
instant crash and flight and sudden death—

        Malaya, Indonesia
        Taiwan, the Philippines, Okinawa
            families sleeping—reaching—
            humans by the millions
            world of breathing flesh.

me in Kyoto.   You in Australia
wasted in the night.
black beard, mad laugh, and sadly serious brow.
        earth lover;   shaper and maker.
            potter, cooker,

        now be clay in the ground.

                                    1964

How Many Times

We walk down streets together
            switching hip globes
            clean skin, neat smell,

why these clothes.
breast, the bra,   stitch & buckle—soft—

(sweaty farm girl on the road to
Yasé   sold me bunch of daikon
nipples brushing bare along
the blue work-jacket seam—)

above the bottom part the hose is browner
              held by funny things.
                 bulge of thigh—softest skin of all—

now   am I all right? ah.
presst down,   open,
       were I   as open,

          we shall do this
                 how
          many times.

Tasting the Snow

The family—the little family—
       table edge and napkin wipe
       the warm   you hold in your arms
       children, saliva, washt clothes
Hand-holds and curves of the palm,
                                all that
Good
       fuss—trust—love—and I
          know not—

Falls away from me now.
Like the two tears from your eyes.
       life and hope had fed, and fed,
       on such,
                 and my pace slacknd.

Out the door:
Icy and clear in the dark.
          once I had thought,

laughing and kissing,
  how cosy to be tuckt in bed—
let them sleep;
Now I can turn to the hunt.

Blade sharp and hair on end
  over the boulders
  eager
          tasting the snow.

Go Round

Plunging donkey   puberty devi
    flings her thighs, swinging long
  legs backward on her mount
hair tosst
          gangle arms but eyes
          her eyes and smile are elsewhere:
swelling out and sailing to the future
  off beyond five-colord clouds.

  we enter this world trailing
          slippery clouds of guts
          incense of our flowery flesh
blossoms;   crusht;   re-turning
  knots of rose meat open out to—over—
  five-hued clouds—
the empty diamond of all space

And into withered, sturdy, body, stalks.
the dry branch dropping seeds.

          plunging donkey
prancing horse and trappings
  her mother watching,
          shopping bag let down
beside her knees, against the bench,
in her eyes too the daughter

whirling
looking outward, knowing,

       having once
        steppt up on the
merry-go-
Round.

[*After Rāmprasād Sen*]

Arms shielding my face
Knees drawn up
Falling through flicker
Of womb after womb,
        through worlds,
Only begging, Mother,
        must I be born again?

Snyder says: you bear me, nurse me
I meet you, always love you,
      you dance
       on my chest and thigh

Forever born again.

— *IV* —
Back

The Old Dutch Woman

The old dutch woman would spend half a day
Pacing the backyard where I lived
                              in a fixed-up shed,
What did she see.
Wet leaves, the rotten tilted-over
                   over-heavy heads
Of domesticated flowers.
                    I knew Indian Paintbrush
Thought nature meant mountains,
Snowfields, glaciers and cliffs,
White granite waves underfoot.

Heian ladies
Trained to the world of the garden,
                         poetry,
      lovers slippt in with at night—

My Grandmother standing wordless
        fifteen minutes
Between rows of loganberries,
      clippers poised in her hand.

New leaves on the climbing rose
Planted last fall.
   —tiny bugs eating the green—

Like once watching
                   mountaingoats:
Far over a valley
Half into the
                   shade of the headwall,
      Pick their way over the snow.

Nature   Green Shit

The brittle hollow stalks of sunflower
    heads broke over full of dusty seed
    peeld, it tastes good, small

Why should dirt be dirty when you clean up.
    stop to like the dead or dying plants,
    twisted witherd grass

Picking the last peppers
Soft and wrinkld; bright green, cool

    what a lump of red flesh *I* am!

Violet dawn sky—no more Arcturus—
    beside the sugi nursery where we
    pulld down vines
    house lights constellations
    still   on the hill.

Heavy frosted cabbage.
    (all night porch bulb—)
    paper boy squealing bike brakes

    hey that's my cat!
Coming home.

To the Chinese Comrades

The armies of China and Russia
Stand facing across a wide plain.
Krushchev on one side and Mao on the other,
Krushchev calls out
      "Pay me the money you owe me!"
Mao laughs and laughs. long hair flops.
His face round and smooth.

The armies start marching—they meet—
Without clashing, they march through each other,
Lines between lines.
All the time Mao Tse-tung laughing.
He takes heaps of money.
He laughs and he gives it to Krushchev.

Chairman Mao's belongings on the March:
"Two cotton and wool mixture blankets,
A sheet, two pants and jackets,
A sweater
A patched umbrella
An enamel mug for a rice bowl
A gray brief-case with nine pockets."

Like Han-shan standing there
        —a rubbing off some cliff
Hair sticking out smiling
    maybe rolling a homegrown
    Yenan cigarette
Took a crack at politics
The world is all one.
—crawling out that hillside cave dirt house—

            (whatever happened to Wong—
                quit Chinese school, slugged his dad
                left the laundry, went to sea
                out the golden gate—did he make AB?—)

black eggshell-thin
pots of Lung-shan
maybe three thousand years B C

You have killed
I saw the Tibetans just down from the passes
Limping in high felt boots
Sweating in furs
Flatland heat.
            and from Almora gazing at Trisul
            the new maps from Peking

call it all China
clear down to here, & the Gangetic plain—

From the Hongkong N.T. on a pine rise
See the other side: stub fields.
Geese, ducks, and children
            far off cries.
Down the river, tiny men
Walk a plank—maybe loading
                                little river boat.
Is that China
Flat, brown, and wide?

The ancestors
what did they leave us.
K'ung fu-tze, some buildings, remain.
    —tons of soil gone.
Mountains turn desert.
Stone croppt flood, strippt hills,
The useless wandering river mouths,
Salt swamps
Silt on the floor of the sea.

Wind-borne glacial flour—
Ice-age of Europe,
Dust storms from Ordos to Finland
The loess of Yenan.
        glaciers
                "shrink
    and vanish like summer clouds . . ."

CROSS THE SNOWY MOUNTAIN
WE SHALL SEE CHAIRMAN MAO!

The year the long march started I was four.
How long has this gone on.
Rivers to wade, mountains to cross—
Chas. Leong showed me how to hold my chopsticks
                            like the brush—
Upstairs a chinese restaurant catty-corner
                        from the police

Portland, oregon, nineteen fifty-one,
Yakima Indian horseman, hair black as crows.
   shovel shaped incisors,
     epicanthic fold.
Misty peaks and cliffs of the Columbia,
Old loggers vanish in the rocks.
They wouldn't tote me rice and soy-sauce
                 cross the dam
"Snyder you gettin just like
   a damned Chinaman."
Gambling with the Wasco and the Wishram
By the river under Hee Hee Butte
& bought a hard round loaf of weird bread
From a bakery in a tent
In a camp of Tibetans
At Bodh-Gaya
Where Gautama used to stay.

On hearing Joan Baez singing "East Virginia"
   Those were the days.
   we strolld under blossoming cherries
   ten acres of orchard
   holding hands, kissing,
   in the evening talkt Lenin and Marx.
You had just started out for Beijing.

   I slippt my hand under her blouse
   and undid her brassiere.
   I passt my hand over her breasts
   her sweet breath, it was too warm for May.
   I thought how the whole world
   my love, could love like this;
   blossoms, the books, revolution
   more trees, strong girls, clear springs;
You took Beijing

Chairman Mao, you should quit smoking.
   Dont bother those philosophers
Build dams, plant trees,
   dont kill flies by hand.

Marx was another westerner.
          it's all in the head.
You dont need the bomb.
          stick to farming.
Write some poems. Swim the river.
          those blue overalls are great.
Dont shoot me, let's go drinking.
          just
Wait.

For the West

I

Europa,
     your red-haired
     hazel-eyed
     Thracian girls
your beautiful thighs
everlasting damnations
and grave insouciance—

a woman's country,
even your fat little popes.
                    groin'd temples
                    groov'd canals
—me too, I see thru
   these green eyes—

the Cowboys and Indians all over Europe
sliding down snowfields on shields.

what next? a farmer's
corner of the planet—
                    who cares if you are White?

2

this universe—"one turn"—turnd over.
   gods of revolution.
sharp beards—fur flap hats—
      kalmuck whip-swingers,

hugging and kissing
white and black,
men, men,
girls, girls,

wheat, rye, barley,
  adding asses to donkeys
  to fat-haunch horses,
it takes tractors and the
  multiple firing of pistons
to make revolution.
still turning. flywheel heavy
   elbow-bending awkward
   flippety drive goes
on, white chicks;

dark skin
   burns the tender lobes.
foggy white skin bleacht out,
pale nipple,
pale breast never freckled,

 they turn and
slowly turn away—

3

Ah, that's America:
the flowery glistening oil blossom
 spreading on water—
it was so tiny, nothing, now it keeps expanding
all those colors,
   our world
 opening inside outward toward us,
each part swelling and turning

who would have thought such turning;
as it covers,
        the colors fade.
and the fantastic patterns
        fade.
I see down again through clear water.

        it is the same
ball bounce rhyme the
        little girl was singing,
        all those years.

7. IV. 64

up at dawn,
sweep the deck and empty garbage
chip paint down below.
all my friends have children
& I'm getting old. at least enough to be
a First Mate or an Engineer.
now I know I'll never be a Ph.D.
dumping oily buckets
in the middle of the ocean—
swirls of dried
paint drips,
white, silver, blue and green
down the outside,
full of oil—rags—
wet paint slosh coils,
marbled grease and cream.

                    pacific near panama

Twelve Hours out of New York after Twenty-five Days at Sea

The sun always setting behind us.
I did not mean to come this far.
 —baseball games on the radio
        commercials that turn your hair—
The last time I saild this coast
Was nineteen forty eight
Washing galley dishes
        reading Gide in French.
In the rucksack I've got three *nata*
Handaxes from central Japan;
The square blade found in China
        all the way back to Stone—
A novel by Kafu NAGAI
About geisha in nineteen-ten
With a long thing about gardens
And how they change through the year;
Azalea ought to be blooming
        in the yard in Kyoto now.
Now we are north of Cape Hatteras
Tomorrow docking at eight.
        mop the deck round the steering gear,
Pack your stuff and get paid.

                        19.IV.1964

Across Lamarck Col

Descending hillsides in
        half morning light, step over
        small down pine,
I see myself as stony granite face.
All that we did was human,
        stupid, easily forgiven,
Not quite right.

A giving stream you give another
        should have been mine
      had I been not me
        —to whom not given—
Who most needed waited,
Stoppt off, my me,—my fault
    your black block mine—our—ours—
Myself as stony granite face—
You giving him because an   other

I also now become another.
              what I
Had not from you, for you,
              with a new lover,
Give, and give, and give, and
              take.

Hop, Skip, and Jump
for Jim and Annie Hatch

    the curvd lines toe-drawn, round cornerd squares
bulge out doubles from its single pillar line, like,
Venus of the Stone Age.
she takes stone,
with a white quartz band for her lagger.
                              she
    takes a brown-staind salt-sticky cigarette
                        butt.
he takes a mussel shell. he takes a clamshell. she takes
a stick.
he is tiny, with a flying run & leap—
shaggy blond—misses all the laggers,
            tumbles from one foot.
            they are dousing
a girl in a bikini down the beach
            first with cold seawater
            then with wine.
double-leg   single-leg   stork stalk turn

on the end-square—   hop, fork, hop, scoop the lagger,
   we have all trippt and fallen.
   surf rough and full of kelp,
  all the ages—
draw a line on another stretch of sand—
                  and—
              everybody try
to do the hop, skip, and jump.

4.X.1964 Muir Beach

August was Foggy
for Sally

August was foggy,
September dry.
October grew too hot.
Napa and Sonoma grasslands,
         brushlands,
      burned.

In November
    then,
We all set back the clock,
    and suddenly it rained.

The first green shoots of grass.
      you
    like some slender
    fresh young plant
turn smooth and cool across me
    in the night.

touch, and taste, and interlace
    deep in the ground.
      new rain.
as we begin our life.

Beneath My Hand and Eye the Distant Hills,
Your Body

What my hand follows on your body
Is the line. A stream of love
   of heat, of light,   what my
   eye   lascivious
         licks
   over, watching
   far snow-dappled Uintah mountains
Is that stream.
Of power.   what my
   hand curves over, following the line.
   "hip" and "groin"
Where "I"
   follow by hand and eye
   the swimming limit of your body.
As when vision idly dallies on the hills
Loving what it feeds on.
   soft cinder cones and craters;
     —Drum Hadley in the Pinacate
       took ten minutes more to look again—
A leap of power unfurling:
     left,   right—right—
My heart beat faster looking
   at the snowy Uintah mountains.

As my hand feeds on you
   runs down your side and curls beneath your hip.
   oil pool; stratum; water—

What "is" within   not known
   but feel it
   sinking with a breath
   pusht ruthless, surely, down.

Beneath this long caress of hand and eye
   "we" learn the flower burning,
       outward, from "below".

The Plum Blossom Poem

Angel island.
The sailboat slipping barely west,
Floating over coiling
                    tongues of filling mud.
East face of the Sierra still is
                    tilting;
Two plums below Buchanan street
                    on Vallejo
Blow blossom petals
                    eastward down the walk.
We hold and caress each other
Where a world is yet unborn;
Long slow swells in the Pacific—
                    the land drifts north.

Through the Smoke Hole
for Don Allen

I

There is another world above this one; or outside of this one;
    the way to it is thru the smoke of this one, & the hole that
    smoke goes through. The ladder is the way through the
    smoke hole; the ladder holds up, some say, the world above;
    it might have been a tree or pole; I think it is merely a way.

Fire is at the foot of the ladder. The fire is in the center. The
    walls are round. There is also another world below or inside
    this one. The way there is down thru smoke. It is not neces-
    sary to think of a series.

Raven and Magpie do not need the ladder. They fly thru the
    smoke holes shrieking and stealing. Coyote falls thru; we rec-
    ognize him only as a clumsy relative, a father in old clothes
    we don't wish to see with our friends.

It is possible to cultivate the fields of our own world without
    much thought for the others. When men emerge from below

we see them as the masked dancers of our magic dreams.
When men disappear down, we see them as plain men going
somewhere else. When men disappear up we see them as
great heroes shining through the smoke. When men come
back from above they fall thru and tumble; we don't really
know them; Coyote, as mentioned before.

II

Out of the kiva come
masked dancers or
plain men.
    plain men go into the ground.

out there out side all the chores
    wood and water, dirt,
wind, the view across the flat,
here, in the round
            no corners
head is full of magic figures—
woman your secrets aren't my secrets
what I cant say I wont
walk round
put my hand flat down.
you in the round too.
gourd vine blossom.
walls and houses drawn up
from the same soft soil.

thirty million years gone
      drifting sand.
  cool rooms pink stone
worn down fort floor, slat sighting
  heat shine on jumna river

dry wash, truck tracks in the riverbed
coild sand pinyon.

        seabottom
        riverbank

sand dunes
the floor of a sea once again.

human fertilizer
underground water tunnels
skinny dirt gods
grandmother berries
out
through the smoke hole.
(for childhood and youth *are* vanity

a Permian reef of algae,

out through the smoke hole
swallowd sand
salt mud
swum bodies,   flap
to the limestone blanket—

lizzard tongue,   lizzard tongue

wha, wha, wha   flying
in and *out* thru the smoke hole

plain men
come out of the ground.

Oysters

First   Samish Bay.
then all morning, hunting oysters

A huge feed on white
wood State Park slab-plank bench-
and table
at Birch Bay
where we picked up rocks
for presents.

And ate oysters, fried—raw—cookt in milk
      rolld in crumbs—
all we wanted.

ALL WE WANTED

& got back in our wagon,
drove away.

— *V* —

Miyazawa Kenji

宮沢賢治

Miyazawa Kenji (1896–1933)

. . . was born and lived most his life in Iwate prefecture in northern Japan. This area, sometimes called the Tibet of Japan, is known for poverty, cold, and heavy winter snows. His poems are all from there.

He was born and lived his life among the farmers: a school-teacher (Chemistry, Natural Sciences, Agriculture) and a Buddhist. His poems have many Buddhist allusions, as well as scientific vocabulary.

The bulk of his work is colloquial and metrically free. His complete work, published after his death, contains seven hundred free-verse poems, nine hundred *tanka* poems, and ninety children's stories.

Refractive Index

This one of the seven forests:
more light than under water—
and vast.
tramping up a frozen rutted road,
rutted snow,
toward those shrivelled zinc clouds—
like a melancholick mailman
        (or Aladdin with his lamp—)
must I hurry so?

The Snow on Saddle Mountain

The only thing that can be relied on
is the snow on Kurakake Mountain.
fields and woods
thawing, freezing, and thawing,
totally untrustworthy.
it's true, a great fuzzy windstorm
like yeast up there today, still
the only faint source of hope
is the snow on Kurakake mountain.

Spring and the Ashura*

From the ash-colored steel of images:
akebia tendrils coil round clouds,
wildrose thicket, swampy leafmold—
everywhere a pattern of flattery

*NOTE
Ashura is a Sanskrit Buddhist term for beings inhabiting one of the six realms
of existence. They are malevolent giants in constant strife, often represented
in art as human warriors, samurai, killing each other. The ashura realm is the
warring, contentious, hostile area of the mind. The other five realms are hell-
dwellers, hungry ghosts, animals, mankind, and devas.

(amber splinters flooding down
  thicker than woodwinds at noon)
the bitter taste of anger, the blueness.
at the depths in the brilliance of this april air
spitting, gnashing, pacing back and forth
I am an Ashura!
  (the scene gets blurred by tears)
smashed bits of cloud cross my vision,
  a holy crystal wind sweeps
    the translucent sea of the sky.
      Zypressen—one line of spring
        blackly draws in ether,
          —through those dark footsteps
           the edge of the mountain of heaven shines.
         (the shimmering mist, white polarization)
       the true words are lost.
      turn, clouds flying
    ah, in the radiant depths of april
  gnashing, BURNING, wander
I am one of the Ashuras:
  (chalcedony clouds flowing
   where is that singing, that spring bird?)
Sun Wheel shimmering blue
  ashura echoing in the forest
    heaven's bowl giddily tilting over
      clusters of giant coal-fern stretch up toward it.
      pitifully dense—those branches
this whole double scene.
flash of a crow flapping
              up from a treetop
      —spiritless woods—
      —the atmosphere clearer and clearer
        cypress trees standing to heaven
            in a dead hush—
a thing in the golden meadow:
just a person.
farmer wearing a straw cape looking at me
can he really see me
at the bottom of this shining sea of air?
    blue over blue, deepening my sadness.

zypressen silently quivering
  bird again cuts the blue
    (my real feelings are not here
     ashura tears on the ground)

breathing anew   in the sky
lungs faintly contracting
    (this body totally dispersed
     mixed with the atoms of space)

twigs of a gingko still reflecting
cypress blacker and blacker
sparks of cloud pour down.

Cloud Semaphore

    Ah, it's great! clear—clean—
    wind blowing
    farm tools twinkling
    vague mountains
      —lava-plug   magma
    all in a dream where there's no time

        when cloud semaphores
        were already hung
        in the stark blue east

    the vague mountains . . .
        wild geese will come
           down to the four
              cedars tonight!

The Scene

Clouds volatile as carbonic acid
blossoming cherries glow in the sun
wind comes again over the grasses
clipped tara trees tremble

    —just finished spreading manure
               in the sandy loam
        now it's all a picture in cobalt glaze.

heedless larks dumdum bullets
suddenly shoot out of the sky—

wind wipes away this blue stupor
gold grass quivering

clouds volatile as carbonic acid
cherry shines white in the sun.

A Break

Up in that gaudy space's
upper section a buttercup is blooming
       (high-class buttercup it is but
       rather than butter, from sulphur and honey)
below that, wild parsley and clover
and a dragonfly of worked tinplate.
rain crackles,
     oriole cries in the
     silverberry tree . . .
stretch out on the grass,
there's white and black both in the clouds;
it all goes shining, seething up.
fling off my hat it's the sooty cap of a mushroom
roll over and tilt my head back
             over the edge of the dike.
yawn; shiny demons come out of space.
   this hay's soft, it's a first-rate bed.

clouds all picked to bits,
the blue becomes eyes in a huge net, an
underlying glimmering steel plate

    oriole without break—
sunshining   crackling

Dawn

    Rolling snow turned peach-color
           the moon
        left alone in the fading night
    makes a soft cry in the heavens
    and once more
    drinks up the scattered light

    (*parasamgate, bodhi, svaha!*)

Some Views Concerning the Proposed Site of a National Park

Well how do you like this lava flow?
not very scenic, is it.
don't know how long ago it was spit out
on a sunny day like this you see the heat waves
just like a huge pan
and the snow up on the peak blue and simmering
say, have a sandwich.
why on earth don't you want to
develop this area?
it's a real good possibility—
mountains all around
crater lakes, hot springs, right there.
Saddle Mountain
well of course Saddle Mountain
and that big crater's probably
older than hell itself.

why sure! you could fix it up like Hell
with a real oriental charm to it, huh
a stockade of red spears
weird-shaped old dead trees put around
and plant flowers here and there,
well, flowers, I mean sort of things like uh
jimsonweed and viper grass
black wolfsbane and such
anyhow, make it gruesome, huh.
tourists will flock from all over.
we could get some mean looking guys
shave their heads
and make gates out of rock here and there
and drag the folks that come, around barefoot
            —you know—
by the "cuckoo singing on the path after death"
and the "ford of the river of the three ways"
"the gate to the new womb" at Yama's office
then, having expiated all their sins
we can sell them certificates for Heaven.
afterwards—at those three wooded hills
we could put on symphonies, huh
first movement: allegro con brio, like springing forth
second movement: sort of "andante"
third movement: like a lament
fourth movement: feeling of death
you know how it goes—at first kind of sorrowful
then bit by bit getting joyous.
at the end, on this side of the hill
hide two field-cannons
shoot them off—live shells—with a bang, by electricity,
just when they're feeling A-1
they'll *really* think they're on the
            River of the Three Ways, huh
us we'll have had lots of practice
we won't be scared at all
I wouldn't be a bit flustered
say, have one of those sandwiches
that hill over there—really drizzling, eh?
like a picture in blue on a porcelain
that fellow will make a good backdrop, huh.

Cow

An ayrshire cow
playing, rubbing her horns in the grass,
                    in the misty soil,
at her back the pulp factory fires
scorch the night clouds.
over low dunes
the sea booms
                    a brass moon
like you could scoop up and swallow

so the cow feels pretty good
playing now
tapping the fence with her horns.

Floating World Picture: Spring in the Kitagami Mountains

I

Nobody at the edge of the firepit
snowboots and jute leggings.
white birch flaming
jetting out sour hot sap
—a child sings the kite song
skinning badgers.
housepillars gleaming with soot
    —like shaped with stone axes—
the sheer ceiling
full of the blue smoke of breakfast
—vault of a temple—
one shaft of sunlight shooting down and
        all is at the bottom in that
                sensual beam of light.

Spring—at the chilly horsebarn
glimmer of dry hay and snow
yearning for sunny hills
the horses stamp their hooves.

2

The willow puts out honey flowers
birds flow over hill after hill
horses hurry:
      hot-breatht Arab
      glistening light-bodies thoroughbred
invisible cuneiform wind
in the stiff gloomy limbs of the walnut—
a dog rustles in bamboo grass.

      heavy work horse
      flashing his tufty tail
      like a monstrous lizard
            navigating in the sun
horses one by one coming,
chewing at the edge of the marl,
climbing along the misty run of snowmelt
under a malachite sky
—bright noisy market—
being led to the
stud inspection center.

Orders

The minus-1 Infantry Company
Leaves bivouac at 1 AM
From the present row of pine advancing
          in a southerly direction
Over there,
That
There uh
That black tree standing alone, proceed
To set your course by the green star visible
          two fingers to the right of the top
          of it
Toward the headwaters,
And attack and destroy the glow of the
          lights from the town.

Leader of Platoon number 1
You can swallow down your great sleepiness
While marching.
Now at the environs of the municipality
In the swamp running along the edge of the
                              roadside trees
Waterlily and Junsai
And swampfire flickering on and off.
No need to bother about that.
Very well. You all understand?
End of orders.

Distant Labor

Beyond the pampas-grass flowers
            and the dark grove
a new sort of wind is blowing
—through dazzling wrinkly cloud fretwork
            and spring sun
with a shiver of strange odors.

And from the hill behind the empty creek
and the barely rising black smoke
of the tileworks
a big cheerful racket.

—listening in the farmers fields
it seems pleasant enough work all right
but every night Chuichi
comes home from there exhausted
            and bad-tempered.

The Politicians

Running around here & there
stirring up trouble and bothering people

a bunch of lushes—
                fern leaves and cloud:
the world was so chilly and dark—

Before long that sort
will up and rot all by themselves
and be washed away by the rain
and afterwards, only green fern.

And when humanity is laid out like coal
somewhere some earnest geologist
will note them in his notebook.

Moon, Son of Heaven

When I was a child
in all sorts of magazines and newspapers
    —how many—photographs of the moon;
face scarred by jagged craters.
I clearly saw that the sun light strikes it.
later I learned it's terribly cold
                and no air.
maybe three times I saw it eclipsed—
the earth's shadow
slipped over it, clearly.
next, that it probably broke off from earth.
and last, a fellow I met during rice planting
    from the Morioka meteorological observatory
    once showed me that heavenly body through
    a something-mm little telescope
    and explained how its orbit and motions
accord with a simple formula.

However. ah,
for me in the end there's no obstacle
to reverently titling that heavenly body
Emperor Moon.
if someone says

man is his body
that's a mistake.
and if someone says
man is body and mind
that too is an error
and if one says man is mind,
still it's wrong.

so—I—
hail the moon as Emperor Moon.
this is not mere personification.

Daydreaming on the Trail

A lonely stretch, in the bind of poor fishing
         & drouth,
following the ocean
crossing pass after pass,
fields of wild reeds,
I've come this far alone.

dozing in the pale sun
on the sand of a dried-up riverbed
back and shoulder chilled
something bothering me—
I think at that last quartzite pass
I left the oak gate in the fence
of the cowpasture open
probably because I was hurrying—
     a white gate—
did I close it or not?

light cool sky,
mistletoe on chestnut floats in vision
manylayered clouds upriver
cool lattice of sunlight
some unknown big bird calling
faintly, crork   crork

The Great Power Line Pole

rain and clouds drift to the ground
susuki-grass red ears washed
fields fresh and live
and the great power line pole of Hanamaki
sparrows on a hundred insulators
then off to pillage a ricefield
whish whish whish whish flying
light of rain and cloud
and nimbly sweeping back to the hundred insulators
at the fork in the Hanamaki road
sparrows

Pine Needles

some raindrops still clinging
—I brought you these pine boughs

—you look like you'd jump up
& put your hot cheek against this green,
fiercely thrust your cheek
into the blue pine needles
greedily
—you're going to startle the others—
did you want to go to the woods
                                        that much?
burning with fever
tormented by sweat and pain

And me working happily in the sunlight
Thinking of you, walking slowly through the trees
        "Oh I'm all right now
        it's like you brought the
        center of the forest right here . . ."

Like a bird or a squirrel
you long for the woods.

how you must envy me,
my sister, who this very day must
    travel terribly far.
can you manage it alone?
      ask me to go with you
        crying—ask me—
your cheeks however
how beautiful they are.

I'll put these fresh pine boughs
on top of the mosquito net
they may drip a little
ah, a clean
smell like turpentine.

Thief

About when the stars of the Skeleton
    were paling in the dawn:
Striding the crackly glitter
    —frozen mud—
The thief who had just stolen a celadon vase
    from the front of a store
Suddenly stopped those long black legs
Covered his ears with his hands
And listened to the humming of his mind.

REGARDING WAVE

FOR MASA

— I —
Regarding Wave

Wave

Grooving clam shell,
         streakt through marble,
      sweeping down ponderosa pine bark-scale
        rip-cut tree grain
            sand-dunes, lava
              flow

Wave   wife.
        woman—wyfman—
"veiled; vibrating; vague"
   sawtooth ranges pulsing;
             veins on the back of the hand.

Forkt out: birdsfoot-alluvium
             wash

       great dunes rolling
Each inch rippld, every grain a wave.

Leaning against sand cornices til they blow away

    —wind, shake
    stiff thorns of cholla, ocotillo
    sometimes I get stuck in thickets—

Ah, trembling spreading radiating wyf
            racing zebra
  catch me and fling me wide
To the dancing grain of things
             of my mind!

Seed Pods

    Seed pods seen inside while high.
    trip of fingers
    to the farthest limits of the thigh

waft of sticky fluid, cypress resin
from peach valley
                    under walls of rock

                    Ferghana horses archt
                    rearing, fucking

tiny seed pods
caught and carried in the fur

        foot-pad   fetlock
                        slipping tongue
A pawtrack windfall
if my seed too—
float into you

colord blood   and apricot

        weavd with thread
    girls
moons
later let it be
        come—
        staind
on their soil ledge tilth
            fucking bed.

seed pod burrs, fuzz, twist-tailed
            nut-babies

    in my fucking head.

All Over the Dry Grasses

Motorburn,   oil sump dirt smell
            brake   drum
once deer kisst, grazed, pranct,
            pisst,

all over
California.

household laps.   gum tea
            buds.
        new houses,
        found wed on block pie.

sa.
bring back thick walls,
        (cools my poison,
                poison,
        scorpio itch, tick—)

        dreaming of

            babies

All over Mendocino County
wrappt in wild iris
            leaves.

Sand

From the desert?
        —when will be sand again.
blowing sand   drifting sand—
    dunes at Bandon
    Oregon   sheltering in a shed of
driftwood, naked,   kelp whip
            "driving sand sends swallows flying—"

shirakawa. "white river" sand.
            what they rake out at Ryōan-ji;
clean crumbled creek-washed rotted granite
            quartz & feldspar   sand.

　　　　—I went there once to check the prices
　　　　　bulk white sand to buy
black-burnt workers spade it thru a flume

　　　　　　the sands of the Ganges
　　　　　　"all the grains of the sands of the sea."

　blowing sand
　running water.
　I slept up on your body;
　walkt your valleys and your hills;

　　　　　　sandbox
　　　　　　sandpaper
　　　　　　sandy.

By the Tama River at the North End of the Plain in April

Round smooth stones
　　　　up here in the weeds
　the air a grey wet,

Across the Tama river
　a screen drum turns sorting gravel:
　　　　dumping loads in
　dump trucks one by one.

Deep in the hills
　　　　the water might be clean

Grilling raw squid over smoky twigs
　a round screen perched on broken bricks

Masa bending on the rocks
Staring close to the water,
Nanao and Nagasawa
　with their lifted cups of shochu,

Friends and poets
Eating, drinking in the rain,
    and these round river stones.

The Wide Mouth

A thick snow
    soft falling
the whole house open.

Snowflakes build up on a
single dark green spray of pine

The sparrow
swung and shrieked
in a swish of snowy clustered points,

Shew
    his wide pink   mouth.
house-cleaning.

Not a sound,
    white world,
great trouble.

In the House of the Rising Sun

Skinny kids in shorts get cups
        full of rice-gruel—steaming
        breakfast—sling
        their rifles, walk
        hot thickets.
        eyes peeled for U S planes.

Kyoto   a bar girl in pink
        with her catch for the night

    —but it's already morning—half-
    dazed, neat suit,
    laugh toward bed,

A guy I worked at logging with in Oregon
    fiddles his new lead-belcher cannons
        in South Yüeh.
    tuned better than chainsaws,
        at dawn,
    he liked mush.   with raisins.

Sleeping out   all night
  in warm rain.
Viet Nam uplands burned-off jungles
  wipe out a few rare birds
Fish in the rice paddy ditches
  stream a dry foul taste thru their gills
New Asian strains of clap
  whip penic   ill in.

Making toast, heating coffee,
    blue as Shiva—
      did I drink some filthy poison
      will I ever learn to love?

Did I really have to kill my sick, sick cat.

White Devils

Strangling a white girl
disembowelled, the insides hid in a shed
the body crushed in earth-working
    under caterpillar tractor treads.

half-done concrete freeway overpass.
digging to bury my own shit
    —a chopped up body
    mixed with shit and towels

and then,
a disembowelled, half-skinned
horse-sized white wolf bitch
lying on its side in a pool of
        half-melted snow,
a snowbank around her,
icy melt water staining red,
the red of blood spreading into the white snow.
        she moved, stirred,

And I thought, my God.
still alive.

— II —

Regarding Wave

Song of the Cloud

Sloped-down shark nose,
        high frilly tail—dorsal fins—
flat sweeping gestures.   Ah, puked out.
sweep the sea.   broom
        my rear is soft—

   Three, and their retinue,
   move up between
slender, with dignity,
       WE
   pile up, pile up, our deep-mounting
   pleasure in our richness
            is not chaos.

scatterings and plains, placings.

   Brothers moving elsewhere
visible and tall,
        but far away.

Song of the Tangle

Two thigh hills hold us at the fork
     round mount center

   we sit all folded
on the dusty planed planks of a shrine
drinking top class saké that was left
     for the god.

        calm tree halls
        the sun past the summit
        heat sunk through the vines,
           twisted sasa

        cicada singing,
           swirling in the tangle

the tangle of the thigh

          the brush
          through which we push

Song of the Slip

     SLEPT
     folded in girls
   feeling their folds; whorls;
        the lips, leafs,
 of the curling   soft-sliding
      serpent-sleep dream.

          roaring and faring
     to beach high on the dark shoal
          seed-prow

moves in and makes home in the whole.

Song of the View

     Line of brow, purst mouth
     blue straight seamless
                    snapless
                    dress

   O!   cunt

     that which you suck in-
          to yourself, that you
                         hold
                      there,
     hover over,
     excellent emptiness your
          whole flesh is wrappt around,
               the

hollow you bear
                   to
               bear,

shows its power and place

in the grace of your glance

Song of the Taste

Eating the living germs of grasses
Eating the ova of large birds

    the fleshy sweetness packed
    around the sperm of swaying trees

The muscles of the flanks and thighs of
                soft-voiced cows
        the bounce in the lamb's leap
        the swish in the ox's tail

Eating roots grown swoll
                inside the soil

Drawing on life of living
    clustered points of light spun
                out of space
hidden in the grape.

Eating each other's seed
                eating
    ah, each other.

Kissing the lover in the mouth of bread:
                lip to lip.

Kyoto Born in Spring Song

Beautiful little children
          found in melons,
          in bamboo,
     in a "strangely glowing warbler egg"
          a perfect baby girl—

baby, baby,
     tiny precious
          mice and worms:

     Great majesty of Dharma turning
     Great dance of Vajra power

lizard baby by the fern
centipede baby scrambling toward the wall
cat baby left to mew for milk alone
mouse baby too afraid to run

          O sing   born in spring
     the weavers swallows babies in Nishijin
          nests below the eaves

          glinting mothers wings
          swoop to the sound of looms

          and three fat babies
     with three human mothers
every morning doing laundry
                    "good
     morning how's your baby?"
Tomoharu, Itsuko, and Kenji—

          Mouse, begin again.
Bushmen are laughing
     at the coyote-tricking
          that made us think machines

wild babies
in the ferns and plums and weeds.

Archaic Round and Keyhole Tombs

One child rides a bike
Her blue dress flutters
    about her gliding
    white-clad hips

The second runs behind
Black hair pulsing
    to the ease of her lope
    bares her pale nape

They pass by a pond of water-lily
and lotusses, a pond with a legend,

Coast out of sight.

— *III* —
Regarding Wave

Burning Island

O Wave God   who broke through me today
    Sea Bream
    massive pink and silver
    cool swimming down with me watching
              staying away from the spear.

Volcano belly Keeper who lifted this island
    for our own beaded bodies adornment
    and sprinkles us all with his laugh—
             ash in the eye
    mist, or smoke,
    on the bare high limits—
          underwater lava flows easing to coral
            holes filled with striped feeding swimmers

O Sky Gods   cartwheeling
    out of   Pacific
    turning rainsqualls over like lids on us
    then shine on our sodden—
         (scanned out a rainbow today at the
           cow drinking trough
            sluicing off
      LAKHS of crystal Buddha Fields
      right on the hair of the arm!)

Who wavers right now in the bamboo:
  a half-gone waning moon.
        drank down a bowlful of shochu
          in praise of Antares
        gazing far up the lanes of Sagittarius
          richest stream of our sky—
  a cup to the center of the galaxy!
        and let the eyes stray
  right-angling the pitch of the Milky Way:
      horse-heads   rings
      clouds   too distant to *be*
      slide free.
         on the crest of the wave.

Each night
O Earth Mother
   I have wrappt my hand
   over the jut of your cobra-hood
                    sleeping;
   left my ear
All night long by your mouth.

O   All
Gods   tides   capes   currents
Flows and spirals of
     pool and powers—

As we hoe the field
   let sweet potato grow.
And as sit us all down when we may
To consider the Dharma
   bring with a flower and a glimmer.
Let us all sleep in peace   together.

Bless Masa and me as we marry
   at new moon   on the crater
This summer.

VIII. 40067

Roots

       Draw over and dig
       The loose ash soil
       Hoe handles are short,
       The sun's course long
       Fingers deep in the earth search
       Roots, pull them out; feel through;
       Roots are strong.

Rainbow Body

Cicada fill up the bamboo thickets:
  a wall of twanging shadow
    dark joints and leaves.
           northwest wind
    from the China sea.

          —

Salt clouds skim the volcano
  mixed with ash and steam
    rumbles downwind
        from the night gleam
    summit, near Algol,
  breathing the Milky Way.

          —

The great drone
In the throat of the hill
The waves drum
The wind sigh.

At dawn the mountain canyons
  spread and rise
  to the falling call of the Akahige
    we half-wake
        in the east light
    fresh

          —

At low tide swim out through a path in the coral
  & into the land of the sea-people:
  rainbows under the foam of the breakers
      surge and streaming
         from the southern beach.
      the lips, where you float
      clear, wave

with the subtle currents
sea-tangle tendrils
outward roil of lava
            —cobalt speckled curling
            mouth of a *shako* clam.

                    ——

Climb delicately back up the cliff
    without using our hands.
    eat melon and steamed sweet potato
    from this ground.
We hoed and fished—
    grubbing out bamboo runners
    hammering straight blunt
    harpoon heads and spears
                Now,
        sleep on the cliff
        float on the surf
        nap in the bamboo thicket
                eyes closed,
        dazzled ears.

Everybody Lying on Their Stomachs, Head toward the Candle, Reading, Sleeping, Drawing

            The corrugated roof
            Booms and fades night-long to

                    million-darted rain
            squalls   and

                    outside

                    lightning

            Photographs in the brain

Wind-bent bamboo.
                    through

        the plank shutter
                    set

Half-open   on eternity

Shark Meat

In the night fouled the nets—
Sonoyama's flying-fish fishing
Speared by the giant trident
        that hung in the net shed
            we never thought used

Cut up for meat on the beach.
At seven in the morning
Maeda's grandson
                    the shy one
                    —a slight harelip
Brought a crescent of pale red flesh
        two feet long, looped on his arm
Up the bamboo lanes to our place.

The island eats shark meat at noon.

Sweet miso sauce on a big boiled cube
        as I lift a flake

                    to my lips,

Miles of water, Black current,
Thousands of days
            re-crossing his own paths
            to tangle our net
                    to be part of
                    this loom.

It Was When

We harked up the path in the dark
            to the bamboo house
                    green strokes down my back
                    arms over your doubled hips
            under cow-breath thatch
                    bent   cool
                                breasts brush my chest
    —and Naga walked in with a candle,
            "I'm sleepy"

Or jungle ridge by a snag—
            banyan canyon—a Temminck's Robin
                    whirled down the waterfall gorge
            in zazen, a poncho spread out on the stones.
                    below us the overturning
                        silvery
                    brush-bamboo slopes—
            rainsqualls came up on us naked
                    brown nipples in needles of ocean-
                        cloud
                            rain.

Or the night in the farmhouse
            with Franco on one side, or Pon
            Miko's head against me, I swung you
                    around and came into you
            careless and joyous,
                        late
                    when Antares had set

Or out on the boulders
            south beach at noon
                    rockt by surf
            burnd under by stone
            burnd over by sun
                    saltwater caked
            skin   swing

hips on my eyes
         burn   between;

That we caught: sprout
      took grip in your womb and it held.
      new power in your breath called its place.
      blood of the moon   stoppt;
      you pickt your steps well.

Waves
    and the
        prevalent easterly
           breeze.
        whispering into you,
           through us,
                the grace.

The Bed in the Sky

Motorcycle strums   the empty streets
Heading home at one a. m.
    ice slicks shine in the moon
        I weave a safe path through

Naked shivering light flows down
Fills the basin over Kyoto
    and the plain
        a ghost glacier dream

From here a hundred miles are clear
The cemetery behind
    Namu   Amida   Butsu
        chiselled   ten thousand times

Tires crackle the mud-puddles
The northern hills gleam white
    I ought to stay outside   alone
        and watch the moon all night

But the bed is full and spread and dark
I hug you and sink in the warm
       my stomach against your big belly

      feels our baby turn

Kai, Today

A teen-age boy in training pants
      stretching by the river
A girl child weeping, climbing
      up her elder sister;
The Kawaramachi Beggar's steady look and
      searching reach of gritty hand
      in plastic sidewalk pail
        with lip of grease

      these fates.

      before Masa and I met
What's your from-the-beginning face?
      Kai.
      born again
To the Mother's hoarse bear-down
      groan and dark red mask:
      spiralling, glistening, blue-white, up

And out from her
        (dolphins leaping in threes
        through blinding silver inter-
        faces, Persian
        Gulf tanker's wave-slip
        opening, boundless
          whap
      as they fall back,
      arcing
      into her—)

      sea.

Not Leaving the House

When Kai is born
I quit going out

Hang around the kitchen—make cornbread
Let nobody in.
Mail is flat.
      Masa lies on her side, Kai sighs,
      Non washes and sweeps
We sit and watch
      Masa nurse, and drink green tea.

Navajo turquoise beads over the bed
A peacock tail feather at the head
A badger pelt from Nagano-ken
For a mattress; under the sheet;
A pot of yogurt setting
Under the blankets, at his feet.

Masa, Kai,
And Non, our friend
In the green garden light reflected in
Not leaving the house.
From dawn til late at night
      making a new world of ourselves
      around this life.

Regarding Wave

The voice of the Dharma
the voice
now

A shimmering bell
through all.

—

Every hill,   still.
Every tree alive. Every leaf.
All the slopes   flow.
          old woods, new seedlings,
          tall grasses plumes.

Dark hollows;   peaks of light.
    wind stirs   the cool side
Each leaf living.
          All the hills.

          —

          The Voice
          is a wife
            to

          him still.

          ──────────

        ōṃ   ah   hūṃ

— *Long Hair* —

Revolution in the Revolution in the Revolution

The country surrounds the city
The back country surrounds the country

"From the masses to the masses" the most
Revolutionary consciousness is to be found
Among the most ruthlessly exploited classes:
Animals, trees, water, air, grasses

We must pass through the stage of the
"Dictatorship of the Unconscious" before we can
Hope for the withering-away of the states
And finally arrive at true Communionism.

———

If the capitalists and imperialists
        are the exploiters, the masses are the workers.
                and the party
                is the communist.

If civilization
        is the exploiter, the masses is nature.
                and the party
                is the poets.

If the abstract rational intellect
        is the exploiter, the masses is the unconscious.
                and the party
                is the yogins.

& POWER
comes out of the seed-syllables of mantras.

What You Should Know to Be a Poet

all you can about animals as persons.
the names of trees and flowers and weeds.
names of stars, and the movements of the planets
                    and the moon.

your own six senses, with a watchful and elegant mind.

at least one kind of traditional magic:
divination, astrology, the *book of changes,* the tarot;

dreams.
the illusory demons and illusory shining gods;

kiss the ass of the devil and eat shit;
fuck his horny barbed cock,
fuck the hag,
and all the celestial angels
                    and maidens perfum'd and golden—

& then love the human: wives   husbands   and friends.

children's games, comic books, bubble-gum,
the weirdness of television and advertising.

work, long dry hours of dull work swallowed and accepted
and livd with and finally lovd.   exhaustion,
                    hunger, rest.

the wild freedom of the dance, *extasy*
silent solitary illumination, *enstasy*

real danger.   gambles.   and the edge of death.

Aged Tamba Temple Plum Tree Song

Firewood under the eaves
    ends trimm'd even

Scaly silver lichen
    on the plum
        bark
Ragged, rough, twisted,
    parts half-rotted

A few blossoms open:
    rich pink tiny petals
        soft and flutter;
Other fat buds.

Fat buds, green twigs,
    flaky gray bark;

        pigeons must all
Flap up together

It

[*Reading Blake in a cowshed during a typhoon
on an island in the East China Sea*]

Cloud—cloud—cloud—   hurls
    up and on over;
Bison herds stamp-
peding   on Shantung

Fists of rain
        flail half down the length of the floor
Bamboo hills
        bend and regain;
                fields follow the laws of waves.

puppy scuds in wet
squats on the slat bed
            —on the edge of a spiral
Centered five hundred miles southwest.

Reading in English:
        the way the words join
        the weights, the warps,

    I know   what it means.
    my language is home.

            mind-fronts meeting
            bite back at each other,
            whirl up a Mother Tongue.
        one hundred knot gusts dump palms
        over somebody's morning cream—

Cowshed skull
Its windows open
        swallows and strains
        gulfs of wild-slung
                quivering ocean air.
                breathe it;
                taste it;   how it

Feeds the brain.

Running Water Music

    under the trees
    under the clouds
    by the river
    on the beach,

    "sea roads."
    whales   great sea-path beasts—

        salt;   cold
        water;   smoky fire.
steam, cereal,
        stone, wood boards.
bone awl, pelts,
        bamboo pins and spoons.
unglazed bowl.
a band around the hair.

        beyond wounds.

sat on a rock in the sun,
watched the old pine
wave
over blinding fine white
        river sand.

Sours of the Hills

barbed seeds   in double ranks
sprung for sending off;

half-moon hairy seeds in the hair of the wrist

majestic fluff
sails . . . rayed and spined . . . up hill at eye level
    hardly a breeze;

amber fruit with veins
on a bending stem,
size of an infant pea.

plumes wave,
seeds spill.

blueblack berry on a bush turned leaf-purple

deep sour, dark tart, sharp
    in the back of the mouth.

in the hair and from head to foot
stuck with seeds—burrs—
     next summer's mountain weeds—

a strolling through vines and grasses:

into the wild sour.

The Wild Edge

Curve of the two steel spring-up prongs on
     the back of the Hermes
     typewriter—paper holders—the same
Curve as the arched wing of a gull:

     (sails through the
     sides of the eyes by white-stained cliffs
     car-park lots and scattered
       pop-top beer tabs in the gravel)

Birds sail away and back.

Sudden flurry and buzz of flies in the corner sun.
Heavy beetle drags stiff legs through moss

Caravans of ants bound for the Wall
     wandering backward—

Harsh Thrush shrieks   in the cherries.
     a murmur in the kitchen
     Kai wakes and cries—

The Trade

I found myself inside a massive concrete shell
     lit by glass tubes, with air pumped in, with
     levels joined by moving stairs.

It was full of the things that were bought and made
    in the twentieth century. Layed out in trays
    or shelves

The throngs of people of that century, in their style,
    clinging garb made on machines,

Were trading all their precious time
    for things.

To Fire

(Goma / Homa)

        I have raised pure flames
        With mystic fists and muttered charms!

All the poems I wrote before nineteen
Heaps of arty cards from Christmas
Straw shoes
Worn clogs
The English Daily—Johnson's, Wilson's Ho Chi Minh
    —face crumpling inward licked by yellow locks

The contracting writhing plastics
And orange skins that shrink and squeak
              peace! peace! grace!

        Using sanctified vajra-tongs of blue
        I turn the mass and let in air

        Those letters forwarded now to Shiva
        the knots of snot in kleenex,
              my offering—my body!

And here the drafts of articles and songs
Words of this and that

Bullshit—renounce
                    the leather briefcase no one wants
                    the holey socks.

As sun moves up and up;
And motorcycles warm the street;
And people at the bus stop steam—

                GREAT BRILLIANT KING
                Unshakeable!
                —halo of flame—

Eat   these   sweets   of   our   house   and   day   :

            Let me unflinching burn
            Such dross within
            With joy
            I pray!

Love

            Women who were turned inside-out
            Ten times over by childbirth

            On the wind-washed lonely islands
            Lead the circle of *obon* dancers
            Through a full moon night in August

            The youngest girl last;

            Women who were up since last night
            Scaling and cleaning the flying fish

            Sing about love.

            Over and over,
            Sing about love.

                        Suwa-no-se Island

The Way Is Not a Way

scattered leaves
    sheets of running
    water.
unbound hair.   loose
    planks on shed roofs.
stumbling down wood stairs
    shirts un done.
children pissing in the roadside grass

In the Night, Friend

Peach blossom
Cling Peaches
Freestone peach.

The Third Engineer meets my wife in the pantry
says "Beards don't make money"
says "I've got two cars"

    (At thirty-five my father had a wife,
    two children, two acres, and two cows.
    he built a barn, fixed the house and added on,
    strung barbed-wire fence,
    planted fruit-trees, blasted stumps,
    they always had a car.
    they thought they were poor—   1935—)

—"the money culture run by Jews"
—"the Africans got all they know from us"

    Etchings of ruins,
    "Interno del Colosseo Scavato nel 1813"
    —Rossini—Roma—1820—
    hung in the passenger lounge.

Fruit tree fields.   orchards.   Santa Clara, San Jose.
          trailer parks in the lemon groves.
Seaman with a few extra bucks:
Talks of stocks, talks of taxes, buy up land.
          the whole state of California
          layed out like meat on a slab.
Growth and investment; development and returns.

—"I think them poets are all just charlatans."

says Dōgen, "every one of us
                    has a natural endowment
                    with provisions for the whole of his life."

———

Off the coast of Oregon
The radio is full of hate and anger.
"Teenagers! getting busted for shoplifting is no joke!"
          phoney friendly cop voice,
"The Ford Foundation is financing revolution—"
"Teach black people to have more self-respect
          and they'll blame the white people more—"

> General Alarm
> When Bell Rings
> Go to Your
> Station

———

After midnight, the "clean time of night"
Rise to see the Morning Star.
Planting the peach tree, mopping the floor.

                    "we all
                    worked hard to get ahead"
                    peach orchard turned roots-up and brush-piled
                    (the unspeakable U S government

cut down the Navajo peach trees
at Canyon de Chelly—)

—

On the face of the waters
A wind moves
Making waves

In the dark
Is a face

Of waters.

A wind moves
Like a word

waves

The face
Is a ground
Land
Looks round

SS Washington Bear
West Coast bound

Beating Wings

Jerky dance of dune weeds
looped-over twigs scribble
wind-and-flower notes
forever,
in the sand—

Hadley   pissing   shakes his cock
in the desert—

Beating wings of a raven just at dawn.

The same first bird chirps at the first light.

    hair, teeth, spit, breath,
backbone, asshole, hip joints, knees,
   ball of the foot.
   knuckles, back of the hands.
   piss-hard-ons at dawn.
Lazy to get up and scuff the chilly sand
                   crap by lantern light.

      —hiss of wings—
          gone.

Comb the sand down from my hair.

"off"
and away.   apart.   separating.   peeling back.
         a-way.   a "ways off"
he's "off"   —*out* of,
        the "offing"

                —hot breath
                  breathing down my neck.

fuzz—burrs—thorns—tiny hairs   stickers,
  fluff—down—stickem.   fly or be carried
        be ate and be shat out.

  moving the seed around.

Two Ravens talk a bit,
Then fly off
In opposite directions.

Poke Hole Fishing after the March

"Those pine shingles—gunpowder dry.
      if you want to save money on shingles
      go up to Petaluma
      a place called Wicks"
on anything; handling; pre-finished plywood;
"I got a house with those kind of walls."

Eel-fishing, poke-holing for blennies
down cliffs through poison oak,
      a minus-two low tide.

      thirty thousand brothers and sisters
      bare-breasted girl on TV
      her braids whipping
      round about her haid,

"A hawk with a fish or a bird, up in the air,
                in his claws."

An older fatter short-haired man
Down fishing too—all catching nothing—
A roofing contractor.
Says "I'd like to stay down here all week."
11.30 AM now, tide's coming back in
                rusty wrecked car on the rocks

After the Peoples' Park march.
Monday, low tide.
      he sits with us down by the fire
      in the truck-high boulders, smoke
      stinging of salt
"Yeah I saw you guys on TV." Laugh, beer.

      as the sea moves in
      we all talk as friends;
      as if America wasn't in a war—

(Gone to the mountains
    gathering herbs
       I do not know
            when he will return—)

High tide.
Where the rocks were
Now there are fish.

N. of Slide Ranch

Brown

black bread, brown sugar

    "all year round"

topsoil,
     obsidian,
          molasses.
   no white places,
   breast or thigh.

oryza: ;genmai (. . . rices . . .)
   "dark and mysterious grain."

okra and cod.
   eggplant purple; heart-wood red.

bare feet, long hair
   sit on the floor,
no meat, no under
   wear.
smoky brun bear

BROWN RICE HEADS

Meeting the Mountains

He crawls to the edge of the foaming creek
He backs up the slab ledge
He puts a finger in the water
He turns to a trapped pool
Puts both hands in the water
Puts one foot in the pool
Drops pebbles in the pool
He slaps the water surface with both hands
He cries out, rises up and stands
Facing toward the torrent and the mountain
Raises up both hands and shouts three times!

Kai at Sawmill Lake VI.69

Before the Stuff Comes Down

Walking out of the "big E"
Dope store of the suburb,
            canned music plugging up your ears
            the wide aisles,
            miles of wares
            from nowheres,

Suddenly it's California:
Live oak, brown grasses

Butterflies over the parking lot and the freeway
A Turkey Buzzard power in the blue air.

A while longer,
Still here.

All the Spirit Powers Went to Their Dancing Place

Floods of men
> on foot, fighting and starving, cans rusted
> by the roadside.

Clouds swirling and spiralling up the sky,
> men fighting with scythes.

Wild beings sweeping on cities—spirits and ghosts—
> cougar, eagle, grizzly bear, coyote, hummingbird
> intelligences
> directing   destructing   instructing;   us all
> as through music:
> songs filling the sky.

The earth lifting up and flying like millions of birds
> into dawn.

Hills rising and falling as music, long plains and deserts
> as slow quiet chanting,

Swift beings, green beings, all beings—all persons;
> the two-legged beings
> shine in smooth skin and their furred spots

Drinking clear water together
> together   turning and dancing
> speaking   new words,
> the first time, for

Air, fire, water, and
> Earth is our dancing place now.

For Jack Spicer

Jack, I heard you died, it was
          the bark chips in the Skagit
          river at Mount Vernon
old Salishan canoes found out
when sandbars opened after heavy thaw and rains—
          all the way up to the hills,
          and Glacier Peak.
You leave us free to follow:
          banks and windings
          forward:
and we needn't *want* to die.   but on, and
          through.

through.

Running Water Music II

     Clear running stream
               clear running stream

     Your water is light
               to my mouth
     And a light to my dry body

                    your flowing
     Music,
                    in my ears. free,

     Flowing free!
     With you
               in me.

Long Hair

Hunting season:

Once every year, the Deer catch human beings. They
do various things which irresistably draw men near them;
each one selects a certain man. The Deer shoots the man,
who is then compelled to skin it and carry its meat home
and eat it. Then the Deer is inside the man. He waits
and hides in there, but the man doesn't know it. When
enough Deer have occupied enough men, they will strike
all at once. The men who don't have Deer in them will
also be taken by surprise, and everything will change
some. This is called "takeover from inside."

———

Deer trails:

Deer trails run on the side hills
            cross country access roads
            dirt ruts to bone-white
            board house ranches,
            tumbled down.

Waist high through manzanita,
Through sticky, prickly, crackling
            gold dry summer grass.

Deer trails lead to water,
Lead sidewise all ways
Narrowing down to one best path—
And split—
And fade away to nowhere.
Deer trails slide under freeways
            slip into cities
            swing back and forth in crops and orchards
            run up the sides of schools!

Deer spoor and crisscross dusty tracks
Are in the house: and coming out the walls:

And deer bound through my hair.

— Target Practice —

Looking for Nothing

Look in the eye of a hawk
The inmost ring of a log

The edge of the sheath and the
Sheath—where it leads—

River sands.
Tārā   "Joy of
Starlight"
         thousand-
         eyed.

       —

    coyote yapping on the ridge
all night sleeping deep
    in the shadow of boulders.
(the saw-whet owl
    calls in the foggy trees)

       —

pack-string of five mules
    winding through the mountain meadow—
watching us: not thirty yards away
a great calm six-point buck
    head up, ears front,
resting deep in flowers.

       —

first the gas engine pops
then the big diesel catches,
roars, and the cat
rumbles off in the
soft green misty light
of the forest at dawn

Stovewood

two thousand years of fog and sucking minerals
    from the soil,
Russian river ox-team & small black train
    haul to mill;
fresh-sawed rough cut by wagon
    and built into a barn;
tear it down and split it up
    and stick it in a stove.

For Will Petersen the Time We Climbed Mt. Hiei Cross-country in the Snow

No trail
    can't be followed:
        wild boar tracks slash
        sidehill through bamboo
            thicket.
Where are we   the hill
Goes up.

——

khaki breeches,
split-toed rubber workshoes,
singing and whistling to a brisk brown bull
dragging the little logs down trail
in a foot of slushy snow
behind the Silver Pavilion.

——

    ranges of hazy hills
    make the heart ache—
tiny flowers in the underbrush,
    winds from Siberia
        in the spring.

Shinkyogoku, Kyoto

in the dusk
between movie halls
the squeak of the chain
of swings

Hiking in the Totsugawa Gorge

pissing

watching

a waterfall

Why I Laugh When Kai Cries

Nothing's to blame:
    daily hunger, baby rage—
                the Buddha's Lion Roar
                and hymns of praise.

Belly and nerves,
    floating gathering mind
                feel pain and wail
                he's getting fat
I have to laugh at that.

———

Masa in the warm dawn
                        naked
    bending over Kai
    laughing,   dripping
                from both breasts

———

The rim of panties rides
    high on the hip
        under cotton dresses,
summer, bending down.

At Kitano Shrine for the Fair

In the washroom I looked in a mirror

And saw the roots of a huge tree.

———

on the night
                of the full moon
mothers with little children
wade home
            in spite of it

The Old Man

His face is the color of the wall
His robe is the same as his cushion
He speaks frog and ox
He laughs up a hill

Some Good Things to Be Said for the Iron Age

A ringing tire iron
            dropped on the pavement

Whang of a saw
brusht on limbs

the taste
of rust.

Cats Thinking about What Birds Eat

the kitten
sniffs deep
old droppings

Four Corners Hopscotch

"Arizona
COL orado
Utah
New MEX ico

AriZOna
U TAH
Colorado &
New MEXico."

Pleasure Boats

Dancing in the offing
Grooving in the coves
Balling in the breakers
Lolling in the rollers
Necking in the ebb
Balmy in the calms
Whoring in the storm
Blind in the wind
Coming in the foam.

Willow

the pussy
of the pussy-willow

unfolds into fuzz on the leaf.
blonde glow on a cheek;
willow pussy hair.

The Good Earth

The empty shell of a snail
By a dry log. Warm grass
seeds in an old cookpot
playing, we were starving,
Playing   "The Good Earth."

Civilization

Those are the people who do complicated things.

they'll grab us by the thousands
and put us to work.
World's going to hell, with all these
villages and trails.
Wild duck flocks aren't
what they used to be.
Aurochs grow rare.

Fetch me my feathers and amber

———

A small cricket
on the typescript page of
"Kyoto born in spring song"

grooms himself
in time with *The Well-Tempered Clavier.*
I quit typing and watch him thru a glass.
How well articulated! How neat!

Nobody understands the ANIMAL KINGDOM.

—

When creeks are full
The poems flow
When creeks are down
We heap stones.

TURTLE ISLAND

FOR LOIS SNYDER HENNESSY
MY MOTHER

INTRODUCTORY NOTE

Turtle Island—the old/new name for the continent, based on many creation myths of the people who have been living here for millenia, and reapplied by some of them to "North America" in recent years. Also, an idea found world-wide, of the earth, or cosmos even, sustained by a great turtle or serpent-of-eternity.

A name: that we may see ourselves more accurately on this continent of watersheds and life-communities–plant zones, physiographic provinces, culture areas; following natural boundaries. The "U.S.A." and its states and counties are arbitrary and inaccurate impositions on what is really here.

The poems speak of place, and the energy-pathways that sustain life. Each living being is a swirl in the flow, a formal turbulence, a "song." The land, the planet itself, is also a living being—at another pace. Anglos, Black people, Chicanos, and others beached up on these shores all share such views at the deepest levels of their old cultural traditions—African, Asian, or European. Hark again to those roots, to see our ancient solidarity, and then to the work of being together on Turtle Island.

— *Manzanita* —

Anasazi

Anasazi,
Anasazi,

tucked up in clefts in the cliffs
growing strict fields of corn and beans
sinking deeper and deeper in earth
up to your hips in Gods
             your head all turned to eagle-down
             & lightning for knees and elbows
your eyes full of pollen

             the smell of bats.
             the flavor of sandstone
             grit on the tongue.

             women
             birthing
at the foot of ladders in the dark.

trickling streams in hidden canyons
under the cold rolling desert

corn-basket   wide-eyed
             red baby
             rock lip home,

Anasazi

The Way West, Underground

             The split-cedar
             smoked salmon
             cloudy days of Oregon,
             the thick fir forests.

Black Bear heads uphill in
Plumas county,
round bottom scuttling through willows—

The Bear Wife moves up the coast.

where blackberry brambles
ramble in the burns.

And around the curve of islands
foggy volcanoes
on, to North Japan. The bears
& fish-spears of the Ainu.
Gilyak.
Mushroom-vision healer,
single flat drum,
from long before China.

Women with drums who fly over Tibet.

Following forests west, and
rolling, following grassland,
tracking bears and mushrooms,
eating berries all the way.
In Finland finally took a bath:
like redwood sweatlodge on the Klamath—
all the Finns in moccasins and
pointy hats with dots of white,
netting, trapping, bathing,
singing holding hands, the while

see-sawing on a bench, a look of love—

Karhu—Bjorn—Braun—Bear

[lightning rainbow great cloud tree
dialogs of birds]
Europa.   'The West.'
the bears are gone
except Brunhilde?

or elder wilder goddesses reborn—will race
    the streets of France and Spain
            with automatic guns—
                in Spain,
Bears and Bison,
Red Hands with missing fingers,
Red mushroom labyrinths;
lightning-bolt mazes,
Painted in caves,

Underground.

Without

        the silence

        of nature

        within.

        the power within.

        the power

        without.

        the path is whatever passes—no

        end in itself.

        the end is,

        grace—ease—

healing,

not saving.

singing

the proof

the proof of the power within.

The Dead by the Side of the Road

How did a great Red-tailed Hawk
    come to lie—all stiff and dry—
        on the shoulder of
            Interstate 5?

Her wings for dance fans

Zac skinned a skunk with a crushed head
    washed the pelt in gas; it hangs,
        tanned, in his tent

Fawn stew on Hallowe'en
    hit by a truck on highway forty-nine
        offer cornmeal by the mouth;
            skin it out.

Log trucks run on fossil fuel

I never saw a Ringtail til I found one in the road:
    case-skinned it with the toenails
        footpads, nose, and whiskers on;
            it soaks in salt and water
            sulphuric acid pickle;

she will be a pouch for magic tools.

The Doe was apparently shot
  lengthwise and through the side—
    shoulder and out the flank
      belly full of blood

Can save the other shoulder maybe,
  if she didn't lie too long—
Pray to their spirits. Ask them to bless us:
  our ancient sisters' trails
    the roads were laid across and kill them:
      night-shining eyes

The dead by the side of the road.

I Went into the Maverick Bar

I went into the Maverick Bar
In Farmington, New Mexico.
And drank double shots of bourbon
      backed with beer.
My long hair was tucked up under a cap
I'd left the earring in the car.

Two cowboys did horseplay
      by the pool tables,
A waitress asked us
      where are you from?
a country-and-western band began to play
"We don't smoke Marijuana in Muskokie"
And with the next song,
      a couple began to dance.

They held each other like in High School dances
      in the fifties;
I recalled when I worked in the woods
      and the bars of Madras, Oregon.
That short-haired joy and roughness—
      America—your stupidity.
I could almost love you again.

We left—onto the freeway shoulders—
                    under the tough old stars—
In the shadow of bluffs
                    I came back to myself,
To the real work, to
                    "What is to be done."

Steak

Up on the bluff, the steak houses
called "The Embers"—called
"Fireside"
with a smiling disney cow on the sign
or a stockman's pride—huge
full-color photo of standing Hereford stud
above the very booth
his bloody sliced muscle is
                    served in;
                    "rare"

The Chamber of Commerce eats there,
the visiting lecturer,
stockmen in Denver suits,
Japanese-American animal nutrition experts
                    from Kansas,
                    with Buddhist beads;

And down by the tracks
in frozen mud, in the feed lots,
fed surplus grain
(the ripped-off land)
the beeves are standing round—
bred heavy.
Steaming, stamping,
long-lashed, slowly thinking
with the rhythm of their
breathing,
frosty—breezy—
early morning prairie sky.

No Matter, Never Mind

The Father is the Void
The Wife   Waves

Their child is Matter.

Matter makes it with his mother
And their child is Life,
                                   a daughter.

The Daughter is the Great Mother
Who, with her father/brother Matter
                                   as her lover,

Gives birth to the Mind.

The Bath

Washing Kai in the sauna,
The kerosene lantern set on a box
      outside the ground-level window,
Lights up the edge of the iron stove and the
      washtub down on the slab
Steaming air and crackle of waterdrops
      brushed by on the pile of rocks on top
He stands in warm water
Soap all over the smooth of his thigh and stomach
      "Gary don't soap my hair!"
      —his eye-sting fear—
      the soapy hand feeling
      through and around the globes and curves of his body
      up in the crotch,
And washing-tickling out the scrotum, little anus,
      his penis curving up and getting hard
      as I pull back skin and try to wash it
Laughing and jumping, flinging arms around,

I squat all naked too,
                    is this our body?

Sweating and panting in the stove-steam hot-stone
        cedar-planking wooden bucket water-splashing
        kerosene lantern-flicker wind-in-the-pines-out
        sierra forest ridges night—
Masa comes in, letting fresh cool air
        sweep down from the door
        a deep sweet breath
And she tips him over gripping neatly, one knee down
        her hair falling hiding one whole side of
        shoulder, breast, and belly,
Washes deftly Kai's head-hair
        as he gets mad and yells—
The body of my lady, the winding valley spine,
        the space between the thighs I reach through,
        cup her curving vulva arch and hold it from behind,
        a soapy tickle   a hand of grail
The gates of Awe
That open back a turning double-mirror world of
        wombs in wombs, in rings,
        that start in music,
                    is this our body?

The hidden place of seed
The veins net flow across the ribs, that gathers
        milk and peaks up in a nipple—fits
        our mouth—
The sucking milk from this our body sends through
        jolts of light; the son, the father,
        sharing mother's joy
That brings a softness to the flower of the awesome
        open curling lotus gate I cup and kiss
As Kai laughs at his mother's breast he now is weaned
        from, we
        wash each other,
                    this our body

Kai's little scrotum up close to his groin,
    the seed still tucked away, that moved from us to him
In flows that lifted with the same joys forces
     as his nursing Masa later,
     playing with her breast,
Or me within her,
Or him emerging,
               this is our body:

Clean, and rinsed, and sweating more, we stretch
    out on the redwood benches hearts all beating
Quiet to the simmer of the stove,
    the scent of cedar
And then turn over,
     murmuring gossip of the grasses,
     talking firewood,
Wondering how Gen's napping, how to bring him in
    soon wash him too—
These boys who love their mother
     who loves men, who passes on
     her sons to other women;

The cloud across the sky. The windy pines.
    the trickle gurgle in the swampy meadow

    this is our body.

Fire inside and boiling water on the stove
We sigh and slide ourselves down from the benches
    wrap the babies, step outside,

black night & all the stars.

Pour cold water on the back and thighs
Go in the house—stand steaming by the center fire
Kai scampers on the sheepskin
Gen standing hanging on and shouting,

"Bao! bao! bao! bao! bao!"

This is our body. Drawn up crosslegged by the flames
   drinking icy water
   hugging babies, kissing bellies,

Laughing on the Great Earth

Come out from the bath.

Coyote Valley Spring

  Cubs
  tumble in the damp leaves
  Deer, bear, squirrel.
  fresh winds scour the
  spring stars.
  rocks crumble
  deep mud hardens
  under heavy hills.

  shifting things
  birds, weeds,
  slip through the air
  through eyes and ears,

  Coyote valley. *Olema*
  in the spring.
  white and solemn toloache flower

  and far out in the *tamal*
  a lost people
  float

  in tiny tule boats.

Spel Against Demons

The release of Demonic Energies in the name of
the People
must cease

Messing with blood sacrifice in the name of
Nature
must cease

The stifling self-indulgence in anger in the name of
Freedom
must cease

this is death to clarity
death to compassion

the man who has the soul of the wolf
knows the self-restraint
of the wolf

aimless executions and slaughterings
are not the work of wolves and eagles

but the work of hysterical sheep

The Demonic must be devoured!
Self-serving must be
cut down
Anger must be
plowed back
Fearlessness, humor, detachment, is power

Gnowledge is the secret of Transformation!

Down with demonic killers who mouth revolutionary
slogans and muddy the flow of change, may they be
Bound by the Noose, and Instructed by the Diamond
Sword of ACHALA the Immovable, Lord of Wisdom, Lord
of Heat, who is squint-eyed and whose face is terrible

with bare fangs, who wears on his crown a garland of
severed heads, clad in a tiger skin, he who turns
Wrath to Purified Accomplishment,

    whose powers are of lava,
      of magma, of deep rock strata, of gunpowder,
          and the Sun.

He who saves tortured intelligent demons and filth-eating
        hungry ghosts, his spel is,

NAMAH SAMANTAH VAJRANAM CHANDA
  MAHAROSHANA
          SPHATAYA HUM TRAKA HAM MAM

Front Lines

    The edge of the cancer
    Swells against the hill—we feel
    a foul breeze—
    And it sinks back down.
    The deer winter here
    A chainsaw growls in the gorge.

    Ten wet days and the log trucks stop,
    The trees breathe.
    Sunday the 4-wheel jeep of the
    Realty Company brings in
    Landseekers, lookers, they say
    To the land,
    Spread your legs.

    The jets crack sound overhead, it's OK here;
    Every pulse of the rot at the heart
    In the sick fat veins of Amerika
    Pushes the edge up closer—

A bulldozer grinding and slobbering
Sideslipping and belching on top of
The skinned-up bodies of still-live bushes
In the pay of a man
From town.

Behind is a forest that goes to the Arctic
And a desert that still belongs to the Piute
And here we must draw
Our line.

Control Burn

What the Indians
here
used to do, was,
to burn out the brush every year.
in the woods, up the gorges,
keeping the oak and the pine stands
tall and clear
with grasses
and kitkitdizze under them,
never enough fuel there
that a fire could crown.

Now, manzanita,
(a fine bush in its right)
crowds up under the new trees
mixed up with logging slash
and a fire can wipe out all.

Fire is an old story.
I would like,
with a sense of helpful order,
with respect for laws
of nature,
to help my land
with a burn. a hot clean
burn.

(manzanita seeds will only open
after a fire passes over
or once passed through a bear)

And then
it would be more
like,
when it belonged to the Indians

Before.

The Great Mother

Not all those who pass

In front of the Great Mother's chair

Get passt with only a stare.

Some she looks at their hands

To see what sort of savages they were.

The Call of the Wild

The heavy old man in his bed at night
Hears the Coyote singing
                    in the back meadow.
All the years he ranched and mined and logged.
A Catholic.
A native Californian.
     and the Coyotes howl in his
Eightieth year.

He will call the Government
Trapper
Who uses iron leg-traps on Coyotes,
Tomorrow.
My sons will lose this
Music they have just started
To love.

———

The ex acid-heads from the cities
Converted to Guru or Swami,
Do penance with shiny
Dopey eyes, and quit eating meat.
In the forests of North America,
The land of Coyote and Eagle,
They dream of India, of
       forever blissful sexless highs.
And sleep in oil-heated
Geodesic domes, that
Were stuck like warts
In the woods.

And the Coyote singing
       is shut away
       for they fear
       the call
       of the wild.

And they sold their virgin cedar trees,
       the tallest trees in miles,
To a logger
Who told them,

"Trees are full of bugs."

———

The Government finally decided
To wage the war   all-out. Defeat
       is Un-American.

And they took to the air,
Their women beside them
        in bouffant hairdos
        putting nail-polish on the
        gunship cannon-buttons.
And they never came down,
        for they found,
        the ground
is pro-Communist. And dirty.
And the insects side with the Viet Cong.

So they bomb and they bomb
Day after day, across the planet
        blinding sparrows
        breaking the ear-drums of owls
        splintering trunks of cherries
        twining and looping
        deer intestines
        in the shaken, dusty, rocks.

All these Americans up in special cities in the sky
Dumping poisons and explosives
Across Asia first,
And next North America,

A war against earth.
When it's done there'll be
        no place

A Coyote could hide.

                        envoy

                I would like to say
                Coyote is forever
                Inside you.

                But it's not true.

Prayer for the Great Family

Gratitude to Mother Earth, sailing through night and day—
  and to her soil: rich, rare, and sweet
    in our minds so be it.

Gratitude to Plants, the sun-facing light-changing leaf
  and fine root-hairs; standing still through wind
  and rain; their dance is in the flowing spiral grain
    in our minds so be it.

Gratitude to Air, bearing the soaring Swift and the silent
  Owl at dawn. Breath of our song
  clear spirit breeze
    in our minds so be it.

Gratitude to Wild Beings, our brothers, teaching secrets,
  freedoms, and ways; who share with us their milk;
  self-complete, brave, and aware
    in our minds so be it.

Gratitude to Water: clouds, lakes, rivers, glaciers;
  holding or releasing; streaming through all
  our bodies salty seas
    in our minds so be it.

Gratitude to the Sun: blinding pulsing light through
  trunks of trees, through mists, warming caves where
  bears and snakes sleep—he who wakes us—
    in our minds so be it.

Gratitude to the Great Sky
  who holds billions of stars—and goes yet beyond that—
  beyond all powers, and thoughts
  and yet is within us—
  Grandfather Space.
  The Mind is his Wife.

    so be it.

        after a Mohawk prayer

Source

To be in
to the land
where croppt-out rock
can hardly see
the swiftly passing trees

Manzanita clans
cluster up and fan out on their soils
in streaks and sweeps
with birds and woodrats underneath

And clay swale keeps wet,
free of trees, the bunch-grass
like no Spaniard ever came

I hear no news

Cloud finger dragons dance and
tremble down the ridge
and spit and spiral snow then pull in
quivering, on the sawtooth
spine

Clears up, and all the stars.
the tree leaves catch
some extra tiny source
all the wide night

Up here
out back
drink deep
that black light.

Manzanita

Before dawn the coyotes
    weave medicine songs
      dream nets—spirit baskets—
    milky way music
        they cook young girls with
        to be woman;
  or the whirling dance of
  striped boys—

At moon-set the pines are gold-purple
Just before sunrise.

The dog hastens into the undergrowth
Comes back panting
Huge, on the small dry flowers.

A woodpecker
Drums and echoes
Across the still meadow

One man draws, and releases   an arrow
Humming, flat,
Missing a gray stump, and splitting
A smooth red twisty manzanita bough.

Manzanita   the tips in fruit,
Clusters of hard green berries
The longer you look
The bigger they seem,

        "little apples"

Charms
for Michael McClure

The beauty of naked or half-naked women,
lying in nothing clear or obvious—not
in exposure; but a curve of the back or arm,
as a dance or—evoking "another world"

"The Deva Realm" or better, the Delight
at the heart of creation.

Brought out for each mammal species
specifically—in some dreamlike perfection
of name-and-form

Thus I could be devastated and athirst with longing
for a lovely mare or lioness, or lady mouse,
in seeing the beauty from THERE
shining through her, some toss of the whiskers
or grace-full wave of the tail

that enchants.

enchants, and thus

CHARMS.

— Magpie's Song —

Facts

1. 92% of Japan's three million ton import of soybeans comes from the U.S.

2. The U.S. has 6% of the world's population; consumes ⅓ the energy annually consumed in the world.

3. The U.S. consumes ⅓ of the world's annual meat.

4. The top ⅕ of American population gets 45% of salary income, and owns about 77% of the total wealth. The top 1% owns 20 to 30% of personal wealth.

5. A modern nation needs 13 basic industrial raw materials. By AD 2000 the U.S. will be import-dependent on all but phosphorus.

6. General Motors is bigger than Holland.

7. Nuclear energy is mainly subsidized with fossil fuels and barely yields net energy.

8. The "Seven Sisters"—Exxon, Mobil, Texaco, Gulf, Standard of California, British Petroleum, Royal Dutch Shell.

9. "The reason solar energy has not and will not be a major contributor or substitute for fossil fuels is that it will not compete without energy subsidy from fossil fuel economy. The plants have already maximized the use of sunlight."
—H. T. Odum

10. Our primary source of food is the sun.

The Real Work
[Today with Zach & Dan rowing by Alcatraz
and around Angel Island]

sea-lions and birds,
sun through fog
flaps up and lolling,
looks you dead in the eye.
sun haze;
a long tanker riding light and high.

sharp wave choppy line—
interface tide-flows—
seagulls sit on the meeting
eating;
we slide by white-stained cliffs.

the real work.
washing and sighing,
sliding by.

Pine Tree Tops

in the blue night
frost haze, the sky glows
with the moon
pine tree tops
bend snow-blue, fade
into sky, frost, starlight.
the creak of boots.
rabbit tracks, deer tracks,
what do we know.

For Nothing

Earth a flower
A phlox on the steep
slopes of light
hanging over the vast
solid spaces
small rotten crystals;
salts.

Earth a flower
by a gulf where a raven
flaps by once
a glimmer, a color
forgotten as all
falls away.

A flower
for nothing;
an offer;
no taker;

Snow-trickle, feldspar, dirt.

Night Herons

Night herons nest in the cypress
by the San Francisco
stationary boilers
with the high smoke stack
at the edge of the waters:
a steam turbine pump
to drive salt water
into the city's veins
mains
if the earth ever
quakes. and the power fails.
and water

to fight fire, runs
loose on the streets
with no pressure.

At the wire gate tilted slightly out
the part-wolf dog
would go in, to follow
if his human buddy lay on his side
and squirmed up first.

An abandoned, decaying, army.
a rotten rusty island prison
surrounded by lights of whirling
fluttering god-like birds
who truth
has never forgot.

I walk with my wife's sister
past the frozen bait;
with a long-bearded architect,
my dear brother,
and silent friend, whose
mustache curves wetly into his mouth
and he sometimes bites it.

the dog knows no laws and is strictly,
illegal. His neck arches and ears prick out
to catch mice in the tundra.
a black high school boy
drinking coffee at a fake green stand
tries to be friends with the dog,
and it works.

How could the
night herons ever come back?
to this noisy place on the bay.
like me.
the joy of all the beings
is in being
older and tougher and eaten
up.

in the tubes and lanes of things
in the sewers of bliss and judgment,
in the glorious cleansing
treatment
plants.

We pick our way
through the edge of the city
early
subtly spreading changing sky;

ever-fresh and lovely dawn.

The Egg

"A snake-like beauty in the living changes of syntax"
—Robert Duncan

Kai twists
rubs "bellybutton"
rubs skin, front and back
two legs kicking
anus a sensitive center
        the pull-together
        between there and the scrotum,
the center line,
with the out-flyers changing
—fins, legs, wings,
feathers or fur,
they swing and swim
but the snake center
fire pushes through:
        mouth to ass,
        root to
        burning, steady,
        single eye.

breeze in the brown grasses
high clouds deep
blue.   white.

blue.   moving
changing

my Mother's old
soft arm. walking
helping up the
path.

Kai's hand
in my fist
the neck bones,
a little thread,
a garland,
of consonants and vowels
from the third eye
through the body's flowers
a string of peaks,
a whirlpool
sucking to the root.

It all gathers,
humming,
in the egg.

The Uses of Light

It warms my bones
            say the stones

I take it into me and grow
Say the trees
Leaves above
Roots below

A vast vague white
Draws me out of the night
Says the moth in his flight—

Some things I smell
Some things I hear
And I see things move
Says the deer—

A high tower
on a wide plain.
If you climb up
One floor
You'll see a thousand miles more.

On San Gabriel Ridges

I dream of—
soft, white, washable country
clothes.
woven zones.
scats
up here on the rocks;
seeds, stickers, twigs, bits of grass
on my belly, pressed designs—

O loves of long ago
        hello again.
all of us together
with all our other loves and children
twining and knotting
through each other—
intricate, chaotic, done.
I dive with you all
and it curls back, freezes;
the laws of waves.
as clear as a canyon wall

as sweet,
as long ago.

woven
into the dark.
squirrel hairs,
squirrel bones crunched,
tight and dry in scats of
fox.

By Frazier Creek Falls

Standing up on lifted, folded rock
looking out and down—

The creek falls to a far valley.
hills beyond that
facing, half-forested, dry
—clear sky
strong wind in the
stiff glittering needle clusters
of the pine—their brown
round trunk bodies
straight, still;
rustling trembling limbs and twigs

listen.

This living flowing land
is all there is, forever

We *are* it
it sings through us—

We could live on this Earth
without clothes or tools!

Black Mesa Mine #1

Wind dust yellow cloud swirls
northeast across the fifty-foot
graded bulldozed road,
white cloud puffs,
juniper and pinyon scattered groves
          —firewood for the People
               heaps of wood for all
               at cross-streets in the pueblos,
ancient mother mountain
pools of water
pools of coal
pools of sand
               buried or laid bare

Solitary trucks go slow on grades
smoking sand
writhes around the tires
and on a torn up stony plain
a giant green-and-yellow shovel
whirs and drags
house-size scoops of rock and gravel

Mountain,
be kind,
it will tumble in its hole

Five hundred yards   back up the road
a Navajo corral
of stood up dried out poles and logs
all leaned in on an angle,
gleaming in the windy April sun.

Up Branches of Duck River

Shaka valley—chickens thousands
    murmur in sheet walls
past plaster house of welder-sculptor
    shakuhachi pond,
dead grass golf-course bulldozed on the hill
    pine Dragon Benten
ridgetop—far off Kyoto on the flat,
turn in to deeper hills toward himuru, "Ice House"—
cut-back Sugi—logger shelter—

Low pass, a snow patch still up here,
they once stored ice for summer,
old women stoking bath fire
white plum bloom

Old man burning brush, a wood sheath for the saw

Over the edge & down to Kamo River
white hills—Mt. Hiei, Hira—cut clean
reseed patchwork, orchard fir

Muddy slipping trail
wobbly twin pole bridges
    gully throat
   forks in
somebody clearing brush & growing tea
& out, turn here for home
along the Kamo River.

hold it close
give it all away.

It Pleases

Far above the dome
Of the capitol—
    It's true!
A large bird soars

> Against white cloud,
> Wings arced,
> Sailing easy in this
> humid Southern sun-blurred
> >   breeze—
> >   the dark-suited policeman
> >   watches tourist cars—
>
> And the center,
> The center of power is nothing!
> Nothing here.
> Old white stone domes,
> Strangely quiet people,
>
> Earth-sky-bird patterns
> >   idly interlacing
>
> The world does what it pleases.

Washington D.C. XI:73

Hemp
for Michael Aldrich

Gravel-bars, riverbanks, scars
of the glaciers,
healing and nursing moraine—
tall hemp plants followed man

> midden   dump heap   roadway slash

To bind his loads and ease his mind
> Moor to Spain, Spain in horse-manure
> and straw, across the sea
> & up from Mexico

—a tiny puff of white cloud far away.
we sit and wait, for days,

and pray for rain.

The Wild Mushroom

Well the sunset rays are shining
Me and Kai have got our tools
A basket and a trowel
And a book with all the rules

Don't ever eat Boletus
If the tube-mouths they are red
Stay away from the Amanitas
Or brother you are dead

Sometimes they're already rotten
Or the stalks are broken off
Where the deer have knocked them over
While turning up the duff

We set out in the forest
To seek the wild mushroom
In shapes diverse and colorful
Shining through the woodland gloom

If you look out under oak trees
Or around an old pine stump
You'll know a mushroom's coming
By the way the leaves are humped

They send out multiple fibers
Through the roots and sod
Some make you mighty sick they say
Or bring you close to God

So here's to the mushroom family
A far-flung friendly clan
For food, for fun, for poison
They are a help to man.

Mother Earth: Her Whales

An owl winks in the shadows
A lizard lifts on tiptoe, breathing hard
Young male sparrow stretches up his neck,
        big head, watching—

The grasses are working in the sun. Turn it green.
Turn it sweet. That we may eat.
Grow our meat.

Brazil says "sovereign use of Natural Resources"
Thirty thousand kinds of unknown plants.
The living actual people of the jungle
        sold and tortured—
And a robot in a suit who peddles a delusion called "Brazil"
        can speak for *them*?

        The whales turn and glisten, plunge
           and sound and rise again,
        Hanging over subtly darkening deeps
        Flowing like breathing planets
           in the sparkling whorls of
               living light—

And Japan quibbles for words on
        what kinds of whales they can kill?
A once-great Buddhist nation
        dribbles methyl mercury
        like gonorrhea
           in the sea.

Père David's Deer, the Elaphure,
Lived in the tule marshes of the Yellow River
Two thousand years ago—and lost its home to rice—
The forests of Lo-yang were logged and all the silt &
Sand flowed down, and gone, by 1200 AD—
Wild Geese hatched out in Siberia
        head south over basins of the Yang, the Huang,
        what we call "China"

On flyways they have used a million years.
Ah China, where are the tigers, the wild boars,
              the monkeys,
                    like the snows of yesteryear
Gone in a mist, a flash, and the dry hard ground
Is parking space for fifty thousand trucks.
IS man most precious of all things?
—then let us love him, and his brothers, all those
Fading living beings—

North America, Turtle Island, taken by invaders
              who wage war around the world.
May ants, may abalone, otters, wolves and elk
Rise! and pull away their giving
              from the robot nations.

Solidarity. The People.
Standing Tree People!
Flying Bird People!
Swimming Sea People!
Four-legged, two-legged, people!

How can the head-heavy power-hungry politic scientist
Government   two-world   Capitalist-Imperialist
Third-world   Communist   paper-shuffling male
         non-farmer   jet-set   bureaucrats
Speak for the green of the leaf? Speak for the soil?

(Ah Margaret Mead . . . do you sometimes dream of Samoa?)

The robots argue how to parcel out our Mother Earth
To last a little longer
              like vultures flapping
Belching, gurgling,
              near a dying Doe.
"In yonder field a slain knight lies—
We'll fly to him and eat his eyes
              with a down
      derry derry derry down down."

An Owl winks in the shadow
A lizard lifts on tiptoe
        breathing hard
The whales turn and glisten
        plunge and
Sound, and rise again
Flowing like breathing planets

In the sparkling whorls

Of living light.

Stockholm: Summer Solstice 40072

Affluence

under damp layers of pine needle
still-hard limbs and twigs
tangled as they lay,
two sixteen foot good butt logs took
all the rest, top, left

and this from logging twenty years ago
(figured from core-ring reading on a tree
still stands, hard by a stump)
they didn't pile the slash and burn then—

fire hazard, every summer day.

it was the logger's cost
at lumber's going rate then

now burn the tangles dowsing
pokey heaps with diesel oil.
paying the price somebody didn't pay.

Ethnobotany

In June two oak fell,
rot in the roots

Chainsaw in September
in three days one tree
bucked and quartered in the shed

sour fresh inner oak-wood smell
the main trunk splits
"like opening a book" (J. Tecklin)

And slightly humping oak leaves
deer muzzle and kick it,
Boletus.
one sort, *Alice Eastwood*
pink, and poison;

Two yellow. *edulus*
"edible and choice."
only I got just so slightly sick—

Taste all, and hand the knowledge down.

Straight-Creek—Great Burn
for Tom and Martha Birch

Lightly, in the April mountains—
                    Straight Creek,
dry grass freed again of snow
& the chickadees are pecking

last fall's seeds
          fluffing tail in chilly wind,

Avalanche piled up cross the creek
          and chunked-froze solid—
water sluicing under; spills out
          rock lip pool, bends over,
          braided, white, foaming,
returns to trembling
          deep-dark hole.

Creek boulders show the flow-wear lines
          in shapes the same
          as running blood
          carves in the heart's main
                    valve,

Early spring dry. Dry snow flurries;
          walk on crusty high snow slopes
—grand dead burn pine—
          chartreuse lichen as adornment
                    (a dye for wool)
angled tumbled talus rock
of geosyncline warm sea bottom
yes, so long ago.
"Once on a time."

Far light on the Bitterroots;
          scrabble down willow slide
changing clouds above,
shapes on glowing sun-ball
writhing,   choosing
          reaching out against eternal
                              azure—

us resting on dry fern and
          watching

Shining Heaven
change his feather garments
          overhead.

A whoosh of birds
swoops up and round
tilts back
almost always flying all apart
and yet hangs on!
together;

never a leader,
all of one swift

empty
dancing   mind.

They arc and loop & then
their flight is done.
they settle down.
end of poem.

The Hudsonian Curlew
for Drum and Diana

The end of a desert track—turnaround—
        parked the truck and walked over dunes.
a cobbly point   hooks in the shallow bay;

        the Mandala of Birds.

pelican, seagulls, and terns,
            one curlew
            far at the end—
they fly up as they see us
                and settle back down.
tern keep coming
                —skies of wide seas—
frigate birds keep swooping

pelicans sit nearest the foam;

tern bathing and fluttering
            in frothy wave-lapping
                        between the round stones.

            we
gather driftwood for firewood
for camping
get four shells to serve up steamed snail

———

            in the top of the cardón cactus
            two vultures
            look, yawn, hunch, preen.
            out on the point   the seabirds
            squabble and settle, meet and leave;
                        speak.
            two sides of a border.
            the margins.   tidewater.   zones.
            up in the void,   under the surface,
            two worlds   touch
            and greet

———

Three shotgun shots as it gets dark;
two birds.
            "how come three shots?"
            "one went down on the water
            and started to swim.
            I didn't want another thing like that duck."

the bill curved in, and the long neck limp—
a grandmother plumage of cinnamon and brown.
the beak not so long—bars on the head;
            by the eye.
            Hudsonian Curlew

                        and those tern most likely
                        "Royal Tern"

with forked tail,
that heavy orange bill.

———

The down
i pluck from the
neck of the curlew
eddies and whirls at my knees
in the twilight wind
from sea.
kneeling in sand

warm in the hand.

———

"Do you want to do it right? I'll tell you."
he tells me.
at the edge of the water on the stones.
a transverse cut just below the sternum
the forefinger and middle finger
                forced in and up, following the
                curve of the rib cage.
then fingers arched, drawn slowly down and back,
forcing all the insides up and out,
toward the palm and heel of the hand.
firm organs, well-placed, hot.
save the liver;
finally scouring back, toward the vent, the last of the
                large intestine.

the insides string out, begin to wave, in the lapping
                waters of the bay.
the bird has no feathers, head, or feet;
                he is empty inside.
the rich body muscle that he moved by, the wing-beating
                muscle
anchored to the blade-like high breast bone,
is what you eat.

The black iron frying pan on the coals.
two birds singed in flame.
bacon, onion, and garlic
browning, then steaming with a lid
put the livers in,
half a bird apiece and bulghour
passed about the fire on metal plates.
dense firm flesh,
dark and rich,
            gathered news of skies and seas.

at dawn
looking out from the dunes
no birds at all but
three curlew

        ker-lew!

        ker-lew!

pacing   and glancing   around.

                Baja: Bahia de Concepción, '69

Two Fawns That Didn't See
the Light This Spring

A friend in a tipi in the
Northern Rockies went out
hunting white tail with a
.22 and creeped up on a few
day-bedded, sleeping, shot
what he thought was a buck.

"It was a doe, and she was
carrying a fawn."
He cured the meat without
salt; sliced it following the
grain.

A friend in the Northern Sierra
hit a doe with her car. It
walked out calmly in the lights,
"And when we butchered her
there was a fawn—about so long—
so tiny—but all formed and right.
It had spots. And the little
hooves were soft and white."

Two Immortals

Sitting on a bench by the Rogue River, Oregon, looking at
a landform map. Two older gents approached and one, with
baseball cap, began to sing: "California Here I Come"—he
must have seen the license. Asked me if I'd ever heard of Texas
Slim. Yes. And he said the song "If I Had the Wings of an
Angel" was his, had been writ by him, "I was in the peniten-
tiary." "Let me shake your hand! That's a good song" I said,
and he showed me his hand: faint blue traces of tattoo on the
back, on the bent fingers. And if I hit you with this hand it's
L-O-V-E. And if I hit you with this hand it's H-A-T-E.
    His friend, in a red and black buffalo check jacket stuck his
hand out, under my nose, missing the forefinger. "How'd I lose
that!" "How?" "An axe!"
    Texas Slim said "I'm just giving him a ride. Last year his wife
died." The two ambled off, chuckling, as Kai and Gen came
running back up from the banks of Rogue River, hands full of
round river stones.
    Looking at the map, it was the space inside the loop of the
upper Columbia, eastern Washington plateau country. "Chan-
nelled Scablands."

Rain in Alleghany

standing in the thunder-pouring
heavy drops of water
              —dusty summer—
drinking beer just after driving
all the way around the
              watershed of rivers

rocky slopes and bumpy cars
its a skinny awkward land
like a workt-out miner's hand
              & how we love it
have some beer and rain,
stopping on our way,
in Alleghany

Alleghany California, home of the
Sixteen to One Mine.

Avocado

The Dharma is like an Avocado!
Some parts so ripe you can't believe it,
But it's good.
And other places hard and green
Without much flavor,
Pleasing those who like their eggs well-cooked.

And the skin is thin,
The great big round seed
In the middle,
Is your own Original Nature—
Pure and smooth,
Almost nobody ever splits it open
Or ever tries to see
If it will grow.

Hard and slippery,
It looks like
You should plant it—but then
It shoots out thru the
          fingers—
gets away.

What Steps

Disciple: "Why is there evil in the universe?"
   Ramakrishna: "To thicken the plot."

What steps.
Philip shaving his head,
Keith looney,
Allen benign,
Dick in charge,
Not magic, not transcendence exactly
but—all created things are of the Mother—
or—the un-created
day by day
stepping in
to the power within.
                    What steps
In the starry night.
    Tārā's eyes
      revolvers clicking
      raccoon eyes shine back
lanterns fading
    (Bhagavan Das like a National Park)

putting chains on
in the mud.

To turn our mad dance partner spinning laughing
        ashes, ashes,
        —all fall down.

Why Log Truck Drivers Rise Earlier
Than Students of Zen

In the high seat, before-dawn dark,
Polished hubs gleam
And the shiny diesel stack
Warms and flutters
Up the Tyler Road grade
To the logging on Poorman creek.
Thirty miles of dust.

There is no other life.

Bedrock
for Masa

Snowmelt pond   warm granite
we make camp,
no thought of finding more.
and nap
and leave our minds to the wind.

on the bedrock, gently tilting,
sky and stone,

teach me to be tender.

the touch that nearly misses—
brush of glances—

tiny steps—
that finally cover worlds
            of hard terrain.
cloud wisps and mists
gathered into slate blue
bolts of summer rain.

tea together in the purple starry eve;
new moon soon to set,
why does it take so
long to learn to
love,
        we laugh
                and grieve.

The Dazzle
for Richard and Michael

    the dazzle, the seduction the
                design
        intoxicated and quivering,
    bees? is it flowers? why does this
            seed move around.
                the one
divides itself, divides, and divides again.
        "we all know where that leads"
        blinding storms of gold pollen.
                —grope through that?
                the dazzle
                and the blue clay.
        "all that moves, loves to sing"
            the roots are at work.
                unseen.

"One Should Not Talk to a Skilled Hunter About What Is Forbidden by the Buddha"
—Hsiang-yen

A gray fox, female, nine pounds three ounces.
39 ⅝" long with tail.
Peeling skin back (Kai
reminded us to chant the *Shingyo* first)
cold pelt. crinkle; and musky smell
mixed with dead-body odor starting.

Stomach content: a whole ground squirrel well chewed
plus one lizard foot
and somewhere from inside the ground squirrel
a bit of aluminum foil.

The secret.
and the secret hidden deep in that.

LMFBR

Death himself,
        (Liquid Metal Fast Breeder Reactor)
        stands grinning, beckoning.
Plutonium tooth-glow.
Eyebrows buzzing.
Strip-mining scythe.

Kālī dances on the dead stiff cock.

        Aluminum beer cans, plastic spoons,
plywood veneer, PVC pipe, vinyl seat covers,
                don't exactly burn, don't quite rot,
                flood over us,

                robes and garbs
                of the Kālī-yūga

                end of days.

Walking Home from "The Duchess of Malfi"

Walking home from "The Duchess of Malfi"
Bellatrix and Rigel gleam out of deep pits
Torn in the sea-cloud
              blown east from the Golden Gate

Months in the cabin: rain,
        cold, hard floor, leaking roof
        beautiful walls and windows—
              feeding birds

              once I
Struck and bit on thought
Of *being*
Being suffering,
Fought free, tearing hook and line
                      (my mind)—
Thus was taught,
Pains of death and love,
Birth and war,
              wreckt earth,

              bless
With more love,

              not less.

Berkeley: 55

Magpie's Song

Six A.M.,
Sat down on excavation gravel
by juniper and desert S.P. tracks
interstate 80 not far off
        between trucks

Coyotes—maybe three
      howling and yapping from a rise.

Magpie on a bough
Tipped his head and said,

> *"Here in the mind, brother*
> *Turquoise blue.*
> *I wouldn't fool you.*
> *Smell the breeze*
> *It came through all the trees*
> *No need to fear*
> *What's ahead*
> *Snow up on the hills west*
> *Will be there every year*
> *be at rest.*
> *A feather on the ground—*
> *The wind sound—*

Here in the Mind, Brother,
Turquoise Blue"

For the Children

O Waters

O waters
wash us, me,
under the wrinkled granite
straight-up slab,

and sitting by camp in the pine shade
Nanao sleeping,
mountains humming and crumbling
snowfields melting
soil
building on tiny ledges
for wild onions and the flowers
Blue
Polemonium

great
earth
sangha

Gen

Gen
little frown
buried in her breast
and long black hair
Gen for milk
Gen for sleep
Gen for looking-over-shoulder
for beyond the waving eucalyptus
limbs and farther dreaming crow
flying slow and steady for the ocean;
eyes over drippy nipple
at the rising shadow sun
whales of cool and dark,
Gen patted-on-the-head by Kai,
"don't cry"

Dusty Braces

O you ancestors
lumber schooners
           big moustache
long-handled underwear
sticks out under the cuffs

tan stripes on each shoulder,
dusty braces—
          nine bows
          nine bows
you bastards
my fathers
and grandfathers, stiff-necked
punchers, miners, dirt farmers, railroad-men

killd off the cougar and grizzly

nine bows. Your itch
in my boots too,

—your sea roving
tree hearted son.

The Jemez Pueblo Ring

Lost in the cracks of the walls or floors in Kyoto
Fell through and missed and sifted out
          when the house was razed,
Foundations poured and apartments raised above it—

In forty ye— ————— ———— ——— torn down.
          scrap wood burned for cooking and
          bath fires—

Another sixty passes, the land is good;
With an ox they snake off concrete shards—

On the tines of the fork
              in the black soil
              the crusted ring.
              wiped with the thumb
              turquoise stone still blue.

The expert looked at it and said,
              this is a ring from the century past.
              when there was travel and trade.
              from across the sea, east,

Silver, and blue of the desert sky.
              the style is old.
              though we never see them now,

Those corn-growing black-haired villagers
              are still there, making such rings,
              I'm told—

Tomorrow's Song

The USA slowly lost its mandate
in the middle and later twentieth century
it never gave the mountains and rivers,
              trees and animals,
                   a vote.
all the people turned away from it
              myths die; even continents are impermanent

              Turtle Island returned.
              my friend broke open a dried coyote-scat
              removed a ground squirrel tooth
              pierced it, hung it
              from the gold ring
              in his ear.

We look to the future with pleasure
we need no fossil fuel

get power within
grow strong on less.

Grasp the tools and move in rhythm side by side
    flash gleams of wit and silent knowledge
            eye to eye
sit still like cats or snakes or stones
   as whole and holding as
          the blue black sky.
gentle and innocent as wolves
        as tricky as a prince.

At work and in our place:

> *in the service*
> *of the wilderness*
> *of life*
> *of death*
> *of the Mother's breasts!*

What Happened Here Before

—300,000,000—

First a sea: soft sands, muds, and marls
    —loading, compressing, heating, crumpling,
    crushing, recrystallizing, infiltrating,
several times lifted and submerged.
intruding molten granite magma
    deep-cooled and speckling,
        gold quartz fills the cracks—

—80,000,000—

sea-bed strata raised and folded,
    granite far below.
warm quiet centuries of rains
    (make dark red tropic soils)

wear down two miles of surface,
lay bare the veins and tumble heavy gold
   in steambeds
       slate and schist rock-riffles catch it—
volcanic ash floats down and dams the streams,
    piles up the gold and gravel—

       —3,000,000—

flowing north, two rivers joined,
    to make a wide long lake.
and then it tilted and the rivers fell apart
    all running west
     to cut the gorges of the Feather,
       Bear, and Yuba.
Ponderosa pine, manzanita, black oak, mountain yew.
    deer, coyote, bluejay, gray squirrel,
   ground squirrel, fox, blacktail hare,
    ringtail, bobcat, bear,
      all came to live here.

    —40,000—

And human people came with basket hats and nets
    winter-houses underground
    yew bows painted green,
     feasts and dances for the boys and girls
       songs and stories in the smoky dark.

    —125—

Then came the white man: tossed up trees and
    boulders with big hoses,
    going after that old gravel and the gold.
horses, apple-orchards, card-games,
    pistol-shooting, churches, county jail.

We asked, who the land belonged to.
      and where one pays tax.
(two gents who never used it twenty years,
and before them the widow
      of the son of the man
      who got him a patented deed
      on a worked-out mining claim,)
laid hasty on land that was deer and acorn
      grounds of the Nisenan?
      branch of the Maidu?
(they never had a chance to speak, even,
      their name.)
(and who remembers the Treaty of Guadalupe Hidalgo.)

      the land belongs to itself.
      "no self in self; no self in things"

      Turtle Island swims
      in the ocean-sky swirl-void
      biting its tail while the worlds go
         on-and-off
            winking

& Mr. Tobiassen, a Cousin Jack,
      assesses the county tax.
(the tax is our body-mind, guest at the banquet
      Memorial and Annual, in honor
      of sunlight grown heavy and tasty
      while moving up food-chains
in search of a body with eyes and a fairly large
         brain—
      to look back at itself
         on high.)

               now,

we sit here near the diggings
in the forest, by our fire, and watch
the moon and planets and the shooting stars—

my sons ask, who are we?
drying apples picked from homestead trees
drying berries, curing meat,
shooting arrows at a bale of straw.

military jets head northeast, roaring, every dawn.
my sons ask, who are they?

> *WE SHALL SEE*
> *WHO KNOWS*
> *HOW TO BE*

Bluejay screeches from a pine.

Toward Climax

I.

salt seas, mountains, deserts—
cell mandala holding water
nerve network linking toes and eyes
fins   legs   wings—
teeth, all-purpose little early mammal molars.
primate flat-foot
front fore-mounted eyes—

watching at the forest-grassland (interface
richness) edge.
scavenge, gather, rise up on rear legs.
running—grasping—hand and eye;
hunting.
calling others to the stalk, the drive.

note sharp points of split bone; broken rock.

brain-size blossoming
on the balance of the neck,
tough skin—good eyes—sharp ears—
move in bands.
milkweed fiber rolled out on the thigh;
            nets to carry fruits or meat.

catch fire, move on.
eurasia tundra reindeer herds
sewn hide clothing, mammoth-rib-framework tent.

Bison, bear,   skinned and split;
        opening animal chests and bellies, skulls,
        bodies just like ours—
pictures in caves.
send sound off the mouth and lips
formal complex grammars transect
        inner structures & the daily world—

big herds dwindle
        (—did we kill them?
        thousand-mile front of prairie fire—)
ice age warms up
learn more plants. netting, trapping, boats.
bow and arrow. dogs.
mingle bands and families in and out like language
        kin to grubs and trees and wolves

        dance and sing.
begin to go "beyond"—   reed flute—
        buried baby wrapped in many furs—
great dream-time tales to tell.

squash blossom in the garbage heap.
        start farming.
cows won't stay away, start herding.
weaving, throwing clay.
get better off, get class,
make lists, start writing down.

forget wild plants, their virtues
lose dream-time
lose largest size of brain—

get safer, tighter, wrapped in,
winding smaller, spreading wider,
lay towns out in streets in rows,
and build a wall.

drain swamp for wet-rice grasses, burn back woods,
herd men like cows.
have slaves build a fleet
raid for wealth—bronze weapons
horse and wagon—iron—war.

study stars and figure central
never-moving Pole Star King.

II.

From "King" project a Law. (Foxy self-
survival sense is Reason, since it "works")
and Reason gets ferocious as it goes for
order throughout nature—turns Law back on
nature. (A rooster was burned at the stake
for laying an egg. Unnatural. 1474.)

III.

science walks in beauty:

nets are many knots
skin is border-guard, a pelt is borrowed warmth;
a bow is the flex of a limb in the wind
a giant downtown building
        is a creekbed stood on end.

detritus pathways. "delayed and complex ways
to pass the food through webs."

maturity. stop and think. draw on the mind's
stored richness. memory, dream, half-digested
image of your life. "detritus pathways"—feed

the many tiny things that feed an owl.
send heart boldly travelling,
on the heat of the dead & down.

IV.

two logging songs

Clear-cut

Forestry. "How
Many people
Were harvested
In Viet-Nam?"

Clear-cut. "Some
Were children,
Some were over-ripe."

Virgin

A virgin
Forest
Is ancient; many-
Breasted,
Stable; at
Climax.

For the Children

The rising hills, the slopes,
of statistics
lie before us.
the steep climb
of everything, going up,
up, as we all
go down.

In the next century
or the one beyond that,

they say,
are valleys, pastures,
we can meet there in peace
if we make it.

To climb these coming crests
one word to you, to
you and your children:

stay together
learn the flowers
go light

As for Poets

As for poets
The Earth Poets
Who write small poems,
Need help from no man.

———

The Air Poets
Play out the swiftest gales
And sometimes loll in the eddies.
Poem after poem,
Curling back on the same thrust.

———

At fifty below
Fuel oil won't flow
And propane stays in the tank.
Fire Poets
Burn at absolute zero
Fossil love pumped back up.

———

The first
Water Poet
Stayed down six years.
He was covered with seaweed.
The life in his poem
Left millions of tiny
Different tracks
Criss-crossing through the mud.

—

With the Sun and Moon
In his belly,
The Space Poet
Sleeps.
No end to the sky—
But his poems,
Like wild geese,
Fly off the edge.

—

A Mind Poet
Stays in the house.
The house is empty
And it has no walls.
The poem
Is seen from all sides,
Everywhere,
At once.

— Plain Talk —

Four Changes

Four Changes was written in the summer of '69 in response
to an evident need for a few practical and visionary sugges-
tions. Michael McClure, Richard Brautigan, Steve Beckwitt,
Keith Lampe, Cliff Humphreys, Alan Watts, Allen Hoffman,
Stewart Brand, and Diane di Prima were among those who
read it during its formative period and offered suggestions and
criticisms. It was printed and distributed widely, free, through
the help of Alan Watts and Robert Shapiro. Several other free
editions circulated, including one beautifully printed version
by Noel Young of Santa Barbara. Far from perfect and in some
parts already outdated, it may still be useful. Sections in brack-
ets are recent commentary.

Whatever happens, we must not go into a plutonium-based
economy. If the concept of a steady-state economy can be
grasped and started in practice by say, 1980, we may be able
to dodge the blind leap into the liquid metal fast breeder reac-
tor—and extensive strip-mining—a path once entered, hard to
turn back.

My Teacher once said to me,
>   —become one with the knot itself,
>   til it dissolves away.
>   —sweep the garden.
>   —any size.

I.   POPULATION

The Condition

Position: Man is but a part of the fabric of life—dependent on
the whole fabric for his very existence. As the most highly devel-
oped tool-using animal, he must recognize that the unknown
evolutionary destinies of other life forms are to be respected,
and act as gentle steward of the earth's community of being.

Situation: There are now too many human beings, and the
problem is growing rapidly worse. It is potentially disastrous
not only for the human race but for most other life forms.

Goal: The goal would be half of the present world population, or less.

Action

Social/political: First, a massive effort to convince the governments and leaders of the world that the problem is severe. And that all talk about raising food-production—well intentioned as it is—simply puts off the only real solution: reduce population. Demand immediate participation by all countries in programs to legalize abortion, encourage vasectomy and sterilization (provided by free clinics)—free insertion of intrauterine loops—try to correct traditional cultural attitudes that tend to force women into child-bearing—remove income tax deductions for more than two children above a specified income level, and scale it so that lower income families are forced to be careful too—or pay families to limit their number. Take a vigorous stand against the policy of the right wing in the Catholic hierarchy and any other institutions that exercise an irresponsible social force in regard to this question; oppose and correct simple-minded boosterism that equates population growth with continuing prosperity. Work ceaselessly to have all political questions be seen in the light of this prime problem.

[The governments are the wrong agents to address. Their most likely use of a problem, or crisis, is to seize it as another excuse for extending their own powers. Abortion should be legal and voluntary, but questions about vasectomy side-effects still come up. Great care should be taken that no one is ever tricked or forced into sterilization. The whole population issue is fraught with contradictions: but the fact stands that by standards of planetary biological welfare there are already too many human beings. The long-range answer is steady low birth rate. Area by area of the globe, the criteria of "optimum population" should be based on the sense of total ecological health for the region, including flourishing wildlife populations.]

The community: Explore other social structures and marriage forms, such as group marriage and polyandrous marriage, which provide family life but many less children. Share the pleasures of raising children widely, so that all need not directly reproduce to enter into this basic human experience. We must hope that no woman would give birth to more than one [two?] child, during this period of crisis. Adopt children. Let reverence for life and reverence for the feminine mean also a reverence for other species, and future human lives, most of which are threatened.

Our own heads: "I am a child of all life, and all living beings are my brothers and sisters, my children and grandchildren. And there is a child within me waiting to be brought to birth, the baby of a new and wiser self." Love, Love-making, a man and woman together, seen as the vehicle of mutual realization, where the creation of new selves and a new world of being is as important as reproducing our kind.

II. POLLUTION

The Condition

Position: Pollution is of two types. One sort results from an excess of some fairly ordinary substance—smoke, or solid waste—which cannot be absorbed or transmitted rapidly enough to offset its introduction into the environment, thus causing changes the great cycle is not prepared for. (All organisms have wastes and by-products, and these are indeed part of the total biosphere: energy is passed along the line and refracted in various ways, "the rainbow body." This is cycling, not pollution.) The other sort is powerful modern chemicals and poisons, products of recent technology, which the biosphere is totally unprepared for. Such is DDT and similar chlorinated hydrocarbons—nuclear testing fall-out and nuclear waste—poison gas, germ and virus storage and leakage by the military; and chemicals which are put into food, whose long-range effects on human beings have not been properly tested.

Situation: The human race in the last century has allowed its production and scattering of wastes, by-products, and various chemicals to become excessive. Pollution is directly harming life on the planet: which is to say, ruining the environment for humanity itself. We are fouling our air and water, and living in noise and filth that no "animal" would tolerate, while advertising and politicians try and tell us we've never had it so good. The dependence of the modern governments on this kind of untruth leads to shameful mind-pollution: mass media and much school education.

Goal: Clean air, clean clear-running rivers, the presence of Pelican and Osprey and Gray Whale in our lives; salmon and trout in our streams; unmuddied language and good dreams.

Action

Social/political: Effective international legislation banning DDT and other poisons—with no fooling around. The collusion of certain scientists with the pesticide industry and agribusiness in trying to block this legislation must be brought out in the open. Strong penalties for water and air pollution by industries—"Pollution is somebody's profit." Phase out the internal combustion engine and fossil fuel use in general—more research into non-polluting energy sources; solar energy; the tides. No more kidding the public about nuclear waste disposal: it's impossible to do it safely, and nuclear-generated electricity cannot be seriously planned for as it stands now. [Energy: we know a lot more about this problem now. Non-polluting energy resources such as solar or tides, would be clearly inadequate to supply the power needs of the world techno-industrial cancer. Five hundred years of strip-mining is not acceptable.

To go into the liquid metal fast breeder reactor on the gamble that we'll come out with the fusion process perfected is not acceptable. Research should continue on nuclear power, but divorced from any crash-program mentality. This means, conserve energy. "Do more with less." "Convert Waste into Treasure."] Stop all germ and chemical warfare research and experimentation; work toward a hopefully safe disposal of the present staggering and stupid stockpiles of H-bombs, cobalt gunk, germ and poison tanks and cans. Laws and sanctions against wasteful use of paper etc. which adds to the solid wastes of cities—develop methods of recycling solid urban wastes.

Recycling should be the basic principle behind all waste-disposal thinking. Thus, all bottles should be reusable; old cans should make more cans; old newspapers back into newsprint again. Stronger controls and research on chemicals in foods. A shift toward a more varied and sensitive type of agriculture (more small-scale and subsistence farming) would eliminate much of the call for blanket use of pesticides.

The community: DDT and such: don't use them. Air pollution: use less cars. Cars pollute the air, and one or two people riding lonely in a huge car is an insult to intelligence and the Earth. Share rides, legalize hitch-hiking, and build hitch-hiker waiting stations along the highways. Also—a step toward the new world—walk more; look for the best routes through beautiful countryside for long-distance walking trips: San Francisco to Los Angeles down the Coast Range, for example. Learn how to use your own manure as fertilizer if you're in the country—as the Far East has done for centuries. There's a way, and it's safe. Solid waste: boycott bulky wasteful Sunday papers which use up trees. It's all just advertising anyway, which is artificially inducing more energy consumption. Refuse paper bags at the store. Organize Park and Street clean-up festivals. Don't work in any way for or with an industry which pollutes, and don't be drafted into the military. Don't waste. (A monk and an old master were once walking in the mountains. They noticed a little hut upstream. The monk said, "A wise hermit must live there"—the master said, "That's no wise hermit, you see that lettuce leaf floating down the stream, he's a Waster." Just then an old man came running down the hill with his beard flying and caught the floating lettuce leaf.) Carry your own jug to the winery and have it filled from the barrel.

Our own heads: Part of the trouble with talking about something like DDT is that the use of it is not just a practical devise, it's almost an establishment religion. There is something in Western culture that wants to totally wipe out creepy-crawlies, and feels repugnance for toadstools and snakes. This is fear of one's own deepest natural inner-self wilderness areas, and the answer is, relax. Relax around bugs, snakes, and your own hairy dreams. Again, we all should share our crops with a

certain percentage of buglife as "paying our dues." Thoreau
says: "How then can the harvest fail? Shall I not rejoice also
at the abundance of the weeds whose seeds are the granary of
the birds? It matters little comparatively whether the fields fill
the farmer's barns. The true husbandman will cease from anx-
iety, as the squirrels manifest no concern whether the woods
will bear chestnuts this year or not, and finish his labor with
every day, relinquish all claim to the produce of his fields, and
sacrificing in his mind not only his first but his last fruits also."
In the realm of thought, inner experience, consciousness, as
in the outward realm of interconnection, there is a difference
between balanced cycle, and the excess which cannot be han-
dled. When the balance is right, the mind recycles from highest
illuminations to the muddy blinding anger or grabbiness which
sometimes seizes us all; the alchemical "transmutation."

III. CONSUMPTION

The Condition

Position: Everything that lives eats food, and is food in turn.
This complicated animal, man, rests on a vast and delicate pyr-
amid of energy-transformations. To grossly use more than you
need, to destroy, is biologically unsound. Much of the produc-
tion and consumption of modern societies is not necessary or
conducive to spiritual and cultural growth, let alone survival;
and is behind much greed and envy, age-old causes of social
and international discord.

Situation: Man's careless use of "resources" and his total depen-
dence on certain substances such as fossil fuels (which are being
exhausted, slowly but certainly) are having harmful effects on
all the other members of the life-network. The complexity of
modern technology renders whole populations vulnerable to
the deadly consequences of the loss of any one key resource.
Instead of independence we have overdependence on life-
giving substances such as water, which we squander. Many spe-
cies of animals and birds have become extinct in the service of
fashion fads—or fertilizer—or industrial oil—the soil is being
used up; in fact mankind has become a locustlike blight on the

planet that will leave a bare cupboard for its own children—all
the while in a kind of Addict's Dream of affluence, comfort,
eternal progress—using the great achievements of science to
produce software and swill.

Goal: Balance, harmony, humility, growth which is a mutual
growth with Redwood and Quail; to be a good member of
the great community of living creatures. True affluence is not
needing anything.

Action

Social/political: It must be demonstrated ceaselessly that a con-
tinually "growing economy" is no longer healthy, but a Can-
cer. And that the criminal waste which is allowed in the name
of competition—especially that ultimate in wasteful needless
competition, hot wars and cold wars with "Communism" (or
"Capitalism")—must be halted totally with ferocious energy
and decision. Economics must be seen as a small sub-branch of
Ecology, and production/distribution/consumption handled
by companies or unions or co-operatives, with the same ele-
gance and spareness one sees in nature. Soil banks; open spaces;
[logging to be truly based on sustained yield; the U.S. Forest
Service is—sadly—now the lackey of business.] Protection for
all scarce predators and varmints: "Support your right to arm
bears." Damn the International Whaling Commission which
is selling out the last of our precious, wise whales; absolutely
no further development of roads and concessions in National
Parks and Wilderness Areas; build auto campgrounds in the
least desirable areas. Consumer boycotts in response to dishon-
est and unnecessary products. Radical Co-ops. Politically, blast
both "Communist" and "Capitalist" myths of progress, and all
crude notions of conquering or controlling nature.

The community: Sharing and creating. The inherent aptness
of communal life—where large tools are owned jointly and
used efficiently. The power of renunciation: If enough Amer-
icans refused to buy a new car for one given year, it would
permanently alter the American economy. Recycling clothes
and equipment. Support handicrafts, gardening, home skills,

midwifery, herbs—all the things that can make us indepen-
dent, beautiful and whole. Learn to break the habit of unnec-
essary possessions—a monkey on everybody's back—but avoid
a self-abnegating anti-joyous self-righteousness. Simplicity is
light, carefree, neat and loving—not a self-punishing ascetic
trip. (The great Chinese poet Tu Fu said, "The ideas of a poet
should be noble and simple.") Don't shoot a deer if you don't
know how to use all the meat and preserve that which you
can't eat, to tan the hide and use the leather—to use it all, with
gratitude, right down to the sinew and hooves. Simplicity and
mindfulness in diet is a starting point for many people.

Our own heads: It is hard to even begin to gauge how much
a complication of possessions, the notions of "my and mine,"
stand between us and a true, clear, liberated way of seeing the
world. To live lightly on the earth, to be aware and alive, to be
free of egotism, to be in contact with plants and animals, starts
with simple concrete acts. The inner principle is the insight that
we are interdependent energy-fields of great potential wisdom
and compassion—expressed in each person as a superb mind,
a handsome and complex body, and the almost magical capac-
ity of language. To these potentials and capacities, "owning
things" can add nothing of authenticity. "Clad in the sky, with
the earth for a pillow."

IV. TRANSFORMATION

The Condition

Position: Everyone is the result of four forces: the conditions
of this known-universe (matter/energy forms and ceaseless
change); the biology of his species; his individual genetic her-
itage and the culture he's born into. Within this web of forces
there are certain spaces and loops which allow to some persons
the experience of inner freedom and illumination. The grad-
ual exploration of some of these spaces is "evolution" and, for
human cultures, what "history" could increasingly be. We have
it within our deepest powers not only to change our "selves"
but to change our culture. If man is to remain on earth he
must transform the five-millennia-long urbanizing civilization
tradition into a new ecologically-sensitive harmony-oriented

wild-minded scientific-spiritual culture. "Wildness is the state of complete awareness. That's why we need it."

Situation: Civilization, which has made us so successful a species, has overshot itself and now threatens us with its inertia. There also is some evidence that civilized life isn't good for the human gene pool. To achieve the Changes we must change the very foundations of our society and our minds.

Goal: Nothing short of total transformation will do much good. What we envision is a planet on which the human population lives harmoniously and dynamically by employing various sophisticated and unobtrusive technologies in a world environment which is "left natural." Specific points in this vision:

—A healthy and spare population of all races, much less in number than today.

—Cultural and individual pluralism, unified by a type of world tribal council. Division by natural and cultural boundaries rather than arbitrary political boundaries.

—A technology of communication, education, and quiet transportation, land-use being sensitive to the properties of each region. Allowing, thus, the Bison to return to much of the high plains. Careful but intensive agriculture in the great alluvial valleys; deserts left wild for those who would live there by skill. Computer technicians who run the plant part of the year and walk along with the Elk in their migrations during the rest.

—A basic cultural outlook and social organization that inhibits power and property-seeking while encouraging exploration and challenge in things like music, meditation, mathematics, mountaineering, magic, and all other ways of authentic being-in-the-world. Women totally free and equal. A new kind of family—responsible, but more festive and relaxed—is implicit.

Action

Social/political: It seems evident that there are throughout the world certain social and religious forces which have worked through history toward an ecologically and culturally enlightened state of affairs. Let these be encouraged: Gnostics, hip Marxists, Teilhard de Chardin Catholics, Druids, Taoists, Biologists, Witches, Yogins, Bhikkus, Quakers, Sufis, Tibetans, Zens, Shamans, Bushmen, American Indians, Polynesians, Anarchists, Alchemists . . . the list is long. Primitive cultures, communal and ashram movements, co-operative ventures. Since it doesn't seem practical or even desirable to think that direct bloody force will achieve much, it would be best to consider this a continuing "revolution of consciousness" which will be won not by guns but by seizing the key images, myths, archetypes, eschatologies, and ecstasies so that life won't seem worth living unless one's on the transforming energy's side. We must take over "science and technology" and release its real possibilities and powers in the service of this planet—which, after all produced us and it.

[More concretely: no transformation without our feet on the ground. Stewardship means, for most of us, find your place on the planet, dig in, and take responsibility from there—the tiresome but tangible work of school boards, county supervisors, local foresters—local politics. Even while holding in mind the largest scale of potential change. Get a sense of workable territory, learn about it, and start acting point by point. On all levels from national to local the need to move toward steady state economy—equilibrium, dynamic balance, inner-growth stressed—must be taught. Maturity/diversity/climax/creativity.]

The community: New schools, new classes, walking in the woods and cleaning up the streets. Find psychological techniques for creating an awareness of "self" which includes the social and natural environment. "Consideration of what specific language forms—symbolic systems—and social institutions constitute obstacles to ecological awareness." Without falling into a facile interpretation of McLuhan, we can hope to use the media. Let no one be ignorant of the facts of biology and related disciplines; bring up our children as part of the wildlife. Some communities can establish themselves in backwater rural areas and flourish—others maintain themselves in urban centers, and the two types work together—a two-way flow of experience, people, money and home-grown vegetables. Ultimately cities may exist only as joyous tribal gatherings and fairs, to dissolve after a few weeks. Investigating new life-styles is our work, as is the exploration of Ways to explore our inner realms—with the known dangers of crashing that go with such. Master the archaic and the primitive as models of basic nature-related cultures—as well as the most imaginative extensions of science—and build a community where these two vectors cross.

Our own heads: Is where it starts. Knowing that we are the first human beings in history to have so much of man's culture and previous experience available to our study, and being free enough of the weight of traditional cultures to seek out a larger identity; the first members of a civilized society since the Neolithic to wish to look clearly into the eyes of the wild and see our self-hood, our family, there. We have these advantages to set off the obvious disadvantages of being as screwed up as we are—which gives us a fair chance to penetrate some of the riddles of ourselves and the universe, and to go beyond the idea of "man's survival" or "survival of the biosphere" and to draw our strength from the realization that at the heart of things is some kind of serene and ecstatic process which is beyond qualities and beyond birth-and-death. "No need to survive!" "In the fires that destroy the universe at the end of the kalpa, what survives?"—"The iron tree blooms in the void!"

Knowing that nothing need be done, is where we begin to move from.

"Energy is Eternal Delight"

A young woman at Sir George Williams University in Montreal asked me, "What do you fear most?" I found myself answering "that the diversity and richness of the gene pool will be destroyed—" and most people there understood what was meant.

The treasure of life is the richness of stored information in the diverse genes of all living beings. If the human race, following on some set of catastrophes, were to survive at the expense of many plant and animal species, it would be no victory. Diversity provides life with the capacity for a multitude of adaptations and responses to long-range changes on the planet. The possibility remains that at some future time another evolutionary line might carry the development of consciousness to clearer levels than our family of upright primates.

The United States, Europe, the Soviet Union, and Japan have a habit. They are addicted to heavy energy use, great gulps and injections of fossil fuel. As fossil-fuel reserves go down, they will take dangerous gambles with the future health of the biosphere (through nuclear power) to keep up their habit.

For several centuries Western civilization has had a priapic drive for material accumulation, continual extensions of political and economic power, termed "progress." In the Judaeo-Christian worldview men are seen as working out their ultimate destinies (paradise? perdition?) with planet earth as the stage for the drama—trees and animals mere props, nature a vast supply depot. Fed by fossil fuel, this religio-economic view has become a cancer: uncontrollable growth. It may finally choke itself, and drag much else down with it.

The longing for growth is not wrong. The nub of the problem now is how to flip over, as in jujitsu, the magnificent growth-energy of modern civilization into a nonacquisitive search for deeper knowledge of self and nature. Self-nature. Mother nature. If people come to realize that there are many nonmaterial, nondestructive paths of growth—of the highest and most fascinating order—it would help dampen the common fear that a steady state economy would mean deadly stagnation.

I spent a few years, some time back, in and around a training place. It was a school for monks of the Rinzai branch of Zen

Buddhism, in Japan. The whole aim of the community was personal and universal liberation. In this quest for spiritual freedom every man marched strictly to the same drum in matters of hours of work and meditation. In the teacher's room one was pushed across sticky barriers into vast new spaces. The training was traditional and had been handed down for centuries—but the insights are forever fresh and new. The beauty, refinement and truly civilized quality of that life has no match in modern America. It is supported by hand labor in small fields, gathering brushwood to heat the bath, well-water and barrels of homemade pickles. The unspoken motto is "Grow With Less." In the training place I lost my remaining doubts about China.

The Buddhists teach respect for all life, and for wild systems. Man's life is totally dependent on an interpenetrating network of wild systems. Eugene Odum, in his useful paper "The Strategy of Ecosystem Development," points out how the United States has the characteristics of a young ecosystem. Some American Indian cultures have "mature" characteristics: protection as against production, stability as against growth, quality as against quantity. In Pueblo societies a kind of ultimate democracy is practiced. Plants and animals are also people, and, through certain rituals and dances, are given a place and a voice in the political discussions of the humans. They are "represented." "Power to all the people" must be the slogan.

On Hopi and Navajo land, at Black Mesa, the whole issue is revolving at this moment. The cancer is eating away at the breast of Mother Earth in the form of strip-mining. This to provide electricity for Los Angeles. The defense of Black Mesa is being sustained by traditional Indians, young Indian militants, and longhairs. Black Mesa speaks to us through an ancient, complex web of myth. She is sacred territory. To hear her voice is to give up the European word "America" and accept the new-old name for the continent, "Turtle Island."

The return to marginal farmland on the part of longhairs is not some nostalgic replay of the nineteenth century. Here is a generation of white people finally ready to learn from the Elders. How to live on the continent as though our children, and on down, for many ages, will still be here (not on the moon). Loving and protecting this soil, these trees, these wolves. Natives of Turtle Island.

A scaled-down, balanced technology is possible, if cut loose from the cancer of exploitation-heavy-industry-perpetual growth. Those who have already sensed these necessities and have begun, whether in the country or the city, to "grow with less," are the only counterculture that counts. Electricity for Los Angeles is not energy. As Blake said: "Energy Is Eternal Delight."

The Wilderness*

I am a poet. My teachers are other poets, American Indians, and a few Buddhist priests in Japan. The reason I am here is because I wish to bring a voice from the wilderness, my constituency. I wish to be a spokesman for a realm that is not usually represented either in intellectual chambers or in the chambers of government.

I was climbing Glacier Peak in the Cascades of Washington several years ago, on one of the clearest days I had ever seen. When we reached the summit of Glacier Peak we could see almost to the Selkirks in Canada. We could see south far beyond the Columbia River to Mount Hood and Mount Jefferson. And, of course, we could see Mount Adams and Mount Rainier. We could see across Puget Sound to the ranges of the Olympic Mountains. My companion, who is a poet, said: "You mean, there is a senator for all this?"

Unfortunately, there isn't a senator for all that. And I would like to think of a new definition of humanism and a new definition of democracy that would include the nonhuman, that would have representation from those spheres. This is what I think we mean by an ecological conscience.

I don't like Western culture because I think it has much in it that is inherently wrong and that is at the root of the environmental crisis that is not recent; it is very ancient; it has been building up for a millennium. There are many things in Western culture that are admirable. But a culture that alienates itself from the very ground of its own being—from the wilderness outside (that is to say, wild nature, the wild, self-contained, self-informing ecosystems) and from that other wilderness, the wilderness within—is doomed to a very destructive behavior, ultimately perhaps self-destructive behavior.

The West is not the only culture that carries these destructive seeds. China had effectively deforested itself by 1000 A.D. India had effectively deforested itself by 800 A.D. The soils of the Middle East were ruined even earlier. The forests that once covered the mountains of Yugoslavia were stripped to build

*Transcript of a statement made at a seminar at The Center for the Study of Democratic Institutions, Santa Barbara, California.

the Roman fleet, and those mountains have looked like Utah ever since. The soils of southern Italy and Sicily were ruined by latifundia slave-labor farming in the Roman Empire. The soils of the Atlantic seaboard in the United States were effectively ruined before the American Revolution because of the one-crop (tobacco) farming. So the same forces have been at work in East and West.

You would not think a poet would get involved in these things. But the voice that speaks to me as a poet, what Westerners have called the Muse, is the voice of nature herself, whom the ancient poets called the great goddess, the Magna Mater. I regard that voice as a very real entity. At the root of the problem where our civilization goes wrong is the mistaken belief that nature is something less than authentic, that nature is not as alive as man is, or as intelligent, that in a sense it is dead, and that animals are of so low an order of intelligence and feeling, we need not take their feelings into account.

A line is drawn between primitive peoples and civilized peoples. I think there is a wisdom in the worldview of primitive peoples that we have to refer ourselves to, and learn from. If we are on the verge of postcivilization, then our next step must take account of the primitive worldview which has traditionally and intelligently tried to open and keep open lines of communication with the forces of nature. You cannot communicate with the forces of nature in the laboratory. One of the problems is that we simply do not know much about primitive people and primitive cultures. If we can tentatively accommodate the possibility that nature has a degree of authenticity and intelligence that requires that we look at it more sensitively, then we can move to the next step. "Intelligence" is not really the right word. The ecologist Eugene Odum uses the term "biomass."

Life-biomass, he says, is stored information; living matter is stored information in the cells and in the genes. He believes there is more information of a higher order of sophistication and complexity stored in a few square yards of forest than there is in all the libraries of mankind. Obviously, that is a different order of information. It is the information of the universe we live in. It is the information that has been flowing for millions of years. In this total information context, man may not be necessarily the highest or most interesting product.

Perhaps one of its most interesting experiments at the point of evolution, if we can talk about evolution in this way, is not man but a high degree of biological diversity and sophistication opening to more and more possibilities. Plants are at the bottom of the food chain; they do the primary energy transformation that makes all the life-forms possible. So perhaps plant-life is what the ancients meant by the great goddess. Since plants support the other life-forms, they became the "people" of the land. And the land—a country—is a region within which the interactions of water, air, and soil and the underlying geology and the overlying (maybe stratospheric) wind conditions all go to create both the microclimates and the large climactic patterns that make a whole sphere or realm of life possible. The people in that realm include animals, humans, and a variety of wild life.

What we must find a way to do, then, is incorporate the other people—what the Sioux Indians called the creeping people, and the standing people, and the flying people, and the swimming people—into the councils of government. This isn't as difficult as you might think. If we don't do it, they will revolt against us. They will submit non-negotiable demands about our stay on the earth. We are beginning to get non-negotiable demands right now from the air, the water, the soil.

I would like to expand on what I mean by representation here at the Center from these other fields, these other societies, these other communities. Ecologists talk about the ecology of oak communities, or pine communities. They *are* communities. This institute—this Center—is of the order of a kiva of elders. Its function is to maintain and transmit the lore of the tribe on the highest levels. If it were doing its job completely, it would have a cycle of ceremonies geared to the seasons, geared perhaps to the migrations of the fish and to the phases of the moon. It would be able to instruct in what rituals you follow when a child is born, when someone reaches puberty, when someone gets married, when someone dies. But, as you know, in these fragmented times, one council cannot perform all these functions at one time. Still it would be understood that a council of elders, the caretakers of the lore of the culture, would open themselves to representation from other life-forms. Historically this has been done through art. The paintings of bison and bears in the caves of southern France were of that order. The animals were speaking through the people and making their point. And when, in the dances of the Pueblo Indians and other peoples, certain individuals became seized, as it were, by the spirit of the deer, and danced as a deer would dance, or danced the dance of the corn maidens, or impersonated the squash blossom, they were no longer speaking for humanity, they were taking it on themselves to interpret, through their humanity, what these other life-forms were. That is about all we know so far concerning the possibilities of incorporating spokesmanship for the rest of life in our democratic society.

Let me describe how a friend of mine from a Rio Grande pueblo hunts. He is twenty-seven years old. The Pueblo Indians, and I think probably most of the other Indians of the Southwest, begin their hunt, first, by purifying themselves. They take emetics, a sweat bath, and perhaps avoid their wife for a few days. They also try not to think certain thoughts. They go out hunting in an attitude of humility. They make sure that they need to hunt, that they are not hunting without necessity. Then they improvise a song while they are in the mountains. They sing aloud or hum to themselves while they are walking along. It is a song to the deer, asking the deer to be willing to die for them. They usually still-hunt, taking a place alongside a trail. The feeling is that you are not hunting the deer, the deer is coming to you; you make yourself available for the deer that will present itself to you, that has given itself to you. Then you shoot it. After you shoot it, you cut the head off and place the head facing east. You sprinkle corn meal in front of the mouth of the deer, and you pray to the deer, asking it to forgive you for having killed it, to understand that we all need to eat, and to please make a good report to the other deer spirits that he has been treated well. One finds this way of handling things and animals in all primitive cultures.

What's Meant by "Here"

The gentle slopes and meadows of the lower ridge—fine deep groves that show what it once was all like, as on the Bureau of Land Management parcel soon to be logged by Yuba River Lumber Company, right next to Wepa land—and the shady, somewhat brushy, but calm and growing woods of the most of the ridge—a human space there. Enough room to fit a few two-legged beings in.

Crackly grass and Blue oak, the special smells of pungent sticky flowers, give way, climbing, through Digger pine and into Black oak and Ponderosa pine; sweet birch, manzanita, kitkitdizze. This is our home country. We dig wells and wonder where the water table comes from.

We wonder where the deer go in the summer heat, and where they come from in the fall. How far east into the high Sierra. In thirty steady climbing miles the ridge contacts the crest, eight thousand feet. Pure granite; little lakes. At zazen, 5:30 AM, the only sound beside the wind in the pines is the empty log-trucks groaning up Tyler road, across the old hydraulic-mining diggings, heading out from coffee-in-the-dark to timber sales far up the ridge in "checkerboard country"—Southern Pacific and Tahoe National Forest sections intermixed.

Down the hogsback little ridge from Chuck and Franco's place (we call it now; but a year ago, it was just "the grassy benches on the way to the river that you can see from the top of Bald Mountain—we looked for Lew Welch there, too") is a trail that was made on a Saturday community work day, a direct route down leading to the great hole and the right-angle bend of the South Fork of the Yuba, (named from Spanish *uva*, grapes). It is, just exactly, where the last clear string-of-bones of true Sierra Granite bares itself, and the river had to take notice of that hardness, she did, she made a bend.

We all went there one Monday in the summer with a ruck-sack of dinner picnic things and spent the afternoon at lazy swimming in the pippin-apple-green waters of the Yuba. Yuba Mā. Her Womb-Realm Mandala center right where we were, with only Bald Mountain (that ascetic) providing space for eyes upstream—rocky brushy slopes.

So, the ridge and the river. Back up again by dark. Under the pine and oak, three thousand feet, it's also cool. And only three miles from a mailbox.

Watershed: west slope of the northern Sierra Nevada, south slope of the east-west running ridge above the south fork, at the level of Black oak mixed with Ponderosa pine.

On "As for Poets"

"Energy is Eternal Delight"—William Blake, in *The Marriage of Heaven and Hell*. What are we to make of this? As the overdeveloped world (the U.S., Japan, etc.) approaches an "energy crisis" with shortages of oil and electric power (and some nations plan a desperate gamble with nuclear generating plants) we must remember that oil and coal are the stored energy of the sun locked by ancient plant-life in its cells. "Renewable" energy resources are the trees and flowers and all living beings of today, especially plant-life doing the primary work of energy-transfer.

On these fuels contemporary nations now depend. But there is another kind of energy, in every living being, close to the sun-source but in a different way. The power within. Whence? "Delight." The delight of being alive while knowing of impermanence and death, the acceptance and mastery of this. A definition:

> Delight is the innocent joy arising
> with the perception and realization of
> the wonderful, empty, intricate,
> inter-penetrating,
> mutually-embracing, shining
> single world beyond all discrimination
> or opposites.*

This joy is continually reflected in the poems and songs of the world. "As for Poets" explores the realm of delight in terms of the five elements that ancient Greek and China both saw

---

*An alternative definition has been suggested by Dr. Edward Schafer of Berkeley, who describes himself as "an imaginative but unreasonable pedant" (but who is really a scholar of the prosody of artifacts, the poetry of tools).

> Delight is the sophisticated joy arising
> with the perception and realization of
> the wonderful, replete, intricate,
> rich-reflecting,
> uniquely aloof, polychrome
> complex worlds beyond all indifference
> to nuances.

as the constituents of the physical world. To which the Buddhist philosophers of India added a sixth, consciousness, or Mind. At one point I was tempted to title this poem "The Five Elements embracing; pierced by; Mind,"—as illustrated in the mūdra (hand position) generally seen on images of Vairocana Buddha (大日如来).

Earth is our Mother and a man or woman goes directly to her, needing no intermediary.

Air is our breath, spirit, inspiration; a flow which becomes speech when "sounded"—the curling back on the same thrust is close to what is meant in the Japanese word *Fushi* (*bushi* 節)—knot, or whorl in the grain, the word for song.

Fire must have a fuel and the heart's fuel is love. The love that makes poetry burn is not just the green of this spring, but draws on the ancient web of sympathetic, compassionate, and erotic acts that lies behind our very existence, a stored energy in our genes and dreams—fossil love a sly term for that deep-buried sweetness brought to conscious thought.

Water is creation, the mud we crawled on; the wash of tides in the cells. The Water Poet is the Creator. His calligraphy is the trails and tracks we living beings leave in each other; in the world; his poem.

But swallow it all. Size is no problem, a little *space* encloses a huge void. There, those great whorls, the stars hang. Who can get outside the universe? But the poem was born elsewhere, and need not stay. Like the wild geese of the Arctic it heads home, far above the borders, where most things cannot cross.

Now, we are both in, and outside, the world at once. The only place this can be is the *Mind*. Ah, what a poem. It is what is, completely, in the past, present, and future simultaneously, seeing being, and being seen.

Can we really do this? But we do. So we sing. Poetry is for all men and women. The power within—the more you give, the more you have to give—will still be our source when coal and oil are long gone, and atoms are left to spin in peace.

AXE HANDLES

This book is for San Juan Ridge

How do you shape an axe handle?
Without an axe it can't be done.
How do you take a wife?
Without a go-between you can't get one.
Shape a handle, shape a handle,
the pattern is not far off.
And here's a girl I know,
The wine and food in rows.

> From *Book of Songs* (*Shih Ching*)
> (Mao no. 158): A folk song from
> the Pin area, 5th B.C.

— *Part One* —
Loops

Axe Handles

One afternoon the last week in April
Showing Kai how to throw a hatchet
One-half turn and it sticks in a stump.
He recalls the hatchet-head
Without a handle, in the shop
And go gets it, and wants it for his own.
A broken-off axe handle behind the door
Is long enough for a hatchet,
We cut it to length and take it
With the hatchet head
And working hatchet, to the wood block.
There I begin to shape the old handle
With the hatchet, and the phrase
First learned from Ezra Pound
Rings in my ears!
"When making an axe handle
            the pattern is not far off."
And I say this to Kai
"Look: We'll shape the handle
By checking the handle
Of the axe we cut with—"
And he sees. And I hear it again:
It's in Lu Ji's *Wên Fu,* fourth century
A.D. "Essay on Literature"—in the
Preface: "In making the handle
Of an axe
By cutting wood with an axe
The model is indeed near at hand."
My teacher Shih-hsiang Chen
Translated that and taught it years ago
And I see: Pound was an axe,
Chen was an axe, I am an axe
And my son a handle, soon
To be shaping again, model
And tool, craft of culture,
How we go on.

For/From Lew

Lew Welch just turned up one day,
live as you and me. "Damn, Lew" I said,
"you didn't shoot yourself after all."
"Yes I did" he said,
and even then I felt the tingling down my back.
"Yes you did, too" I said—"I can feel it now."
"Yeah" he said,
"There's a basic fear between your world and
mine. I don't know why.
What I came to say was,
teach the children about the cycles.
The life cycles. All the other cycles.
That's what it's all about, and it's all forgot."

River in the Valley

We cross the Sacramento River at Colusa
follow the road on the levee south and east
find thousands of swallows nesting
on the underside of a concrete overhead
roadway? causeway? abandoned. Near
                    Butte Creek.

    Gen runs in little circles looking up
    at swoops of swallows—laughing—
                they keep
    flowing under the bridge and out,

    Kai leans silent against a concrete pier
    tries to hold with his eyes the course
    of a single darting bird,

    I pick grass seeds from my socks.

The coast range. Parched yellow front hills,
blue-gray thornbrush higher hills behind,

and here is the Great Central Valley,
drained, then planted and watered,
    thousand-foot deep soils
    thousand-acre orchards

    Sunday morning,
only one place serving breakfast
in Colusa, old river and tractor men
sipping milky coffee.

From north of Sutter Buttes
we see snow on Mt. Lassen
and the clear arc of the Sierra
south to the Desolation peaks.
One boy asks, "where do rivers start?"

in threads in hills, and gather down to here—
but the river
is all of it everywhere,
all flowing at once,
all one place.

Among

Few Douglas fir grow in these pine woods
One fir is there among south-facing Ponderosa Pine,

Every fall a lot of little seedlings sprout
                    around it—

Every summer during long dry drouth they die.
Once every forty years or so
A rain comes in July.

Two summers back it did that,
The Doug fir seedlings lived that year

The next year it was dry,
A few fir made it through.

This year, with roots down deep, two live.
A Douglas fir will be among these pines.

            at the 3000-foot level
            north of the south fork
            of the Yuba river.

On Top

All this new stuff goes on top
turn it over   turn it over
wait   and water down.
From the dark bottom
turn it inside out
let it spread through, sift down,
even.
Watch it sprout.

A mind like compost.

Berry Territory
(Walking the woods on an early spring dry
day, the slopes behind Lanes Landing Farm
on the Kentucky River, with Tanya and Wendell)

Under dead leaves Tanya finds a tortoise
      matching the leaves—legs pulled in—

And we look at woodchuck holes that dive
      under limestone ledges
      seabottom strata,
who lives there brushes furry back
on shell and coral,

Most holes with leaves and twigs around the door,
      nobody in.

Wendell, crouched down,
    sticks his face in a woodchuck hole
    "Hey, smell that, it's a fox!"
I go on my knees,
    put the opening to my face
    like a mask. No light;
    all smell: sour—warm—
    Splintered bones, scats? feathers?
    Wreathing bodies—wild—

Some home.

Bows to Drouth

Driest summer,
The hose snakes under the mulch
    to the base of a gravenstein apple
    three years old,
And back to the standpipe
    where it dives underground.

At the pump,
    the handle extended with pipe
    sweeps down
    six strokes to a gallon,
    one hundred and fifteen feet deep
    force pump, the cylinder set in the water
Sucker-rod faintly clangs in the well.

Legs planted,
    both hands on the handle,
    whole body bending,
    I gaze through the trees and
    see different birds,
    different leaves,
    with each bow.

No counting,
    all free—
    deep water softly lifts out—
    over there—
At the base of an apple.

Drouth of the summer of '74

The Cool Around the Fire

Drink black coffee from a thermos
    sitting on a stump.

      piles burn down, the green limb
      fringe edge
      picked up and tossed in
To the center: white ash mound
    shimmering red within.
    tip head down
    to shield face
    with hat brim   from the heat;

The thinning, pruning, brush-cut
    robbed from bugs and fungus—
    belly gray clouds
    swing low soft over
    maybe rain, bring an end
    to this drouth;

Burn brush to take heat
    from next summer's wildfires
    and to bring rain on time,
    and fires clear the tangle.

    the tangle of the heart.
Black coffee, bitter, hot,
    smoke rises straight and calm
    air
Still and cool.

Changing Diapers

How intelligent he looks!
    on his back
    both feet caught in my one hand
    his glance set sideways,
    on a giant poster of Geronimo
    with a Sharp's repeating rifle by his knee.

I open, wipe, he doesn't even notice
    nor do I.
Baby legs and knees
    toes like little peas
    little wrinkles, good-to-eat,
    eyes bright, shiny ears,
    chest swelling drawing air,

No trouble, friend,
    you and me and Geronimo
    are men.

Beating the Average

Odd rain in August,
    Gen with asthma in the night kept us awake
    entered our bed, wheezing,
    scratching poison oak—

So tired today.
All morning down at Rod's and help
    adjust the valves,
    fix the back trunk lock.
More rain.

Zucchini recipes from Patty,
    and back home now,
    nap, try to forget,
    get head ready for state work tomorrow,

fly early to L.A.,
Arts Council meet.

Half asleep on the top bunk
        thinking of mushrooms that this rain will bring.
And the two boys five and seven
        race around the house
        shrieking, laughing, weeping, wailing,

        calls of kids
        echoing through the woods:
        calls of play.

The weather record says for August,
        O.OOO
        is the average rainfall here.

Painting the North San Juan School

White paint splotches on blue head bandanas
Dusty transistor with wired-on antenna
        plays sixties rock and roll;
Little kids came with us are on teeter-totters
        tilting under shade of oak
This building good for ten years more.
The shingled bell-cupola trembles
        at every log truck rolling by—

The radio speaks:
        today it will be one hundred degrees in the valley.
—Franquette walnuts grafted on the
        local native rootstock do o.k.
        nursery stock of cherry all has fungus;
Lucky if a bare-root planting lives,

This paint thins with water.
This year the busses will run only
        on paved roads,
Somehow the children will be taught:

How to record their mother tongue
   with written signs,

Names to call the landscape of the continent
                         they live on
Assigned it by the ruling people of the last
   three hundred years,
The games of numbers,
What went before, as told by those who
   think they know it,

A drunken man with chestnut mustache
Stumbles off the road to ask if he can help.

Children drinking chocolate milk

Ladders resting on the shaky porch.

All in the Family

For the first time in memory
heavy rain in August
   tuning up the chainsaw
     begin to cut oak
Boletus by the dozen
   fruiting in the woods
Full moon, warm nights
   the boys learn to float
Masa gone off dancing
   for another thirty days
Queen Anne's Lace in the meadow
   a Flicker's single call

Oregano, lavender, the *salvia* sage
   wild pennyroyal
   from the Yuba River bank
All in the family
   of Mint.

Fence Posts

It might be that horses would be useful
On a snowy morning to take the trail
Down the ridge to visit Steve or Mike and
Faster than going around the gravelled road by car.

So the thought came to fence a part of the forest,
Thin trees and clear the brush,
Ron splits cedar rails and fenceposts
On Black Sands Placer road where he gets
These great old butt logs from the Camptonville sawmill
Why they can't use them I don't know—
They aren't all pecky.
He delivers, too, in a bread van
His grandfather drove in Seattle.

Sapwood posts are a little bit cheaper than heartwood.
I could have bought all heartwood from the start
But then I thought how it doesn't work
To always make a point of getting the best which is why
I sometimes pick out the worse and damaged looking fruit
And vegetables at the market because I know
I actually will enjoy them in any case but
Some people might take them as second choice
And feel sour about it all evening.

With sapwood fenceposts
You ought to soak to make sure they won't rot
In a fifty-five gallon drum with penta 10 to 1
Which is ten gallons of oil and a gallon of
Termite and fungus poison.
I use old crankcase oil to dilute
And that's a good thing to do with it but,
There's not really enough old crank to go around.
The posts should be two feet in the ground.

So, soaking six posts a week at a time
The soaked pile getting bigger week by week,
But the oil only comes up one and a half feet.
I could add kerosene in

At seventy cents a gallon
Which is what it costs when you buy it by the drum
And that's $3.50 to raise the soaking level up
Plus a half a can of penta more, six dollars,
For a hundred and twenty fence posts
On which I saved thirty dollars by getting the sapwood,
But still you have to count your time,

A well-done fence is beautiful.
And horses, too.
Penny wise pound foolish either way.

Spring, '77

So Old—

Oregon Creek reaches far back into the hills.
Burned over twice, the pines are returning again.
Old roads twist deep into canyons,
      hours from one ridge to the next
The new road goes straight on the side of the mountain,
      high, and with curves ironed out.
A single hawk flies leisurely up,
      disturbed by our truck
Down the middle fork-south fork opening,
      fog silver gleams in the valley.
Camptonville houses are old and small,
      a sunny perch on a ridge,
Was it gold or logs brought people to this spot?
      a teenage mother with her baby stands by a pickup.
A stuffed life-size doll of a Santa Claus
      climbs over a porch-rail.
Our old truck too, slow down the street,
      out of the past—
It's all so old—the hawk, the houses, the trucks,
      the view of the fog—
Midwinter late sun flashes through hilltops and trees
      a good day, we know one more part of our watershed,

And have seen a gorge with a hairpin bend
    and followed one more dirt road to its end.
Chilling, so put on jackets
    and take the paved road out
Back to our own dirt road, iron stove,
    and the chickens to close in the dusk.
And the nightly stroll of raccoons.

Look Back

Twice one summer
I walked up Piute mountain,
our trailcrew was camped at Bear Valley.
I first had chainsaw practice
cutting wood there for the cook.
Piute mountain. And scanned the crest
of the Sawtooths, to the east.
A Whitebark pine relict stand
cut off from friends
by miles of air and granite—me
running out ridges.
Jimmy Jones the cook said "I
used to do that, run the ridges
all day long—just like a coyote."
When I built a little sweatlodge
one Sunday by the creek
he told me to be careful,
and almost came in too.

Today at Slide Peak in the Sawtooths
I look back at that mountain
twenty-five years. Those days
when I lived and thought all alone.

I was studying Chinese
preparing for Asia
every night after trail crew work
                       from a book.

Jimmy Jones was a Mariposa Indian.
One night by the campfire
drinking that coffee black
he stood there looking down at my
H. G. Creel, "Those letters Chinese?"
"Yes," I said. He said, "Hmmmmm.
My grandpa they say was Chinese."

And that year I quit early.
told the foreman I was headed for Japan.
He looked like he knew, and said "Bechtel."
I couldn't tell him something strange as Zen.

Jimmy Jones, and these mountains and creeks.
The up and down of it
stays in my feet.

VII, '78, The Sawtooths.

Soy Sauce
for Bruce Boyd and Holly Tornheim

Standing on a stepladder
          up under hot ceiling
tacking on wire net for plaster,
a day's work helping Bruce and Holly on their house,
I catch a sour salt smell and come back
          down the ladder.

"Deer lick it nights" she says,
and shows me the frame of the window she's planing,
clear redwood, but dark, with a smell.

"Scored a broken-up, two-thousand-gallon redwood
soy sauce tank from a company went out of business
down near San Jose."
Out in the yard the staves are stacked:
I lean over, sniff them, ah! it's like Shinshu miso,

the darker saltier miso paste of the Nagano
uplands, central main island, Japan—
it's like Shinshu pickles!

I see in mind my friend Shimizu Yasushi and me,
one October years ago, trudging through days of snow
crossing the Japan Alps and descending
the last night, to a farmhouse,
taking a late hot bath in the dark—and eating
        a bowl of chill miso radish pickles,
        nothing ever so good!

Back here, hot summer sunshine dusty yard,
        hammer in hand.

But I know how it tastes
        to lick those window frames
        in the dark,
                        the deer.

Delicate Criss-crossing Beetle Trails
Left in the Sand

    Masa's childhood village
    the bus takes us through it again;

    soaked drooping bamboo groves
    swaying heavy in the drizzle,
    and perfectly straight lines of rice plants
    glittering orderly mirrors of water,
    dark grove of straight young Sugi trees
    thick at the base of the hill,

    a crow flaps, a
    cluster of yellow-hat children
    marching to kindergarten,
    right by the bus in the rain

Walking out on the beach, why I know this!
   rode down through those pines once
   with Anja and John

And watch bugs in their own tiny dunes.

   from memory to memory,
   bed to bed and meal to meal,
   all on this road in the sand

Summer, '81, Tango, Japan Sea

Walking Through Myoshin-ji

Straight stone walks
   up lanes between mud walls

. . . the sailors who handled the ships
   from Korea and China,
the carpenters, chisels like razors,

   young monks working on *mu,*

   and the pine trees
      that surrounded this city.
      the Ancient Ones, each one
anonymous.
      green needles,
         lumber,
            ash.

VII, 81, Kyoto

Fishing Catching Nothing off the Breakwater near the Airport, Naha Harbor, Okinawa

Self-defense-force jets in pairs
scream out over the bay
lay a track of smoke and whine
on the Kumé islands

Clouds sailing right on the sea
clouds and waters
prairie of wavelets

Jet plane outriders—scouts—
Displaying with Soviet pilots
who's weak?   who's strong?

Burning millions of gallons of kerosene

Screaming along.

At the Ibaru Family Tomb Tagami Village, Great Loo Choo: Grandfathers of My Sons

Weeds in the stone courtyard
        stone door plastered shut,
        washed bones within
        ranked in urns,

We drink and sing in the courtyard:
        songs of a beautiful reef,
        songs of a grove
        they walked through long ago,

Drinking with the ancestors
        singing with their sons.

VI, '81, Okinawa

Strategic Air Command

The hiss and flashing lights of a jet
Pass near Jupiter in Virgo.
He asks, how many satellites in the sky?
Does anyone know where they all are?
What are they doing, who watches them?

Frost settles on the sleeping bags.
The last embers of fire,
One more cup of tea,
At the edge of a high lake rimmed with snow.

These cliffs and the stars
Belong to the same universe.
This little air in between
Belongs to the twentieth century and its wars.

VIII, 82, Koip Peak, Sierra Nevada.

Eastward Across Texas

In a great cave of minerals and
    salts-in-shapes
Gen said he saw a Ringtail
    with a bat in its mouth

Out of mountains onto flat high land
    phosphate diggings,
And subtly down, eastward, dry wide plains
    till we come
    to a warm eve in Snyder, Texas.

Kai says to a waitress, "our name is Snyder too."
    She says, "Yeah, there's some Vietnamese
    refugees near here."
His black hair?

obsidian in graves.

gifts to the future
    to remember us.

Working on the '58 Willys Pickup
For Lu Yu

The year this truck was made
I sat in early morning darkness
Chanting sūtra in Kyoto,
And spent the days studying Chinese.
Chinese, Japanese, Sanskrit, French—
Joys of Dharma-scholarship
And the splendid old temples—
But learned nothing of trucks.

Now to bring sawdust
Rotten and rich
From a sawmill abandoned when I was just born
Lost in the young fir and cedar
At Bloody Run Creek
So that clay in the garden
Can be broken and tempered
And growing plants mulched to save water—
And to also haul gravel
From the old placer diggings,
To screen it and mix in the sand with the clay
Putting pebbles aside to strew on the paths
So muddy in winter—

I lie in the dusty and broken bush
Under the pickup
Already thought to be old—
Admiring its solidness, square lines,
Thinking a truck like this
would please Chairman Mao.

The rear end rebuilt and put back
With new spider gears,
Brake cylinders cleaned, the brake drums
New-turned and new brake shoes,
Taught how to do this
By friends who themselves spent
Youth with the Classics—

The garden gets better, I
Laugh in the evening
To pick up Chinese
And read about farming,
I fix truck and lock eyebrows
With tough-handed men of the past.

Getting in the Wood

The sour smell,
       blue stain,
              water squirts out round the wedge,

Lifting quarters of rounds
       covered with ants,
       "a living glove of ants upon my hand"
the poll of the sledge a bit peened over
so the wedge springs off and tumbles
       ringing like high-pitched bells
              into the complex duff of twigs
              poison oak, bark, sawdust,
              shards of logs,

And the sweat drips down.
       Smell of crushed ants.
The lean and heave on the peavey
that breaks free the last of a bucked
       three-foot round,
              it lies flat on smashed oaklings—

Wedge and sledge, peavey and maul,
    little axe, canteen, piggyback can
    of saw-mix gas and oil for the chain,
knapsack of files and goggles and rags,

All to gather the dead and the down.
    the young men throw splits on the piles
    bodies hardening, learning the pace
and the smell of tools from this delve
    in the winter
        death-topple of elderly oak.
Four cords.

True Night

Sheath of sleep in the black of the bed:
From outside this dream womb
Comes a clatter
Comes a clatter
And finally the mind rises up to a fact
Like a fish to a hook
A raccoon at the kitchen!
A falling of metal bowls,
    the clashing of jars,
    the avalanche of plates!
I snap alive to this ritual
Rise unsteady, find my feet,
Grab the stick, dash in the dark—
I'm a huge pounding demon
That roars at raccoons—
They whip round the corner,
A scratching sound tells me
    they've gone up a tree.

I stand at the base
Two young ones that perch on
Two dead stub limbs and
Peer down from both sides of the trunk:

Roar, roar, I roar
you awful raccoons, you wake me
up nights, you ravage
our kitchen

As I stay there then silent
The chill of the air on my nakedness
Starts off the skin
I am all alive to the night.
Bare foot shaping on gravel
Stick in the hand, forever.

Long streak of cloud giving way
To a milky thin light
Back of black pine bough,
The moon is still full,
Hillsides of Pine trees all
Whispering; crickets still cricketting
Faint in cold coves in the dark

I turn and walk slow
Back the path to the beds
With goosebumps and loose waving hair
In the night of milk-moonlit thin cloud glow
And black rustling pines
I feel like a dandelion head
Gone to seed
About to be blown all away
Or a sea anemone open and waving in
cool pearly water.

Fifty years old.
I still spend my time
Screwing nuts down on bolts.

At the shadow pool,
Children are sleeping,
And a lover I've lived with for years,
True night.
One cannot stay too long awake

In this dark

Dusty feet, hair tangling,
I stoop and slip back to the
Sheath, for the sleep I still need,
For the waking that comes
Every day

With the dawn.

— *Part Two* —

Little Songs for Gaia

across salt marshes north of
San Francisco Bay
cloud soft grays
blues little fuzzies
illusion structures—pale blue of the edge,
    sky behind,

hawk dipping and circling
over salt marsh

ah, this slow-paced
system of systems, whirling and turning

a five-thousand-year span
    about all that a human can figure,

grasshopper man in his car driving through.

———

Look out over
This great world
Where you just might walk
As far as the farthest rim

There's a spring, there
By an oak, on a dry grass slope,
Drink.   Suck deep.

And the world goes on

———

The manzanita succession story—

Shady lady,
    makes the boys
        turn gray.

———

trout-of-the-air, ouzel,
bouncing, dipping, on a round rock
round as the hump of snow-on-grass beside it
between the icy banks, the running stream:
and into running stream

right in!

you   fly

—

As the crickets' soft autumn hum
is to us,
so are we to the trees

as are they

to the rocks and the hills.

—

Awakened by the clock striking five
Already light,
I still see the dream
Three Corn Maidens in green
Green leaves, skirt, sleeves—
Walking by.
        I turned my eyes, knowing not to stare.

And wake thinking
I should have looked more
To see the way they were
Corn Maidens in green.
Green leaf face, too
Eyes turned aside.

But then I'm glad for once I knew
Not to look too much when
Really there.

        Or try to write it down.

The stylishness of winds and waves—
nets over nets of light
reflected off the bottom
nutcracker streaks over,
        hollering

Nature calls.
bodies of water
     tuned to the sky.

"Find a need and be filled by it."

Red-shafted
Flicker—
        sharp cool call

The smell of Sweet Birch blooms
Through the warm manzanita

And the soft raining-down
Invisible, crackling dry duff,

        of the droppings of oak-moth caterpillars.
        nibbling spring leaves

High in the oak limbs above.

Red hen on her side
     flips dust under her wing
     the free leg powerful,
        levering leaves and dirt,

In the afternoon manzanita shade
     her sisters too,

this joy of dust and scrabble
after morning's

Brisk scratch of bugs and weeds—
they are all "seventeen"
just into a life
of egg-bearing pride,

May health, beauty,
long life and wisdom
come to the barnyard fowl,
with humans to serve them:

World made for Red Hens.

———

Hear bucks skirmishing in the night—

the light, playful rattle
of antlers
in a circle of moonlight
between the pond and the barn,
and the dancing-pushing-
stamping—and off running,
open the door to go out
to the chickencoop for eggs

———

Deep blue sea baby,
Deep blue sea.
Ge, Gaia
Seed syllable, "ah!"

Whirl of the white clouds over blue-green land and seas
bluegreen of bios   bow—curve—

Chuang-tzu says the Great Bird looking down,
all he sees is
blue . . .

Sand hills. blue of the land, green of the sky.
      looking outward
      half-moon in cloud;

Red soil—blue sky—white cloud—grainy granite,
             and
Twenty thousand mountain miles of manzanita.
   Some beautiful tiny manzanita
   I saw a single, perfect, lovely,
      manzanita

              Ha.

———

      One boy barefoot
         swinging madly
         in the driving rain
         I stand by the pond
         the hiss
      Of rain into itself

———

    Log trucks go by at four in the morning
       as we roll in our sleeping bags
         dreaming of health.
    The log trucks remind us,
       as we think, dream and play

    of the world that is carried away.

———

    Steep cliff ledge, a pair of young raptors
       their hawklet-hood hanging
       over blue lake   over space

    The flat green hayfields
       gleaming white *playa*   below

Hawks, eagles, and swallows
   nesting in holes between
                layers of rock

Life of,
   sailing out over worlds up and down.
   blue mountain desert,
   cliff by a blue-green lake.

              The Warner Range

———

Dead doe lying in the rain

        on the shoulder
        in the gravel

I see your stiff leg

        in the headlights
        by the roadside

Dead doe lying in the rain

———

I dreamed I was a god

last night. Melting the winter snows
with my warm breath. Bending low over
snowy mountains with the black sharp
scattered fir and pine, breathing,
"Haaaaaah"

———

Snowflakes slip into the pond
        no regrets.
Thin shoots of new-sprouted grass,
        it grows.

Two children learning Chinese checkers
And grownups sipping whiskey,
Spring evening snow.

—

THE FLICKERS

sharp clear call

THIS!

THIS!

THIS!

in the cool pine breeze

—

Hers was not a
Sheath.
It was
A
Quiver.

—

I am sorry I disturbed you.

I broke into your house last night
To use the library.
There were some things I had to look up;
A large book fell
        and knocked over others.
Afraid you'd wake and find me
and be truly alarmed
                I left
Without picking up.

I got your name from the mailbox
As I fled, to write you and explain.

— *Part Three* —
Nets

NETS

I

Walked Two Days in Snow, Then It Cleared for Five

Saw a sleek gray bullet-body, underwater,
    hindfeet kicking, bubbles trailing,
    shoot under bushes on the bank;

A tawny critter on the gravel bar—
    first morning sunlight, lay down, ears up,
    watch us from afar.

And two broad graceful dark brown leaf-eaters with
    humped shoulders, flopping ears, long-legged,
    cross the creekbed and enter the woods.

A white and black bird soars up with a fish
    in its claws.

A hawk swings low over slough and marsh, cinnamon
    and gold, drops out of sight

A furred one with flat tail hung floating
    far from shore, tiny green wavelets, waiting;

And I saw: the turn of the head, the glance of the eye,
    each gesture, each lift and stamp

Of your high-arched feet.

IX, '74, Thoroughfare Meadow,
Upper Yellowstone River

Geese Gone Beyond

In the cedar canoe gliding and paddling
on mirror-smooth lake;
    a carpet of canada geese
afloat on the water
who talk first noisy   then murmur

we stop paddling, let drift.
yellow larch on the shores
morning chill, mist off the
cold gentle mountains beyond

I kneel in the bow
in *seiza,* like tea-ceremony
      or watching a Nō play
kneeling, legs aching, silent.

One goose breaks and flies up.

      a rumble of dripping water
      beating wings
      full honking sky,

A touch across,
      the trigger,

The one who is the first to feel to go.

                    X, 79, Seeley Lake, Montana

Three Deer One Coyote Running in the Snow

            First three deer bounding
and then coyote streaks right after
                  tail   *flatout*

I stand dumb a while   two seconds
blankly black-and-white of trees and snow

            Coyote's back!
            good coat, fluffy tail,
sees me: quickly gone.

Later:
I walk through where they ran

to study how that news all got put down.

White Sticky

Glancing up through oaks
    dry leaves still hanging on,
    some tilt
    and airy wobble down, dry settles.
Pale early sun,
    standing in damp leaf ground
    pine needles, by dirt road,
    holding Gen's hand,
    waiting for his ride to school.

We talk about mushrooms.
This year was good
    but most got eaten by the worms.
There, under manzanita, more white stickies.
Can't find the bookname—
    glowing white and gooey cap,
    an unknown
    that we call "White Sticky" which is good
    as any name.

He goes off in Mike's old car to school,
    I walk back to the house
    try once more the mushroom book.

    (*Hygrophorus?*)

Old Pond

Blue mountain white snow gleam
Through pine bulk and slender needle-sprays;
    little hemlock half in shade,
    ragged rocky skyline,

    single clear flat nuthatch call:
    down from the treetrunks

    up through time.

At Five Lakes Basin's
Biggest little lake
    after all day scrambling on the peaks,
    a naked bug
    with a white body and brown hair

    dives in the water,

Splash!

24:IV:40075, 3:30 PM, n. of Coaldale, Nevada, A Glimpse through a Break in the Storm of the Summit of the White Mountains

O Mother Gaia

sky   cloud   gate   milk   snow

wind-void-word

I bow in roadside gravel

—

I: VI: 40077

Ceanothus blossoms
   and the radiator boiling
      smells of spring

Fat rear haunches
   toes, tail,
   half a mouse
      at the door at dawn.
         our loving cat.

Setting sugar water
   feeder jars for bees out—
         hum of mosquitoes at dusk.

This year, the third
   of the bullfrog,
   he rarely speaks.
      Is it drouth and low water
     or age?

Kid coming out of the outhouse
   at dusk in pajamas
      still tucking them in,
        "how many eggs?"

Last night, the first time,
   raccoons opened
   the refrigerator.
      You can't slow down
       progress.

"Aphids giving birth
   to ninety live babies
    a day."

NETS
II

The Grand Entry

The many American flags
Whip around on horseback,
Carried by cowgirls.
            the whirling lights of pleasure rides,
            the slow whine of an ambulance.

Two men on horseback roping head and leg of a calf:
Held immobile, from each end,
            a frieze;
            the crowd's applause;
            released, and scamper off.

Grassland biome technicians.
More spirit than those alluvial delta
High biomass priest-accountants
Who invented writing—

The announcer speaks again of the flag.
            the flag's like a steak: cowboys
            are solar energy-
            grass-to-protein
            conversion-magic priests!

Hamburger offerings all over America
Red, white,
and Blue.

Year of the bicentennial,
Nevada County Fair rodeo

Under the Sign of Toki's

Is this Palo Alto?
"No, Wisconsin."
so gentle—distant older woman's voice—
                faint accent—Swede?
"Where are you?"   "This is Wisconsin."
Area code was wrong.
                what stream sipped from
                together in another life, to touch base
                ten seconds here in this?

                Toki's
snack bar
juice bar
        ice
worms

And the operators
Keep asking me what do I want?
Sacramento, San Diego, Indiana, Ohio
        as I stand here with lists and letters,
        outside, cold feet in the slush,
        at the pay phone
        (my office)

phone truck comes and takes coins while we talk
about art in LA
        under the ice sign
        next to the high way
talking,   ice   worms

        And snow
falls off the limbs
down my notebook
down into my neck
                drip drip
        red brick   iron doors   stone walls
old town run down

at Toki's
              ice
worms

The year I served as
chair for the California
Arts Council without a
phone at home and
twelve miles from the
pay phone next to
Toki's Okinawan Noodle
and Bait Shop

Talking Late with the Governor about the Budget
for Jerry Brown

Entering the midnight
Halls of the capitol,
Iron carts full of printed bills
Filling life with rules,

At the end of many chambers
Alone in a large tan room
The Governor sits, without dinner.
Scanning the hills of laws—budgets—codes—
In this land of twenty million
From desert to ocean.

Till the oil runs out
There's no end in sight.
Outside, his car waits with driver
Alone, engine idling.
The great pines on the Capitol grounds
Are less than a century old.

Two A.M.,
We walk to the street
Tired of the effort

Of thinking about "the People."
The half-moon travels west
In the elegant company
Of Jupiter and Aldebaran,

And east, over the Sierra,
Far flashes of lightning—
Is it raining tonight at home?

"He Shot Arrows, But Not
at Birds Perching"
Lun yü, VII, 26

The Governor came to visit in the mountains
    we cleaned the house and raked the yard that day.
He'd been east and hadn't slept much
    so napped all afternoon back in the shade.

Young trees and chickens must be tended
    I sprayed apples, and took water to the hens.
Next day we read the papers, spoke of farming,
    of oil, and what would happen to the cars.

And then beside the pond we started laughing,
    got the quiver and bow and strung the bow.
Arrow after arrow flashing
    hissing under pines in summer breeze

Striking deep in straw bales by the barn.

Summer, '76

Arts Councils
for Jacques Barzaghi

Because there is no art
There are artists

Because there are no artists
We need money

Because there is no money
We give

Because there is no we
There is art

What Have I Learned

What have I learned but
the proper use for several tools?

The moments
between hard pleasant tasks

To sit silent, drink wine,
and think my own kind
of dry crusty thoughts.

   —the first Calochortus flowers
   and in all the land,
        it's spring.
   I point them out:
   the yellow petals, the golden hairs,
        to Gen.

Seeing in silence:
never the same twice,
but when you get it right,

   you pass it on.

NETS
III

A Maul for Bill and Cindy's Wedding

Swung from the toes out,
Belly-breath riding on the knuckles,
The ten-pound maul lifts up,
Sails in an arc overhead,
And then lifts *you*!

It floats, you float,
For an instant of clear far sight—
Eye on the crack in the end-grain
Angle of the oak round
Stood up to wait to be split.

The maul falls—with a sigh—the wood
Claps apart
            and lies twain—
In a wink. As the maul
Splits all, may

You two stay together.

Alaska

Frozen mist sheets low along the ground
        but outside town, at Gold Stream Vale
        forty below zero in the sun, stamp feet,
        chilled people in thick clothes,

Read what somebody sprayed on the yard-wide
        elevated tube, the shining pipe
        the heated crude oil travels,

    "Where will it all end?"

Drive back to stuffy rooms:
        lawyers, teachers, plant ecologists,

energy visionaries, peoples' land managers
cross minds

And then fly on to other towns
      dozing in planes
      the mountains

Soaring higher yet, and quite awake.

Dillingham, Alaska, the Willow Tree Bar

Drills chatter full of mud and compressed air
all across the globe,
      low-ceilinged bars, we hear the same new songs

All the new songs.
In the working bars of the world.
After you done drive Cat. After the truck
            went home.
            Caribou slip,
            front legs folded first
            under the warm oil pipeline
            set four feet off the ground—

On the wood floor, glass in hand,
            laugh and cuss with
            somebody else's wife.
            Texans, Hawaiians, Eskimos,
            Filipinos, Workers, always
            on the edge of a brawl—
            In the bars of the world.
            Hearing those same new songs
                        in Abadan,
            Naples, Galveston, Darwin, Fairbanks,
            White or brown,
Drinking it down,

the pain
of the work
of wrecking the world.

Removing the Plate of the Pump
on the Hydraulic System
of the Backhoe
for Bert Hybart

Through mud, fouled nuts, black grime
it opens, a gleam of spotless steel
machined-fit perfect
swirl of intake and output
relentless clarity
at the heart
of work.

Glamor

A man who failed to master his Ally correctly
when young, and was out seeking power,

so heard there were "white people" and left
his own to go there,

and became infected with greed, went home
with trade goods, they saw he was crazy.

Greedy, and crazy, the relatives should kill
such a man, but this time no one did.

Crazy and greedy, he lives on. To the damage
of his people.
Civilization spreads: among people who are generous,
who know nothing of "ownership,"
like a disease. Like taking poison.

A glamorous disease
a dazzling poison

"overkill."

Uluru Wild Fig Song

1

Soft earth turns straight up
curls out and away from its base
hard and red—a dome—five miles around
                    Ayers Rock, Uluru,

we push through grasses, vines, bushes
along the damp earth wash-off watershed margin
        where vertical rock dives
                into level sand,

Clustering chittering zebra finches on the
                    bone-white twigs,
red-eyed pink-foot little dove,

push on, into caves of overhangs,
painted red circles in circles,
black splayed-out human bodies,
painted lizards, wavy lines.

skip across sandy peels of clean bent bedrock
stop for lunch and there's a native fig tree
        heavy-clustered, many ripe:
        someone must have sat here, shat here
                    long ago.

2

Sit in the dust
        take the clothes off. feel it on the skin
        lay down. roll around
        run sand through your hair.
        nap an hour

bird calls through dreams
now
you're clean.

sitting on red sand ground with a dog.
breeze blowing, full moon,
women singing over there—
men clapping sticks and singing here

eating meaty bone,
hold the dog off with one foot

stickers & prickles in the sand—

clacking the boomerang beat,
a long walk
singing the land.

3
naked but decorated,
scarred.
white ash   white clay,
scars on the chest.
lines of scars on the loin.
the scars: the gate,
the path, the seal,
the proof.

white-barred birds under the dark sky.

4
singing and drumming at the school
a blonde-haired black-skinned girl
watching and same time teasing a friend
dress half untied, naked beneath,
young breasts like the *mulpu*
mushroom,
swelling up through sand.

stiff wind close to the ground,

trash lodged in the spinifex, the fence,
the bottles, broken cars.

                    5

Sit down in the sand
          skin to the ground.
          a thousand miles of open gritty land
          white cockatoo on a salt pan

hard wild fig on the tongue.

          this wild fig song.

Fall of 40081, Uluru, Amata, Fregon,
Papunya, Ilpili, Austral.

NETS
IV

Money Goes Upstream

I am hearing people talk about reason
Higher consciousness, the unconscious,
 looking across the audience
 through the side door
 where hot sunshine blocks out
 a patch of tan grass and thorny buckbrush

There are people who do business within the law.
And others, who love speed, danger,
Tricks, who know how to
Twist arms, get fantastic wealth,
Hurt with heavy shoulders of power,
And then drink to it!
 they don't get caught.
 they *own* the law.
Is this reason? Or is it a dream.

I can smell the grass, feel the stones with bare feet
 though I sit here shod and clothed
 with all the people. That's my power.
And some odd force is in the world
Not a power
That seeks to own the source.
It dazzles and it slips us by,
It swims upstream.

Breasts

 That which makes milk can't
     help but concentrate
 Out of the food of the world,
 Right up to the point
     where we suck it,
 Poison, too

 But the breast is a filter—
 The poison stays there, in the flesh.

Heavy metals in traces
                    deadly molecules hooked up in strings
                    that men dreamed of;
Never found in the world til today.
                    (in your bosom
                    petrochemical complex
                    astray)

So we celebrate breasts
We all love to kiss them
                    —they're like philosophers!
Who hold back the bitter in mind
To let the more tasty
Wisdom slip through
                    for the little ones.
                    who can't take the poison so young.

The work that comes later
After child-raising
For the real self to be,
Is to then burn the poison away.
Flat breasts, tired bodies,
That will snap like old leather,
                    tough enough
                    for a few more good days,

And the glittering eyes,
Old mother,
Old father,
                    are gay.

Old Rotting Tree Trunk Down

Winding grain
Of twisting outer spiral shell

Stubby broken limbs at angles
Peeled off outer layers askew;
A big rock
Locked in taproot clasp
Now lifted to the air;
Amber beads of ancient sap
In powdery cracks of red dry-rot
                    fallen away
From the pitchy heartwood core.

Beautiful body we walk on:
Up and across to miss
                the wiry manzanita mat.
On a slope of rock and air,
Of breeze without cease—

     If "meditation on decay and rot cures lust"
     I'm hopeless:
     I delight in thought of fungus,
     beetle larvae, stains
             that suck the life still
             from your old insides,

Under crystal sky.
And the woodpecker flash
     from tree to tree
     in a grove of your heirs
On the green-watered bench right there!

     Looking out at blue lakes,
     dripping snowpatch
             soaking glacial rubble,
     crumbling rocky cliffs and scree,

Corruption, decay, the sticky turnover—
Death into more of the
Life-death same,

A quick life:
and the long slow
feeding that follows—
the woodpecker's cry.

VII, '78, English Mountain

For a Fifty-Year-Old Woman in Stockholm

Your firm chin
straight brow
tilt of the head

Knees up in an easy squat
your body shows how
You gave birth nine times:
The dent in the bones
in the back of the pelvis
mother of us all,
four thousand years dead.

*X, '82, The Bäckaskog woman, Stockholm
Historic Museum*

Old Woman Nature

Old Woman Nature
naturally has a bag of bones
tucked away somewhere.
a whole room full of bones!

A scattering of hair and cartilage
bits in the woods.

A fox scat with hair and a tooth in it.
a shellmound
a bone flake in a streambank.

A purring cat, crunching
the mouse head first,
eating on down toward the tail—

The sweet old woman
calmly gathering firewood in the
moon . . .

Don't be shocked,
She's heating you some soup.

*VII, '81, Seeing Ichikawa Ennosuke in
"Kurozuka"—"Demoness"—at the Kabuki-za
in Tokyo*

The Canyon Wren
for James and Carol Katz

I look up at the cliffs
But we're swept on by   downriver
the rafts
Wobble and slide over roils of water
boulders shimmer
under the arching stream
Rock walls straight up on both sides.
A hawk cuts across that narrow sky
hit by sun,

We paddle forward, backstroke, turn,
Spinning through eddies and waves
Stairsteps of churning whitewater.
above the roar
hear the song of a Canyon Wren.

A smooth stretch, drifting and resting.
Hear it again, delicate downward song

       ti ti   ti ti tee tee tee

Descending through ancient beds.
A single female mallard flies upstream—

Shooting the Hundred-Pace Rapids
Su Shih saw, for a moment,
     it all stand still
"I stare at the water:
     it moves with unspeakable slowness"

Dōgen, writing at midnight,

     "mountains flow

     "water is the palace of the dragon
     "it does not flow away.

We beach up at China Camp
Between piles of stone
Stacked there by black-haired miners,
     cook in the dark
     sleep all night long by the stream.

These songs that are here and gone,
Here and gone,
To purify our ears.

———

The Stanislaus River runs through Central Miwok country and down to the San Joaquin valley. The twists and turns of the river, the layering, swirling stone cliffs of the gorges are cut in nine-million-year-old latites. For many seasons lovers of rocks and water have danced in rafts and kayaks down this dragon-arm of the high Sierra. Not long ago Jim Katz and friends, river runners all, asked me to shoot the river with them, to see its face once more before it goes under the rising waters of the New Mellones Dam. The song of the Canyon Wren stayed with us the whole voyage; at China Camp, in the dark, I wrote this poem.

April, 40081, Stanislaus River, Camp 9 to
Parrott's Ferry

For All

Ah to be alive
            on a mid-September morn
            fording a stream
            barefoot, pants rolled up,
            holding boots, pack on,
            sunshine, ice in the shallows,
            northern rockies.

Rustle and shimmer of icy creek waters
stones turn underfoot, small and hard as toes
            cold nose dripping
            singing inside
            creek music, heart music,
            smell of sun on gravel.

            I pledge allegiance

I pledge allegiance to the soil
            of Turtle Island,
and to the beings who thereon dwell
            one ecosystem
            in diversity
            under the sun
With joyful interpenetration for all.

LEFT OUT IN THE RAIN

— Introduction —
I
1947–1948

Elk Trails

Ancient, world-old Elk paths
Narrow, dusty Elk paths
Wide-trampled, muddy,
Aimless . . . wandering . . .
Everchanging Elk paths.

I have walked you, ancient trails,
Along the narrow rocky ridges
High above the mountains that
Make up your world:
Looking down on giant trees, silent
In the purple shadows of ravines—
Above the spire-like alpine fir
Above the high, steep-slanting meadows
Where sun-softened snowfields share the earth
With flowers.

I have followed narrow twisting ridges,
Sharp-topped and jagged as a broken crosscut saw
Across the roof of all the Elk-world
On one ancient wandering trail,
Cutting crazily over rocks and dust and snow—
Gently slanting through high meadows,
Rich with scent of Lupine,
Rich with smell of Elk-dung,
Rich with scent of short-lived
Dainty alpine flowers.
And from the ridgetops I have followed you
Down through heather fields, through timber,
Downward winding to the hoof-churned shore of
One tiny blue-green mountain lake
Untouched by lips of men.

Ancient, wandering trails
Cut and edged by centuries of cloven hooves
Passing from one pasture to another—
Route and destination seeming aimless, but
Charted by the sharp-tempered guardian of creatures,

Instinct. A God coarse-haired, steel-muscled,
Thin-flanked and musky. Used to sleeping lonely
In the snow, or napping in the mountain grasses
On warm summer afternoons, high in the meadows.
And their God laughs low and often
At the man-made trails,
Precise-cut babies of the mountains
Ignorant of the fine, high-soaring ridges
And the slanting grassy meadows
Hanging over space—
Trails that follow streams and valleys
In well-marked switchbacks through the trees,
Newcomers to the Elk world.

(High above, the Elk walk in the evening
From one pasture to another
Scrambling on the rock and snow
While their ancient, wandering,
Aimless trails
And their ancient, coarse-haired,
Thin-flanked God
Laugh in silent wind-like chuckles
At man, and all his trails.)

Mt. St. Helens, Spirit Lake

"Out of the soil and rock"

Out of the soil and rock,
the growing season and spring, death
and winter,
out of the cold and rain, dust and sunshine,
came the music of cities and streets.
The people who take that music
                    into themselves,
creatures of salt, carbon, nitrogen, water,
may sometimes hang on the point of it,

hunger, an instant,
the world round the edge.

This city smoke and building steel
already is no more;
The music and cities of the future wait beyond the edge.

New York City

— On the Doab of the Columbia —
and the Willamette
II
1949–1952

Lines on a Carp

old fat fish of everlasting life
in rank brown pools discarded by the river
soft round-mouth nudging mud
among the reeds, beside the railroad track

you will not hear the human cries
but pines will grow between those ties
before you turn your belly to the sun

A Sinecure for P. Whalen

Whalen, curious vulture,
Picked the Western mind,
Ate the cataracted eyes
That once saw Gwion race the hag
And addle gentlemen

Still unfilled, he skittered to
The sweet bamboo
Fed green on yellow silt
And built a poem to dead Li Po.
The Drunkard taught him how to dance,
Leave dead bodies to the plants,
Sleep out nights in rain.

For George Leigh-Mallory

Escaping Cambridge,
He turned away from London
With austere passion faced the seas.

Accompanied by numbered boxes
Crossed the plains in teeming summer

Soft eyes avoiding sores and hunger
And came to cool Darjeeling.

Hundreds of sleepy Sherpas
Hired at dawn, to carry
Tea and socks to Chomolungma.

Here, disregarding whimpered warnings
With practised skill maintained his life
In that translucent cold
And still had strength to breathe, and climb:

And found a hideous demon there
Waiting in a golden chair
With drums

This is what the simplest nomad knows.

Spring Songs

Out the building's shadow
A seagull bursts
Caught in slanted sunbeam,
Wing-slanted windward, head cocked sideways—
Eyeing the broil of cars
Within the shadow—

     what noise, what beasts rush
     on those ordered paths
     what ugly visions in this cubic tangle?

Early Spring afternoon. Befuddled bird,
Away!

Sky, high wind flowing
Hair, wind blown back
Water, black mud bank

Green growing
Wild things, free sowing
Wind-blown seed plants
Curl
Sprout
Tissue-tearing out

Message from Outside

I am the one who gnawed the blanket through
Peeped in the hole and saw with my left eye
The one-leg sliver man put out the fire.

I dug like mice below the cabin's floor
Crawling through oil and rotted hides, I broke
Into that curious handsewn box. Pursued by birds,
Threw my comb, my magic marbles to the wind,
Caught the last bus, and made it here on time.

Stop chewing gum, I show you what I stole—
Pine-marten furs, and box within each box,
The final box in swallow tendons tied,
Inside, an eye! It screws into
The center of your head.

But there they call me urine-boy,
And this deserted newsstand is quite safe.
Peer through this and watch the people spawn:
It makes me laugh, but Raven only croaks.

I saw Coyote! And I'll buy a gun,
Go back and build a monstrous general fire,
Watch the forests move into this town.

You stand cracking sunflower seeds and stare.

A Change of Straw

Flickering eye
Peers from a birdcage
       shivering lips of bone
       scratch, and a taste of shell

Feathers cram the mouth.
Birdtalk, loose claw curved
       on a stained bough
Slick eyes sleep
       in a dungheap

Ruffle of dusty wings.

Creep to the fence
Crisscross chickenwire screens at the sun
     crickets and plums
             wither dry

Caught in a barnyard!
       with a pocketful of straw.

Under the Skin of It

Naturally tender, flesh and such
Being entirely mortal, fragile
And complex as a model plane.
Demanding attention, in its unfair ways

Getting, of course, the pleasure that it seeks.

But is it pleased?
Flesh being a type of clay (or dust);
Spirit, the other, like a gas,
Rising and floating in the hollow
Of the Skull—

Which is to know the other's real delight?

Both under the skin, which stretches
As we grow, sagging a trifle
In the pinch of time. Enchanting
The thought of pleasure pleasing flesh and bone.

"dogs, sheep, cows, goats"

dogs, sheep, cows, goats
and sometimes deer, hear loud noises
crackling in bushes, and they flick
fly or creep, as rabbits do
does too, into warm nests. no talk
but chatters there, small throat sounds
ear-pricks, up or back. hooves
tinkle on creekbeds. who fears a talk-
less landscape, crowded with creatures
leaves. falls. undergrowth
crawls all night, and summer smells
deep in the bushes. crouch!
at the thorny stalks.

Birth of the Shaman
for Phil Whalen

—well there he is. six a.m.
rhythmic flutter of the guts, now he's
born
in a drizzle of rain
     apple blossoms at Hood river,
smoke along water.
at river's mouth
tide frets the pilings.

here he is.
back of the clearing, cedar drips.
clouds are breaking, Wy-east shines through
          —the white summit—
a truck honks, crossing the logging-road
in the valley.
          he is here.

Atthis

1.

The painful accumulation of our errors
In dry summer, and her loneliness
And that distracted weeping
Of hot endless afternoons
Foretold the famine

Her swimming fondness
Stretched taut in sterile time
Contracted into dusty fractions
And now the crops are failing.

Since my sorcery has failed
My blood must feed the soil.
Let no delirious priest proclaim
A second coming;
          these fragments will stay scattered.

2.

Her life blew through my body and away
I see it whirling now, across the stony places.

I lost her softly through my fingers,
Between my ribs in gentle gusts she
Sifted free, polishing the small bones.

The mute, thin framework takes the winds
That blow across the stony places.

3.

". . . Still, she reproached all lands,
calling them ungrateful
and unworthy of the gift of corn"

She shall not be mollified
Til men go mad, and trees have died
For no known reason on the heights
And cornfields withered overnight;
Til Elk have groaned with thirst
And flower buds refuse to burst
Til rivers turn the fish to stone
And rocks are heard again to moan:
Until the sun has been re-tied
To Machu Picchu, men who die
Will be but corpses dressed in frocks
Who cannot speak with birds or rocks.

4. TIGER SONG

I gnaw the body of delight
Spit the knotted gristle out
Lap the blood left lie by night

O see your joy digested here
Splintering to the bones of life
That torture with their fractured points
Your concupiscence into strife
Your love into a ball of hair
That cuts me worse than any knife

5.

Poorness and the pride we shared
Our mutual vicious natures bared
Made a jungle of a bed
Gnawed and comforted we fled.
It should have birthed a human child,
Instead our intellects ran wild.

My bitter foe, O sterile lover,
Stranded in my brain, you

Are loved, still loved, there
Which is nowhere, and leaves me
Strangled, bound and dangled, yet
Me, yet of most men most free.

6.

You've gone cold, I suppose
In the prosperous East, with a good job,
Your bright mind turned all brain,
Your wild dancing feet and eyes
Held still, fear
Finally running it all
Under some fancy name.
The summer I hitchhiked from New York
In the hottest week of August
Over the desert and into sea-fog
San Francisco and took you
From your Mother's place, and we hiked
Over Tamalpais, caught a ride
To Tomales Bay, and camped under pines.
You remember it now and put it down,
Turning hard. But I know
How clear and kind your love was
At eighteen, how keen your heart and eye,
How you wrote me of your downtown job,
Sandpipers at Stinson Beach, an old
German you met on a lonely hike
With freckles on his back—the sunburn
On your breasts. Even then
I had a terrible thought of time,
And age, and the death
Of our dream-like young love.
It began too soon,
Was too strong too soon,
And it's gone.

7.

Love me love, til trees fall flat
      their trunks flail down the berries
Til ripe sharp vines crawl through the door
      and the air is full of sparrows

I loved you love, in halls and homes
            and through the long library;
I loved you in the pine and snow
            now I love blackberry

8.

Half-known stars in the dawn sky
Purple Finch at the feed-tray
A broom beat on a back porch,
                        tea,
My bent legs, love of you.

9. UP THE DOSEWALLIPS

In the ruins of a CCC shelter
            cooking stew,
rain thru the broken shakes
gorge a low roar,
            rain and creeks—

A doe in the meadow
hair plastered to steaming flanks
            —hoofprints down gullies
wind whipping rain against cliffs

The trail fades in the meadow,
            cairns at each rise to the pass.
ash-scars, a ring of stone
            —we camped here one other
            summer—

rainsoaked and shivering
            kneedeep in squaw grass,

two days travel from roads.

                    Olympic Mountains

10. SEAMAN'S DITTY

I'm wondering where you are now
Married, or mad, or free:

Wherever you are you're likely glad,
But memory troubles me.

We could've had us children,
We could've had a home—
But you thought not, and I thought not,
And these nine years we roam.

Today I worked in the deep dark tanks,
And climbed out to watch the sea:
Gulls and salty waves pass by,
And mountains of Araby.

I've travelled the lonely oceans
And wandered the lonely towns.
I've learned a lot and lost a lot,
And proved the world was round.

Now if we'd stayed together,
There's much we'd never've known—
But dreary books and weary lands
Weigh on me like a stone.

Indian Ocean

— The Broad Roads of the West —
III
1952–1956

Bakers Cabin on Boone's Ferry Road

Frogs all night
> three white ducks
> chanting down the pond
> the yowling of the Siamese in heat
> the hot iron thud on spitting shirts
Dampish firewood squeaks and burns.
> four kittens and a baby squall
> in boxes by the kitchen stove.

Portland

Numerous Broken Eggs

Ejected from such pleasaunce,
Naturally some snivelling is expected.
Dalliance, in the old sense, these days rare;
One is not unaffected. Repair to symbols—
Fracture of the nerve. Keeping the word inflected
When monosyllabic pain would be the cure.

Nauseous, although inspired.
"Experience" had been the guide; freedom inflicted
By one's dismissal, proved to be the snare.
A dangling pink-eyed rodent could learn more
From such a death; retired for meditation
One sometimes wonders on the morpheme "pure."

In fact, the work was good.
When used the art is Art; dissected,
Each fragment starts anew, and resurrected,
A thousand baby starfish swarm the sea.
Perhaps not wisdom, but a certain gain—
Freedom is painless, pleasure not the lure.

And grammar is not the goal.
An insight into "structure" is the point—

Without a method—but a sudden stare
Refracted into objects, each Delight.

A junkyard neat as Nature, or a Bronze.
Unstuck from objects, meanings are unsure.

Gazing on unzoned stars the mind takes flight—
The Astrolabe precisely marks each place,
Moving on jewelled pinions, rimmed in brass
(Implicit order is the error here)
What fills the sky is keening of Swift wings!
All things seen by the naked eye, when closed.

The Lookouts

Perched on their bare and windy peaks
They twitter like birds across the fractured hills
Equipped by Science with the keenest tool—
A complex two-way radio, full of tubes.

The most alone, and highest in the land,
We trust their scrupulous vision to a man:
Assume their eyes are slitted to the sun
Searching each gorge and ridge-slope for a sign;

They are the ones to fix a point in sight
Reveal the azimuth of a distant flame,
Define the range and township of its light
And send us tramping blindly to the scene.

What we perceive on maps, in scale, is theirs:
Enormous and sprawling, falling on every side
Off to a rough horizon, scoured by ice,
Poking through clouds, and snowbound half the year.

Should we envy how they peer above
Over our rainy valleys, peak to peak,

Sending triumphant warnings out of space
That blare and startle, on the speaker box?

We need not listen. With a toggle switch
All that they say is stopped, our time is ours;
Or if that complex radio should break down—
Taught how to use, but not to fix, its tubes—

For all their artful watching, they are dumb.
Totally useless, lost to human speech,
They mutely have to make the long hike down.

History Must Have a Start
Upper Skagit country

Took all day to find it:
Mine cabin on Canyon Creek,
Looking for good tools, or an old brass
Safety razor with teeth.

Grown over with berries,
In a rubble of tailings,
Doorframe broke, roof sagged in,
Logs all skewed
About ready to fall.
Wheelbarrow, gears, a pick
Rusted by the door;
Inside, chairs broken, the mouse-proof
Chest filled with dry pellets and the
Shredded remains of a blanket.
Rusty crosscuts hung from the rafters.
Less than 20 years
Since the claim was abandoned,
But isolated: mice had moved in,
Plants poked through the puncheon.
Tools of our time, nothing for an
Archeologist, unless washboards are rare—

The whole works packed in on muleback
In pieces, and never enough gold to pay.

(No ceramics or statues
Like Harappa or Knossos,
These are from civilized times.)

Poem Left in Sourdough Mountain Lookout*

I the poet Gary Snyder
Stayed six weeks in fifty-three
On this ridge and on this rock
& saw what every Lookout sees,
Saw these mountains shift about
& end up on the ocean floor
Saw the wind and waters break
The branched deer, the Eagle's eye,
& when pray tell, shall Lookouts die?

Geological Meditation

Rocks suffer,
          slowly,
Twisting, splintering scree
Strata and vein
          writhe
Boiled, chilled, form to form,
Loosely hung over with
Slight weight of trees,
          quick creatures
Flickering, soil and water,
Alive on each other.

* (A later lookout told me this poem was still pinned up in the cabin in 1968.)

Matter
Bent into life,
Has hallucinations, astonished
Molecules informing in chains
            at last,
Incredible, the torture is known,
Called ideas.
            are they real?
Mountains are squashed like slugs.
Perception a chemical trick,
            dreams—
Men and beasts dream
Of pleasure.

Sourdough Mountain

Fording the Flooded Goldie River

Clamped to the log by the current
Stream breaking over my pack,
Fighting edging across,
Footholds wash out, felt
My body give way: to be
Swept beneath log and downstream,
Down the rocks, to the gorge.
Looked up from the rush of the torrent—
Sunlight in fir-boughs,
Midges in a sunpatch, a bird breaking up,
Cloud on the ridge,
Sky
Blue
I fought death:
        got across it
            alone.

Olympic Mountains

"Svāhā a Feminine Ending for Mantra"

Under the lilac, svāhā girl
eating the plum-pit, crunch.
bees buzz, green apples by watering holes
wet leaves and spiders in shadows.
green scum on the pond, beside
cement cisterns, moss green, what smells?
lift the rotted lid, smell it dark water.
they are breeding and feeding there
still water waits where, of a breeding day,
someone lets it out to seep
seep away.

"Wind has blown . . ."

Wind has blown
the blossoms down

no use dodging puddles
when your feet are soaked
      —scum of petals
slip on the wet walk;
a soft rain rides my skull.

I never loved you,
this spring or another.
rain in the plum bough

deer on the mountain
trout in the creek.

Berkeley

Song for a Cougar Hide*

The Fully Human time is nigh,
Alas, the other beasts must die.

Sea lions beat and snort and dive.
Left no mottled fawn alive.
A black bear winters in his cave,
Coyote's bottled in his grave.

I have heard the fat buck snort
Gut-shot—winchester ninety-four
The Doe that winds a sitting sage,
Flees in such a fearful rage.

Wang Wei built his own Deer Park,
Chao-chou left no gate ajar
Murasaki rose at dawn and
Let the snow come blowing in.

I have logged and I have planted
Killed and birthed in measure
Forgot what I learned to learn
A cougar hide's my treasure.

"Plum petals falling . . ."

Plum petals falling
cherry still hard buds
drinking wine
in the garden
The landlady comes out
            in the twilight
and beats a rug.

---

* *(The cougar hide was carried off by an enterprising lad in San Francisco in 1970.)*

The Rainy Season

Rain,
A steady drip from the eaves;
A trickle leaks down the wall,
Blankets piled in a dry corner
Wet jeans hang from the toe
                        of a corkt boot
Perched on the redwood tokonoma.

Reading Rexroth's *Japanese Poems*.
The wet bike dries on the porch.
Walt Whitman, Hitomaro, Han Shan,
                        here
In Berkeley December twentieth-
Century rain, in this city-
                        world-war age,
And *of* it,
                        the jazz of
Late nights streets and all these people
Springs from the same love
And cool eyes now
                        as then.

Granite sierras, shelves of books,
Holy teachings, scatter
Aimlessly tumbling through
Years and countries—
Aristotle's herd of formal stars
                        stampedes—
The diamond-point mercy
Of this timeless rain.

The Genji Story

I once had a gray brindle tomcat named Genji
who would run off for days at a time

& come back to my pad & I'd feed him
                    with horsemeat
& put medicine in his swoll eye.
His ears tattered up & his hide
                    full of scratches
he'd sit on my lap while I read,
then he'd go through a gap in the window
& he made out much better than I.

I went off to a job in the mountains
and Genji got left with a friend
after a week Genji ran off
& was never seen ever again.
                    that was some years ago,
at the moment I wonder
since I raised him from a kitten and fed him
                    quite well,
if he's healthy & strong from the horsemeat
                    we shared then
now living on scraps in wild streets
                    where he dwells

Late October Camping in the Sawtooths

Sunlight climbs the snowpeak
                    glowing pale red
Cold sinks into the gorge
                    shadows merge.
Building a fire of pine twigs
                    at the foot of a cliff,
Drinking hot tea from a tin cup
                    in the chill air—
Pull on sweater and roll a smoke.
                    a leaf
                    beyond fire
Sparkles with nightfall frost.

Point Reyes

Sandpipers at the margin
              in the moon—
Bright fan of the flat creek
On dark sea sand,
              rock boom beyond:
The work of centuries and wars,
              a car,
Is parked a mile above
              where the dirt road ends.
In naked gritty sand,
Eye-stinging salty driftwood campfire
              smoke, out far,
It all begins again.
Sandpipers chasing the shiny surf
              in the moonlight—
By a fire at the beach.

April

I lay on my back
Watching the sun through the
Net glitter of your gold hair
Our naked selves on a
Steep grassy slope
Your third child in your belly
Your face by mine
Your husband's blessing
On our brief, doomed love
All of us in the heat of
April wine and sun
And sex and many friends
Our bodies flaring hot
Where we touch,
The sun burns the
Writhing snakebone
Of your back.

Makings

I watched my father's friends
Roll cigarettes, when I was young
Leaning against our black tarpaper shack.
The wheatstraw grimy in their hands
Talking of cars and tools and jobs
Everybody out of work.
    the quick flip back
And thin lick stick of the tongue,
And a twist, and a fingernail flare of match.
I watched and wished my overalls
Had hammer-slings like theirs.

The war and after the war
With jobs and money came,
My father lives in a big suburban home.
It seems like since the thirties
I'm the only one stayed poor.
It's good to sit in the
Window of my shack,
Roll tan wheatstraw and tobacco
Round and smoke.

                              Marin-an

— Kyoto, and the Sappa Creek —
IV
1956–1959

Longitude 170° West, Latitude 35° North
For Ruth Sasaki

This realm half sky half water,
    night black with white foam
    streaks of glowing fish
    the high half black too lit with
    dots of stars,
The thrum of the diesel engine twirling
    sixty-foot drive shafts of twin screws,
Shape of a boat, and floating
    over a mile of living seawater, underway,
    always westward, dropping
    land behind us to the east,
Brought only these brown Booby birds that trail
    a taste of landfall feathers in the craw
    hatchrock barrens—old migrations—
    flicking from off stern into thoughts,
Sailing jellyfish by day, phosphorescent
    light at night,
    shift of current on the ocean floor
    food chains climbing to the whale.

Ship hanging on this membrane infinitely
    tiny in the "heights" the "deep"
    air-bound beings in the realm of wind
    or water, holding hand to wing or fin
Swimming westward to the farther shore,
    this is what I wanted? so much
    water in the world and so much crossing,
    oceans of truth and seas of doctrine
Salty real seas of our westering world,
    Dharma-spray of lonely slick on deck
Sleepy, between two lands, always a-
    floating world,
                I go below.

M. S. Arita Maru

For Example

There was an old Dutch lady
Lived in a room in the house
In front of my small shack
Who sat all day in the garden
By my door and read.
She said she knew the East
And once had seen a book
On Buddhist monks. "And you
Gott no business going to
Japan. The thing to be
Is life, is young and travel
Much and love. I know
The way you are, you study hard
But you have friends that
Come and stay, and bike, and
There's the little tree you
Planted by the wall" As I
Filled my water bucket from
A hose. The sun lit up
Her thin white hair a bird
Squawked from the Avocado at the air
& Bodhisattvas teach us everywhere.

Chion-In
Temple of the Pure Land

        hot blue
high clouds pile
flicker-eave pigeons under dark wood
clink bells and wood clack chant
        gold, wood, incense,
trees behind—
        stop here
on the granite step
foot-polished and eat a plum.

Bomb Test

The fish float belly-up, for real—
Uranium in the whites
                    of their eyes
They've been swimming
Deep down where it's black when a
Silvery snow of something queer
                    glinted in
From cirrus clouds to the seamounts,
Through all the food chains,
Shrimp to tuna, the currents,
Riding the waves.

                                        Kyoto

Dullness in February: Japan

The high-class families
Teach their virgin daughters
English, flowers, and Tea:
Culture of the East—poor girls
Ride boys' bikes balancing noodles.

Brutal sergeants, vicious aesthetes,
                    the meeting
Of the worst of East and West.
Silly priests in temples
Far too fine for now.
Discipline for what end?
We gave up wisdom long ago,
Enlightenment is kicks
                    —but there is better.
Cold smooth wood floors
And doves, stone pools, moss
Under maples, silent frosty rooftiles
Slanting high—what sense
The old boys made—

Confucius, Lao-tzu, Tu Fu, Sesshu
                    and the rest,
Through the centuries, peed off
By politicians in their robes.
Perhaps some flame remains.
                    I hope
Again some day
To hit the night road in America
Hitchhiking through dark towns
Rucksack on my back,
To the home of a
Poverty-stricken witty
Drunkard friend.

Map

A hill, a farm,
A forest, and a valley.
Half a hill plowed, half woods.
A forest valley and a valley field.

Sun passes over;
Two solstices a year
Cow in the pasture
Sometimes deer

A farmhouse built of wood.
A forest built on bones.
The high field, hawks
The low field, crows

Wren in the brambles
Frogs in the creek
Hot in summer
Cold in snow

The woods fade and pass.
The farm goes on.

The farm quits and fails
The woods creep down

Stocks fall you can't sell corn
Big frost and tree-mice starve
Who wins who cares?
The woods have time.
The farmer has heirs.

The Feathered Robe
For Yaeko Nakamura

On a clear spring windless day
Sea calm, the mountains
        sharp against the sky,
An old man stopped in a sandy
        seashore pine grove,
Lost in the still clear beauty.
Tracing a delicate scent
        he found a splendid robe
Of feathers hanging on a bough.

            Robe over his arm
            He heard   alarm
            Stop, and there he saw
            A shining Lady,
                    naked from her swim.

            Without my feathered robe
            that useless-to-you a human,
            Robe, I cannot,
            Home, I
            Cannot fly,
                    she cried

And for a dance
        he gave it back.
A dance,

she wore it glinting in the sun
Pine shadow breeze
Fluttering light sleeves—

old man watching saw
all he dreamed in youth
the endless springtime
morning beauty
of the world
                as

She, dancing, rose
Slow floating over pines
High beyond the hills
               a golden speck
In blue sky haze.

Nō play "Hagoromo"

On Vulture Peak

All the boys are gathered there
Vulture Peak, in the thin air
Watching cycles pass around
From brain to stone and flesh to ground,
Where love and wisdom are the same
But split like light to make the scene,
Ten million camped in a one-room shack
Tracing all the causes back
To Nothing which is not the start
(Now we love, but   here we part)
And not a one can answer why
To the simple garden in my eye.

I.

J.K. & me was squatting naked and sandy
At McClure Beach steaming mussels, eating,

Tossing the shells over our shoulders,
A pair of drunk Siwash starting a shellmound.
Neuri sleeping off a hangover face down
At the foot of a cliff; sea lions off shore

II.

Are bums and drunks truly Angels?
Hairy Immortals drinking poorboys in doorways?
Poor Abelard, thou'rt clipped!
                    the vomit
& prickles of a gritty desert drug
                    sweat and fire
Berry lather & lapping dogs—
                    All babies
Are unborn; tracking the moon through
Flying fenceposts a carload of groceries, home—
What home, pull in park at, and be known?

III.

                "the little cloud"
A nebula seen slantwise by the naked eye.
The curse of man's humanity to man. "My hair
        is in a pony-tail, I run!"
Each day a lunchpail and a shirtful of sawdust.
Old women dry pods fry corn in the cinders.
The head is a hawk on a boulder
The boulder a nest of coiled snakes

IV.

Nearer than breathing
Closer than skin
                    smack in the earballs
nosehalls, brainpans, tongueclucks
eyeholes, prickbones,
answer! answer! why!
                "with lowered lids
                i have entered
                            nibbana"

V.

Wisdom of the Arab:
  a camel lets her milk down
when tickled in the snatch.
philosophers are horrified
because there is no cause
because everything exists
because the world is real and so are they
and so is nothing is, not nothing save us—
    bony jungle spring
     Shakya in the boondocks.
  a broken start,
    sprout,
   is REALLY gone
        wow, he
always been standin there
   sweatin' and explainin'?

VI.

  gone where.
Nowhere, where he came from
  thus that thing
  that thus thing
     where were you born from
     born from, born from—
Did you fall fall fall
        fall
  from the salmonberry bough?
Are you the reborn soul
  of a bitter cheated chief?
      —I came out my mammy
Slick & yapping like a seal
My uncle washed me in the brine
I was a hero & a hunter in my time
A badger gave me visions
A whale made me pure
I sold my wife & children
& jumped into a mirror

VII.

Hot wispy ghosts blown
　　　　down halls between births,
　　　　　　　hobo-jungles of the void—
—Where did we meet last? where
Were you born? Wobblies of the Six
Realms—huddling by some campfire
　　　　　　　　　　in the stars
Resting & muttering before a birth
On Mars,

VIII.

What can be said about a Rabbit
Solitary and without context
Set before the mind. Was it born?
Has it horns? Dream people walking around
In dream town
　　　　　　—the city of the Gandharvas—
　　　　　not a real city, only the
　　　　　　　　　　memory of a city—
"The mind dances like the dancer
The intellect's the jester
The senses seem to think the world's a stage—"

IX.

For forty years the Buddha begged his bread
And all those years said nothing, so he said,
& Vulture Peak is silent as a tomb.

The Bodhisattvas

Some clap hands, some throw flowers,
Pat bread, lie down, sell books,
Do quaint dance steps, jingling jewels,
Plant wild Thyme in engine-blocks,
Make dark grimace stroking mules,
Fall backward into tom-tom thumps;
& cheer and wave and levitate

And pass out lunch on Vulture Peak
Enlightening gardens, parks, & pools.

A Monument on Okinawa

"One hundred twenty schoolgirls
Committed suicide together here."
Dead now thirteen years.
Those knot-hearted little adolescents
In their fool purity
Died with a perverse sort of grace;
Their sisters who lived
Can be seen in the bars—
The agreeable hustlers of peace.

Straits of Malacca 24 oct 1957

a.
   Soft rain on the
   gray ocean, a tern
   still glides low over
   whitecaps
   after the ship is gone

b.
   Soft rain on
                        gray sea
   a tern
        glides brushing
                           waves
   The ship's silent
                        wake

c. Fog of rain on
                        water
   Tern glides

Over waves,
         the
  wake

The Engine Room, S.S. Sappa Creek

Cool northern waters
Walk around the engine room where
Seven months I worked.

Changing colors
Like seasons in the woods
One week the rails and catwalks all turned red
Valve wheels grow green
Fade with soot and oil,
And bloom again bright yellow after weeks

Paintbrush, pots, & walking round.
The overhead line
Big enough to crawl through
        like I did in Ras Tanura,
Three months ago was white. & now it's
Gray.
Under rusty floorplates
        bilges lap
Venture there in slop of oil & brine
To clean out filters in the fuel oil line.

The engineer said
Paint the hot-lines silver.
I stood on ladders with a silver brush.
Skittering gauges tacked up everywhere
Pressure, pressure on each pump and pipe;
Heat of the steam, heat of the oil,
Heat of the very water where we float
Wrote down in the log book every hour,

Boilers, turbines, nest of bulkheads,
Hatches, doorways, down & sidewise, up,
But no way out.
Sweeping & changing all of it by bits.
—A yard of pipe replaced
A bearing in the trash can.
Me changing less by far—

All that time
Chipping, painting, fixing, this machine.
Lugging wrenches take off manhole covers
Polish tubes, and weld and gasket
        til the damn thing goes,

On land nobody off this ship
Will ever be so free or gay
Though in San Pedro we will
        each man get paid off about
            three thousand dollars cash
In two more days.

Hills of Home

I.

Today is like no day that
came before
I'll walk the roads and trails to Tamalpais.
        one clear day of fall,
        wind from the north
        that cleans the air a hundred
                miles

A little girl in a dark garage:
her home in the redwood shade,
            her father there
            he saws
        a board
(across the hill is

        nothing but sunshine,
liveoak, hardscrabble, hot little
            lizards)
                  wet shade
made those huge damp trees.
At my sister's house
at the foot of the trail,
I stop
drink coffee, tell her of my walk.

II.

I know nothing
of planes: I have seen pictures
           of the bomb:
It is beautiful to watch
jets skim by Richmond
            and the prison, pass the
            mountain, out
on a shining endless ocean
lift up on clouds and gleam
            even the noise is
interesting to hear and how if
            echoes across these
            manzanita hills.

III.

Stop the sailing sailboats:
            they are still.
just west of Alcatraz,
beyond them San Francisco town
            bonewhite in blue sea bay
            two major jails
            an oil refinery
sailboats all the way.
I eat my lunch on
sharp rocks at the top.

IV.

to see your own tracks climbing
up the trail that you go down.

the ocean's edge is high
it seems to rise and hang there
halfway up the sky.

V.

sun goes down.
on the dark side of the hill
       through pecker redwood trees
       in gloom and chill
       a small red blossom
       agitates the shade.
              the pipeline trail.
weave forward
carried on these feet
feel of the body
& abstract recollection held in time.
abandoned house at road's end:
       gray and real the
       glassless square holes
black/the steps all sidewise
and the wise inside.

I walk back to my cabin door
And leave this day behind.

The North Coast

Those picnics covered with sand
No money made them more gay
We passed over hills in the night
And walked along beaches by day.

Sage in the rain, or the sand
Spattered by new-falling rain.
That ocean was too cold to swim
But we did it again and again

— The Wide Pacific —
V
1959–1969

One Year

The hills behind
        Santa Barbara
           from the sea.
Pedro at midnight.
          three thousand dollars
Cash in hundred dollar bills
          —the Wakayama hills—
           each time
A ship hits land the land
        is new.
April. Oakland at eight A.M.
          hotcakes in San Francisco, ten
(Pago a month gone by)
          —jukebox tunes in
           far-off foreign towns;
Mt. Hiei. Tamalpais.
          June. The Desolation
           Valley snow.
She read her poems.
          Sierras in August, always
"Will I ever see those hills again?"
          rain. lightning
           on Whitney
Crackling hair on end.
          Once
           on the coast,
I heard of "Sticky Monkey Flower"
          "It makes you high"
Seals laugh
          in the seaweed—
The mind aches
          seeing a tanker passing
           out at sea.
At Port Townsend on the Sound
          I didn't stop
           to see Aunt Minnie:
Who gave cookies to my father
          1910. On Mt. St. Helens

Rotten glaciers turned us back.
           Hitching home,
                a German boy from BC
In one sweep drove me down.
           Columbus Street San Francisco
The bed falls on the floor.
           months of Marin-an
Learning again the names of birds & trees;
I saw the sea
           from Santa Barbara,
January. The water always warm.
           Big Sur in the fog;
In February packed my sleeping bag.
           Piers, blast
                whistle & the ship
Backs back & all
           we never stop to do
            & think of then
Can cry—lightship, albatross,
           the ocean like a friend,
Yokohama, Fuji, where its always been—
Mt. Hiei. On the river.
           settled here.
Today, America, Japan,
           one year.

Housecleaning in Kyoto *

This red washrag
           full of holes
faded grayish-pink
from scouring smoky
pots—before I throw it out,
           we found it:
camping
Potrero Meadows 1956

* (Jack Kerouac and I took a three day hike on the far slopes of Tamalpais just before I left for Asia—the washrag salvaged there got somehow to Japan.)

Seeing the Ox

Brown ox
Nose snubbed up
Locking his big head high
    against telephone pole
    right by Daitoku   temple—
Slobbering, watching kids play
    with rolling eye,

Fresh dung pile under his
    own hind hooves.

Kyoto

After the Typhoon

Rain whipped up the umbrella
The river was boiling down trees.
I stood on the bridge in a puddle
And crossed to the Yase zoo.
Three monkeys on top of a rock
Made a house for the new baby,
Hawk plucking a soggy old fish—
And the bear asleep: a brown muzzle
Deep in a damp cement cave.

Three Poems for Joanne

I. LOVING WORDS

Her big basket
    blonde hair drawn back
    over the ears
a directoire, or jacobean feel
    last summer, on crutches
hobbling down the steep hill trail.

sitting beside the geraniums
marking the eucalyptus rustle—sea wind—
                listening
i was chopping wood around the corner
down the hill.
          axe-sound
          the bird
          the wind
     the snorting horses & the starting cars,

loving words—
        "be true
to the *poem*"
nothing will shake that
        fine commitment down.

2. THE HEART OF THE WOOD

The cool
    clearing.
We have never seen
Such trees or
     flowers.
We are bare
In the open.
     here make
     our love
No one will
Watch us.
This place is
  Too far
In.

3. JOANNE MY WIFE

Joanne my wife
why frown
long legs are lovely
    I like yr
    freckld breast
    you butt me at night
        asleep

cry out for mother
hurt wild
like child
in dreams
          I cd write you
     no "love" poem
               so long.

     fights and the frown
                    at dawn.

Tenjin

We had ten Zen monks
          down for lunch—
"tenjin" the head monk said:
in China it was just a bun ("t'ien-hsin")
means "that the heart"
it means a real feed
               in Japan today.
"they still have buns in China
called 't'ien-hsin'"—
Dimsum, in Cantonese.

Joanne, Aronowitz, and I
once had tenjin (dim-sum)
on a quiet San Francisco
Sunday morning, chinatown.

Parting with Claude Dalenberg

Why don't we get drunk
          sit all night facing the moon
     "opening our hearts"
          as men did long ago?

last night was full moon, but
                    too cloudy.
one bottle of saké
              soon gone.
at lunchtime today you stopped by
your ship sails from Kobe at six.

eight years: San Francisco, the
beaches, the mountains,
                    Japan.

Quiet talk and slow easy pace.
with your rucksack to India,
Europe, return

ease of the world, the light
                    rain
as though we might
somewhere be
          parting again.

                              Kyoto

Crash

An old man riding his slow bike
Right down the center of the gravel road
At walking pace to talk to two old women
Bundled firewood balanced on their heads,
Distracted or intense in other mind
I picked the space between him and the two
Without a horn-honk tried to ride
Straight through, he swerved inside,
We soft collided in slow motion,
Motorcycle, man, and bike.
In grooved and rutted gravel powder dirt.
He red-faced cursed me in the local way
As I responded in a fair polite

Level of language, Ohara busses,
Waiting at our rear,
The peasant women waited down the road.
My fault. And he recalled he knew my face
And house, a Yase dweller too,
He said he would be madder,
But knew me now. It was not real
Even while kicking back the crash-bars into line.
Where was my mind.
Hieizan over, and the stream,
And all the cherry trees around
About to bloom—and us not hurt—
He rode away, his old brown overcoat
And rubber work shoes puffing dirt.
I overtook him. Later at the temple
My hands began to tremble:
I saw my inattention,
Tiny moment in the thread,
Was where the whole world could have turned
And gone another way.

Kyoto

Two Comments

I.

I walk the oldest culture on earth & hold
concrete & asphalt concordances.
childhood of flush and propellor
always a bored eye on the factories
I tell you shoes
what can I elaborate of doorknob?
privacy always.
your railway timetable spells.
we were raised in a warehouse
& teach the archaic
way of Technique.
        I know the whole of my time.

my people half-lidded drive their machines
what other people from birth
             have known orgies and tigers?
                         my heart?

II.

Kennedy, Krushchev, & Nixon
your little children will all be destroyed
& the potsherds heap over them
nobody follows the
Logic of this to its end.

"Riding the hot electric train"

Riding the hot electric train
Between temples and companies,
Trading my mother tongue
For the means to stay here,

I know what
Dante meant
Entering that cave
In a forest when faced by wolves.

I must not keep forgetting
I am still travelling
The land between here
And the sea.

The man on the mountain is wise,
In town he is
Jackrolled and
Gets clap from good-hearted whores.

Foreigners

tall
yellow teeth
deep voices
pimples.
walk like policemen
hands in their pockets,
always wanting girls.
music hard and fast
getting drunk
fighting with their fists

laughing at each other.
their eyes
aren't really blue.

Kyoto Vacation

Down from the country, old train bogies,
Piled up with plaid country quilt
They've been travelling days,
Purple flag says "Hokkaido"
Lined up on the platform in groups
Loads wrapped in furoshikis,
Red-faced geezer with white fringe-beard
All dowdy, shabby,
From cold pebble saltshore towns
And sugarbeet fields.
This is their Kyoto
        (who's that foreigner—)
Busy, with someplace to go.
Teapots and bedding,
A bunch of old lambs in their huddles
They get told where to go and have fun—

This Is Living

Who's that old lady?
She's going to get her
Nice kimono all dirty
Being sick
In the station
Of the train

In Tokyo: At Loose Ends

all those books and those clothes
            are forgotten.
how could we have cared.
those plans, those evenings
            all over.
the whole world is here—
paste in the postoffice,
            paintings in museums
people in houses,
            me on my feet through the town.
liking it,
            ready to leave.

English Lessons at the Boiler Company

The western hills curve down from Mt. Atago
Toward Osaka plains and the inland sea.
Sun, snow, clouds, flurry and glitter,

From long high sheds comes the rivetting,
Shriek of steam pressure tests,
They make boilers—

File into the small, heated, carpetted,
Office room: start teaching language,

Strange feeling sounds, odd puffs and buzzes,
Bend tongues, re-wrap the brain,

Over the plains,   snow-whirling clouds.

From Below

turkey buzzards wheeling
            wheeling

quivering inter-crossing
        zag   fern fronds

high blue two
    supersonic feathery ice-
        tracks sail south

rear jet trail plumes crossing
            with the leader

sun flashes the buzzard breast
        over shingle corners
        this old redwood house.

The Fruit

More sour, more bitter than lemon
It had seemed a sweet coarse orange,

Even bananas with seeds.
Huge blooms of no odor

Brook water warm to the touch.
Dreaming but not quite sleeping,
Wakened but not awake.

The Ride

To
Force to the furthest edge where
    it still holds up

Riding Visions isn't fun
    must be done.

Only
When children and friends
All in a whirl go wild for a while—
Lips drawing over our mouths—hair in our eyes—
    can we rest and smile.

Riding the edge makes one crude.
The Chinese poets
    I have no heart to read.

We trap dreams
And club them,
Skin them out, tools are few,
The guts and the shit can be used—
To keep up this work
    poison is food.

To draw the times over the edge
To go where we could.

Then

When everybody in the world has a car
and nobody knows the smell
people will be amazed at our carpentry
all the deer in zoos
they'll remember wild animals and trees
call their housecats "tiger"
dream of the days

when men were poor and dirty—
it was great—
beggars, the wine-red saris
of outcaste Indian girls
lean hunger in the rain
—we were
alive, then

Saying Farewell at the Monastery after Hearing the Old Master Lecture on "Return to the Source"

At the last turn in the path
        "goodbye—"
          —bending, bowing,
        (moss and a bit of
          wild
            bird—)
down.

Daitoku-ji Monastery

Farewell to Burning Island

A white bird lands on the ship
—The smoking island from afar
Feet scorch on the white deck
—Sailing east across the ocean
Once more.

Suwa-no-se Island, East China Sea

— Shasta Nation —

VI

1968–1985

First Landfall on Turtle Island

Crossing eastward the Pacific on the Washington Bear
The high route, just under the Aleutians
Twelve days storms and heavy seas
Kai laughs in his playpen hanging on
Rough or gentle weather, it's all one to him—
Masa seasick, naps in the daytime,
Last morning early: blue and smooth.
Watch for Gray Whales from the flying deck
A whale blows over by the lightship
    brisk winds, Ah, Ah,
Masa in her yellow parka, "the SKIN
    of the California hills!"
Seagull sails in, hangs there, a yard off my eye
Past the port side the flash of the Point Reyes lighthouse—
A whale rolls up, doesn't blow, just by the ship.

The long dawn chilly curve blue-purple,
    that's Bolinas, that's the oak in the
    meadow on the ridge under Tam
    I sat with Lew at—

A long land, a smooth land, clear sky,
    a whale,
    a gull,
To say hello.

Alabaster

    The leather fringes
        swing on the thighs.
        ah   so hot
        only beads to wear are cool

    And the girls chests like the mens
        are bare
        in the shade
        but the girls differ though the men are same.

Tanya's bosom like a drawn bow
    Holly like a load of flowers
    Ann's gracious fruits
    Masa brown and slimming down
        from milky dark-veined weight
    and, slighter than the rest,

But strongly dappled in the
    sweltering-shady mind,
    Edie's alabaster breasts.

                For the women carpenters of Kitkitdizze

The Years

The years seem to tumble
    faster and faster
    I work harder
    the boys get larger
    planting apple and cherry.

In summer barefoot,
    in winter rubber boots.

Little boys bodies
    soft bellies, tiny nipples,
    dirty hands

New grass coming
    through oakleaf and pine needle
    we'll plant a few more trees
    and watch the night sky turn.

Burned Out

An ancient incense cedar stump to burn
Against which piled the limbs
Of gnarly wolf-tree pine
Those limbs that burn black smoke
And dripping pitch
Along with other trunks and twigs
And heaps of manzanita, set fire to,
In February on a day when rain
Will just start after nine dry days.
Brush pile burning is a time to sit
Or nap by the big fire glow
Then pile on more
Dragged out from toppled beetle-kills.
Next day it rained some lightly
Then all night rain and wind that woke us
Heavy rain lashes and cascades
On the buddha-like seven-ton tile roof
And stout pine-pillared body of our *kum*,
Even after rain
The cedar stump still flickering in the wind
Smoking through the storm
Turned to a hole in the ground,
Black lips hissing jets of steam
From white ash mounds
Fire reaching deeper to its end
In narrow pitchy roots
It arrives at the beginning
Where a cone-flaked seed
Made its sprout.
Leaves a ghost-root hole,
A perfect cast of what's below,
So above. Cool.
Burned out. Again.

O
For Ed Schafer

O
Mistress of Bobcats
Lady of Sagebrush
    why do you fool me?
   showing me
          you
In a thousand shapes.
Groin, eyes, flank, toes,
Arches,
Lifts of the arm,
Hollow soft of the back of the knees,

    sweets and salts of
    lips and gulfs,
    halls of deep flesh song—
Why do you trick me
Queen of Taste?
    whose real beauty

    is none.

To Meet with Agaricus Augustus

    Back up the ridge
    at Bloody Run
    is an old time sawmill
    fifty years gone,

    At Bloody Run
    in the sawmill ruin
    we found a mushroom
    one foot wide.

    I felt small.
    To see that one,

So rare and great,
and good to eat,

"The Prince"

Too Many Chickens Gone

Bobcat paws. Bobcat pelt
        bobcat bobtail tail-bone;
                tufted ears.
Glazed eyes   heaving belly
        kicking chicken-dusty
                dirt

        wire fencing fenced him in
        his fur in puffs on wire
        where up he jumped,
                and fell.

For Alan Watts

He blazed out a new path for all of us
And came back and made it clear.
Explored the side canyons and deer trails
And investigated cliffs and thickets.
Many guides would have us travel
Single file, like mules in a pack-train;
And never leave the trail.
Alan taught us to move forward like the breeze;
Tasting the berries—greeting the bluejays—
Learning and loving the whole terrain.

                                    on his death

Original Vow

pollen, eagle down
light-on-the-water
bird-rising

    rattlesnake nose-pits
sense heat
    "See" the heart in a
        mouse
        beating;
    strike for the meat.

No Shoes No Shirt No Service

Padding down the street, the
Bushmen, the Paiute, the Cintas Largas
    are refused.
The queens of Crete,
The waiting-ladies of the King of Bundelkhand.
Tārā is kept out,
Bare-breasted on her lotus throne.

    (officially, no one goes through
    unofficially, horses go through,
    carriages go through—)

The barefoot shepherds, the bare-chested warriors

    (what is this gate,
    wide as a highway
    that only mice can enter?)

The cow passed through the window nicely—
Only the tail got stuck,

And the soils of this region will be fertile again
After another round of volcanoes

Nutrient ash—
     Shiva's dancing feet
     (No shoes)

Kine

Eight cows
         on a hillside
One stands,
         the brown
Grass around them flattened down.
Cows rest
         nestled on jut of hip
         springy rib and skin,
A huge taut sigh
         from the road,
         passing by

"The Trail Is Not a Trail"

I drove down the Freeway
And turned off at an exit
And went along a highway
Til it came to a sideroad
Drove up the sideroad
Til it turned to a dirt road
Full of bumps, and stopped.
Walked up a trail
But the trail got rough
And it faded away—
Out in the open,
Everywhere to go.

Poetry Is the Eagle of Experience

All the little mice of writing letters,
Sorting papers,
And the rabbits of getting in the wood,
The big Buck of a lecture in town.

Then, walk back into the brush
To keep clearing a trail.
High over even that,
A whistle of wings!
Breath of a song.

Calcium

The doe munches on rotten cow-skull
bone, she is pregnant.
Back of the woodshed
hooves rustling dry poison oak.

Cement hardens up at the footings
poured for the barn.

Molecule by molecule
drawn in and saved by
single swimming cells,
a few sparks of Calcium
like Blue Whales
far apart, and streaming through the sea.

High Quality Information

A life spent seeking it
Like a worm in the earth,
Like a hawk. Catching threads
Sketching bones

Guessing where the road goes.
Lao-tzu says
To forget what you knew is best.
That's what I want:
To get these sights down,
Clear, right to the place
Where they fade
Back into the mind of my times.
The same old circuitry
But some paths color-coded
Empty
And we're free to go.

The Arts Council Meets in Eureka

We held a meeting in Eureka
  far in the corner of the state.
  some flew, but I drove it straight—
  east beside Clear Lake
  through level valleys first,
  then chaparral,
  until we reach the cooler coastal air
  and camped the first night under
  tanbark oak.

Next day saw the tallest tree of all:
clapped our hands and asked for longer life.

Eureka by the bay:
  a nuclear power plant; heaps of chips.
  the sawmills owned by men from far away,
  the heaped up kerf
  of mountainsides of logs.
  stand at the edge of sea air fog,

No one who lives here
  has the power
  to run this town.

Ordering Chile Verde in Gallup

Wet lips sidewise,
lightly chewing gum,
half parted, combed out bangs
earrings almost to the shoulder
calm wide eyes,
large soft
wide-moving body swinging
out-pointed breasts
in her white waitress dress,
she tosses head and
calls back to the kitchen,

"Green, with"

Getting There

Padma Sambhava, the furry tail
Lin-chi, tooth and claws
Buddha-nature, smoke blown through passes
Ezra Pound, the purple-white Jimson Weed
            trumpet flower.

Lion roar splitting dumb ears.

The turned up oak-leaf duff scoop
Left hollow, empty, damp, where a doe
            found out and ate a mushroom.
Snowflakes settle in on coiling millipede
At edge of rotten pine.

The summit of the world.
We were always climbing,
Sometimes resting,
Stopping to talk or to take a drink—

The summit always there.
How many steps, how many bows,

Deep sighs, sturdy frowns,
Brothers and sisters all the way:
              no matter who goes or who stays.

Sustained Yield
For the treeplanters

Spain, Italy, Albania, Turkey, Greece,
once had hills of
oak and pine

This summer-dry winter-wet
              California
manzanita, valley oak, redwood,
              sugar pine, our folk
sun, air, water,
              our toil,

Topsoil, leafmold, sifted dirt,
hole-in-the-ground

Hold the whip of a tree
steady and roots right
somebody tamp the
              earth, as it's slipped in,
down.

Keep trees growing in this
              Shasta nation alta California
              Turtle island
ground.

"Low winter sun . . ."

Low winter sun. Kai sits on the *engawa*
reading, next to him Ediza—and steady
drips off the eaves, of melting snow.

He looks, she looks,
          through a veil of waterdrops
off the edge of the eaves—snow melts
          in the warm brief winter sun slant—
                    he's reading; at me

lunch pail in hand down the path.
          Him ten,
                    cat six,
                              me forty-eight.

The Weave

Walking the Yuba canyon
          through buckbrush, berberis,
          water-curling wilderness

          all the lines sending
          realms overlapping

Human projects break their weave.
          they re-group
          knitting and probing,
          don't miss a beat.

Hear, walking the wilderness
          steady rivers hissing over boulders
          Nuthatch, Peewee,
                    peeeeeeeeeee

Enforcement

Low planes—
          the government has eyes
                    in the sky.

Fast cars—
        the county police
                are on the dirt roads.

When the people were poor
        they were left alone

Now, with more money,
        the police and the thieves
                both come for the crop.

Yuba Country Autumn

Today is the first day of autumn
        long shadows—cool wind—

A squirrel scolds and chatters
        from up in a pine at the cat.
        chickens out of the coop
        scratching dry leaves,

A government plane breaks the quiet.
        flies over the treetops
        searching again,

So many arrested
        for growing some plants.
        A hard winter coming
        for the back-country families;

        the squirrel scolds and chatters
A big green acorn,
        whack! on the woodshed roof.

The Spirits Wait and Sing
Beneath the Land
"Lassen's one big sweat lodge"

Under the hills the *Kukini* gamble
          hand-games, marked bones
          whose bones?
          waiting

Land tilting, streams cutting,
The People, to change,
          Kukini gamble,
          who'll win?
Will the People
          come back again?

A mountain like a sweat lodge
Smoke Hole smoking
Red rock running
Rivers flapping off in steam.

Bear

Kai was alone by the pond in the dusk. He heard
          a grunt and felt, he said, his hair tingle.
          He jumped on a bike and high-tailed it down
          the trail, to some friends.

Scott stood alone in the dark by the window. Clicked
          on his flashlight and there out the window, six
          inches away, were the eyes of the bear.

Stefanie found her summer kitchen all torn up.

I went down the hill to the beehives next morning—
          the supers were off and destroyed, chewed comb
          all around, the whole thing tipped over, no
          honey, no larvae, no bees,

But somewhere, a bear.

Arktos

(Pythagoras: She-bears are the hands of Rhea)

Sighing, bursting: steam—sulfur—lava—
Rolling and bubbling up, falls out,
Back in on itself
        curling and licking
            getting hard.

Lichens, oak groves, float in up like cloud shadows
Soft, soft,
Loving plant hands.

Tendrils slip through til they meet
        it pulls taut
Green and quick—sap call swells the hills

            changing cloud mountain
            changing cloud gate

Rainbow glimmering with swallows, looping cranes.

        icefields and snowfields ring
        as she comes
        gliding down the rainbow bridge

        Joy of the Mountains
        "The Great She Bear"

Fear Not

    Will Dallas grow, or wither?
        said the paper.
    "Let the bastards freeze in the dark."

            dead or alive?
            knocking at the stone door.
    "Goat ropers need love too."

embracing more than "being"
　　the stone door knocks back.

Two women masturbate a corpse,
　　　　　　　　　in clay,
One holds his chin—

The Fox-girls switch from
　　human to fox-form
　　right during the party!
　　　　one man
who was doing cunnilingus on his friend,
　　now finds a mouth
　　of fur.
The saké bottles clatter down.
　　and daylight; all's well,
　　just a little sore—

Who's there?
No one who

I See Old Friend Dan Ellsberg
on TV in a Mountain
Village of Japan

His familiar youthful face
　　as I stand with my back
　　to the open-door dark
　　looking into the TV light,

In the Yura valley, Honshu,
　　ricefields and cedars,
　　an owl calls
　　in from the night.

Dan's message is good,
　　stop arming, put the missiles away,
　　Japan shouldn't join in.

the owls hoot again,
The whole nation of owls
In all the dark trees
calls in and agrees.

Waikiki
For Chris Pearce

A steep reef of concrete, steel, and glass
Owned by one man forty percent
Whose ex-lover watches the scene for him
While tending a classy bar,
And white people get a touch of symbolic brown
          at the shore,
Brown people get their symbolic touch of white,

Twenty-five thousand rooms, on a swamp.
In the heart of it all a Banyan:
Arching and spreading,
          surrounded by buildings,
Is the god of the place. Is a ghost of the past,
The life of the present,
          the hope of the future.
(A fortune-teller booth
          tucked away in a nook in the roots.)

"She dreamed . . ."

She dreamed she was a cougar,
          a panther,
          A great cat bounding,
          and she is.
          Young, slim, nullipara,
          a wild cat like that
          in the dark, in the night.
Feeling the whap of the forepaw,

Making the turn,
        springing aside—right—left—
        bounding and curving.
Long loins stretched out behind.
Graceful tail arching and following
As she told it—
        as we walked on a dark
        mountain road.

Her eyes laughed as she danced how she
        leaped in the dream
        as she showed me,

Later, and back under a shelter
We curled up in a corner
I kissed her small nipples
        and bit her a little, and we
        growled and purred.

We Make Our Vows
Together with All Beings

Eating a sandwich
At work in the woods,

As a doe nibbles buckbrush in snow
Watching each other,
        chewing together.

A Bomber from Beale
over the clouds,
Fills the sky with a roar.

She lifts head, listens,
Waits til the sound has gone by.

So do I.

At White River Roadhouse in the Yukon
For Gary Holthaus

At White River Roadhouse   in the Yukon
A bell rings   in the late night:
A lone car   on the Alaska highway
Hoping to buy gas   at the shut roadhouse.

For a traveller sleeping   in a little room
The bell ring   is a temple in Japan,
In dream I put on   robes and sandals
Chant sūtras   in the chilly Buddha-hall.

Ten thousand miles   of White Spruce taiga.
The roadhouse master   wakes to the night bell
Enters the dark   of ice and stars,
To sell the car some gas.

The Persimmons

In a cove reaching back between ridges
the persimmon groves:
leaves rust-red in October
ochre and bronze
scattering down from the
hard slender limbs of this
slow-growing hardwood
that takes so much nitrogen
and seven years to bear,
and plenty of water all summer
to be bearing so much and so well
as these groves are this autumn.
Gathered in yard-wide baskets
of loose open weave
with mounds of persimmons just picked
still piled on the ground.
On tricycle trucks
pedaled so easy and slow down the lanes,

"Deep tawnie cullour" of sunset
each orb some light left from summer
glowing on brown fall ground,
the persimmons are flowing
on streams of more bike-trucks
til they riffle and back up
alongside a car road
and are spread on the gravel by sellers.
The kind with a crease round the middle,
Tamopan, sweet when soft,
ripening down from the top to the base.
Persimmons and farmers
a long busy line on the roadside,
in season, a bargain, a harvest
of years, the peace of
this autumn again, familiar,
when found by surprise at
the tombs of the dead Ming emperors.
Acres of persimmon orchards
surrounding the tumuli
of kings who saw to it they kept on consuming
even when empty and gone.
The persimmons outlive them,
but up on the hills
where the Great Wall wanders
the oaks had been cut for lumber or charcoal
by Genghis Khan's time.
People and persimmon orchards prevail.
I walked the Great Wall today,
and went deep in the dark of a tomb.
And then found a persimmon
ripe to the bottom
one of a group on a rough plaited tray
that might have been drawn by Mu Ch'i,
tapping its infant-soft skin
to be sure that it's ready,
the old man laughing,
he sees that I like my persimmons.
I trade him some coin
for this wealth of fall fruit

lined up on the roadside to sell to the tourists
who have come to see tombs,
and are offered as well
the people and trees that prevail.

Beijing, Peoples Republic

— Tiny Energies —
VII
1970–1984

For such situations of a few combinations found in messages, the energy content as a fuel is far too negligible to measure or consider compared to the great flows of energy in the food chain. Yet the quality of this energy (tiny energies in the right form) is so high that in the right control circuit it may obtain huge amplifications and control vast flows of power.

H. T. Odum, *Environment Power and Society*

Dragonfly

Dragonfly
Dead on the snow
How did you come so high
Did you leave your seed child
In a mountain pool
Before you died

Evolution Basin IX 69

Through

The white spot of a Flicker
  receding through cedar

Fluttering red surveyors tapes
  through trees, the dark woods

Spring

bees humming

tires spinning

spring mud

For Berkeley

City of buds and flowers

Where are your fruits?

Where are your roots.

The Songs at Custer's Battlefield

Crickets and meadowlarks today;

that day—

"Some lovers wake one day"

Some lovers wake one day
To a stone wall in the way
—I should be free to choose—
Mutually accuse.
The rest is years to tell:
Domestic hell.

"What history fails to mention is"

What history fails to mention is

Most everybody lived their lives
With friends and children, played it cool,
Left truth & beauty to the guys
Who tricked for bigshots, and were fools.

Channelled Scablands

Asleep on an eight foot strip of grass
In Eastern Washington
A thousand square miles
Of plowed wheatfield.

The Taste

I don't know where it went
Or recall how it worked
What one did
What the steps were
Was it hands?
Or the words and the tune?
All that's left
Is a flavor
That stays

Home on the Range

Bison rumble-belly
Bison shag coat
Bison sniffing bison body
Bison skull looking at the sweat lodge.
Bison liver warm. Bison flea
Bison paunch stew.
Bison baby falls down.
Bison skin home. Bison bedding,
"Home on the Range."

The Forest Fire at Ananda

A skunk walks out of a thicket
        of burning blackberries

And down the hill come hundreds of
        yellow-clad firefighters

After fire, green
sprouts

many children

of the same old roots

The Route

We didn't go so much to the south
As to the west.
Following the hills
Beating the bad
Greeting the good.

The Other Side of Each Coin

The head of a man of the ruling elite
And a very large building.
One on each side of the coin

Serves

A human arm
bone is the best
bone for a
bone chisel.
A corn cob
serves as a cork.*

W

in every house there is a wife
in every wife there is a womb
in every womb there is a waif
in every waif there is a wail
in every wail there is a will

* *(As stated by: Captain Cook, and an elder lady of Zuni.)*

The Net

A man in a canoe
Catching fish by dancing—

    "hey, fish by casting with a net!"

Women in the evening circle
casting, round a fire

A man in a canoe
Dances with a net.

Tibetan Army Surplus Store

—The Tibetan Army knife,
With a special patented
Mind-opener,

Used Dorjes,
With the wrong number of prongs.

"Lots of play"

Lots of play

in the way things work,
in the way things are.

History is made of mistakes.

yet—on the surface—
the world looks OK

lots of play.

The Orchard

Writhing, wreathing,
The twang of a fence drawn up tight.

Pound, pound, the staples go in
Gates on hinges—

Sakura to bloom, persimmon leafing out.

Know

The trees know
stars to be sources

Like the sun,
of their life;

But many   and tiny
sprinkled through the dark

When,
where has the sun gone—

Gatha for All Threatened Beings

Ah Power that swirls us together
Grant us bliss
Grant us the great release
And to all beings
Vanishing, wounded,
In trouble on earth,
We pass on this love
May their numbers increase

"There are those who love to get dirty"

There are those who love to get dirty
    and fix things.
They drink coffee at dawn,
    beer after work,

And those who stay clean,
    just appreciate things,
At breakfast they have milk
    and juice at night.

There are those who do both,
    they drink tea.

Lizards, Wind, Sunshine, Apples

a plane circling in the distance

a football game on the radio in the barn

an axe chopping in the woods

a chicken pecking catfood in the kitchen.

How Zen Masters Are Like Mature Herring

So few become full grown
And how necessary all the others;
    gifts to the food chain,
    feeding another universe.

These big ones feed sharks.

— Satires, Inventions, & Diversions —
VIII
1951–1980

Villanelle of the Wandering Lapps

We seek the hidden lair
Where the strange beast goes—
The honey-footed bear.

With a cruel gold snare
We track him in the snow—
We seek the hidden lair.

The bleak winds blare
Where the bald moon glows
The honey-footed bear,

Was born, soft and fair,
With a wet pink nose.
We seek the hidden lair.

But he ate the bright glare,
So fierce did he grow
The honey-footed bear,

Of the sun in the air.
And the grassland froze.
We seek the hidden lair
Of the honey-footed bear.

The Professor as Transformer

That ugly infant who stole sunshine
from the Old Man's lodge
dances in impotent rage: children,
feed him! lest he loose light,
        blinding us with imponderables.
who could have guessed his love
for putrid fish?

That Greasy Boy with knowledge,
naked, and dull as mush,

a REAL SEDUCER
The outraged girl protests—
"But Mother, he———"
"Hush child, he cured you didn't he?"
        (we wash our hair in urine in this town)

"I am enormous,
Wonders cower in my beak
Come, guess what I will say!"
Feed him. he ate the belly of his slave.

caw
caw
the bleak didactic cry

                                        Bloomington

The Elusiad
Or Culture Still Uncaught
IN HEROICKS

Fair *Clio,* of the muses most severe,
Calliope, Erato, my song hear:
Of *Culture,* and her various complex ways
That tangle *Man* in folly all his days.

Each soul from dawn to dark each act behaves
In *Culture*'s net, unseen; yet he who braves
Some deed beyond her shaping soon will know
Sad guilt, remorse, and social outcast's woe.

Stout *Lowie* "rags and patches" thus described
Of *Culture*'s various workings, *Benedict* bribed
By false *Gestalt* and ugly *Structure*'s name
Proclaimed a *Pattern* in her all the same;
But brave *Sapir* a manly tear once shed;
Saw *Culture* as man's most Procrustean bed.

Hence *Students*, bending all their thoughts to map
Bleak *Culture*'s Protean name will find mayhap
Their subject swift transform from hideous hag
To shining youth, a fire, a leathern bag
And leave them sunk in ign'rance as before—
Perplex'd, bewilder'd, seldom knowing more.
But lo! The hunters have a happy thought,
To trap dim *Culture*'s form, say what she's not!
Restrictions six are cunningly designed—
A noose to drop on *Culture* from behind.
Behaviour then becomes the Goddess' name
And her confusing shapes are called the same.

But in the bosky wood a figure lurks—
'Tis *Language* still untrapp'd, who does her works
In *Culture*'s guise, applies a mantic frame
To lines & figures, making charms to tame
Rude uncouth sounds to *Meaning* cruel and clear,
So man a moral in all chatt'ring hears.
This mystick force of *Language* sure must prove
It false to put her in *Behaviour*'s groove—
Yet *Language* often goes in *Culture*'s dress;
The two are but one Goddess, this distress
Allows our captur'd *Culture* to escape
And join the lurking figure; in one shape
A radiant Maiden stands, and students gape.

"Bring more restrictions!" is the hearty cry
And armed with spears of "never, no, & why"
They scatter through the land, proclaim in glee
At ev'ry new glimps'd figure, "That's not she!"
Poor pious madmen, seeking all their days,
When ev'n the search is under *Culture*'s gaze.

For she, cruel Goddess! Speaks to our surprise—
"Ev'n seeking me, you see through Mine own eyes."

The Third Watch

He is the pard that pads on two bare feet,
Plucks the sacred seventh of his bow
Twangs air to ashes in a heat.

Then rising tide-wash lips the clean cool rocks:
Who but the Lover floats off-shore in surf?
Her cockle-shell is but a pudding crust,

Her known erotic zone a source of mirth.
Or change the trope: with water, night, and dream
Select the mythical fable of your "soul."

No one will snicker if you toss and scream
At monsters of the amniotic brain—
But if a barefoot stranger in their midst,

Sacred lions, swans, and limping bull
Choose him to charge: who wanders through their den
And turns the rose, or idol, or slow chant

Into a mock of that mock-awful night.
Furious Aphrodite casts her glance
Beyond Eorthan Modor's steamy lair

Where he, the Buddha, walks. Rattle of hooves and horns,
Nets and knives, falls on an empty air
—Something is awake once walked in there.

Sestina of the End of the Kalpa

You joyous Gods, who gave mankind his Culture,
And you, brave nymphs, who taught him love of Nature,
You sturdy Mountains, Prairies, in your Pattern
Breeding from Uncouth Ape the various Races,
Give ear to what I sing, of place and Structure,
Troubling the simple air with blushing Language.

Because, astride his horse, a Siouan's Language
As well as painted steed, is part of Culture,
We soon find Substance melted into Structure.
And pitying poor Mankind's silly Nature—
An equal meagre blandness in all Races:
We look beyond mere Man to find a Pattern.

Each blotch and wiggle has distinctive Pattern,
And order lurks within each mumbling Language.
Hermes the sneaky watcher of the Races,
If caught might tell the sins of every Culture.
Each bungles life according to its Nature,
Which is to say, each has a faulty Structure.

But Man is taught necessity of Structure,
And Birth and Death whirl in a single Pattern;
The bleating Dewey says, "But this is Nature"—
And Law and Order, if you know the Language.
To have a God (The Possum sez) is Culture,
And God is Order, for most Human Races.

Apollo: let us wander through the Races,
Sifting each hiss and glottal for its Structure,
And come to make conclusion of all Culture.
Poor Kwakiutl! Tangled in their Pattern;
Stern Indo-Aryans; slaves to Language.
And somehow through this, Science fingers Nature.

A use is found for every law of Nature,
The future planned (humanely) for all Races,
Wisdom wallows in decay of Language.
Fierce *Siva*! These Greeks defend their "Structure,"
The God of Christians, in the same old Pattern
Perpetuates the form and force of Culture,

Destroyer: with fire inform the Races
That Chaos is the Pattern under Structure.
Language and Culture burn! and death to Nature.

Berkeley

Epistemological Fancies

My friend Hoodlatch used to ask,
"Can these five senses know the real?"
Perceive the Ground, or God, or What
Is felt when these five senses feel?"

And two would do, I used to say,
To crack through what illusions might
Out-side our senses to wrong scent
Or baffle heard or heart insight—

"And just what two?" He'd often jeer:
Profundity and clear precept
Obstructed by (we thought) the sense
That wades in superficial depth—

Why any two, or all, or none,
Will do to put the Noumenon
In its right place: which is in front
Of wispy, frail phenomenon.

For all that's real, or ought to be,
Is what one can, or cannot, see.

A War of Dwarfs and Birds Beyond the Sea

Feeble breakers, the loose kelp slop
Slopping in swarm of squid, a warm beach.
Care, carry it in your head without words,
We have ways, waves of talking about the sea.

Apprehensive, in to the waist,
The shy ones urinate in the sea.

What we file, defile, is tern-pipe
Seasnipe, drowned mews, bird fright:
A grammar of scattered cries.
One tells a file, a system, to the sea.

This utterance is oblivious of the sea
Wet, of course, but water? in the sea?

It takes a net, a swatch of labels wagging
With the jawbone, the *Sea* is made tongue
Tickling a rush of air behind the teeth,
A high front moan; and now you understand.

Exclamations Gone to the Twin Breasts of Maya

Terence! Ovid! Nothing is satisfactory.
Bleeding the fluvial ground to raise grape, pay tax—
Vag rap sufferings, the hard bust rock,
And all who knew you gone on the last witch-
Angel Diesel-hike, the metaphysical
Home gate she made wild.

Ballad of Rolling Heads

Here's the last drunk song I'll sing
Of all the balls we had this Spring.
Swigging Akadama Port,
Holding my Kyoto fort
Against the waves of squares and scholars
That truss me up in ties and collars;
Shavehead Roshis put to bed
Like babies simple in the head;
An arty nation plunged in squalor
That never learned to jump or holler—
In my wine I'll gently float
Back to where I caught the boat
Leaving T and addled brains
In that last campfire in the rain—
Clear back to ancient lost November
High and swinging nights remember:
Jack Kerouac in smoky flame

Blazing bright at Buddha's name,
Sputtering in his jug of port
Cursing Cowley's last report,
Burning hot & bright again
With poems and notes beneath his pen
While Whalen talked precise and clear
Drunk and barefoot on the floor;
Naked Allen, naked Peter,
Neuri in her shoes and sweater,
Montgomery peering through the screen,
Jinnie lovely as a Queen,
The toothless grin of Du Peru
Who saw the whole of wisdom through
And ended wholly baffled simple
Concerned with shoes and socks & pimples,
La Vigne who painted in his head
The orgies held on floors and beds
And who of all of us shall be
The one who saves poor Natalie—
Who finished off this round of pain,
I tracked her through the Bardo plane
Peyote-sick but seeing clear
The hells & heavens we are near.
Neal with pockets full of T
Dirty pictures on his knee
Spread out to view by candlelight—
McCorkle's shack, an April night,
Locke getting off the kids to bed
With sips of Casanova red—
The wine, the wine, the wine is gone!
And Kerouac has left for town
To buy another gallon jug
We'll all be rolled out on the rug—

The wilderness is in the heart
Where babies books & orgies start
With jugs & blankets, dressed in rags
The whole wild tribe is on the vag
From book to book & town to town
& cops or books can't put us down

Until beyond all cures & beds
On floors, on floors we bang our heads
& sing with angels drunk as we
Hung up in the Christmas tree
Of Golden Boughs and Buddha-eyes,
Fertility to make us wise!
This thunderbolt is hard as jewel,
A swinging dink both hot and cool
The opposites are all congealed
& squares and fools will be revealed
By Whalen's calm and classic glance,
Allen Ginsberg's naked dance.

After T'ao Ch'ien

"Swiftly the years, beyond recall:
Solemn the stillness of this Spring morning."
I'll put on my boots & old levis
& hike across Tamalpais.
Along the coast the fog hovers,
Hovers an hour, then scatters.
There comes a wind, blowing from the sea,
That brushes the hills of spring grass.

marin-an

After the Chinese

She looked like a fairy
All dressed in shaky cheesecloth,
And ran off with a fairy poet
Back to town. Her hair
Was black as a mud-snail's bowels
Her skin was like chilled grease.
My sleeves are sopping wet
From crying. My white hair scraggly

& my eyes all red. Pour another
Cup of wine for this poor
Bureaucrat stuck out in the sticks.

Versions of Anacreon

On his Own Loves
If you can tell the leaves on all the trees
And know all the sands of the sea,
You alone can calculate my loves.
First, for Athens put down twenty and add fifteen;
Great lists of loves for Corinth, which is Achaia,
Where women are fair.
Then put my Lesbian, and the far Ionians,
And Caria and Rhodes—two thousand loves.
                    You say What? Add more:
I haven't mentioned my Syrian, my passions at Canopus,
Or those of Crete—where everything happens—
Love holds orgies in the streets.
                    What?
You want the count of those beyond Gadira,
And the Bactrians, and the Indians,
Loves of my soul?

To a Girl
Don't run off because my hair is gray
Don't put me down because your
                    first fresh flower-young beauty's with you.
Look: even in garlands
It is good to see the white lilies
Twined with roses.

On Himself
                    WHEN I drink wine,
My warmed heart hears the Muses.
                    When I drink wine,
Cares fall away, and busy thinking
And contriving becomes wind beating the sea.

When I drink wine,
Sorrow-melting Bacchus whirls me
In flowery breezes, charmed and delirious.
When I drink wine,
I weave rings of flowers and
Put them on my head, and sing the calm-of-life.
When I drink wine,
My body sprinkled in perfume,
Clasping a girl in my arms, I sing of Venus.
When I drink wine,
Out of embossed cups, soothing my soul,
I delight in a choir of youths.
When I drink wine,
This is the only gain. I've taken it,
And I'll carry it away.
For after all, we have to die.

On Love
It hurts to love
It hurts not to love
It hurts worst to fail at love.
Birth is nothing to love:
Wisdom, genius, get tramped down.
They look to money alone.
Money breaks up brothers,
Money breaks up parents,
Causes wars and murders.
What is worse,
Money kills us lovers.

A Little Ode on Lovers
Horses have the print of fire
                    on their haunches:
Anyone can tell a Parthian by his turban.
And I can tell lovers on sight:
They have a certain delicate
Impress of the soul
Within.*

* *(From John Taylor's literal interlinear.)*

Tree Song

Between dirt dark and giddy sky
Straight, twisted, mountains, mudflats,
Where we bloom,
        limbs that wait and wave,
Noble Silence for a lifetime's talk.

        across the hill the pollen blows
        a cloud of orgies in the boughy air—

Are we our black wet roots
Or do we live by light?
One hand grips, the other makes a sign.
Scanning slope or gully where it soon must lie.

        I lay
This punky mossy gnarled and
Useless scab-barked worm-ate
Seedless wore out loggy body
—with a great crash—
                        down.
My secret heartwood no bud ever knew.

                                    Kyoto

Joe Hill Fragment

"The copper bosses shot you Joe—"

        sheets of color shift like northern lights.
        the tiger grumbles in the bamboo grove
        streetcars squeak to carbarns in the night.
        sending signals, scaring fish,
        tankers wallow in the sea
        the Hungry Ghosts and Demons out on strike—

"I never died" said he.

Prepotent

Justin Morgan
    was powerful and large.
J.M. didn't look a
    bit like his Maw or Paw.
He was born Springfield Mass
    about 1790,
He once won a gallon of rum
    on a bet.
He made love
    all over New England.
All his children grew up
    strong and strange as he.
We still see them sometimes,
    those Morgans.

Hieiharu-maru

A Work for Burke *

"Moveable type" indeed has spread the Word
& printers' devils mightier than swords.
In China first, the Diamond Sutra pressed
With type of clay, all Sentient Beings Blessed.

Gunpowder & compass, to Europe gift
Along with printing, brought about a shift
From Feudal to Bourgeois. From Asia
On Mongol ponies' backs. The phase you

See us enter now, post-industry
Replete with glamorous technology
Will nonetheless need PRINTING all the more
For keeping track, and evening the score.

* *(written at the eminent Printer's request)*

Printing, with beauty, craft and skill,
In any age brings deep aesthetic thrills
To watchful minds. We must not shirk
Support of Cranium Press, & Clifford Burke.

smog

smog

smog   smog

smog   smog   smog

smog   smog   smog   smog   smog

smog   smog   smog   smog   smog

smog smog smog smog smog smog smog smog

smog smog smog smog smog smog smog smog smog

smog smog smog smog smog smog smog smog smog
smog smog smog smog smog smog smog smog smog

Sherry in July

Julius Caesar, cut from his mother's womb
        Caedare to cut off (caesura)
        Sanskrit *khidāti*—tear—
(Jack Wilson, Wovoka, Paiute "Cutter")
Caesar to Kaiser to Tsesari, Tsar.
        and a town in Spain, Caesaris
        —Xeres—Jerez—
        have some sherry.

Coyote Man, Mr. President, & the Gunfighters

Mr. President was fascinated by gunfighters. Expert gun-
fighters were invited to his White House, three thousand of
them, like guests in the house. Day and night they practiced
fast-draw and shootouts in his presence until the dead and
wounded men numbered more than a hundred a year.

The Senator from the Great Basin was troubled by this, and
summoning his aides, said, "I'll give a basket of turquoise
and a truckload of compost to any man who can reason
with Mr. President and make him give up these gunfights!"
"Coyote Man is the one who can do it!" said his aides.

Pretty soon Coyote Man turned up, but he refused the tur-
quoise. He said, "If Mr. President should get angry, I might
go to jail. What could I do with turquoise then? And if I do
persuade him, then you'd owe a million wild ducks."

"The trouble is," said the Senator, "Mr. President refuses
to see anybody but gunfighters." "Fine!" said Coyote Man,
"I'm good with revolvers."

"But the kind of gunfighters Mr. President receives," said
the Senator, "all wear starched uniforms and have shaved
cheeks; they glare fiercely, and speak in staccato sentences
about ballistics and tactical deployment. Men like that he
loves! If you go in to see him in your overalls you'd be
wrong from the start."

"I'll get me the uniform of a gunfighter," said Coyote Man.
After a couple of days he had his gunfighter's costume ready
and arranged an appointment with Mr. President. Mr. Pres-
ident's guards had their big Magnum revolvers on Coyote
Man as he entered calm and soft. "Now that you got the
Senator to get you an appointment what do you think you
can tell me?" said Mr. President.

"I heard Mr. President likes guns, and so I have come to
demonstrate my skill to you."

"What's special about your skill?" said Mr. President. "My shooting strikes and kills at every shot, and doesn't miss at nine hundred miles," said Coyote Man.

Mr. President was pleased and said, "I'd like to see you shoot it out." Coyote Man said, "He who draws the revolver plucks out emptiness, teases on with hopes of dominance. Leaves last, arrives first. Allow me to show my capacity."

Mr. President spent a week checking out his gunfighters. Three dozen were wounded or died in the trials. The survivors were instructed to appear on the lawn and Mr. President sent for Coyote Man.

"Today let's see you reach for the revolver with these fine officers. What will you shoot? A long or a short barrel?"

"I'll use any type," said Coyote Man. "It happens I have three revolvers. You tell me which to use—but first I'll explain them."

"Let's hear about your three revolvers," said Mr. President.

"There is the revolver of the cosmos, the revolver of mankind, and the revolver of state."

"What is the revolver of the cosmos?" asked Mr. President. —"The revolver of the cosmos? The Milky Way is its grip; the solar winds, the barrel. Its bullets are stars, it sights by the beams of pulsars. It spits out planets and bathes them, spinning, in heat and light. The ninety-two elements aim it; the secrets of fusion fire it. Wield it, and countless beings leap into life and dance through the void. Conceal it, and whole galaxies rush into nothingness. When this revolver is manifested the whole earth flourishes, the skies clear, the rivers sing, the gardens are full of squash and corn, the high plains rich with Bison. This is the revolver of the cosmos."

Mr. President was at an utter loss. "So what is the revolver of mankind?"

"The revolver of mankind? The twelve races are the grip; the three thousand languages, the barrel. Forged in the Pliocene, finished in the Pleistocene, decorated with civilization, it aims for knowledge and beauty. The cylinder is the rise and fall of nations, the sights are the philosophies and religions and sciences, the bullets are countless men and women who have pierced through ignorance and old habits, and revealed the shining mirror of true nature. It takes its model from life itself, and trusts in the four seasons. Its secret power is the delight of the mind. Once grasped it brings harmony and peace to the planet; like a thunderbolt it destroys exploiters, and dictators crumble like sand. This is the revolver of mankind."

Mr. President said, "What is the revolver of the State?"

"The revolver of the State? It is used by men in starched uniforms with shaved chins who glare fiercely and speak in staccato sentences about ballistics and tactical deployment. On top it blows out brains and splinters neckbones; underneath it spits out livers and lungs. Those who use this revolver are no different from fighting cocks—any morning they may be dead or in jail. They are of no use in the councils of mankind. Now you occupy the office of Mr. President, and yet you show this fondness for gunfighters. I think it is rather unworthy of you."

Mr. President took Coyote Man to the dining room and the waiter brought lunch. But Mr. President just paced around the room. "Hey!" said Coyote Man, "Eat your lunch! The affair of the gunfighters is over and finished!"

After that Mr. President didn't come out of the Oval Room for three months. All his gunfighters secretly took off their uniforms and sneaked away, back to the businesses and offices in various towns around the land from which they had come.*

   special thanks to Burton Watson.

*(After the "Discourse on Swords" in the Third Century BC Chinese Chuang-tzu text.)

from NO NATURE

How Poetry Comes to Me

It comes blundering over the
Boulders at night, it stays
Frightened outside the
Range of my campfire
I go to meet it at the
Edge of the light

On Climbing the Sierra
Matterhorn Again
After Thirty-one
Years

Range after range of mountains
Year after year after year.
I am still in love.

4 X 40086, On the summit

Kušiwoqqóbɨ

Did it come from
The ice age lakes and streams?
Flows of liquid rock
The salt of seas,
Wind on hills for years,
This day's sun and trees?
Or this one nose?
The smell in the bark of
                    Jeffrey Pine.

My nose poked in the bark
Went a million years—
Sweet smell of the pine.

Delicious! Like pineapple!
What did the Piute children think of,
Smelling *Kušiwoqqóbɨ*,
What did they say?

Sun glittering on obsidian,
Wind on a hundred peaks,
Hugging a tree, smelling the bark,
I thought I heard "Kušiwoqqóbɨ"
A soft voice from across,

From the dust, from the breeze.

> *VII 82, Trip with Kai down the east side*
> *near Mammoth*

The Sweat
For John and Jan Straley

Now I must sit naked.

Socks and glasses tucked into my moccasins,
Wearing only earrings and a faded tattoo—

On a cedar bench too hot to touch,
Buttocks take it—legs fold,
Back eases on to the burning wall
Sweating and the in-breath cooled
Through a wet-soaked towel
—old Aleut trick—
And look out the small window
On a snow-capped volcano
And inside toward the stove, the
Women who sweat here
And groan and laugh with the heat,

The women speak of birth at home.
Of their children, their breasts hang
Softer, the nipples darker,
Eyes clear and warm.
Naked. Legs up, we have all raised children,

I could love each one,
Their ease, their opened—sweet—
    older—still youthful—
    womanly being bodies—

And outside, naked, cooling on the deck
Midsummer's far northern soft dusk eve,
Bare skin to the wind;
Older is smarter and more tasty.
Minds tough and funny—many lovers—
At the end of days of talking
Science, writing, values, spirit, politics, poems—

Different shoes and shirts,
In little heaps—sit naked, silent, gaze
On chests and breasts and knees and knobby feet
    in the tide smell, on the bleached deck planks,
Like seals hauled out for sunning,

Crinkles by the eyes,
Limber legs crossed,
Single mothers—past parenting—
Back to college—running a business—
Checking salmon for the Fish & Game,
Writing a play, an article, a novel,
Waitressing and teaching,
In between men friends, teen-age son—
Doing a dissertation on the Humpbacked Whales,
Doing tough-assed poems—

Naked comfort, scant fear,
Strong soul, naught to hide,

This life:
We get old enough and finally really like it!
Meeting and sweating
At a breezy beach.

VI 87, Baranoff Island, Alaska

Building

We started our house midway through the Cultural
    Revolution,
The Vietnam war, Cambodia, in our ears,
    tear gas in Berkeley,
Boys in overalls with frightened eyes, long matted hair, ran
    from the police.
We peeled trees, drilled boulders, dug sumps, took sweat baths
    together.
That house finished we went on
Built a schoolhouse, with a hundred wheelbarrows,
    held seminars on California paleo-indians during lunch.
We brazed the Chou dynasty form of the character "Mu"
    on the blacksmithed brackets of the ceiling of the lodge,
Buried a five-prong vajra between the schoolbuildings
    while praying and offering tobacco.
Those buildings were destroyed by a fire, a pale copy rebuilt
    by insurance.

Ten years later we gathered at the edge of a meadow.
The cultural revolution is over, hair is short,
    the industry calls the shots in the Peoples Forests,
Single mothers go back to college to become lawyers.

Blowing the conch, shaking the staff-rings
    we opened work on a Hall.
Forty people, women carpenters, child labor, pounding nails,
Screw down the corten roofing and shape the beams
    with a planer,

The building is done in three weeks.
We fill it with flowers and friends and open it up.

Now in the year of the Persian Gulf,
Of Lies and Crimes in the Government held up as Virtues,
    this dance with Matter
Goes on: our buildings are solid, to live, to teach, to sit,
To sit, to know for sure the sound of a bell—
This is history. This is outside of history.
Buildings are built in the moment,
    they are constantly wet from the pool
        that renews all things
    naked and gleaming.

The moon moves
Through her twenty-eight nights.
Wet years and dry years pass;
Sharp tools, good design.

Surrounded by Wild Turkeys

Little calls   as they pass
    through dry forbs and grasses
Under blue oak and gray digger pine
In the warm afternoon of the forest-fire haze;

Twenty or more, long-legged birds
    all alike.

So are we, in our soft calling,
    passing on through.

Our young, which trail after,

Look just like us.

Off the Trail
for Carole

We are free to find our own way
Over rocks—through the trees—
Where there are no trails. The ridge and the forest
Present themselves to our eyes and feet
Which decide for themselves
In their old learned wisdom of doing
Where the wild will take us. We have
Been here before. It's more intimate somehow
Than walking the paths that lay out some route
That you stick to,
All paths are possible, many will work,
Being blocked is its own kind of pleasure,
Getting through is a joy, the side-trips
And detours show down logs and flowers,
The deer paths straight up, the squirrel tracks
Across, the outcroppings lead us on over.
Resting on treetrunks,
Stepping out on the bedrock, angling and eyeing
Both making choices—now parting our ways—
And later rejoin; I'm right, you're right,
We come out together. *Mattake,* "Pine Mushroom,"
Heaves at the base of a stump. The dense matted floor
Of Red Fir needles and twigs. This is wild!
We laugh, wild for sure,
Because no place is more than another,
All places total,
And our ankles, knees, shoulders &
Haunches know right where they are.
Recall how the *Dao De
Jing* puts it: the trail's not the way.
No path will get you there, we're off the trail,
You and I, and we chose it! Our trips out of doors
Through the years have been practice
For this ramble together,
Deep in the mountains
Side by side,
Over rocks, through the trees.

Word Basket Woman

Years after surviving
the Warsaw uprising,
she wrote the poems of ordinary people
building barricades while being shot at,
small poems were all
that could hold so much
close to death   life
without making it false.

Robinson Jeffers, his tall cold view
quite true in a way, but why did he say it
as though he alone
stood above our delusions, he also
feared death, insignificance,
and was not quite up to the inhuman beauty
of parsnips or diapers, the deathless
nobility   at the core of all ordinary things

I dwell
in a house on the long west slope
of Sierra Nevada, two hundred mile
swell of granite,
bones of the Ancient Buddha,
miles back from the seacoast
on a line of fiery chakras
in the deep nerve web of the land,

Europe forgotten now, almost a dream—
but our writing
is sidewise and roman, and the language
a compote of old wars and tribes from some
place overseas. Here
at the rim of the world
where the *panaka* calls in the *chá*—the heart
words are Pomo, Miwok, Nisenan,
and the small poem word baskets
stretch to the heft of their burden.

I came this far to tell
of the grave of my great-
grandmother Harriet Callicotte
by itself on a low ridge in Kansas.
The sandstone tumbled,
her name almost eaten away,
where I found it in rain drenched grass
on my knees, closed my eyes
and swooped under the earth
to that loam dark, holding her emptiness
and placed one cool kiss
on the arch of her white
pubic bone.

VI 85, Carneiro Kansas
XII 87, Kitkitdizze

At Tower Peak

Every tan rolling meadow will turn into housing
Freeways are clogged all day
Academies packed with scholars writing papers
City people lean and dark
This land most real
As its western-tending golden slopes
And bird-entangled central valley swamps
Sea-lion, urchin coasts
Southerly salmon-probes
Into the aromatic almost-Mexican hills
Along a range of granite peaks
The names forgotten,
An eastward running river that ends out in desert
The chipping ground-squirrels in the tumbled blocks
The gloss of glacier ghost on slab
Where we wake refreshed from ten hours sleep
After a long day's walking
Packing burdens to the snow
Wake to the same old world of no names,

No things, new as ever, rock and water,
Cool dawn birdcalls, high jet contrails.
A day or two or million, breathing
A few steps back from what goes down
In the current realm.
A kind of ice age, spreading, filling valleys
Shaving soils, paving fields, you can walk it
Live in it, drive through it   then
It melts away
For whatever sprouts
After the age of
Frozen hearts. Flesh-curved rock
And gusts on the summit,
Smoke from forest fires is white,
The haze above the distant valley like a dusk.
It's just one world, this spine of rock and streams
And snow, and the wash of gravels, silts
Sands, bunchgrasses, saltbrush, bee-fields,
Twenty million human people, downstream, here below.

Right in the Trail

Here it is, near the house,
A **big** pile, fat scats,
Studded with those deep red
Smooth-skinned manzanita berries,
Such a pile! Such droppings,
Awesome. And I saw how
The young girl in the story,
Had good cause to comment
On the bearscats she found while
Picking blueberries with her friends.
She laughed at them
Or maybe **with** them, jumped over them
(Bad luck!), and is reported
To have said "wide anus!"
To amuse or annoy the Big Brown Ones
Who are listening, of course.

They say the ladies
Have always gone berrying
And they all join together
To go out for the herring spawn,
Or to clean green salmon.
And that big set of lessons
On what bears really want,
Was brought back by the girl
Who made those comments:
She was taken on a year-long excursion
Deep in the mountains,
Through the tangled deadfalls,
Down into the den.
She had some pretty children by a
Young and handsome Bear.

Now I'm on the dirt
Looking at these scats
And I want to cry not knowing why
At the honor and the humor
Of coming on this sign
That is not found in books
Or transmitted in letters,
And is for women just as much as men,
A shining message for all species,
A glimpse at the Trace
Of the Great One's passing,
With a peek into her whole wild system—
And what was going on last week,
(Mostly still manzanita)—

Dear Bear: do stay around. Be good.
And though I know
It won't help to say this,

Chew your food.

Travelling to the Capital

I put on my travelling clothes
        and went up to the Capital
        to see the blooming cherries—

Elderly sakura blossoming
        east of the huge library
        loosing petals to the winds.

We walked by miles of buildings
        past sheets of clear pool water
        men begging on the street
        where people come to eat

We stand in the grass in the open—
        hear jet plane takeoff rumble
        fill the whole downtown.
        go read poems with friends
        in a theater made for Shakespeare,
        have a party with the crowd—

An elderly black man caterer
        pours drinks at a table,
        I ask him why the channel-locks?
        he says "For the Perrier"

This our little nation,
        —our capital, its blossoms—
        its library for the people
        our nation of bison and grass. Those
        days of woods and glades,

Those days are gone.
        we get,
        This dolphin-drowned,
        This waste-tormented sea.

Spring 89, Washington

Thoughts on Looking at a Samuel Palmer
Etching at the Tate

Moonlight landscape, sheep,
　　　and shepherds watching eerie beauty

The broad sheep backs
　　　resting bunched up under leafy oaks
　　　or hid in black moon shadow,

Lives of cows and sheep—
　　　calf mouth that sucks your finger
　　　the steer that pokes his head through
　　　pipe iron gate
　　　to lick lapel, and lightly
　　　touch and taste
　　　the buttons of your coat,

Cows that trail you as you cross the meadow;
　　　& silent sheep　　slow heads turning
　　　solemn faces
　　　hooves fringed in dewy grass.

They stamp and steam in chilly morn
　　　and gaze at length on clouds and hills

　　　　before they board the truck.

82, Devon & London

Kisiabaton

Beat-up datsun idling in the road
shreds of fog
almost-vertical hillsides drop away
huge stumps fading into mist
soft warm rain

Snaggy, forked and spreading tops, a temperate cloud-forest
  tree

> *Chamaecyparis formosiana*—
>   Taiwan hinoki,
>   hung-kuai   red cypress

That the tribal people call   *kisiabaton*

>   this rare old tree
>   is what we came to see.

IX 90, Ali-shan, Taiwan

For Lew Welch in a Snowfall

Snowfall in March:
I sit in the white glow reading a thesis
About you. Your poems, your life.

The author's my student,
He even quotes me.

Forty years since we joked in a kitchen in Portland
Twenty since you disappeared.

All those years and their moments—
Crackling bacon, slamming car doors,
Poems tried out on friends,
Will be one more archive,
One more shaky text.

But life continues in the kitchen
Where we still laugh and cook,
Watching snow.

III 91, Kitkitdizze

Ripples on the Surface

"Ripples on the surface of the water—
were silver salmon passing under—different
from the ripples caused by breezes"

A scudding plume on the wave—
a humpback whale is
breaking out in air up
gulping herring
          —Nature not a book, but a *performance*, a
high old culture

Ever-fresh events
scraped out, rubbed out, and used, used, again—
the braided channels of the rivers
hidden under fields of grass—

The vast wild
          the house, alone.
The little house in the wild,
          the wild in the house.
Both forgotten.

No nature

Both together, one big empty house.

MOUNTAINS AND RIVERS
WITHOUT END

This book is for

Gen,
Kai,
Mika,
Kyung-jin

The notion of Emptiness engenders Compassion.

Milarepa

An ancient Buddha said "A painted rice cake does not satisfy hunger." Dōgen comments:

"There are few who have even seen this 'painting of a rice cake' and none of them has thoroughly understood it.

"The paints for painting rice cakes are the same as those used for painting mountains and waters.

"If you say the painting is not real, then the material phenomenal world is not real, the Dharma is not real.

"Unsurpassed enlightenment is a painting. The entire phenomenal universe and the empty sky are nothing but a painting.

"Since this is so, there is no remedy for satisfying hunger other than a painted rice cake. Without painted hunger you never become a true person."

Dōgen, "Painting of a Rice Cake"

— *I* —

Endless Streams and Mountains
Ch'i Shan Wu Chin

Clearing the mind and sliding in
      to that created space,
a web of waters streaming over rocks,
air misty but not raining,
      seeing this land from a boat on a lake
      or a broad slow river,
      coasting by.

The path comes down along a lowland stream
slips behind boulders and leafy hardwoods,
reappears in a pine grove,

no farms around, just tidy cottages and shelters,
gateways, rest stops, roofed but unwalled work space,
      —a warm damp climate;

a trail of climbing stairsteps forks upstream.
Big ranges lurk behind these rugged little outcrops—
these spits of low ground rocky uplifts
      layered pinnacles aslant,
flurries of brushy cliffs receding,
far back and high above, vague peaks.
A man hunched over, sitting on a log
      another stands above him, lifts a staff,
a third, with a roll of mats or a lute, looks on;
a bit offshore two people in a boat.

The trail goes far inland,
      somewhere back around a bay,
lost in distant foothill slopes
          & back again
at a village on the beach, and someone's fishing.

Rider and walker cross a bridge
above a frothy braided torrent
that descends from a flurry of roofs like flowers
      temples tucked between cliffs,
        a side trail goes there;

a jumble of cliffs above,
ridge tops edged with bushes,
valley fog below a hazy canyon.

A man with a shoulder load leans into the grade
the trail goes up along cascading streambed
no bridge in sight—
comes back through chinquapin or
liquidambars;
another horse and a hiker.
Trail's end at the edge of an inlet
below a heavy set of dark rock hills.
Two moored boats with basket roofing,
        a boatman in the bow looks
            lost in thought.

            Hills beyond rivers, willows in a swamp,
            a gentle valley reaching far inland.

            The watching boat has floated off the page.

                    ——

At the end of the painting the scroll continues on with seals
and poems. It tells a further tale:

"—Wang Wen-wei saw this at the mayor's house in Ho-tung
  town, year 1205. Wrote at the end of it,

                'The Fashioner of Things
                        has no original intentions
                Mountains and rivers
                        are spirit, condensed.'

                '. . . Who has come up with
                        these miraculous forests and springs?
                Pale ink
                        on fine white silk.'

Later that month someone named Li Hui added,

> '. . . Most people can get along with the noise
>   of dogs and chickens;
> Everybody cheerful in these peaceful times.
> But I—why are my tastes so odd?
> I love the company of streams and
>   boulders.'

T'ien Hsieh of Wei-lo, no date, next wrote,

> '. . . The water holds up the mountains,
>   The mountains go down in the water . . . '

In 1332 Chih-shun adds,

> '. . . This is truly a painting worth careful
>   keeping.
> And it has poem-colophons from the Sung and
> the Chin dynasties. That it survived dangers of
> fire and war makes it even rarer.'

In the mid-seventeenth century one Wang To had a look at it:

> 'My brother's relative by marriage, Wên-sun, is
> learned and has good taste. He writes good prose
> and poetry. My brother brought over this painting of
> his to show me . . .' "

The great Ch'ing dynasty collector Liang Ch'ing-piao owned it, but didn't write on it or cover it with seals. From him it went into the Imperial collection down to the early twentieth century. Chang Ta-ch'ien sold it in 1949. Now it's at the Cleveland Art Museum, which sits on a rise that looks out toward the waters of Lake Erie.

—

> Step back and gaze again at the land:
>   it rises and subsides—

ravines and cliffs like waves of blowing leaves—
    stamp the foot, walk with it, clap! turn,
the creeks come in, ah!
strained through boulders,
mountains walking on the water,
water ripples every hill.

—I walk out of the museum—low gray clouds over the lake—
chill March breeze.

———

Old ghost ranges, sunken rivers, come again
    stand by the wall and tell their tale,
walk the path, sit the rains,
grind the ink, wet the brush, unroll the
    broad white space:

lead out and tip
the moist black line.

Walking on walking,
          under foot   earth turns.

Streams and mountains never stay the same. *

Old Bones

Out there walking round, looking out for food,
a rootstock, a birdcall, a seed that you can crack
plucking, digging, snaring, snagging,
    barely getting by,

* Note: A hand scroll by this name showed up in Shansi province, central China, in the thirteenth century. Even then the painter was unknown, "a person of the Sung Dynasty." Now it's on Turtle Island. Unroll the scroll to the left, a section at a time, as you let the right side roll back in. Place by place unfurls.

no food out there on dusty slopes of scree—
carry some—look for some,
go for a hungry dream.
Deer bone, Dall sheep,
        bones hunger home.

Out there somewhere
a shrine for the old ones,
the dust of the old bones,
        old songs and tales.

What we ate—who ate what—
        how we all prevailed.

Night Highway 99

*Only the very poor, or eccentric, can surround themselves with
shapes of elegance (soon to be demolished) in which they are forced
by poverty to move with leisurely grace. We remain alert so as not to
get run down, but it turns out you only have to hop a few feet to one
side and the whole huge machinery rolls by, not seeing you at all.*
                                                        Lew Welch

We're on our way

                        man
                out of town
                go hitching down
                that highway 99

Too cold and rainy to go out on the Sound
Sitting in Ferndale drinking coffee
Baxter in black, been to a funeral
Raymond in Bellingham—Helena Hotel—
Can't go to Mexico with that weak heart
Well you boys can go south. I stay here.
Fix up a shack—get a part-time job—
                (he disappeared later
                maybe found in the river)
In Ferndale & Bellingham

Went out on trail crews
Glacier and Marblemount
There we part.

          Tiny men with mustaches
          driving ox teams
          deep in the cedar groves
          wet brush, tin pants, snoose—

Split-shake roof barns
          over berry fields
                    white birch chicken coop

Put up in Dick Meigs cabin
          out behind the house—
Coffeecan, PA tin, rags, dirty cups,
Kindling fell behind the stove, miceshit,
          old magazines,

               winter's coming in the mountains
               shut down the show
               the punks go back to school
               and the rest hit the road—

          strawberries picked, shakeblanks split
          fires all out and the packstrings brought
          down to the valleys:
                    set loose to graze.

Gray wharves and hacksaw gothic homes
Shingle mills and stump farms

                         overgrown.

                    —

Fifty weary Indians   Mt. Vernon
Sleep in the bus station
Strawberry pickers speaking Kwakiutl
          turn at Burlington for Skagit & Ross Dam

under apple trees by the river
banks of junked cars

BC Riders give hitchhikers rides

"The sheriff's posse stood in double rows   Everett
        flogged the naked Wobblies down
        with stalks of Devil's Club
        & run them out of town"

While shingle weavers lost their fingers
        in the tricky feed and take
                of double saws.

Dried, shrimp   Seattle
        smoked, salmon
—before the war old Salish gentleman came
& sold us kids rich hard-smoked Chinook
from his flatbed model T
        Lake City,

        waste of trees & topsoil, beast, herb,
        edible roots, Indian field-farms & white men
        dances   washed, leached, burnt out
        minds blunt, ug! talk twisted

        a night of the long poem
        and the mined guitar
        "Forming the new society
        within the shell of the old"
                mess of tincan camps and littered roads.

The Highway passes straight through every town
        at Matsons washing bluejeans
                hills and saltwater

                        ack, the woodsmoke in my brain

        (high Olympics—can't go there again)

East Marginal Way the hitchhike zone
Boeing down across Duwamish slough
and angle out   & on.

———

Night rain wet concrete headlights blind   Tacoma

        salt air / bulk cargo / steam cycle / AIR REDUCTION

        eating peanuts I don't give a damn
        if anybody ever stops   I'll walk
        to San Francisco   what the hell

            "that's where you going?
            why you got that pack?"

            "well man I just don't feel right
            without something on my back"

                & this character in milkman overalls
                "I have to come out here
                every once in a while, there's a guy
                blows me here"

                        way out of town.

Stayed in Olympia with Dick Meigs
        —this was a different year & he had moved—
        sleep on a cot in the back yard
        half the night watch shooting stars

These guys got babies now
        drink beer, come back from wars,
        "I'd like to save up all my money
        get a big new car, go down to Reno

        & latch onto one of those rich girls—
        I'd fix their little ass"—nineteen yr old
        North Dakota boy fixing to get married next month.

To Centralia in a purple Ford.

>   Carstruck dead doe
>   by the Skookumchuck river

Fat man in a Chevrolet
>   wants to go back to L.A.   "too damned poor now"

Airbrakes on the log trucks hiss and whine
>   stand in the dark by the stoplight
>   big fat cars tool by
>   drink coffee, drink more coffee
>   brush teeth back of Shell

>   hot shoes
>   stay on the rightside of that
>   yellow line

Mary's Corner, turn for Mt. Rainier
>   —once caught a ride at night for Portland here.
Five Mexicans ask me "chip in on the gas."
>   I never was more broke & down.

>   Got fired that day by the USA
>   (the District Ranger up at Packwood
>   thought the Wobblies had been dead for
>   forty years
>   but the FBI smelled treason
>   —my red beard)

That Waco Texas boy
>   took A.G. and me through miles of snow
>   had a chest of logger gear
>   at the home of an Indian girl
>   in Kelso hadn't seen since fifty-four

Toledo, Castle Rock, free way four lane
>   no stoplights and no crossings, only cars,
>   & people walking, old hitchhikers
>   break the laws. How do I know . . .

the state cop
told me so.

Come a dozen times into
Portland
on the bum or
hasty lover
late at night.

———

Portland

Dust kicking up behind the trucks—night rides—
Who waits in the coffee stop
night highway 99

Sokei-an met an old man on the banks of the
Columbia growing potatoes & living all alone,
Sokei-an asked him the reason why he lived there,
he said

Boy, no one ever asked me the reason why,
I like to be alone.
I am an old man.
I have forgotten how to speak human words.

All night freezing in the back of a truck
dawn at Smith River
battering on in loggers' pickups
prunes for lunch
The next night, Siuslaw.

Portland sawdust down town
Buttermilk corner all you want for a nickel
(now a dime)   —Sujata gave
Gautama buttermilk.
(No doubt! says Sokei-an, that's all it was:
plain buttermilk)

rim of mountains,
pulp bark chewed snag papermill
tugboom in the river
—used to lean on bridge rails
dreaming up eruptions and quakes—

Slept under juniper in the Siskiyou   Yreka
a sleeping bag, a foot of snow
black rolled umbrella
ice slick asphalt

Caught a ride the only car come by
at seven in the morning
chewing froze salami
riding with a passed-out L.A. whore
glove compartment full of booze,
the driver a rider,
nobody cowboy,
sometime hood,
Like me picked up to drive,
& drive the blues away.
We drank to Portland
and we treated that girl good.
I split my last two bucks with him in town
went out to Carol & Billy's in the woods.

Foggy morning in Newport
housetrailers
under the fir.

———

An old book on Japan at the Goodwill
unfurled umbrella in the sailing snow
sat back in black wood
barber college
chair, a shave

On Second Street in Portland.
        What elegance. What a life.
        Bust my belly with a quart of
        buttermilk
        & five dry heels of French bread
        from the market cheap
                clean shaved, dry feet,

We're on our way
        man
            out of town

Go hitching down that
        highway 99.

—

Oil pump broken, motor burning out   Salem

Ex-logger selling skidder cable
      wants to get to San Francisco,
      fed and drunk   Eugene

Guy just back from Alaska—don't like
      the States now—too much law   Sutherlin

A woman with a kid & two bales of hay   Roseburg

Sawmill worker, young guy thinking of
      going to Eureka for redwood logging
      later in the year   Dillard

Two Assembly of God Pentecostal boys from
      a holy-roller high school. One had
          spoken in tongues   Canyonville

      (LASME Los Angeles–Seattle Motor Express)
        place on highway 20
        LITTLE ELK
        badger & badger

South of Yoncalla burn the engine
        run out of oil (a different car)
(Six great highways; so far only one)

Jumpoff Joe Creek &
        a man carrying nothing, walking sort of
        stiff-legged along, blue jeans & denim jacket
        wrinkled face, just north of
        Louse Creek

                —Abandon really means it
                the network womb stretched loose all
                        things slip through

        Dreaming on a bench under newspapers
        I woke covered with rhododendron blooms
                alone in a State Park in Oregon.

                        ——

        "I had a girl in Oakland who worked
        for a doctor, she was a nurse, she let him
        eat her. She died of tuberculosis
        & I drove back that night to Portland
        nonstop, crying all the way"   Grants Pass

        "I picked up a young mother with two
        children once, their house had just burned down"

        "I picked up an Italian tree-surgeon
        in Port Angeles once, he had all his
        saws and tools all screwed & bolted on
        a beat-up bike."

Oxyoke, Wolf Creek, a guy
Coming off a five-day binge to   Phoenix
An ex-bartender from Lebanon to   Redding
Man & wife on a drinking spree, to   Anderson

Snow on the pines & firs around Lake Shasta
        —Chinese scene of winter hills and trees

us "little travelers" in the bitter cold
six-lane highway slash & D–9 Cats—
bridge building   squat earth-movers
—yellow bugs
                    I speak for hawks. Creating
"Shasta" as I go—

The road that's followed goes forever;
        in half a minute crossed and left behind.

Out of the snow and into red-dirt plains
                blossoming plums

Each time you go that road it gets more straight
        curves across the mountain lost in fill
        towns you had to slow down all four lane
                Azalea, Myrtle Creek

    watch out for deer.

At Project City Indian hitcher
Standing under single tarpole lamp
        nobody stopped
                we walked four miles
                to an oak fire left by the road crew,
                        shivered the night away.

                        ——

Going to San Francisco
Yeah San Francisco
Yeah we came from Seattle
Even farther north
Yeah we been working in the mountains
        in the spring
        in the autumn
                    I always go this highway 99—

    "I was working in a mill three weeks there
    then it burned down & the guy didn't even

pay us off—but I can do anything—
I'll go to San Francisco—tend bar—"

Sixteen speeds forward   windows open
Stopped at the edge of Willows for a bite
              grass shoots on the edge of
              drained rice plains
                        —where are the Sierras—

———

        standing in the night   in the world-end winds
        by the overpass bridge
              junction US 40   and highway 99

              trucks, trucks,   roll by
              kicking up dust   dead flowers

        level, dry,
Highway 99 turns west.
                Miles gone, speed still
                pass through lower hills
                heat dying
                toward Vallejo
                gray on the salt baywater
                      brown grass ridges
                            buckbrush blue.

Herons in the tideflats
        have no thought for
States of Cars

              —I'm sick of car exhaust

                      City
                gleaming far away
              we make it into town tonight
              get clean and drink some wine—

              SAN FRANCISCO

                        NO
                   body
                   gives a shit
                                man
                        who you are
                   or what's your car
                                there
                   IS no   99

Three Worlds, Three Realms, Six Roads

Things to Do Around Seattle

Hear phone poles hum
Catch garter snakes. Make lizard tails fall off;
Biking to Lake Washington, catch muddy little fish.
Peeling old bark off madrone to see the clean red new bark
Cleaning fir pitch off your hands
Reading books in the back of the University District
     Goodwill.
Swim in Puget Sound below the railroad tracks
Dig clams
Ride the Kalakala to Bremerton
See Mt. Constance from the water tower up by the art
     museum
Fudgsicles in Woodland Park zoo, the eagle and the camel
The mummy Eskimo baby in the University Anthropology
     museum.
Hung up deep sea canoes, red cedar log.
Eating old-style oatmeal mush cooked in a double boiler
     or cracked-wheat cereal with dates.
Sway in the wind in the top of the cedar in the middle of
     the swamp
Walk through the swamp and over the ridge to the pine
     woods,
Picking wild blackberries all around the stumps.
Peeling cascara

Feeding chickens
Feeling Penelope's udder, one teat small.
Oregon grape and salal.

Things to Do Around Portland

Go walk along the Sandy when the smelt run
Drink buttermilk at the Buttermilk Corner
Walk over Hawthorne Bridge the car tires sing
Take the trolley out to Sellwood when cherries are in
    bloom
Hiking the woods below Council Crest, a tree house
    high in a Douglas fir near the medical school.
Bird watching and plant hunting on Sauvies Island in May
Vine maple leaves in the slopes above St. John's Bridge in
    autumn
Wading the Columbia out to sandbars
Himalayan blackberries tangle at the base of steel high-
    tension Bonneville transmission tower—your fingers
    stained
Get married in Vancouver without the three-day wait.
Cash paychecks at the Pastime
Beer in Ericson's, hamburgers at Tic Tock.
Led down narrow corridors of Court House, City Hall,
    the newspapers, the radios, the jail.
Parking in the Park blocks
Sunburned skiing
Shivering at the ocean
Standing in the rain

Things to Do Around a Lookout

Wrap up in a blanket in cold weather and just read.
Practice writing Chinese characters with a brush
Paint pictures of the mountains
Put out salt for deer
Bake coffee cake and biscuit in the iron oven
Hours off hunting twisty firewood, packing it all back up
    and chopping.

Rice out for the ptarmigan and the conies
Mark well sunrise and sunset—drink lapsang soochong.
Rolling smokes
The flower book and the bird book and the star book
Old Reader's Digests left behind
Bullshitting on the radio with a distant pinnacle like you
    hid in clouds
Drawing little sexy sketches of bare girls
Reading maps, checking on the weather, airing out
    musty Forest Service sleeping bags and blankets
Oil the saws, sharpen axes,
Learn the names of all the peaks you see and which is
    highest—there are hundreds—
Learn by heart the drainages between
Go find a shallow pool of snowmelt on a good day, bathe in
    the lukewarm water
Take off in foggy weather and go climbing all alone
The rock book—strata, dip, and strike
Get ready for the snow, get ready
To go down.

Things to Do Around San Francisco

Catch eels in the rocks below the Palace of the Legion of
    Honor.
Four in the morning—congee at Sam Wo.
Walk up and down Market, upstairs playing pool,
Turn on at Aquatic park—seagulls steal bait sardine
Going clear out to Oh's to buy bulghur.
Howard Street Goodwill
Not paying traffic tickets; stopping the phone.
Merry-go-round at the beach, the walk up to the cliff
    house, sea lions and tourists—the old washed-out
    road that goes on—
Play chess at Mechanics'
Dress up and go looking for work
Seek out the Wu-t'ung trees in the park arboretum.
Suck in the sea air and hold it—miles of white walls—sun-
    set shoots back from somebody's window high in the
    Piedmont hills

Get drunk all the time. Go someplace and score.
Walk in and walk out of the Asp
Hike up Tam
Keep quitting and starting at Berkeley
Watch the pike in the Steinhart Aquarium: he doesn't
    move.
Sleeping with strangers
Keeping up on the news
Chanting sutras after sitting
Practicing yr frailing on guitar
Get dropped off in the fog in the night
Fall in love twenty times
Get divorced
Keep moving—move out to the Sunset
Get lost—or
Get found

Things to Do Around a Ship at Sea

Go out with a small flashlight and a star chart on a clear
    night and check out the full size of Eridanus.
Sunbathe on a cot on the boatdeck
Go forward and talk with the lookout, away from the
    engines, the silence and shudder
Watch running lights pass in the night.
Dolphins and sharks.
Phosphorescing creatures alongside the shipside, burning
    spots in the wake.
Stag, Argosy, Playboy, and Time.
Do pushups.
Make coffee in the galley, telling jokes.
Type letters to his girlfriend in Naples for the twelve-to-
    four Oiler
Sew up jeans.
Practise tying knots and whipping
Watch the Chief Cook singing blues
Tell big story lies
Grow a beard
Learn to weld and run a lathe
Study for the Firemans Oilers and Watertenders exam

Tropic- and sea-bird watching
Types of ships
Listening to hours of words and lifetimes—fuck and
    shit—
Figuring out the revolution
Hammer pipes and flanges
Paint a picture on a bulkhead with leftover paints
Dream of girls, about yr girlfriend, writing letters, wanting
    children,
Making plans

Things to Do Around Kyoto

Lie on the mats and sweat in summer,
Shiver in winter, sit and soak like a foetus in the bath.
Paikaru and gyoza at Min Min with Marxist students full
    of China
Look for country pothooks at the Nijo junk store
Get dry bad red wine to drink like a regular foreigner,
    from Maki's
Trudging around with visitors to gardens

Pluck weeds out of the moss. Plant morning glories
Walk down back alleys listening to looms
Watching the flocks of sparrows whirling over trees on
    winter sunsets
Get up at four in the morning to go meet with the Old
    Man.
Sitting in deep samadhi on a hurting knee.
Get buttered up by bar girls, pay too much
Motorcycle oil change down on Gojo
Warm up your chilly wife, her big old feet.

Trying to get a key made
Trying to find brown bread
Hunting rooms for Americans
Having a big meeting, speaking several tongues.

Lose your way in the bamboo brush on Hiei-zan in winter
Step on a bug by mistake
Quiet weeks and weeks, walking and reading, talking and

weeding
Passing the hand around a rough cool pot
Throwing away the things you'll never need
Stripping down
Going home.

Jackrabbit

Jackrabbit,
black-tailed Hare
by the side of the road,
hop, stop.

Great ears shining,
you know me
a little. A lot more than I
know you.

The Elwha River

I was a girl waiting by the roadside for my boyfriend to come
in his car. I was pregnant. I should have been going to high
school. I walked up the road when he didn't come, over a
bridge: I saw a sleeping man. I came to the Elwha River—the
grade school—classes—I went and sat down with the children.
The teacher was young and sad-looking, homely; she assigned
us an essay: "What I Just Did." I wrote,

"I was waiting for my boyfriend by the Elwha River
bridge: the bridge was redwood, a fresh bridge with inner
bark still clinging on some logs—it smelled good. There
was someone sleeping under redwood trees. He had a box
of flies by his head and he was on the ground. The Elwha
River bridge is by a meadow; there's a rocky bar there
where the river forks . . ."

thinking this would please the teacher. We handed all the papers
in, and got them back—mine was C minus. The children then
went home. The teacher came to me and said "I just don't
like you."
—"Why?"
—"Because I used to be a man."

The Elwha River, I explained, is a real river, and different
from the river I described. Where I had just walked was real,
but I wrote a dream river—actually the Elwha doesn't fork at
that point.

As I write this now I must remind myself that there is
another Elwha, the actual Olympic peninsula river, which
is not the river I took pains to recollect as real in the dream.

There are no redwoods north of southern
        Curry County, Oregon.

Bubbs Creek Haircut

High ceilinged and the double mirrors, the
        calendar a splendid alpine scene—scab barber—
in stained white barber gown, alone, sat down, old man
a summer fog gray San Francisco day
I walked right in. On Howard Street
                haircut a dollar twenty-five.
Just clip it close as it will go.
        "Now why you want your hair cut back like that."
        —Well I'm going to the Sierras for a while
Bubbs Creek and on across to upper Kern.
                He wriggled clippers
"Well I been up there, I built the cabin
        up at Cedar Grove. In nineteen five."
                Old haircut smell.

Next door, Goodwill
        where I came out.

A search for sweater and a stroll
            in the board & concrete room of
            unfixed junk downstairs—
all emblems of the past—too close—
      heaped up in chilly dust and bare-bulb glare
of tables, wheelchairs, battered trunks & lamps
& pots that boiled up coffee nineteen ten, things
swimming on their own & finally freed
                  from human need. Or?
      Waiting a final flicker of desire
to tote them out once more. Some freakish use.
The Master of the limbo drag-legged watches
                  making prices
            to the people seldom buy.
The sag-asst rocker has to make it now. Alone.

            A few days later drove with Locke
down San Joaquin, us barefoot in the heat
stopping for beer and melon on the way
            the Giant Orange,
rubber shreds of cast truck retreads on the pebble
shoulder, highway 99.
            Sierras marked by cumulus in the east.
Car coughing in the groves,   six thousand feet
down to Kings River Canyon; camped at Cedar Grove.
      Hard granite canyon walls that
      leave no scree.

Once tried a haircut at the Barber College too—
sat half an hour before they told me
            white men use the other side.
Goodwill, St. Vincent de Paul,
            Salvation Army up the coast
for mackinaws and boots and heavy socks
      —Seattle has the best for logger gear
once found a pair of good tricouni boots
            at the under-the-public market store,
            Mark Tobey's scene,
                  torn down I hear—
and Filson jacket with a birdblood stain.

A.G. and me got winter clothes for almost nothing
        at Lake Union, telling the old gal
            we was on our way
to work the winter out up in B.C.
                    hitchhiking home the
green hat got a ride (of that more later).
Hiking up Bubbs Creek saw the trail crew tent
in a scraggly grove of creekside lodgepole pine
            talked to the guy, he says

"If you see McCool on the other trail crew over there
tell him Moorehead says to go to hell."
Late snow that summer. Crossing the scarred bare
                shed of Forester Pass
        the winding rock-braced switchbacks
dive in snowbanks, we climb on where
            pack trains have to dig or wait.
A half-iced-over lake, twelve thousand feet
            its sterile boulder bank
but filled with leaping trout:
            reflections wobble in the
mingling circles always spreading out
        the crazy web of wavelets makes sense
        seen from high above.
A deva world of sorts—it's high
            —a view that few men see, a point
        bare sunlight
        on the spaces
empty sky
            molding to fit the shape of what ice left
of fire-thrust, or of tilted, twisted, faulted
                cast-out from this lava belly globe.

The boulder in my mind's eye is a chair.
                    . . . why was the man drag-legged?
King of Hell
        or is it a paradise of sorts, thus freed
from acting out the function some
                creator / carpenter

thrust on a thing to think he made, himself,
        an object always "chair"?
                Sinister ritual histories.
        Is the Mountain God a gimp?
The halting metrics   and the ritual limp,
                            Good   Will?

Daughter of mountains, stooped
        moon breast Parvati

                mountain thunder speaks
                hair tingling static as the lightning lashes
                is neither word of love nor wisdom;
                though this be danger: hence thee fear.
                        Some flowing girl
                whose slippery dance
                en trances Shiva
                        —the valley spirit / Anahita,
                                Sarasvati,
                dark and female gate of all the world
                water that cuts back quartzflake sand
                            soft is the dance that melts the
                mat-haired mountain sitter
                                to leap in fire
                & make of sand a tree
                    of tree a board, of board (ideas!)
                    somebody's rocking chair.
                A room of empty sun of peaks and ridges
                beautiful spirits
                    rocking lotus throne
                a universe of junk, all left alone.

The hat I always take on mountains:
When we came back down through Oregon
                (three years before)
at nightfall in the Siskiyou few cars pass.

A big truck stopped a hundred yards above
        "Siskiyou Stoneware" on the side
the driver said

he recognized my old green hat.
I'd had a ride
                    with him two years before
a whole state north
                    when hitching down to Portland
                        from Warm Springs.

Allen in the rear on straw
forgot salami and we went on south
all night—in many cars—to Berkeley in the dawn.

            Upper Kern River country now after nine days walk
            it finally rain.
                    We ran on that other trail crew
            setting up new camp in the drizzly pine
            cussing & slapping bugs, four days from road,
            we saw McCool, & he said tell that Moorehead
                    kiss my ass.

        We squatted smoking by the fire.
                "I'll never get a green hat now"
        the foreman says fifty mosquitoes sitting on the brim

                    they must like green.
        & two more days of thundershower and cold
                    (on Whitney hair on end
                    hail stinging bare legs in the blast of wind
                    but yodel off the summit echoes clean)

            all this comes after:

purity of the mountains and goodwills.
The diamond drill of racing icemelt waters
            and bumming trucks & watching

buildings raze
            the garbage acres burning at the Bay
            the girl who was the skid-row
cripple's daughter—

out of the memory of smoking pine
the lotion and the spittoon glitter rises
chair turns and in the double mirror waver
the old man cranks me down and cracks a chuckle

"Your Bubbs Creek haircut, boy."

Boat of a Million Years

The boat of a million years,
        boat of morning,
sails between the sycamores of turquoise,

Dawn white Dutch freighter
in the Red Sea—with a red stack—
heads past our tanker, out toward Ras Tanura,
        sun already fries my shoulder blades, I
        kneel on ragged steel decks chipping paint.
Gray old T-2 tanker and a
        white Dutch freighter,

        boat of the sun,
the abt-fish, the yut-fish,
        play in the waves before it,

salty Red Sea
        dolphins rip sunlight
streak in, swirl and tangle
        under the forward-arching wave roll
of the cleaving bow

        Teilhard said "seize the tiller of the planet" he
        was joking,

We are led by dolphins toward morning.

The Blue Sky

"Eastward from here,
    beyond Buddha-worlds ten times as
    numerous as the sands of the Ganges
there is a world called
            PURE AS LAPIS LAZULI
its Buddha is called Master of Healing,
            AZURE RADIANCE TATHAGATA"

            it would take you twelve thousand summer vacations
            driving a car due east all day every day
            to reach the edge of the Lapis Lazuli realm of
            Medicine Old Man Buddha—
            East. Old Man Realm
            East across the sea, yellow sand land
            Coyote old man land
            Silver, and stone blue

            —

Blue	blāew, bright	flāuus	flamen, brāhman

Sky.	sky⁻ scūwo "shadow"

Sanskrit skutās   "covered"
skewed (pied)
            skewbald (. . . "Stewball")
skybald / Piebald
    Horse with lightning feet, a mane like
    distant rain, the Turquoise horse,
    a black star for an eye
    white shell teeth
    Pony that feeds on the pollen of flowers
    may he
    make thee whole.

Heal.   hail   whole   (khailaz . . . kail . . .koil I. E. r)

The Spell of the Master of Healing

> Namo bhagavate bhaishajyagura-vaidurya-
> prabharajaya tathagata arhate samyak
> sambuddhaya tadyatha *om* bhaishajye
> > bhaishajye bhaishajya samudgate
> > svāhā.

> "I honour the Lord, the Master of Healing,
> shining like lapis lazuli, the king, the
> Tathagata, the Saint, the perfectly enlightened
> one, saying *OM* TO THE HEALING
> > TO THE HEALING   TO THE HEALER
> > HAIL!
> > > svāhā.

—

Shades of blue through the day

T'u chüeh   a border tribe near China
Türc
Turquoise: a hydrous phosphate of aluminum
                 a little copper
                 a little iron—

> Whole, Whole, Make Whole!
> Blue Land Flaming Stone—
> Man
> > Eastward—
> > > sodium, aluminum, calcium, sulfur.

—

In the reign of the Emperor Nimmyō
when Ono-no-Komachi the strange girl poet
was seventeen, she set out looking for her father
who had become a Buddhist Wanderer. She took ill
on her journey, and sick in bed one night saw

AZURE RADIANCE THUS-COME MEDICINE MASTER

in a dream. He told her she would find a hotsprings
on the bank of the Azuma river in the Bandai mountains
that would cure her; and she'd meet her father there.

———

      "Enchantment as strange as
      the Blue up above"   my rose of San Antone

Tibetans believe that Goddesses have Lapis Lazuli hair.

Azure.   O. F. azur
      Arabic lāzaward
      Persian lāzhward   "lapis lazuli"
  —blue bead charms against the evil eye—

(*Hemp.* ". . . Cheremiss and Zyrjän word . . . these two
  languages
      being Finno-Ugric—
      a wandering culture word
      of wide diffusion.")

      Tim and Kim and Don and I were talking about
      what an awful authoritarian garb Doctors
      and Nurses wear, really, how spooky it is.
      "What *should* they wear?"

      —"Masks and Feathers!"

———

Ramana Maharshi Dream

I was working as a wood cutter by a crossroads—Ko-san
was working with me—we were sawing and splitting the
firewood. An old man came up the lane alongside a mud
wall—he shouted a little scolding at some Zen monks who
were piling slash by the edge of the woods. He came over
and chatted with us, a grizzled face—neither eastern or
western; or both. He had a glass of buttermilk in his
hand. I asked him "Where'd you get that buttermilk?"
I'd been looking all over for buttermilk. He said,
"At the O K Dairy, right where you leave town."

—

Medicine. mederi, Indo-european me- "to measure"
   "Maya"— Goddess illusion-wisdom fishing net

Celestial. arched cover. . . . *kam.*
Heaven. heman . . . *kam.*
Comrade: under the same sky / tent / curve. *kam*, a bent
curved bow,
Kama, God of Love   "Son of Maya"
          bow of flowers.

> *sky blue*
> *right in the rocks too—*
> *lazuli bunting*
> *sea-blue*
> *hazy-hills blue*
> *huckleberry, cobalt*
> *medicine-bottle*
>   *blue*

—

:Shakyamuni would then be the lord of the present
world of sorrow; Bhaishajyaguru / Yao-shih Fo /

Yakushi; "Old Man Medicine Buddha" the lord of the
Lost Paradise.

Glory of morning,
        pearly gates,
        tlitliltzin, the "heavenly blue."

———

Thinking on Amitabha in the setting sun,
        his western paradise—
        impurities flow out away, to west,
        behind us, *rolling*

        planet ball forward turns into the "east"
        is rising,
        azure,
        two thousand light years ahead

        Great Medicine Master;
        land of blue.

        The Blue Sky

        The Blue Sky

        The Blue Sky

        is the land of

OLD MAN MEDICINE BUDDHA

                where the Eagle
                that Flies out of Sight

                flies.

— *II* —

The Market

Heart of the city
                down town
the country side.

John Muir   up before dawn
packing pears in the best boxes
        beat out the others—to Market
                the Crystal Palace
on the morning milk-run train.

Me, milk bottles by bike
Guernsey milk, six percent butterfat
raw and left to rise natural
                ten cents a quart
slipped on the ice turning
                in to a driveway
        and broke all nine bottles.
When we had cows . . .
        a feathery hemlock out back
        by manure pile where
one cow once
        lay with milk fever
        confusions & worries until the vet come
we do this still dark in the morning—

To town on high thin-wheeled carts.
Squat on the boxtop stall.
Papayas banana sliced fish grated ginger
fruit for fish, meat for flowers
        french bread for ladle
                steamer, tea giant

rough glaze earthware
        —for brass shrine bowls.

Push through fish
bound pullets lay on their sides
                wet slab
watch us with glimmering eye
                slosh water.
A carrot, a lettuce, a ball of cooked noodle.
        Beggars hang by the flower stall
        give them all some.

Strong women.   Dirt from the hills
                in her nails
valley thatch houses
        palmgroves for hedges
ricefield and thrasher
        to white rice
        dongs and piastre
to market, the
                changes, how much
                is our change:

                —

                                Kathmandu

Seventy-five feet hoed rows equals
one hour explaining power steering
equals two big crayfish =
        all the buttermilk you can drink
= twelve pounds cauliflower
= five cartons greek olives = hitchhiking
        from Ogden Utah to Burns Oregon
= aspirin, iodine and bandages
= a lay in Naples = beef
= lamb ribs = Patna
        long grain rice, eight pounds
equals two kilogram soybeans = a boxwood
                geisha comb

equals the whole family at the movies
equals whipping dirty clothes on rocks
        three days some Indian river
= piecing off beggars two weeks
= bootlace and shoelace
        equals one gross inflatable
        plastic pillows
= a large box of petit-fours, chou-crèmes,
        mangoes, apples, custard apples, raspberries
= picking three flats strawberries
= a christmas tree = a taxi ride
carrots, daikon, eggplant, green peppers
oregano white goat cheese
        = a fresh-eyed bonito, live clams
a swordfish
a salmon
        a handful of silvery smelt in the pocket;
        whiskey in cars   out late after dates
        old folks eating cake in secret
        breastmilk enough,
                if the belly be fed—

& wash down   hose off aisles
reach under fruit stands
        green gross rack
                meat scum on chop blocks
                bloody butcher concrete floor
        old knives sharpened down to scalpels
        brown wrap paper rolls, stiff
                push-broom back
wet spilled food
        when the market is closed
                the cleanup comes
                        equals

a billygoat pushing through people
stinking and grabbing a cabbage
arrogant, tough,
he took it—they let him—
Kathmandu—the market

I gave a man seventy paise
in return for a clay pot
of curds
was it worth it?
How can I tell

—

                              Varanasi

They eat feces
        in the dark
        on stone floors
one-legged monkeys, hopping cows
        limping dogs   blind cats
crunching garbage in the market
        broken fingers
                cabbage
        head on the ground.

Who has young face
        open pit eyes
between the bullock carts and people
        head pivot with the footsteps
                passing by
dark scrotum spilled on the street
        penis laid by his thigh
                torso
turns with the sun.

I came to buy
        a few bananas by the Ganges
while waiting for my wife.

Journeys

Genji caught a gray bird, fluttering. It
was wounded, so I hit it with a coal shovel;
it stiffened, got straight and symmetrical,
and began to grow in size. I took the bird by
the head with both hands and held it as it
swelled, turning the head from side to side.
The bird became a woman, and I was embracing
her. We walked down a dim-lighted stairway
holding hands, then walking more and more swiftly
through an enormous maze, all underground.
Occasionally we touched surface, and redescended.
As we walked I held a map of our route in
mind—but it became increasingly complex—and
just when I was about to lose the picture,
the woman transferred a piece of fresh-tasting apple
from her mouth to mine. Then I woke.

—

Through deep forests to the coast,
and stood on a white sandspit looking in:
over lowland swamps and prairies
where no one had ever been
to a view of the Olympic Mountains in a chill clear wind.

—

We moved across dark stony ground to the great
wall: hundreds of feet high. What was beyond
it, cows?—then something began to lift up from behind.
I shot my arrows, shot arrows at it, but it came—
until we turned and ran. "It's too big to
fight"—the rising thing a quarter mile across—
it was the flaming pulsing sun. We fled and
stumbled on the bright lit plain.

—

Where were we—
A girl in a red skirt, high heels,
going up the stairs before me in a made-over barn.
Whitewash peeling, we lived together in the loft,
on cool bare boards.
—Lemme tell you something kid—
        back in 1910.

———

Walking a dusty road through plowed-up fields
at forest-fire time—the fir tree hills dry,
smoke of the far fires blurred the air—
& passed on into woods along a pond,
beneath a big red cedar
to a bank of blinding blue wildflowers
and thick green grass on leveled ground
of hillside where our old house used to stand.
I saw the footings damp and tangled,
and thought my father was in jail,
and wondered why my mother never died,
and thought I ought to bring my sister back.

———

High up in a yellow-gold
dry range of mountains—
brushy, rocky, cactussy hills
slowly hiking down—finally can see below,
a sea of clouds.

Lower down, always moving slowly over the
dry ground descending, can see through the breaks
in the clouds: flat land.
Damp green level rice fields, farm houses,
at last to feel the heat and damp.

Descending to this humid, clouded level world:
now I have come to the LOWLANDS.

—

Underground building chambers clogged with refuse
discarded furniture, slag, old nails,
rotting plaster, faint wisps, antique newspapers
rattle in the winds that come forever down the hall;
passing, climbing ladders, and on from door to door.
One tiny light bulb left still burning
        —now the last—
locked *inside* is hell.
Movies going, men milling round the posters
        in shreds
        the movie always running
—we all head in here somewhere;

—years just looking for the bathrooms
huge and filthy, with strange-shaped toilets full of shit.
Dried shit all around, smeared across the walls of the
adjoining room,
and a vast hat rack.

—

With Lew rode in a bus over the mountains—
rutted roads along the coast of Washington
through groves of redwood. Sitting in the
back of an almost-empty bus,
talking and riding through.
Yellow leaves fluttering down. Passing
through tiny towns at times. Damp cabins
set in dark groves of trees.
Beaches with estuaries and sandbars. I brought
a woman here once long ago,
but passed on through too quick.

—

We were following a long river into the mountains.
Finally we rounded a ridge and could see deeper in—
the farther peaks stony and barren, a few alpine trees.

Ko-san and I stood on a point by a cliff, over a
rock-walled canyon. Ko said, "Now we have come to
where we die." I asked him—what's that up there,
then—meaning the further mountains.
"That's the world after death." I thought it looked
just like the land we'd been traveling, and couldn't
see why we should have to die.
Ko grabbed me and pulled me over the cliff—
both of us falling. I hit and I was dead. I saw
my body for a while, then it was gone.
Ko was there too. We were at the bottom of the gorge.
We started drifting up the canyon. "This is the
way to the back country."

Mā

Hello Boy—

I was very glad to hear from you
I know by the way you write and what you said
That you was just ok.
Yes I know you all have been busy working long hours.
$15.00 isn't bad at all.
I never made but $5.00 a day.
I thought that was good.
Try your damdest to hang on to a little of it
So if you quit you will have a little to go on.
Glad you are satisfied thats all you need.
Guess you need good saws.
I hope you can get them.
They cost a lot too—gee those boots are high.
They should wear real good.
Sounds like you like it up there and like to work in the
    timber.
I am glad.
One thing don't be drinking too much cut down once
    in a while.
Ray talked like Walter charged too much a week,
Don't let him cheat you.

Food is getting higher every place.
You buy a couple calves and I'll raise them for you
I am going to raise some more this year.
The little mare looks much better and she leads.
So you cook.
You don't mind that do you.
Just so you had plenty to cook.
Cooking always looked like it was easy for you.
Do your best thats all you can do.

I been planting some more stuff.

After this month I'll quit.
Getting late to plant even now

But I want to see how it works out.
According to the Almanac it isn't too late.
We had a few corn.
Ruby didn't plant anything so she comes over and takes
 what she wants.
Vino did get in once, she got in by the dead tree.
Then I had to fix fence.
She hasn't been in since but sure watches my gates.
I am up here at Ray's place right now watering flowers and
 trees—they have a few garden stuff.
Few beans, squash, potatoes and couple hills of watermelon.
I told Ruby that Mel and Shafer were up they left last night.
They killed quite a few rabbits.
Mel dried the meat cut it in small pieces—tasted pretty
 good.
Zip ate some of it and liked it she said, said she was going
 to make some.
She has a .22—keeps it with her all the time.
My old .22 won't even shoot, just snaps.
Guess there is something wrong with it but I sure don't
 know anything about it.
But I can shoot.
I killed several rabbits in my garden.

We had a few funerals here lately.
First Pablo died then Gracie Quarto got word her boy
 was killed in Viet-Nam.
So the two were buried the same day.
Just lately 9th Sabrina died and was buried here.
There were quite a few from all over.
Frank and his wife sang—that was nice.

Wish I was there to eat some of those wild berries.
I can't see where you will find time to go pick them.
If some one would pick them then you might make some
 jelly.

All our cattle are falling off.
We had a thunder shower ruined the grass.
A big fire at Antelope Wells, sure was smoky here.

Said lightning started it.
Pretty clear now so they must of put it out.
Been hot here the last couple days.
Rained all around us not a drop fell here.
I am pretty busy since everyone here is gone watering things.

Will Stark told me to tell you he wanted you to go to
    Oklahoma with him.
Said he wanted you to stay with him.
He is going to start moving in September—taking a bull and
    horses first.
He will have to make about 3 trips before his family goes.
They are all going but the big boy.
Will said you was real good when you were with them.
Said I don't mind drinking but I can't stand a drunk.
Mabie the work is hard.
Nothing here same old thing
People allways drinking then dieing.
Don't seem to mind tho.

Well Boy I'll quit writing for now—write when you can.
Be careful. Drink but don't get drunk. (huh).
Tell all hello—all said hello to you—
Charley was telling me she got a letter from you.

                    By Boy
                      as ever

                      Ma.

Instructions

Fuel filler cap
> —haven't I seen this before? The
> sunlight under the eaves, mottled
> shadow, on the knurled rim of
> dull silver metal.

Oil filler cap
> bright yellow,
> horns like a snail
> —the oil's down there—
> amber, clean, it
> falls back to its pit.

Oil drain plug
> so short, from in to out. Best
> let it drain when it is hot.

Engine switch
> off, on. Off, on. Just
> two places. Forever,
>
> or,   not even one.

Night Song of the Los Angeles Basin

            Owl
        calls,
        pollen dust blows
    Swirl of light strokes writhing
    knot-tying light paths,

        calligraphy of cars.

Los Angeles basin and hill slopes
Checkered with streetways. Floral loops
Of the freeway express and exchange.

            Dragons of light in the dark
            sweep going both ways
            in the night city belly.
            The passage of light end to end and rebound,
            —ride drivers all heading somewhere—
            etch in their traces to night's eye-mind

            calligraphy of cars.

Vole paths. Mouse trails worn in
On meadow grass;
Winding pocket-gopher tunnels,
Marmot lookout rocks.
Houses with green watered gardens
Slip under the ghost of the dry chaparral,

            Ghost
            shrine to the L. A. River.
            The *jinja* that never was there
            is there.
            Where the river debouches
            the place of the moment
            of trembling and gathering and giving
            so that lizards clap hands there
            —just lizards
            come pray, saying
            "please give us health and long life."

A hawk,
a mouse.

Slash of calligraphy of freeways of cars.

Into the pools of the channelized river
the Goddess in tall rain dress
tosses a handful of meal.

Gold bellies roil
mouth-bubbles, frenzy of feeding,
the common ones, the bright-colored rare ones
show up, they tangle and tumble,
godlings ride by in Rolls Royce
wide-eyed in brokers' halls
lifted in hotels
being presented to, platters
of tidbit and wine,
snatch of fame,

churn and roil,

meal gone   the water subsides.

A mouse,
a hawk.

The calligraphy of lights on the night
            freeways of Los Angeles

will long be remembered.

            Owl
calls;
            late-rising moon.

Covers the Ground

"When California was wild, it was one sweet bee-garden . . ."

John Muir

Down the Great Central Valley's
blossoming almond orchard acres
lines of tree trunks shoot a glance through
        as the rows flash by—

And the ground is covered with
cement culverts standing on end,
house-high & six feet wide
culvert after culvert far as you can see
        covered with
mobile homes, pint-size portable housing, johnny-on-the-spots,
concrete freeway, overpass, underpass,
        exit floreals, entrance curtsies, railroad bridge,
long straight miles of divider oleanders;
scrappy ratty grass and thistle, tumbled barn, another age,

yards of tractors, combines lined up—
new bright-painted units down at one end,
old stuff broke and smashed down at the other,
cypress tree spires, frizzy lonely palm tree,
steep and gleaming
fertilizer tank towers fine-line catwalk in the sky—

        covered with walnut orchard acreage
irrigated, pruned and trimmed;
with palleted stacks of cement bricks
        waiting for yellow fork trucks;
quarter-acre stacks of wornout car tires,
dust clouds blowing off the new plowed fields,
taut-strung vineyards trimmed out even on the top,

cubic blocks of fresh fruit loading boxes,
long aluminum automated chicken-feeder houses,
        spring furz of green weed
        comes on last fall's hard-baked ground,
            beyond "Blue Diamond Almonds"

come the rows of red-roofed houses
& the tower that holds catfood
with a red / white checkered sign

crows whuff over almond blossoms
beehives sit tight between fruit tree ranks
eucalyptus boughs shimmer in the wind—a pale blue
    hip-roof
house   behind a weathered fence—
crows in the almonds
        trucks on the freeways,
            Kenworth, Peterbilt, Mack,
            rumble diesel depths,
like boulders bumping in an outwash glacial river

      drumming to a not-so-ancient text

      "The Great Central Plain of California
      was one smooth bed of honey-bloom
          400 miles, your foot would press
      a hundred flowers at every step
      it seemed one sheet of plant gold;

      all the ground was covered
      with radiant corollas ankle-deep:
      bahia, madia, madaria, burielia,
      chrysopsis, grindelia,
         wherever a bee might fly—"

us and our stuff just covering the ground.

The Flowing

Headwaters

Head doused under the bronze
    dragon-mouth jet
    from a cliff
    spring—headwaters, Kamo

River back of Kyoto,
    Cliff-wall statue of Fudo
Blue-faced growling Fudo,

Lord of the Headwaters, making
Rocks of water,
Water out of rocks

Riverbed

Down at the riverbed
    singing a little tune.
    tin cans, fork stick stuck up straight,
    half the stones of an old black campfire ring,

The gypsy actors, rags and tatters,
    wives all dancers,
    and the children clowns,
    come skipping down
    hop on boulders,
        clever—free—

Gravel scoop bed of the Kamo
    a digger rig set up on truck bed with
    revolving screen to winnow out the stones
    brushy willow—twists of sand

At Celilo all the Yakima
    Wasco, Wishram, Warmspring,
    catching salmon, talking,
        napping scattered through the rocks

Long sweep dip net held by a
foam-drenched braced and leaning man
on a rickety scaffold rigged to rocks

the whole Columbia River thunders
beneath his one wet plank

the lift and plume
of the water curling out and over,

Salmon arching in the standing spray.

———

Falls

Over stone lip
  the creek leaps out as one
  divides in spray and streamers,
  lets it all   go.

Above, back there, the snowfields
  rocked between granite ribs
  turn spongy in the summer sun
  water slips out under
  mucky shallow flows
  enmeshed with roots of flower and moss and heather
  seeps through swampy meadows
  gathers to shimmer sandy shiny flats
  then soars off ledges—

Crash and thunder on the boulders at the base
  painless, playing,
  droplets regather
  seek the lowest,
       and keep going down
  in gravelly beds.

There is no use, the water cycle tumbles round—

Sierra Nevada
  could lift the heart so high
  fault block uplift
  thrust of westward slipping crust—one way
to raise and swing the clouds around—
thus pine trees leapfrog up on sunlight

trapped in cells of leaf—nutrient minerals called together
like a magic song
to lead a cedar log along, that hopes
    to get to sea at last and be
        a great canoe.

A soft breath, world-wide, of night and day,
  rising, falling,

The Great Mind passes by its own
  fine-honed thoughts,
  going each way.

Rainbow hanging steady
  only slightly wavering with the
  swing of the whole spill,
      between the rising and the falling,
        stands still.

I stand drenched in crashing spray and mist,
and pray.

——

Rivermouth

Mouth
you thick
vomiting outward sighing prairie
    muddy waters
    gathering all and
    issue it
    end over end
        away from land.
The faintest grade.
Implacable, heavy, gentle,

—O pressing song
    liquid butts and nibbles

between the fingers—in the thigh—
against the eye

curl round my testicles
drawn crinkled skin
        and lazy swimming cock.

Once sky-clear and tickling through pineseeds
        humus, moss fern stone
        but NOW

the vast loosing
                of all that was found, sucked, held,
                born, drowned,

sunk sleepily in
to the sea.

        The root of me
        hardens and lifts to you,
        thick flowing river,

        my skin shivers. I quit

        making this poem.

The Black-tailed Hare

A grizzled black-eyed jackrabbit showed me

        irrigation ditches, open paved highway,
                        white line
        to the hill . . .
        bell chill blue jewel sky
                        banners,

banner clouds flying:
the mountains all gathered,

juniper trees on their flanks,
                              cone buds,
    snug bark scale
    in thin powder snow
over rock scrabble, pricklers, boulders,

pines and junipers
singing.

The mountains   singing
to gather the sky and the mist
    to bring it down snow-breath
                              ice-banners—
    and gather it water
sent from the peaks
    flanks and folds
down arroyos and ditches by highways the water

the people to use it, the
    mountains and juniper
do it for us

            said the rabbit.

With This Flesh

"Why should we cherish all sentient beings?
Because sentient beings
            are the roots of the tree-of-awakening.
The Bodhisattvas and the Buddhas are the flowers and fruits.
Compassion is the water for the roots."
                              Avatamsaka Sūtra

I   A BEACH IN BAJA

". . . on the twenty-eighth day of September 1539, the very
excellent Señor Francisco de Ulloa, lieutenant of the Governor
and captain of the armada by grace of the most illustrious Señor

Marques de Valle de Oaxaca, took possession of the bay of San
Andres and the Bermeja Sea, that is on the coast of this new
Spain toward the north, at thirty-three and a half degrees, for
the said Marques de Valle in the name of the Emperor our
King of Castile, at the present time and in reality,

> placing a hand on the sword,
> saying, that if anyone contradicts this
>   he is ready to defend it;
> cutting trees with his sword,
> uprooting grass,
> removing rocks from one place to another,
> and taking water from the sea;

all as a sign of possession.
. . .—I, Pedro Palenzia, notary public of this armada, write what
happened before me."

II   SAN IGNACIO, *Cadacaaman,* "REED CREEK"

Señora Maria Leree is ninety-eight years old,
rests in a dark cool room at full noon.
A century-old grapevine covers the house. Casa Leree.
"She still tries to tell me what to do"
—her daughter Rebecca
lived fifty-five years in Los Angeles,

Dagobert drives beer truck all day every day
and some nights,
from Guerrero Negro to San Ignacio.
Says the salt works at Guerrero Negro
sell most of their salt to Japan;

Rebecca plays a mandolin
"I need some music down here."
Dagobert trucks beer to ranches
all through central Baja
over those rutted roads.
"I have six kids in Guaymas. I
get over to see them three days a month"

South of El Arco
a hummingbird's nest with four eggs;
    four Mexican black hawks
a caracara on the top of a cardón
a bobcat crossing the truck track at twilight
a wadi full of cheeping evening birds

Cats walk the fan-palm roof.
    Her two sons are painters.
    —"I am a poet."
"You came down here to Baja for
—inspiration? Poeta?"
Yes, on these tracks. Rising early
Dry leather. Deep wells.
  Where we breathe, we bow.

III   THE ARROYO

The bulls of Iberia—Europa loves the Father;
India loves the big-eyed Mother Cow,

In the Thyssen Collection in Madrid there is a painting by
Simon Vouet—*The Rape of Europa*—from about 1640. The
white bull is resting on the ground, the woman sweetly on
his back. A cheerful scene, three serving women, two cherubs,
stand by to help this naked lady and the handsome eager bull.
His round eyes looking up and back, flowers twined around his
horns. The Goddess thinks there's nothing she can't handle?
Leaving us with modern Europe and its states and wars.

    The bony cows of Baja.
Body of grass, forbs, brush, browse.
Dried meat. Charqui "jerky";
(Little church up the arroyo,
Leathery twisted ropy Christ
figure racked to dry)
Quechua *ch'arki*:
dried to keep, good years and bad—
    With this flesh—

skinny cow scratching
horny forehead on a mesquite limb—
Sweet breath spiraling outward,

the MUSCLE   jerky.
the SKIN   shoes, saddles, sheaths
the BONES   buttons
the FAT   buckets of lard
HORNS & HOOVES   glue.
Loose vulva, droopy udder;
the MILK   buttermilk babes

      (the hoof of the cow is a trace of the grasslands
      —the print in the grass is the hoof of a cow)

      Mother *Bos*
in her green-grass body at
  Arroyo de Camanjue—arroyo of reeds—

(Five thousand native people lived here,
temedegua, valiant people, Cochimi,
      old rancherias called
Aggvacaamanc—creek of the hawks
Camané caamanc—creek of the cardón cactus
Cahelulevit—running water
Vaba cahel—water of the camp
Cunitca cahel—water of the large rocks
Cahelmet—water and earth.
        cadéu: reed. *aggava*: hawk.)

      A ragged white-bearded vaquero
rides up the dust track, calls
"A su servicio!" with elegance

      Says, "Adiós!"   "Go with God!"

with this meat   I thee feed
with this flesh   I thee wed.

The Hump-backed Flute Player

The hump-backed flute player
    walks all over.
    Sits on the boulders around the Great Basin
    his hump   is a pack.

Hsüan Tsang
    went to India 629 AD
    returned to China 645
    with 657 sūtras, images, mandalas,
    and fifty relics—
    a curved frame pack with a parasol,
    embroidery, carving,
    incense censer swinging as he walked
    the Pamir   the Tarim   Turfan
    the Punjab   the doab
    of Ganga and Yamuna,

Sweetwater, Quileute, Hoh
Amur, Tanana, Mackenzie, Old Man,
Big Horn, Platte, the San Juan

    he carried
        "emptiness"
    he carried
        "mind only"
        vijñaptimātra

The hump-backed flute player
Kokop'ele

    His hump is a pack.

In Canyon de Chelly on the north wall up by a cave is the hump-backed flute player lying on his back, playing his flute. Across the flat sandy canyon wash, wading a stream and breaking through the ice, on the south wall, the pecked-out pictures of some mountain sheep with curling horns. They stood in the icy shadow of the south wall two hundred feet away; I sat with my shirt off in the sun facing south, with the hump-backed flute player just above my head. They whispered. I whispered. Back and forth across the canyon, clearly heard.

———

In the plains of Bihar, near Rajgir, are the ruins of Nalanda. The name Bihar comes from "vihara"—Buddhist temple—the Diamond Seat is in Bihar, and Vulture Peak—Tibetan pilgrims still come down to these plains. The six-foot-thick walls of Nalanda, the monks all scattered—books burned—banners tattered—statues shattered—by the Türks. Hsüan Tsang describes the high blue tiles, the delicate debates—Logicians of Emptiness—worshippers of Tārā, "Joy of Starlight," naked breasted. She who saves.

———

Ghost bison, ghost bears, ghost bighorns, ghost lynx, ghost pronghorns, ghost panthers, ghost marmots, ghost owls: swirling and gathering, sweeping down, in the power of a dance and a song.

> Then the white man will be gone.
> butterflies on slopes of grass and aspen—
> thunderheads the deep blue of Krishna
> rise on rainbows
> and falling shining rain
> each drop—
> tiny people gliding slanting down:
> a little buddha seated in each pearl—
> and join the million waving grass-seed-buddhas
> on the ground.

———

> Ah, what am I carrying? What's this load?
> Who's that out there in the dust

sleeping on the ground?
With a black hat, and a feather stuck in his
sleeve?

—It's old Jack Wilson,
Wovoka, the prophet,

Black Coyote saw the whole world
In Wovoka's empty hat

the bottomless sky

the night of starlight, lying on our sides

the ocean, slanting higher

all manner of beings
may swim in my sea
echoing up conch spiral corridors

the mirror: countless ages back
dressing   or laughing
what world today?

      pearl crystal jewel
      taming and teaching
      the dragon in the spine

      spiral, wheel,
      or breath of mind

      —desert sheep with curly horns.
      The ringing in your ears

      is the cricket in the stars.

———

Up in the mountains that edge the Great Basin

it was whispered to me
by the oldest of trees.

By the Oldest of Beings
the Oldest of Trees

Bristlecone Pine.

And all night long sung on
by a young throng

of Pinyon Pine.

— III —

The Circumambulation of Mt. Tamalpais

Walking up and around the long ridge of Tamalpais, "Bay Mountain," circling and climbing—chanting—to show respect and to clarify the mind. Philip Whalen, Allen Ginsberg, and I learned this practice in Asia. So we opened a route around Tam. It takes a day.

STAGE ONE

Muir Woods: the bed of Redwood Creek just where the Dipsea Trail crosses it. Even in the dryest season of this year some running water. Mountains make springs.

> Prajñāpāramitā-hridaya-sūtra
> Dhāranī for Removing Disasters
> Four Vows

Splash across the creek and head up the Dipsea Trail, the steep wooded slope and into meadows. Gold dry grass. Cows—a huge pissing, her ears out, looking around with large eyes and mottled nose. As we laugh. "—Excuse us for laughing at you." Hazy day, butterflies tan as grass that sit on silver-weathered fenceposts, a gang of crows. "I can smell fried chicken" Allen says—only the simmering California laurel leaves. The trail winds crossed and intertwining with a dirt jeep road.

TWO

A small twisted ancient interior live oak splitting a rock outcrop an hour up the trail.

> Dhāranī for Removing Disasters
> The Heat Mantra

A tiny chörten before this tree.

Into the woods. Maze fence gate. Young Douglas fir, redwood, a new state of being. Sun on madrone: to the bare meadow knoll. (Last spring a bed of wild iris about here and this time too, a lazuli bunting.)

THREE

A ring of outcropped rocks. A natural little dolmen-circle right where the Dipsea crests on the ridge. Looking down a canyon to the ocean—not so far.

> Dhāranī for Removing Disasters
> Hari Om Namo Shiva

And on to Pan Toll, across the road, and up the Old Mine Trail. A doe and a fawn, silvery gray. More crows.

FOUR

Rock springs. A trickle even now—

> The Sarasvatī Mantra
> Dhāranī for Removing Disasters

—in the shade of a big oak spreading out the map on a picnic table. Then up the Benstein Trail to Rifle Camp, old food-cache boxes hanging from wires. A bit north, in the oak woods and rocks, a neat little saddhu hut built of dry natural bits of wood and parts of old crates; roofed with shakes and black plastic. A book called *Harmony* left there. Lunch by the stream, too tiny a trickle, we drink water from our bota. The food offerings are swiss cheese sandwiches, swede bread with liverwurst, salami, jack cheese, olives, gomoku-no-moto from a can, grapes, panettone with apple-currant jelly and sweet butter, oranges, and soujouki—greek walnuts in grape-juice paste. All in the shade, at Rifle Camp.

FIVE

A notable serpentine outcropping, not far after Rifle Camp.

> Om Shri Maitreya
> Dhāranī for Removing Disasters

SIX

Colier Spring—in a redwood grove—water trickling out a pipe.
  Dhāranī of the Great Compassionate One

California nutmeg, golden chinquapin the fruit with burrs, the chaparral. Following the North Side Trail.

SEVEN

Inspiration Point.

Dhāranī for Removing Disasters
Mantra for Tārā

Looking down on Lagunitas. The gleam of water storage in the brushy hills. All that smog—and Mt. St. Helena faintly in the north. The houses of San Anselmo and San Rafael, once large estates . . . "Peacock Gap Country Club"—Rocky brush climb up the North Ridge Trail.

EIGHT

Summit of Mt. Tamalpais. A ring of rock pinnacles around the lookout.

Prajñāpāramitā-hridaya-sūtra
Dhāranī for Removing Disasters
Dhāranī of the Great Compassionate One

Hari Krishna Mantra
Om Shri Maitreya
Hari Om Namo Shiva

All about the bay, such smog and sense of heat. May the whole planet not get like this.
Start the descent down the Throckmorton Hogback Trail. (Fern Canyon an alternative.)

NINE

Parking lot of Mountain Home. Cars whiz by, sun glare from the west.

> Dhāranī for Removing Disasters
> Gopala Mantra.

Then, across from the California Alpine Club, the Ocean View Trail goes down. Some yellow broom flowers still out. The long descending trail into shadowy giant redwood trees.

TEN

The bed of Redwood Creek again.

> Prajñāpāramitā-hridaya-sūtra
> Dhāranī for Removing Disasters
> Hari Om Namo Shiva
> Hari Krishna Mantra
> Four Vows

—standing in our little circle, blowing the conch, shaking the staff rings, right in the parking lot.

The Canyon Wren

> I look up at the cliffs
> but we're swept on by downriver
> the rafts
> wobble and slide over roils of water
> boulders shimmer
> under the arching stream
> rock walls straight up on both sides.
> A hawk cuts across that narrow sky hit by sun,
>
> we paddle forward, backstroke, turn,
> spinning through eddies and waves

stairsteps of churning whitewater.
Above the roar
hear the song of a Canyon Wren.

A smooth stretch, drifting and resting.
Hear it again, delicate downward song

ti ti ti ti tee tee tee

descending through ancient beds.
A single female mallard flies upstream—

Shooting the Hundred-Pace Rapids
Su Tung P'o saw, for a moment,
it all stand still.
"I stare at the water:
it moves with unspeakable slowness."

Dōgen, writing at midnight,
"mountains flow
water is the palace of the dragon
it does not flow away."

We beach up at China Camp
between piles of stone
stacked there by black-haired miners,
cook in the dark
sleep all night long by the stream.

These songs that are here and gone,
here and gone,
to purify our ears.

Arctic Midnight Twilight
Cool North Breeze With Low Clouds
Green Mountain Slopes, White Mountain Sheep

Dibée

Song

Green mountain walls in blowing cloud
white dots on far slopes, constellations,
slowly changing   not stars   not rocks
"by the midnight breezes strewn"
cloud tatters, lavender arctic light
on sedate wild sheep grazing
tundra greens, held in the web of clan
and kin by bleats and smells to the slow
rotation of their Order living
half in the sky—damp wind up from the
whole north slope and a taste of the icepack—

the primus roaring now,
here, have some tea.

    A broad bench, slate surfacing
    six sheep break out of the gorge
    skyline brisk trot scamper

        Pellet piles in moss
        a spiral horn in the grass
        long tundra sweeps and the rise of slopes
        to a peak of Doonerak,
        white sheep dots on the far green

One chases one, they run in circles
three move away. One cuts a tangent.
On the shade side canyon wall
scree patch rock slides, serried stepped-up
ledges, a host of sheep hang out.
Sunshine across the valley, they choose

the chilly shade. Perched on cliffs
napping, scratching,
insouciant white head droops
over gulfs of air;

Low sun swings through the twenty-four hours
never high, never gone, a soft slant light,
miles of shadows, ever-dappling clouds,

    a sheepskull forehead with its horn prongs
    sitting on a boulder—
    an offer of the flower of a
    million years of nibbling forbs

    to the emptiness of intelligence,

    sheep impermanence, sheep practice,
    sheep shapeshifting—vows of beings—
    Vajra Sheep teaching the Koyukuk waters
    suchness for each—

"The beat of her unseen feet"
which the wild sheep hear
at the roof of the planet, the warp
of the longitudes gathered,
rips in the wind-built tent
of sky-sea-earth cycles, eating the
green of the twenty-four hours,
breaking the cloud-flock flight
with floods of rising, falling,
warmer, cooler, air-mass swirls
like the curls
of Dall sheep horns. The "feet"
of the onward paces of skulls and pellets—
clouds sublimate to pure air
blowing south through passes
feeding the white dot Dall sheep—dew.

    A sheep track followed by a wolf track
    south of the lake.

A ewe and lamb in the sunshine, the lamb
tries to nurse, it's too old,
she lies down.
In the scoured-out gullies
thirty-one sheep.

Climbing Midnight Mountain sliding rock
find a sheep trail goes just right:
on the harder scree at the bases of faces,
follow it out, over ledges, find their hidden
sheltered beds.

Sweet rank smell makes the heart beat,
dusty and big pebbles whisked out
so it's softer, shaped,
sheep dreaming place—

        Sheep time.
        All over the world.
        At rest in a sheep bed
        at the cliff-edge of life and death
        over endless mountains
        and streams like strips of the sky.

Up the knife ridge
the trail crosses over and heads down a glacier,
tracks fade in the snow.

Sheep gone, and only endless twilight mountains.
Rest awhile among the rocks
arise to descend   to unbuild it again,

    and hear the Koyukon riddle:

    "It really snowed hard
    in opposite directions
    on my head

        who am I?"

—dibée

a mountain sheep.

Under the Hills Near the Morava River

She lay there midst

Mammoth, reindeer, and wolf bones:

Diadem of fox teeth round her brow

Ocher under her hips

26,640 plus or minus 110 years before "now."

Burnt reindeer-pelvis bone bits
        in her mouth,

Bones of two men lying by her,
        one each side.

Walking the New York Bedrock
Alive in the Sea of Information

Maple, oak, poplar, gingko
New leaves, "new green" on a rock ledge
Of steep little uplift, tucked among trees
Hot sun dapple—
        wake up.

Roll over and slide down the rockface
Walk away in the woods toward
A squirrel, toward
Rare people! Seen from a safe distance.
A murmur of traffic approaching,

Siren howls echoing
Through the gridlock of structures,
Vibrating with helicopters,
    the bass tone
            of a high jet.

       Leap over the park stone wall
       Dressed fast and light,
       Slip into the migrating flow.

New York like a sea anemone
Wide and waving in the Sea of Economy,
Cadres of educated youth   in chic costume
Step out to the nightlife, good food, after work—
In the chambers of prana-subtle power-pumping
Heartbeat buildings   fired
Deep at the bottom, under the basement,
Fired by old merchant marine
Ex-fire-tenders   gone now from sea
    to the ships stood on end on the land:
    ex-seamen stand watch at the stationary boilers,
    give way to computers,
That monitor heat and the power
    webs underground;   in the air;
In the Sea   of Information.

Brisk flesh, keen-eyed, streams of people
Curve round the sweep of street corners
    cardboard chunks tossed up in truckbed.
Delicate jiggle, rouge on the nipple,
       kohl under the eye.

Time and Life buildings—sixty thousand people—
Wind ripples the banners
    stiff shudder shakes limbs on the
    planted trees growing new green,

Glass, aluminum, aggregate gravel,
Iron. Stainless steel.
Hollow honeycomb brain-buildings owned by

Columbia University, the landlord of
Anemone
       colony
Alive, in the Sea of Information

  "Claus the Wild man"
  Lived mostly with Indians,
  Was there as a witness when the old lady
  "Karacapacomont"
  Sold the last bit of Washington Heights, 1701

  Down deep grates hear the watercourse,
  Rivers that never give up
  Trill under the roadbed, over the bedrock.
  A bird angles way off a brownstone
  Couloir that looks like a route.

Echo the hollowing darkness.
Crisscrossing light threads
Gleam squeals up the side streets,
One growl shadow
  in an egg of bright lights,
Lick of black on the tongue.
Echoes of sirens come down the walled canyons
Foot lifts to the curb and the lights change—

And look up at the gods.
Equitable god, Celanese god, noble line,
Old Union Carbide god,
Each catching   shares of the squared blocked shadow
Each swinging in sundial arc of the day
           more than the sum of its parts.
The Guggenheims, the Rockefellers, and the Fricks,
Assembling the art of the world, the plate glass
Window lets light in on "the water lilies"
Like fish or planets, people,
Move, pause, move   through the rooms,
White birch leaves shiver in breezes
While guards watch the world,
Helicopters making their long humming trips

Trading pollen and nectar
In the air
    of the
Sea of   Economy,

    Drop under the streetworld
    Steel squeal of stopping and starting
    Wind blows through black tunnels
      spiderwebs, fungus, lichen.

Gingko trees of Gondwanaland. Pictographs,
Petroglyphs, cover the subways—
Empty eye sockets of buildings just built
Soulless, they still wait the ceremony
    that will make them too,
      new, Big
      city Gods,
Provided with conduit, cable and plumbing,
They will light up, breathe cool air,
Breathe the minds of the workers who work there—
The cloud of their knowing
As they soar in the sky, in the air,
Of the Sea
Of Information,

    Cut across alleys and duck beneath trucks.
    "Under Destruction"—trash chair at the curb—
    Stop to gaze on the large roman letters
    Of writing on papers that tell of Economy,

Skilsaw whine slips through the windows
Empty room—no walls—such clear air in the cellar
Dry brick, cooked clay, rusty house bodies
Carbide blade Skilsaw cuts bricks. Squalls
From the steps leading down to the subway.
Blue-chested runner, a female, on car streets,
Red lights block traffic but she like the
Beam of a streetlight in the whine of the Skilsaw,
    She runs right through.

A cross street leads toward a river
North goes to the woods
South takes you fishing
Peregrines nest at the thirty-fifth floor

Street people rolling their carts
    of whole households
Or asleep wrapped in light blue blanket
    spring evening, at dusk, in a doorway,
Eyeballing arêtes and buttresses rising above them,
    con domus, dominion,
        domus,
    condominate, condominium
Towers, up there the
Clean crisp white dress white skin
    women and men
Who occupy sunnier niches,
Higher up on the layered stratigraphy cliffs, get
More photosynthesis, flow by more ostracods,
    get more sushi,
Gather more flesh, have delightful
Cascading laughs,

    —Peregrine sails past the window
    Off the edge of the word-chain
    Harvesting concepts, theologies,
    Snapping up bites of the bits bred by
    Banking
        ideas and wild speculations
    On new information—
        and stoops in a blur on a pigeon,

As the street bottom-feeders with shopping carts
Slowly check out the air for the fall of excess,
Of too much, flecks of extra,
From the higher-up folks in the sky

    As the fine dusk gleam
    Lights a whole glass side of
    Forty some stories

Soft liquid silver,

Beautiful buildings we float in, we feed in,

Foam, steel, gray

Alive   in the Sea of Information.

Haida Gwai North Coast, Naikoon Beach, Hiellen River Raven Croaks

Twelve ravens squawk, squork, crork
over the dark tall spruce
  and down to the beach.
Two eagles squabbling, twitter, meeting,
bumping flying overhead

amber river waters
dark from muskeg acids, irons,
murk the stream of tide-wall eagre coming up
over the sandspit, through the drumming surf,
eagles, ravens, seagulls,   over surf,
Salal and cedar at the swelling river,

  wheeling birds make comment:

on gray skies, big swells, storms,
the end of summer, the fall run—
humpy salmon waiting off the bar
  and when they start upstream—

comment
on the flot and jet of sea crud
and the downriver wash of inland
hard-won forest natural trash
from an older wildness, from a climax lowland,
  virgin   system,

Mother
              Earth
loves to love.

Love hard, playing, fighting,
rough and rowdy love-rassling
she can take it, she gives it,

kissing, pounding, laughing—

up from old growth mossy bottoms
twa corbies rork and flutter

  the old food
  the new food

tangled in fall flood streams.

New Moon Tongue

        Faint new moon arc, curl,

        again in the west. Blue eve,

        deer-moving dusk.

        Purple shade in a plant-realm—

        a million years of sniffs,

              licks, lip and

        reaching tongue.

An Offering for Tārā

I

Have you seen my companion
With her moon-like forehead
Has she passed this way?

Senge Chhu, the Indus River.
Some land from Gondwana,

crossed the Tethys Sea
and fetched up against Eurasia,
ranges warping out—
Indus, Sutlej, rivers even from before
sat their seats
as mountains rose around them million-yeared.

Now town of Leh.
Tattered prayer flags on the house-roofs—
built on a bajada, a
glacier-flour and outwash gravel fan down from the hills,
built up to be fields for the barley,
all crisscrossed with ditches—

(Some questions rise:
Glaciers, and how high must they be to catch snow and make
year-round streams in a land of no rain?
Where was the hearth of high altitude barley and when did it
spread?
Did these people move here to escape some tyrant, or because
they were crazy and bold?)

Water from the icefields,
"The long wide tongue of the Buddha" led into asides,
divided down to little rock-edged channels—

wanders on the terraces,
passes through barley plots
apples and apricots, poplar stands:
finds its way back to the gorge.

Wild sheep whose horns and skulls
make a woven rooftop shrine,
—hunters came for sheep before farmers or lamas,
   but now they move rocks.

Marpa had Milarepa build stone houses many times. People
raising gravel outwash into walls and houses. Walls built within
walls, terrace stepped above terrace—mixing mud, drying
brick, moving rock: to build a *gompa* on some peak or cliff.

Alluvium carried up the slope
shaped into *gompas*, temples,
confidence, patience, good humor
in the work of hands with the stone and grit of the world.

Tabletop mandalas made
by the monks over weeks—
screek screek, goes the rasp as the sand tube
is played like a brush—sand colors,
fine-ground minerals from
cut-banks and outcroppings,
pulverized rocks from the canyons,
monk-artists making vision palaces,
maps of stages of the soul and all its pathways,
out of mountain dust. For the
puja, the ritual, the offering, the meal,

Marpa purifying Milarepa,
"Build it again!" Snapping
snap-lines, setting levels, placing stones.

II

In the lofty sky
Is the nest of a vulture
May it remain unchanged.
The unchanged bird,
May you remain unchanged.

Angdu's parents were still out in the fields so we stepped into
a half-built house up the hill, and were served both butter tea

and black tea. A little Tārā shrine in a corner, a floor-sitters
table and a small blue rug. Catty-corner on a torn-out tarp
was something drying, twiggy bunches, caraway seed-heads,

We do the Tārā mantra for the shrine—

Om tāre tuttāre ture swāhā   tāre tāre tāre
     Om tāre tuttāre ture swāhā   tāre tāre tāre
Om tāre tuttāre ture swāhā   tāre tāre tāre

———

Tārā's Vow

"Those who wish to attain supreme enlightenment
in a man's body are many . . .
therefore may I,
          until this world is emptied out,
serve the needs of beings
with my body of a woman."

These steep eroding mountains,
no place for lakes or meadows
newest mountains,
Baby Krishna Himalaya,
snowy Storehouse Mountains,
snow-basket Mountains,

Baby Himalaya loves butter,
loves dirt,

baby mountains—Ancient Buddhas—
naked Blue Samantabhadra,
Kalachakra, Yamantaka,
young eroding
Himalaya,

alpine fields of blue sheep meadow
          blue sheep love the Himalayas—

each one thinks the Himalaya
    is hers alone.

Rock stuff always folding
turned back in again, re-folded,
wrapping, twisting in and out like dough.

"Black as bees are the plaits of your hair"

III

The great Indus river's running
just there by the wall.
        (The far shore
wild salmon spawning
in old mine-tailing gravels down the Yuba)

Led to the kohlrabi, peas and potatoes,
gold-dry barley,
come songbirds,
a village with flat-roofed houses
and a flag in the breeze
always murmuring,

        Space of joy
        in the life of the moment
        Om, Mind, in Phenomena, Hum

The crooked sickle topples alfalfa,
and the sheaves are packed on their backs
husband and wife walk singing
song bounced between voices
down the stone-paved walk
to the storehouse and stables,

        and give some away.

Up in the stone towers and walkways,
apartments and chambers,
wide-ranging cloud chaos
silvery Senge Chhu curving below

fields by the river, white dot houses
        barley laid drying.

Conch blows from the rooftop
monks in maroon
chant, grin and glance,
and a boy who plays leader
makes all the bows,
Tārā, cross-legged, head tilted smiling,
hands shaping "the giving"
red body, gold body, green,

a puja, a potluck
for the whole Himalayan plateau,
—drop of chang on the tongue,
barley dough pinch,
salt tea and sliced apple—
In the temple built above the Indus
demons trample,
intestines tangling, men and women dancing screwing
head of a horse, a bull, all
painted on shadowy walls in the
Buddha hall in the sky.

—

(Tārā's love magic

From the boy's heart a red beam of light goes out through his
right ear, enters the nock of his arrow, comes out the arrow-
head, and shines straight to his loved one's vagina—menstrual
blood trickles down, he enters her mind, she becomes full of
desire.)

—

Cross-legged,
we sit on the wood floor taking
puja, the offering for Tārā,
old monks and a boy bring food

to the music of shawms.
Ibex, antelope, argali sheep, golden eagle,
over mountains and valley,
(summer sleeping on the rooftops,
Indo-Tibetan army unit
camps beside the airport
jeeps clatter up the hill toward Leh)

> *space of joy*
> *in the heart of the moment*
> prayer spins in the crankcase,

Baby Himalaya
loves butter, loves a little taste of dirt,
loves the herdgirls, loves the ibex,

> Tārā lady of the stars:

grimy-handed cutting barley,
leading water,
moving stones.

> *On the lofty mountain*
> *Is the nest of a hawk;*
> *On the lofty rock,*
> *The nest of a white hawk;*

> *The unchanged bird,*
> *May you remain unchanged.*

The Bear Mother

She veils herself
        to speak of eating salmon
    Teases me with
        "What do you know of my ways"
    And kisses me through the mountain.

Through and under its layers, its
gullies, its folds;
Her mouth full of blueberries,
We share.

Macaques in the Sky

Walking the trail with Wang Ch'ing-hua, Red Pine, Lo Ch'ing,
and Carole from Nanren Lake, we see a clear spot in the jungle
canopy of leaves—a high point arch of heavy limbs, a lookout
on the forest slope—

A mother monkey sits and nurses,

A couple perching side by side,

A face peeks from another leaf screen, pink cheeks,
shining eyes,

An old male, silver belly, furrowed face,
laid back in a crotch

harsh little cough-calls echo

faces among the leaves,
being ears and eyes of trees
soft hands and haunches pressed on boughs and vines

Then—*wha!*—she leaps out in the air
the baby dangling from her belly,

they float there,

—she fetches up along another limb—
and settles in.

Her
arching like the Milky Way,
mother of the heavens,
        crossing realm to realm
        full of stars

as we hang on beneath with all we have

enjoy her flight.
Drink her light.

Rhesus macaque.

— IV —

Old Woodrat's Stinky House

The whole universe is an ocean of dazzling light
On it dance the waves of life and death.
                                    a service for the spirits of the dead

—

Coyote and Earthmaker whirling about in the world winds
found a meadowlark nest floating and drifting; stretched it to
cover the waters and made us an earth—

Us critters hanging out together
something like three billion years.

Three hundred something million years
the solar system swings around
with all the Milky Way—

Ice ages come one hundred fifty million years apart
last about ten million
then warmer days return—

A venerable desert woodrat nest of twigs and shreds
plastered down with ambered urine
a family house in use eight thousand years,
        & four thousand years of using writing equals
the life of a bristlecone pine—

A spoken language works
for about five centuries,
lifespan of a douglas fir;
big floods, big fires, every couple hundred years,
a human life lasts eighty,
a generation twenty.

Hot summers every eight or ten,
four seasons every year
twenty-eight days for the moon
day / night   the twenty-four hours

& a song might last four minutes,

a breath is a breath.

———

      all this in 5,086 coyote scats:
Pocket gopher, elk, elk-calf, deer, field mouse,
snowshoe hare, ground squirrel, jackrabbit, deer mouse,
pine squirrel, beaver.
Jumping mouse, chipmunk, woodrat, pika.
House cat, flying squirrel. Duck, jay, owl, grebe,
fish, snake, grasshopper, cricket, grass.
Pine nuts, rose seeds, mushrooms, paper, rag, twine, orange
peel, matches, rubber, tinfoil, shoestring, paint rag, two
      pieces of a shirt—
         —The Greater Yellowstone Ecosystem—

—And around the Great Basin
people eating cattail pollen,
bullrush seeds, raw baby birds,
cooked ducks and geese,
antelope, squirrel, beetles, chub, and suckers—
ten thousand years of living
      —thousands of paleo human droppings in the
         Lovelock Cave—

Great tall woodrat heaps. Shale flakes, beads, sheep scats,
flaked points, thorns,
piled up for centuries
placed under overhangs—caves in cliffs—
at the bottom, antique fecal pellets;
orange-yellow urine-amber.
Shreds of every bush that grew eight thousand years ago;
      another rain, another name.

Cottontail boy said "Woodrat makes me puke!
Shitting on his grandmother's blankets—
stinking everything up—pissing on everything—
yucky old woodrat!
Makes his whole house stink!"

—Coyote says "You people should stay put here,
     learn your place,
               do good things. Me, I'm traveling on."

Raven's Beak River
At the End

Doab of the Tatshenshini River and the Alsek Lake, a long spit
of gravel, one clear day after days on the river in the rain, the
glowing sandy slopes of Castilleja blooms & little fox tracks
in the moose-print swales, & giant scoops of dirt took out by
bears around the lupine roots, at early light a rim of snowy
mountains and the ice fields slanting back for miles, I find
my way

                    To the boulders
                         on the gravel   in the flowers
                    At the end of the glacier
                         two ravens
                    Sitting on a boulder
                         carried by the glacier
                    Left on the gravel
                         resting in the flowers
                    At the end of the ice age
                         show me the way
                    To a place to sit
                         in a hollow on a boulder
                    Looking east, looking south
                         ear in the river
                    Running just behind me
                         nose in the grasses
                    Vetch roots scooped out
                         by the bears in the gravels
                    Looking up the ice slopes
                         ice plains, rock-fall
                    Brush-line, dirt-sweeps
                         on the ancient river
                    Blue queen floating in
                         ice lake, ice throne, end of a glacier

Looking north
   up the dancing river
Where it turns into a glacier
   under stairsteps of ice falls
Green streaks of alder
   climb the mountain knuckles
Interlaced with snowfields
   foamy water falling
Salmon weaving river
   bear flower   blue sky singer
As the raven leaves her boulder
   flying over flowers
Raven-sitting high spot
   eyes on the snowpeaks,
Nose of morning
   raindrops in the sunshine
Skin of sunlight
   skin of chilly gravel
Mind in the mountains, mind of tumbling water,
   mind running rivers,
Mind of sifting
   flowers in the gravels
At the end of the ice age
   we are the bears, we are the ravens,
We are the salmon
   in the gravel
At the end of an ice age

Growing on the gravels
   at the end of a glacier
Flying off alone
   flying off alone
   flying off alone

Off alone

Earrings Dangling and Miles of Desert

Sagebrush *(Artemisia)*, is of the sunflower family *(Astera-ceae)*. (Sage *[Salvia]* is in the family of mint.) The Great Basin sagebrush, our biggest artemisia, *Artemisia tridentata*, grows throughout the arid west. Sagebrush often lives with rabbit-brush *(Chrysothamnus)*, saltbush *(Atriplex)*, and greasewood *(Sarcobatus)*. As a foursome they typify one of the largest plant communities in North America.

> —brushy, bushy, stringybark cobwebby tangle
> multi-stemmed, forking,
> twiglets jut sidewise, a scatter of silky tiny leaves,
> dry twigs stick up straight;
>   a lizard scooting in the frizzy dust—

It is eaten by sagebrush voles, pygmy rabbits, sage grouse, and pronghorn (which can browse it: the plant contains an oil that inhibits microbes in the rumen of cows so that they cannot digest it. Sheep can eat a little. Elk eat it and belch a lot). It is a home to mourning doves, night hawks, sage thrashers, shrikes, and sage sparrows.

The bark has been used by humans for tens of thousands of years. The shreddy fiber makes bags, nets, shawls, and sandals. It is used by ranchers and Indians alike for firewood. The leaves are burned as a purifying incense or a mosquito-repellant smoke. It is used as a tea for stomach disorders by the Hopi, who call it *wi:'kwapi*. The edible seeds are gathered by the Cahuilla, who also make an herbal tea from it. They call it *wikwat*. Another smaller artemisia, *Artemisia californica*, is used by the Cahuilla for a women's tonic.

Sagebrush: in northern Paiute called *sawabi*, in southern Paiute *sangwabi*.

> Artemisia,
> who lives across the ranges,
> stretching for miles,
>   she's always there:

with saltbush and greasewood, with rabbitbrush
and all the little grasses.
Her blue-gray-green—

In Europe, plants of the sagebrush group are known as worm-
wood. The wormwood *absinthium* gives the flick of danger
to the drink absinthe—"sagebrush of the glaciers," said Rim-
baud. Pernod is the same drink minus wormwood. Tarragon's
a wormwood—

Artemisia is worldwide—thirty species in Japan alone. It's the
mugwort and moxa of China. Wormwood is sacred to Artemis.
Narrow leaves glow silver in her moonlight—

> "She loves to hunt
> in the shadows of mountains
> and in the wind"——

Artem in Greek meant "to dangle" or "earring."
(Well-connected, "articulate," art. . . .)

> Her blue-gray-green
> stretching out there
> sagebrush flats reach to the edge
> bend away—
> emptiness far as the mind can see—

> Raincloud maidens come walking
>   lightning-streak silver,
> gray skirts sweeping and trailing—

Hail, Artemisia,
aromatic in the rain,
I will think of you in my other poems.

Cross-Legg'd
for Carole

Cross-legg'd under the low tent roof,
dim light, dinner done,

drinking tea. We live
in dry old west

lift shirts bare skin
lean   touch lips—

old touches.
Love made, poems, makyngs,

always new, same stuff
life after life,

as though Milarepa
four times built a tower of stone

like each time was the first.
Our love is mixed with

rocks and streams,
a heartbeat, a breath, a gaze

makes place in the dizzy eddy.
Living this old clear way

—a sizzle of ash and embers.
Scratchy breeze on the tent fly

one sip tea, hunch on bones,
we two be here   what comes.

Afloat

Floating in a tiny boat
lightly on the water, rock with every ripple,

another skin that slides along the water
hung by sea and sky

green mountains turn to clouds
and slip slow by

two-mile saltwater channel
sucks and coils   with the tide,

kayak like a cricket husk—
        like an empty spider egg case,
like dried kelp fronds,
like a dry cast skin of a snake,
like froth on the lip of a wave,

trembles on the membrane
paddling forward, paddling backward

crossing at an angle to the
roiling shallow bars

the mountain slides, the moon slides,
the waters churn together,
the near bank races onward,

twin kayak paddles turn and glint like wings
casting spume,
there is no place we are
but maybe here

sky and water stitched together
with the oystercatchers screaming steady flight
the kittiwakes deliberate beat of wing
the murres bob up from underworlds
the seals heads dip back to it
the terns erratic dive and splash

the ravens tweet and croak and gurgle in the far-off
outflow alders;

wind ripples westward, the tide goes east,
we paddle east southeast
the world a rush of wings and waters,

up the slopes the mountain glacier
looses icemelt over gravel in a soft far roar
that joins the inlet-basin world of cries and whistles

(and all this realm was under icefields ten miles long,
when my grandfather drove his team
to pick berries at Port Orchard)

the glaciers shift and murmur like the tides
under the constant cross-current
steady drum of bird wings
full of purpose, some direction,
all for what
in the stroke
in the swirl of the float

we are two souls in one body,
two sets of wings, our paddles swing
where land meets   water   meets   the sky,

where judges and speechmakers, actresses and carpenters,
drop their masks and go on as they were,
as
petrels, geese, oystercatchers, murrelets,
and small fish fry,

in the tide-suck dark draft sea,
floating in the weaving

of clouds, ice, tides, calls
—only to be here!

The tiny skin boat.

The Dance

"Against its will, energy is doing something productive,
like the devil in medieval history. The principle is that
nature does something against its own will and,
by self-entanglement, produces beauty."

Otto Rössler

Izanami
gave birth to rocks, trees, rivers, mountains, grass
and last, a blazing child
        so burned she died.

    In the land of darkness
    a mass of pollution.

    Ah wash her clear stream

    —skinny   little   girl   with   *big* ears
    we have passed through
            passed through,   flesh out of flesh.

                        ⸺

"Shining Heavens," Goddess of the Sun,
        her brother flung
                mud and shit and a half-skinned pony through
                the palace,
    so she entered a cave—shut it up with a rock—
        made the world dark.

                        ⸺

Ame-no-uzume, "Outrageous Heavenly Woman," wrapped
the numinous club-moss of Mt. Kagu round her hips, made
a headband from the leaves of nishikigi, bound bamboo grass
for her wristlets, and put a sounding-board down before the
cave where the Sun Goddess stayed.
    She danced and she stamped til it echoed around, she danced
like a goddess possessed, pulled out her nipples, pushed her
sash down til she showed herself down below, and the Plain

of High Heaven shook with the laughs and the cheers and the
whistles of thousands of gods who were gathered to watch.

Jean Herbert

———

The whole river. Clear back to each creeklet
rock-rimmed,
    all one basin drawing in the threads
pacing down dry riverbeds the dance,
    mai, stomping, stepping on the gravelly bar
step, stop, stamp of the foot. Glide and turn,

        headwaters, mountains,
            breathing icy bliss

diamond-glittered bitty snowcreek
eating the inorganic granite down.

Trees once cooled the air, and clouds, ah, ghost of
    water
    springs gone dry. Hills of Yugoslavia clearcut
        for the Roman fleet
    —don't think all that topsoil's gone
        it only waits.

    —slept on river sidebars
        drank from muddy streams
        grains cooked in rock-flour glacier water,
        —dirt left on boulders
        for a sandy heap of years,

and creeks meander   just because they swing.

Stamp of the masked dancer
    pacing tangled channels
        putting salt and gold dust in the sea.

———

Ame-no-uzume-no-mikoto bound up her sleeves with a cord
of heavenly *hi-kage* vine, tied around her head a head-band
of the heavenly *ma-saki* vine, bound together bundles of sasa
leaves to hold in her hands, and overturning a bucket before
the heavenly rock-cave door, stamped resoundingly upon it.
Then she became divinely possessed, exposed her breasts, and
pushed her skirt-band down to her genitals.

Allan Grapard

—

Laughter roared like thunder
        through the plains of heaven
and the hidden
        Goddess of the Sun,
        Amaterasu,
        peeked out round the rock.

All the little faces of the gods gleamed
        white   in the light!

omoshiri.

—

	Herbert	*Grapard*
Around her head:	nishikigi leaves	masaki vines
In her hands:		sasa
As wristlets:	bamboo grass	
sleeves tied w/:		hi-kage vine
around her hips:	club moss	

—

Ame no uzume.
What did she wear?
What leaves in her hair?

How far did she push her skirt down?

We Wash Our Bowls in This Water
"The 1.5 billion cubic kilometers of water on the earth are
split by photosynthesis and reconstituted by respiration
once every two million years or so."

A day on the ragged North Pacific coast get soaked by whip-
ping mist, rainsqualls tumbling, mountain mirror ponds,
snowfield slush, rock-wash creeks, earfulls of falls, sworls of
ridge-edge snowflakes, swift gravelly rivers, tidewater crumbly
glaciers, high hanging glaciers, shore-side mud pools, icebergs,
streams looping through the tideflats, spume of brine, distant
soft rain drooping from a cloud,

sea lions lazing under the surface of the sea—

> We wash our bowls in this water
> It has the flavor of ambrosial dew—

> Ga shi sempasui
> Nyoten kanro mi

———

Beaching the raft, stagger out and shake off wetness like a
        bear,
stand on the sandbar, rest from the river   being

upwellings, sideswirls, backswirls
curl-overs, outripples, eddies, chops and swells
wash-overs, shallows   confluence turbulence   wash-seam
wavelets, riffles, saying

"A hydraulic's a cross between a wave and a hole,
  —you get a weir effect.
Pillow-rock's a total fold-back over a hole,
    it shows spit on the top of the wave
a haystack's a series of waves at the bottom of a tight
    channel
    there's a tongue of the rapids—the slick tongue—the
    'v'—
some holes are 'keepers,' they won't let you through;
eddies, backflows, we say 'eddies are your friends.'
Current differential, it can suck you down
vertical boils are straight-up eddies spinning,
herringbone waves curl under and come back.
Well, let's get going, get back to the rafts."
        Swing the big oars,
              head into a storm.

      We offer it to all demons and spirits
      May all be filled and satisfied.
      Om makula sai svaha!

      Seyo kijin shu
      Shitsuryô toku hôman
      Om makura sai sowaka

                    ——

Su Tung-p'o sat out one whole night by a creek   on the slopes
of Mt. Lu. Next morning he showed this poem to his teacher:

    The stream with its sounds   is a long broad tongue
    The looming mountain   is a wide-awake body
    Throughout the night   song after song
    How can I   speak at dawn.

Old Master Chang-tsung approved him. Two centuries later
Dōgen said,
    "Sounds of streams and shapes of mountains.
    The sounds never stop and the shapes never cease.
    Was it Su who woke

or was it the mountains and streams?
Billions of beings see the morning star
and all become Buddhas!
If *you*, who are valley streams and looming
mountains,
can't throw some light on the nature of ridges and rivers,

who can?"

The Mountain Spirit

Ceaseless wheel of lives
ceaseless wheel of lives

red sandstone;
gleaming dolomite

ceaseless wheel of lives

red sandstone and white dolomite.

Driving all night south from Reno
through cool-porched Bridgeport,
past Mono Lake's pale glow,
past tongues of obsidian flow stopped chill,
and the angled granite face
of the east Sierra front—

                    Ah. Here I am arrived in Bishop,
Owens Valley, called Payahu Nadu not so long ago.

Ranger Station on main street,
"I'm a traveler.
I want to know the way
to the White Mountains,
& the bristlecone pines."
She gives me maps. "Here. The trail
to the grove at timberline

where the oldest living beings
thrive on rock and air."

"—Thank you for your help."

> I go to the pass, turn north,
> end of day, climbing high,
> find an opening where a
> steep dirt side road halts.
> A perch in the round dry hills,
> prickly pinyon pine boughs shade,
> a view to the Last Chance range,
> & make a camp.

Nearby, a rocky point.
            Climb it,
passing a tidy scat-arrangement on a ledge,
stand on a dark red sandstone strata outcrop at the edge.
Plane after plane of desert ridges
darkening eastward into blue-black haze.

A voice says

"You had a bit of fame once in the city
for poems of mountains,
            here it's real."

What?

"Yes. Like the lines

> *Walking on walking*
> *under foot   earth turns*

But what do you know of minerals and stone.
For a creature to speak of all that scale of time—what for?

Still, I'd like to hear that poem."

            I answer back,
"—Tonight is the night of the shooting stars,

Mirfak the brilliant star of Perseus
      crosses the ridge at midnight

I'll read it then."

      Who am I talking to? I think,
walk back to camp.

—

Evening breeze up from the flats
from the valleys "Salt" and "Death"—
Venus and the new moon sink in a deep blue glow
      behind the Palisades to the west,
needle-clusters shirring in the wind—
listen close, the sound gets better.

Mountain ranges violet haze back fading in the east
puffs of sailing dark-lit cloud, a big owl's
swift soft whip between the trees,
unroll the bedding, stretch out blankets on the
crunchy dry pine needles sun-warm
      resinous ground.

Formations dip and strike my sleep.

. . . .

—Approaching in a dream:

      "Bitter ghosts that kick their own skulls like a ball
      happy ghosts that stick a flower
            into their old skull's empty eye—
      'good and evil'
            —that's another stupid dream—
      for streams and mountains
            clouds and glaciers,
        is there ever an escape?

      Erosion always wearing down;
      shearing, thrusting, deep plates crumpling,

still uplifting—ice-carved cirques
dendritic endless fractal streambed riffs on hillsides

—bitter ghosts that kick their own skulls like a ball
what's it all for?"

A meteor swift and streaking
like a tossed white pebble
arcing down the sky—

the Mountain Spirit stands there.
Old woman? white ragged hair?
in the glint of Algol, Altair, Deneb,
Sadr, Aldebaran—saying, "I came to hear—"

I can't say no: I speak

THE MOUNTAIN SPIRIT

Walking on walking,
under foot   earth turns

Streams and mountains never stay the same.

Walking on walking,
under foot   earth turns

Streams and mountains never stay the same.

Into earth   rock dives.

As the mountains lift and open
underground out,
        dust over seashell, layers of ooze,
display how it plays.

Buttresses fractured, looming,
friction only, soon to fall, each face
a heap of risks

talus slopes below
flakes weathered off the buried block,
            tricked off an old pluton,
and settle somewhere, ever lower down—
gives a glimpse
of streaks and strains, warp and slide,
abraded gritty mudwash glide
        where cliffs lean
                to the raven-necklace sky—

        Calcium spiraling shells,
no land plants then when
sands and stones flush down the
barren flanks of magma-swollen uplands
slurry to the beach,
ranges into rubble, old shores buried by debris
a lapping trough of tide flats and lagoons
lime-rich wave-wash soothing shales and silts
a thousand miles of chest-deep reef
seabottom riffled, wave-swirled, turned and tilled
by squiggly slime-swimmers many-armed,
        millions of tiny different tracks
        crisscrossing through the mud—

trilobite winding salt sludge,
calcite ridges, diatom babies drifting home,
swash of quartzy sand
        three hundred million years
                be rolling on   and then

ten million years ago an ocean floor
glides like a snake beneath the continent crunching up
old seabed till it's high as alps.
Sandstone layers script of winding tracks
        and limestone shines like snow
        where ancient beings grow.

"When the axe-strokes stop
        the silence grows deeper—"

Peaks like Buddhas   at the heights
        send waters streaming down
to the deep center of the turning world.

And the Mountain Spirit always wandering
            hillsides fade like walls of cloud
            pebbles smoothed off sloshing in the sea

        old woman mountain hears
shifting sand
        tell the wind
                "nothingness is shapeliness"

Mountains will be Buddhas then

        when—bristlecone needles are green!
        Scarlet penstemon
                flowers are red!

(Mountains feed the people too
stories from the past
        of pine-nut gathering baskets quickly full
        of help at grinding, carrying, healing—)

Ghosts of lost landscapes
        herds and flocks,
                towns and clans,
great teachers from all lands
tucked in Wovoka's empty hat,
        stored in Baby Krishna's mouth,
                kneeling for tea
in Vimalakīīrti's one small room.

Goose flocks
        crane flocks
                Lake Lahontan come again!

        Walking on walking,
        under foot   earth turns.

The Mountain Spirit whispers back:
"All art and song
is sacred to the real.
As such."

Bristlecone pines live long

on the taste of carbonate,
                    dolomite,

spiraled standing coiling
dead wood with the living,
four thousand years of mineral glimmer
spaced out growing in the icy airy sky
white bones under summer stars.

—The Mountain Spirit and me

like ripples of the Cambrian Sea

dance the pine tree

old arms, old limbs, twisting, twining

scatter cones across the ground

stamp the root-foot DOWN

                and then she's gone.

Ceaseless wheel of lives
red sandstone and white dolomite.

            A few more shooting stars
            back to the bedroll, sleep till dawn.

Earth Verse

Wide enough to keep you looking

Open enough to keep you moving

Dry enough to keep you honest

Prickly enough to make you tough

Green enough to go on living

Old enough to give you dreams

Finding the Space in the Heart

I first saw it in the sixties,
driving a Volkswagen camper
with a fierce gay poet and a
lovely but dangerous girl with a husky voice,

we came down from Canada
on the dry east side of the ranges. Grand Coulee, Blue
Mountains, lava flow caves,
the Alvord desert—pronghorn ranges—
and the glittering obsidian-paved
dirt track toward Vya,
seldom-seen roads late September and
thick frost at dawn; then
follow a canyon and suddenly open to
        silvery flats that curved over the edge

> *O, ah! The*
> *awareness of emptiness*
> *brings forth a heart of compassion!*

We followed the rim of the playa
to a bar where the roads end
and over a pass into Pyramid Lake
from the Smoke Creek side,
by the ranches of wizards

who follow the tipi path.
The next day we reached San Francisco
in a time when it seemed
the world might head a new way.

And again, in the seventies, back from
Montana, I recklessly pulled off the highway
took a dirt track onto the flats,
got stuck—scared the kids—slept the night,
and the next day sucked free and went on.

Fifteen years passed. In the eighties
With my lover I went where the roads end.
Walked the hills for a day,
looked out where it all drops away,
discovered a path
of carved stone inscriptions tucked into the sagebrush

"Stomp out greed"
"The best things in life are not things"
—DeWayne Williams

words placed by an old desert sage.

Faint shorelines seen high on these slopes,
long gone Lake Lahontan,
cutthroat trout spirit in silt—
Columbian Mammoth bones
four hundred feet up on the wave-etched
        beach ledge; curly-horned
            desert sheep outlines pecked into the rock,

and turned the truck onto the playa
heading for know-not,
bone-gray dust boiling and billowing,
mile after mile, trackless and featureless,
let the car coast to a halt
on the crazed cracked
flat hard face where
winter snow spirals, and

summer sun bakes like a kiln.
Off nowhere, to be or not be,

    all equal, far reaches, no bounds.
    Sound swallowed away,
    no waters, no mountains, no
    bush no grass and
        because no grass
    no shade but your shadow.
    No flatness because no not-flatness.
    No loss, no gain. So—
    nothing in the way!
    —the ground is the sky
    the sky is the ground,
    no place between, just

    wind-whip breeze,
    tent-mouth leeward,
    time being here.
    We meet heart to heart,
    leg hard-twined to leg,
        with a kiss that goes to the bone.
    Dawn sun comes straight in the eye. The tooth
    of a far peak called King Lear.

Now in the nineties desert night
    —my lover's my wife—
old friends, old trucks, drawn around;
great arcs of kids on bikes out there in darkness
    no lights—just planet Venus glinting
by the calyx crescent moon,

and tasting grasshoppers roasted in a pan.

    They all somehow swarm down here—
    sons and daughters in the circle
    eating grasshoppers grimacing,

singing sūtras for the insects in the wilderness,

—the wideness, the
foolish loving spaces

full of heart.

> *Walking on walking,*
> *under foot   earth turns*

> *Streams and mountains never stay the same.*

The space goes on.
But the wet black brush
tip drawn to a point,
lifts away.

Marin-an 1956–Kitkitdizze 1996

The Making of *Mountains and Rivers Without End*

As a student at Reed College I had the good fortune to study with the brilliant polymath Lloyd Reynolds, who was—among many things—a remarkable calligrapher in the Renaissance Italic mode. It was from Lloyd I learned to appreciate the pen, whether reed, turkey feather, or carefully hand-ground alloy steel tip. One of Lloyd's students was Charles Leong, a Chinese-American veteran back from World War II and studying on the GI Bill. He was already an accomplished seal carver and brush calligrapher of Chinese; with Charlie as my guide, I learned to hold the brush as well as the pen.

I had been introduced to the high snow peaks of the Pacific Northwest when I was thirteen and had climbed a number of summits even before I was twenty: I was forever changed by that place of rock and sky. East Asian landscape paintings, seen at the Seattle Art Museum from the age of ten on, also presented such a space. While at Reed I stumbled onto Ernest Fenollosa's *Epochs of Chinese and Japanese Art*, which gave me further guidance into Asian art. Fenollosa also led me to the translations of Ezra Pound.

After a brief spell of graduate study in anthropological linguistics, I entered graduate school in Oriental languages at the University of California at Berkeley. I also signed up for a class in sumi—East Asian brush painting—in the art department. The instructor was an intense, diminutive Japanese man named Chiura Obata. Obata had us grinding ink seriously and working with an array of brushes; we learned by trying to match his fierce, swift strokes that made pine needles, bamboo stalks, eucalyptus leaves appear as if by magic on the white paper. He was a naturalized citizen who had been in an internment camp—I learned little else about him. Though I lacked talent, my practice with soot-black ink and brush tuned my eye for looking more closely at paintings. In museums and through books I became aware of how the energies of mist, white water, rock formations, air swirls—a chaotic universe where everything is in place—are so much a part of the East Asian painter's world. In Hugo Munsterberg's little book on Chinese landscape painting I came upon a reference to a hand scroll *(shou-chuan)* called *Mountains and Rivers Without End.* The name stuck in my mind.

While a student at Berkeley I spent summers working in the mountains, in National Parks or Forests. Two seasons on lookouts (Crater Mountain in 1952, Sourdough Mountain in 1953) in what was then the Mount Baker National Forest, not far south of the Canadian border, gave me full opportunity to watch the change of mood over vast landscapes, light moving with the day—the countless clouds, the towering cumulus, black thunderstorms rolling in with jagged lightning strikes. The prolonged stay in mountain huts also gave me my first opportunity to seriously sit cross-legged, in the practical and traditional posture of Buddhist meditation. Back in Berkeley, I became acquainted with the warm, relaxed, familial, and devotional Buddhism of traditional Asia in the atmosphere of the Berkeley Buddhist church, presided over by Reverend Kanmo Imamura and his gracious and tireless wife, Jane. Their Jodoshin, or "Pure Land," Buddhism is one of infinite generosity that had come to California with the Japanese immigrants of the early twentieth century. In Berkeley it was open to all. Jodoshin and Zen are both in the Mahayana tradition; I soaked up Mahayana sūtras and traditional commentaries, Chinese and Japanese Ch'an texts, and Vajrayana writing through those years, taking delight in their scale of imagination and their fearless mytho-psychological explorations.

Thoughts of that time, along with a half year spent working as a logger in eastern Oregon, took shape in a poem sequence I called *Myths and Texts.* This sequence was my first venture into the long poem and the challenge of interweaving physical life and inward realms. While studying literary Chinese and modern Japanese languages and practicing traditional calligraphy with the brush, I was also finishing up *Myths and Texts.* The final touches were done in a small abandoned cabin I found in Marin County, California, in early 1956.

My interest in Zen led me to the lectures of Alan Watts, founder of the Academy of Asian Studies in San Francisco, and we came to be friends on the basis of our shared taste for Italic calligraphy as much as our Buddhist interests. In the winter of 1955–56 a remarkable artist from Japan, Saburo Hasegawa, was in residence at the Academy of Asian Studies. I attended some of Hasegawa's lectures. I never saw him wearing West-ern clothes: He was always in formal kimono and *hakama*. He spoke of East Asian landscape painting as a meditative exercise. I think he once said that the landscape paintings were for Zen as instructively and deeply Buddhist as the tankas and mandalas are for Tibetan Buddhism.

At some point Hasegawa heard that I had never tasted the ceremonial powdered green tea, and he delightedly invited me to his apartment. I still remember the day, April 8, 1956, because it was also the Buddha's birthday. He frothed up the tea with a bamboo whisk, we chatted, and he talked at length about the great Japanese Zen monk painter Sesshū. As I left that day I resolved to start another long poem that would be called *Mountains and Rivers Without End*.

One month later I headed west for the East on a Japanese passenger-freighter. In Kyoto I lived in the Rinzai Zen temple compound of Shokoku-ji. I immediately hiked the local hilly forests, found the trails and shrines, and paid my respects to the local *kami*. In my small spare time I read geology and geomor-phology. I came to see the yogic implications of "mountains" and "rivers" as the play between the tough spirit of willed self-discipline and the generous and loving spirit of concern for all beings: a dyad presented in Buddhist iconography as the wisdom-sword-wielding Manjushri, embodying transcendent insight, and his partner, Tārā, the embodiment of compassion, holding a lotus or a vase. I could imagine this dyad as paralleled in the dynamics of mountain uplift, subduction, erosion, and the planetary water cycle.

I began to attend Nō performances, and became an aficio-nado of Nō history and aesthetics. Over ten years I was able to attend a large number of plays, seeing some of them several times over. Nō is a gritty but totally refined high-culture art that is in the lineage of shamanistic performance, a drama that by means of voice and dance calls forth the spirit realms. I began to envision *Mountains and Rivers* through the dramatic strategies of Nō. The great play *Yamamba* ("Old Mountain Woman") especially fascinated me. But I never lost my sense of belonging to North America, and I kept nourishing the images and practices that kept me connected to a sense of the ancient, sacred Turtle Island landscape.

Most of the sixties I spent in Japan. One break was to work nine months on a tanker that went between Persian Gulf and mid-Pacific oil ports. When I got back to Kyoto, Cid Corman was there and had started publishing *Origin* Magazine. Early sections of *Mountains and Rivers* appeared there. Others came out in James Koller's *Coyote's Journal*. A visit to the United States in 1964 got me back into the High Sierra, a refreshing return to the realm of rock and ice. In the course of that visit I showed Donald Allen, the editor, translator, and publisher, what I had been up to. He brought out a small book of the sections to date, under the title *Six Sections from Mountains and Rivers Without End*.

Although my main reason for being in Kyoto was to do Zen Buddhist practice, I was also fortunate enough to make contact with Yamabushi, the Mountain Buddhists, and I was given a chance to see how walking the landscape can become both ritual and meditation. I did the five-day pilgrimage on the Omine ridge and established a tentative relationship with the archaic Buddhist mountain deity Fudo. This ancient exercise has one visualizing the hike from peak to valley floor as an inner linking of the womb and diamond mandala realms of Vajrayana Buddhism.

I was now studying under the Rōshi of Daitoku-ji and had moved into my own place, a ten-minute walk from the monastery. I shared the little house with a highly cultured, mature woman named Yaeko Hosaka Nakamura, a student of Nō singing. For more than five years I was soaked in the *utai* chants from *Yamamba* and other Nō plays. Her full, strong voice belted out the eerie melodies from her room upstairs. I even tried chanting with her, but soon gave up.

I got to see rare Japanese and Chinese scrolls in the richly endowed Buddhist temples of Kyoto, especially those of Daitoku-ji. Poems for *Mountains and Rivers* kept showing up at the rate of about one a year. I was writing other poems at the same time, but in a different and more lyrical mode.

In 1969 I returned to live on Turtle Island. More sections got written and they often appeared in Clayton Eshleman's *Caterpillar*. (Eshleman had been a number of years in Kyoto and it was there I first met him.) Later sections have appeared in his magazine *Sulfur*. I moved with my family to the northern Sierra

Nevada in the Yuba River country and developed a farmstead in the pine-oak forest.

I supported my family through the seventies and eighties by giving readings and talks around the country. Along with that I was able to visit most of the major collections of East Asian paintings in the United States, and several in Europe and Asia. In Cleveland I saw the anonymous Sung Dynasty *Streams and Mountains Without End*, the one that is described in the poem by that name. In earlier years the curators at the Freer generously let me have two private viewings of Lu Yüan's Ch'ing scroll called *Mountains and Rivers Without End*—most likely the very one that first came to my attention in Munsterberg's book, but it was too large to bring over into this poem. I roamed the Nelson Gallery in Kansas City, the Honolulu Academy of Arts, the Boston Museum of Fine Arts; and in Europe the British Museum and the Stockholm National Museum. I had always made good use of The Asian Art Museum of San Francisco. Finally I managed to get to the Palace Museum in Beijing and the huge Palace Museum in Taipei, where I was deeply moved to see calligraphy from the hand of Su Shih himself. Gazing at these many paintings was each time a mysteriously enlarging experience.

In the late seventies my thinking was invigorated by the translations from Dōgen's *Treasury of the True Dharma Eye* just then beginning to come out. His *Mountains and Waters Sūtra* is a pearl of a text. It made me think more about rivers. What with mountaineering and seasonal labor I had plenty of firsthand experience with mountains, so now I studied waters, spinning and dashing down many a rapids in rowdy and convivial company. And, starting from when I returned to the Pacific coast, I gradually extended my range of walked-in landscapes. North to Alaska, as far as the Brooks Range and the Arctic Sea; south to the Southwestern U.S. and the length of Baja California. Overseas I spent time in the Central Australian Desert; traveled in the Himalayan nation of Ladakh; visited China; and made a brief visit to the wilder parts of Taiwan. I crossed the pass and went east into the Great Basin frequently. I went back into old High Sierra haunts and took some sweet and reflective treks.

At some point I became aware of the powerful light-filled watercolor paintings and color woodblocks of California mountain landscapes that had been done by my old teacher Chiura Obata. It turned out that he had explored and sketched the Sierra high country many times, beginning in the 1920s.

During the last twenty years my sense of the poem has also been enlarged by several other experiences: walking visits to major urban centers; working alongside my brilliant and cranky neighbors in the Sierra foothills; laboring hands-on at forest and ecosystem management chores; studies of landscape and forest ecology; the lessons of our local watershed, getting down to the details of its tiniest rivulets and hillocks; and the joys and teachings that come with family life—my wife Carole and my sons Kai and Gen and daughters Mika and Robin.

By the 1990s I was teaching part-time at the University of California at Davis, 108 miles away in the broad Sacramento Valley. I turned my full attention to the thought of *Mountains and Rivers*. In April 1996, on the fortieth anniversary of that tea with Saburo Hasegawa, a few of us old mountain-Buddhist-poetry types got together again in San Francisco: to remember old comrades, to declare this project ended, and to lift a cup to "the supreme theme of art and song." The T'ang poet Po Chü-i said, "I have long had the desire that my actions in this world and any problems caused by my crazy words and extravagant language *[kyōgen kigo]* will in times to come be transformed into a clarification of the Dharma, and be but another way to spread the Buddha's teachings." May it be so!

People used to say to me, with a knowing smile, "*Mountains and Rivers* is endless, isn't it?" I never thought so. Landscapes are endless in their own degree, but I knew my time with this poem would eventually end. The form and the emptiness of the Great Basin showed me where to close it; and the boldness of my young people, who ate unlikely manna in the wilderness, how. This poem, which I have come to think of as a sort of sūtra—an extended poetic, philosophic, and mythic narrative of the female Buddha Tārā—is for them.

Notes

Endless Streams and Mountains

Colophons, reproduction of the handscroll, and commentary can be found in Sherman Lee and Wen Fong, *Streams and Mountains Without End* (1967). Most of the colophon/poem translations are my own.

The East Asian landscape paintings invite commentary. In a way the painting is not fully realized until several centuries of poems have been added.

A note on Chinese landscape paintings: There were very early scenes of hills and woods in China, on silk or plastered walls, but they were full of deer and other animals, or dream creatures, or people, or some combination. Paintings of large vistas did not appear until around the tenth century. This was after two and a half millennia of self-aware civilization in the basins of the Ho and Chiang. They are at their most vigorous from mid-Sung through the Yüan and early Ming—exactly when much of China was becoming deforested.

After the Yüan dynasty large-scale "Mountains and Waters" paintings became less important, and the painter's eye moved closer; some call them "Rocks and Trees" paintings. Later paintings drew even closer to give us pictures of "Birds and Flowers," *hua-niao*, precise and lovely, and superb sumi sketches of insects, gourds, melons, and leaves.

Old Bones

This poem is for Paul Shepard.

Three Worlds, Three Realms, Six Roads

The title derives from Buddhist terms. The "three worlds" are periods of time: past, present, and future. The "three realms," *triloka*, describe the universe in terms of desire, form, and formlessness. The "six paths" are territories of psychological passage: the hells, the animals, the humans, delightful gods and goddesses, angry warrior-geniuses, and hungry ghosts.

Bubbs Creek Haircut

This poem is for Locke McCorkle.

Shiva, the "Destroyer" of the Hindu trinity, is practicing in the mountains. His lover and yogic partner is Parvati.

The Blue Sky

This section is an exploration of some of the lore of healing as found in Mahayana Buddhism and in Native North America. Bhaishajyaguru (Sanskrit)—the "Medicine Buddha"—is known in Japan as Yakushi Nyorai. He holds a tiny medicine bottle in the palm of one hand. Eons ago he made a vow to work for the welfare and healing of all sentient beings.

Another element is the ancient lore of the protective and healing powers of the color blue and of certain blue stones.

The character *k'ung*, used for the Buddhist term *shunyata* or "emptiness" in Chinese, also means "sky." I was once told by a Native California elder that the diagnostic and healing hand of a "trembling-hand healer's hand" was guided by an eagle so high up in the sky as to be out of sight.

The Hump-backed Flute Player

Ancient rock art—petroglyphs—of a walking flute-playing figure, sometimes with a hump on his back, are found widely in the Southwest and into Mexico. These images are several thousand years old. There is a Hopi secret society that takes the Flute-player as its emblem. Some of the figures have an erect penis, and some have feelers on their heads that look like insect antennae.

It has been suggested that the hump is possibly a pack, and that the figure may represent Aztec or Toltec wandering traders, who once came up into the Southwest with trade items. In Peru even today you can see young men with a sort of sling-pack on their backs, carrying a load and playing the flute while walking.

Gary Paul Nabhan and I were reflecting on Kokop'ele a few years ago, and were entertained by the thought that it might be *seeds* that he was carrying! As a possible emblem of genetic diversity his work is not over: guardianship and preservation, not just of plants and animals, but of peoples and cultures as well.

Hsüan Tsang, the Buddhist scholar-pilgrim, brought back the famed "Heart Sutra"—the one-page condensation of the whole philosophy of transcendent wisdom—in his pack. Once he had translated it into Chinese it was set in movable type—the first text to be printed this way, it is said.

Note: "White man" here is not a racial designation, but a name for a certain set of mind. When we all become born-again natives of Turtle Island, then the "white man" will be gone.

The Circumambulation of Mt. Tamalpais

This poem is for Philip Whalen and Allen Ginsberg.

Walking meditation, circumambulation, *pradakshina*, is one of the most ancient human spiritual exercises. On such walks one stops at notable spots to sing a song, or to chant invocations and praises, such as mantras, songs, or little sūtras.

The Canyon Wren

This poem is for James and Carol Katz.

The Stanislaus River comes out of the central Sierra. The twists and turns of the river, the layering, swirling stone cliffs of the gorges, are cut in nine-million-year-old latites. We ran the river to see its face once more before it went under the rising water of the New Melones Dam. The song of the canyon wren stayed with us the whole time.

Arctic Midnight Twilight . . .

This poem is for Peter Coyote.

Under the Hills Near the Morava River

Excavations by Bohuslav Klima at the Dolni Vestonice site in the Pavlovske Kopce hills of southern Moravia (Czech Republic).

Haida Gwai North Coast, Naikoon Beach

This poem is for Sherman Paul.

An Offering for Tārā

Out of the upper Indus River watershed, on the Western Tibetan Plateau, around Ladakh and its main town of Leh.

Tārā, "She Who Brings Across," is a female Buddha of both Compassion and Wisdom. She is one of the most revered figures in Buddhism, especially in Tibet, Mongolia, and Nepal.

Old Woodrat's Stinky House

Coyote diet from Adolph Murie, *Ecology of the Coyote in the Yellowstone* (Washington, D. C.: U. S. Government Printing Office *Conservation Bulletin* 4, 1940).

Human diet from David Perlman, "An Earthly Approach," the research of Robert Heizer and students on six thousand ancient human droppings found in the Lovelock Cave north of Fallon, Nevada (*San Francisco Chronicle*, July 14, 1969).

Prehistory of woodrat nests in the Great Basin from Julio Betancourt, Thomas Van Devender, and Paul Martin, eds., *Packrat Middens* (Tucson: University of Arizona Press, 1990).

Cottontail boys and woodrat, part of a tale from William Shipley, ed., *The Maidu Myths and Tales of Hanc'ibyjim* (Berkeley: Heyday, 1991).

Raven's Beak River

This poem is for Edward Schafer.

Earrings Dangling and Miles of Desert

This poem is for Ursula Le Guin.

The Dance

Otto Rössler as cited in James Gleick, *Chaos: Making a New Science* (1987), 142.

Jean Herbert's *Kojiki* translation from his *Shinto* (1967).

Allan Grapard's translation from the same episode in "Visions of Excess," *Japanese Journal of Religious Studies* 18:1 (March 1991).

We Wash Our Bowls in This Water

This poem incorporates a Zen training-hall meal verse. Su Shih (Su Tung-p'o) was the great eleventh-century Chinese poet and Zen adept. This was his "enlightenment poem." The translation is my own. Dōgen gave a lecture on it to his students some two centuries later.

"Two million years": Preston Cloud and Aharon Gibor, "Oxygen Cycle," *Biosphere* (San Francisco: Scientific American Books/Freeman, 1970).

The Mountain Spirit

This poem somewhat follows the Nō play *Yamamba* (Old
Mountain Woman), a play of the "supernatural being" class,
written in the "aged style" of "quiet heart and distant eye."

There are stands of bristlecone pine, *Pinus longaeva*, in the
mountains at the western edge of the Great Basin that contain
individual trees that are dated as more than four thousand
years old. They are thought to be the oldest living beings.

Wovoka was the visionary founder of the Ghost Dance
religion. He had a big hat that he sometimes let his followers
peek inside: They said it contained all the wildlife and native
homelands of the pre-white world.

Lord Krishna, when a baby, sometimes ate dirt. Once when
his Mother tried to take a lump of dirt off his tongue, he play-
fully let her see the whole universe with its stars and planets,
all in his mouth.

And a Zen story: When Huang-bo bid goodbye to Nan-
ch'üan, who saw him off at the door, Nan-ch'üan held out
Huang-bo's straw hat and said: "Your body is unusually big.
Isn't your straw hat too small?" Huang-bo said "Although my
hat is small the entire universe is in it."

Vimalakīrti was an enlightened Buddhist layman from
north India who fell sick. In the sūtra named for him an
incredible number of beings of all categories from all over the
various universes come at the same time to pay him a sick call.
No matter how many keep arriving, they all fit into his one
small room, "ten feet square."

At various times over the recent periods of glacial advance
there has been a vast inland sea, Lake Lahontan, covering
much of the Great Basin. At the moment it is almost entirely
dry.

By Way of Thanks

I thank the fellow writers who helped me shape this poem's idea from earliest on: Philip Whalen, Allen Ginsberg, Michael McClure, Jack Kerouac, and Lew Welch.

And my Dharma Teachers: Isshū Miura Rōshi, Sessō Oda Rōshi, and So(ko) Morinaga Rōshi. Nine bows.

Hosts of poets and writers, scientists, scholars, craftspersons, rivers-and-mountain people, fields-and-orchards people, and streets-and-buildings people have befriended and instructed this work. They are too numerous to thank by name. My gratitude to you all.

Thanks to the John Simon Guggenheim Foundation, the University of California at Davis (Research Grants), and the Foundation for Deep Ecology.

I am grateful for the readings and suggestions given the almost-finished manuscript by Peter Coyote, Alan Williamson, Scott McLean, Michael McClure, Jon Halper, David Padwa, and especially the witty and demanding Jim Dodge.

And thanks to Jack Shoemaker, friend of more than thirty years, advisor, publisher, and editor. I am indebted to his warmth, skill, and encouragement.

And finally, great thanks to my wife, lover, and partner, Carole Koda—at home in the world, at home at home, and a *dakini* of mountains and rivers.

DANGER ON PEAKS

FOR CAROLE

". . . danger on peaks."

— *I* —
Mount St. Helens

LOOWIT

from Sahaptin / lawilayt-Lá / "Smoker, Smoky"

The Mountain

From the doab of the Willamette and the Columbia, slightly higher ground, three snowpeaks can be seen when it's clear— Mt. Hood, Mt. Adams, and Mt. St. Helens. A fourth, Mt. Rainier, farther away, is only visible from certain spots. In a gentle landscape like the western slope, snowpeaks hold much power, with their late afternoon or early morning glow, light play all day, and always snow. The Columbia is a massive river with a steady flow. Those peaks and the great river, and the many little rivers, set the basic form of this green wooded Northwest landscape. Whether suburban, rural, or urban the rivers go through it and the mountains rise above.

Mt. St. Helens, "Loowit" (said to be the "Indian name")—a perfect snowcapped volcanic cone, rising from almost sea level to (back then) 9,677 feet. I always wanted to go there. Hidden on the north side in a perched basin is a large deep lake.

Spirit Lake

When I first saw Spirit Lake I was thirteen. It was clear and still, faint wisps of fog on the smooth silvery surface, encircled by steep hills of old fir. The paved road ended at the outlet, right by the Spirit Lake Lodge. A ways down the dirt road was a little shingle Forest Service Ranger Station. Farther down was a camp.

Looking out on the lake and across, only forested hills. Cool silence. South of the ranger station a dirt road climbed steadily up to a lighter drier zone. It was three miles to timberline. The mountain above the lake: they reflected each other. Maybe the mountain in the lake survives.

The camp had tent platforms under the big trees in a web of soft fir-floor trails. They were all near the water. It was so dark on the forest floor that there was almost no undergrowth, just a few skinny huckleberries. The camp had a big solid wood and stone kitchen building, and a simple half-open dining hall. There was one two-story lodge in the rustic stone and log construction that flourished (making work for skilled carpenters) during the Depression.

From the camp by the lake we went out on several-day hikes. Loading Trapper Nelson packboards, rolling our kapok sleeping bags tight, and dividing the loads of groceries and blackened #10 can cook pots with wire bail handles. The trails took us around the lake and up to the ridges: Coldwater Mt. Lookout and on to Mt. Margaret and beyond, into a basin of lakes and snowfields nestled below. From the ridges we could look back to Spirit Lake and the mountain with its symmetry and snowfields. We walked through alpine flowers, kicked steps traversing snowfields, glissaded down and settled in by rocky lakes to boisterous campsites and smoky crusty tincan meals all cooked by boys.

The Climb

Walking the nearby ridges and perching on the cliffs of Coldwater Mountain, I memorized the upper volcano. The big and little Lizards (lava ridges with their heads uphill), the Dogshead, with a broad bulge of brown rock and white snowpatches making it look faintly like a St. Bernard. The higher-up icefields with the schrund and wide crevasses, and the approach slopes from timberline. Who wouldn't take the chance to climb a snowpeak and get the long view?

Two years later the chance came. Our guide was an old-time Mazama from Tigard in Oregon. His climbing life went back to World War One. Then he got a big orchard. He wore a tall black felt hunting hat, high corked loggers-boots, stagged-off pants, and carried the old style alpenstock. We put white zinc oxide paste on our noses and foreheads, each got our own alpenstock, and we wore metal-rimmed dark goggles like Sherpas in the thirties. We set out climbing the slidey pumice lower slopes well before dawn.

Step by step, breath by breath—no rush, no pain. Onto the snow on Forsyth Glacier, over the rocks of the Dogshead, getting a lesson in alpenstock self-arrest, a talk on safety and patience, and then on to the next phase: ice. Threading around crevasses, climbing slow, we made our way to the summit just like Issa's

> "Inch by inch
> little snail
> creep up Mt. Fuji"
> ISSA

West Coast snowpeaks are too much! They are too far above the surrounding lands. There is a break between. They are in a different world. If you want to get a view of the world you live in, climb a little rocky mountain with a neat small peak. But the big snowpeaks pierce the realm of clouds and cranes, rest in the zone of five-colored banners and writhing crackling dragons in veils of ragged mist and frost-crystals, into a pure transparency of blue.

St. Helens' summit is smooth and broad, a place to nod, to sit and write, to watch what's higher in the sky and do a little dance. Whatever the numbers say, snowpeaks are always far higher than the highest airplanes ever get. I made my petition to the shapely mountain, "Please help this life." When I tried to look over and down to the world below—*there was nothing there.*

And then we grouped up to descend. The afternoon snow was perfect for glissade and leaning on our stocks we slid and skidded between cracks and thumps into soft snow, dodged lava slabs, got into the open snowfield slopes and almost flew to the soft pumice ridges below. Coming down is so fast! Still high we walked the three-mile dirt road back to the lake.

Atomic Dawn

The day I first climbed Mt. St. Helens was August 13, 1945.

Spirit Lake was far from the cities of the valley and news came
slow. Though the first atomic bomb was dropped on Hiro-
shima August 6 and the second dropped on Nagasaki August
9, photographs didn't appear in the *Portland Oregonian* until
August 12. Those papers must have been driven in to Spirit
Lake on the 13th. Early the morning of the 14th I walked over
to the lodge to check the bulletin board. There were whole
pages of the paper pinned up: photos of a blasted city from
the air, the estimate of 150,000 dead in Hiroshima alone, the
American scientist quoted saying "nothing will grow there
again for seventy years." The morning sun on my shoulders,
the fir forest smell and the big tree shadows; feet in thin
moccasins feeling the ground, and my heart still one with the
snowpeak mountain at my back. Horrified, blaming scientists
and politicians and the governments of the world, I swore a
vow to myself, something like, "By the purity and beauty and
permanence of Mt. St. Helens, I will fight against this cruel
destructive power and those who would seek to use it, for all
my life."

Some Fate

Climbed Loowit—Sahaptin name—three more times.
July of '46 with sister Thea
(went to Venezuela & Cartagena as a seaman summer of
1948)
June of '49 with dear friend Robin who danced shimmering
in the snow, and again with her late that summer

> This wide Pacific land   blue haze edges
> mists and far gleams   broad Columbia River
> eastern Pacific somewhere west
> us at a still place   in the wheel of the day
> right at home at   the gateway to nothing
> can only keep going.

Sit on a rock and gaze out into space
leave names in the summit book,
prepare to descend

on down to some fate in the world

1980: Letting Go

Centuries, years and months of—

let off a little steam
cloud up and sizzle
growl   stamp-dance
quiver   swell, glow
glare   bulge

swarms of earthquakes, tremors, rumbles

she goes
                8.32 AM   18 May 1980

superheated steams and gasses
white-hot crumbling boulders lift and fly in a
burning sky-river wind of
searing lava droplet hail,
huge icebergs in the storm, exploding mud,
shoots out flat and rolls a swelling billowing
cloud of rock bits,
crystals, pumice, shards of glass
dead ahead blasting away—
a heavenly host of tall trees goes flat down
lightning dances through the giant smoke

a calm voice on the two-way
ex-navy radioman and volunteer
describes the spectacle—then
says, the hot black cloud is
rolling toward him—no way
but wait his fate

a photographer's burnt camera
full of half melted pictures,
three fallers and their trucks
chainsaws in back, tumbled gray and still,
two horses swept off struggling in hot mud
a motionless child laid back in a stranded ashy pickup

roiling earth-gut-trash cloud tephra twelve miles high
ash falls like snow on wheatfields and orchards to the east
          five hundred Hiroshima bombs

in Yakima, darkness at noon

Blast Zone

Late August 2000.
An early plane from Reno to Portland, meet Fred Swanson
at the baggage claim. Out of the Portland airport and onto
these new streets, new highways, there's a freeway bridge goes
right across the Columbia, the 205, piers touch down on the
mid-river island, but there's no way onto it. This is the skinny
cottonwood island that Dick Meigs and I used to sail to and
camp on the sandbars. Blackberries growing around the trans-
mission towers.

In an instant we're in Washington State, and swinging north
to join the main 5. Signs for Battleground, Cougar. Crossing
the Lewis River, the Columbia to the left, the Kalama River,
the old Trojan nuke plant towers, then on to Castle Rock.
Freeway again, no sign of the towns—they're off to the west—
and we turn into the Toutle River valley on a big new road.
Old road, old bridges most all swept away.

(Remembering two lane highway 99, and how we'd stop for
groceries in Castle Rock, a hunter/logger's bar with walls
covered solid by racks of antlers. The road east toward Spirit
Lake first climbed steeply out of town and then gradually up
along the river. It was woodlots and pasture and little houses

and barns, subsistence farms, farmer-loggers.) Air cool, clear day, bright green trees.

The new Silver Lake Mt. St. Helens Visitors Center is close enough to the freeway that travelers on the 5 can swing by here, take a look, and continue on. It's spacious, with a small movie theater in back and a volcano model in the center large enough to descend into, walk through, and at the center look down a skillful virtual rising column of molten magma coming up from the core of the earth.

The Center's crowded with people speaking various languages. Gazing around at the photographs and maps, I begin to get a sense of what transformations have been wrought. The Toutle River *lahar* made it all the way to the Columbia River, some sixty miles, and deposited enough ash and mud into the main channel to block shipping until it was dredged, weeks later.

We go on up the highway. Swanson explains how all the agencies wanted to get in on the restoration money that was being raised locally (and finally by Congress). They each put forth proposals: the Soil Conservation Service wanted to drop $16.5 million worth of grass seed and fertilizer over the whole thing, the Forest Service wanted to salvage-log and replant trees, and the Army Corps of Engineers wanted to build sediment retention dams. (They got to do some.) The Forest Ecology Mind (incarnated in many local people, the environmental public, and some active scientists) prevailed, and within the declared zone, zero restoration became the rule. Let natural succession go to work and take its time. Fred Swanson was trained as a geologist, then via soils went into forest and stream ecology research in the Andrews Forest in Oregon. He has been studying Mt. St. Helens from the beginning.

The Corps of Engineers went to work along the Toutle with hundreds of giant trucks and earth movers. Swanson takes a turn off the main road, just a few miles on, to a view of an earthwork dam that was built to help hold back further debris floods in the new river channel. The lookout parking lot had clearly been more of a tourist destination in the past than it is now, partly closed and getting overgrown with alders. Once the dump trucks stopped, the people didn't come so much to look. But there it is, lots of earth holding back what further mud and gravel might be coming down—for a while.

The color of the dam, the riverbanks, the roads, is "volcano-ash-gray." New bridges, new road, this has all been rebuilt. Swanson says that for some years after the eruption there was no access into the west side of Spirit Lake. To get closer to the lake and the mountain, people were driving a string of small roads north and around. You could drive up from the east to Windy Ridge. And then a new state highway from the 5 to the west side ridge above the lake got built. You still can't drive to the edge of the lake—all pumice, ash, and broken rock.

The new road is an expensive accomplishment. It runs above the old Toutle riverbed along the hillside with fancy bridges, then into the Coldwater Creek drainage (I hiked down this when it was old-growth forest, and trail was the only access); makes a big curve around the head of the valley and does a long switchback climb. In that upper cirque of Coldwater Creek there are plenty of old gray logs lying tossed about on the ground. Between and around the logs the hills are aflower in fireweed and pearly everlasting *Anaphalis marga-ritacea*. Little silver fir three to ten feet high are tucked in behind the logs, mixed in with the tall flowers.

Finally pull up to the high ridge, now named Johnston after the young geologist who died there, and walk to the edge. The end of the road. Suddenly there's all of Loowit and a bit of the lake basin! In a new shape, with smoking scattered vents in this violet-gray light.

> The white dome peak whacked lower down,
> open-sided crater on the northside, fumarole wisps
> a long gray fan of all that slid and fell
> angles down clear to the beach

dark old-growth forest gone   no shadows
the lake afloat with white bone blowdown logs
scoured ridges round the rim, bare outcrop rocks
squint in the bright
ridgetop plaza packed with puzzled visitor gaze

no more White Goddess
but,   under the fiery sign of Pele,
and Fudo—Lord of Heat
who sits on glowing lava with his noose
lassoing hardcore types
from hell against their will,

Luwit, lawilayt-lá—*Smoky*
is her name

To Ghost Lake

Walk back down from the west side view ridge and drive back
to Castle Rock and the 5. Start a drive-circumambulation
of the mountain, going north and then east up the Cowlitz
Valley. The Cowlitz River gets some of its water from the
south side glaciers of Mt. Rainier and the northwest side of
Mt. Adams. Dinner at "Carter's Roadhouse"—old place, slow
and funky service, a bar, small press local history books for
sale. Then swing south on a forest road to the Iron Creek
Campground on the Cispus River and lay out groundsheet in
the dark.

Next morning walk the gravelly bar of the little Cispus, duck
under droops of moss from old-growth cedar, hot tea on the
fir needles. Drive to the Boundary Trail, winding higher on
ridgerunning tracks, break out around a corner and there's
the mountain and then suddenly we are in the Blast Zone.

In a great swath around the lake basin, everything in direct
line to the mountain is flat down: white clear logs, nothing
left standing. Next zone of tree-suffering is dead snags still

upright. Then a zone called "ashed trees" blighted by a fall
of ash, but somehow alive. Last, lucky to be out of line with
the blast, areas of green forest stand. A function of distance,
direction, and slope. Finally, far enough back, healthy old
forest stretches away.

New patterns march in from the edges, while within the zone
occasional little islands of undamaged vegetation survive. In
some cases a place still covered with snow and down in a dip.
From Windy Ridge the carpet of floating logs on the lake is
mostly at the north end.

Go out several miles walking along the ridge and onto slopes
of the volcano. It's all ash and rock now, no forest regrowth
here, and the sun as hot and dry as Arizona.

At the car again and drive to the Norway Pass road turnoff
(from the mountain road see an arrow, shot and sticking in
a dead tree, up high, and from the downslope side. Why?
How?) and go north for a look down at the Green River val-
ley and beyond that the high Goat Mountain ridge. Too far
north up there to be affected. Down in the Green River valley
one can see the distinct boundary between the unmanaged
"ecological zone" of the Volcanic Monument where natural
succession rules, and the adjacent National Forest land that
had soon been logged and planted. The planting took hold
well. In the natural succession blast zone the conifers are
rising—not quite tall enough to shade out down logs and
flowers, but clearly flourishing. But over into the "planted"
zone it's striking to see how much taller and denser the grow-
ing plantation is. Well, no surprise. Wild natural process takes
time, and allows for the odd and unexpected. We still know
far too little about it. This natural regeneration project has
special values of its own, aesthetic, spiritual, scientific. Both
the wild and the managed sides will be instructive to watch
for centuries to come.

Baby plantlife, spiky, firm and tender,
stiffly shaking in the same old breeze.

We camped for the night on a ridgetop with long views both
ways. A tiny fire, a warm breeze, cloudless starry sky. The
faint whiffs of sulfur from the fumaroles. In the morning,
cloud-fog rising covers the sun. Fog comes up the Columbia
Valley and fills the deep-cut side-canyons clear back to here—
floats awhile past our nearby truck.

Sit on folded groundsheets on the ashy pumice hard-packed
soil and pick up our conversations again. Fred clarifies distinc-
tions such as "original" and "restored." What's old? What's
new? What's "renew"? I then held forth on the superiority of
the Han'-gul writing system of Korea over all other alphabets,
but what got me started on that? Our hissing Primus stove. I
talked about ten years of living in Japan, "Two hundred miles
of industrial city-strip along the railroad, and tenth-growth
forest mountains far as you can see. Went twice through
Hiroshima, great noodles, full of activists, green and leafy—
doing fine."

Fred's mind is as open as a summer morning in the Sierra.
We talk about a lot. But when we come back to forests,
eruptions, and the balance of economy and ecology, I shut
up and listen.

Green tea hotwater
Sunball in the fog
Loowit cooled in white
New crater summit lightly dusted
Morning fumarole summit mist-wisps—"Hah" . . . "Hah"

One final trip before leaving: a walk to Ghost Lake: pearly
everlasting, huckleberries and fireweed, all the way.

    Out to Ghost Lake through white snags,
      threading down tree deadfalls, no trail work lately here,
      light chaco sandals leaping, nibbling huckleberries,
        walking logs
      bare toed dusty feet
      I worked around this lake in '49
      both green then

Pearly Everlasting

Walk a trail down to the lake
mountain ash and elderberries red
old-growth log bodies blown about,
whacked down, tumbled in the new ash *wadis.*
Root-mats tipped up, veiled in tall straight fireweed,
fields of prone logs laid by blast
in-line north-south down and silvery
limbless barkless poles—
clear to the alpine ridgetop all you see
is toothpicks of dead trees
thousands of summers
at detritus-cycle rest
—hard and dry in the sun—the long life of the down
    tree yet to go
bedded in bushes of pearly everlasting
dense white flowers
saplings of bushy vibrant silver fir
the creek here once was "Harmony Falls"
The pristine mountain
just a little battered now
the smooth dome gone
ragged crown

the lake was shady *yin*—
now blinding water mirror of the sky
remembering days of fir and hemlock—
no blame to magma or the mountain
& sit on a clean down log at the lake's edge,
the water dark as tea.

I had asked Mt. St. Helens for help
the day I climbed it,   so seems she did

The trees all lying flat like,   after that big party
Siddhartha went to on the night he left the house
    for good,

crowd of young friends whipped from sexy dancing
dozens crashed out on the floor

angelic boys and girls, sleeping it off.
A palace orgy of the gods but what
"we" see is "Blast Zone" sprinkled with
clustered white flowers

"Do not be tricked by human-centered views," says
   Dogen,
And Siddhartha looks it over, slips away—for another
   forest—
—to really get right down on life and death.

If you ask for help it comes.
But not in any way you'd ever know
—thank you Loowit, lawilayt-lá, *Smoky Mâ*
          gracias   xiexie   grace

Enjoy the Day

   One morning on a ridgetop east of Loowit
   after campstove coffee

   looking at the youthful old volcano
   breathing steam and sulfur
   sunrise lava
   bowls of snow

   went up behind a mountain hemlock
   asked my old advisors where they lay

   what's going on?

   they say

   "New friends and dear sweet old tree ghosts
      here we are again. Enjoy the day."

— *II* —
Yet Older Matters

Brief Years

HANGING OUT BY PUTAH CREEK WITH YOUNGER POETS

Sitting on the dusty
dry-leaf crackly ground,
freeway rumble south,
black walnut shade,
crosslegged, hot,
       exchanging little poems

YET OLDER MATTERS

A rain of black rocks   out of space
onto deep blue ice   in Antarctica
nine thousand feet high   scattered for miles.

Crunched inside   yet older matter
from times before our very sun

(from a conversation with Eldridge Moores
& Kim Stanley Robinson)

FLOWERS IN THE NIGHT SKY

I thought, forest fires burning to the north!
yellow nomex jacket thrown in the cab, hard-hat, boots,
I gunned the truck up the dirt-road scrambling,
and came out on a flat stretch with a view:
shimmering blue-green streamers and a red glow down
   the sky—
Stop. Storms on the sun. Solar winds going by

(The night of the red aurora borealis:
seen as far south as northern California, April 2001)

A Dent in a Bucket

Hammering a dent out of a bucket
        a woodpecker
                answers from the woods

Baby Jackrabbit

Baby jackrabbit on the ground
thick furry brindled coat
little black tailtip
back of the neck ate out,
life for an owl.

Work Day

They want—
Short lengths of 1" schedule 40 PVC
A 10' chimney sweeping brush
someone to grind the mower blades
a log chain,
my neighbors' Spring work.

        Chainsaw dust
        clay-clod stuck spade
        apple blossoms and bees

Asian Pear

The slender tender Asian pear
unpruned, skinny, by the zendo
never watered, ragged,
still puts out fruit
                fence broken,

trunk scored with curls of bark,
bent-off branches, high-up scratches—
pears for a bear

COOL CLAY

In a swarm of yellowjackets
a squirrel drinks water
feet in the cool clay, head way down

GIVE UP

Walking back from the Dharma-Talk
summer dry madrone
leaves rattle down

"Give up! give up!
Oh sure!" they say

HOW

small birds   flit
from bough
to bough to bough

to bough to bough to bough

WHACK

Green pinecone flakes
pulled, gnawed clean around,
wobbling, slowly falling

scattering on the ground,
    whack the roof.
Tree-top squirrel feasts
—twitchy pine boughs.

YOWL

Out of the underbrush
a bobcat bursts chasing a housecat.
Crash—yowl—silence.
Pine pollen settles again.

APRIL CALLS AND COLORS

Green steel waste bins
flapping black plastic lids
gobbling flattened cardboard,
far off, a backup beeper

STANDUP COMICS

A parking meter that won't take coins
a giant sprinkler valve wheel chained and locked
a red and white fire hydrant
a young dandelion at the edge of the pavement

SKY, SAND

Cottonwoods streambank
    splashing fording up the creekbed
black phoebe calling *pi pi pi* here, near—

Mexican blackhawk cruising—squint at the sky,
shoes full of sand

(Aravaipa Canyon, Arizona)

MIMULUS ON THE ROAD TO TOWN

Out of cracks in the roadcut rockwalls,
clumps of peach-colored mimulus
spread and bloom,
      stiffly quiver in the hot
log-truck breeze-blast
always going by—
they never die.

A TERCEL IS A YOUNG MALE HAWK

Falconers used to believe that the third hawk egg in
a clutch would be a male. So they call a young male
hawk a "tercel" from *tertius*, "third." Who knows why
carmakers name their cars the way they do.

    Taking the gas cap off
        stick it in my work vest pocket
    I see a silver Tercel parked
    by a hedge and a waste bin full of bottles

    —filling my old Toyota pickup.

BRIGHTER YELLOW

An "Ozark Trucking" bigrig pulls up
by me on the freeway, such a vivid yellow!
a brighter yellow than bulldozers.

This morning James Lee Jobe was talking
        of the wild blue bonnets
and the dark red Indian paintbrush down in Texas.
Said, "from a distance—them growing all together
        makes a field of solid purple."
Hey—keep on the right side
of that yellow line

To the Liking of Salmon

Spawning salmon dark and jerky
just below the surface ripple
shallow lower Yuba

River bed—old mining gravels
mimicking a glacier outflow
perfect for the redds below Parks Bar.

*(how hydraulic mining made the Yuba Goldfields
like a post-glacial river in Alaska)*

Glacier Ghosts

Late July: Five Lakes Basin & Sand Ridge, Northern Sierra

A lake east of the east end of Sand Ridge, a sleeping site tucked
under massive leaning glacial erratic propped on bedrock,
bed of wood bits, bark, and cones.

Gravelly bed below a tilted erratic,
        chilly restless night,
        —ants in my hair

Nap on a granite slab
half in shade, you can never hear enough
sound of   wind in the pines

—

Piko feared heights
went up the steep ridge on all fours.
But she went

—

Catching grasshoppers for bait
attaching them live to the hook
—I get used to it

—

a certain poet, needling
Allen Ginsberg by the campfire
"How come they all love *you*?"

—

Clumsy at first
my legs, feet, and eye   learn again to leap,
skip through the jumbled rocks

—

Starting a glissade
down a steep snowfield
they say, "Gary, don't!"
but I know my iceaxe

—

Diving in the perched lake, coming up
can see right over the outlet waterfall
distant peaks   Sierra Buttes

———

Tired, quit climbing at a small pond
made camp, slept on a slab
til the moon rose

———

ice-scrape-ponds, scraggly pines,
long views, flower mud marshes,
so many places
for a wandering boulder to settle,
forever.

———

A gift of rattlesnake
meat—packed in—
cooked on smoky coals
how did it taste?

———

Warm nights,
the lee of twisty pines—
high jets crossing the stars

———

Things spread out
rolling and unrolling, packing and unpacking,
—this painful impermanent world.

———

Exploring the Grouse Ridge—crossing through
manzanita mats from
peak to peak—scaring up grouse

———

Creek flowing out of Lake Fauchery
old white dog
caught in the fast current
—strong lads saved him

———

Coming back down the
trail from Glacier Lake
KJ lifts her T-shirt
"look, I'm getting boobs"
two tiny points, age nine.

———

Down in the meadow
west end of Sand Ridge
the mosquitos bite everyone
but Nanao and me—why?

———

SAND RIDGE

How you survived—
gravelly two mile lateral moraine of
sand and summer snow and hardy flowers
always combing the wind
that crosses range and valley from the sea.
Walk that backbone path
ghosts of the pleistocene icefields
stretching   down and away,
both sides

— *III* —
Daily Life

What to Tell, Still

Reading the galley pages of Laughlin's *Collected Poems*
with an eye to writing a comment.
How warmly J speaks of Pound,
        I think back to—

At twenty-three I sat in a lookout cabin in gray
    whipping wind
at the north end of the northern Cascades,
high above rocks and ice, wondering
            should I go visit Pound at St. Elizabeth's?

And studied Chinese in Berkeley, went to Japan instead.

J puts his love for women
his love for love, his devotion, his pain, his causing-
    of-pain,
            right out there.

I'm 63 now & I'm on my way to pick up my ten-year-
    old stepdaughter
            and drive the car pool.
I just finished a five-page letter to the County
    Supervisors
dealing with a former supervisor,
            now a paid lobbyist,
who has twisted the facts and gets paid for his lies. Do I
have to deal with this creep? I do.

James Laughlin's manuscript sitting on my desk.
Late last night reading his clear poems—
and Burt Watson's volume of translations of Su Shih,
            next in line for a comment.

September heat.
The Watershed Institute meets,
            planning more work with the B.L.M.
And we have visitors from China, Forestry guys,
        who want to see how us locals are doing with
            our plan.

Editorials in the paper are against us,
        a botanist is looking at rare plants in the marsh.

I think of how J writes stories of his lovers in his poems—
        puts in a lot,
        it touches me,

So recklessly bold—foolish?—
to write so much about your lovers
when you're a long-time married man. Then I think,
what do I know?
        About what to say
        or not to say, what to tell, or not, to whom,
        or when,

        still.

                                          (1993)

Strong Spirit

Working on hosting Ko Un great Korean poet.
I was sitting on the floor this morning in the dark
At the Motel Eco, with my steel cup full of latte from
   the Roma
calendar template sketched in pencil:
student lunches, field trips in the Central Valley
waterfowl? Cold Canyon? State Library with Kevin Starr?
Charlie wants to help with speakers money so he gave us some
a cultural visitor for a week at Aggie Davis
in the flat plain valley just by Putah Creek,
which was re-routed by engineers a hundred years ago.
I'm on the phone and on the e-mail working all this out
students and poets to gather at the Cafe California
the Korean graduate student too.
His field is Nineteenth Century Lit and he's probably a
   Christian,
but says he'll do this. Delfina, wife of Pak, a Korean Catholic,

looks distasteful at the book and says
Ko Un's a Buddhist!—I don't think she'll come to the
    reading.
Drive the car through a car wash—get Sierra mud off,
about to meet him at the airport, his strong wife Sang-wha
with him in flight from Seoul.
First drive to Albany and pick up Clare Yoh,
Korean Studies at Berkeley, lives near an
old style eucalyptus grove, the smell surprised me
when I visited California as a kid—I like it still.

Down to the airport meet at Customs
and now to pay respects to our friend
poet, translator, Ok-ku died last fall
her grave on the ridgetop near the sea.
Straight up a hill due west
walk a grassy knoll in the wind,
Ko Un pouring a careful trickle of *soju* on her mound,
us bowing deep bows
—spirits for the spirit, bright poet gone
then pass the cup among the living—

strong.

(2001)

Sharing an Oyster with the Captain

"On June 17, 1579, Captain Francis Drake sailed his ship,
The Golden Hinde, into the gulf of the Farallones of the bay
that now bears his name. He sighted these white cliffs and
named the land Nova Albion. During his 36 day encampment
in California, Drake repaired his ship, established contact with
local Indians, explored inland, took on supplies and water,
and claimed the region for Queen Elizabeth."

Along the roadside yarrow, scotch broom, forbs,
hills of layered angled boughs like an Edo woodcut,
rare tree—bishop pine—storm-tuned,

blacktop roadbed over the native Miwok path
over the early ranches "M" and "Pierce"
          —a fox dives into the brush,
wind-trimmed chaparral and
estuary salt marsh, leaning hills,
technically off the continent,
out on the sea-plate, "floating island."

—Came down from inland granite and
gold-bearing hills   madrone and cedar;
& from ag-fields laser land-levelers,
giant excavators—subdivision engineers
"California" hid behind the coastal wall of fog

Drake saw a glimpse of brown dry grass and gray-
     green pine,
came into a curve of beach. Rowed ashore,
left a scat along the tideline, cut some letters in an oak.

The "G" Ranch running Herefords,
Charley Johnson growing oysters
using a clever method from Japan,
and behind the fog wall
sunny grassy hills and swales
filled with ducks and tules.

Cruising down the narrow road-ridge
one thing we have together yet:
this Inglis—this Mericano tongue.
—Drake's Bay cliffs like Sussex—
gray and yellow siltstone, mudstone, sandstone,
undulating cliffs and valleys—days of miles of fog.

Gray-mottled bench boards lichen.
Sea gulls flat down sun-warmed
parking lot by cars.
We offer to the land and sea,
a sierra-cup of Gallo sherry,
and eat a Johnson's oyster from the jar,

offer a sip of Sack to the Captain
and an oyster raw:
a salute, a toast to Sir Francis Drake
from the land he never saw.

Summer of '97

West of the square old house, on the rise that was made
    when the pond was dug; where we once slept out;
            where the trampoline sat,

                Earth spirit please don't mind
                If cement trucks grind
                And plant spirits wait a while
                Please come back and smile

                Ditches, lines and drains
                Forms and pours and hidden doors
                The house begins:

                Sun for power
                Cedar for siding
                Fresh skinned poles for framing
                Gravel for crunching and
                Bollingen for bucks—

                Daniel peeling
                Moth for singing
                Matt for pounding
                Bruce for pondering
                Chuck for plumbering
                David drywalling
                        staining, crawling;
                Stu for drain rock
                Kurt for hot wire
                Gary for cold beer
                Carole for brave laugh
                        til she leaves,
                        crew grieves,

Gen for painting
            each window frame
            Gen-red again

Garden cucumbers for lunch
Fresh tomatoes crunch
Tor for indoor paints and grins
Ted for rooftiles
Tarpaper curls
Sawdust swirls
Trucks for hauling
Barrels for burning
Old bedrooms disappearing

Wild turkeys watching
Deer disdainful
Bullfrogs croaking,

David Parmenter for bringing
            flooring oak at night
Though his mill burned down
He's still coming round.

Cyndra tracing manzanita
On the tile wall shower,
Sliding doors
Smooth new floors—

Old house a big hall now
Big as a stable
To bang the mead-stein on the table
Robin got a room to write a poem,
& no more nights out walking to the john.

Carole finally coming home
Peeking at her many rooms.
Oak and pine trees looking on
Old Kitkitdizze house now
Has another wing—

So we'll pour a glass and sing—
This has been fun as heaven
Summer of ninety-seven.

Really the Real
for Ko Un and Lee Sang-wha

Heading south down the freeway making the switch
from Business 80 east to the I-5 south,
watch those signs and lanes that split
duck behind the trucks, all going 75 at 10 am
I tell Ko Un this is the road that runs from Mexico to
    Canada,
right past San Diego—LA—Sacramento—Medford—
    Portland—Centralia—
Seattle—Bellingham, B.C. all the way,
the new suburban projects with cement roof tiles
neatly piled on unfinished gables,
turn onto Twin Cities Road, then Franklin Road
pull in by the sweet little almost-wild Cosumnes River
right where the Mokelumne meets it,
(*umne* a Miwok suffix meaning river)
walking out on a levee trail through cattail, tule,
    button-brush,
small valley oaks, algae on the streams. Hardly any birds.
Lost Slough, across the road, out on the boardwalk
—can't see much, the tules all too tall. The freeway roar,
four sandhill cranes feeding, necks down, pacing slow.
Then west on Twin Cities Road til we hit the river.
Into Locke, park, walk the crowded Second Street
all the tippy buildings' second stories leaning out,
gleaming bikes—huge BMW with exotic control panel
eat at the Locke Gardens Chinese place, Ko Un's choice,
endless tape loop some dumb music, at the next table one
    white couple,
a guy with a beard; at another a single black woman
with two little round headed clearly super-sharp boys.

Out and down to Walnut Grove til we find road J-II
    going east
over a slough or two then south on Staten Island Road.
    It's straight,
the fields all flat and lots of signs that say
no trespassing, no camping, no hunting, stay off the levee.
Driving along, don't see much, I had hoped, but about to
    give up.
Make a turn around and stand on the shoulder, glass the
    field:
flat farmland—fallow—flooded with water—
full of birds. Scanning the farther sections
hundreds of sandhill cranes are pacing—then,
those gurgling sandhill crane calls are coming out of the
    sky
in threes, twos, fives, from all directions,
circling, counter-spinning, higher and lower,
big silver bodies, long necks, dab of red on the head,
chaotic, leaderless, harmonic, playful—what are they doing?
Splendidly nowhere thousands

And back to Davis, forty miles, forty minutes
shivering to remember   what's going on
just a few miles west of the 5:
in the wetlands, in the ongoing elder   what you might
    call,
really the real,   world.

(*October 2001, Cosumnes and Staten Island*)

Ankle-deep in Ashes

Ankle-deep gray muddy ash   sticky after rain
walking wet burnt forest floor
(one-armed mechanic working on a trailer-mounted
    generator
a little barbecue by a parked trailer,
grilling steak after ten hours checking out the diesels)

—we're clumping through slippery ashes to a sugar pine
—a planner from a private timber company
a fire expert from the State, a woman County Supervisor
a former Forest Service line officer, the regional District
    Ranger,
a businessman-scientist who managed early retirement
    and does good deeds,
the superintendent of the county schools,
& the supervisor of one of the most productive public
    forests in the country—
pretty high back in the mountains
after a long hot summer wildfire and a week of rain.
Drove here through miles of standing dead trees
gazed across the mountain valley,
the sweep of black snags with no needles,
stands of snags with burnt needles dangling,
patches of green trees that still look live.
They say the duff layers glowed for weeks as the fire sank
    down.
This noble sugar pine we came to see is green
seven feet dbh, "diameter at breast height"
first limb a hundred feet above.
The District Ranger chips four little notches
round the trunkbase, just above the ashy dust:
cambium layer dry and brown
cooked by the slow duff burn.
He says, "Likely die in three more years
but we will let it stand."
I circumambulate it and invoke, "Good luck—long life—
Sarvamangalam—I hope you prove him wrong"
pacing charred twigs crisscrossed on the ground.

(Field trip to the aftermath of the Star Fire, 5 November 2001)

Winter Almond

Tree over and down
its root-rot clear to the air, dirt tilted

trunk limbs and twiglets crashed
on my mother's driveway—her car's barricaded
up by the house—she called last night
"I can't get out"

I left at dawn—freezing and clear,
a scatter of light snow from last week still
little Stihl arborist's chainsaw (a thrasher)
canvas knapsack of saw gear
and head for town   fishtailing ice slicks

She's in the yard in a mustard knit hat and a shawl cerise
from her prize heap of woolens
from the world's Goodwills
The tree's rotten limbs and whippy sprouts both
in a damn near dead old frame

my mother eighty-seven (still drives)
worries the danger,
the snarl of the saw chases her into the house
in the fresh clear air I move with the limbs and the trunk
crash in a sequence and piled as it goes, so,
firewood rounds *here,* and the brushpile *there.*
rake down the drive for the car—in three hours.

Inside where it's all too hot
drink chocolate and eat black bread with smoked
     oysters,
Lois goes over her memory of my jobs as a youth
that made me do this sort of work
when I'm really "So intellectual. But you always worked
     hard as a kid."

She tells me a story: herself, seventeen, part-time clerk in
     a store
in Seattle, the boss called her in for a scolding.
"how come you shopped there?"—a competitor's place.
—her sister worked there (my Aunt Helen)
who could get her a discount as good
 as what they had here.

The boss said "o.k. That's o.k. then," and Lois said "also
it's time for a raise." I asked did you get it?
      "I did."
So many hours at this chair
hearing tales of the years.
"I was skinny. So thin."
With her great weight now.

"Thank you son for the tree.
You did it quick too.
The neighbors will say
He came right away."

Well I needed a change.
A few rounds of sound almond wood—
maybe my craft friend Holly will want them
you won't be just firewood—a bowl or a salad fork
old down
almond tree

(1993)

Mariano Vallejo's Library

Mariano Vallejo's library
was the best in the Eastern Pacific
he was reading Rousseau, Voltaire
(some bought from the ship *Leonor*)
The Yankees arrived and he welcomed them
though they drove off his horses and cattle
then one year the Casa, books and all, burned to the ground.

The old adobe east of the Petaluma River still stands.
Silvery sheds in the pastures once were chicken-coops
the new box mansions march up the slope.
At my sister's *Empty Shell* book party some retired
chicken growers walked in cuddling favorite birds.
Vallejo taught vine-growing tricks to Charles Krug

and Agostin Haraszthy—the vineyards are everywhere
but the anarchist egg growers gone.

The bed of the Bay all shallowed by mining
pre–ice age Sierra dry riverbeds
upturned for gold and the stream gravel washed off by hoses
swept to the valley in floods.
Farmers lost patience, the miners are now gone too.
New people live in the foothills.
pine-pitch and dust, poison oak.

The barnyard fence shades jimson weed,
datura, toloache, white trumpet flower, dark leaf.
The old ones from the world before taught care:
whoever's here, whatever language—
race, or century, be aware
that plant can scour your mind,

put all your books behind.

Waiting for a Ride
for Gary Holthaus

Standing at the baggage passing time:
Austin Texas airport—my ride hasn't come yet.
My former wife is making websites from her home,
one son's seldom seen,
the other one and his wife have a boy and girl of their own.
My wife and stepdaughter are spending weekdays in town
so she can get to high school.
My mother ninety-six still lives alone and she's in town too,
always gets her sanity back just barely in time.
My former former wife has become a unique poet;
most of my work,
such as it is   is done.
Full moon was October second this year,
I ate a mooncake, slept out on the deck
white light beaming through the black boughs of the pine

owl hoots and rattling antlers,
Castor and Pollux rising strong
—it's good to know that the Pole Star drifts!
that even our present night sky slips away,
not that I'll see it.
Or maybe I will, much later,
some far time walking the spirit path in the sky,
that long walk of spirits—where you fall right back into the
"narrow painful passageway of the Bardo"
squeeze your little skull
and there you are again

waiting for your ride

(October 5, 2001)

— *IV* —
Steady, They Say

Doctor Coyote When He Had a Problem

Doctor Coyote when he had a problem
took a dump. On the grass, asked his turds where they lay
what to do? They gave him good advice.

He'd say "that's just what I thought too"
And do it.   And go his way.

Claws / Cause
for Zenshin

"Graph" is the claw-curve, carve—
        grammar a   weaving

paw track, lizard-slither, tumble of
a single boulder down. Glacier scrapes across the bedrock,
        wave-lines on the beach.

Saying, "this was me"
        scat sign of time and mood and place

language is   breath, claw, or tongue

"tongue" with all its flickers
might be a word for

hot love, and   fate.
A single kiss   a tiny cause [claws]

—such grand effects [text].

How Many?

Australia, a group of girls at a corroboree
Lapland, reindeer herdgirls

China, the "yaktail"

Greece, the seven daughters, sisters,
or "the sailing stars"

a cluster of faint stars in Taurus,
the Pleiades,

name of a car in Japan—
"Subaru"

in Mayan—A fistful of boys—

Loads on the Road

Stu's stubby heavy tough old yellow dump truck
parked by his place   "For Sale"
he's fine, but times and people change.

Those loads of river-run and crushed blue mine rock
in our roadbed   Stu and me
standing talking   engine idling
those days gone now,

days to come.

Carwash Time

Looking at a gray-pine,
chunky fire-adapted cones
bunched toward the top,
a big tree there behind the tire shop

—I'm sitting on a low fence
while a wild gang does a benefit
wash-job on my daughter's car.

Tattooed and goateed white dudes,
brown and black guys,
I say "What you raising money for?"

—"The drug and alcohol halfway
house up the street"
old Ridge sedan
never been this neat

To All the Girls Whose Ears I Pierced Back Then
for Maggie Brown Koller
(among others)

Sometimes we remember that moment:
you stood there attentive with clothespins
dangling, setting a bloodless dimple in each lobe
as I searched for a cork & the right-sized needle
& followed the quick pierce with a small gold hoop.
The only guy with an earring
back then

It didn't hurt that much
a sweetly earnest child
and a crazy country guy
with an earring and a
gray-green cast eye
and even then,
this poem.

She Knew All About Art

She knew all about art—she was fragrant, soft,
I rode to her fine stone apartment, hid the bike in the hedge.
—We met at an opening, her lover was brilliant and rich,
first we would talk, then drift into long gentle love.
We always made love in the dark. Thirty years older than me.

Coffee, Markets, Blossoms

My Japanese mother-in-law
born in America
tough with brokers
a smart trader
grew up working barefoot
in the Delta, on the farm.
Doesn't like Japan.
Sits in the early morning
by the window, coffee in hand,

gazing at cherry blossoms.
Jean Koda
needing no poem.

In the Santa Clarita Valley

Like skinny wildweed flowers sticking up
hexagonal "Denny's" sign
starry "Carl's"
loopy "McDonald's"
eight-petaled yellow "Shell"
blue-and-white "Mobil" with a big red "O"

growing in the asphalt riparian zone
by the soft roar of the flow
                    of Interstate 5.

Almost Okay Now

She had been in an accident: almost okay now,
but inside still recovering,
bones slow-healing—she was anxious
still fearful of cars and of men.
As I sped up the winding hill road

she shuddered—eyes beseeching me—
I slowed the car down.
Out on a high meadow under the moon,
With delicate guidance she showed me
how to make love without hurting her
and then napped awhile in my arms,

smell of sweet grass
warm night breeze

Sus

Two pigs in a pickup sailing down the freeway
stomping with the sway,
        gaze back up the roadbed
                on their last windy ride.

Big pink ears up   looking all around,
taut broad shoulders   trim little legs,
bright and lively with their parsnip-colored skin
wind-washed earth-diggers
        snuffling in the swamps

they're not pork, they are forever *Sus:*
        breeze-braced and standing there,
                                velvet-dusty pigs.

Day's Driving Done

Finally floating in cool water
red sun ball sinking
through a smoky dusty haze

rumble of bigrigs,
constant buzz of cars on the 5;
at the pool of Motel 6

in Buttonwillow,
south end of the giant valley,
ghost of ancient Lake Tulare

sunset   splash.

Snow Flies, Burn Brush, Shut Down

A wide line of men in the open pine woods
diesel torches   dripping flame
lava soil   frost on the sagebrush
loggers walking from brushpile to brushpile
dark sky reddish from brushpiles burning.
At Sidwalter Butte three men on horseback
torches mounted on slender lances
crisscrossing miles of buttes and canyons

hundreds of brushpiles aflame
steady light snow.

(end of the season, Warm Springs, Oregon, 1954)

Icy Mountains Constantly Walking
for Seamus Heaney

Work took me to Ireland
          a twelve-hour flight.
The river Liffey;
          ale in a bar,
So many stories
          of passions and wars—
A hilltop stone tomb
          with the wind across the door.
Peat swamps go by:
          people of the ice age.

Endless fields and farms—
> the last two thousand years.

I read my poems in Galway,
> just the chirp of a bug.
And flew home thinking
> of literature and time.

The rows of books
> in the Long Hall at Trinity
The ranks of stony ranges
> above the ice of Greenland.

(March 1995)

For Philip Zenshin Whalen
d. 26 June 2002

(and for 33 pine trees)

Load of logs on
chains cinched down and double-checked
the truck heads slowly up the hill

I bow *namaste* and farewell
these ponderosa pine
whose air and rain and sun we shared

for thirty years,
struck by beetles   needles
turning rusty brown,
and moving on.

—decking, shelving, siding,
stringers, studs, and joists,

I will think of you   pines from this mountain
as you shelter people in the Valley
years to come

For Carole

I first saw her in the zendo
at meal time   unwrapping bowls
head forward folding back the cloth
        as server I was kneeling
to fill three sets of bowls each time
up the line
                Her lithe leg
                proud, skeptical,
                passionate, trained
                by the
                heights   by the
                danger on peaks

Steady, They Say

Clambering up the rocks of a dry wash gully,
warped sandstone, by the San Juan River,

look north to stony mountains
shifting clouds and sun

—despair at how the human world goes down

Consult my old advisers

"steady" they say

"today"

*(At Slickhorn Gulch on
the San Juan River, 1999)*

— *V* —

Dust in the Wind

Gray Squirrels

Three squirrels like,   dash to the end of a pine limb, leap, catch
an oak bough angling down—jump across air to another pine—
and on—forest grove canopy world "chug - chug" at each other—
scolding empty space

Follow their path by the quivering oak leaves
and a few pine needles floating down

One Day in Late Summer

One day in late summer in the early nineties I had lunch with
my old friend Jack Hogan, ex-longshore union worker and
activist of San Francisco, at a restaurant in my small Sierra
town. The owner had recently bought and torn down the
adjoining brick building which had been in its time a second-
hand bookstore, "3Rs," run by a puckish ex-professor. Our
lunch table in the patio was right where his counter had been.
Jack was married to my sister once. We all hung out in North
Beach back in the fifties, but now he lives in Mexico.

This present moment
that lives on

to become

long ago

(1994)

Spilling the Wind

The faraway line of the freeway faint murmur of motors, the
slow steady semis and darting little cars; two thin steel towers
with faint lights high up blinking; and we turn on a raised dirt
road between two flooded fallow ricefields—wind brings more
roar of cars

> hundreds of white-fronted geese
> from nowhere
> spill the wind from their wings
> wobbling and sideslipping down

(Lost Slough, Cosumnes, February 2002)

California Laurel

The botanist told us
"Over by Davis Lumber, between house furnishings and
plumbing, there's a Grecian laurel growing—not much
smell, but that's the one that poets wore. Now California
laurel's not a laurel. It can drive off bugs or season a
sauce, and it really clears your sinus if you take a way deep
breath—"

> Crushed leaves, the smell
> reminds me of Annie—by the Big Sur river
> she camped under laurel trees—all one summer
> eating brown rice—naked—doing yoga—
> her chanting, her way deep breath.

Baking Bread

Warm sun of a farmyard   a huge old chestnut tree   just
     yesterday
the woman said   been raided by wild rhesus monkeys
we had boar meat, *inoshishi*, stewed with chestnuts   for
     lunch.
Deer, boar, monkeys, foxes   in these mountains
and lots of dams   little trucks on narrow winding roads

Four hours from Tokyo
brightly colored work clothes
living on abandoned farms
fighting concrete dams
"I am hippy" says this woman
baking bread

*(early October 2000 in the headwaters
of the Mibu River, Southern Japan Alps)*

One Empty Bus

Jirka's place, a two-story farmhouse, the only one left in this
narrow mountain valley. Drive into the yard of cars and little
trucks. Several families sitting on the floor by the firepit,
heavy board tables loaded with local food. It's great to see
Jirka again—he's Czech. He and his Japanese wife have been
here five years. Their daughter comes in, lovely young woman
glancing. Jirka says "she's shy"—she answers firmly back in
English, "Dad, I'm not shy!" Her name's "Akebi," flowering
vine. I swap stories with the back country friends that came to
say hello, after years away. Upstairs was once a silk-worm loft.
Jirka and Etsuko weave rugs using goat hair from Greece.
A Rinzai priest from the nearby town drops in, planning a
poetry reading with our old friend Sansei. Bobbu sings Oki-
nawan folksongs with that haunting falling close. Children sit
closest to the fire. Polished dark wood, sweet herb tea. Old

house, new songs. After eating and singing, it's dark. Need to
keep moving—back to the car—

> On the night mountain canyon wall road
> construction lights flash
> we wait til the other lane comes through
>
> one empty bus

*(early October 2000 in the headwaters
of the Mibu River, Southern Japanese Alps)*

No Shadow

My friend Deane took me into the Yuba Goldfields. That's at
the lower Yuba River outflow where it enters the Sacramento
valley flatlands, a mile-wide stretch between grass and blue
oak meadows. It goes on for ten miles. Here's where the min-
ing tailings got dropped off by the wandering riverbed of the
1870s—forty miles downstream from where the giant hoses
washed them off Sierra slopes.

We were walking on blue lupine-covered rounded hundred-
foot gravel hills til we stood over the springtime rush of
water. Watched a female osprey hunting along the main river
channel. Her flight shot up, down, all sides, suddenly fell feet
first into the river and emerged with a fish. Maybe fooling
the fish by zigzagging, so—no hawk shadow. Carole said later,
that's like trying to do zazen without your self entering into
it.

> Standing on a gravel hill by the lower Yuba
> can see down west a giant airforce cargo plane from Beale
> hang-gliding down to land
> strangely slow over the tumbled dredged-out goldfields

—practice run
shadow of a cargo jet—soon gone

no-shadow of an osprey

still here

Shandel

I gave a talk one outdoor evening to some students at a park.
After, sitting on the bench and drinking juice, crowd chatting,
a slender woman with dark hair came by and flashed a smile.

She had her daughter with her, maybe nine. Also dark short
hair. Introduced her, "This is Shandel." I said "Please—
tell me about the name Shandel." The mother sat on the
bench beside me. "Shandel," she said, "is Yiddish—it means
beautiful."

And then she pulled her daughter toward her, cupped her
head in her hands and said "like a *shandel* head." And then
she put her hands on the girl's cheeks and said "or a *shan-
del* face"—the young girl stood there smiling sweetly at her
mother.

"Why did you want to know?" the woman asked me. I told
her "I once had a dear friend named Shandel who grew up
in Greenwich Village. She was talented and lovely. I never
heard the name again."—"It's not common—and Yiddish isn't
either. I liked your talk—my daughter too."—they strolled
away.

> People leaving in the dusk
> lights coming on, someone drumming in a cabin
> I remember Shandel saying
> "We were radicals and artists,
> I was the little princess of the Village—"

at her home in San Francisco
half a century ago.

Night Herons

At Putah Creek a dense grove of live oaks. Step out of the
sun and into the leafy low opening—from within the tree
comes a steady banter, elusive little birds—they shift back,
move up, stay out of sight. It's a great dark hall arched over
with shimmering leaves—a high network of live oak limbs and
twigs—four or five big trees woven together. Then see:
a huge bird on a limb, head tucked under, motionless, sleep-
ing. Peering deeper, seeing others—it's night herons! Roost
by roost, settled in. One shifts a little, they know someone's
here. Night herons passing the daylight hours in this hall of
shadowy leaves.

Driving the 80 East, on the Bryte Bend bridge
high over the Sacramento River
wind-whipped by passing bigrigs,
        thinking of night herons
in a leafy palace, deep shade, by a pool.

*(Family Ardeidae, the black-crowned
night heron, Nycticorax nycticorax)*

The Acropolis Back When

Toula Siete meets me on the street, she translates into Greek
from German and Italian. She and I are off to the Acropolis.
We walk through winding back streets and around the east
end to the south side walls and cliffs, go west past the semi-
standing theater of Dionysus. Reach up and pick some rotten
shriveled olives—so bitter!

Up the steps to an outlook ledge, a glint of sunshine, and
we are above Athens. The modern city starts to fade. Toula's
friend arrives and leads us on steeper steps past the small
shrine to Bear-girl Artemis and into the territory of big clean
slabs, pentelian marble, old stone newly stacked—lintels
perched on blocks, old talus tumble.

Walk the porch edge of the soaring Parthenon, sacred to
gray-eyed Athena. Slip into the restoration office by the
cliff for tea. He is the director of the restoration project for
the whole show, especially the Parthenon, Taso Tanoulas.
He explicates the structures ruin by ruin, and explains the
calibrated aesthetics of just "leaving be." The city racketing
around below. Chilly breeze—now see the housecat tribe
gone wild in the scattered heaps of big stone blocks. This
whole hilltop a "palimpsest," Taso says, of buildings: Neo-
lithic, Mycenean, Periclean, and after. Then I'm thinking,
here's a good place for a bivouac—there's a spring, they say,
a few yards down—people must have camped here when—

> Lifetimes ago
> drawn to this rock
> I climbed it
> watched the clouds and the moon,
> slept the night.
>
> Dreamed of a gray-eyed girl
> on this rocky hill
> no buildings
> then

(1998)

The Emu

Driving out of the foothills heading west—there's a high
layer of cloud that's thin enough to let a lot of light through,
not exactly sunshine but it showed up as 5 amps on the solar

charge-controller at home. At about Truxell Road I slip ser-
iously under the fog/cloud cover. Coming from up high like
this, one knows that there are two layers of clouds, a high one
and this low one. Closer to Davis, the belly of the cloud is
almost on the ground and now it's fog.

In this drippy gloom I manage to pick up my laser printer,
which has been repaired, buy a copy of *The Economist* at
Newsbeat, get Korean-style ramen at the Asian store, and
then cruise down to Red Rum Burger to try eating Ostrich.

Thinking back to the Emu: there it was last summer, an Emu
in the yard with a green garter (probably an identification
band, maybe with a serial number and a record of its shots).
Our place surrounded by a dozen miles of forest. It soon ran
off. I told Shawna about that—and she changed it into an
Ostrich in her mind. As an Ostrich its picture got into a zine/
comic poem, garter and all.

I'm recollecting all this as I eat my Ostrich burger at the
place that now calls itself "Red Rum," which is "murder"
backwards. Because for years it was called Murder Burger,
until, I guess, there were just too many murders happening
out there. The Ostrich burger is delicious. It's big, with lots
of lettuce, onions, hot mustard, Swiss cheese, and sesame
bun. In the midst of all those, you really don't taste Ostrich as
anything special—it's just nice and chewy. I don't think they
cook it rare. It is supposed to be good for you, low fat. And
they don't use feedlots, so Ostriches probably eat lower on
the food chain than steers that are being fattened on milo or
corn for the slaughterhouse.

It certainly tastes just like Emu! Or vice versa. The Emu, a
case of parallel evolution developing in far-off New Zealand.
No garters there. But hold! Maoris might have tattooed some
green designs right around those handsome thighs.

Lost Emu wandering the Sierra pine woods
        I have dressed you, tattooed you,
eaten you, spread wide your fame,
        in the time it takes to eat lunch

The Hie Shrine and the "One-Tree" District

The Hie Jinja in Akasaka is on a rocky tree-covered *kopje*—
skull-shaped little rocky hill and surrounded by an ocean of
metropolis that stretches kilometers in all directions: urban
buildings all sizes, broad traffic roads, narrow-lane neigh-
borhoods, elevated speedways, criss-crossed underground
subways. The great Diet buildings are to the north and
beyond that the moated island of the Imperial Palace. The
upscale Capital Tokyu Hotel just abutting the jinja is built on
some land the shrine sold off. A giant ginkgo tree at the foot
of the broad shrine stairs leads up into a forest of evergreen
broad-leaved hardwoods and dense underbrush. At the top of
the steps is a flat white gravel yard in front of the main shrine
structure, wood all painted red.

Quarreling crows and crisp hopping sparrows, a dash of liz-
ard. Green hill in the urban desert, "Island biogeography"—the
shrews and geckos holed-up in the shrine-protected little for-
est, waiting for their time to come again. Down another set of
steep steps and across the street below you go into the crowded
"One-Tree" district with its many tiny multi-story buildings.
Countless young Leisure Workers put out food and drink in
thousands of bars til almost dawn.

            From the One-Tree bar district
            to the politics of parliament
            there's a shortcut over the hill
            up broad steep steps like
            crossing a pass
            and down the other side

            "Even though you may be busy
                  stop

and make a little bow to the
San O, the Mountain God
of the Shrine"
says a sign

Cormorants

Dropping down rock ledges toward the breakers see a long
flat point spiked with upright black cormorants and a few
gulls gray and white. Rocks dabbed with threads and dribbles
of bird-white. "White writing" like Mark Tobey did—drawn in
loops and splatters—lime-rich droppings pointing back to the
fishy waves.

Some rocks more decorated than others. A dark stink as the
breeze rises, whiffs of ammonia—stabs you in the back brain—
the only place worse once was on a fishing boat in the Gulf
of Alaska—came alongside sea lion rocks and the whole thing
blew in our face and whipped us with awful offal gassy blast.

Each bird-scholar has its own stone chair and the long full
streaks below. Some rocks are unoccupied, unwritten.

Pelicans flap slow by. Cormorants fly clumsy—taking off from
the water, drag their toes in the waves flap flap flap leaving
scratch lines in the froth until they get just barely up and
never fly much higher. Cormorants on a cliff launch out and
fly downward til they drag their toes and then gain height
again. Underwater they are fast as jets and full of grace.

Toes writing in water
rocks drawn with dribbles
scat incense in the wind
cormorants open their thin black wings
talk about art, lecture the
clouds of tiny fish

To Go

Slopes of grassy mountains rise steep up from the narrow
town of Gorman north of LA on the route of the 5. Clusters
of bush and spans of spring wildflowers in bloom: California
poppy, lupine, paintbrush, fiddlenecks—blue, orange, and yel-
low—arching across the slopes above. Afternoon angle to the
sun. "Gorman" painted on a hillside water tower. At Carl's Jr.
in Gorman, getting coffee, I say to the truck driver just parked
on a slant and walked in behind me, "those things are huge,
how the hell do you drive them." He says, "they're really
easy."—"still, you have to find a place to park"—He laughs,
"yeah, you do."

> Heading north toward Tejon Pass
> humming ant-column vehicles
> six, eight lanes wide
> curving through a gap in the vertical
> cowflank-tan mountains, tops out of sight
> sprinkled with spring flowers
>
> bigrig parked by the water tower
> sun, cars, hills, coffee—all
> to go

One Thousand Cranes

When Carole had a bad cancer prognosis some years back,
several of her relatives got together and started folding the
little *origami* called "cranes." They made one thousand paper
cranes in different colors and sent them to us, it's a loving
custom, to help one get well. Carole got better, though not
cured, and they now hang in swooping strings like flowers
on a wall in the house.

In East Asia cranes are noble birds of good fortune,

suggesting long life, health, good luck, and troth. They are much in art. Most of the cranes of the world are now centered in Siberia and East Asia—they summer in the north, and winter in north India, eastern China, central Korea, and Japan's big south island, Kyushu.

There are two crane species in North America. One is the endangered whooping crane and the other the gray-beige sandhill crane. One group of sandhill cranes comes down to the Great Central Valley of California: an estimated 30,000 winter over in the area around Lodi, Cosumnes, Thornton, and west toward Walnut Grove. In late February I went with a friend to Cosumnes to look at the flocks of waterfowl one more time before they went back north. We found a place of flooded ricefields full of swimming white-fronted geese, ring-necked ducks, old squaws, teals, coots, and a few tundra swans. And then looking beyond them to a far levee there were rows of cranes pacing, eating, doing their leaping and bowing dance. "Staging up to go back north," they say.

A month later Carole and I were in Berkeley down on 4th Street where we saw an Asian crafts store called "One Thousand Cranes." It had that subtle incense and hinoki-wood aroma of old Japan. I asked the handsome Japanese woman "How do you say one thousand cranes?" She laughed and said "*senbazuru.*" "Oh yes: one thousand *wings* of *tsuru,* cranes." And I told her that my wife and I lived in the Sierra Nevada and watch the cranes flying directly over our place. I remembered back to early March—Carole had been outside, I was in the shop. We began to hear the echoing crane calls. We saw a V—a V made of sub-Vs, flying northeast. They were way high but I did a count of a subsection and it came to eighty birds. They kept coming, echelon after echelon—the cranes just specks, but the echoing calls are loud. More grand flying wedges all afternoon—at least a thousand cranes.

So I told the lady of the store, "Not long ago we watched the cranes go over heading north. They came by all afternoon, at least a thousand." The woman smiled. "Of course. Real life cranes. Good luck for all of us, good luck for you."

From the shady toolshed
hear those "gr r u gr u u   g rr ruu"
calls from the sky
step out and squint at the bright
            nothing in sight
just odd far calls
echoing, faint,
grus canadensis
heading north
                one mile high

For Anthea Corinne Snyder Lowry
1932–2002

She was on the Marin County Grand Jury, heading to a meet-
ing, south of Petaluma on the 101. The pickup ahead of her
lost a grassmower off the back. She pulled onto the shoulder,
and walked right out into the lane to take it off. That had
always been her way. Struck by a speedy car, an instant death.

            White egrets standing there
                always standing there
                    there at the crossing

            on the Petaluma River

The Great Bell of the Gion

"The great bell of the Gion Temple reverberates into every
human heart to wake us to the fact that all is impermanent and
fleeting. The withered flowers of the sâla trees by Shakyamuni's
deathbed remind us that even those flourishing with wealth
and power will soon pass away. The life of fame and pride is as
ephemeral as a springtime dream. The courageous and aggres-
sive person too will vanish like a swirl of dust in the wind."

—The Heike Monogatari, 12th century

Heading back to our little house in Murasakino from the
Gion Shrine on New Year's eve, with a glowing wick handout
from a priest—lit in the New Year sacred fire started anew
by bow drill, purified. Walking and lightly swinging the long
wick to keep it aglow, in a crowd of people whirling wicks and
heading home, finally catch a taxi. Once home start a propane
gasplate from the almost-gone wick. Now, a sacred fire in the
house. The Gion's huge bell still ringing in the new year: as
soft, as loud, at the house three kilometers away as it was at
the temple.

Up along the Kamo River
northwest to higher ground.
After midnight New Year's eve:
the great bell of the Gion
one hundred eight times
deeply booms through town.
From across the valley
it's a dark whisper
echoing in your liver,
mending your
         fragile heart.

*(Gion Park, Shrine, & Temple in Eastern Kyoto,
named for the park, monastery, and bell of Jetavana in India,
south of Shravasti, where the Buddha sometimes taught)*

— VI —

After Bamiyan

After Bamiyan

March 2001

The Chinese Buddhist pilgrim Hsüan Tsang described the giant, gleaming, painted carved-out Buddhas standing in their stone cave-niches at the edge of the Bamiyan Valley as he passed through there on foot, on his way to India in the seventh century CE. Last week they were blown up by the Taliban. Not just by the Taliban, but by woman-and-nature-denying authoritarian worldviews that go back much farther than Abraham. Dennis Dutton sent this poem around:

> Not even
> under mortar fire
> do they flinch.
> The Buddhas of Bamiyan
> Take Refuge in the dust.

May we keep our minds clear and calm and in the present moment, and honor the dust.

—

April 2001

From a man who writes about Buddhism

> Dear Gary:
>> Well, yes, but, the manifest Dharma is intra-samsaric, and will decay.
>> —R.
> —I wrote back,
>> Ah yes . . . impermanence. But this is
never a reason to let compassion and focus slide, or to pass off the sufferings of others because they are merely impermanent beings. Issa's haiku goes,

> *Tsuyu no yo wa   tsuyu no yo nagara   sarinagara*

—

"This dewdrop world
is but a dewdrop world
and yet—"

That *"and yet"* is our perennial practice. And
maybe the root of the Dharma.

A person who should know better wrote, "Many credulous
and sentimental Westerners, I suspect, were upset by the
destruction of the Afghan Buddha figures because they
believe that so-called Eastern religion is more tender-hearted
and less dogmatic . . . So—is nothing sacred? Only respect
for human life and culture, which requires no divine sanction
and no priesthood to inculcate it. The foolish veneration of
holy places and holy texts remains a principal obstacle to that
simple realization."

—"This is another case of 'blame the victim'" I answered.
"Buddhism is not on trial here. The Bamiyan statues are
part of human life and culture, they are works of art, being
destroyed by idolators of the book. Is there anything 'cred-
ulous' in respecting the art and religious culture of the past?
Counting on the tender-heartedness of (most) Buddhists,
you can feel safe in trashing the Bamiyan figures as though
the Taliban wasn't doing a good enough job. I doubt you
would have the nerve to call for launching a little missile at
the Ka'aba. There are people who would put a hit on you and
you know it."

——

September 2001

The men and women who
died at the World Trade Center
together with the
Buddhas of Bamiyan,
Take Refuge in the dust.

Loose on Earth

A tiny spark, or
the slow-moving glow on the fuse
creeping toward where
ergs held close

in petrol, saltpeter, mine gas,
buzzing minerals in the ground,
are waiting.

Held tight in a few hard words
in a dark mood,
in an old shame.

Humanity,
        said Jeffers, is like a quick

explosion on the planet
we're loose on earth
half a million years
our weird blast spreading—

and after,
rubble—millennia to weather,
soften, fragment,
sprout, and green again

Falling from a Height, Holding Hands

What was *that*?
storms of flying glass
& billowing flames

a clear day to the far sky—

better than burning,
hold hands.

We will be
two   peregrines   diving

all the way down

The Kannon of Asakusa,
Sensō-ji   Short Grass Temple
Sumida River

At the Buddha-hall of Sensō-ji
hundreds of worshippers surge up the high stone steps,
into the hall dropping coins in the bin—
look into the black-and-gold chambers, somewhere a statue
of Kannon, Kuan-yin, Kwanum, Goddess of Mercy,
Avalokiteshvara Bodhisattva,
peace and compassion for all in this world-realm
        this particular time,
old and young people swirl by. Incense in clouds.
We follow the flow out the south side steps,
white gravels, and back down the pilgrim
stone walkway that leads there
lined with street shops and stalls, packed with
babies in strollers, old folks in wheelchairs, girls in their
    tanktops
back to the gate at the entrance.

Gold Dragon Mountain, Thunder Gate,
red tree pillars and sweeping tile eaves—
back out to the streets: traffic, police, taxis,
tempura restaurants of Edo.
Cross to the riverside park space,
men cross-legged on cardboard under the shade tree
and step into the long slender riverboat water-bus
that runs down the Sumida River.

I came here unwitting, the right way,
ascending the Sumidagawa, approaching Sensō-ji from the sea.
Under the Thunder Gate, walking the pilgrim path,

climbing the steps to
Avalokiteshvara, Bodhisattva of Compassion,
asking: please guide us through samsara.

> ("Form, sensation, thought, impulse, consciousness,
> are not born, not destroyed,
> without gain, without loss
no hindrance! Thus no fear.")

For all beings
living or not,   beings or not,

inside   or   outside of time

Envoy

A Turning Verse for the Billions of Beings

We have spoken again the unknown words of the spell
that purifies the world
turning its virtue and power back   over
to those who died in wars—in the fields—on the seas
and to the billions of spirits in the realms of
form, of no-form, or in the realm of hot desire.

Hail all true and grounded beings
in all directions,   in the realms of form,
of no-form, or of hot desire

hail all noble woke-up big-heart beings;
hail—great wisdom of the path that goes beyond

Mahāprajñāpāramitā

(from the Chinese)

Notes

"Letting Go"

The person who was calmly calling radio information in on his
two-way radio was Gerald Martin at a site two miles north of
Coldwater II station and seven miles from the crater. He was
a retired navy radioman volunteer from Southern California.
The very first victim of the blast was volcanologist David
Johnston, who was on watch at the Coldwater II Observation
Post. He radioed the famous message "Vancouver! Vancou-
ver! This is it!" at 8:32 AM on May 18, 1980. His station was
vaporized. The viewpoint is now known as Johnston Ridge.

"Pearly Everlasting"

". . . that big party Siddhartha went to on the night he left the
house for good" is a reference to a passage in Ashvaghosha's
Acts of the Buddha (Skt *Buddhacharita*), second century
CE, describing the conclusion of an evening's entertainment
in the palace. Siddhartha's many beautiful companions had
finally all fallen asleep on the floor in various relaxed postures.
Siddhartha, still awake, paced among them thinking, "Even
the liveliest pleasures of privileged young people come to
this!" or somesuch, and went down to the stable, got a horse,
and rode into the forest. Cutting off his hairdo, practicing
yoga and austerities, and learning to meditate, he eventually
accomplished realization and became the "Enlightened
One"—"The Buddha."

"One Thousand Cranes"

With regard to the sandhill crane color "gray-beige," the clos-
est color in the Methuen *Handbook of Color* would be saruk
(6E3), from *Saruq*, an Iranian village where it is a traditional
color for rugs. The French derivation is *saroque*, or *saroq*.

"The Great Bell of the Gion"

The large Gion Park, shrine, and temple complex is one of the
loveliest features of the eastern edge of Kyoto, the old capital
of Japan. It stretches along the lower slopes of the hills. It
is named for the grounds and monastery of Jetavana that
were on the outskirts of the ancient Indian city of Shravasti.

Jetavana was a favorite stopping place of the historical
Buddha: he spent nineteen rainy seasons there. Jetavana
was a site of many teachings, and is said to have had
a great bell.

"Sensō-ji"

This popular Buddhist temple is commonly referred to as the
"Asakusa Kannon-dera," that is, the "Kannon temple of the
Asakusa district." Asakusa means "short grass" as does the
"sensō" in "Sensō-ji." The whole neighborhood, on the right
bank of the Sumida River, has long been famous for its count-
less little shops, temples, parks, and popular amusements.

In the seventh century three fishermen pulled in their net
and found a Kannon image in it. They first enshrined it in a
little hut. This was the beginning of what was to become a
great temple, the earliest in Edo (old Tokyo). Soon there were
many other Buddhist images on the altar besides the first lit-
tle one (supposedly only 2.1 inches tall)—a Kannon, a Fudo,
an Aizen, and much more. All of it went up in flames during
World War II. The rebuilt temple has the old-style power and
beauty. Throngs of pilgrims and visitors are constantly coming
and going.

Thanks To

Especially:
—Carole Koda, ever so
Jack Shoemaker—comrade and publisher
Fred Swanson—scientist, philosopher, walker

Aki Tamura and the people of Oshika village
Bob Uchida, poet-musician
Chizu Hamada, for One Thousand Cranes
Deane Swickard
Dennis Dutton for his Bamiyan poem
Eldridge Moores
Gary Holthaus
Henry Zenk, for his help with Sahaptin place names
    and the name "Loowit"
Isabel Stirling for research help and advice
Jean Koda
Jirka Wein, of Praha and the Southern Japan Alps
Kai Snyder
Katsu Yamazato of Naha
Ko Un of Seoul
Lee Gurga
Liana Sakeliou of Athens
Misa Honde of Kobe
Morio Takizawa of Tokyo
Nanao Sakaki, for his translation of Issa's "snail," nine bows
Peter Matthiessen
Satoru Mishima of the Kanto Plain
Shawna Ryan for ostrich and emu
Shige Hara
Steve Antler and Carla Jupiter, and the house above the river
Steve Eubanks for the Star Fire
Ursula Le Guin for her fine rare book on Mt. St. Helens,
    In the Red Zone
Young poets of Putah-toi, sitting on the summer dust

THIS PRESENT MOMENT

FOR MY FEARLESS SISTER
ANTHEA CORINNE HOGAN LOWRY SNYDER

— *I. Outriders* —

Gnarly

Splitting 18" long rounds from a beetle-kill
pine tree we felled
so it wouldn't smash a shed
—with a borrowed splitter briggs & stratton
twenty-ton pressure
wedge on a piston push-rod
some rounds fall clean down split in two,
some tough and thready, knotty,
full of frass and galleries, gnarly
gnarly!—my woman
              she was sweet

The Earth's Wild Places

Your eyes, your mouth and hands,
the public highways.
Hands, like truck stops,
semis rumbling in the corners.
Eyes like the bank clerk's window
foreign exchange.
I love all the parts of your body
friends hug your suburbs
farmlands are given a nod
but I know the path
to your wilderness.
It's not that I like it best,
but we're almost always
alone there,
and it's scary but also calm.

Siberian Outpost

What are these deserts? Sheep overgrazed them years ago?
A sweeping gallery forest and a gentle five mile ridge
   of foxtail pine

Tom and I walk up the arid slope

Caught in lightning crashes—
Siberian Outpost meadow
bunchgrass tufts and gopher holes—
shelter in the space beneath a huge old edge-zone foxtail pine;
hail storm and heavy showers;
big root trees, red bark chunks—stay barely dry

Lifetimes ago this same tree sheltered me
on Thornapple Island.
I was a junior bodhisattva then named
"No More Tricks"
and was sent to sit with the boulders here
an aeon or two
til the soil came up to my eyes.
I shook and yanked and stood, said,

OK Tom let's head back to the camp

The desert smells like rain

2 August 2007 / 8 VIII 08

Walking the Long and Shady Elwha

After many years the two dams on the Elwha River of the Olympic Peninsula came down. The Elwha Klallam tribe rejoiced and a little book of poems was gathered. One year I walked, alone, the full length of that stream.

Elwha, from its source.
Threadwhite falls
out of snow-tunnel mouths with
cold mist-breath
saddles of deep snow on ridges—

o milky confluence, bank cutter

                    alder toppler
                    make meander,
swampy acres   elk-churned mud—

The big Doug fir in this valley,
deep grooved bark, it adapts, where
Sitka spruce often can't.
Three days on trail,

—Trail crew foreman says they finally got wise
to making trails low on the outside, so water
can run off good—before they were worried because
pack stock always walks the outside of the trail
because they don't want to bump their loads on rocks
or trees.   "Punchin out all the way from N Fork
over Low Divide & clear back here, this punchin gets
mighty old"

Puncheon slab saw-cut *wowed*

"They got rip-cut chains now maybe different rakers
         this here punchin gets old"

          About 12:30 come to Whiskey Bend.
          That lowland smell—

Charles Freer in a Sierra Snowstorm
(little did I know)

Charles Freer made a fortune building railroad cars.
What he most loved in all the world was art.
He bought East Asian Art—China – Japan—
when things were cheap
and built a fine stone building for his works right on the Mall,
a lot's in storage, underground.

—After two seasons up on
Lookouts in the North Cascades,

a few years in Japan,
and many climbs on the snowpeaks of the west,
I found myself once in DC and asked to see
a sidewise handscroll mentioned in a book
"Rivers and Mountains Without End" or was it "Streams"?
kept at the Freer. I wanted to study
just how an artist might take on
the size of a range of mountains,
the landscape of the world.

They let me roll it out a meter at a time
and always kept an eye—allowed to write notes only with a
    pencil
—I think it was three hours.

Then slowly rolled the scroll back to the start.

Why I Take Good Care of My Macintosh

Because it broods under its hood like a perched falcon,

Because it jumps like a skittish horse and sometimes
    throws me,

Because it is pokey when cold,

Because plastic is a sad strong material that is charming
    to rodents,

Because it is flighty,

Because my mind flies into it through my fingers,

Because it leaps forward and backward, is an endless
    sniffer and searcher,

Because its keys click like hail on a boulder,

And it winks when it goes out,

And puts word-heaps into hoards for me, dozens of
    pockets of gold under boulders

in streambeds, identical seedpods strong on a vine,
  or it stores bins of bolts;

And I lose them and find them again,

Because whole worlds of writing can be boldly laid
  out and then highlighted and vanish in a flash at
  "delete,"

so it teaches of impermanence and pain;

And because my computer and me are both brief in
  this world,

both foolish, and we have earthly fates,

Because I have let it move in with me right in the tent,

And it goes with me out every morning;

We fill up our baskets, get back home,

Feel rich, relax,

I throw it a scrap and it hums.

Artemis and Pan

"The wildness of the savage is but a faint symbol
of the awful ferity with which good men and lovers meet."
                                        —HD Thoreau

          The "field" of the wild
                    Ainu, *iworu*,

          feeling the field; outback the ears;
outside the eyes, faint whiff—loose knees

Two fluff gray-squirrel tails whip round an oak's
          gray bark
Wildly horny   ferociously aloof
          the ferity of lovers

Pan and Artemis
        bow-twang   or
        open-sight .270 barks a puff

bring down a deer
and skin it together
eat fresh liver
        cooked over embers

In the silvery light of the moon

Anger, Cattle, and Achilles

Two of my best friends quit speaking
one said his wrath was like that of Achilles.
The three of us had traveled on the desert,
awakened to bird song and sunshine under ironwoods
        in a wadi south of the border.

They both were herders. One with cattle and poems,
the other with business and books.

One almost died in a car crash but slowly recovered
the other gave up all his friends,
        took refuge in a city
and studied the nuances of power.

One of them I haven't seen in years,
I met the other lately in the far back of a bar,
musicians playing near the window and he
sweetly told me "listen to that music.

The self we hold so dear will soon be gone."

A Letter to M.A. Who Lives Far Away

Dear Melissa,
I do remember you
You had curly hair
And stood by the stair
Up there on Quadra Isle
With a shy smile
Say hello to your mother Jean
I don't remember your sister's name
And that's a shame
But I sort of remember her face
And natural grace
Not all poetry has to rhyme
But this time
I'm writing back, the way you did it
It's to your credit
You got me to write this form
Since real poetry is born
From a formless place
Which is our Original Face
Zen Buddhists say,
In play.
So if this helps you to be a writer
It will please your new friend
Gary Snyder.

24. XI. 1986

First Flight

The Names of Actaeon's Hounds

Black-foot
Trail-follower
Voracious
Gazelle
Mountain-ranger
Fawn-killer
Hurricane
Hunter
Winged
Sylvan
Glen
Shepherd
Seizer
Catcher
Runner
Gnasher
Spot
Tigress
Might
White
Soot
Spartan
Whirlwind
Swift
Cyprian
Wolf
Grasper
Black
Shag
Fury
White-tooth
Barker
Black-hair
Beast-killer
Mountaineer

Old New Mexican Genetics

Santa Fe, at the Palace of the Governors, this 18th century listing of official genetic possibilities:

> *Español.* White. But maybe a Mestizo, or anyone who has enough money and the right style
>
> *Indio.* A Native American person
>
> *Mestizo.* One Spanish and one Indio parent
>
> *Color Quebrado.* "Broken color"—a rare category of 3-way or more mix. White / African / Indio
>
> *Mulatto.* White/African ancestry
>
> *Coyote.* Indio parent with Mestizo parent
>
> *Lobo.* One Indio plus one African parent
>
> *Genizaro* (Janissary). Plains Indian captives sold and used as slaves

Polyandry

The following castes practice polyandry:

Nayars, Thandanes, and Thiyyas:

Kammalane such as goldsmiths,
Blacksmiths, carpenters, laterite cutters,
bell-metal smiths and braziers,

also the castes allied to those of Kolla-kurupe—

shampooers, masseurs, and leather shield-makers

bow-makers, leather workers,
astrologers, washermen and barbers,
exorcists and umbrella-makers,
herbalists and *nag*-worship songsters.

All follow patriliny but the Nayars:
who are *marumakkathayam*, followers
of the mother-lineage,

from one end of Kerala to the other.

Stages of the End of Night and Coming Day

Halving of the night
frogs croaking
cock crowing
morning and night together
crow cawing
bright horizon.
glimmer of day

colors of cattle can be seen.
sunrise
dew dries
cattle go out

—Antananarivo of Madagascar

— II. Locals —

Why California Will Never Be Like Tuscany

There must have been huge oaks and pines, cedars,
                    maybe madrone,
in Tuscany and Umbria long ago.
A few centuries after wood was gone, they began to build
    with brick and stone.

Brick and stone farmhouses, solid, fireproof,
steel shutters and doors.

But farming changed.
60,000 vacant solid fireproof Italian farm houses
on the market in 1970,
scattered across the land.
Sixty thousand affluent foreigners,
to fix them,
learn to cook, and write a book.

But in California, houses all are wood—
roads pushed through, sewers dug, lines laid underground—
hundreds of thousands, made of strandboard, sheetrock,
    plaster—.

They won't be here 200 years from now—they'll burn or rot.

No handsome solid second homes for
Thousand-year later wealthy
Melanesian or Eskimo artists and writers here,

—oak and pine will soon return.

Sunday

Well I know Sunday is Sabbath
but who ever does it?
Except Berry. Nice poems.
It just happens I'm free

the first time in weeks from
chores and promises,
cracked valves, late bills,
and I think I'll take time
to brush the dog. She likes that.
& oil dry hard leather for sheath for shears,
for the tape rule, hatchet—
read a recipe for an aubergine salad,
this isn't work—

Then go for a hike
toward the bobcat dens and gravels,
hope no wildfires start today
—I'll get there and back
and just for a second,
maybe play.

Michael des Tombe
at the edge of the Canyon
the Killigrew Place

The Michael Killigrew des Tombe place
on a fine ledge of land out over the steep south canyon
drops off to a far river roar through the brush
huge old oaks and once was a small worn house
where a logger and family with kids all lived and then left
A year-round spring on the slope up so high, welcome
    surprise—
Michael and Tove, Theo and Mike, Julie and Za
all made it work. With cows and chickens and gardens
    and ponds
and barn and studio, books and paintings,
all made again and again, and the grandfather's sword
    from Japan
the Emperor had given him!
Over the canyon, just down from Bald Mountain,
paintings of slopes and of clouds and the deep blue sky,
the echoing conch, the mantras, the smiles and the hikes.

Mad Michael a genius, a leader, a visionary English-Dutch-
Turtle Island Elder,
here in this room where he lay with his cancer,
his friends and his *mala*,
calming them, easing them, utterly sane

Utterly sane, and then slipped away.

Chiura Obata's Moon

Walking along the noisy busy north Lake Tahoe shoreline
    highway 7 PM—
early October, late dusk, rickety houses, old motels
on the lakeshore side of the street a plastic
orange fencing keeps out
those who would try to get to the beach where they're
    building
some whole new set of structures for the tourists.
I'm at the Firelight Lodge, cramped for space and built
    around a pool
    that's empty, the clerk a slender blonde with an accent,
Polish she says, but she's been here now for years
and plans to stay. She's pretty,
she knows the life of youth, in the water and snow world of
    Lake Tahoe.
Walking up on a sign says Sancho's Tacos, a tiny storefront in
    a house.
Off to the southwest planet Venus, really bright,
sky so clear and purple-violet tonight,
two pine trunks and that early crescent moon—
the silhouetted ponderosa pine mature and tall
I make my way into Sancho's—I hadn't planned to—
but it's got a menu more than tacos.
Three youthful outdoor-clad enthusiasts just back from
some ridgetop hike are laughing and drinking in the corner.
Sancho's an anglo! With a little beard and sardonic smile.
I decide to go for a dinner—a whole cooked tilapia,
never saw that on a Mexican menu before.

Shades of Jack and Nancy Todd. Some article 30 years ago
on the fresh water fish tilapia, cousin of minnows,
first from Africa, you could raise in your greenhouse in tubs—
the fish that might help all us back-to-the-landers
get virtuous protein, maybe feed the world as well.
Looking south toward the darkening lake and the murmur of
trail gossip just at my back, it's the right place to be—
The tilapia-rice-and-beans dinner comes hot and it's good.
Outside on the deck the moon and Venus have shifted:
I see Chiura Obata's woodblock of dusk at Yosemite,
dated 1930—the soaring blue cliff, the pines, the new moon.

How to Know Birds

The place you're in
The time of year

How they move and where in the meadows, brush, forest,
          rocks, reeds, are they hanging out
               alone or in a group or little groups?

Size, speed, sorts of flight

Quirks. Tail flicks, wing-shakes, bobbing—
Can you see what they're eating?

Calls and songs?

Finally, if you get a chance, can you see their colors,
details of plumage—lines, dots, bars

That will tell you the details you need to come up with a name
but

You already know this bird.

Starting the Spring Garden
and Thinking of Thomas Jefferson

Turning this cloddish soil still damp and cold
with a heavy curved crofters spade

finally I've read the life of Thomas Jefferson
here we are about the same age
—eighty—except I'm living alone with my dog
and spading a tiny spring garden
and he had hundreds of workers
on the farm and fixing the house while he
mostly wrote letters and thinking—thinking
true democracy is to help everyone
do for themselves. Which means
we must think with the help of the whole
neighborhood, bullshit detectors in place but
cleanly and clearly forgiving
—to be free is to get past too much lonely stubborn
deluded private thirst for what?
for things? for some small perk?
So give and take. Where was Jefferson in this—I wonder—
whacking clods, tossing clumps of winter grass roots
                                    to the side
scooping out and heeling in some Asian aubergine
—the long thin kind you grill with grated ginger

Everyone free to decide to join in on the work
and the play
empowered to be free of "me"
in a world which both has and has not
hierarchy. But he had slaves
and never thought that through.

& Tom had friends like Madison and Adams
to honestly argue him down and explain
the cracks in his dream;

Now—out on the far west coast of the continent
this rough mountain pine tree land

two hundred years later,
putting another turn on
whatever he thought we could do
Tom Jefferson: never too late,
never be through,
you always can pick up a hoe—

let your people go—

Log Truck on the 80

Heading west down the 80
last slope before the valley,
pass a loaded log truck
incense cedars with that stringy bark
Mind watching lanes ahead
roams back to the mountains.
On the left side across the river
out toward Forest Hill,
or back toward Duncan Canyon,
or south to Sailor Meadow—
dark forests pass in mind.
See a shady canyon, tangled gully,
under old pine and fir and,
there: the fresh cut stumps of cedar.

Someone napping with his chainsaw
after lunch

Stories in the Night
In Native California the winter was storytelling time

Yesterday I was working most of the day with a breakdown in
   the system.
Generator 1, Generator 2, old phased-out Generator 3,

the battery array, the big Trace inverter—solar panels—
they had all stopped—cold early morning in the dark—
back to the old days, kerosene lamp—candles—woodstoves
   always work—
the back up generator #3 Honda, cycles wrong? Tricking
   inverter relay that starts the bulk charge?

Big Green Onan—fueled by propane—wouldn't start—
(one time turned out there was a clogged air cleaner; oil-
   drops blow back up from deep inside.)

(I try to remember machinery can always be fixed—but be
ready to give up the plans that were made for the day—go
back to the manual—call up friends who know more—make
some tea—relax with your tools and your problems, start
enjoying the day.)

First fifteen years we lived here, kerosene lamps. Heavy tile
roof in the shade of a huge pre-contact black oak;

Cheri, Siegfried's long-time woman friend and partner, is due
at any time with a 9-ton truck of ¾ inch crushed rock. Wet
dirt every winter eats up gravel, keeping a few hard roads
for drenching winter rains and melting snows takes plan-
ning.   You have to ditch them too.

In 1962 going all through Kyushu with Joanne, walked
around Hiroshima. Busy streets and coffee shops, green
leafy trees and gardens, a lively place. But at Mt. Aso, great
caldera in the center of the island, crater 30 miles across, saw
sightseers from Nagasaki with the twisted shiny scarred
burn-faces of survivors from those days. And then read
Barefoot Gen.

What got to me about the Bomb was *too much power*.
And then temptation there to be . . . the first.
The first to be "The Emperor of the World."
Yet to be done. So change our course around, or there we
   head.

I could never be a Muslim, a Christian, or a Jew because the
Ten Commandments fall short of moral rigor. The Bible's
"Shalt not kill" leaves out the other realms of life,

How could that be? What sort of world did they think this is?
With no account for all the wriggling feelers and the little
fins, the spines, the slimy necks—eyes shiny in the night—paw
prints in the snow.

And that other thing, can't have "no other god before
   me"—like,
profound anxiety of power and jealousy and envy,
what sort of god is that?
worrying all the time?
Plenty of little gods are waiting to begin their practice and
learn just who they are.

In North India, Fourth Century AD, some Buddhist
Tantrick Teacher Lady said, "That God called Yahweh to
the west, he's really something. But too bad, he has this
nutty thing that he's
Creator of the world."
A delusion that could really set you back.

But returning to energy. I'll fix the Onan, give up on # 3, it's
too far gone and next time get a backup with a cast iron block
and water cooling and a warranty good for centuries—put in
a bunch more panels for the sun—

The old time people here in warm earth lodges thirty feet
   across
burned pitchy pinewood slivers for their candles,
snow after snow for all those centuries before—
lodgefire light and pitchy slivers burning—

don't need much light   for stories in the night.

III.09

Morning Songs, Goose Lake

Orion, Pleiades, in the east, then
white glow on the hills,
try to count the stars inside the corral of Capella
they fade as light from the east comes on

wild goose-calls wake us awake

crows, robins, woodpeckers   truck-rumbles
we diurnal daylight eyebright beings

hear goose-calls greet the star-fade
far-off cows begin the morning Moo.

Travelling to the Malheur Lake Wildlife Preserve
in the Oregon High Desert, slept the first night at a little
campground by Goose Lake on the Oregon-California Line.
With Carole, Mika, and Robin—August 1990

Second Flight

Fixing the System

Under the topless, bottomless,
        empty blue sky
hands and knees,
        looking down a little hole

leaky gate-valve   drip drip

Young surfers on the
        frothy shallow beach
        ecstatic dogs bite waves
log truck rumbles on the bridge.

        Big River, Mendocino

Watching a tiny bird flit down and
perch on a standpipe hose bib
dipping drinking drops of drip

every valve
leaks a little
there is no

stopping the flow.

"Reinventing North America"

Living on the western edge of Turtle Island
in Shasta Nation
Whose people are Native, Euro-, African, Asian, Mestizo,
Pacific and Nuevo Americano—Turtle Islanders—
Where the dominant language is still Mericano
In the Homo sapiens year 50,000.

From the Sky

The sandhill cranes are leaving
soundings from the sky
songbirds from Central America
begin to arrive.
Flitting through the bushes
                    snowpatches on the ground
truck still in four-wheel drive.

Here

In the dark
(The new moon long set)

A soft grumble in the breeze
Is the sound of a jet so high
It's already long gone by

Some planet
Rising From the east   shines
Through the trees

It's been years since I thought,

Why are we here?

30. VIII. 09

— *III. Ancestors* —

Eiffel Tundra

Graceful. Several million rivets, as it arcs up a lath-work of steel riveted webs. The first level ascended either by the stairway or a slightly inclined funicular lift that has an upper and lower section to carry passengers in. Up to the first level, which has a full-scale quality restaurant, as well as a sort of "bistro" and some exhibits on the construction of the tower. Then the next level up another few hundred feet is a somewhat smaller area with outlook platforms, some glassed-in and another not; and a stand-up coffee place. From there you get into the direct elevator to the *sommet*. It's a fast elevator considering how much it gains, and at the top there are two levels. The lower level is glassed-in; step up to the next level and you're out in the wind. Above that is another 100 feet or so with a control room connected to it. A high mast is studded with electronic equipment, repeaters, what-all. When they built the Eiffel Tower they had no idea of what use it would be to electronics in the future. Everyone's bundled up, the usual complement of a few East Asians, not crowded but—these are hardy people! And I take my time to gaze down from behind the protection of a glass enclosure, out of the wind, on each section of the city—half an hour of studying each block and section while referring back to the map. It's nowhere a kind of a grid town although there are repetitions of the radiating star road motif, particularly outward from the Arc de Triomphe. This entire tower is repainted they say every five years.

chill wind, air gray and misty,
looking down on tundra, frost-heave-shapes, polygons,

faint aurochses and mammoths browsing in the fog.

Kill

The women share in the kill

The women are first at the kill

The women kill the kill

Three straight vertical lines   tattooed

On the shaved plucked mons.

pass through   *go past*

life, past death.

Kalahari Desert dream, Botswana 1994

Claws / Cause
for Zenshin Whalen

"Graph" is graceful claw-curve,
        grammar a   weaving carving

paw track, lizard-slither, tumble of
a single boulder down. Glacier scrapes across the bedrock,
wave-lines on the beach.

Saying, "this was me"
scat sign of time and place

language is   shit, claw, or tongue

"tongue" with all its flickers
might be a word for

sex, and   fate.
A single kiss   a tiny cause [claws]

—such grand effects [text]

                                        2000

Hai-en Temple South Korea
Home of the Total Tripitaka
Set of Printing Blocks

Four a.m. sandy courtyard, Orion rising

The great drum   booms
from the painted bell-tower
        And the bell then bongs

morning sutra chanting
in the Great Hall up another flight of stairs
        & one more terrace further up the slope,
        is the hall of all
        the birchwood blocks.
        that print the thousand-volume *Triple Basket*   .
        Eighty thousand carved blocks rank on rank.
        Cooled by grillwork open windows

—one block page says it,

        "*live* the wisdom   gone beyond:
        consciousness   is shapely,
        being, empty   formal;
        form,   is freedom,

these fast deep bows

                        South Korea X. '00

Young David in Florence, Before the Kill

Michelangelo's David's not a warrior,
not just a clever boy—he's a cool young man.
Weight on the right leg, eyes left
brow crinkled, calculating, estimating
         the text says Goliath is already down.

Left arm to his left shoulder and the stone-pouch,
right hand down at his side,
holds the ends
         long leather sling straps—he has *not*
thrown it yet. Stands still, in a deep place
a hinge in time

modesty
and naked grace.

Firenze 2004

Mu Ch'i's Persimmons

On a back wall down the hall

lit by a side glass door

is the scroll of Mu Ch'i's great
sumi painting, "persimmons"

The wind-weights hanging from the
axles hold it still.

The best in the world, I say,
of persimmons.

Perfect statement of emptiness
no other than form

the twig and the stalk still on,
the way they sell them in the
market even now.

The original's in Kyoto at a
lovely Rinzai temple where they
show it once a year

this one's a perfect copy from Benrido
I chose the mounting elements myself
with the advice of the mounter

I hang it every fall.

And now, to these over-ripe persimmons
from Mike and Barbara's orchard.
Napkin in hand,
I bend over the sink

suck the sweet orange goop
that's how I like it
gripping a little twig

those painted persimmons

sure cure hunger

(Dôgen: ". . . there is no remedy for satisfying hunger
other than a painted rice-cake." November 1242.)

The Bend in the Vlatava

On a stone bridge in Praha
watching water swirl and splash below
scouring stone millrace

darkly frothy,
thinking soon I leave and go,
this place for birds, this town,

all its stairs and walkways,
drains and gates
leading water to the river

sweeping toward the Elbe,
Hamburg, North Sea,
curving little river

I have seen your water
everywhere I walk
—your big wide bend at the Hrad—

> *I will remember you Vlatava River*
> *as I streak on winged sandals*
> *west to the rivers of home.*

The Shrine at Delphi

The shrine compound is located eight or ten miles inland
and about 1500' above sea level. Above are rock steeps. The
hills are rocky outcrops and a kind of chaparral. Neatly
arranged and lavish, extensive, "European Cultural Center"
we stay at. Delphi oracle power lasted about 2000 years,
finally shut down by Theodosius in AD 385.

A stream comes down a ravine reaching back to Mt. Par-
nassus, waters the "Castalian Spring" of pilgrim-purification.
In a rocky cleft, a chosen place, I leave an offering from
Turtle Island: a large quartz crystal, a *panaka* feather, a black-
bear claw, a Bodhi-tree bead; and native tobacco. And chant
the *Daihishu*. That night we share poems.

I'm in the Tourist Guest House
Together with Greek poets, teachers, writers,
at the ruins of the Shrine of Delphi
on a rocky slope of chaparral

and a lovely young poet reads aloud
in Greek translation

my poems for you,
takes me first back to Kyoto,

the room in the temple by the old plum tree
where one night I dreamed of you
forty years ago

And eight years even further back,
to an apple orchard,
us making love in the shadow of leaves
curled up together, happy, green

I knew even then
I'd never feel quite like that
with anyone,
ever again.

5.XII.98

Wildfire News

For millions,

for hundreds of millions of years

there were fires. Fire after fire.

Fire raging forest or jungle,

giant lizards dashing away

big necks from the sea

looking out at the land in surprise—

fire after fire. Lightning strikes

by the thousands, just like today.

Volcanoes erupting, fire flowing over the land.

Huge Sequoia   two foot thick fireproof bark

fire pines, their cones love the heat,

how long to say,

that's how they covered the continents

ten lakhs of millennia or more.

I have to slow down my mind.

slow down my mind

Rome was built in a day.

Otzi Crosses Over

I concluded that he was crossing the range to get to a settle-
ment on the other side where his daughter lived. He had
unfinished arrows in his quiver that he could finish over the
winter, and he'd return to the south side of the range next
spring.

Moretti and I had spent the day in Bolzano studying his
tools, clothes, herbs, flints, everything about him—and then
when we were up on the Dolomite ridge near Sella Pass
I realized we were looking far at the range he had indeed
walked over—and it all fell into place.

On his Way

He walks steady up the slope—bedrock and plant clumps—
wind in his ear, beard waving a bit in the breeze—low clouds

from the west in puffs—passing over and through the high
peak points; blue sky gaps seen—farther on a set of white
and gray cloud puffs hides a ridge. View through a notch to
farther blue cloud-shadow patches and sunshine—breeze soft-
ens—getting into snow now, sun behind clouds but still lots
of light,

Sore knee, and painful shoulder—but—about to step out on
the icefield, cross it and go down the other side, more snow
and rock and alpine fir below. This moment sun and wind—
my little knife, my fire-kit, my settled daughter, this lonely
route.

5500 years ago. 22 Sept 2004.

Third Flight

Inupiaq values

HUMOR

SHARING

HUMILITY

HARD WORK

SPIRITUALITY

COOPERATION

FAMILY ROLES

AVOID CONFLICT

HUNTER SUCCESS

DOMESTIC SKILLS

LOVE FOR CHILDREN

RESPECT FOR NATURE

RESPECT FOR OTHERS

RESPECT FOR ELDERS

RESPONSIBILITY FOR TRIBE

KNOWLEDGE OF LANGUAGE

KNOWLEDGE OF FAMILY TREE

On the walls of a classroom in a tiny school in Kobuk Alaska
just a bit south of the tree-line.

Seven Brief Poems from Italia

Roma

Built back, of old stones from old buildings,
old bricks and stones on even older stones
—always-changing languages
broken tumbled talus slopes again

Victory Monument

Piled onto Roman Forum ruins
—dust on dust of days

Roma

Acquapendente Forest

Cowbarn on the mountainside
wooden hay-fork museum
life-size plastic cows in the yard,
"Michelangelo's Cow Sculpture Piazza"

Tuscany

The Maremma

Mesa-cliff edges of the lands of the Maremma
white cows, white horses,
fluffy white slow-walking dogs

Pitigliano

Commercial Poplar by the River Po

> pulp-for-paper groves
>   so cool, so woodsy!
>   cut every twelve years

Isola Boschina / Woodsy Isle

> Dense deep woods
> Creeper vines everywhere,
>   over the Po   herons, and
> small hawk   *geppio*
> large hawk   *poliana*

Po Valley

Alongside the Road just Below Sella Pass

> leaning back on a
>   bench look straight up
>   at the blue sky duomo
>
> all the church we'll ever need

Alto Adige

Askesis, Praxis, Theôria of the Wild

The shining way of the wild

—its *theôria*

is,   that the world is unrelenting, brief, and often painful

and its *askesis*,

cold, hunger, stupid mistakes, bitterness, delusions, loneliness;

hard nights and days   are unavoidable

to find the *praxis* is to

hang in, work it out, watch for the moment,

coiled and gazing,   the shining way of the wild

from before, & 4. IX. 94

— *IV. Go Now* —

Go Now

You don't want to read this,
reader,
be warned, turn back
from the darkness,
go now.

—about death and the
death of a lover—it's not some vague meditation
or a homily, not irony,
no god or enlightenment or
acceptance—or struggle—with the
end of our life,

it's about how the eyes
sink back and the teeth stand out
after a few warm days.
Her last
breath, and I still wasn't ready
for *that* breath, that last, to come
at last. After ten long years.
So thin that the joints showed through,
each sinew and knob
Shakyamuni coming down from the mountain
after all that fasting
looked plumper than her.
          "I met a walking
                    skeleton, his name was Thomas Quinn"—
we sang
back then
she could barely walk, but she did.
I gave her the drugs every night and we always
kissed sweetly and fiercely after the push;
kissed hard, and our teeth clacked, her
lips dry, fierce, she was all
bones, breath and eyes.

We hadn't made love in eight years
she had holes that drained all the time

in her sides, new ones that came,
end game—and she talked when she could.

Daughters, mother, sister, cousins, friends
in and out of the room. Even the
hardened hospice nurse in tears.

"Goodnight sweetheart, well it's time to go."
our duet, cheek to cheek,
for that last six weeks

She watched the small nesting birds
in the tree just outside.
Then she died.
I sponged her and put on a blouse
with sleeves to cover gaunt elbows,
a long gauzy skirt
like Mumtaz Mahal—

I was alone. Then they came.
One daughter cried out
"She's a corpse!" and stood fixed
outside on the deck. It was warm.
The third day
the van from the funeral home came for her,
backing up close to the door,
I helped roll her into the sheets
slid on a gurney and wheeled to the car
and they drove up the rough gravel hill
our family group standing there silent
as I turned, held my breath,
closed my eyes to the sky.

Five days of heat and they called me,
just Kai and me, to come witness cremation.
It cost extra. Only the two of us
wanted to be there, to see.
We followed the limousine
through a concrete-yard with hoppers of gravel
through a gate beyond that

to an overgrown
sheet metal warehouse that once was a body-shop
to the furnace and chimney room,
it looked like a kiln for a potter,
there were cardboard coffins
stacked up   empty around.

The young man at a desk and a table
filling out papers, sweating, as we
set out the incense and bell, the candle,
and I went to the light cardboard coffin
and opened the lid. The smell hit like a blow.
I had thought that the funeral home
had some sort of cooling
like a walk-in
maybe they did. But it didn't much help.
Her gaunt face more sunken, dehydrated,
eyes still open but dull, teeth bigger, her body,
her body for sure, my sweet lady's body
down to essentials, and I placed two books on
her breast, books she had written,
to send on her way, looked again
            and again,
and closed it   and nodded.

He rolled it up close, slid the
box in the furnace, locked down the door,
like loading a torpedo
we burned incense and chanted the
texts for impermanence and all beings who have lived
or who ever will yet; things writ only in magic
and just for the dead—*not for you dear reader*—
watching the temperature gauge on the furnace,
firing with propane, go steadily up.

So now we can go.
Maybe I know where she's gone—

Kai and I one more time
take a deep breath

—this is the price of attachment—

"Worth it. Easily worth it—"

Still in love, being there,
seeing and smelling and feeling it,
thinking farewell,

worth even the smell.

This present moment
that lives on

to become

long ago

Notes and Acknowledgments

PART I. OUTRIDERS

Gnarly

Versions 2002 to 2012, then revised and sent to Glenn Storhaug for a broadside in Sept of 2014. Still in the works, January 2015.

The Earth's Wild Places

This poem was lost for some years and then turned up again. I don't remember any publishing history for it other than as a fugitive broadside maybe in the seventies.

Siberian Outpost

This poem was composed in the far southern high Sierra. First published in *The American Scholar* along with several others. Siberian Outpost is a bleak post in the ground along the Pacific Crest Trail, not far from Siberian Pass. There are no Foxtail Pine in Siberia.

Elwha River

The major river coming right out of the Olympic Mountains of Washington State. The Elwha tribe had been working for the removal of dams from it for years. Finally in 2011 the river was opened and salmon instantly swam the long distance to the headwaters. A longer version of this poem is with my unpublished 1964 notes for "Mountains and Rivers Without End." This version is now published in *Where the Thunderbird Rests His Head and Waits for the Songs of Return*, Kate Reavey and Alice Derry, eds. Sequim, WA: Rhymestone Arts, 2011.

Charles Freer in a Sierra Snowstorm

Published in *Catamaran*.

My Macintosh

This poem too lived the life of a stray cat for several years and was rediscovered by somebody at the *NY Times*. Like Sappho's poems it had apparently been used to wrap fresh fish.

Artemis and Pan
First published in Ann Kjellborg's *Little Star*.

Anger, Cattle, and Achilles
It always surprises me how many people in the audience know the name "Briseis"—the young woman that Achilles loved so dearly. First published in *Little Star*.

A Letter to M.A. Who Lives Far Away
This young woman lived on one of the islands in the Straits of Georgia in British Columbia. Since she had written a letter about poetry to me all in rhyme I tried to reciprocate. She was about thirteen then. She now works as a "Clown Adventurer Busker" in Vancouver, BC. This also was first published in *The American Scholar*.

First Flight (for "flight" think of a set of wine-tastings)

> *Actaeon's Hounds.* As translated from Ovid's Latin by Frank Justus Miller.

> *Old New Mexican Genetics* from the Palace of the Governors. On display in the museum.

> *Polyandry*, from a book on that topic based on the State of Kerala in SW India.

> *Stages of the End of Night*, from Madagascar.

PART II. LOCALS

Why California Will Never Be Like Tuscany
Published first in *The American Scholar*.

Sunday
for Wendell Berry

Stories in the Night
First published in *The American Scholar*.

PART III. ANCESTORS

Claws / Cause
for Philip

Mu Ch'i's Persimmons
Published in *The New Yorker*.

The Bend in the Vlatava

Wildfire News
Published in *Tree Rings*.

Thanks To

An incomplete list of the many people about the planet who
have been challengers, teachers, and friends to my various
works—

East Asia—
My thanks to Bei Dao; Yamazato Katsunori, Hara Shigeyoshi,
Bruce Bailey, Oe Kenzaburo, and Tanikawa Shuntaro for
insights and conversations; and the great South Korean poet
Ko Un.

Eurasia—
A special thanks to Irina Dyatlovskaya for her help in under-
standing Russian and Buryat visions of recent decades; Czech
thinker and writer Lubos Snizek; Italian bioregionalist editor,
translator, and farmer Giuseppe Moretti; the selfless and
dedicated translators Rita degli Esposti and Chiara D'Ottavi,
also of Italy.

Africa—
Julia Martin

The Spanish and Catalonian translator and tireless human
rights advocate Jose Luis Regojo of Barcelona; Ignacio Fer-
nandez of Madrid; Estonian poet Jaan Kaplinski who I finally
met in Tokyo.

Mid-Pacific—
Shawna Yang Ryan

Turtle Island—
John Schreiber of Vancouver Island and the Chilcotin coun-
try; Jan Zwicky and Robert Bringhurst, a formidable team
based in the Straits of Georgia;

Puget Sounders Kate Reavey, Tim McNulty, and Red Pine;

Columbia River people Jarold Ramsey, Bill Baker, Richard
Blickle, Rosemary Berleman, and Ursula Le Guin; Deschutes

country forester Michael Keown; and north coastal California sages Jim Dodge, Freeman House, and Jerry Martien;

Montana poet Roger Dunsmore and songwriter Greg Keeler; Rockies linguist-poet Andrew Schelling, southern Colorado Rockies tipi-maker and beadworker Nosaka Kazuko; Southwest Plateau ethnomusicologist wanderer Jack Loeffler; potter and river-runner Joe Bennion; J B Bryan the publisher; scholar and jaguar-conservationist Diana Hadley; the guardian of the Los Angeles River Lewis MacAdams; rancher-poet of the southern Sierra John Dofflemeyer; Eliot Weinberger.

Right in the middle of it all: Wendell Berry.

Northern California—
Multi-faceted poet/actor/priest Peter Coyote; Brenda Hillman; the Grand Acharya of Mt. Tamalpais Matthew Davis; inspiring collaborator-artist Tom Killion; razor-sharp Rebecca Solnit; poet and explorer Dale Pendell; Robert Hass; and Malcolm Margolin with his tireless vision; precise and often hilarious Joanne Kyger; scientist-shaman-rebel Kim Stanley Robinson.

And always, Jack Shoemaker.

UNCOLLECTED POEMS, DRAFTS, FRAGMENTS, AND TRANSLATIONS

Reed College Poems

a poem

walking lonely on a fall day
in a long meadow, slanting open to the woods
where the frost chilled
the dead grass, a year ago.

peer sharply through the brown grass:
the slim thin white thing rotted
long ago.

build now a squat stone tablet
for ants to sun on
and hide it in the dead grass:
"Here Lie My Children."

The Death of Rhea

"Behold, behold!" the Bowman said
With a fearful falling cry
While the man in black
With his blue jowls slack
Like a fluttering moth came wheeling back
From the pitiless velvet sky.

An Autumn Poem

This distraught season
Sunlight shivers on the grass
Like a pale genius in his bathrobe
Barefoot, wavering up the stairs.

All the lovely vicious women
Seeking Orpheus through the halls,
The poet cowering in the Men's Room:
A dead leaf, withered.

See his veins,
O daughters of Jerusalem.

Kasina Song

Dallying in pleasant verdure
One warm Monday afternoon
Forming circles in the sand
With wet red clay, you cried,
"Insatiable are the lusts!"
A vision then appeared.

So I departed, bowl in hand
To live in this transcendent land.

"Escaping Cambridge"

Escaping Cambridge,
He turned away from London
With austere passion faced the seas

Accompanied by numbered boxes
Crossed the plains in teeming summer
Soft eyes avoiding sores and hunger

Stood sorrowful in cool Darjeeling:
Above the tea-brush Kanchenjunga falls unfurled
Placenta of the soil created
Strewn beyond Cathay

Through rank valleys, thirsty plains
Rising early—frost chilling sandalled feet—
Sleepy men muttering in an unknown tongue
Pack loaded, far from villages
So he could venture

Indus, Brahmaputra, silver shreds at glacier snout
Wheels of fluttering paper creaking turn

He fell beyond the mists of Chomolungma
Where even nomads shun to die
      Who is to say that demons did not kill him
Far from Tea and Cambridge?

1950–51

"Dear Mr. President"

Dear Mr. President:

There is no bomb in Gilead.
The red Chinese are not red Indians:
You could have saved the Sioux.
Please stop them building roads
In the North Cascades.

There were great white birds
In the tops of the banyan trees
Calling across the town,
When I was in Saigon.

      Respectfully yours,
      Gary Snyder

c. 1955

Hymn to the Goddess San Francisco in Paradise
If you want to live high get high—Nihil C.

I

up under the bell skirt
caving over the soil
white legs flashing
         —amazed to see under their clothes they are
                        naked
         this makes them sacred
& more than they are in their own shape
                free.

the wildest cock-blowing
         gang-fucking foul-tongued
                head chick
         thus the most so—

II

high town
high   in the dark   town
         dream   sex   church
         YAHWEH   peyote spook
         Mary the fish-eyed
                spotless,
                lascivious,
vomiting molten gold.

san fran sisco
hung over & swing down
                dancers on water
         oil slick glide
         shaman longshoremen
         magical strikes—
howls of the guardians rise from the waterfront.
—state line beauties those switcher engines
         leading waggons
warehouz of jewels and fresh fur

car leans
    on its downhill springs
        parked on mountainsides.
white minarets in the night
    demon fog chaos.
bison stroll on the grass.
    languid and elegant, fucking while standing
        young couples in silk
          make-up on.

crystal towers   gleam for a hundred miles
    poison oak hedges, walld child garden
& the ring mountains holding a cool
    basin of pure evening fog
    strained thru the bridge
    gold and orange,
beams of cars wiser than drivers
stream across promenades, causeways
    incensed exhaust.

smiling the City Hall Altar to Heaven
    they serve up the cock   tail,
there is higher than nature in city
    it spins in the sky.

III

quenching the blue flame
tasting the tea brought from China
cracking the fresh duck egg on white plate

passed out the gates of our chambers
over the clear miles, ships.
forever such ecstasy
    wealth & such beauty
    we live in the sign of Good Will . . .
(the white-robed saint trim my locks for
    a paltry sum . . . life is
    like free)
rolling lawns clippt and the smell of gum tree.

boiled crab from a saltwater vat.
                              rhine wine.
bison and elk of Chrysopylae
eels in those rocks in the wave
olive oil, garlic, soy, hard cheese.

Devas of small merit in Jambudvipa
Plucking sour berries to eat:
shall ascend to an eminence,
scanning the scene
                              fog in
            from the Farallones
long ship low   far below
            sliding under the bridge
            bright white   red-lead.
                              —blue of the sea.
            on that ship is me.

                              IV
—smilers all on the nod nap on cots
but the slither   & breakfree
            tosst slipper up on the toe
                        & the white thighs open
                                    the flesh of the wet flower
                              LAW
crossed eyes gleam   *come*
            flowery prints and
            yellow kettles in a row
            breast weight swelld down

kind chairmen smile around.
generals and presidents swallow
                        hoping   they too   can come . . .
            THERE IS NO WAY

            turn back dead tourist
            drop your crumb your funny passport
—fall back richer spenders
            think you make with wild teenager

on hard forever
crust in jewel
—*you are too old.*
the san francisco fake front strip tease
phony, sweaty,
last a minute and they stink and die

THIS LAND IS FOR THE HIGH
    & love is for ten thousand years.
        (damnd square climbers give me pains)
them wilty blossoms on her sweaty brow—
    the flute and lute and drums

    policecars sireen down on Fillmore
    fog clears back away
    the police close in
       & shoot the loose
    & clouds are slipping by

& hide it in your pockets.

It all becomes plain sky.

                       1965

The Elwha River

I

I was a girl waiting by the roadside for my boyfriend to come in his car. I was pregnant, I should have been going to high school. I walked up the road when he didn't come, over a bridge; I saw a sleeping man. I came to the Elwha River— grade school—classes—I went and sat down with the children. The teacher was young and sad-looking, homely; she assigned us an essay:
"What I Just Did."

"I was waiting for my boyfriend by the Elwha bridge. The
bridge was redwood, a fresh bridge with inner bark still
clinging on some logs—it smelled good. There was a man
there sleeping under redwood trees. He had a box of flies by
his head; he was on the ground. I crossed the Elwha River
by a meadow; it had a flat stony prong between two river
forks . . ."

Thinking this would please the teacher. We handed all the
papers in, and got them back—mine was C minus. The chil-
dren then went home; the teacher came to me and said
"I don't like you."
"Why?"
—Because I used to be a whore."

The Elwha River, I explained, is a real river, but not the river
I described. Where I had just walked was real but for the
dream river—actually the Elwha doesn't fork at that point.

As I write this I must remind myself that there is another
Elwha, the actual Olympic peninsula river, which is not the
river I took pains to recollect as real in the dream.

There are no redwoods north of southern
Curry County, Oregon.

21.X.1958

II

Marble hollow-ground hunting knife;

        pigleather tobacco pouch
      left on the ground at Whiskey Bend along
      the Elwha, 1950—

Sewing kit. Blown off the cot beside me
on the boatdeck by a sudden wind
                South China Sea;

A black beret Joanne had given me for my birthday
left in some
Kawaramachi bar.

Swiss army knife stole from my pants
        at Juhu Beach outside Bombay,
                            a fine italic pen,

Theodora, Kitty-chan,
                bottle of wine got broke.
                things left on the sand.

    Lost things.

III

Elwha, from its source. Threadwhite falls
out of snow-tunnel mouths with
cold mist-breath
saddles of deep snow on the ridges—

        o wise stream—o living flow
    o milky confluence, bank cutter
                alder toppler
                make meander
swampy acre   elk churned mud

    The big Douglas fir in this valley.
    Nobly groovd bark, it adapts: where Sitka spruce
    cannot.
            Redwood and sequoia
    resisting and enduring, as against adaptation;
    one mind.

        Trail crew foreman says they finally got wise
    to making trails low on the outside, so water
    can run off good—before they were worried because
    packstock always walks the outside of the trail
    because they don't want to bump their loads on rocks
    or trees   "punching out all the way from N Fork

over Low Divide & clear back here, this punchin gets
    mighty old"

Puncheon slab saw cut *wowed*

"They got rip-cut chains now maybe different rakers
    this here punchin gets old"

    About 12:30 come to Whiskey Bend.
    That lowland smell.

21.VIII.1964

A Lion Dream

I

Dressed up in slacks & good shoes I was going walking with
two friends along a road a ways above a river. To get down,
we found an opening in the bushes and a stairway made
of stone. Slippery and some parts muddy, thick with moss.
Down by the river I went out on a gravel-bar and looking
back, I saw a lion coming up behind my friends. I shouted
out a warning, and then waded in the river, thinking lions
wouldn't swim. Clothes and all. I started swimming at an
angle to the current—a fast, fairly shallow mountain river—

The lion started swimming too. Scrambling up the far bank,
I threw rocks at the lion; one hit it on the nose. It changed
into a girl. I kept on throwing rocks and she turned over in
the water, one glancing off her belly. I ran to a house on the
riverbank and rang the doorbell, getting scared. It sounded
like the people in the house were trying to open up the door
but it was stuck.

The Lion-girl was standing in the water wading out of the
shallows. She was very young and slender; very high, very
small, breasts; and no pubic hair. She was carrying a book.
She came up on the porch and said "I live here." I said,
"You ought to let the neighbors know."

II

HAIL

to the Goddess in the LION FORM
    who swims rivers
high-breasted, slender,
    no body hair.

SHE who carries a book and
DWELLS
    on the opposite shore,

    svāhā

        1967

A Curse
on the Men in Washington, Pentagon

OṂ A KA CA ṬA PA YA ŚA   SVĀHĀ

As you shoot down the Vietnamese girls and men
    in their fields
    burning and chopping,
    poisoning and blighting,

So surely I hunt the white man down
    in my heart.
The crew-cutted Seattle boy
The Portland boy who worked for U.P.
        that was me.

I won't let him live. The 'American'
    I'll destroy. The 'Christian'
        has long been dead.

They won't pass onto my children.
I'll give them Chief Joseph, the Bison herds,

Ishi, sparrowhawk, the Fir trees
The Buddha, their own naked bodies,
Swimming and dancing and singing
                    instead.

As I kill the white man,
              the 'American'
              in me
And dance out the Ghost dance:
To bring back America, the grass and the streams,

To trample your throat in your dreams.

This magic I work, this loving I give
              that my children may flourish

And yours won't thrive.

                HI'NISWA' VITA'KI'NI

                                    June 1967

Smokey the Bear Sutra

Once in the Jurassic, about 150 million years ago,
the Great Sun Buddha in this corner of the Infinite
Void gave a great Discourse to all the assembled elements
and energies: to the standing beings, the walking beings,
the flying beings, and the sitting beings—even grasses,
to the number of thirteen billion, each one born from a
seed, were assembled there: a Discourse concerning
Enlightenment on the planet Earth.

"In some future time, there will be a continent called
America. It will have great centers of power called
such as Pyramid Lake, Walden Pond, Mt. Rainier, Big Sur,
Everglades, and so forth; and powerful nerves and channels
such as Columbia River, Mississippi River, and Grand Canyon.

The human race in that era will get into troubles all over
its head, and practically wreck everything in spite of
its own strong intelligent Buddha-nature."

"The twisting strata of the great mountains and the pulsings
of great volcanoes are my love burning deep in the earth.
My obstinate compassion is schist and basalt and
granite, to be mountains, to bring down the rain. In that
future American Era I shall enter a new form: to cure
the world of loveless knowledge that seeks with blind hunger;
and mindless rage eating food that will not fill it."

And he showed himself in his true form of

SMOKEY THE BEAR

A handsome smokey-colored brown bear standing on his
hind legs, showing that he is aroused and watchful.

Bearing in his right paw the Shovel that digs to the
truth beneath appearances; cuts the roots of useless attach-
ments, and flings damp sand on the fires of greed and war;

His left paw in the Mudra of Comradely Display—
indicating
that all creatures have the full right to live to their limits
and that deer, rabbits, chipmunks, snakes, dandelions,
and lizards all grow in the realm of the Dharma;

Wearing the blue work overalls symbolic of slaves and
laborers, the countless men oppressed by a civilization
that claims to save but only destroys;

Wearing the broad-brimmed hat of the West, symbolic of
the forces that guard the Wilderness, which is the Natural
State of the Dharma and the True Path of man on earth;
all true paths lead through mountains—

With a halo of smoke and flame behind, the forest fires
of the kali-yuga, fires caused by the stupidity of those

who think things can be gained and lost whereas in truth all
is contained vast and free in the Blue Sky and Green Earth
of One Mind;

     Round-bellied to show his kind nature and that the great
earth has food enough for everyone who loves her and trusts
her;

     Trampling underfoot wasteful freeways and needless
suburbs; smashing the worms of capitalism and
totalitarianism;

     Indicating the Task: his followers, becoming free of cars,
houses, canned foods, universities, and shoes, master the
Three Mysteries of their own Body, Speech, and Mind; and
fearlessly chop down the rotten trees and prune out the
sick limbs of this country America and then burn the leftover
trash.

Wrathful but Calm, Austere but Comic, Smokey the Bear
will Illuminate those who would help him; but for those who
would hinder or slander him,

              HE WILL PUT THEM OUT.

Thus his great Mantra:
     Namah samanta vajranam chanda maharoshana
     Sphataya hum traka ham mam

"I DEDICATE MYSELF TO THE UNIVERSAL DIAMOND
BE THIS RAGING FURY DESTROYED"

And he will protect those who love woods and rivers,
Gods and animals, hobos and madmen, prisoners and sick
people, musicians, playful women, and hopeful children;

And if anyone is threatened by advertising, air pollution,
or the police, they should chant SMOKEY THE BEAR'S
WAR SPELL:

DROWN THEIR BUTTS
CRUSH THEIR BUTTS
DROWN THEIR BUTTS
CRUSH THEIR BUTTS

And SMOKEY THE BEAR will surely appear to put the
enemy out with his vajra-shovel.

Now those who recite this Sutra and then try to put it in
    practice will accumulate merit as countless as the sands
    of Arizona and Nevada,
Will help save the planet Earth from total oil slick,
Will enter the age of harmony of man and nature,
Will win the tender love and caresses of men, women, and
    beasts,
Will always have ripe blackberries to eat and a sunny spot
    under a pine tree to sit at.

AND IN THE END WILL WIN HIGHEST PERFECT
ENLIGHTENMENT.

thus have we heard.

(may be reproduced free forever)

February 1968

Kumarajiva's Mother
From Mountains & Rivers

Who was Kumarajiva's mother.
            giva-giva
            jiva-jiva   "some mysterious bird
        with a lovely call. It has a human face
        and two heads—a bird's body—"

    princess of the royal line of Kucha

"I don't know anything about it.   So I can't."
"I never met the lady . . . I don't know—I remember
          you telling a story about him the other day."

      she had freckles. she
      became a nun? She took him to Kashmir
      they met an arhat with a piercing glance

What do you mean by that?
      year by year his Chinese prose style grew—

"first great revolutionist in prose the next is
      Mao Tse-tung"

      he ate needles
      in China
      in front of all the monks, ah,
he liked girls.
      save innumerable people a scholar-master
              brilliant talent
        his mother?

Kumari
a girl about twelve
          "the girl without corsets
          "the lady of the mammoth

              Lakshmi is still riding elephants

She was a Kumari virgin.
A virgin of 11–12–or 13 "north Indian
          tantric gambit
      again a variation"

Did she *produce* him?
"She gave him the insight:
But not the consciousness
         of the Mother:
      she's sprinkling water
      into his eyes"

Nobody has ever lifted my veil

>The Mother . . . that's all.
>Nothing more about her.
>She was great, wasn't she,
>the sister of the emperor
>Her name was *Giva*.

1969

Song to the Raw Material

"I am one with my food"
            eskimo dreaming of the game
            they've killed,
    afraid it don't want to be reborn
    in edible form no more—

production, distribution, consumption.
the meat body's "changing   body"—

space is fucking with time on the
            edge   of things!

            meta-ecology or meta-economics

society / economics / politics / fucking
the meat—"changing body"—but fucking
crosses up all the lines:

            a process ticked off.

chewing peanuts.

April 1970

Down

Back to where it started.
Over the fields, looks level,
Begins to go down.
Thicker trees in this shade
A few ranches on benches
                what river? valley
Lower, shadier, the trail less worn,
Rougher gulch,
Rockier, brushier,
Opening out on bare stone hogsback
        arching bull hump forward
        over and tilting, opening,
        gorge,
Switchbacking down to that edge and around it,
Steeper, darker,
Cliffs breaking *under*,   closer,
        A cool   a well
of nothing
        happening beneath,   and to the lips
        there's no   stream
                             there
It keeps going:
        old tree trunk ladders,
        rusty iron stakes
    driven into cracks,   descending.
A rock falls.
Wind blowing softly *up*.

I swallow, lean forward, look down:
My balls and belly turn over

      can   I   make   it?

It pulls—I hold—I hang *on*
Freezing—the chill—the pulse roar in the skull

      ah, gone   off

BLACK   TANGLE   MOTHER   EAGLE

    ah   bottomless blessing, gulping

    FALL

beyond   behind beyond   below beyond

EMPTY   BELLY   VOMIT   MUSIC   WHIRLING

stars!

Fall 1970

Swimming Naked in the Yuba River

> White, shining, boulders in the sun.
> Light and water
> Gathered in the gorge,
> The world
> In every grain of sand.
> To step into this flowing
> With a suit on
> Would be a sin.

1971

The California Water Plan

Thunderstorm downpours on 395—south of Bridgeport—
and looking down into Mono Lake,
crackling

that fiery spirit, dark fist mudras
                    two crossed fists
lightning jagged lines.

           in man too, no purpose
           but dark playful power.

Up the sandy trail   *in a sacred way we come*
Up the sandy trail   *in a sacred way we come*

creeks rush down through banks of flowers
              wild onions   lupines

                  inbreath   hold   the snow
                  outbreath, summer, let   them go

                  middle fork, south fork, the san joaquin

Lined with flowers, the waters dancing gaily down;
the lacy leaves all wave goodbye! cascading toward
the gorges
cutting through the snake-dry foothills,
out into diversion ditches of the
tractor plains—

          sPhat!

ACHALA
"Immovable"

or Caṇḍamahāroṣaṇa   "Lord of Heat"

color—yellow   arms—two   tools—sword and noose

"Four Sādhanas are devoted to his worship and he is
always represented in yab-yum. The worshipper should
think of himself as Caṇḍamahāroṣaṇa, whose color is like
that of the Atasī flower and whose second name is Achala.
He is one-faced, two-armed, and is squint-eyed. His face

appears terrible with bare fangs. He wears a jeweled head-
dress, bites his lips, and wears on his crown a garland of
severed heads. His eyes are slightly red, and he carries the
sword in his right hand and the noose round the raised
index finger against the chest in the left. His sacred thread
consists of a white snake; he is clad in tiger-skin and he
wears jewels. He is radiant as the sun and bears on his
crown the effigy of Akṣobhya. Thus he should be meditated
upon. His worship is performed in secret . . ."
Benoytosh Bhattacharyya, *The Indian Buddhist Iconography*
       "Mainly based on the Sādhanamālā and cognate
       Tantric Texts of Rituals"

In this iconography he is considered an "emanation" of
Akṣobhya, who is one of the five "Victors" or "Vectors"
. . . one of the "five cosmic rays of evolution" . . . in the
Vajradhātu Maṇḍala (Diagram of the Irreducible Space)
Akṣobhya is green and maintains the East.

In Japan, where Achala is called Fudo, he is considered a
direct emanation of Vairocana, the Great Sun Buddha, who
is at the center of the five-spot mandala, the Unconditioned
Body-of-Dharma represented, amazingly, WITH form, as
"Lord of Forms" and in human form, Fudo statues to be
found in cliffs, on peaks, by waterfalls, in mossy grottos and
everywhere that rock crops out.
    He stands in a halo of raging flame, or sits, his vehicle
is rough rock, maybe half-molten magma. Thus he rides
out wrath, and like a craggy peak his lover is Kwannon, the
creeks that flow and keep back "nothing" til they "empty"
in the sea.

ALL HAIL THE NOBLE UPLIFT OF THE JURASSIC
       CALLED SIERRA GRANITE

AND THOSE SINUOUS CLEFTS AND WINDING
WATERS THE DAKINIS WHO FLY IN SWIRLING
       CLOUD MIST BRIGHTNESS

THOSE GODDESSES CALLED YUBA, BEAR AND
FEATHER, FIERY FIST AND THEIR GENTLE
DOWNHILL GLIDING BE ONE GIFT TO ALL

& death to all dams.

November 1971

Greasy Boy

Dirt & tatters—dirt rubs off.
             rags, rags, rags
        tear it up
             tear it up
                  over and over—
dirt, rags—tatters.
the sand blown grim soot
                  caking under eyes

Tear it up,
dirt and rags,
        —tattered—

Let them fly, dirt bits
             through the air.
across scab land.

I, I,
for "one"
        —not afraid of
dirt, and,
ragged,
me——death.

June 1973

"I saw the Mother once"

I saw the Mother once
at Pondicherry, morning darshan, looking up
til our necks were stiff, as she stared down at the little crowd
dawn street, with a fixed hypnotic smile and painted eyes,
finally backing off the balcony away.
Last night I dreamed again: "the Mother"
in her room upstairs, sitting on a concrete floor
her legs stuck out in front
like proper Navajo women used to do,
no cushion, someone said,   "The Mother."
I went forward and bowed low,
as I was once taught long ago
put my forehead to the floor.
She rubbed my ears,
stroked the neck, and said
....
....
....
I forget.
& then showed me a letter which I read,
one side of the page about myself.
I think it said, "keep calm."
And the other side was all about my wife.
Much about Masa
....
          ....
....................and,
finally,
"dark powers."

June 1973

Tomorrow's Song

*in the service
of the wilderness*

of life
of death
of the Mother's breasts!
in the service
of the wilderness
of life
of Death
of the Mother's breaths!

Spring 1974

Gold, Green

Let it be
On a day in March
California;
When the grass is green
On the rolling hills
And the snow
Is deep in the mountains—

Let it be
On a day like this
That we plant a tree
California
For the years to come
For the little ones
and the lakes
Will be pure in the mountains—

Let it be gold and green
California;
That we touch the ground
That we heal the land
From the mountains to the sea.

c. March 1978

"The delicacy of the mountains"

The delicacy of the mountains
      "you lead me into dry pasture
I eat thistle"

The art of maintenance,
ends curled back
               toward home
     passing through.

     balance of power,

     O Father Sun

1979

"Emptiness, anti-entropy ultimate"

Emptiness, anti-entropy ultimate

     no friction whatever.

     let it all slide.

The holy, the perfect, transcendent,

       "grease"

1979

"The dried out winter ricefields"

The dried out winter ricefields
men far off loading junks in the river
bales of rice on their shoulders

a little boat poles out
    —roosters and geese—
    –looking at China

       1983

"At Sarnath"

At Sarnath
    a Rongbuk, and a
twisty-horned white-bellied
      antelope, some
     elk and deer
       behind barbed wire.
a Lama tries
to sell Tibetan coin
the Grove where Buddha spoke.

       1983

haiku

baby monkey taking first steps
    top of the wall
back of the tourist bungalow.

the tonga-wallah   (ponycart driver)
pinches the scab on his
     pony's haunch
instead of the whip

a sikh boy
like a wild little girl
   combs his long hair

monkeys wrestle
            in the thorny tree

on top of vulture peak
   nobody all morning
selling flowers.

               scrub jungle and monkeys,
                  rajagriha
barefeet on cold marble
   naked Jain genitals   (Sarnath)
      in the shadows.

letting tourists off his back
the painted elephant craps   (Amber)

lady in a nice sari
   walks quickly, not looking too much
at Khajuraho

                                    1983

on the train

Sikhs and Punjabis
tired of looking at Joanne
      put their heads
between their knees
            and sleep.

                  1983

"nothing at the center"

nothing at the center
a huge old tree lives
spring by spring

1984

Needles Country of the Canyonlands

Down I-15 to Spanish Fork, thence Soldier Pass—Green
River—Moab. Turn off into Needles district of the Canyon-
lands. Camp at Squaw Flat. Wine, crackers, up on the butte;
almost half moon. Scramble down to sleep at the foot of the
rock under a juniper.

Saturday

  Walk over Butte 1, across a flat, into a canyon and over
slickrock, from the crest the wall of needles. Northerly around
some ends—across a small flat, and a pass, notch, defile.
Lunch on a ledge through a gap looking down. ["woven
bamboo burden basket"]—descend into Elephant Canyon
and across, up, through a low pass, into   Chesler park.
                    camp in a cove
on a soil-building ledge.
Wingate—Navajo—Chinle formations. Ages of sand. What
were the parent materials? Sandstone locks in much of the
world's oxygen.   Layers. Soft parts under wear back leav-
ing hard upper over-hanging. Layers laid bare.   —Packed
all our water in. Then, Saturday afternoon, explore out the
S. end through a gap, down into "joint canyon" a walk in
vertical-walled slots stemmed into—what echo—not echo,
but reverberation, muffled and low. Gaté gaté paragaté
parasamgaté   svāhā.

Come down on sandy wash-bottom (used as a jeeproad) and rest with Tom Dickman under a giant elderly Juniper. Return to camp to cook and drink.

Sunday

(Gale Dick my companion speaks of his early college days—drive to grasp, master, the scientific view of the universe—what is it, "views of the universe" and our efforts to master them—the men in the kiva.)
    —to master "cultural lore"
    —via that, mastering as aspect of inborn
    psychological structuring, both individual and universal
    —via both above, master natural world fact &
    process.   Three overlapping questions. The
last phase having almost always been done through myth, a point of "view"
           leaving us with that question, is any view not just a view & objectivity another variety of myth.

wake to morning of snow. the firewood floating in a stream.   —from dry twigs under Juniper make a fire in tree-shelter on the kicked-out sand. Tea and *familia*—wet legs. Then   down a direct way into Elephant Canyon—stash the packs—go upstream.
(and quite suddenly streamwater starts running—comes rushing down, not rushing but rustling along, filling each pool then spilling onward—)
Up on a ledge overlooking Druid Arch. Hailstorm while drifting sheets blow in swiftly as we race for shelter in an alcove overhang. Eat lunch, then step out into sunshine, of the arch, like a complex part of some machine, or set of inner earbones.

       no route

         to the summit cap.
            remembering: roughly:

& Back down E. Canyon skipping side-to-side; mushy sand
steps mixed with rock slab or loose sub-surface boulder; but
never a   slip—duck under Juniper limb—(sometimes by
the trail *Mahonia fremontii* [who later discovered re-named
Berberis . . .]) and retrieving packs proceed downstream to
the squaw flat trail.   a yellow flower / paintbrush / a
lupine / in bloom

[to master so much of the world.]

—So then, returning, sun-and-cloud—and long views over
"Ernie's country" crosst the Colorado; and up there, THE
MAZE. Such land. A dream of mudpies, sandboxes, slapped,
whopped, dried out, hosed down, scuffed, leaving tricky runs
of structures; following hard—and soft—the blow and flow of
wind-and-water; years
        (seconds?) gone by, in which we wander like tentative
exploring ants. What of this do the petroglyphs say, those ants
who rambled here before.
        The long distant front of layered cliff. Surface: this is
where it's at now; but cut crosswise, the cliff, "This is what
we've done."
        Back over the humps, benches, slots, and flats, to the car.
        A fenced-off tumble of logs near the car is an oldstyle Diné
hogan ruin; I presume.
        In cloud and blue sky.   Rainpools, glittering on the rocks,
wind whipping at the top of every rise.   Soft reddish sand, in
every place that's dished and low.

the last weekend in March, '74

Spring 1990

from *"A Single Breath"*

Teasing the demonic
Wrestling the wrathful
Laughing with the lustful

Seducing the shy
Wiping dirty noses and sewing torn shirts
Sending philosophers home to their wives in time for dinner
Dousing bureaucrats in rivers
Taking mothers mountain climbing
Eating the ordinary

1991

from *"Coming into the Watershed"*

California is gold-tan grasses, silver-gray tule fog,
olive-green redwood, blue-gray chaparral,
silver-hue serpentine hills.
Blinding white granite,
blue-black rock sea cliffs.
—Blue summer sky, chestnut brown slough water,
steep purple city streets—hot cream towns.
Many colors of the land, many colors of the skin.

March 1–2, 1992

Ravynes Fly East

A volcano erupting under the sea
  becomes quartz porphyry

Hundreds of millions of years
  makes a peak

In a place of snow
  and careen of birds

Black, not vultures,
  croak and their tail-

Feathers swoop back upwards
  ten thousand feet

Ravens! a gang
  tangling, tumbling, rising

Then shoot up past us
  (shivering on the summit)

Eastward toward the desert,
  dots sailing off away.

                    Spring 1994

Daconstruction

They're slogging through the worksite,
rubber boots, pumps running, foot-wide hose
gushing steely water in a frothy pond

the link-belt crane turns like a Nō stage dance
dangles a trembling sixty-foot pipe.
Young guys in hardhat and T-shirts
hand-signal as it swings

To lower it tenderly
into a three-foot-wide casing
—a whomping cement truck backs in and
dumps down the pipe.

Eight at night—job lights glaring—
shrieks and whistles—
soupy mudponds—rebar and wire snipper trash
a high-rise building start
chain-linked off from the gridlocked streets,

another "economic miracle" of Asia,
smoking cigarettes and shouting—

laying new horizons on old swampy soils,
long-lost wetlands,
rainy noisy sticky city night,

Taipei.

Autumn 1994

Mountains Walk on Water

Sunrise a rose-red crack below the clouds, above the fog;
     folds of ranges north   edges burning

Shadow hollows, dropt-out dewy rounded cliffs,
     layer on layer—rock, cloud—

Snaky ridges wriggle the abyss   mountain wall mist tatters,
cloud veil thins and peels,
     a rush of water running down there rising—

Rose light leaping hill to hill—dark down gorges have no
end;

     no bottom to the bottom.

Taiwan's twenty million people
live below these mountain depths,

soaking cliffs and drippy elder trees.

c. 1995

from *"Allen Ginsberg Crosses Over"*

Cherry blossoms falling
     Young girls rising
         Us on the deck.

—

Raw tuna, saké,
     And blossoms.
         Spilled shoyu.

—

READING BASHŌ ON THE PLANE

Between lectures,
     This little seat by the window
     My hermitage.

1997

from *"The Cottonwoods"*

Deaf Smith. I remember that   *wheat*
   back in the sixties   drive out to the co-op for it
"Deef Smith County whole wheat berries"

      and grind it ourselves.

Fall 1998

Where the Sammamish, the Snohomish, and the Skykomish All Come In

The sweet insipid taste of *salal*
and the sharp sour Oregon grape

bland salmonberry
spit-bugs inside

grasshoppers under dry
cowpies   China pheasant flies up

broad white dogwood bloom
we tried smoking shredded cedarbark

bubbles of pitch in the bark
pull bracken ferns to throw like spears

cows, they
shit as they walk
plop   plop

July–September 2005

from *"Writers and the War Against Nature"*

Soaring just over the sea-foam
riding the wind of the endless waves
albatross, out there, way

away,   a far cry
down from the sky

Winter 2006

What a life!

the single fly
in the spotless Forest Service
campground
toilet

Candle Creek, Oregon

c. September 2007

nine frags

"Don't twist my hair"

Don't twist my hair
old bear

Three-inch teeth
good grief

Vows

The voice (vow)
is a breath (brother),
a spirit, a spiral, a sphere,
it woos (waves—wives,)

the wild

White Rumps

Northern flickers

Pronghorns

Dwarf stars

Receding.

Out West

There's all the time in the universe,

And plenty of wide open space

Country & Western

Loving, hurting,

Cheating, flirting,

Drinking, lying,

Laughing, crying

songs.

(seen on the side of a bus in Louisville Kentucky
April '83. Station WINN)

A buzzy huddle

of shiny flies on the trail

Ah, twisty carcass of a worm.

in Hokkaido

Doctors will be Protected

"Write down" I said to the child who was writing
what I told her,

"That from the notch

carved on the vine between the maple and the
flowering peach,

along the trail and the whole way down to here,

Doctors will be protected. By us."

As I knelt and carved the notch.

Minutes

He wears his warm wig an hour
And mountains of minutes
press his feet between his skull

IAMBICS

The tautology:
  I AM THAT I AM

The paradox:
  I AM NOT THAT   I AM

The practice
  NOT

The fruit
  NOT I   I AM

July–August 2009

The Dancer is a Weaver

Her dance is   daily life   transformed

holding a spinner's spindle
face a calm still mask
wheeling slow as the night sky

kimono plain and perfect   robe of dawn
dressed for work
in heaven   in deva space
spindle in hand

moving like the moon   reflecting
brief like   craft   long time

eyes down   face pure   slow

as she goes

Taira Mari's Ryukyu Court Dance performance
Naha, Okinawa, 4.III.2003
2010

The Goosenecks of the San Juan

The goosenecks of the San Juan
river   turn, turn, and turn again
this old meander
is entrenched.
500 feet down
in the rock   cliffs,
float and look up at the sky
past   stars   murmuring

—"there you are"—and
"we are here"

2010

Where

Shoot an arrow into the
secret heart of the monster
I once said. But the Airports
Skyscrapers   Markets had no secrets
just more places that won't die.

No use shooting there—

Seek the *secret heart.*
The core, the center, of the monster's power
—not where you thought. It's elsewhere,
hidden in a harmless-looking spot

If you've wiped somebody's nose,
untied a knot, looked for a lost key
maybe a little bird
or mouse   will point
and   whisper in your ear,

shoot there

July 3, 2018

Victoria Falls and Zimbabwe

In 1993 my older son Kai was contracted with the World
Wildlife Fund to do GIS mapping of elephant habitat in Zam-
bia. In time he continued this work in Botswana and Zimba-
bwe. Spring of 1994 my other son Gen and I decided to visit
him, and we found ourselves in the northerly town of Maun in
Botswana. Maun is at the edge of the big network of wetlands
and waterways known as the Okavango marshes—fed by the
Chobe River. It hosts a huge population of African wildlife
including what is probably the largest herd of wild free-ranging
elephants in the world. Kai borrowed an elderly Toyota Land
Cruiser and with very little gear and rudimentary maps, we

packed up and drove across to Zimbabwe, to the big town of Victoria Falls. This is right at the edge of the Zambezi River, which is the northern boundary of Zimbabwe and Botswana. South of the Zambezi it is known as "Southern Africa" with the nation of South Africa at the bottom of the continent. Victoria Falls (in the days when Zimbabwe was called "Rhodesia" and Brits ran the show) was a very classy tourist town, with its elegant Victoria Falls Hotel.

Today it is a bit run down. Young European backpackers with shaved heads (to avoid lice, they say) make it feel a bit like Kathmandu. One of the marvels of the world, the sublime Victoria Falls, is just down the hill. It is known as "Mosi oa Tunya"—"Smoke that Thunders."

I walk back the half-mile or so out of the park around Victoria Falls and decide "unfinished"—did it too fast—need another trip to the place where it roars, so go down there again.

The Zambezi River (which is huge) comes in a broad sweep, approaches this edge of basalt, lays itself across some ancient volcanic flow, shallows and stretches out on the tableland to a mile wide then drops abruptly over the system of ledges to fall anywhere from 300 to 360 feet down, along that face.

It spills into a narrow channel that runs at right angles to the direction of the falls-flow; it hits a trough and cuts sharp north in a great turmoil. Finally makes a complete sharp bend, turns south again, and from the map (I couldn't see this all on foot) I see it makes another sharp U-bend, turns north. After a few more turns and curves becomes at last a channel—and flows on toward the Indian Ocean.

One walks from the south end out along the first tongue of the table land opposite the falls so you can look right across at falling water, only a few hundred feet from you, the whole way. As one goes farther out the cool moist air wells up in one's face, misting through the increasingly thicker canopy and undergrowth, and then as you step out at a viewing point, you get hit by a blast of cloud and spray and a sight of a perpetual rainbow.

There's first one great cataract coming down, then north
a little, a kind of island juts out with some falls dropping off
behind that, and this "island" has forest on it with cliffs and
water on all sides and then another broad stretch of falls with
a great flow first and then a thinner flow over a rocky jumble,
then an increased flow again, then another small point of dry
land and then another very long arc of breaking water going
directly over it and down.

I make my way, point by point, out to the far end, taking my
shirt off and putting it in my pack as I am getting drenched
now, and the few other tourists walking this far out, black and
white alike, are also drenched. Two white girls in high-thigh
bathing suits looking totally un-African in their bareness—but
I know they'll put on clothes again as soon as they get back
towards the entrance. And finally I'm approaching the last rock
point where the rising water of the falls is falling in a heavy
drenching rain back down on us. The path is awash with a
constant flow of inch-deep water flooding back out, sideways
over to the edge. The grass here is a marsh and the rocks are
covered with moss. The drenching downpour comes in pulses
as do waves of mist rising up.

I find myself standing in a cloud of spray and—shades of the
penitential warrior priest Mongaku—chanting the Fudo man-
tra, doing the Yamabushi waterfall practice (hands in gassho,
standing straight in the cold downpour, meditating in the
midst of the downpour, eyes closed. For days and days—the
meeting of the ceaseless flow and stubborn hardness—)

And the energy-package all this represents—volcanism, tec-
tonics, subduction and the globe, the planetary "heat engine"
that makes the cycles of weather and water.

Finally, sopping, I'm looking over the edge at the very far
point of this, half off the cliff, hanging onto a share of a piece
of a boulder, I can see straight down into the whirling, froth-
ing channels below. I recall my Yamabushi teacher saying as he
hung me over the cliffs of Mt. Omine (in Japan) "just tell the
truth." Reticulate foam shows up in a quick shaft of sunlight

between the mist—huge raindrops falling, while between and through them, fine mist is rising, all at the same time. The natural magic of the planet.

And walk back beyond the reach of the heavy rains, only a few hundred yards away by path and it gets much drier. Take off my canvas shorts and wring them out and then walk slowly back up trail again, listening to the roar, touching from time to time on mist.

I've seen a mother and daughter, 11-year-old girl, the daughter in swimming suit who is ecstatically jumping up and down, waving her arms, getting wet—thoroughly taken by the whole scene, at the junction of the trails, see the ecstatic look on the little face.

She's still doing jumping jacks and waving her arms and rubbing the water on her skin and on her chest. I say to the mother, "This is a place you can't stay dry, isn't it. I was here yesterday and I couldn't help but come back again." And she laughs, and speaks (an American accent), "Well we were here this morning and did all of this one time and my daughter insisted we come back again."

As I walk back toward the gate, note the gradual change in vegetation away from the almost cloud forest that has formed along the lip where the spray rises from the Falls into the more common acrid crackly dry leaves on the ground, trees, and bushes. Trees: red-leaf fig and *Acacia galpinii*, with big vines on it. By the time I get to the gate my chest has already dried off, my hair is half dry, I put my t-shirt back on. In wet shorts and dry t-shirt, little day pack, walk back up by trail taking the Victoria Falls Hotel branch, a trail spattered by elephant droppings. And ran into an elephant! Close, also out for a walk.

Go through the backside of the old colonial Victoria Falls Hotel with its broad clipped lawn, its starched waiters, its patio laid out for tea or dinner, and pass right through the lobby and reception room in a décor of white and light green and

on down the steps to the limousine stop, and down the gated
driveway of the Hotel to the broad half-dirt main street that
runs between town proper and the waterfalls. Head for our
tent-site out in the public camping-ground. A continuous
stream of variously-dressed people, walking, walking, every-
where. No whites.

Zimbabwe 1994
c. 2016–20

By the Chobe River

Botswana. Zambia border

The new moon crescent settles in a lavender dusk

An elephant shadow slides beyond the rise

Bathing by a faucet with a bucket,

sitting on a shattered concrete block

The old Landcruiser engine cooling

Just before hyenas come.

c. 2016–20

For Robert Duncan

Walking down Grant Street just short of the Place
        late at night
ran into Robert Duncan, we embraced,
        nineteen fifty five.
        He said, "Gary your number."
Gave me a copy

of *Letters*, signed it standing in the streetlight.
number 69. The gleam
in Robert's sidelong eye

    And I think of Neuri,
whose elbows and jaw-juts and knees all jangling
I wrapped up in my arms and packed into the car,
'37 Packard,
her so drunk, she beat my
face and eye—mean and sweet—
and in the poem I wrote for her I said
"because I once beat you up"
when it was me got whacked.
    Old "male chivalry"
and a literary scholar trots it out
    because I'm "Allen's friend"
slender girl I never slept with
you liked women.

And I loved Robert for his teaching
Some crime.

c. 2016–20

Song for Wrecked Cars

cars   wrecked, washed
strewn through the desert,
trash   space
        ironwood limbs lit by the moon
        mesquite twig   breeze
cars
rusting to death
while alive

c. 2016–20

After Dōgen

Mimulus on the cliffside in April
Nuthatches in the summer pines
Cranes calling south in September
Winter pond-ice crackling bright

c. 2016–20

Having Seen on Earth

The Taj Mahal, cool marble upward space, a uterine
emptiness edged
        with tracework, for the love of Mumtaz Mahal

Nanda Devi appearing from behind the cloud, as we stood
under blossoming
        rhododendron at Kausani, in Almora

The Zambezi river topple and crash, Victoria Falls,
        soaked in spray

The Southern Cross in the night—through tangled hair—
from under a
        woman on a beach in Samoa

The Buddha's seat at Bodh Gaya still shaded by a giant Fig

The Temple of the Sixth Patriarch of Zen, Hui-Neng, in
Guangzhou city, well-
        kept but now an "educational park" with a picture of
him splitting wood

The complex Lama Temple in Beijing, being repainted and
touched up by art
        students from the University

The six great snowpeaks of the Northwest—all—Koma
Kulshan, Tahoma, Klickitat, Loowit, Shuksan,
     Wyeast
     above the clouds at dawn

Looking into the lava cauldron of Smoking Island, Ten
Islands Archipelago,
     East China Sea

A huge shark's shadow passing over, as I spearfished deep
in the green water
     alone off the reef of Suwa-no-se Island

An elephant black and shining, bathing in a pool in the
Chobe savannah—
     water streaming off her as she rose.

c. 2016–20

Bai Juyi's "Long Bitter Song"

The "Long Bitter Song" (Chang hen ge) of Bai Juyi (Po Chü-I) is probably the best known and most widely popular poem in the whole Chinese cultural-sphere. Bai and his friend Wang Shifu (Wang Shih-fu) were visiting the Xienfu Chan Buddhist training center in 806, and were talking one night of the events of the reign of Emperor Xuanzong (Hsüan Tsung) and the An Lushan rebellion, sixty years earlier. Xuanzong was one of China's better rulers and presided over what has since been considered the golden age of both Chan Buddhist creativity and Chinese poetry. He took power in 712 and led a strong and innovative administration up to about 745. At that time he became totally infatuated with Yang Gui Fei (Yang Kuei-fei), the wife of one of his many sons. She became his concubine, the Sogdian-Turkish general An Lushan became an intimate of the couple and perhaps also a lover of Yang, the restive Northeast revolted under An, he led his troops into the capital, Xuanzong, Yang Gui Fei and the palace guard fled the city, and outside town at Horse Cliff the troops stopped, refused to go on, and insisted on putting Yang Gui Fei to death. That was in 755. The rebellion was quelled by 762, about the same time Xuanzong died. This rebellion marked a watershed in the fortunes of the Tang dynasty, beginning a period of somewhat more decentralized power, a rise of Chinese cultural chauvinism and contempt for the "third world" border peoples, and a greater weakness in relation to the borders.

The story of the Emperor and his lovely concubine had become legend. After that evening's reminiscences, Bai was inspired to write the story as a long poem. Within his own lifetime he then heard it sung on the canals and in the pleasure quarters by singing-girls and minstrels. Bai lived from A.D. 772 to 846. He was born in a poor family, passed the examinations partly on the strength of his literary brilliance, and became a lifelong political functionary of great integrity and compassion who wrote many stirring poems on behalf of the common people. He was a Chan Buddhist, and studied under the master Wei Kuan, who was a disciple of the outstanding Chan teacher Mazu (Ma-tsu).

This poem is in the seven character line, which gives it (in Chinese) this sort of rhythm:

tum tum / tum tum: tum tum tum

I have tried to keep this beat as far as possible in my translation. I did the first version of it with the aid of Ch'en Shih-hsiang who was my teacher in graduate seminars at U.C. Berkeley in Tang poetics, in the early fifties. I must take full responsibility, however, for idiosyncratic aspects of the translation—cases of both stripped-down literalism, and occasional free flights. My debt to his gracious, learned, unquenchable delight in all forms of poetry is deep indeed, and I am pleased to honor his memory with this publication of a poem that we took much pleasure in reading together.

28.X.86

Long Bitter Song

I

Han's Emperor wanted a Beauty
          one to be a "Destroyer of Kingdoms"
Scouring the country, many years,
          sought, but didn't find.
The Yang family had a girl
          just come grown;
Reared deep in the inner-apartments,
          men didn't know of her.
Such Heaven-given elegance
          could not be concealed
One morning she was taken to
          the Emperor's household.
A turn of the head, one smile,
          —a hundred lusts were flamed
The Six Palaces rouge-and-eyebrow
          without one beautiful face.
In the Spring cold she was given a bath
          at the Flower-pure Pool

Warm pool, smooth water,
          on her cold, glowing skin
Servant girls helping her rise,
          languorous, effortless beauty—
This was the beginning of her new role:
          glistening with Imperial favour.
Hair like a floating cloud, flower-face,
          ripple of gold when she walked.
—In the warm Hibiscus curtains
          they spent the Spring night.
Spring night is bitterly short
          it was noon when they rose;
From this time on the Emperor
          held no early court.
Holding feasts and revels
          without a moment's rest
Spring passed, Spring dalliance,
          all in a whirl of nights.
Beautiful girls in the outer palace:
          three thousand women:
Love enough for three thousand
          centered in one body.
In Gold House, perfectly attired
          her beauty served the night;
In the Jade Tower the parties ended
          with drunk, peaceful Spring.
Here sisters and brothers
          all given land,
Splendor and brilliance
          surprised her humble family.
Following this, on all the earth,
          fathers & mothers hearts
No longer valued bearing males
          but hoped to have girls.
The high-soaring Li palace
          pierces blue clouds
Delights of Immortals, whirled on wind
          were heard of everywhere.
Slow song, flowing dance,
          music like frost-crystal
          sifting from the lute-strings—

The Emperor could exhaust a day
                watching—and still not full

II

Then Yuyang war drums,
                approached, shaking the earth;
Alarming, scattering, the "Rainbow Skirt"
                the "Feathered Robe" dances.
From the nine great City-Towers,
                smoke, dust, rose.
Thousands of chariots, ten thousand horsemen
                scattered Southwest—
Kingfisher banner fluttering, rippling,
                going and then stopping;
West out the city walls
                over a hundred li
And the six armies won't go on:
                nothing can be done—
Writing, twisting, Moth-eyebrows
                dies in front of the horses.
Her flower comb falls to the ground
                not a man will pick it up—
Kingfisher feathers, "little golden birds",
                jade hair-pin;
The Emperor hides his face
                no way to help
Turns, looks, blood, tears,
                flow, quietly mingle.
Yellow dust eddies and scatters.
                Desolate winds blow.
Cloud Trail winds and twists
                climbing to Sword-point Peak
Under Omei Shan
                the last few came.
Flags, banners, without brightness,
                a meagre-coloured sun.
Shu river waters blue
                Shu mountains green
And the Emperor, days, days,
                nights, nights, brooding.

From the temporary palace, watching the moon
              colour tore his heart
The night-rain bell-tinkle
                 —bowel-twisting music.

III

Heaven turns, earth revolves,
              The Dragon-Chariot returned.
But he was irresolute,
              didn't want to go;
And at the foot of Horse Cliff,
              in the sticky mud,
    Couldn't find the Jade Face
                  at her death-place.
    Court officials watching him
                  soaked their clothes with tears.
    Looking east to the Capital walls,
                  they returned on horses
    Came back to Pond Park
                —all was as before.
    Taiye Hibiscus,
              Weiyang Willow.
    But Hibiscus flowers were like her face,
              the Willows like her brow:
    Seeing this, how could he
              keep tears from falling.
    Spring wind, peach, plum,
              flowers open in the sun;
    Autumn rain, Wutong trees,
              leaf-fall time.
    Western palace, the inner court,
              many autumn grasses.
    Falling leaves fill the stairs
              red: and no one sweeps.
    The Pear-garden players
              white-haired young.
    Pepper-court eunuchs
              watched beautiful girls age.
    Evening, palace, glow-worm flight,
              —his thoughts were soundless.

He picked his single candle-wick down,
        couldn't reach sleep.
Slow, slow, the night bell
        begins the long night,
Glimmering, fading, the Milky Way,
        and day about to dawn.
Silent tile roof-ducks
        are heavy with frost-flowers
The Kingfisher quilt is cold—
        who will share his bed?
Far, far, the living and the dead
        and the light years—cut apart.
Her spirit already dissolving,
        not even entering dreams.

IV

A Linqiong Daoist priest
        of the Hongdu school
Was able to deeply concentrate
        and thus call up the spirits.
Hearing this, the Emperor
        —troubled, twisting thoughts.
Ordered the Daoist priest
        to make a thorough search.
Pushing the sky, riding air,
        swift as a thunderbolt,
Harrowing the heavens, piercing Earth,
        he sought everywhere
Above exhausting the blue void,
        below, the Yellow Springs.
The ends of earth—vast, vast,
        and nowhere did he find her.
Then he heard—that out on the ocean—
        was a mountain of Immortals
A mountain at—nowhere—
        a cloudy, unreal place.
Palace towers, tinkling gems,
        where Five Clouds rise.
Within—lovely, wanton, chaste,
        many faery people.

There was there one faery
        called Taizhen;
Snow skin, flower appearance,
        it had to be her.
At the Gold Tower of the West Wing,
        he knocked on the Jade door:
Announcing himself to Little Jade
        —and she told Shuang Cheng,
That the Emperor of the people of Han
        had sent an envoy.
In the nine-flowered canopy
        the faery's dreams were broken;
Holding her clothes, pushing the pillow,
        she rose, walking unsteady.
Winding, opening the pearl door,
        the inlaid silver screens.
Her cloud-like hair, floating on one side,
        —just brought from sleep.
Her flower-cap unadjusted
        she came down the hall,
Wind blew her elegant sleeves
        floating, floating up—
Seemed like the "Rainbow Skirt",
        the "Feathered Robe" dance.
Her jade-like figure small and alone,
        she scattered her sad tears:
As though one branch of a blossoming pear
        was holding the whole Spring's rain.
Restraining her feelings, cooling her look,
        she told him to thank the Emperor;
"With that parting our two forms
        were split by the World's vast shifting;
After Zhaoyang temple,
        our love was cut off.
Here in Raspberry-tangle Palace
        the days and months are long—
I look down, hoping to see
        lands where humans dwell,
I never see Chang'an
        but only dusty haze."

Then taking some ancient treasures
          rich in deep feeling,
An inlaid box, a gold hairpin,
          to be delivered back,
Keeping a leg of the hairpin,
          keeping half the box,
Breaking the gold of the hairpin,
          box cut in two—
"If only our hearts are strong as
          this gold hairpin,
Above in heaven, or among men,
          we will somehow meet.
Go back swiftly
          tell him this message:
For it tells of one Vow
          that two hearts know,
In the seventh month on the seventh day
          in Long-Life Temple.
At midnight, no one about,
          we swore together
If in heaven, to fly as
          the 'paired-wing' birds;
If on earth, to grow as
          one joined branch."
Heaven lasts, Earth endures,
          —and both will end;
This sorrow stretches on
          forever, without limit.

Sixteen T'ang Poems

Note for Sixteen T'ang Poems

In the early fifties I managed to get myself accepted into the
Department of Oriental Languages at UC Berkeley as a gradu-
ate student. I took seminars in the reading of T'ang and Sung
poems with Professor Ch'en Shih-hsiang, a remarkable scholar,
calligrapher, poet, and critic who had a profound appreciation
for good poetry of any provenance. Ch'en hsien-sheng intro-
duced me to the Han-shan poems, and I published those trans-
lations back in the sixties. The poems translated here also got
their start in those seminars, but I never considered them quite
finished. From Berkeley I went to Japan and for the subse-
quent decade was working almost exclusively with Ch'an texts.
Another twenty years went into developing a farmstead in the
Sierra Nevada and working for the ecological movement. In
the last few years I have had a chance to return to my readings
in Chinese poetry and bring a few of the poems I started back
then to completion. This little collection is dedicated to the
memory of Ch'en Shih-hsiang.

14.I.93

Two Poems by Meng Hao-jan

SPRING DAWN

Spring sleep, not yet awake to dawn,
I am full of birdsongs.
Throughout the night the sounds of wind and rain
Who knows   what flowers fell.

MOORING ON CHIEN-TE RIVER

The boat rocks at anchor by the misty island
Sunset, my loneliness comes again.
In these vast wilds the sky arches down to the trees,
In the clear river water, the moon draws near.

Five Poems by Wang Wei

DEER CAMP

Empty mountains:
   no one to be seen.
Yet—hear—
    human sounds and echoes.
   Returning sunlight
   enters the dark woods;
Again shining
   on green moss, above.

BAMBOO LANE HOUSE

Sitting alone, hid in bamboo
Plucking the lute and gravely whistling.
People wouldn't know that deep woods
Can be this bright   in the moon.

SAYING FAREWELL

Me in the mountains   and now you've left.
Sunset,   I close the peephole door.
Next spring   when grass is green,
Will you   return once more?

THINKING OF US

Red beans grow in the south
In spring they put out shoots.
Gather a lapful for me—
And doing it, think of us.

POEM

You who come from my village
Ought to know its affairs
The day you passed the silk window
Had the chill plum bloomed?

Three Poems for Women in the Service of the Palace

AUTUMN EVENING
Tu Mu

A silver candle in the autumn gloom
  by a lone painted screen
Her small light gauze fan
  shivers the fireflies
On the stairs of heaven, night's color
  cool as water;
She sits watching the Herd-boy,
  the weaving-girl, stars.

The Herd-boy is Altair, in Aquila.
The Weaving-girl in Vega, in Lyra.

THE SUMMER PALACE
Yuan Chen

Silence settles on the old Summer Palace
Palace flowers   still   quiet   red.
White-haired concubines
Idly sit and gossip   of the days of Hsüan Tsung.

PALACE SONG
Po Chü-i

Tears soak her thin shawl
  dreams won't come.
In the dark night, from the front palace,
  girls rehearsing songs.
Still fresh and young,
  already put down,
She leans across the brazier
  to wait the coming dawn.

Spring View
Tu Fu

The nation is ruined,   but mountains and rivers remain.
This spring the city   is deep in weeds and brush.
Touched by the times   even flowers weep tears,
Fearing leaving   the birds tangled hearts.
Watch-tower fires   have been burning for three months
To get a note from home   would cost ten thousand gold.
Scratching my   white hair thinner
Seething hopes   all in a trembling hairpin.

Events of the An Lushan rebellion.

Parting from Ling Ch'e
Liu Ch'ang-ch'ing

Green, green
        bamboo-grove temple
Dark, dark,
        the bell-sounding evening.
His rainhat catches
        the slanting sunlight,
Alone returning
        from the distant blue peaks.

Climbing Crane Tower
Wang Chih-huan

The white sun has gone over the mountains
The yellow river is flowing to the sea.
If you wish to see a thousand *li*
Climb one story higher in the tower.

River Snow
Lo Tsung-yuan

These thousand peaks cut off the flight of birds
On all the trails, human tracks are gone.
A single boat—coat—hat—an old man!
Alone   fishing   chill   river   snow.

Parting with Hsin Chien at Hibiscus Tavern
Wang Ch'ang-ling

Cold rain on the river
        we enter Wu by night
At dawn I leave
        for Ch'u-shan, alone.
If friends in Lo-yang
        ask after me, I've
"A heart like ice
        in a jade vase."

Two Poems Written at Maple Bridge
Near Su-chou

MAPLE BRIDGE NIGHT MOORING
Chang Chi

Moon set, a crow caws,
        frost fills the sky
River, maple, fishing-fires
        cross my troubled sleep.
Beyond the walls of Su-chou
        from Cold Mountain temple
The midnight bell sounds
        reach my boat.

(circa 765 AD)

AT MAPLE BRIDGE
Gary Snyder

Men are mixing gravel and cement
At Maple bridge,
Down an alley by a tea-stall
From Cold Mountain temple;
Where Chang Chi heard the bell.
The stone step moorage
Empty, lapping water,
And the bell sound has travelled
Far across the sea.

1984 AD

CHRONOLOGY

NOTE ON THE TEXTS

NOTES

INDEX OF TITLES AND FIRST LINES

Chronology

1930–32   Born Gary Sherman Snyder in San Francisco, California, on May 8, 1930, the first child of Harold Alton Snyder, 29, and Ethel Lois Wilkie Snyder, 24. Father, a native of Seattle whose parents Henry W. Snyder and Missouri L. Snyder came to Washington as homesteaders, is employed as a telephone salesman. After enlisting in the Marines in 1918 and serving at the Mare Island Naval Shipyard, he worked until about 1925 as a purser on the West Coast passenger ship *H.F. Alexander*. Mother, born in Palestine, Texas, to Rob Wilkey and Lula Callicotte Wilkey, moved to Seattle with her mother around 1919. She graduated from Queen Anne High School in 1922 (her yearbook motto "what man dares, I dare"), afterwards working as a clerk before enrolling at the University of Washington in 1925. They married at St. James Presbyterian Church in Bellingham, Washington, on July 11, 1929. On October 13, 1932, having settled just north of Seattle in rural Lake City, Washington, they have a daughter, Anthea Corinne Snyder. The family lives on a subsistence farm where they tend a small orchard and a few dairy cows, keep chickens, and make cedar-wood shingles.

1933–38   Without regular work for much of the Great Depression, father takes whatever odd jobs he can find. Mother reads poetry aloud before bedtime, including Edgar Allan Poe's "The Raven" and Robert Louis Stevenson's anthology *A Child's Garden of Verses*. At seven, walking accidentally over some hot ash, burns his feet and is unable to walk for several months; reads voraciously while he recuperates, his parents borrowing books from the Seattle Public Library.

1939–40   Spends the summer of 1939 with an aunt in Richmond, California, travelling there alone by train; they visit the Golden Gate International Exposition, Muir Woods, Muir Beach, and Mt. Tamalpais. Father finds work as an interviewer for Washington state Employment Security Service.

1941–42   At age 11 or 12, is impressed by Chinese landscape paintings at the Seattle Art Museum: "It looks just like the Cascades." Makes frequent visits to the University of Washington's

Anthropology Museum. Moves with mother and sister to Portland, Oregon, father now a housing administrator in San Francisco; parents soon divorce. Later recalls: "At that time I was intensely concerned with American Indians. I was sewing my own moccasins and spending as much time as possible out in the woods around the Columbia River, or south of Portland, camping and hiking."

1943–44   Attends nearby St. John's High School, but soon transfers to the more academically demanding Lincoln High in downtown Portland. Joins staff of the school paper, *The Cardinal*, and gets a job as a copyboy on the graveyard shift for the Portland *Oregonian*, where his mother, an aspiring journalist, works in the circulation department. Spends summers at a YMCA camp in Spirit Lake, Washington, working on the trail crew.

1945   Climbs Mount St. Helens in August, starting from Spirit Lake.

1946   Earns membership in the Mazamas, a Portland mountaineering club, after climbing Mt. Hood; publishes "A Young Mazama's Idea of a Mount Hood Climb" in *Mazama*, the club's annual journal, and frequents the clubhouse library.

1947   Graduates from Lincoln High. Joins an informal group of young mountain climbers, the Youngsteigers; climbs Mt. Rainier and other peaks. Attends Reed College beginning in the fall, with a grant-in-aid; unable to afford board and too far from home to commute regularly, sometimes camps out in the dorm rooms of friends. In December, publishes essay "The Youngsteigers" in *Mazama*.

1948   Mother marries Douglas Hennessy in Portland on January 24. In May, appears in the Reed student revue "Nobody Else Has Frances." Over the summer, hitchhikes to New York City, obtains his seaman's papers, and, as a member of the Marine Cooks and Stewards Union, ships out to the Caribbean, visiting Colombia and Venezuela. Hitchhikes back to Portland by way of Los Angeles and San Francisco; in September, hikes and camps on Mt. Tamalpais with Reed girlfriend Robin Collins. Moves into a basement room in an off-campus apartment building at 1414 Lambert Street in Portland, working as a part-time custodian in exchange for reduced rent; meets several lifelong friends among the building's student tenants and visitors, including poets Lew Welch and Philip Whalen.

1949   Teaches himself sitting meditation. Over the summer, works on a trail crew for the U.S. Forest Service in the Columbia National Forest (now the Gifford Pinchot Forest).

1950   Publishes poems in Reed student magazine *Janus*. On June 5 marries Alison Gass, a fellow student, but they separate six months later. During the summer, works for the U.S. Park Service excavating the archaeological site of old Fort Vancouver in Washington state. Meets William Carlos Williams, who visits Reed in November; Williams reads his poems and offers encouragement.

1951   Graduates from Reed with a B.A. in anthropology and literature, completing a senior thesis on "The Dimensions of a Haida Myth." Over the summer works as a timber scaler on the Warm Springs Indian Reservation; attends Warm Springs berry feast. Backpacks in the Olympic Mountains. In the fall, with the aid of a scholarship, begins graduate study in anthropology and linguistics at the University of Indiana; reads D. T. Suzuki's *Essays in Zen Buddhism* while hitchhiking to Bloomington, where he shares an apartment with Reed friend Dell Hymes.

1952   Decides against a career in anthropology, leaving Indiana after one semester and moving to San Francisco in March. Moves in with Philip Whalen. Works as an installer of burglar alarms and in a film-processing lab. Attends study sessions at the Berkeley Buddhist Church, where he meets visiting speaker Alan Watts, and at the American Academy of Asian Studies in San Francisco. Over the summer months works as a U.S. Forest Service lookout on inaccessible Crater Mountain, in Mt. Baker National Forest. Divorce from Alison Gass is finalized. In the fall, applies for U.S. Customs Service and Coast Guard jobs in San Francisco.

1953   Father, in the wake of son's job applications, is questioned by government agents who claim Snyder was "closely associated with members or supporters of the Communist Party during the past several years." Corresponds with Ruth Fuller Sasaki of the First Zen Institute of America in June about how he might begin Zen Buddhist study in Japan. In the summer, works once more as a Forest Service lookout, this time on Sourdough Mountain in Mt. Baker

National Forest. Moves to Berkeley in the fall, enrolling as a graduate student in the Oriental Languages Department at the University of California; studies Chinese and Japanese language, literature, and art. Meets poet Kenneth Rexroth in November and begins attending his Friday evening workshops.

1954   In February, learns that he has been blacklisted from U.S. Forest Service jobs because of his membership in the Communist-linked Marine Cooks and Stewards Union. Finds another summer job as a choker-setter for the Warm Springs Lumber Company, returning to Berkeley in mid-October.

1955   Tries peyote for the first time on January 1: "An astonishing experience," he writes Philip Whalen. In April, with the help of Alan Watts, meets Ruth Fuller Sasaki; she offers him a yearlong scholarship to study Zen in Kyoto. Unable to obtain a passport because of alleged Communist ties, even after submitting an affidavit and signing a loyalty oath, loses his Zen Institute scholarship; Sasaki promises legal help and a job in Kyoto as her assistant. (A later ACLU case resolves his and others' passport problems.) Despite his blacklisting, obtains a National Park Service job at Yosemite, working on a trail crew beginning in July. At UC–Berkeley in the fall, studies Chinese poetry with Chen Shih-hsiang; translates the "Cold Mountain" poems of Han-Shan. In October, at Kenneth Rexroth's suggestion, is invited by Allen Ginsberg to read at the Six Gallery in San Francisco, along with Philip Lamantia, Michael McClure, and Philip Whalen; follows Ginsberg's "Howl" with "A Berry Feast." Is introduced by Ginsberg to Jack Kerouac, with whom he climbs Yosemite's Matterhorn Peak later that month. Moves into a Mill Valley cabin he names "Marin-an."

1956   At the beginning of the year, hitchhikes with Ginsberg through the Pacific Northwest, mountaineering and giving poetry readings along the way. In April, while conversing over tea with visiting artist Saburo Hasegawa, is inspired to begin *Mountains and Rivers Without End*. Hikes Mt. Tamalpais with Jack Kerouac, who lives at Marin-an during the spring. About to depart for Kyoto, entrusts his only manuscript of *Myths & Texts* to Robert Creeley, who promises to find it a publisher. On May 6, after a three-day farewell party, sails for Japan aboard the freighter *Arita*

Maru. Awaiting the arrival of his teacher, Miura Isshu Roshi, climbs Mt. Atago and Mt. Hiei; attends first Noh performances; assists Ruth Fuller Sasaki with Japanese translations, joining her staff of a half dozen at Daitoku-ji. Begins formal Zen training in July at Shokoku-ji temple complex.

1957   Leaves Kyoto in August, taking a job in the engine room of the S.S. *Sappa Creek*; over the next eight months travels through the Persian Gulf, the Red Sea, the Suez Canal, the Mediterranean, the Bay of Bengal, and the Pacific.

1958   Returns to the United States in April, staying briefly with friend Locke McCorkle in San Francisco and with his father in Corte Madera before settling in Marin-an. Meets Joanne Kyger, a bookstore clerk and poet, at a San Francisco poetry reading in June, and they become a couple. Essay "Spring *Sesshin* at Sokoku-ji" is published in a special summer Zen issue of the *Chicago Review*, and his "Cold Mountain" translations in the fall *Evergreen Review*. Backpacks in the Sierras with Locke McCorkle. Appears as "Japhy Ryder" in Jack Kerouac's semi-fictional novel *The Dharma Bums*, published in October; one of Kerouac's early titles for the book was "Visions of Gary." Camps out with Philip Whalen on the Olympic Peninsula in Oregon; hikes in Sequoia National Park with other friends. Toward the end of the year, improvises a tiny zendo at Marin-an, hosting and teaching meditation.

1959   In January, after a farewell poetry reading at Bread & Wine Mission in San Francisco, returns to Kyoto, renting a house in suburban Yase. Begins studies under Oda Sesso Roshi, abbot at Daitoku-ji. Attends Noh performances with Cid Corman and Will Petersen, the former a poet and publisher of the magazine *Origin*, the latter an artist. In August, travels along the coast of the Sea of Japan. *Riprap* is published by Corman's Origin Press and printed in Kyoto; Lawrence Ferlinghetti of San Francisco's City Lights Bookstore underwrites the publication, and the first printing quickly sells out.

1960   Marries Joanne Kyger on February 23 at the American Consulate in Kobe, a few days after her arrival in Japan. (Ruth Fuller Sasaki objects to her employee and his girlfriend living together out of wedlock.) In June they move into a larger house in Kyoto; she works as an English tutor, learns flower arranging, and writes poetry (her journals of 1960–64 later published as *Strange Big Moon*). With British potter John Chappell and his wife Anya, they spend two weeks at the beach near Kurayoshi and visit the island of Nishijima. In September, *Myths & Texts* is published in New York by LeRoi Jones's Totem Press in association with Corinth Books.

1961   In May, after a fight between Ruth Fuller Sasaki and his fellow translator Philip Yampolsky, resigns from the First Zen Institute; takes English-teaching jobs to pay rent. Climbs Mt. Omine the following month with *yamabushi* mountain monks and becomes an honorary initiate; acquires a *yamabushi* conch horn. Works on Japanese translation of *Riprap*. Sketches Japanese farmhouses, imagining he might build one in America. With Joanne, sails from Yokohama on December 12 heading for India by way of Hong Kong, Saigon, and Sri Lanka, where they arrive two weeks later. On the last day of the year, in Kandy, rides an elephant.

1962   Travels with Joanne throughout India, and to Nepal, from January through April, later publishing an account of their journey as *Passage Through India*. They visit the Sri Aurobindo and Sri Ramana Maharishi Ashrams; temples at Konarak; Bodh Gaya, where the Buddha achieved enlightenment; the ruins at Nalanda; Kathmandu; and the Taj Mahal. At the end of February, they connect with Allen Ginsberg and Peter Orlovsky, continuing to Almora in the Himalayas, where they meet Lama Govinda, author of *The Foundations of Tibetan Mysticism*. On March 31 they have an audience with the Dalai Lama at Dharamshala; Ginsberg and Orlovsky ask about drugs and meditation (offering to send psilocybin), Kyger asks about meditation practices for Westerners, and the Dalai Lama asks Snyder about Zen practices in Japan. Returning to Kyoto in May, resumes English teaching and Zen training; receives his dharma name, "Chofu" ("Listen to the Wind"). Gives a dinner party for a group of Daitoku-ji monks in July, serving spaghetti, jello, and ice cream; socializes with John and Anya Chappell, Will and Ami Petersen, Philip Yampolsky, Burton Watson, and others. Blows his *yamabushi* horn at a party ringing in the new year.

1963   With Joanne, travels to Kyushu in March, visiting Nagasaki and Kagoshima. They host Allen Ginsberg, who arrives in mid-June for a monthlong stay. Tibald, one of five cats in the house (the others Fudo, Henry, Nansen, and Theadora), has kittens. Meets poet Nanao Sakaki. Spends time with Alan Watts and his girlfriend Mary Jane King, attending Noh performances, drinking sake, and taking LSD.

1964   Returns to the United States in April, renting an apartment in San Francisco; wife Joanne, who left Japan in January, lives separately. Reads with Lew Welch and Philip Whalen at the Pacific Longshoremen's Memorial Hall in San Francisco; in the same month, tours Native American sites in the Southwest with Donald Allen (founder of the Four Seasons Foundation and Grey Fox Press) and visits Robert Creeley in Texas. Hikes in Kings Canyon National Park, up the Bubbs Creek Trail. Teaches freshman composition and poetry writing at UC–Berkeley during the fall. Wins *Poetry* magazine's annual Bess Hokin Prize for poems from the sequence "Six Years." Reads with Robert Duncan at UCLA, and lectures on "Buddhist Practices" at the Berkeley Buddhist Temple.

1965   Continues teaching at Berkeley during the spring. Leads weekend meditation seminar in March at the Esalen Institute in Big Sur. On June 22, with Philip Whalen and a half dozen others, sits in meditation outside the Oakland Army Terminal, departure point to Southeast Asia for many U.S. troops, as part of a larger protest against the war in Vietnam. Reads at the Berkeley Poetry Conference in July. The Four Seasons Foundation publishes *Riprap and Cold Mountain Poems* and *Six Sections from Rivers and Mountains Without End*. Hikes with Drum Hadley and Philip Whalen to States Lake Basin in Kings Canyon National Park, and in September, with Martine Algier and Allen Ginsberg, hikes up Glacier Peak in the North Cascades. On October 2, circumambulates Mt. Tamalpais with Ginsberg and Whalen, chanting at points from Hindu and Buddhist texts. Returns to Kyoto at the end of October for another year of Buddhist study, this time with a grant from the Bollingen Foundation. Divorce from Joanne Kyger is finalized.

1966   While living in Kyoto, *A Range of Poems* is published in London by Fulcrum Press, and the documentary *USA: Poetry*, featuring Snyder and Whalen, airs on American television. Meets Masa Uehara, a recent graduate of Kobe University, at a dinner party; they begin to see each other frequently. Hosts writer Pupul Jayakar—an acquaintance from Bombay, now cultural adviser to Indira Gandhi—introducing her to Oda Sesso Roshi, abbot of Daitoku-ji, and touring Nara. Oda dies in September. Reads with Franco Beltrametti, Nanao Sakaki, Tetsuo Nagasawa, and Sansei Yamao at a "Bum Academy Festival" in Tokyo. Back in the United States in October, settles in Mill Valley. Hikes through Sequoia National Park; spends time in San Francisco ("the dance-joy-costume-love-acid scene is too beautiful," he writes Ginsberg). Visits a 160-acre property near Nevada City, California, which he purchases with Ginsberg, Richard Baker Roshi, and J. Donald Waters (Swami Kriyananda), envisioning a future home. Reads widely: at UC–Berkeley, the Houston Poetry Festival, New Mexico State, the Guggenheim in New York (with David Ignatow), and elsewhere. Travels with Drum Hadley in the Pinacate Desert in Sonora, Mexico.

1967   Reads at the January 8 opening of the Unicorn Bookshop, co-owned by future publisher Jack Shoemaker, in Isla Vista, California. Blowing a *yamabushi* conch-shell trumpet, opens the Human Be-In, a "Gathering of the Tribes" held in San Francisco's Golden Gate Park on January 14 with approximately 20,000 in attendance; performs a ritual circumambulation of the event with Allen Ginsberg. Joins Ginsberg, Timothy Leary, and Alan Watts in a conversation published in February in the counterculture newspaper the *City of San Francisco Oracle*. Departs for Kyoto on March 23. Kenneth Rexroth and Nanao Sakaki visit for much of May. The following month, with girlfriend Masa Uehara, helps Sakaki build one of two ashrams Sakaki has planned for his "Bum Academy" (later *Buzoku*, "the Tribe"). Hitchhikes with Masa to Tokyo, where he reads for the Bum Academy magazine *Psyche*. In July they sail to Suwanosejima, a volcanic island in the Ryukyus that is home to Sakaki's Banyan Ashram. Marries Masa there on August 6. *The Back Country* is published in London by Fulcrum Press. Wins *Poetry* magazine's Frank O'Hara prize for "Three Worlds, Three Realms, Six Roads." During the winter months, studies with Nakamura Sojun Roshi at Daitoku-ji.

1968   *The Back Country* is published in the United States in March by New Directions. Wins a Guggenheim Fellowship for poetry the following month; hopes to complete *Mountains and Rivers Without End* "in the next two years." Son Kai is born in Kyoto on April 17. ("Fatherhood is like having a Zen Master in the house all the time," he writes Ginsberg. "Talk about dignity, demands, non-verbal communication; and a mirror held up to yourself.") In June joins *yamabushi* mountain pilgrims on five-day ritual hike. Presents essay "Poetry and the Primitive" at Kanto Gakuin University in Yokohama. Beginning in August spends six weeks at Banyan Ashram, Masa and Kai remaining in Kyoto. In November wins *Poetry* magazine's Levinson Prize for his sequence "Eight Songs of Cloud and Water." Father dies on December 23 in Palma de Mallorca, Spain. Returning to the U.S. after a long trip at sea, the family stays with sister Thea in San Anselmo.

1969   At the end of January, leaving Kai with Thea, drives to Tucson with Masa in their new Volkswagen camper van to join Drum and Diana Hadley for a three-week trip through Baja California. Attends the Sierra Club Wilderness Conference in San Francisco in March, distributing copies of his "Smokey the Bear Sutra" and giving interviews: "Ecology radicals should call for Green Studies programs at universities—teaching emergency planet information and the non-negotiable demands of nature if the biosphere is to remain intact." *Earth House Hold*, a collection of essays and journal entries, is published by New Directions the next month, followed in June by *Regarding Wave*, in a limited edition from Windhover Press. Rents a house in Mill Valley, near Muir Woods, while planning a move to "Kitkitdizze" (the family's land in Nevada County, California—its name taken from the Miwok word for Bear Clover, a native shrub). Hikes in the High Sierra with Nanao Sakaki ("one of my most important teachers," he writes Ginsberg), who stays with the family. Alan Watts visits. Gen, his second son, is born early on November 1, his father in Minnesota for a reading.

1970   Reads and lectures across Canada in March and gives an Earth Day speech at Colorado State. Moves with family to Kitkitdizze where, with the aid of many friends, they begin building a home, borrowing features from Native American earth lodges and Japanese farmhouses. *Six Sections from Mountains and Rivers Without End Plus One* is published by Four Seasons Press in June and an expanded *Regarding Wave* by New Directions in October. By the end of the year, the house at Kitkitdizze is inhabited and almost done; a group of those who helped to build it join together to buy an adjacent property.

1971 Teaches at the University of California–Riverside from January to early March, and travels for readings throughout the year: to the University of California at Santa Cruz, Washington University, Iowa State University, Goucher College, Sonoma State College, Boston College, and elsewhere. Reads "The Wilderness" at the Center for the Study of Democratic Institutions in Santa Barbara. In May, Lew Welch, camping near Kitkitdizze during a bout of depression, disappears, leaving his car and a suicide note behind. Despite a five-day community search, his body is never found. Helps fight a forest fire on a neighbor's land. At sunrise on the day of the fall equinox, as part of a multimedia "ecological service" at San Francisco's Grace Cathedral, presents "Prayer for the Great Family" with Masa and children.

1972 Along with Theodosius Dobzhansky and Loren Eiseley, serves as writer-in-residence at the University of Redlands in March. In June, with the support of the *Whole Earth Catalog*, attends United Nations Conference on the Human Environment in Stockholm ("full of groups of people who came to argue over the spoils, not to quit spoiling," he writes Ginsberg). Travels to Hokkaido, climbing in the Daisetsuzan mountains; studies Ainu culture and the local Ussuri brown bear. *Manzanita*, a chapbook, is published by Four Seasons.

1973 Spends three weeks in Montana in April as guest lecturer for the Round River Experiment in Environmental Studies, a University of Montana program; Masa attends, teaching Asian dance. Visits Wendell Berry and his wife Tanya at their farm, Lanes Landing, in Port Royal, Kentucky, amid end-of-year readings in the Midwest. Shaman Drum publishes his chapbook *The Fudo Trilogy*.

1974 Lectures on "The Incredible Survival of Coyote" at Utah State College, and on "The Yogin and the Philosopher" at the Conference on the Rights of the Nonhuman in Claremont, California; reads poetry at the University of North Carolina and the University of Utah. In May the "Ring of Bone" zendo, a Mahayana Buddhist *sangha*, is formally declared at Kitkitdizze, its meetings held in a small barn (the "barndo"). In November, New Directions publishes *Turtle Island*, the title an "old/new name" for North America, "based on many creation myths of the people who have been living here for millennia." Reads with Allen Ginsberg, Michael McClure, and Nanao Sakaki at a Berkeley benefit for the Banyan Ashram.

1975   In February, is appointed to the California Arts Council by newly elected governor Jerry Brown, an admirer of *Turtle Island*. Wins the Pulitzer Prize in Poetry for *Turtle Island* in May, donating his $1,000 prize money toward the completion of Oak Tree School, a new elementary school and community project on San Juan Ridge. Mother moves to nearby Grass Valley, California.

1976   Reads at a Berkeley benefit for Balasaraswati Music and Dance Company, of which his wife is a member. Bob Steuding's *Gary Snyder*, the first book-length study of the poet's work, is published in Twayne's United States Authors Series. Writes to the editor of the *Sacramento Bee* on August 1, defending the work of the California Arts Council amid criticism of its nontraditional and multi-cultural funding priorities. Joins Governor Brown, Joni Mitchell and other musicians, conservationists, and whale researchers at a "California Celebrates the Whale" event at the Sacramento Memorial Auditorium.

1977   Reads poems with Wendell Berry at the San Francisco Museum of Modern Art in March; attends symposium on "Chinese Poetry and the American Imagination" in New York the following month. *The Old Ways*—"six brief approaches to the old ways via poetry, myth, and sense of place"—is published by City Lights. In the fall, goes backpacking with his sons in the Olympic Mountains; joins Olga Broumas, Carolyn Kizer, and others at a poetry teaching symposium in Port Townsend, Washington, and lectures at the Church of the Holy Communion in New York, home of the Lindisfarne Association.

1978   With Nelson Foster, Robert Aitken Roshi, Anne Aitken, Jo-anna Macy, Jack Kornfield, Al Bloom, and others, becomes a member of the newly formed Buddhist Peace Fellowship. Visits with Tanya and Wendell Berry on their Kentucky farm in March, amid many readings and speaking engagements, one of them a San Francisco benefit for Greenpeace. Receives the ongoing support of Governor Brown as critics of the California Arts Council introduce legislation to abolish it; Brown is an occasional guest at Kitkitdizze and considers buying a nearby property. Begins an annual Ring of Bone zendo summer tradition, the "Mountains and Rivers" sesshin, combining hiking and meditation; later describes it as the zendo's singular "contribution to Zen practice." Backpacks with friends in the high country of Yosemite in August. Co-edits and writes an introductory statement for the *Journal for the Protection of All Beings*, a special issue of *CoEvolution Quarterly*.

1979   *Songs for Gaia*, a chapbook illustrated with Michael Corr's woodblock prints, is published by Copper Canyon, and *He Who Hunted Birds in His Father's Village: The Dimensions of a Haida Myth*, based on his Reed College thesis, by Grey Fox Press. In July, with Masa, participates in a symposium on "Poetry and Dance of Life and Place" at the University of Hawaii; meets W. S. Merwin, reading with him at a Honolulu benefit for Robert Aitken Roshi's Diamond Sangha. Joins Wendell Berry at a Menninger Foundation conference in Topeka, Kansas, reading essay "Poetry, Community, and Climax." Discusses "Zen and Contemporary Poetry" with Robert Bly, Richard Brautigan, Lucien Stryk, and Philip Whalen at a Modern Language Association meeting in San Francisco.

1980   Reads from his poems in Sitka, Alaska; at Berkeley; at a San Francisco benefit for Fay Stender, an activist lawyer paralyzed after a shooting; and on Earth Day at Purdue. *The Real Work: Interviews & Talks, 1964–1979* is published in August by New Directions. In October, Robert Aitken Roshi leads a sesshin at Kitkitdizze.

1981   Reads in Newport, Brookings, and Astoria, Oregon, telling one audience: "First thing I do here when I get up into the Northwest is get out of the car and go a few yards off into the woods and just sniff that distinctive moldy underbrush. Nothing like it anywhere else." Takes a rafting trip down the Stanislaus River. Travels to Japan with Masa, Kai, and Gen over the summer, visiting Masa's extended family. In September and October spends six weeks in Australia with Nanao Sakaki, reading poems in cities and outback Aboriginal communities throughout the country; meets Aboriginal poet Kath Walker on North Stradbroke Island in Queensland and in Tasmania reconnects with potter Les

Blakebrough, a friend from his years in Kyoto. Installs solar panels at Kitkitdizze.

1982 Gives talk "Sacred Land: A Cross-Cultural Perspective" in Wyoming in February; speaks at the University of Montana with Native American activist Russell Means. Spends the summer at Kitkitdizze helping to build a community hall for the Ring of Bone zendo. In a friendly letter published in *Earth First!* in August, urges environmental activist Dave Foreman to reconsider his advocacy of violent "monkey-wrenching" (the destruction of machines or property in defense of wild nature). Hosts a Nevada City benefit for Gene Covert, a candidate for Nevada County supervisor running on an environmental platform. In October travels to Sweden where *The Old Ways* has recently been translated. Meets up with Wendell Berry in Edinburgh; they read together in London and address the Schumacher Society in Bristol (Snyder on "Good, Wild, and Sacred Land"). Attends the annual meeting of the Lindisfarne Association in Crestone, Colorado. Reads with poet-anthropologist Stanley Diamond at the New School in New York and at the annual meeting of the American Anthropological Association in Washington, D.C.

1983 Appears at a San Francisco benefit for the new Rainforest Action Network in March with activists Dave Foreman and John Seed; the following month, reads from his poetry with Drummond Hadley at the University of Kentucky and the University of Louisville. Lectures at the Naropa Institute in Boulder over the summer. Tanya and Wendell Berry visit Kitkitdizze. In October, publishes a new collection of poems, *Axe Handles*, from North Point Press, followed at the end of the year by an edition of his journals and travel writings of 1962, *Passage Through India*.

1984 Reads throughout Alaska in April and May—in Sitka, Kenai, Unalaska, Anchorage, Haines, Shungnak, Kobuk, and elsewhere—in association with the Alaska Humanities Forum. Attends community meetings on San Juan Ridge to protest the proposed development of a local mine. Visits Oregon's Willamette National Forest, speaking at the Cathedral Forest Rendezvous. In October, sponsored by the Chinese Writers Association and the University of California–Los Angeles, travels with Ginsberg, Maxine Hong Kingston, Toni Morrison, and others to Beijing for a conference on "The Sources of Creativity"; visits Hanshan Temple in Suzhou, giving the head priest a copy of his "Cold Mountain" translations. Wins an American Book Award for *Axe Handles*.

1985   Reads from his poems at UCLA, the California Institute of the Arts, and the Herbst Theater in San Francisco. In Kansas in June for the Kansas Prairie Festival, tracks down and visits the grave of his great-grandmother, Harriet Callicotte. In August, sponsored by the University of Alaska–Fairbanks, teaches a course on "Nature Literature: Gates of the Arctic National Park" at Summit Lake and Chimney Lake in central Brooks Range. Travels to Hawaii in October as a guest of the Hawaii Literary Arts Council. Joins Wendell Berry at the University of Montana for "On Common Ground," a conference on the relationship between wilderness and agriculture.

1986   Teaches "The Literature of the Wilderness" at the University of California–Davis in the spring, joining the English Department there. Rafts down the Tatshenshini River in British Columbia with Gen in July; later Kai joins them for a trip exploring the headwaters basin of the Noatak River in northern Alaska. Receives the Poetry Society of America's Shelley Memorial Award. Publishes poetry collection *Left Out in the Rain* with North Point Press.

1987   Gives talk "Recollections of Early Zen" at Green Gulch Farm Zen Center in Muir Beach, California, in April; the following month, is inducted into the American Academy of Arts and Letters. Visits Sitka, Alaska, with son Gen and Nanao Sakaki, staying with anthropologist Richard Nelson; reads at the Sitka Summer Writers Symposium. Climbs and hikes on Baranof Island, Alaska, in the Yukon ranges, and, back in California, in the Sierra Nevada. In the fall, reads in Vermont with novelist Jim Dodge. Celebrates the centennial of Robinson Jeffers's birth with William Everson, Czesław Miłosz, Diane Wakoski, and others. Kai, recovering from a serious car accident, resumes his studies at the University of California–Santa Cruz.

1988   Writes to friends in March: "Masa and I are realigning our lives," she beginning a relationship with Zen teacher Nelson Foster while remaining at Kitkitdizze, he a relationship with Carole Koda, a physician's assistant and avid hiker and climber. Arranges for Allen Ginsberg to speak at UC–Davis and the North Columbia Cultural Center. Joins Ginsberg,

Joanne Kyger, Michael McClure, and Nanao Sakaki at an
August "Eco Poetry Round Up" in San Francisco to ben-
efit conservation of the Shiraho reef in the Ryukyu Islands;
over 1,000 attend. In September, with friend David Padwa
and others, travels across Tibet.

1989   Divorce from Masa Uehara is finalized; in June, Carole
Koda moves to Kitkitdizze with her daughters Mika (b.
1978) and Kyung-jin Robin (b. 1983). Travels with Carole
in southeast Alaska in July, following the route of John
Muir; they take sea-kayaks to the base of Muir Glacier.
Back home, suffers from apparent asthma or bronchitis,
later diagnosed as pneumonia; an x-ray reveals a lesion on
his lung. Returning from a speaking engagement at the
University of the Ryukyus in Okinawa, undergoes surgery
to remove the growth, which on biopsy proves benign.

1990   Recovering slowly from surgery, drives with Carole to Ari-
zona in February, where they visit with Dave Foreman and
Drum Hadley. Gives an Earth Day lecture at Bridgeport,
on the South Yuba River; in May, circumambulates Mt.
Tamalpais. Works with Nanao Sakaki at Kitkitdizze on a
new Japanese translation of *Turtle Island*. In July travels
with Carole to the Naropa Institute where they meet with
Ginsberg. *The Practice of the Wild*, an essay collection, is
published in September by North Point Press. With Nevada
County neighbors, helps to establish the Yuba Watershed
Institute; they reach an agreement with the Bureau of Land
Management, taking cooperative responsibility for over
2,000 local forest acres. In October gives talk on "Medita-
tion, (Chan), and Poetry" at a conference on literature and
religion at Fu Jen University in Taipei.

1991   Marries Carole Lynn Koda in Kitkitdizze Meadow on
April 18; they travel widely in Alaska in July, climb in the
Palisades region of the Sierras with Kai in August, and
in October hike in Japan with Nanao Sakaki. Reads with
Sakaki in Kyoto and, as part of a protest against nuclear
energy, in Obama, a city in Fukui Prefecture with many
nuclear power stations. Is described as the "poet laureate
of Deep Ecology" in Max Oelschlaeger's influential book
The Idea of Wilderness. Toward the end of the year, Carole
is diagnosed with a rare cancer, pseudomyxoma.

1992   Buys Bedrock Mortar, Allen Ginsberg's cabin adjoining
Kitkitdizze. Helps to establish an annual "Art of the Wild"
writers' conference at UC–Davis. In September travels to

Leh in the Indian territory of Ladakh, presenting essay "A Village Council of All Beings." *No Nature: New and Selected Poems* is published by Pantheon the same month; it is a National Book Award finalist. Joins Sue Halpern, William Kittredge, Bill McKibben, and Terry Tempest Williams for a November "Evening with Nature Writers" at Miami-Dade Community College. Reads in Spain in December.

1993   Co-founds the Nature and Culture Program at UC–Davis, supporting an undergraduate major for students of society and the environment. In June, quietly resigns from the board of advisors of *Tricycle: The Buddhist Review*, explaining to its editor Helen Tworkov: "So much time has elapsed and nothing has yet been done to address the question of the role of Asian-Americans in the evolution of American Buddhism, and how they are feeling about Caucasian Buddhist assumptions."

1994   Reads from his poems at Butler University in Indianapolis. In April, with Gen, flies to Botswana to meet with Kai, who is working there; they travel through Tanzania, Kenya, and Zimbabwe. Tanya and Wendell Berry visit Kitkitdizze in May; with Carole, they camp out in the Black Rock Desert of Nevada. Attends a tribute to Allen Ginsberg at the Naropa Institute in Boulder, and the Geraldine R. Dodge Poetry Festival in Bryam Township, New Jersey.

1995   Speaks on "Rediscovering Turtle Island" at the University of Arizona in April; reads with Stanley Kunitz and Denise Levertov at the National Poetry Festival in Des Moines, Iowa. Is featured on the PBS television program *The Language of Life with Bill Moyers*, which premieres in July, and at a September benefit for the Sonoma Land Trust. In the fall, travels to Nepal with Carole; they trek to Sagarmatha (Mt. Everest) Base Camp. Essay collection *A Place in Space: Ethics, Aesthetics, and Watersheds* is published by Counterpoint in October.

1996   Teaches "The Making of the Long Poem" at UC–Davis in the spring. Joins other noted writers in Washington, D.C., for conference "Watershed: Writers, Nature and Community," organized by poet laureate Robert Hass and the Orion Society. With Carole, travels to France in June and July to study cave art, visiting Peche-merle, Cougnac, Niaus, El Portel, Lascaux, and Trois-Frères. In September, *Mountains and Rivers Without End* is published by

Counterpoint Press, representing the culmination of four decades of writing and revision. Reads selections from the book at the Library of Congress the following month. Carole undergoes surgery and chemotherapy.

1997   Wins the Bollingen Prize in Poetry from Yale University Library in January, and in April both the John Hay Award for Nature Writing, presented by the Orion Society, and the 1996 Robert Kirsch Award for lifetime achievement, from the *Los Angeles Times.* Allen Ginsberg dies on April 5. Is diagnosed with prostate cancer and begins treatment. Travels to Japan over the summer, reading at the Tokyo Summer Festival. With the aid of his $50,000 Bollingen award, builds a 600-square-foot addition onto the house at Kitkitdizze, including its first indoor toilet.

1998   Travels to Japan in March to receive the thirty-second Bunka-Sho (Buddhism Transmission Award) from the Bukkyo Dendo Kyokai (Society for the Propagation of Buddhism), the first American to be thus honored. Also wins a Lila Wallace–Reader's Digest Fund award, supporting both his own writing and a program of readings at the nearby North Columbia Schoolhouse Cultural Center. Reads in Hawaii, Greece, and the Czech Republic. In October, amid controversy over a state ballot measure that would ban forest clearcutting and pesticide use, and an attempt to prevent him from speaking on campus, addresses an audience of over 1,000 at Oregon State University on "Gratitude to Trees: Buddhist Resource Management in Asia and California." Visits new granddaughter, Kiyomi, and son Kai, a graduate student in forestry at Oregon State. Lectures at Westminster College in Salt Lake City and at the Connecticut Museum of Natural History in Hartford; reads with Mexican poet Alberto Blanco at the Art Institute of Chicago.

1999   Appears with cultural historian Mike Davis and state senator Tom Hayden in April in a program to benefit the Friends of the Los Angeles River. *The Gary Snyder Reader: Prose, Poetry, and Translations, 1952–1998* is published by Counterpoint in June. Reads with Wendell Berry in Santa Fe, hosted by the Lannan Foundation; the two are interviewed onstage by their publisher, Jack Shoemaker.

2000   Visits Hawaii in February; appears with Nanao Sakaki and Albert Saijo at the Volcano Arts Center. Is named Faculty Research Lecturer at UC–Davis, the university's highest peer honor; receives an honorary degree at Colby College commencement. As co-host, joins environmental leaders traveling through the Tongass region of southeast Alaska aboard the *Catalyst*, a restored 1930s wooden ship. In August, accompanied by San Juan Ridge musicians Ludi Hinrichs and Daniel Flanigan, reads from *Mountains and Rivers Without End* for an audience of over 500 in the amphitheater of the North Columbia Schoolhouse Cultural Center. In September, attends "Writing Across Boundaries" symposium in Seoul, South Korea. Presents lecture "Zen and Ecology" at Komazawa University in Tokyo.

2001   Receives the California State Library Gold Medal for Excellence in the Humanities and Social Sciences.

2002   In January, sister Thea is killed after being struck by a car in Novato, California. Formally retires as Professor Emeritus from UC–Davis; donates his papers to the university library. Philip Whalen dies in June. Reads from *Mountains and Rivers Without End* at the Tokyo Summer Festival, accompanied by San Juan Ridge musicians. Prepares a short selection of his writings, *Look Out*, published by New Directions in November. Heyday Books publishes *The High Sierra of California*, with selections from his journals and woodblock prints by Tom Killion. Reads from *Mountains and Rivers Without End* in December at the Maison de la Culture du Japon in Paris, accompanied by Noh musicians.

2003   Gives keynote speech—"Ecology, Literature, and the New World Disorder"—at a "Literature and the Environment" conference at the University of the Ryukyus in April, and reads poetry in Tokyo. Is elected a chancellor of the Academy of American Poets.

2004   Receives the Masaoka Shiki International Haiku Awards Grand Prize from the Ehime Cultural Foundation in Matsuyama City, Japan; in his acceptance speech, highlights "the influence from haiku and from the Chinese" on his poetry. Mother dies in Grass Valley on August 13, at ninety-eight. Visits Italy with Carole in the fall, but she returns home early, in declining health. *Danger on Peaks*, a new poetry collection, is published by Shoemaker & Hoard in September.

2005   *Danger on Peaks* is named a National Book Critics Circle award finalist. Reads from the book at Iowa State

University, and in May speaks on "Lessons from Mount St. Helens" in Portland alongside ecologist Jerry Franklin. The same month, with Carole, visits Death Valley, where the wildflowers are blooming. Attends "Writing for Peace" conference in Seoul as a guest of the Daesan Foundation, and reads at a year-end exhibition celebrating the Black Rock Desert at the Nevada Museum of Art.

2006　　On June 29, Carole Koda dies at home from cancer.

2007　　*Back on the Fire*, a collection of essays, is published by Shoemaker & Hoard in February; reads from the book, and from *Danger on Peaks*, in Santa Fe, Charlotte, and Chicago. Attends the Prague Writers Festival in June.

2008　　Wins the Ruth Lilly Poetry Prize from the Poetry Foundation, and $100,000. In June, in San Francisco, introduces a program of his poems set to music by Fred Frith, Allaudin Mathieu, Robert Morris, and Roy Whelden, and performed by contralto Karen Clark and the Galax Quartet.

2009　　Counterpoint publishes *The Selected Letters of Allen Ginsberg and Gary Snyder, 1956–1991*, edited by Bill Morgan, and a fiftieth-anniversary edition of *Riprap and Cold Mountain Poems*; Heyday Books publishes *Tamalpais Walking: Poetry, History, and Prints*, a collaboration with artist Tom Killion.

2010　　*The Practice of the Wild*, a documentary about Snyder directed by John J. Healey and produced by Jim Harrison and Will Hearst, premieres at the San Francisco Film Festival on May 3. A companion book—*The Etiquette of Freedom: Gary Snyder, Jim Harrison, and "The Practice of the Wild,"* edited by Paul Ebenkamp—is published by Counterpoint later in the year. Reads with Ursula K. Le Guin in Portland, on the thirtieth anniversary of the Mount St. Helens eruption.

2011　　Contributes a foreword to the anthology *The Nature of This Place: Investigations and Adventures in the Yuba Watershed*, and discusses the book with environmental journalist David Lukas at UC–Davis.

2012　　Wins the Wallace Stevens Award for lifetime achievement from the Academy of American Poets, and a $100,000 stipend. In April, receives the Henry David Thoreau Prize for Literary Excellence in Nature Writing from PEN New England. Reads at the Folger Shakespeare Library. On August 30, writes to Wendell Berry: "I'm beset, as I'm sure you are, by numerous requests, but I try to hold the line so that I can finish up a couple more writing projects before I get too close to (as Gore Vidal put it) the exit."

2013   Reads with Kashaya Pomo poet Martina Morgan at Fort Ross State Historic Park in Sonoma County, to benefit the Fort Ross Conservatory, and at the twelfth annual Quivira Coalition Conference, "Inspiring Adaptation," in Albuquerque.

2014   *Distant Neighbors: The Selected Letters of Wendell Berry and Gary Snyder*, edited by Chad Wriglesworth, is published by Counterpoint in June, and in November *Nobody Home: Writing, Buddhism, and Living in Places* by Trinity University Press, the latter gathering Snyder's conversations and correspondence with South African scholar Julia Martin.

2015   Publishes *This Present Moment* with Counterpoint, and a third collaboration with artist Tom Killion, *California's Wild Edge: The Coast in Prints, Poetry, and History.* The Center for Gary Snyder Studies at Hunan University in Changsha, China, hosts an "International Symposium on Ecopoetics, Ekphrasis, and Gary Snyder Studies."

2016   Lectures on "Scholars, Hermits, and People of the Land" at Cornell University. Counterpoint publishes *The Great Clod: Notes and Memories on the Natural History of China and Japan* in March—a collection of environmental essays—and in November *Dooby Lane: Also Known as Guru Road, a Testament Inscribed in Stone Tablets by DeWayne Williams*, a celebration of the Nevada folk artist DeWayne Williams, with photographs by Peter Goin.

2017   Travels to Santa Fe in May, giving a keynote address as part of the New Mexico History Museum's exhibit "Voices of Counterculture in the Southwest." At the end of the year is inducted into the California Hall of Fame by Governor Jerry Brown.

2018   Talks with students and reads from his poems at Macalester College in October, and at the University of California–Santa Cruz the following month.

2019   Contributes a foreword to *Karst Mountains Will Bloom* by Hmong American poet Pos Moua, a former student.

2020   Joins poet Jane Hirshfield for a reading at Mill Valley Public Library.

2021   Hikes in the High Sierra with Kim Stanley Robinson, the
            novelist, and David Robertson, the photographer. Visits
            northern California's Giant Sequoia groves with Tom
            Killion; they meet with foresters and ecologists.

Note on the Texts

This volume gathers all of the poems Gary Snyder has collected in book form up to 2022, along with a selection of previously uncollected poems, drafts, fragments, and translations, including 9 poems believed to be published in the present volume for the first time. The poems appear in the order in which they are arranged in his original collections, which are presented chronologically: *Riprap and Cold Mountain Poems* (1959/1965), *Myths & Texts* (1960), *The Back Country* (1968), *Regarding Wave* (1970), *Turtle Island* (1974), *Axe Handles* (1983), *Left Out in the Rain* (1986), from *No Nature* (1992), *Mountains and Rivers Without End* (1996), *Danger on Peaks* (2004), and *This Present Moment* (2015). *Riprap* was first published separately, in 1959, and "Cold Mountain Poems" in periodical form in 1958; they have been published together since 1965. *No Nature* presented a selection of Snyder's poetry up to 1992, along with a group of new poems; the new poems are included here in the section "from *No Nature*."

The texts of Snyder's books have been taken from their most recent American trade editions, in the most recent printings known to be available: for *Myths & Texts, The Back Country, Turtle Island*, and *Regarding Wave*, from New Directions in New York; for *No Nature*, from Pantheon Books in New York; and for *Riprap and Cold Mountain Poems, Axe Handles, Left Out in the Rain, Mountains and Rivers Without End, Danger on Peaks*, and *This Present Moment*, from Counterpoint Press in Berkeley. Snyder has often corrected and revised poems in later printings of these editions. Many of his poems have also appeared, sometimes in different form, in small press editions, British and Canadian editions, and selected editions, as well as in a wide variety of periodicals and broadsides, but these editions and periodical printings do not consistently reflect his latest intentions in regard to particular poems and arrangements of poems. The texts of Snyder's uncollected poems, drafts, fragments, and translations have been taken from a variety of sources, as described below.

Snyder has approved the contents of the present volume and its choices of texts, and guided the selection and arrangement of his previously uncollected works. For further information about the publication history of individual poems in periodical, broadside, and chapbook form, see Katherine McNeil's *Gary Snyder: A Bibliography* (New York: Phoenix Bookshop, 1983), and the 2010 second edition of John Sherlock's "Bibliography of Works by and about Gary Snyder," published online at https://www.library.ucdavis.edu/wp-content/

uploads/2017/03/bib-garysnyder-2ed.pdf by the Special Collections Department of the Library of the University of California, Davis.

Riprap and Cold Mountain Poems. Riprap, Snyder's first collection of poems, was published by Origin Press in 1959, in a printing of 500 copies. Origin was ordinarily headquartered in Ashland, Massachusetts, but its owner and proprietor, Cid Corman, was then visiting Kyoto, where Snyder was living and where *Riprap* was assembled, designed, edited, and printed during the summer and fall. Lawrence Ferlinghetti of City Lights Books in San Francisco underwrote the costs of publication and distributed the book; its first printing rapidly sold out, and a second, including corrections of typographical errors and minor revisions, appeared in 1960.

In July 1965, the Four Seasons Foundation of San Francisco published *Riprap and Cold Mountain Poems* in combined form, adding Snyder's "Cold Mountain Poems," from the Autumn 1958 *Evergreen Review*, to the Origin Press *Riprap* by photo-offset. A second Four Seasons edition, newly typeset, appeared in 1969, and went through five additional printings, the last in 1976. Separate editions of *Cold Mountain Poems* were published in 1968 by A. Shiller in Santa Barbara (in a printing of 5 copies, on clay tablets), and by Press 22 in Portland, Oregon, the latter notable for its calligraphic rendering of Snyder's text. In 1980 Grey Fox Press of San Francisco reprinted the second Four Seasons edition. A new edition published in 1990 by North Point Press in San Francisco added titles to two previously untitled poems, "At Five a.m. off the North Coast of Sumatra" and "Goofing Again." Subsequent editions published by Shoemaker & Hoard in Washington, D.C., in 2004, and by Counterpoint Press in Berkeley in 2009, added notes and an afterword.

All of the individual works in *Riprap and Cold Mountain Poems* were included, sometimes in slightly different order, in a collected edition of Snyder's poetry, *A Range of Poems*, published by Fulcrum Press in London in 1976; selections appear in *No Nature: New and Selected Poems* (New York: Pantheon, 1992) and *The Gary Snyder Reader* (Berkeley: Counterpoint, 1999). The text of *Riprap and Cold Mountain Poems* in the present volume is that of the most recent printing of the Counterpoint edition of 2009, supplied by Counterpoint in digital form on May 25, 2021.

Myths & Texts. First published in September 1960, Snyder's second collection of poems, *Myths & Texts*, was actually the first he finished writing, in the fall of 1955. Leaving his manuscript with Robert Creeley when he departed for Kyoto the following spring, Snyder hoped

Creeley and other friends would help him to publish the book in his absence from the United States. As it happened, his manuscript spent "a long time," he later recalled, in the trunk of Creeley's car. LeRoi Jones in New York eventually obtained a copy and proposed *Myths & Texts* as the first book in a new cooperative series to be jointly published by his imprint, Totem Press, and Corinth Books, also in New York. The first Totem/Corinth printing was followed by at least five additional printings through 1975; the third printing, in 1965, corrected typographical errors, including the omission of two lines. The complete text of the book also appeared in the United Kingdom, as part of *A Range of Poems* (London: Fulcrum Press, 1966).

New Directions in New York published a new edition of the book, including revisions and an introduction by Snyder, on April 1, 1978. The text of *Myths & Texts* in the present volume is that of the undated seventh printing of the New Directions edition.

The Back Country. The Back Country was first published by Fulcrum Press in London in October 1967. About half of the poems included in the first edition had previously appeared, in March 1966, in *A Range of Poems*, also published by Fulcrum Press; Snyder's work had not yet been collected in the United Kingdom in 1966, and Fulcrum's publisher Stuart Montgomery asked to be allowed to publish as much of *The Back Country* as possible as soon as possible, though the book was not, Snyder felt, "entirely ready." The first U.S. edition of the collection—published by New Directions in New York on March 21, 1968—was offset from the 1967 Fulcrum edition, with some alterations: section titles were added between groups of poems, and within the final section, "Miyazawa Kenji," Snyder revised poems and added a new final poem, "Thief." These revisions also appear in New Directions' newly typeset second edition of *The Back Country*, published on January 17, 1971. The text of *The Back Country* in the present volume is that of the second New Directions edition of 1971, in its seventeenth printing.

Regarding Wave. The first complete edition of *Regarding Wave*, containing five groups of poems ("Regarding Wave I," "Regarding Wave II," "Regarding Wave III," "Long Hair," and "Target Practice"), was published by New Directions in New York on October 21, 1970. A Canadian *Regarding Wave*, identical in its contents, was published simultaneously by McClelland & Stewart in Toronto, and a British edition, from Fulcrum Press in London, followed later in the year. Prior to these trade press editions, on June 25, 1969, a preliminary version of the collection, containing its first three sections, was printed at The Windhover Press, a private press of the English Department at the University of Iowa. The text of *Regarding Wave* in the present

volume is that of the New Directions first edition of 1970, in its un-
dated ninth printing.

Turtle Island. First published by New Directions in New York on
November 27, 1974, *Turtle Island* contains three sections of poetry
("Manzanita," "Magpie's Song," and "For the Children") and a con-
cluding section of prose ("Plain Talk"). The poems in "Manzanita"
had previously appeared in *Manzanita*, published by the Four Seasons
Foundation in Bolinas, California, on September 13, 1972. (Snyder
left one *Manzanita* poem out of *Turtle Island*, "Song to the Raw
Material"; it is included among the "Uncollected Poems" in this vol-
ume, on page 889.) One of the prose items in "Plain Talk," the essay
"Four Changes," had been printed in several broadside and pamphlet
editions from 1969 to 1974.

Snyder did not make corrections or revisions to two subsequent edi-
tions of *Turtle Island*, one a bilingual Japanese-English edition, with
translations by Nanao Sakaki, published by Yamaguchi Bookstore in
1991, and the other a "pocket classics" edition published by Shambhala
in Boston in 1993. The text of *Turtle Island* in the present volume is
that of the undated twenty-seventh printing of the New Directions
edition of 1974.

Axe Handles. Axe Handles was first published by North Point Press
in San Francisco in October 1983. Parts of the book's second section,
"Little Songs for Gaia," had previously appeared in the chapbook
Songs for Gaia (Port Townsend, WA: Copper Canyon Press, 1979). A
second edition was published by Shoemaker & Hoard in Washington,
D.C., on January 28, 2005; subsequent printings of this edition have
been published by Counterpoint Press, which subsumed Shoemaker
& Hoard. The text of *Axe Handles* in the present volume is that of
the most recent Counterpoint printing of the Shoemaker & Hoard
edition of 2005, supplied by Counterpoint in digital form on May
25, 2021.

Left Out in the Rain. First published by North Point Press in San
Francisco on November 20, 1986, *Left Out in the Rain* gathered
poems both old and new, as reflected in the book's subtitle, *Poems,
1947–1985*; Snyder selected, arranged, and in some cases revised his older
poems for the book. Counterpoint Press published a new edition
of the collection on December 9, 2005, shortening the subtitle to
Poems and adding a new preface by Snyder. The text of *Left Out in
the Rain* in the present volume is that of the most recent printing of
the Counterpoint first edition of 2005, as supplied by Counterpoint
in digital form on May 25, 2021.

From *No Nature*. On September 25, 1992, Pantheon Books in New York published the first career-retrospective selection of Snyder's poetry, *No Nature*; Jack Shoemaker, Snyder's former editor at North Point Press, had become West Coast editor at Pantheon. Along with published works from *Riprap* through *Left Out in the Rain*, *No Nature* presented a concluding section of 15 recent and previously uncollected poems, also titled "No Nature"; this section has not appeared in its entirety since. The text of "No Nature" in the present volume has been taken from an undated fourth printing of *No Nature*, believed to be the last printing to which Snyder may have sought to make corrections and revisions.

Mountains and Rivers Without End. Snyder's long poem *Mountains and Rivers Without End* was first published in its complete form on October 1, 1996, by Counterpoint Press in Washington, D.C. By his own account, the poem was over forty years in the making: on April 8, 1956, having finished *Myths & Texts*, and after a conversation with visiting artist Saburo Hasegawa in San Francisco about the Japanese painter Sesshū, he "resolved to start another long poem that would be called *Mountains and Rivers Without End*."

By 1965, Snyder felt that his evolving work was strong enough to be printed in book form: that July, the Four Seasons Foundation in San Francisco published *Six Sections from Mountains and Rivers Without End* (as "Writing 9" in a series edited by Donald Allen), including "Bubbs Creek Haircut," "The Elwha River," "Night Highway Ninety-Nine," "Hymn to the Goddess San Francisco in Paradise," "The Market," and "Journeys." All of these sections, other than "The Elwha River," had previously appeared in magazines, beginning with "Bubbs Creek Haircut" in *Origin* in July 1961. Five of the six are included, in revised form, in the first complete *Mountains and Rivers Without End* of 1996: "Hymn to the Goddess San Francisco in Paradise," which Snyder omitted, is gathered among the "Uncollected Poems" in this volume (see pages 876–79), as is "The Elwha River" (see pages 879–82), of which Snyder retained only the first of three parts.

Six Sections from Mountains and Rivers Without End was published in England as well as in the United States—by Fulcrum Press in London, in 1967—and in 1970 it was revised, expanded, and reset in a new Four Seasons edition titled *Six Sections from Mountains and Rivers Without End, Plus One*. The newly included section, "The Blue Sky," is also included in the complete poem of 1996, in revised form.

As of 1970, Snyder "decided not to publish any more sections in books" until he "finished the whole thing," though he continued to work on the poem sporadically, and turned his "full attention" to it in the 1990s. Several poems that he published in magazines and small press editions during the intervening years as sections of *Mountains and Rivers Without End*—including "Down," "The California Water Plan," and "Greasy Boy," all gathered in the "Uncollected Poems" section of the present volume—he ultimately omitted from the completed work. Others that he subsequently included in *Mountains and Rivers Without End* were retitled and/or substantially revised. A typescript draft of the poem shared with the editors of the present volume in 1995 contained the draft poem "Mountains Walk on Water," also omitted from the published edition of 1996; this draft poem appears herein on page 905. For a more detailed account of the publication history of individual sections of *Mountains and Rivers Without End* in periodical, broadside, and chapbook form, see the relevant appendix in Anthony Hunt's *Genesis, Structure, and Meaning in Gary Snyder's "Mountains and Rivers Without End"* (Reno: University of Nevada Press, 2004).

A second complete edition of *Mountains and Rivers Without End*, including textual corrections, was published by Counterpoint Press in Berkeley on March 3, 2008. The text of *Mountains and Rivers Without End* in the present volume is that of the 2008 Counterpoint edition in its most recent printing, supplied by Counterpoint in digital form on May 25, 2021.

Danger on Peaks. Danger on Peaks was published by Shoemaker & Hoard in Washington, D.C., on August 24, 2004, and on April 21, 2016, in a "deluxe audio" edition, featuring a book and CD, by Counterpoint Press and Audible Studios. The text of the book in the present volume is that of the Shoemaker & Hoard edition of 2004 in its most recent Counterpoint printing, supplied by Counterpoint in digital form on May 25, 2021.

This Present Moment. This Present Moment was first published by Counterpoint Press in Berkeley on April 14, 2015, and has not appeared in subsequent editions. The text of *This Present Moment* included here has been taken from the most recent printing of the Counterpoint edition, supplied by Counterpoint in digital form on May 25, 2021.

Uncollected Poems, Drafts, Fragments, and Translations. This volume gathers 48 uncollected poems, drafts, and fragments by Snyder, arranged in approximate chronological order of first publication, or, for manuscript poems, composition. Following these uncollected poems are 17 poems in translation, and an additional poem by Snyder ("At Maple Bridge"), written in response to Chang Chi's "Maple Bridge Night Moon." It is believed that 9 poems within this section—marked with an asterisk (*) below—are published in the present volume for the first time. For untitled poems, titles have been supplied by enclosing their opening lines in quotation marks, or (in cases where poems have been taken from essays by Snyder) by quoting the essay title (as in "from 'A Single Breath'").

The following is a list of sources from which texts of these uncollected works have been taken. All typescripts listed are from the private collections of the editors of the present volume:

Reed College Poems. Title for this group supplied for the present volume. It includes "a poem," *Janus* (Reed College), January 1950; "The Death of Rhea," *Janus*, November 1950; "An Autumn Poem," *Janus*, November 1950; "Kasina Song," *Janus*, May 1951; and "'Escaping Cambridge'," in Robert Ian Scott (ed.), "The Uncollected Early Poems of Gary Snyder," *North American Review*, Fall 1977. "Kasina Song" was originally published as the first poem in the group "Three Mantic Poems," the second and third poems of which were subsequently published, in slightly revised form, in *Left Out in the Rain*, as sections 3 and 4 of the poem "Atthis," included on page 467 of the present volume. "'Escaping Cambridge'" was first published as a broadside at Reed College, c. 1950–51.

"Dear Mr. President." Broadside (San Francisco: C. Plymell and Ari Publications, 1965).

Hymn to the Goddess San Francisco in Paradise. *Six Sections from Mountains and Rivers Without End* (San Francisco: Four Seasons Foundation, 1965).

The Elwha River. *Six Sections from Mountains and Rivers Without End* (San Francisco: Four Seasons Foundation, 1965).

A Lion Dream. *Coyote's Journal* #8, 1967.

A Curse on the Men in Washington, Pentagon. Broadside (San Francisco: Communications Company, 1967).

Smokey the Bear Sutra. Broadside (San Francisco: The Author, 1969).

Kumarajiva's Mother. *In Transit* ("The Gary Snyder Issue"), 1969.

Song to the Raw Material. *Caterpillar*, April 1970.

Down. *Iowa Review*, Fall 1970.

Swimming Naked in the Yuba River. Broadside (Berkeley: Maidu Press, 1971).

The California Water Plan. First published in *Clear Creek*, November 1971; text from *The Fudo Trilogy* (Berkeley: Shaman Drum, 1973).

Greasy Boy. *Caterpillar*, June 1973.

"I saw the Mother once." *Caterpillar*, June 1973.

Tomorrow's Song. *Espejo*, Spring 1974.

Gold, Green. Broadside (Sacramento, s.n.: c. March 1978).

"The delicacy of the mountains." *Songs for Gaia* (Port Townsend, WA: Copper Canyon, 1979).

"Emptiness, anti-entropy, ultimate." *Songs for Gaia* (Port Townsend, WA: Copper Canyon, 1979).

"The dried out winter ricefields." *Passage Through India* (San Francisco: Grey Fox Press, 1983).

"At Sarnath." *Passage Through India* (San Francisco: Grey Fox Press, 1983).

haiku. *Passage Through India* (San Francisco: Grey Fox Press, 1983).

on the train. *Passage Through India* (San Francisco: Grey Fox Press, 1983).

"nothing at the center." (with D. Steven Conkle), *Tree Zen* (Columbus, OH: The Broken Stone, 1984).

Needles Country of the Canyonlands. *Petroglyph*, Spring 1990.

From "A Single Breath." First published (as from "Just One Breath: The Practice of Poetry and Meditation") in *Tricycle: The Buddhist Review*, Fall 1991; text from *A Place in Space: Ethics, Aesthetics, and Watersheds* (Washington, D.C.: Counterpoint, 1995).

From "Coming into the Watershed." First published in *San Francisco Examiner*, March 1–2, 1992; text from *A Place in Space: Ethics, Aesthetics, and Watersheds* (Washington, D.C.: Counterpoint, 1995).

Ravynes Fly East. *Princeton University Library Chronicle*, Spring 1994.

Daconstruction. *Antaeus*, Autumn 1994.

*Mountains Walk on Water. Typescript (from an unpublished draft of *Mountains and Rivers Without End*), c. 1995.

From "Allen Ginsberg Crosses Over." First published in *Woodstock Journal*, May 2–16, 1997; text from *Back on the Fire* (Washington, D.C.: Counterpoint, 2007).

From "The Cottonwoods." First published in *Terra Nova*, Fall 1998; text from *Back on the Fire* (Washington, D.C.: Counterpoint, 2007).

*Where the Sammamish, the Snohomish, and the Skyhomish All Come In. Typescript, July–September 2005.

From "Writers and the War Against Nature." First published in *Kyoto Journal*, Winter 2006; text from *Back on the Fire* (Washington, D.C.: Counterpoint, 2007).

*What a life! Typescript, c. September 2007.

nine frags. *American Poetry Review*, July/August 2009.

The Dancer is a Weaver. *Columbia: A Journal of Literature and Art*, 2010.

The Goosenecks of the San Juan. *Columbia: A Journal of Literature and Art*, 2010.

Where. *Alta Journal*, July 3, 2018.

*Victoria Falls and Zimbabwe. Hand-emended typescript, c. 2016–20.

*By the Chobe River. Typescript, c. 2016–20.

*For Robert Duncan. Typescript, c. 2016–20.

*Song for Wrecked Cars. Typescript, c. 2016–20.
*After Dogen. Hand-emended typescript, c. 2016–20.
*Having Seen on Earth. Hand-emended typescript, c. 2016–20.
Long Bitter Song. *The Gary Snyder Reader: Prose, Poetry, and Transla-*
    tions, 1952–1998 (Washington, D.C.: Counterpoint, 1999).
Sixteen T'ang Poems. *The Gary Snyder Reader: Prose, Poetry, and*
    Translations, 1952–1998 (Washington, D.C.: Counterpoint, 1999).
At Maple Bridge. *The Gary Snyder Reader: Prose, Poetry, and Transla-*
    tions, 1952–1998 (Washington, D.C.: Counterpoint, 1999).

This volume presents the texts of the original printings and typescripts
chosen for inclusion here, but it does not attempt to reproduce features
of their typographic design. The texts are reprinted without change,
except for the correction of typographical errors. Spelling, punctua-
tion, and capitalization are often expressive features, and they are not
altered, even when inconsistent or irregular. The following is a list of
typographical errors corrected, cited by page and line number: 119.8,
Dalenburg; 149.22, hataké; 156.27, the the; 164.6, you; 261.8, blinnies;
319.18, *Aldritch*; 355.6, Diane de Prima; 362.12, guage; 362.36, millenia;
376.10, thrust"; 399.15, *Nevada,*; 437.7, *Burt*; 530.12, berberia; 555.13,
'Tis; 596.8, liquidabars; 606.27, Lost; 756.29, too; 761.19, Mokulumne;
804.32, LeGuin; 820.10, *Mulato*; 831.31, Empeor; 874.15, transcendant;
874.21, ion; 881.20, selk; 902.3, *fremontia*; 902.4, *Berberia*; 907.1,
Samamish; 913.9, work; 914.21, Yambushi; 914.24, hardness—; 915.6,
11-year old; 915.22, *acacia*; 918.19, at Both; 918.20, Patriach; 918.24,
"Lama; 929.18, peelpole.

Notes

Notes and acknowledgments included in Snyder's original books of poetry are presented in their original form and location. For his notes to his "Cold Mountain" translations see page 38 in the present volume; for his notes to *Mountains and Rivers Without End* see pages 717–22; for *Danger on Peaks* see pages 802–4; for *This Present Moment* see pages 865–67.

In the notes below, the reference numbers denote page and line of this volume (the line count includes headings but not blank lines). Biblical references are keyed to the King James Version. For further information on Snyder's life and works, and references to other studies, see Bert Almon, *Gary Snyder* (Boise: Boise State University Press, 1979); David Stephen Calonne, ed., *Conversations with Gary Snyder* (Jackson: University Press of Mississippi, 2017); Mark Gonnerman, ed., *A Sense of the Whole: Reading Gary Snyder's "Mountains and Rivers Without End"* (Berkeley: Counterpoint, 2015); Timothy Gray, *Gary Snyder and the Pacific Rim: Creating Countercultural Community* (Iowa City: University of Iowa Press, 2006); Jon Halper, ed., *Gary Snyder: Dimensions of a Life* (San Francisco: Sierra Club, 1991); Anthony Hunt, *Genesis, Structure, and Meaning in Gary Snyder's "Mountains and Rivers Without End"* (Reno: University of Nevada Press, 2004); Howard McCord, *Some Notes to Gary Snyder's "Myths & Texts"* (Berkeley: Sand Dollar, 1971); Katherine McNeil, comp., *Gary Snyder: A Bibliography* (New York: Phoenix Bookshop, 1983); Bill Morgan, ed., *The Selected Letters of Allen Ginsberg and Gary Snyder* (Berkeley: Counterpoint, 2009); Patrick D. Murphy, ed., *Critical Essays on Gary Snyder* (Boston: G. K. Hall, 1991); Patrick D. Murphy, *A Place for Wayfaring: The Poetry and Prose of Gary Snyder* (Corvallis: Oregon State University Press, 2000); Bob Steuding, *Gary Snyder* (Boston: Twayne, 1976); John Suiter, *Poets on the Peaks: Gary Snyder, Philip Whalen, & Jack Kerouac in the North Cascades* (Washington, D.C.: Counterpoint, 2002); Chad Wriglesworth, ed., *Distant Neighbors: Selected Letters of Wendell Berry and Gary Snyder* (Berkeley: Counterpoint, 2014).

RIPRAP AND COLD MOUNTAIN POEMS

2.2–13 SPEED MCINTURFF . . . CRAZY HORSE MASON] Snyder's fellow workers in jobs he held, c. 1948–58, on trail crews, as a fire lookout, and as a merchant seaman.

5.1   *Sourdough Mountain*] 6,111-foot mountain in Whatcom County, Washington, within North Cascades National Park; Snyder worked as a fire lookout on Sourdough in the summer of 1953.

5.15   gypos] In the Pacific Northwest, loggers seeking work during a strike, or working as independent contractors.

5.24   Shuksan] Mountain in North Cascades National Park in Washington state.

6.5   green-chain] A system used in a sawmill to collect, grade, and sort processed lumber.

6.14   contra naturam] Latin: against nature.

7.29   kali/shakti] Kali is a Hindu goddess, a destroyer of evil and a universal mother; she manifests shakti, a female principle of divine energy.

8.1   *Piute Creek*] A tributary of the Tuolumne River, in Yosemite National Park.

9.3–4   "O hell . . . behold?"] See *Paradise Lost*, IV.358, by John Milton (1608–1674).

9.21   Han River] A tributary of the Yangtze River, in central China.

10.4   *Pate Valley*] Ravine in Yosemite National Park, beside the Tuolumne River.

11.33   *Sandra Gilbert*] Gilbert (b. 1936) is a poet and literary critic often remembered for *The Madwoman in the Attic* (1979), written with Susan Gubar.

12.12   Zimmer's book of Indian Art] Heinrich Zimmer's *Myths and Symbols in Indian Art and Civilization* (1946).

14.14   99] The main north–south highway on the U.S. West Coast until 1964, running from Calexico, California, to Blaine, Washington; it was decommissioned in 1972.

15.27–28   Jack Kerouac . . . *Diamond Sutra*] Kerouac (1922–1969) later published an account of his friendship with Snyder in *The Dharma Bums* (1958), casting Snyder as "Japhy Ryder." The Sanskrit Diamond Sutra, probably written around the second century, is a central Buddhist text, and presents a philosophical exchange between the Buddha and his followers.

15.29   *Migration of Birds*] Probably Frederick C. Lincoln's book, first published as *The Migration of North American Birds* in 1935 and revised as *Migration of Birds* in 1950, rather than *The Migration of Birds* (1912) by Thomas A. Coward.

16.10   Kobo Daishi . . . tall] Also known as Kūkai, the Shingon Buddhist monk Kōbō Daishi (774–835) was head of Tōji temple, where he is now represented by a large statue.

16.15   Avalokita] Also known as Avalokitesvara, a Buddhist bodhisattva or enlightened being who appears in multiple avatars, both male and female.

17.1   *Higashi Hongwanji*] Shinshu Buddhist temple in Kyoto, first constructed in 1658.

17.27   Mt. Hiei] Also referred to as Hiei-zan or Hieizan, a mountain northeast of Kyoto.

18.11   hinoki] *Chamaecyparis obtusa* or Japanese cypress, a native Japanese tree known for its rot-resistant timber.

19.20   Narihira's lover] Ariwara no Narihira (825–880), a courtier-poet of Heian-era Japan.

19.25   Yakamochi] Ōtomo no Yakamochi (c. 718–785), poet and politician.

20.7   *Sappa Creek*] A T-2 class oil tanker aboard which Snyder worked as a wiper, in the engine room, from August 1957 to April 1958.

22.17   rabbit on its face] In East Asian folklore, the moon's face is said to resemble a rabbit.

23.1   *blala*] Pidgin Hawaiian: brother, comrade.

23.19   d'antan] Of years gone by—an allusion to François Villon's sixteenth-century refrain "Mais où sont les neiges d'antan?" ("But where are the snows of yesteryear?").

27.1–2   *Preface . . . Lu Ch'iu-Yin*] Also spelled Lüqiu Yin, a Tang dynasty contemporary of Hanshan known principally for this "Preface," and probably fictional.

27.7   *Hu Shih*] Chinese philosopher and literary critic (1891–1962).

27.8–9   *Tu Fu . . . Po Chü-i*] Other prominent Tang dynasty poets, Tu Fu (712–770) also known as Du Fu, Li Po (701–762?) as Li Bai, and Po Chü-i (772–846) as Bai Juyi.

27.18   li] Traditional Chinese unit of distance, now standardized at 500 meters.

27.20   Kuo-ch'ing Temple] Also spelled Guoqing, a Buddhist temple in present-day Taizhou, Zhejiang province.

29.7   Amitabha] A major Buddha of Esoteric Buddhism, Amitabha is often depicted sitting on his throne beneath a flowering tree of jewels in his paradise, Sukhavati, the Western Pure Land.

33.5   the Yellow Springs] Huangquan, the underworld or hell in Chinese mythology.

34.22   sword of wisdom] The bodhisattva Mañjuśrī carries a sword of wisdom with which to cut through obstacles to enlightenment.

39.9   the Whorfian hypothesis] The idea, named after linguist Benjamin Lee Whorf (1897–1941), that language structure determines or influences thought and worldview.

40.18   zendo] Meditation hall.

MYTHS & TEXTS

44.1–2 LLOYD REYNOLDS AND DAVID FRENCH] Reynolds (1902–1978) and French (1918–1994) were among Snyder's professors at Reed College; Reynolds taught calligraphy and creative writing and French taught anthropology and linguistics.

49.4 Io] In Latin poetry, a ritual interjection of strong emotion; in Greek mythology, a princess who is transformed by Zeus into a white heifer and condemned to wander.

49.7–10 "The May Queen . . . rutting season"] A quotation from Géza Róheim's *Animism, Magic, and the Divine King* (1930).

49.18 Young girls . . . pine bough] In Greek mythology, ecstatic female followers of Dionysus known as maenads ("raving ones") carried a thyrsus, a long stick wrapped in vine leaves and tipped with a pinecone.

49.26 log dogs] Equipment used to hold logs in place while cutting or shaping them.

50.10 crummy-truck] In logging jargon, a vehicle used to carry workers and supplies to the worksite.

50.11 the Cat] Short for Caterpillar, a manufacturer of heavy equipment.

50.12–13 "Pines grasp the clouds . . . rising from sleep"] From a poem by the Chinese landscape painter Shi Tao (1642–1707), as translated by Osvald Sirén (see "Shih-T'ao, Painter, Poet and Theoretician," *Bulletin*, The Museum for Far Eastern Antiquities, Stockholm, 1949).

50.18–24 "Lodgepole Pine . . . springs up."] See George B. Sudworth, *Forest Trees of the Pacific Slope* (1908).

50.26 choker] A cable or heavy chain attached to a log.

50.28 piss-firs] White fir (*Abies concolor*), said to smell like urine when burned; not commercially valuable to loggers.

51.1 Hsü Fang . . . pumpkins.] Chinese landscape painter and poet (1622–1694), also known as Xu Fang. (See Osvald Sirén, "Shih-T'ao, Painter, Poet and Theoretician," *Bulletin*, The Museum for Far Eastern Antiquities, Stockholm, 1949: "Other painters of the same generation retired into far away mountain huts . . . This was the case . . . of Hsü Fang, who subsisted on leeks and pumpkins which he raised in a small garden.")

51.18 Seami Motokiyo] Japanese actor, playwright, and philosopher, known to have written at least a dozen Noh plays, and credited, less certainly, for many others; also transliterated as Zeami or Kanze Motokiyo (c. 1363–c. 1443).

51.19 The Doer] The *shite* or main actor and character of a Japanese Noh play.

51.22 Takasago] A city in southern Japan, and the title of a major Noh play involving a sacred pine tree.

51.22   Ise] A city in Japan, site of the Grand Shinto Shrine dedicated to Amaterasu, which is completely rebuilt with new lumber every twenty years.

51.25   Tomales Bay] Long, narrow bay in Marin County, California, north of San Francisco.

52.1   "Today's wind moves in the pines"] From the Noh play *Nishikigi* by Zeami Motokiyo (c. 1363–c. 1443), as translated by Ernest Fenollosa and published in *Poetry* in May 1914.

52.4   Olallie Butte] Shield volcano in the Cascade Range of northern Oregon, located within the Warm Springs Indian Reservation; its summit was the site of a fire lookout tower from 1915 to 1967.

52.5   the Schoolie flat] An Oregon lake, located within the Warm Springs Indian Reservation.

52.8   Seami, Kwanami] Seami Motokiyo (see note 51.18) and his father Kan'ami Kiyotsugu (1333–1384), the former credited as reviser and the latter as author of the Noh play *Matsukaze* (*Wind in the Pines*).

52.28   be-Homburged] The Homburg hat, named after the German town of Bad Homburg, was introduced to men's semi-formal attire in England in the late nineteenth century and was worn by businessmen and politicians on both sides of the Atlantic until the 1960s.

53.12–54.6   "In that year . . . three days."] In correspondence with Howard McCord (see *Some Notes to Gary Snyder's Myths & Texts*, 1971), Snyder commented: "'In that year, 1914' is my father talking about his childhood in Kitsap county. He & I were drinking together. I copied his words down w/out him noticing it."

53.22   Puncheon] A split log or rough piece of timber with one finished flat surface, used for log roads, boardwalks over marshy ground, and occasionally for flooring.

54.8–15   Felix Baran . . . November 5 1916] On November 5, 1916, approximately 300 members of the Industrial Workers of the World, an international labor union founded in 1905 in Chicago, also known as the Wobblies, left Seattle on the steamers *Verona* and *Calista* to support striking members of the shingle-weavers union in Everett, Washington, where they were met by over 200 policemen and "citizen deputies." In a confrontation that has since become known as the Everett Massacre, the five I.W.W. members Snyder lists were killed.

54.16   Ed McCullough] One of Snyder's fellow workers at the Warm Springs, Oregon, logging camp in the summer of 1951.

54.24   Hooverville, Sullivan's Gulch] Depression-era homeless encampments, including one in the Sullivan's Gulch area of Portland, Oregon, were nicknamed "Hoovervilles" after President Herbert Hoover, whose policies were blamed for economic hardship.

54.31   "Soldiers of Discontent"] See Charles Ashleigh's poem "Everett, November Fifth," first published in the *International Socialist Review* in February 1917.

55.15   D8] A bulldozer model produced by Caterpillar beginning in 1937.

55.31   Taurus] A constellation visible in the winter sky of the Northern Hemisphere, often figured as a bull.

56.22   stagged pants] A logger's pants with cuffs cut off to avoid catching on forest debris.

56.27   Bindlestiff] A tramp or hobo with his bundle of clothes and/or bedding.

56.28   poor bastards at Nemi] High priests of the Temple of Diana Nemorensis, built around 300 BCE on the site of an older sacred grove near present-day Nemi, Italy, succeeded to their positions—as Sir James Frazer describes this cycle, in *The Golden Bough* (1890)—by murdering their predecessors, and then were murdered in turn.

57.13   Ray Wells] One of Snyder's fellow workers at the Warm Springs, Oregon, logging camp in the summer of 1951.

57.13   Nisqually] Native American tribe from western Washington state.

57.20   Wasco] A Native American tribe, part of the Confederated Tribes of Warm Springs since 1938 and living principally on the Warm Springs Indian Reservation in northern Oregon.

58.8–12   "You shall live . . . Drinkswater.] In *Black Elk Speaks* (1932) by John G. Neihardt, Black Elk (Heȟáka Sápa, 1863–1950) attributes the quotation to "Drinks Water," a "Lakota holy man" of his grandfather's generation "who dreamed what was to be."

58.14   Crazy Horse] Crazy Horse (c. 1840–1877), a Lakota war leader of the Oglala band.

58.22   "He-at-whose-voice-the-Ravens-sit-on-the-sea"] See "Big-tail," a Haida tale told by Job Moody and recorded by John R. Swanton in *Haida Texts and Myths: Skidegate Dialect* (1905).

58.30   Han Shan] Chinese poet (fl. ninth century CE); see "Cold Mountain Poems" on pages 25–38 of the present volume.

58.31   scissorbill stooge] A worker who refused to join a union or who colluded with management.

59.2   T 36N   R 16E   S 25] Township, Range, and Section information describing an area within the Okanogan-Wenatchee National Forest in Washington state.

59.21   Groves of Ahab, of Cybele] See 1 Kings 16:33; Cybele was a Phrygian mother goddess.

59.25   Haida] Native American tribe, known for their cedar woodwork, living on Haida Gwaii (formerly Queen Charlotte Islands), British Columbia.

59.31   Luther and Weyerhaeuser] Martin Luther (1483–1546), German Protestant theologian, and the Weyerhaeuser Company, a forestry and pulp-paper conglomerate founded in 1900.

60.1   squareheads and finns] Derogatory term for German and Scandinavian immigrants.

60.17   What mad pursuit! . . . escape!] See "Ode on a Grecian Urn" by John Keats (1795–1821).

60.20–21   "A seed pod . . . meeting together."] See note 52.1.

60.27   Shiva . . . kalpa] A principal Hindu deity who destroys the universe in order to create it, at the end of an immense measure of time.

60.33   Gautama] Siddhartha Gautama (fl. c. fifth–fourth century BCE), founder of Buddhism and referred to after his death as the Buddha ("Awakened One" or "Enlightened One").

61.3–8   Pa-ta Shan-jen . . . lost."] The Chinese painter Shan-jen (c. 1626–1705), also known as Zhu Da or Bada Shanren, is quoted in Sirén (see note 51.1).

65.19   waterdogs] Salamanders.

65.22–24   Atok . . . seals] Inuit seal-hunting techniques: *atok* or *utok* (creeping over sea ice) and *maupok* (waiting at a breathing hole).

65.30–66.2   "Upon the lower slopes . . . Fenollosa] See *Epochs of Chinese and Japanese Art: An Outline History of East Asiatic Design* (1912) by Ernest F. Fenollosa (1853–1908), an American art historian and student of East Asian literature and culture.

66.3   Shang] In China, the Shang dynasty ruled from 1600 to 1046 BCE.

66.5   Yang Kuei Fei] Also known as Yang Yuhan or Yang Guifei (719–756 CE), imperial consort to Emperor Xuanzong of Tang (Tang Ming Huang), strangled on his command at the insistence of his guards.

66.13–15   "You who live . . . in my mouth."] See "The Winnebago Hare Cycle" in Paul Radin's *The Trickster: A Study in American Indian Mythology* (1956).

67.7–9   Vaux Swifts . . . wing-whistle] Snyder adapted these lines from his "Lookout Journal" of August 10, 1953, subsequently published in *Caterpillar* 3/4 (1968).

67.20–21   "We pull out . . . drifts away."] See "The Skunk. Her Story," as translated by Franz Boas in *Chinook Texts* (1894).

67.23–24   "my children . . . log"] See "Rabbit," a Cowlitz tale recounted by Mary Iley in 1926 and published by Thelma Adamson in *Folk-Tales of the Coast Salish* (1934).

NOTES

67.30–32 San Francisco . . . the Farallones] In his correspondence with How-
ard McCord (see *Some Notes to Gary Snyder's* Myths & Texts, 1971), Snyder
commented: "in Meiji period Japan, S.F. was called Sōkō, 'Mulberry Harbor.'
During the 1850's in S.F. there were no chicken eggs to eat; but every day some
boatmen went out to the Farallon Islands—just some rocks actually—twenty
miles out the Golden Gate, and gathered various sea-bird eggs which were
sold in the food stores of the city—they were all different sizes and colors and
specklings."

68.18–20 Raven . . . bird-book] Ravens have symbolic or mythological
significance in many cultures, ancient and modern; they are often trickster or
transformative figures in Native American folklore.

68.23–69.5 *the making* . . . laxeq] See "The Making of Horn Spoons (1)" in
Franz Boas's *Ethnology of the Kwakiutl* (1921), which translates the final line as
"Now the black horn spoon is finished after this."

69.7 *this poem is for bear*] In his correspondence with Howard McCord (see
Some Notes to Gary Snyder's Myths & Texts, 1971), Snyder pointed out that this
poem refers to "Marius Barbeau's Bella-Coola collection. plus an article on the
circumpolar Bear Cult by A. O. Hallowell, about 1914. & my own encounters
with Bears."

69.8 "As for me . . . the mountains."] See John Batchelor's *The Ainu and
Their Folk-Lore* (1901), which offers the statement as typical of Ainu members
of the bear clan.

70.13 (Odysseus was a bear)] By some folkloric accounts (but not according
to the *Iliad* or the *Odyssey*), Odysseus had ursine ancestry through his grand-
father Arkeisios, child of Kephalos and a she-bear.

71.25 Coyote] A mythological trickster figure in a variety of Native American
cultures.

71.28 Shuswap] Native tribal group living primarily in British Columbia.

72.3–6 "I dance on . . . five mountains"] See note 67.23–24.

72.18 Picasso's fawn, Issa's fawn] Pablo Picasso (1881–1973), the Spanish
painter, and Kobayashi Yatarô (Issa, 1763–1828), the Japanese poet, both
produced several works depicting fawns.

73.11 hunter's belt] The belt of stars found in the constellation of Orion, also
known as "the hunter."

74.28–33 "I kill everything . . . chief's tail"] See "Cougar and Skunk," a
Cowlitz tale recounted by Mary Iley in 1926 and published by Thelma Adam-
son in *Folk-Tales of the Coast Salish* (1934). The Cowlitz is a river in Washington
state, a tributary of the Columbia River.

75.1–3 "We carry deer-fawns . . . blackened."] See "The Skunk—Her Story,"
a myth recounted by Charles Cultee in 1890 or 1891 and published by Franz
Boas in *Chinook Texts* (1894).

75.5–7   "If I were a baby seal . . . toward shore—"] See "Crow Doctors Raven," a Skokomish tale recounted by Mary Adams in 1926 and published by Thelma Adamson in *Folk-Tales of the Coast Salish* (1934).

75.9–26   *songs for a four-crowned . . .* human beings?"] From the myth "Bigtail," told by Job Moody of the Witch people during the winter of 1900–1901 and published by John R. Swanton in *Haida Texts and Myths: Skidegate Dialect* (1905).

75.10–14   Prajapati . . . The Boar!] A lord of creation in Vedic texts, sometimes associated with the Hindu god Brahma; in one legend Prajapati assumes the shape of a boar in order to raise the earth up out of the primeval waters.

75.25–26   "What will you . . . beings?"] See note 58.22.

77.13–18   Where are you going . . . 1887] See Franz Boas, "Chinook Songs," *Journal of American Folk-Lore*, October–December 1888.

77.16   Kwakiutl] Native American tribe principally inhabiting Vancouver Island, British Columbia, and its environs; many tribal members prefer the name Kwakwa̱ka̱'wakw, meaning "Kwak'wala speaking peoples."

77.20   vajra-hitch] A vajra is an Indo-Tibetan ritual object believed to have the force of lightning and the indestructibility of diamond, and a diamond hitch a lashing method used to attach loads to pack animals.

77.28–30   "Stalk lotusses . . . sevens."] See "The Attainment of Buddhaship," a translation by Henry Clarke Warren of an introduction to the Jataka tales, collected in his *Buddhism in Translations* (1922).

78.14   Maudgalyâyana] One of the Buddha's principal disciples.

78.30   Chao-chou] Also known as Zhaozhou Congshen (778–897), Zen master most often remembered for the first koan in the thirteenth-century *Mumonkan* or *Gateless Gate*: a monk asked Chao-chou, "Has the dog Buddha nature or not?" Chao-chou said "Mu."

84.31   Bardo] In Tibetan Buddhism "the Bardo" refers to the undecided state of the soul between death and rebirth.

85.20   *Maitreya*] In Mahayana Buddhist eschatology, a Buddha who will appear in the future to succeed the historic one.

85.27   Wheel] As a cross represents Christianity or a Star of David Judaism, the Dharma Wheel or *dharmachakra* (Sanskrit) is one of the oldest symbols of Buddhism.

86.6   *jimson weed*] *Datura stramonium*, a weedy plant with psychoactive properties.

86.15   Vulture Peak] Mountain on the outskirts of Rajagaha, India (now Rajgir), a favorite retreat of the Buddha.

86.16   calor/canor/dulcor] Heat, song, sweetness: the three moods or phases of spiritual illumination described by English hermit and mystic Richard Rolle (c. 1300–1349) in his treatise *Incendium Amoris (The Fire of Love)*.

86.30–31   "Jesus was a great . . . United States"] See Jaime de Angulo's essay "The Background of the Religious Feeling in a Primitive Tribe" (*American Anthropologist*, April 1926), in which the quotation is attributed to Likely Ike, an American Indian of the Pit River tribe explaining the religion of the Christian converts of the Klamath tribe.

86.32–87.2   At Hakwinyava . . . Blue] From a Mohave song quoted in "The Mohave: Dream Life," chapter 51 of A. L. Kroeber's *Handbook of the Indians of California* (1925).

87.20   Chao-chu's *wu*] See note 78.30.

87.22   Ananda] One of the Buddha's principal disciples.

88.6–7   "byrdes sing . . . every bough"] See Ovid's "Elegy XIII," as translated by Christopher Marlowe (1564–1593).

88.9   Duke of Chou] Also known as Zhougong, Chinese ruler (fl. eleventh century BCE) esteemed by Confucius as a paragon of political virtue.

88.12–13   the statue . . . from Java] The Prajñāpāramitā of Java, a thirteenth-century depiction of the bodhisattva known as the "Great Mother," now in the National Museum of Indonesia.

88.18–21   "Earthly Mothers . . . Universe."] In "The Psychology of Hindu Religious Ritual," a lecture delivered by Sir John Woodroffe (1865–1936) and collected in the third edition of *Shakti and Shâkta: Essays and Addresses on the Shâkta Tantrashâstra* (1928), these words are attributed to "the 'mad,' wine-drinking Sadhu Bhâma" (Bamakhepa, 1837–1911), who addressed them to a man of Woodroffe's acquaintance whose mother had died.

88.23–89.17   John Muir . . . at all to do.] Quoted, with slight variations, from Muir's essay "A Near View of the High Sierra," collected in *The Mountains of California* (1894).

89.24–26   "Forming the New . . . the Wobbly Hall] The motto is adapted from the 1908 "Preamble" to the Industrial Workers of the World's constitution; I.W.W. meeting halls were known as Wobbly Halls.

90.1   Bodhidharma] A semi-legendary Indian Buddhist monk credited with establishing Chan (Zen) Buddhism in China.

90.3   Hsüan Tsang] Xuanzang (fl. 602–664), Chinese Buddhist monk who traveled overland between China and India to obtain Buddhist scriptures, which he translated into Chinese.

90.4   Joseph] Chief Joseph (1840–1904), also known as Hin-mah-too-yah-lat-kekt, a leader of the Wallowa band of the Nez Perce who resisted the forcible removal of his people from their homeland by the U.S. government before surrendering in October 1877.

90.8   Lao-tzu] Semi-legendary philosopher (fl. sixth century BCE) credited with founding the philosophical system of Taoism.

90.13   *Amitabha's*] See note 29.7.

91.25–26   Coyote . . . Earthmaker] In Maidu mythology, Coyote and Earth-maker create the world by singing together.

92.10   The city of the Gandharvas] In Hindu and Buddhist cosmology, the Gandharvas are musical deities. Snyder noted, in his correspondence with Howard McCord, that "'city of the Gandharvas' is an Indian trope for 'a mirage.'"

92.22   fifty-stringed *seh*] A zither-like instrument of ancient China.

92.27   "Herrick . . . to love"] See "The Vision," a poem collected by Robert Herrick (1591–1674) in his *Hesperides* (1648).

93.3   Nootka] Now referred to as the Nuu-cha-nulth, an indigenous tribal group of the Pacific Northwest, especially Vancouver Island.

93.27–29   At Nyahaim-kuvara . . . my land] From a Mohave *yellaka* or "goose" song translated in "The Mohave: Dream Life," chapter 51 of A. L. Kroeber's *Handbook of the Indians of California* (1925); Nyahaim-kuvara refers to a place in the San Francisco Mountains of northern Arizona.

94.2   symplegades] Rocky islands at the mouth of the Bosphorus fabled to squeeze together to crush passing ships.

94.2   *mumonkwan*] The "Gateless Barrier" or "Gateless Gate," an early thirteenth-century collection of 48 koans used for practice in the Rinzai School of Zen.

94.5   "Leap through an Eagle's snapping beak"] See Robert H. Lowie's essay "The Test-Theme in North American Mythology," published in the April–September 1908 *Journal of American Folk-Lore*: "In a Bella Coola legend five brothers escape from the pursuing ogre by leaping through an eagle's snapping beak into their savior's hut."

94.6   Actaeon saw Dhyana] In Greek mythology, Actaeon is turned into a stag when he encounters chaste Artemis, goddess of the hunt, wild animals, and the moon, known to the Romans as Diana. *Dhyana*, a Buddhist term, refers to meditation.

94.7–9   it was nothing special . . . low tide] These lines adapt the conclusion of a Chinese lyric by Su Tung-po (1037–1101), "Mt. Baker" replacing "Mount Lu," and "Neah Bay" the Chinese "River Che."

94.27   manzanita] Literally "little apple" in Spanish, common name for a variety of shrubs and trees in the genus *Arctostaphylos*, native to the western United States.

94.28   Tamalpais] Mountain in Marin County, California, north of San Francisco.

95.13   Siwash] Term in the Chinook jargon of the Pacific Northwest, and in regional English usage, from the French *sauvage*, for Native American; it is now considered derogatory.

95.23   Mt. Sumeru L.O.] Mount Sumeru (or Meru) is a sacred mountain in Buddhist cosmology, the center of the earth and the pillar of the universe, and "L.O." an abbreviation for a fire lookout tower.

96.16–18   "Get foggy . . . Buttercup roots"] See "The Sharptailed Man," a Skokomish tale recounted by Mary Adams in 1926 and published by Thelma Adamson in *Folk-Tales of the Coast Salish* (1934).

97.21   troy's burning] In Homer's epic poem, the *Iliad*, the Greeks ultimately burn the city of Troy.

98.3   The sun is but a morning star] The final sentence of Henry David Thoreau's *Walden; or, Life in the Woods* (1854).

98.5   Marin-an] A cabin on the rented Mill Valley, California, property of poet-carpenter Locke McCorkle (b. 1930) where Snyder lived in 1956 and again in 1958, and which he named "horse grove hermitage," from the Chinese *ma* (horse) and *rin* (grove) and the Japanese *an* (hermitage).

THE BACK COUNTRY

100.1   KENNETH REXROTH] Snyder met Rexroth (1905–1982), a poet, translator, and leading figure of the San Francisco Renaissance, in the fall of 1953, and remains an admirer of his work.

100.2–7   So—when it was . . . Basho] See the opening of *Narrow Road to the Deep North* (*Oku no Hosomichi*) by Matsuo Bashō (1644–1694), as translated by Cid Corman and Kamaike Susumi (*Roads to Far Towns*, 1968).

103.1–2   *Berry Feast . . . Matson*] Joyce Matson (1930–2008) and her husband Homer (1926–1992), both Reed College anthropology students with a newborn baby, hosted Snyder in their cabin at Schoolie Flats, on the Warm Springs Indian Reservation, in the summer of 1951. They attended the Warm Springs berry feast in late August.

103.20–21   "Where I shoot . . . sunflower's shade] See "Coyote's People Sing," collected in *Wishram Texts*, vol. 2 (1909), by Edward Sapir.

104.17   derry derry down] A conventional refrain in early English ballads.

104.28   oxen of Shang] Oxen shoulder blades, with carved symbols, called Oracle Bones, were used in the Shang dynasty (c. 1600–1046 BCE) to foretell the future.

106.28   *Marin-an*] See note 98.5.

107.16   rakers] Gauges used to control the cutting depth of teeth on a chainsaw.

108.10   bitchmo] Bitumen or asphalt.

108.30   Benson Lake] Lake in the northern wilderness of Yosemite National Park, California.

109.6   stemmed] A climbing technique: to ascend using a wide enough vertical opening in the surface, the right foot pushes against one wall while the left foot pushes against its opposite.

109.34   Piute Mountain] A 10,541-foot peak in Yosemite National Park.

111.3   mt. Ritter] A 13,149-foot peak in the Ansel Adams Wilderness of California's Sierra Nevada range.

111.12   buckbrush] *Ceanothus cuneatus*, a species of flowering shrub and one of the most common and widespread native plants in California.

112.6   mush pot] Pot used for cooking, especially while camping.

112.18   *Foxtail Pine*] *Pinus balfouriana*, a rare, high-elevation pine endemic to California.

112.19   Jeffries] *Pinus jeffreyi*, a North American pine tree mainly found in California.

112.20   Ponderosa] *Pinus ponderosa*, commonly known as Ponderosa pine, is a very large pine tree native to mountainous regions of western North America.

112.24   high lead riggers] A rigger's job, in the logging industry, is to climb trunks to the top of the tallest trees in order to place cables, winches, and/or pulleys to manage the movement of logs.

112.26   doug fir] An evergreen conifer species in the pine family, *Pseudotsuga menziesii* is native to western North America. Despite its common name, "Douglas fir," it is not a true fir.

112.28   cascara] The dried bark of cascara (*Frangula purshiana*) was used as a laxative by the indigenous peoples of the Pacific Northwest. It is native to western North America.

113.1   tanbark oak] *Notholithocarpus densiflorus*, commonly known as the tanoak or tanbark-oak, is a broadleaf tree native to the western United States.

113.2   myrtlewood] *Umbellularia californica*, commonly known as California bay or Oregon myrtlewood.

113.4–6   baby girl . . . daughter of the moon] See the Japanese folktale "Kaguyahime" ("The Tale of the Bamboo Cutter" or "The Tale of Princess Kaguya").

114.18   *Sourdough*] See note 5.1.

114.18   Dick Brewer] Snyder's friend Richard Caldwell Brewer (1923–2014), an abstract expressionist painter.

115.3   the Bonins] Officially known as the Ogasawara Islands, a Japanese island group about 600 miles south of Tokyo.

116.9   *Sappa Creek*] See note 20.7.

117.4   Phil Whalen] Whalen (1923–2002), like Snyder, graduated from Reed College in 1951 and presented his poetry at the 1955 Six Gallery reading, a major event of the San Francisco Renaissance. In 1973 he was ordained as a priest at the San Francisco Zen Center, eventually receiving the dharma name Zenshin Ryufu. His *Collected Poems* was published posthumously in 2007.

117.7   skidders] Four-wheeled tractors used to haul logs.

117.24   Fu Manchu] A mustache style like that of Dr. Fu Manchu, villainous title character of a series of novels by Sax Rohmer, published from 1913 to 1959 and widely adapted for film and other media.

117.25   Queets Indian Reservation] Located on the Pacific coast of the Olympic Peninsula, in Washington state.

118.3   Smoke Creek desert] An arid region of northwestern Nevada, north of Pyramid Lake.

118.5   Elko] A small city in northern Nevada.

118.22   *Thomas L. Hoodlatch*] Snyder's friend and Reed College classmate Bob Allen (1928–2000) nicknamed himself "Hoodlatch" during their undergraduate years.

119.1–2   Ithaca . . . bowstring] At the end of Homer's *Odyssey*, Penelope, Ulysses's wife, agrees to marry whoever wins a contest using Ulysses's bow.

119.8   *Bob Greensfelder and Claude Dalenberg*] Snyder met Robert J. Greensfelder (1923–2018)—a longtime neighbor, who worked as a film producer and distributor—while the two were students at Reed College. He attended the American Academy of Asian Studies and meditation sessions with Dalenberg (1927–2008), who appears in Jack Kerouac's novel *The Dharma Bums* (1958) as "Bud Diefendorf."

119.13   Timber Gap] A hiking destination in Sequoia National Park, California.

119.18   Hood river] A town east of Portland, Oregon, along the Columbia River.

119.20   Willapa Bay] A large estuarial bay on the southwest coast of Washington state.

121.1   *Pinacate Desert*] Volcanic region within the Sonoran Desert in Sonora, Mexico.

121.2   *Locke & Drum*] Snyder met Locke McCorkle (b. 1930) in San Francisco around 1955, while both were students at the American Academy of Asian Studies, and later lived in a cabin on property McCorkle leased in Mill Valley, California (see note 98.5); McCorkle appears as "Sean Monahan" in Jack Kerouac's roman à clef *The Dharma Bums* (1958). Drummond Hadley (1938–2015) was a poet, rancher, and conservationist who lived most of his life along the Arizona–New Mexico borderlands with Mexico.

121.3   A. J. Bayless] Now known as AJ's Fine Foods, an Arizona supermarket chain.

121.9   Diana] Diana Hadley (b. 1939), Drum Hadley's wife; she later directed the Arizona State Museum's office of ethnohistorical research.

122.26   snoose] A powdered form of tobacco, also known as snuff.

123.7   *Dodger Point*] Site of a U.S. Forest Service fire lookout cabin in Olympic National Park, Washington.

123.9   *my first wife*] Snyder married Alison Gass (1931–2013), a fellow student at Reed College, in 1950; they separated after only a few months and were divorced in 1952. She married Martin E. Murie later the same year.

123.20   Swan Maiden] A widespread mythological tale with many variations among different cultures. Typically, the swan maiden removes her swan skin to bathe and so appears briefly in human form. A hidden male observer then steals her feathered garment to prevent her from flying away.

127.1   *Yase*] A northern suburb of Kyoto where Snyder lived briefly after he returned to Japan in 1959.

127.2   Mrs. Kawabata] Snyder's landlady in Yase.

127.13   *Tetsu*] Kanetsuki Gutetsu, co-author with Snyder of *The Wooden Fish: Basic Sutras and Gathas of Rinzai Zen*, a small, limited-edition book published in Kyoto by the First Zen Institute of America in 1961.

127.15   Matsue castle] Castle in Shimane Prefecture completed in 1611 and occupied by the Matsudaira family from 1637 to 1927.

128.15   *Daitoku-ji*] A Rinzai Zen Buddhist temple in Kyoto, Japan, where Snyder studied and practiced in 1959–60.

128.16   *Mt. Hiei*] See note 17.27.

128.30   Aldebaran] The brightest star in the zodiac constellation of Taurus; one of the brightest stars in the entire night sky.

129.10   deodar] *Cedrus deodara*, Himalayan cedar.

129.22   *Ami*] Ami Petersen, one of Snyder's friends in Kyoto; along with her husband Will and the poet Cid Corman (1924–2004), she published the literary magazine *Origin*.

131.10   *silent night*] The popular Christmas carol, composed by Franz Xaver Gruber (1787–1863) in 1818.

132.12–16   J. Robert Oppenheimer . . . Los Alamos] An American theoretical physicist, Oppenheimer (1904–1967) led the Los Alamos Laboratory in New Mexico where the atomic bomb was developed beginning in 1943.

132.17   Takano River] A shallow river running through the Yase section of Kyoto.

134.15 *Robin*] Robin Collins Coffee (1930–2019), Snyder's college classmate, girlfriend, and soulmate, the subject or muse of several of his poems.

134.16 *Siwashing . . . Siuslaw Forest*] To *siwash* is to camp out using only natural shelter; the Siuslaw National Forest is located in western Oregon.

135.1 *Shokoku-ji*] Rinzai Zen Buddhist temple in Kyoto where Snyder studied and practiced with Isshu Miura Roshi (1903–1978) in 1956.

135.8 the old capital] Kyoto, the capital city of Japan for more than 1,000 years, until 1868.

135.9 Yugao] A character in Murasaki Shikibu's eleventh-century Japanese novel, *The Tale of Genji*, Yugao, a delicate beauty and one of Genji's lovers, is suddenly possessed and dies mysteriously. Her spirit is also the focus of a Noh play of the same name.

137.11 Les Blakebrough . . . Chappell] Blakebrough (b. 1930), an Australian, and Chappell (1931–1964), an Englishman, were both potters Snyder met in the early 1960s in Kyoto, where they were studying with Japanese potter Kawai Takeichi; Chappell died in 1964 in a motorcycle accident in Sydney.

137.14 showa thirty eight] Japanese calendar year equivalent to 1963 in the Western calendar.

137.15–16 Shiga . . . Lake Biwa] Lake Biwa, Japan's largest lake, is located in Shiga Prefecture just east of Kyoto.

137.17–19 Domura . . . Shigaraki] Japanese towns east of Kyoto, the latter famous for its pottery.

137.21 Yamanashi wine "St. Neige"] Sainte Neige wines have been produced from grapes grown in Yamanashi Prefecture since 1957.

137.29 saggars . . . segers] Devices used during the firing of ceramics.

138.2 Tokuri . . . black chawan] *Tokuri* refers to tall, slender sake bottles, and black chawan to a type of tea bowl.

138.22–23 Kamo river . . . Uji hills] A river running through Kyoto, Japan, and hills to the south of it.

138.28 *Nansen*] One of Snyder's cats when he lived in Kyoto, its name probably an allusion to the thirteenth-century *Mumonkan* koan "Nansen kills the cat."

140.4 shoji] Wooden frames covered with translucent paper, used as doors, windows, or room dividers.

140.10 kama] A traditional Japanese cooking pot.

140.11 Mrs. Hosaka's] The landlady of the house in Kyoto where Snyder lived with his wife Joanne Kyger.

140.13 kotatsu] A heated table frame covered by a blanket or futon.

140.22   genkan] In Japan, the entryway to a dwelling.

140.30   *Liberation*] Probably the New Left journal *Liberation*, published from 1956 to 1977.

141.1   doboroku] Home-brewed sake.

141.11   Kato, Nagasawa, me, Sakaki] Mamoru Kato, Tetsuo Nagasawa, and Nanao Sakaki (1923–2008), friends of Snyder's from Tokyo who organized the countercultural "Bum Academy" (later "the Tribe," *Buzoku*) and led experiments in communal living; Sakaki (1923–2008), a poet, later translated Snyder's *Turtle Island*, and traveled with him.

141.12   awamori] An Okinawan alcoholic beverage.

141.24   Zojoji] Buddhist temple in Tokyo.

142.24   zokin] Rags for cleaning.

142.29–30   *go . . . sho*] Traditional Japanese measures of volume, one *go* the approximate equivalent of 180 milliliters, and 10 *go* making one *sho*.

142.35–36   Dai-Hannya . . . Wisdom] *Dai-Hannya* is a Japanese Buddhist ritual that features the chanting of the Great Sutra on the Perfection of Wisdom.

143.1   Dragon Cloud Temple] Probably Tenryū-ji, a fourteenth-century Buddhist temple in Kyoto featuring a cloud dragon painting on the ceiling of its dharma hall.

143.14–15   Yokkawa . . . Ohara] Yokkawa or Yokawa is one of three areas of the Enryaku-ji temple complex atop Mt. Hiei, and Ohara village at its base.

143.16   sugi] *Cryptomeria japonica* or Japanese cedar, a large evergreen cypress species.

143.18–19   Lute/Lake] Lake Biwa (see note 137.15–16).

143.27   Shaka-dō] A building enshrining a statue of Buddha.

143.29   jikatabi] Traditional Japanese two-toed, boot-like footwear.

144.3   Jakko-in] A small temple in the village of Ohara.

144.4   Jizo] A Buddhist bodhisattva ("enlightened being") often depicted holding a staff in his right hand used to warn insects and small animals of his approach.

144.22   Atago Mountain] A mountain in the northwestern sector of Kyoto.

145.5   Keith Lampe's] Snyder met Lampe (1931–2014), later known for his environmental activism, in Japan, and was interviewed by him for *The Berkeley Barb* in 1968.

145.12   sasa] A genus of bamboo, also known as broad-leaf bamboo.

148.2   Lake Biwa] See note 137.15–16.

148.3 Fukui] Japanese prefecture bordering on the Sea of Japan, north of Kyoto Prefecture.

148.8 ryokan] A traditional Japanese inn.

148.11 yukata] A Japanese bathrobe.

148.19 Eihei-ji] One of two main temples of the Sōtō school of Zen Buddhism, located east of Fukui in Fukui Prefecture.

149.14 *mikan*] A Japanese citrus fruit, also known as satsuma mandarin.

149.15 Kshatriya] One of four Vedic social classes, traditionally the warrior or ruling class.

149.20 Dharma Kings] A Tibetan phrase, referring to several historical defenders of Buddhism.

149.22 hatake] Japanese: field, garden.

149.32 gobo] *Arctium lappa* or greater burdock, a root vegetable.

150.23 Ko] Sōkō Morinaga (1925–1995), also known as Kō-san or Ko, was the head monk at Daitoku-ji meditation hall. (See also the poem "The Blue Sky" on pages 622–26 of the present volume.)

150.26 hondo . . . Gi:] A hondo is the entrance hall of a Buddhist temple; *gi*, the third character in the Immeasurable Meanings Sutra, pertains to observing the mind at work.

150.28 sanzen] An appointed meeting with a Zen master for instruction.

150.30 Shukuza] Breakfast time at a Zen temple.

151.8 Saiza] Lunch, the main meal of the monastic day.

151.20 jiki] Jikijitsu, the monk in charge of meditation in the zendō.

151.27 kinhin] A term that refers to walking meditation (to go straight).

152.8 Soogy] A nautical term, the act of wiping down the oil sump with rags.

153.2 Kālī] A Hindu goddess of time who has powers of destruction and creation, often depicted as dark, red-eyed, and bloodstained, with a necklace of skulls.

154.2 *sea-lion town*] Kay Llnagaay, site of a historic Haida village in present-day Skidegate, British Columbia.

155.1 *Alysoun*] Alison Gass (see note 123.9); "Alysoun" is a Middle English spelling.

155.2 Robin] Robin Collins (see note 134.15).

156.1 *Sanchi*] Buddhist monument and temple site near Bhopal in Madhya Pradesh, India; Snyder visited in April 1962.

157.7 Hatch] Jim Hatch, also known as "Steamboat," was a friend of Snyder's at Reed College and later at Berkeley.

157.9 *Alba*] An Old Occitan lyric genre featuring lovers who must separate when morning comes.

157.15 tamalpais] See note 94.28.

157.27 Yellow corn woman] A mythical goddess figure in southwestern Pueblo culture.

160.15 Lady Komachi] Ono no Komachi (c. 825–c. 900) a renowned Japanese *waka* poet known for her beauty; she is the subject of several Noh plays.

160.25 Danae] In Greek mythology, Danaë's father imprisons her in a room with no doors or windows to keep her from conceiving a child. Zeus impregnates her in the form of golden rain that seeps through the roof of her chamber.

163.1 *The Manichaeans*] Followers of a religion established in third-century Persia, known for its extreme dualism, or more loosely, those who tend to see things in terms of black and white absolutes.

163.2 *Joanne*] Joanne Kyger (1934–2017), a poet to whom Snyder was married from 1960 to 1965.

163.5 Tun-huang fragments] Important religious and secular documents, dating from the late fourth to early eleventh centuries, discovered in China in the early twentieth century.

163.17 Ourabouros] The ancient circular symbol of a snake biting its own tail.

163.18 Naga King] In East Asian mythology, nagas are divine or semi-divine deities of half-human, half-serpent form.

163.32 Pier 41] A ferry terminal on Fisherman's Wharf in San Francisco.

164.15 Shiva and Shakti] In Hindu thought, the merging of Shiva–Shakti represents the unification of masculine and feminine principles of the universe.

164.17 *Artemis*] In Greek myth, Artemis, goddess of wild animals and the moon, is seen bathing by the hunter Actaeon. She transforms him into a stag who is then killed by his own hounds.

165.19 cutting your own . . . kybele] In Greco-Roman mythology, the goddess Cybele causes Attis to castrate himself after she discovers he has been unfaithful to her; her priests carry out a yearly emasculation ritual to commemorate Attis's castration.

165.20 Graves] Robert Graves (1895–1985), English poet, novelist, and classicist, known especially for *The White Goddess* (1948), a study of poetry and mythology.

165.24 infibula] A clasp used in female circumcision.

166.21   HO] Mescalero Apache: peyote (*Lophophora williamsii*).

167.13   slave-of-god-dancer] In an Indian practice begun in the sixth or seventh century but now outlawed, young girls known as devadasis (Sanskrit for "slaves of god") were "married" to a deity and trained in devotional song and dance.

167.17   calamus] *Acorus calamus*, also known as sweet flag, a plant used in traditional medicine.

168.15   fiddley] The space above the engine room of a ship.

168.23   soogying] See note 152.8.

169.1   Maya] Derived from a Sanskrit term, *maya* refers to the illusory nature of all elements of the surrounding physical world.

169.2   *Peter Orlovsky*] Snyder and his wife Joanne Kyger traveled with Orlovsky (1933–2010), a poet, and his partner Allen Ginsberg, in India in 1962.

169.12–30   *Mother of the Buddhas . . . Bihar*] In his *Passage Through India* (1983), Snyder describes a January 29, 1962, visit to the ruins of Nalanda: "The Nalanda site is notable for the number of buildings, each on a similar plan, open center courtyard with outer rim of cells for the monks . . . While studying through this, Bhikku Ghosananda, a youthful Cambodian, came across the fields holding his robe over his head, and climbed the high Chaitya to join us, then led us out across some farmland to view a statue of Marichi ('Mother of the Buddhas') a big stone slab leaning over in a field—exotic Mahayana Goddess, bare-breasted (as they all are), holding a noose, a flower, a sword, and riding a flock of pigs, haloed in fire. Close-grained gray stone; from there we walked through an Untouchable village, to the noise of a squealing pig getting shaved." Ghosananda (1913?–2007), then a graduate student at Nalanda University, was elected *sangharaja* or patriarch of Cambodian Buddhism in 1988.

170.4   Evtushenko] Yevgény Yevtushénko (1933–2017), Soviet Russian poet.

170.13   Komsomol] The youth division of the Soviet All-Union Communist Party.

170.17   *khol*] Also spelled *kohl*, a black powder used as eye makeup.

170.22   *Khajuraho*] A group of Hindu and Jain temples and monuments in Madhya Pradesh, India.

171.1   pice] The smallest unit of Indian currency, renamed *paisa* in 1957.

171.3   Bundelkhand] An Indian geographical and cultural region within the present-day states of Uttar Pradesh and Madhya Pradesh.

171.10   *Anuradhapura*] City in Sri Lanka, a longtime center of Theravada Buddhism and the site of ancient Sinhalese ruins.

171.11   Joanne] Joanne Kyger (see note 163.2).

172.1   *Circumambulating Arunachala*] Arunachala is a sacred mountain in Tamil Nadu, India, around which pilgrims walk in a clockwise direction as a devotional act.

173.10   mohenjo-daro] A Pakistani archaeological site.

173.19   Nanao Sakaki] See note 141.11.

175.2   Ali Akbar Khan] Khan (1922–2009), an Indian Hindustani classical composer and musician, was an influential popularizer of Indian classical music in the United States.

175.26   madrone] *Arbutus menziesii*, an evergreen tree common on the Pacific coast of North America.

175.27   *John Chappell*] See note 137.11.

176.7   Tango] A seaside town in the north of Kyoto Prefecture, now part of the city of Kyōtango.

177.2   Yasé] See note 127.1.

178.10   devi] Sanskrit: goddess.

178.24   empty diamond] A reference to the Vajracchedika ("Diamond") Sutra, an influential work in the Mahayana Buddhist tradition, which discusses, among other ideas, the emptiness of all phenomena.

179.7   *Rāmprasād Sen*] Sadhak Rāmprasād Sen (c. 1723–c. 1775), a poet and saint of eighteenth-century Bengal; many of his poems are addressed to the Hindu goddess Kali.

183.9   Indian Paintbrush] *Castilleja*, a flowering plant genus containing approximately 200 species.

183.13   Heian ladies] Heian Japan (794–1185) was noted for its sophisticated court culture.

185.7   *the March*] In October 1934, Chinese Communist forces began a yearlong, 5,000-mile retreat from the army of the nationalist Kuomintang, evading capture and defeat; Mao Zedong emerged as a leader during this "Long March."

185.14   *Han-shan*] Ninth-century Chinese poet; see "Preface to the Poems of Han-Shan" on pages 27–29 of the present volume.

185.18   Yenan cigarette] Chinese Communists celebrate Yan'an as the birthplace of the revolution; cigarette production is a major industry of the area.

185.25   AB] Able-bodied seaman, a rank in the merchant marine.

185.27   Lung-shan] A late Neolithic culture in the middle and lower Yellow River valley areas of northern China from about 3000 to 1900 BCE.

185.34   from Almora gazing at Trisul] Trisul, a group of three Himalayan mountain peaks that resemble a trident, may be seen from Almora, a town in the state of Uttarakhand, India.

186.3   N.T.] The New Territories, one of the three main regions of Hong Kong, along with Hong Kong Island and the Kowloon Peninsula.

186.14   K'ung fu-tze] Confucius (551–479 BCE), one of China's principal philosophers.

186.23   Ordos] A desert region in northwest China; to its south is the Loess Plateau, named for its yellowish, glacial till soil.

186.33   Chas. Leong] Charles Leong (1905–1986), a veteran of World War II who joined the Reed College class of 1953 on the G.I. Bill, taught Snyder Chinese calligraphy.

187.11   Wasco and the Wishram] Closely related Chinook Indian tribes from the Columbia River region in Oregon.

187.16   Bodh-Gaya] A religious site in the Indian state of Bihar, notable as the place where Gautama Buddha is said to have attained Enlightenment under what became known as the Bodhi Tree.

187.18   *Joan Baez . . . Virginia"*] Baez (b. 1941) sings "East Virginia," a folk song about a young man who meets a "fair pretty maiden," on her self-titled 1960 debut album.

187.31   dont kill flies by hand] In 1958, Chairman Mao inaugurated a program to eradicate "four pests": rats, flies, mosquitoes, and sparrows.

188.12   Europa] In Greek mythology, a Phoenician princess abducted by Zeus in the form of a bull.

188.15   Thracian] An Indo-European people who inhabited large parts of eastern and southeastern Europe in ancient history.

189.5   kalmuck] A nomadic Mongol people living primarily in southwestern Russia who raise horses, cattle, sheep, and goats.

191.10   Gide] André Gide (1869–1951), French novelist and winner of the 1947 Nobel Prize in Literature.

191.15–18   A novel by Kafu NAGAI . . . the year] See *Geisha in Rivalry*, a novel first published in Japanese in 1918 and in English translation in 1963; Nagai was a pseudonym of Japanese writer Nagai Sōkichi (1879–1959), most often remembered for depictions of life in the entertainment districts of early twentieth-century Tokyo.

191.26   *Lamarck Col*] A high mountain pass southwest of Bishop, California.

192.20   Venus of the Stone Age] Paleolithic "Venus" figurines often have heavily rounded breasts, stomachs, and buttocks.

192.22   lagger] In hopscotch, an object or token thrown by a player into the squares on the court.

193.9   *Muir Beach*] A beach in Marin County, California, north of San Francisco.

193.11   Sally] Sally ("Shandel") Parks (1916–2005), co-owner of a San Francisco art gallery, helped to found the American Academy of Asian Studies, where she and Snyder met in the early 1950s.

194.9   Uintah mountains] A mountain range in northeastern Utah, part of the Rocky Mountains.

194.20   Drum Hadley] See note 121.2.

195.2   Angel island] An island in San Francisco Bay, site of a military installation until 1962.

195.16   *Through the Smoke Hole*] This poem describes a ceremony of the Pueblo peoples of the American Southwest, especially the Hopi. A kiva is a subterranean room, usually round, with a single ladder used for entry to the room from above; the hole through which the ladder is extended may also double as an escape for smoke coming from the fire below. Village elders descend into the pit house, later to emerge from the hole as various masked supernatural beings.

195.17   Don Allen] Allen (1912–2004), an editor, publisher, and translator, established Grey Fox Press and the Four Seasons Foundation, two literary presses that published works from Beat, San Francisco Renaissance, Black Mountain, and New York School writers, including several by Snyder.

196.30   jumna river] Also known as the Yamuna, a tributary of the Ganges.

197.22–27   Samish Bay . . . Birch Bay] Bays in the North Puget Sound region of Washington state.

200.12   *tanka*] A Japanese poetic form consisting of 31 syllables, usually presented, in translation, in five lines of 5, 7, 5, 7, and 7 syllables.

201.11–13   *Saddle Mountain* . . . Kurakake] *Kurakake-yama*, a saddle-shaped mountain south of Hakone, in Kanagawa Prefecture.

201.23   akebia] A flowering plant genus. The Japanese term *akebi* refers to the species *Akebia quinata*, also known as the five-leaf chocolate vine.

202.11   *Zypressen*] German: cypress trees.

204.5   tara trees] *Tara spinosa*, a small, thorny shrub native to Peru and invasive in arid regions of Africa, Asia, and the Middle East.

204.9   dumdum bullets] Bullets designed to expand on impact.

205.13   *parasamgate, bodhi, svaha!*] Mantric phrase concluding the Heart Sutra and expressing the essence of Mahayana Buddhist teaching; it is a cry of joy (*svaha*) and a recognition of enlightenment (*bodhi*) in that "everyone has gone over to the other shore" (*parasamgate*).

206.16–18   cuckoo singing . . . Yama's office] In his 2007 edition of Kenji,

Miyazawa Kenji: Selections, translator Hiroaki Sato explains these lines as follows: "After death one is destined to spend the first seven days climbing up and down a steep path, where the cuckoo, the messenger of death, calls. Then one crosses a river in one of three ways, depending on the sins one committed while alive, before reaching the world of the dead, where Yama is the presiding deity. This notion seems to derive from the Ten King Sutra, the 'fake sutra,' concocted toward the end of the Tang Dynasty by combining Buddhist elements with Taoism. When it came to Japan it incorporated Shinto elements. *Sanzu no kawa*, the Three-Way River, is often compared with the River Styx. The practice of *tainai-kuguri*, 'ducking through the womb,' may be largely of Shinto origins, with some Buddhist elements. One may cleanse the body and spirit by passing through a narrow passage like a cave or hole."

207.14   *Floating World Picture*] *Ukiyo-e* or "pictures of the floating world" is a Japanese artistic style that began in paintings and woodblock prints of late seventeenth-century Edo depicting life in the city's pleasure districts, and that evolved into the twentieth century in works of various genres.

207.15   *Kitagami Mountains*] A mountain range in northeastern Honshu, northern Japan, located primarily within eastern Iwate Prefecture.

209.7   Junsai] *Brasenia schreberi* or watershield, a traditional Japanese vegetable grown in shallow ponds.

209.13   pampas-grass] *Miscanthus sinensis*, also known as susuki-grass, Chinese silver grass, or Japanese pampas grass, grows wild over much of Japan.

212.5   Hanamaki] A city in Iwate Prefecture, Japan, and Kenji Miyazawa's birthplace.

213.2   my sister] Miyazawa's younger sister Toshiko died in November 1922 at the age of 24.

REGARDING WAVE

215.1   *Regarding Wave*] Asked by bibliographer Katherine McNeil what he meant by his title, Snyder answered: "That's a riddle—I'll explain it, though. If you translate the Bodhisattva Avalokitesvara or Kuan Yin's name literally, it means 'Regarding the Sound Waves.' '*Kuan*' means 'to regard intently,' and '*on*' is 'sound waves.' That is because in this kalpa . . . it is the sense of hearing by which people become enlightened most directly. This is the universe of the sense of hearing."

216.1   MASA] Snyder married Masa Uehara (b. 1942), a recent graduate of Kobe University, on August 6, 1967. They had two children—Kai in 1968 and Gen in 1969—and divorced in 1989.

219.9   wyfman] Old English "wyf" or "wif" meant a "female person"; the combination of "wyf" or "wif" with "man" (meaning "a human being") produced "wyfman" or modern-day "woman" (an adult female person).

220.4 Ferghana horses] Horses from the Ferghana Valley in Central Asia were imported into China during the Han dynasty; known as "heavenly horses," both Genghis Khan and Alexander the Great were said to ride them.

220.20 tilth] Soil suitable for planting.

221.24 "driving sand . . . flying"] See Snyder's poem "Hunting" on page 67, line 33, of the present volume.

221.25 shirakawa] Shirakawa-suna or "white river sand," gathered from the Shirakawa River, is in common use in Japanese rock gardens.

221.26 Ryōan-ji] A Kyoto Rinzai Zen temple, the site of Japan's most famous dry landscape garden.

222.13 *Tama River*] River flowing from the foothills of Yamanashi Prefecture into Tokyo Bay.

222.28 Nanao & Nagasawa] See note 141.11.

222.29 shochu] A Japanese alcoholic beverage, usually distilled from barley, rice, or sweet potatoes.

223.19 *In the House of the Rising Sun*] The folk song "House of the Rising Sun," about a young man who comes to ruin in a New Orleans brothel, has been recorded by many artists, including the British rock band The Animals in 1964; Japan is proverbially referred to as "the land of the rising sun."

224.6 South Yüeh] Han Chinese term for non-Chinese peoples of what is now southeastern China and northern Vietnam; "South Yüeh" implies "South Vietnam."

224.19 blue as Shiva] One of the principal Hindu deities, the creator, preserver, and destroyer of the universe; by one account, Shiva turned blue after drinking a deadly poison but his consort, Parvati, intervened to control its spread.

229.28 sasa] See note 145.12.

232.2–5 Beautiful little children . . . warbler egg"] See the Japanese folktales Urikohime ("Princess Melon"), Kaguyahime ("The Tale of the Bamboo Cutter"), and Uguisuhime ("Princess Nightingale").

232.10 Dharma] In Buddhism, cosmic law or universal truth as expressed by the Buddha.

232.11 Vajra] See note 77.20.

232.17 Nishijin] A famous Kyoto weaving district.

232.26 Tomoharu, Itsuko, and Kenji] Japanese given names.

233.3 *Archaic Round and Keyhole Tombs*] Found all across Japan, "kofun" are distinctly shaped megalithic burial grounds (c. third–seventh century CE), ranging in size from several meters to over 400 meters long.

237.1 *Burning Island*] Snyder spent the parts of the summer of 1967 and 1968 living in the Banyan Ashram on Suwanosejima, a small volcanic island in the Ryūkyūs; local fishermen (he explained in his 1967 essay "Suwa-no-se Island and the Banyan Ashram") "call it 'Yake-jima'—Burning Island. Because much of the time the volcano is smoking."

237.22 LAKHS of crystal Buddha Fields] Countless paradisiacal realms purified by the presence of a Buddha.

237.27 Antares] In his essay "Suwa-no-se Island and the Banyan Ashram," Snyder describes Antares as "our patron star."

238.21 40067] In some of his early works, Snyder marked time on a 40,000-year scale, "reckoning roughly" (as he put it in his essay "Suwa-no-se Island and the Banyan Ashram") "from the earliest cave paintings." 40067 is 1967.

239.1 *Rainbow Body*] In Tibetan Buddhist tradition, a transformation of the body in the wake of transcendent meditation practice, ultimately into radiance.

239.19 Akahige] The Japanese robin, *Larvivora akahige*, a small passerine bird.

240.5 *shako* clam] *Shakogai*: large, blue-lipped reef clams in the genus *Tridacna*.

242.12 Temminck's Robin] The Ryukyu robin, *Larvivora komadori*, originally described by Dutch zoologist Coenraad Jacob Temminck (1778–1858) in 1835 and endemic to the Ryūkyū Islands.

242.14 zazen] Prolonged meditation in a prescribed, cross-legged posture.

243.26 Namu Amida Butsu] An invocation of the Buddha Amitābha, meaning "Hail to Amitābha Buddha"; it is chanted or recited by Japanese Pure Land Buddhists in order to gain rebirth into the Pure Land after death.

244.5 *Kai*] Kai Snyder (see note 216.1).

244.10 Kawaramachi] A street in central Kyoto.

244.16 from-the-beginning face?] Original face, a Zen Buddhist concept presented in one of the koans of the *Gateless Gate* (and elsewhere): "Quickly, without thinking good or evil, what is your original face before your parents were born?"

245.13 Nagano-ken] A mountainous inland prefecture of Japan, on the main island of Honshū.

246.10 The Voice] See Snyder's essay "Poetry and the Primitive: Notes on Poetry as an Ecological Survival Technique," collected in *Earth House Hold* (1969): "In mantra chanting, the magic utterances, built of seed-syllables such as OM and AYNG and AH, repeated over and over, fold and curl on the breath until—when most weary and bored—a new voice enters, a voice speaks through you clearer and stronger than what you know of yourself; with a sureness and melody of its own, singing out the inner song of the self, and of the planet."

246.14 ōṃ ah hūṃ] A mantra from the Tibetan tradition, to help clarify, or purify, body, speech, and mind.

249.4 "From the masses to the masses"] A slogan attributed to Mao Zedong (Mao Tse Tung, 1893–1976); see "Some Questions Concerning Methods of Leadership," June 1943.

249.25 seed-syllables] In Hinduism and Vajrayana Buddhism, mantras may have mystical "seed syllables" with spiritual power but no precise meaning; *om* is a well-known example.

250.8 the *book of changes*] The *I Ching*, an ancient Chinese divinatory text.

251.1 *Tamba*] Also spelled Tanba, a historical Japanese province that included parts of present-day Kyoto and Hyogo Prefectures.

251.23 Shantung] A Chinese coastal province (now Shandong) bordering the East China Sea, and a silken fabric historically produced there.

255.9 (Goma / Homa)] Buddhist and original Vedic (Sanskrit) terms for a ritual in which offerings are sacrificed in fire.

255.21 vajra-tongs] See note 77.20.

256.19 *obon* dancers] During Japanese *obon* festivals, members of the community dance to honor ancestral spirits.

257.27–28 "Interno del Colosseo . . . 1820] *Interior of the Colosseum Excavated in 1813*, an etching by Luigi Rossini (1790–1857).

258.9 Dōgen] Dōgen Zenji (1200–1253) was a Japanese Buddhist priest, writer, poet, philosopher, and founder of the Sōtō school of Zen in Japan.

258.16 The Ford Foundation] Established in 1936 by Edsel and Henry Ford, the organization's stated purpose is "to reduce poverty and injustice, strengthen democratic values, promote international cooperation, and advance human achievement."

258.29–259.2 the unspeakable . . . Canyon de Chelly] In 1864, U.S. troops destroyed approximately 3,000 peach trees in the Canyon de Chelly, then a Navajo agricultural area, as part of a scorched earth campaign to displace the tribe; the canyon is now part of the Canyon de Chelly National Monument in northeastern Arizona.

259.24 Hadley] Drum Hadley (see note 121.2).

260.24 Two Ravens talk a bit] See the traditional Lowland Scots ballad "The Twa Corbies," in which two ravens morbidly discuss the meal they will make of a slain knight's corpse.

261.8 poke-holing for blennies] Fishing for blenny eels (*Cebidichthys violaceus*, also known as monkeyface prickleback) with a long stick, poked into holes in rocky jetties and intertidal zones.

261.23   Peoples' Park march] On May 30, 1969, approximately 30,000 people marched in Berkeley, California, to "Defend People's Park"—an improvised community garden on university-owned land—and to protest the killing and wounding of students in clashes with police on May 15.

262.8   *Slide Ranch*] A former dairy farm north of Muir Beach, California, purchased by The Nature Conservancy in 1969 and now part of the Golden Gate National Recreation Area.

262.17   *oryza: :genmai*] *Oryza* is the plant genus encompassing most edible rice species, and *genmai* a Japanese generic term for whole-grain brown rice.

263.13   *Sawmill Lake*] A small lake near Truckee, California, in the Sierra Nevada Mountains.

263.15   the "big E"] The Emporium, a California department store chain with a flagship store, opened in 1896 in San Francisco; it went out of business in 1996.

265.1   *Jack Spicer*] Spicer (1925–1965), a poet often associated with the San Francisco Renaissance, cofounded the Six Gallery in San Francisco where Allen Ginsberg first read *Howl* and Snyder "A Berry Feast" in October 1955.

271.7–8   Tārā . . . "Starlight"] A Buddhist deity, Tārā represents the female counterpart of the bodhisattva Avalokiteśvara and embodies the feminine aspect of compassion. Known in Tibet as the Great Savioress, Tārā is said to represent the very essence of loving devotion; "joy of starlight" is one of her many epithets

271.24   the cat] See note 50.11.

272.4   Russian river] River flowing south through Sonoma and Mendocino Counties in northern California.

272.10   Will Petersen] Petersen (1928–1994) was a lithographer, painter, and poet who lived for a time in Kyoto and studied Japanese calligraphy, printmaking, and Noh performance. His drawings appear in the first edition of Snyder's *Myths & Texts* (1960).

272.10   Mt. Hiei] See note 17.27.

272.24   Silver Pavilion] Ginkakuji, or the Silver Pavilion, is a Zen temple in the foothills of eastern Kyoto.

273.1   *Shinkyogoku*] A shopping district in central Kyoto.

273.6   *Hiking in the Totsugawa Gorge*] Snyder later published a prose recollection about a hike in this gorge—in Nara Prefecture, in June 1968—in "Walking the Great Ridge Omine on the Womb-Diamond Trail," *Kyoto Journal*, December 9, 2011.

273.13 the Buddha's Lion Roar] A metaphor used to express happiness due to faith and trust in the profound truths of Buddhism.

274.5 *Kitano Shrine . . . Fair*] A Shinto shrine in Kyoto, site of a regular flea market.

275.7 *Four Corners*] The unique point at which the borders of Arizona, Colorado, New Mexico, and Utah meet.

275.17 offing] That part of the sea that remains in view from shore, beyond anchorages or inshore navigational dangers.

276.12 "The Good Earth."] A 1937 American film about Chinese farmers who struggle to survive, based on the 1931 novel of the same title by Nobel laureate Pearl S. Buck.

276.21 Aurochs] Large wild cattle, the ancestors of modern domestic cattle, that inhabited Asia, Europe, and North Africa. The last known individuals died in Poland in 1627.

276.25 "Kyoto born in spring song"] See pages 232–33 in this volume.

277.2 *The Well-Tempered Clavier*] A collection of two sets of preludes and fugues for keyboard, composed in 1722 and 1742 by Johann Sebastian Bach (1685–1750).

TURTLE ISLAND

285.1 *Manzanita*] See note 94.27.

287.1 *Anasazi*] Ancient Native American peoples, also known as Ancestral Puebloans, inhabiting parts of present-day Arizona, Colorado, New Mexico, and Utah.

287.23 *The Way West, Underground*] Introducing this poem during a reading at Portland State University on November 11, 1974, Snyder commented: "This is a little bit of bear religion poetry dealing with the circumpolar bear cult . . . a religion that used to run from Utah around through northern California, the Pacific Northwest, and out across northern Japan, all the way across Siberia and into Finland and Lapland, and anciently, like Middle Paleolithic or earlier, down into Europe too. Man's oldest religion, possibly; or at least the earliest thing we have any evidence of that has the appearance of being magical is the way bear skulls were treated in some of those caves in Bavaria. So how'd it get back to Europe, was the question that I put to myself."

288.2 Plumas county] A county in the northern Sierra Nevada of California, principally inhabited (before the Gold Rush of 1849) by the indigenous Mountain Maidu.

288.4 The Bear Wife] Snyder retells and analyzes the story of "The Woman Who Married a Bear" in an essay of the same title, collected in *The Practice of the Wild* (1990).

288.10   Ainu] The indigenous inhabitants of the Japanese island of Hokkaido and of nearby areas of Russia.

288.11   Gilyak] Also known as the Nivkh, an indigenous group inhabiting the north of Sakhalin Island and nearby mainland Russia.

288.15   Women with drums who fly over Tibet.] Probably a reference to a type of sacred female spirit in Hinduism and Buddhism known as a "dākinī"; in Sanskrit the term means "to fly" and in Tibetan it means "skygoer." They carry *damaru* drums.

288.27   Karhu—Bjorn—Braun] *Bear* in Finnish and Dutch; *brown* in German.

288.32   Brunhilde] A princess deceived by her lover Siegfried in the German epic the *Nibelungenlied* (c. 1200) and earlier Icelandic eddas.

290.12   Zac] Zac H. Reisner, Jr. (b. 1947), an outdoorsman, writer, and painter who helped Snyder build his house at Kitkitdizze in the summer of 1970 and worked as his "right-hand man" for a couple of years thereafter.

290.21   case-skinned] A method in taxidermy whereby the skin is peeled from the animal from a single aperture.

291.24   "We don't smoke . . . Muskokie"] Opening line of the 1969 country hit "Okie from Muskogee," written by Merle Haggard (1937–2016) and Roy Edward Burris (1931–2011) as a reproach to protesters of the Vietnam War.

292.6   "What is to be done."] English-language title of a 1902 pamphlet by Vladimir Lenin (1870–1924), advocating the spread of Marxist political ideas among workers.

294.20   double-mirror world] In a 1978 interview with Ekbert Fass, Snyder mentioned the double mirror as "a key image in *Avatamsaka* philosophy, Buddhist interdependence philosophy. Multiple reflections in multiple mirrors, that's what the universe is like."

295.16   Gen's] Gen Snyder (see note 216.1).

296.19   *Olema*] A town on Point Reyes Peninsula in Marin County, California; the name, from the Coast Miwok, means "coyote valley."

296.21   toloache] Mexican common name for flowering plants in the genus *Datura*, also known as moonflowers, thornapples, jimsonweeds, or devil's trumpets; all species in the genus have toxic, hallucinogenic, or medicinal properties.

296.22   *tamal*] Miwok: bay.

296.25   tule] *Schoenoplectus acutus*, also known as hardstem bulrush, a marsh plant used by a variety of Native American tribes to make baskets, clothing, boats, houses, and other items.

297.29   ACHALA] In Buddhist tradition, a wrathful deity who cuts through veils of ignorance; known in Japan as Fudō Myō-ō.

298.9–11 NAMAH . . . TRAKA HAM MAM] Sanskrit "Mantra of Acala." In his "Smokey the Bear Sutra" (see pages 884–87 in the present volume), Snyder translates it thus: "I dedicate myself to the universal diamond / be this raging fury destroyed."

298.28 Amerika] A variant spelling of "America," used by dissenters beginning in the 1960s to suggest an authoritarian, fascist state.

299.19 kitkitdizze] Miwok name for *Chamaebatia foliolosa*, an aromatic shrub endemic to the mountains of central California, also known as "mountain misery" and "bearclover"; Snyder borrowed the term for the name of his home on the San Juan Ridge.

306.2 Michael McClure] Introducing McClure (1932–2020) at a reading on the San Juan Ridge in August 1999, Snyder commented: "Michael and I have been conspirators in the cultural rebellion of our times since we were both in our twenties. Both of us performed at the Six Gallery reading in 1955, which marked the west coast beginning of the Beat Generation, and we have stayed in close touch ever since."

306.7 "The Deva Realm"] Devas, in Buddhist mythology, are godlike beings who live in hierarchical realms according to their merits; ultimately they are subject to mortality.

309.1 *Facts*] Introducing this poem at a reading on March 20, 1974, at the University of North Dakota Writers Conference, Snyder commented: "This is a 'found' poem. I found most of these facts in one issue of the *Christian Science Monitor* eighteen months ago, reading it at random because it was put in my mailbox by mistake."

309.22 H.T. Odum] Howard Thomas Odum (1924–2002), American ecologist.

310.2–3 Alcatraz . . . Angel Island] Islands in San Francisco Bay.

312.9–10 An abandoned . . . island prison] The Presidio, an army post overlooking San Francisco Bay, was transferred to the National Park Service in 1994. Alcatraz, now a tourist attraction, was the site of a federal penitentiary from 1934 to 1963.

312.17–18 a long-bearded . . . brother] Bruce E. Boyd (b. 1948) helped to design and build Snyder's home at Kitkitdizze, as an apprentice architect, in the summer of 1970; he was a founding member of the Yuba Watershed Institute, a local forest advocacy group, and served as editor for the journal *Tree Rings*.

313.12–13 "A snake-like beauty . . . Duncan] See "The Structure of Rime I," collected in *The Opening of the Field* (1960) by Robert Duncan (1919–1988).

313.26–31 the snake center . . . single eye.] In Tantric Buddhism and elsewhere, kundalini ("coiled snake") refers to a vital energy force that, when awakened, will rise up from the base of the spine toward the crown of the head.

315.7–9 If you climb . . . miles more.] Snyder's rhyming version of a widely known and variously translated Chinese proverb: "Climb mountains to see lowlands."

315.10 *San Gabriel Ridges*] The San Gabriel Mountains, now a National Monument, are located in southern California between the Los Angeles Basin and the Mojave Desert.

316.9 *Frazier Creek Falls*] A 176-foot cascade located near the Sierra Buttes in the Plumas National Forest, north of Snyder's home at Kitkitdizze.

317.1 *Black Mesa Mine #1*] Black Mesa, on Hopi and Navajo lands in north-eastern Arizona, was the site of controversial large-scale coal-mining operations beginning in the late 1960s.

318.1 *Duck River*] "Kamo-gawa," the Japanese name for the Kamo River, in Kyoto, literally translates into English as "Duck River."

318.5 shakuhachi] A Japanese bamboo flute.

318.7 Benten] Japanese Buddhist goddess, a patron of literature and music, often depicted in association with snakes or dragons and playing a *biwa* lute.

319.18 Michael Aldrich] Aldrich (b. 1942) edited *The Marijuana Review* from 1968 to 1973 and co-directed Amorphia, a Mill Valley, California, nonprofit promoting marijuana legalization.

321.9 Brazil says . . . Natural Resources"] Snyder spoke at the United Nations Conference on the Human Environment in Stockholm in June 1972, and reports the Brazilian delegate's opposition to any international restriction of its resource use.

321.24 methyl mercury] In 1956, the first cases of what became known as Minamata disease were characterized in Minamata, Japan; mercury, discharged into the ocean in industrial wastewater beginning in the 1930s, had accumulated in shellfish and other marine organisms, slowly poisoning the local population and causing over 2,000 deaths.

321.27 Père David's Deer, the Elaphure] *Cervus davidianus,* an endemic Chinese deer, was probably extinct in the wild when the first specimens were sent to Europe by Armand David, a French missionary, in the 1860s; populations bred from a handful of individuals surviving in zoos have been reintroduced in Chinese nature parks beginning in 1985.

322.25 Margaret Mead . . . Samoa?] Mead (1901–1978), an anthropologist, published *Coming of Age in Samoa: A Psychological Study of Primitive Youth for Western Civilization,* in 1928.

322.31–34 "In yonder field . . . down down"] An amalgamation of "Twa Corbies," a traditional Lowland Scots ballad, and "Three Ravens," an earlier English ballad.

324.9 bucked] Trees felled and delimbed into usable lengths.

324.12   J. Tecklin] Jerry Tecklin (b. 1938), an ecologist and former civil rights activist, has been a member of the San Juan Ridge community since the 1970s.

324.15–16   Boletus . . . *Eastwood*] *Boletus eastwoodiae*, named for the botanist Alice Eastwood (1859–1953) and since included in the genus *Rubroboletus*, is a highly poisonous mushroom native to western North America.

324.18   *edulis*] *Boletus edulis,* an edible mushroom species.

324.22   *Straight-Creek—Great Burn*] The Great Burn is an area in the Bitterroot Mountains of Montana; Straight Creek flows out of it.

324.23   Tom and Martha Birch] Thomas H. Birch, Jr. (b. 1937), taught philosophy for many years at the University of Montana.

326.15   *Hudsonian Curlew*] Now known as the Hudsonian whimbrel (*Numenius phaeopus hudsonicus*), a migratory coastal wading bird.

326.16   Drum and Diana] Drum and Diana Hadley (see notes 121.2 and 121.9).

326.20   Mandala] Sanskrit for "circle"; more broadly a vibrant geometric design organized around a central point used symbolically for meditation in Hindu and Buddhist cultures.

327.8   cardón cactus] *Pachycereus pringlei*, also known as elephant cactus, is native to deserts in Baja California and the coastal region of the Mexican state of Sonora; it is the largest cactus species in the world.

327.31   "Royal Tern"] The royal tern, *Thalasseus maximus*, is a seabird that nests on islands and isolated beaches.

330.17   "California Here I Come"] 1921 popular song written by Buddy DeSylva (1895–1950), Joseph Meyer (1894–1987), and Al Jolson (1886–1950), sometimes considered an unofficial California anthem.

330.19–20   "If I Had the Wings of an Angel"] A line from "The Prisoner's Song," a popular song first recorded by Vernon Dalhart in 1924 and said to have been written by a relative of Dalhart's, while in prison.

330.33–34   "Channelled Scablands."] A region in eastern Washington crisscrossed by canyons, channels, and rock basins produced by immense, erosive Ice Age flooding.

331.27   Original Nature] In Zen Buddhism, seeing one's original mind (or original nature) directly, without the intervention of the intellect, is a path to achieve enlightenment.

332.9   Ramakrishna] Sri Ramakrishna Paramahamsa (1836–1886), Bengali Hindu mystic and religious leader.

332.23   Tārā's] See note 271.7–8.

333.27   Bhagavan Das] Born Kermit Michael Riggs in 1945, a yogic and spiritual teacher who lived as an ascetic and initiate of various sages in Nepal, India, and Sri Lanka for six years beginning in 1964.

333.4–5   ashes, ashes . . . fall down.] Lines from an English nursery rhyme and playground game—"Ring a Ring o' Roses"—that first appeared in print in 1881 but was known earlier as a folk song. Some have associated the lines with the Great Plague of 1665 in England.

334.15   Richard and Michael] Richard Sisto (b. 1945), a jazz percussionist and meditation teacher who had a house on the San Juan Ridge in the 1970s, set some of Snyder's poetry to music; Michael Killigrew (1941–2003), another member of the San Juan Ridge community, was a painter, writer, and activist against nuclear weapons.

335.3   Hsiang-yen] The author of the poem's title quote ("One Should Not . . . by the Buddha"), Hsiang-yen (d. c. 900) was a Buddhist scholar and Zen master famous for his association with the "Original Face" kōan.

335.7   *Shingyo*] The *Hannya Shingyo* or Heart Sutra is a core teaching about "emptiness" (the impermanence and interdependence of all things) common to many forms of Buddhism.

335.23   Kālī] See note 153.2.

335.29   Kālī-yūga] In Hinduism, the fourth and present age of the world cycle of *yūgas* ("ages"). Known as the "dark age," this fourth *yūga* will culminate in the destruction of the present world followed by the creation of a new cycle.

336.1   *"The Duchess of Malfi"*] An English Renaissance revenge tragedy about political and moral corruption written by John Webster (c. 1580–c. 1632) and first performed in 1613 or 1614.

336.3   Bellatrix and Rigel] Stars in the constellation Orion.

336.27   S.P.] The Southern Pacific Railroad operated in the western United States from 1865 to 1996.

341.7   Nanao] Nanao Sakaki (see note 141.11).

341.14   Polemonium] A genus of flowering plants, also known by the common name Jacob's ladder, often producing blue flowers.

341.17   sangha] A Buddhist community of religious and laypeople.

342.9   nine bows] A ritualistic act of respect in Buddhism.

345.12–13   the Feather . . . Yuba] Rivers in northeastern California forming part of the watershed near Snyder's home on the San Juan Ridge.

346.13   Treaty of Guadalupe Hidalgo] The 1848 treaty ending the Mexican-American War (1846–48); it rearranged borders between the two countries and established conditions for determining citizenship.

346.21   Tobiassen] A common surname in Nevada County, California, political and civic life.

346.32   the diggings] The Malakoff Diggins, site (near Snyder's home Kitkit-dizze) of extensive nineteenth-century hydraulic mining operations.

347.11   *Climax*] Snyder commented on the ecological sense of this term in an April 1977 interview collected as "The *East West* Interview" in *The Real Work* (1980): "Every given natural region has a potential top situation where all of the plants that will grow there have grown up now and all of those that will push out something else have pushed out something else, and it reaches a point of stability. . . . This condition, called 'climax,' is an optimum condition of diversity—optimum stability. When a system reaches climax, it levels out for centuries or millennia. . . . almost half the energy that flows in the system does not come from annual growth, it comes from the recycling of dead growth."

349.20–21   A rooster . . . 1474] See Johannis Gross, *Kurze Basler Chronik* (1624).

349.33   "detritus pathways"] Routes by which organic waste is decomposed into its constituent elements and returned to the environment.

355.9   Robert Shapiro] Shapiro (1911–2005), a lawyer and manufacturing executive active in the Human Potential movement, published Snyder's "Four Changes" in booklet form in Chicago in 1969.

357.24   "the rainbow body"] See note 239.1.

360.1–9   Thoreau says . . . last fruits also."] From the conclusion of "The Bean-Field," chapter 7 of Thoreau's *Walden; or, Life in the Woods* (1854).

364.34   McLuhan] Marshall McLuhan (1911–1980), Canadian author of *The Gutenberg Galaxy* (1962), *Understanding Media: The Extensions of Man* (1964), and other books.

370.3   latifundia] Large, landed estates producing agricultural commodities for sale.

373.5   Wepa land] Land held by the cooperative Wepa Land Association, part of the San Juan Ridge community; *Wepa* is the Niesnan word for coyote.

373.26   Lew Welch] Lewis Barrett Welch (1926–1971?) graduated from Reed College, where he was one of Snyder's roommates and a fellow poet, in the class of 1950; the two shared a Marin County cabin for some months in 1958. In May 1971, while visiting Snyder at Kitkitdizze, he disappeared into the Sierra Nevada leaving a note behind, a probable suicide though his body was never found. Welch published several collections of poetry, including *Wobbly Rock* (1960), *On Out* (1965), and *The Song Mt. Tamalpais Sings* (1970).

375.1   *"As for Poets"*] See page 351–52 in the present volume.

AXE HANDLES

383.15–30   Ezra Pound . . . Shih-hsiang Chen] Pound's translation—in *Confucius: The Unwobbling Pivot & The Great Digest*, first published in *Pharos*, Winter 1947—reads "Cutting ax-handle / Cutting an ax-handle / The model is not far off." Chen (1912–1971) was professor of Chinese and Comparative

Literature at Berkeley, and Snyder, in the fall of 1953, one of his graduate students; he published his translation of Lu Ji's *Essay on Literature* in 1953.

384.2 Lew Welch] See note 373.26.

384.16 Colusa] A small city in Colusa County, California, approximately 125 miles north of San Francisco.

386.18–19 *Lanes Landing Farm . . . Wendell*] Tanya Berry (b. 1936) and her husband Wendell Berry (b. 1934), a novelist, poet, and farmer-philosopher, purchased Lanes Landing Farm, on the western bank of the Kentucky River near Port Royal, Kentucky, in 1965, and have lived there ever since. Snyder's correspondence with Wendell Berry was published in 2014 as *Distant Neighbors*.

389.6–7 a giant poster of Geronimo . . . his knee] Geronimo (Goyaalé, 1829–1909), a leader of a band of the Apache tribe, carried out numerous raids against soldiers of the U.S. and Mexico during the prolonged years of Apache-U.S. conflict. A photograph of him kneeling with a rifle, taken by A. Frank Randall around 1884, was widely reproduced in the 1960s and '70s as a symbol of revolutionary action.

390.2 Arts Council] Snyder served as the first chairperson of the California Arts Council, established by Governor Jerry Brown in 1976.

390.14 *North San Juan School*] Beginning in the 1970s, the design, construction, and maintenance of the North San Juan School has been a focal point for San Juan Ridge community activities.

390.25 Franquette walnuts] An old French walnut variety, preferred for its frost tolerance.

391.26 Flicker's single call] The northern flicker, *Colaptes auratus*—the only flicker commonly found in the San Juan Ridge area—has a loud, single-note call.

391.30–31 the family / of Mint] The mint family, *Lamiaceae*, includes over 7,000 species, many of them aromatic.

392.10 Camptonville] A small town in Yuba County, California.

392.26 penta] Volvo Penta, a brand of engine oil.

393.13 Oregon Creek] A creek located approximately 10 miles from Nevada City, California.

395.5 H.G. Creel] Herrlee Glessner Creel (1905–1994), longtime professor of Chinese at the University of Chicago and author of many books on Chinese language, history, and philosophy.

395.10 "Bechtel."] A multinational engineering and construction firm founded in San Francisco in 1908.

395.17 Bruce Boyd and Holly Tornheim] Boyd (see note 312.17–18) and Tornheim (b. 1948) both participated in the construction of Snyder's home at Kitkitdizze in 1971; Tornheim has since become a fine art woodworker, exhibiting in galleries and museums.

396.25 Sugi trees] See note 143.16.

397.3 Anja and John] Anja Chappell, a Swedish-born potter, and her husband John Chappell (see note 137.11); Snyder met the couple in Kyoto around 1960.

397.8 *Tango*] See note 176.7.

397.9 *Myoshin-ji*] A temple complex in Kyoto, Japan, and head temple of the associated branch of Rinzai Zen Buddhism.

398.15 *mu*] See note 78.30.

399.15–16 *Ibaru Family Tomb . . . Great Loo Choo*] Okinawans gather at family tombs periodically to celebrate the spirits of their ancestors; the island of Okinawa was once Anglicized as "Great Loo Choo."

400.4 *Willys*] Brand name of Willys-Overland Motors, founded in 1908 and merged in 1963 into the firm Kaiser-Jeep.

400.5 Lu Yu] Song dynasty poet (1125–1210), also known as Lu You or by his literary name Fang-weng.

400.18 Bloody Run Creek] A stream north of Snow Tent, an abandoned gold-mining and lumbering town on San Juan Ridge in Nevada County, California.

401.21 the poll of the sledge] One face of a sledgehammer's metal head, a poll, is flattened and designed to drive a wedge into wood for splitting it.

401.29 peavey] A lumberman's 5-foot lever with a pivoting hooked arm and metal spike at one end principally used for turning logs over.

402.1 maul] A heavy hammer with a wedge-shaped end especially used to split wood.

405.2 Gaia] A mother goddess personifying Earth in Greek mythology, and, in the "Gaia hypothesis" first proposed by environmentalist James Lovelock in 1972, the idea of Earth as a single, complex, self-regulating system.

408.16 Corn Maidens] See note 157.27.

410.23 Ge] Greek: Earth.

410.24 seed syllable] See note 249.25.

410.27–29 Chuang-tzu . . . blue] The *Zhuangzi*, a classic Taoist text by Chinese philosopher Chuang-tzu (also known as Zhuang Zhou, c. fourth century BCE), recounts the myth of the Kun Peng, a giant fish (K'un) who changes into a giant bird (P'eng). Flying south, P'eng sees only blue above and below.

412.8 *Warner Range*] An 85-mile-long mountain range running north–south in northeastern California and south-central Oregon.

420.6 *seiza*] Traditional Japanese formal seated posture, kneeling with the buttocks resting on the heels.

421.26 *Hygrophorus?*] A genus of gilled mushrooms, commonly known as "waxy caps"; many species are sticky when wet.

422.12–13 a naked bug . . . brown hair] See Snyder's "Cold Mountain Poems" on page 34, lines 16–17, of the present volume.

422.17 *Coaldale*] A ghost town in Esmarelda County, Nevada.

423.2 Ceanothus] A North American flowering plant genus; Californian *Ceanothus* species are commonly referred to as California lilacs.

427.1 *The Grand Entry*] Introducing this poem at an August 1983 reading at the Naropa Institute, Snyder commented: "In the rodeo world, there is something called 'the grand entry.' During the bicentennial year, they had quite a pageant at the Nevada County Fair . . . they had all of the cowgirls in the county, practically, riding in patterns, carrying American flags (each one of the flags being one of the different flags, you know, from the thirteen-star flag, up to the fifty-star flag)."

429.14 Jerry Brown] Brown (b. 1938) served as governor of California from 1975 to 1983 and again from 2011 to 2019, holding positions in the interim as mayor of Oakland, California (1999–2007), and California attorney general (2007–2011); he sought the Democratic presidential nomination in 1976, 1980, and 1992. He appointed Snyder to the newly formed California Arts Council in 1976, and inducted him into the California Hall of Fame in 2017.

430.10 Lun yü] Also known as the *Analects of Confucius*, a 20-book anthology of the sayings of Confucius (551–479 BCE), collected posthumously.

431.2 Jacques Barzaghi] Barzaghi (1938–2021), a former actor and soldier who emigrated from France to the U.S. in the late 1960s, served as an advisor and confidant of Jerry Brown (see note 429.14) from the early 1970s until 2004.

431.19 Calochortus] A native North American flowering plant genus.

435.20–24 Gold Stream Vale . . . shining pipe] A section of the Trans-Alaska pipeline, constructed from 1975 to 1977, is on public view in the Goldstream Valley north of Fairbanks, Alaska.

437.7 Bert Hybart] Hybart (1905–1981) worked at various jobs on the San Juan Ridge, including "driving dump truck, backhoe, grader, and Cat," Snyder noted in his essay "The Place, the Region, and the Commons," collected in *The Practice of the Wild* (1990): "Roads, ponds, and pads are his sculpture, shapes that will be left on the land long after the houses have vanished."

438.9 Ayers Rock, Uluru] English and Pitjantjatjara names for a large, iconic sandstone rock formation in the south of Australia's Northern Territory.

439.29   *mulpu*] Pintupi term referring to "a plant or fungus breaking through the soil or to a girl's prepubescent breasts."

440.1   spinifex] Common name for Australian tussock grasses in the genus *Triodia*.

440.10–11   *Uluru . . . Ilpili*] Aboriginal communities in South Australia and the Northern Territory.

446.8   *English Mountain*] An 8,300-foot peak in Nevada County, California.

446.20   *The Bäckaskog woman*] Stone Age skeleton (c. 7010–6540 BCE) unearthed in Barum, Sweden, in a sitting position, in 1939, and thought to be the remains of a woman of 40 to 50 years old who had given birth to a large number of children.

447.12–13   *Ichikawa Ennosuke . . . "Kurozuka"*] Ennosuke, a stage name of kabuki actor Masahiko Kinoshi (b. 1939), played the demonic old woman Iwate in the dance-drama *Kurozuka* (1939), written by Kimura Tomiko (1890–1944).

447.16   James and Carol Katz] James Katz (b. 1947), owner of James Henry Wilderness and River Tours, and his wife Carol Katz (b. 1943) hosted Snyder on a rafting trip down the Stanislaus River in April 1981.

448.7–10   Su Shih . . . slowness"] See "The Hundred-Pace Rapids" by the Song dynasty poet Su Shih (1037–1101), also known as Su Tung P'o.

448.11–14   Dōgen . . . flow away.] See the Mountains and Rivers Sutra of Japanese Buddhist writer Dōgen (1200–1253).

LEFT OUT IN THE RAIN

452.1   DONALD ALLEN . . . LAUGHLIN] Allen was an editor and publisher (see note 195.17). Laughlin (1914–1997) founded New Directions, one of Snyder's publishers, in 1936.

456.23   *Mt. St. Helens, Spirit Lake*] Prior to the eruption of Mount St. Helens in 1980, Spirit Lake, located north of the mountain, was a popular tourist destination; in 1945, Snyder climbed the mountain starting from the YMCA camp at Spirit Lake.

459.1–2   *the Doab . . . Willamette*] *Doab* is a South Asian term for the land between two confluent rivers; the doab of the Columbia and the Willamette is the site of much of Portland, Oregon, and of Reed College, where Snyder was an undergraduate from 1947 to 1951.

461.9   *P. Whalen*] See note 117.4.

461.13   Gwion race the hag] Gwion, in Celtic mythology, is the servant and ultimately the child of the shapeshifting witch goddess Ceridwen; he is later reborn as the poet Taliesin.

461.18   Li Po] See note 27.8–9.

461.22   *George Leigh-Mallory*] Mallory (1886–1924), an English mountaineer, took part in the first three British expeditions to Mount Everest in the early 1920s. In 1924, he and his climbing partner disappeared just below Everest's summit.

462.5   Chomolungma] Tibetan name for Mt. Everest, meaning "Goddess Mother of Mountains."

463.21   urine-boy] A figure in Cowlitz mythology.

466.3   Wy-east] Multnomah name for Mount Hood, the highest peak in Oregon, southeast of Portland.

466.8   *Atthis*] A lost love of the Greek poet Sappho (630–570 BCE), named in several of her fragmentary lyrics. At points within this sequence of poems, Snyder recalls his relationship with Robin Collins (see note 134.15).

467.2–4   *". . . Still, she reproached . . . gift of corn"*] These lines—from Ovid's *Metamorphoses*, V.474–86—refer to the famine in Sicily instigated by the goddess Ceres when she cannot find her lost daughter, Proserpina.

468.25   Stinson Beach] Now part of the Golden Gate National Recreation Area, a beach about 20 miles north of San Francisco.

469.11   DOSEWALLIPS] The Dosewallips River has its source in the Olympic Mountains of Washington state.

469.12   CCC] The Civilian Conservation Corps, a Depression-era public works program (1933–42).

473.1   *Bakers Cabin . . . Road*] After graduating from Reed College, Snyder's friends Carol and Bill Baker lived on Boone's Ferry Road, south of Portland.

476.4   Harappa or Knossos] Harappa, in the Indus River valley in Pakistan, and Knossos, an ancient city in Crete, were early centers of civilization.

476.16   *Geological Meditation*] When Snyder first published this poem—in *The Fates of Rocks and Trees*, a small press edition, in 1986—he dated it "1953."

479.12–14   Wang Wei . . . Murasaki] Wang Wei (699–759) was a Tang dynasty poet, musician, painter, and politician; Chao-chou (778–897), a leading Zen master in China; and Lady Murasaki Shikibu (c. 973 or 978–c. 1014 or 1031), the Japanese author of the eleventh-century novel *The Tale of Genji*.

480.8   tokonoma] A recessed space in a Japanese reception room, often with a raised floor, in which items for artistic appreciation are displayed.

480.9   Rexroth's *Japanese Poems*] Kenneth Rexroth (1905–1982) published *100 Poems from the Japanese* in 1955.

480.11   Hitomaro] Kakinomoto no Hitomaro (c. 653–655–c. 707–710), a prominent Japanese *waka* poet.

481.21 *the Sawtooths*] A mountain range in central Idaho, attaining a maximum elevation of almost 11,000 feet.

482.1 *Point Reyes*] A peninsula approximately 30 miles northwest of San Francisco.

487.1 *Longitude . . . North*] A point in the North Pacific, roughly halfway between San Francisco and Kobe, Japan.

487.2 *Ruth Sasaki*] Sasaki (1892–1967), who sponsored Snyder's first trip to Japan, oversaw the translation of Zen texts into English, and beginning in 1958 was the first foreigner to serve as a priest of a Rinzai Zen temple.

487.33 floating world] See note 207.14.

487.35 M.S. *Arita Maru*] Cargo ship aboard which Snyder traveled from San Francisco to Japan in May 1956.

488.24–25 *Chion-In . . . Pure Land*] Kyoto temple headquarters of the Jōdo-shū or Pure Land sect founded by Hōnen (1133–1212), who taught that chanting the name of Amida Buddha (Sanskrit: Amitabha) will lead to salvation in Buddha's Western Paradise or "Pure Land."

490.1 Tu Fu, Sesshu] Tu Fu (712–770), also known as Du Fu, was a leading poet of the Tang dynasty, and Sesshū Tōyō (1420–1506) a Japanese painter.

491.8 *The Feathered Robe*] A popular Noh play—*Hagoromo*, in Japanese—of unknown authorship, in which a fisherman steals a magical robe belonging to a celestial spirit while she is bathing, promising to return it only after she dances for him.

491.9 *Yaeko Nakamura*] A student of Noh singing with whom Snyder shared a house in Kyoto in the 1950s; see his recollection of her on page 714 of the present volume. She later taught at Green Gulch Farm Zen Center in Marin County, California.

492.16 Vulture Peak] A mountain in Bihar, India, traditionally a site at which the Buddha gathered with his followers.

492.23 Ten million camped in a one-room shack] A reference to Vimalakīrti's 10-foot-square-hut, which was said to accommodate 10,000 bodhisattvas; Vimalakīrti, a contemporary of Gautama Buddha, was a Buddhist lay practitioner.

492.30 J.K.] Jack Kerouac.

492.31 McClure Beach] Also known as McClures Beach, now part of Point Reyes National Seashore, north of San Francisco.

493.3 Neuri] Marilyn Arnold (b. 1926), a woman Snyder dated before he left for Japan in 1956; she appears as "Psyche" in Jack Kerouac's *The Dharma Bums*.

493.7 poorboys] In the 1950s, especially in the writing of Jack Kerouac, a "poorboy" referred to a jug of cheap wine.

493.8   Abelard, thou'rt clipped!] Peter Abelard (1079–1142), a medieval French scholastic philosopher, musician, and poet, was considered a heretic in his defense of women's education; he was famously castrated as a result of his relationship with Héloïse.

493.9–10   vomit . . . desert drug] Peyote, a small cactus (*Lophophora williamsii*) found in the southwestern United States and northern Mexico, has long been consumed for its psychoactive effects, and often acts as an emetic.

493.35   nibbana] Nirvana, a state of liberation from suffering and cycles of rebirth.

494.11   Shakya] Shakyamuni or "Sage of the Shakyas," an epithet applied to the Buddha.

494.27   salmonberry] *Rubus spectabilis*, a bramble species native to western North America.

495.17   city of the Gandharvas] See note 92.10.

495.20–22   "The mind dances . . . a stage—"] See the Lankāvatāra Sūtra (c. 350–400 CE), chapter V.

496.3   *A Monument on Okinawa*] The Himeyuri Monument & Peace Museum in southern Okinawa commemorates the fate of schoolgirls who were conscripted to work in a Japanese underground army field hospital. As U.S. forces advanced during the Battle of Okinawa the girls were not only abandoned by the Japanese military but ordered to commit suicide. Out of a total of 240 only 14 girls survived.

499.6   my sister's house] Snyder's younger sister Anthea Snyder Lowry (1932–2002) lived in Mill Valley, California, near Mt. Tamalpais.

500.21   my cabin] See note 98.5.

503.5–8   Pedro . . . Wakayama hills] As San Pedro is one of the first sightings of land when approaching the Port of Los Angeles from the sea, so the Wakayama Hills are seen as one approaches Osaka Bay and Kobe Harbor.

503.14   Pago] Pago Pago, the territorial capital of American Samoa.

503.28   "Sticky Monkey Flower"] *Diplacus aurantiacus*, a flowering plant native to California and southern Oregon; its resinous leaves were sometimes used by Native Americans for medicinal purposes.

504.34–36   Potrero Meadows . . . *before I left for Asia*] Potrero Meadows is one of several camping areas on the slopes of Mt. Tamalpais in Marin County, California. Kerouac presents a semi-fictional version of the hike in his novel *The Dharma Bums* (1958).

505.12   *the Typhoon*] Probably a reference to typhoon Vera, a tropical cyclone that struck Japan in September 1959.

505.22   *Joanne*] Joanne Kyger (see note 163.2).

506.11–12 "be true/to the *poem*"] In a letter of May 5, 1959, Joanne Kyger wrote to Snyder in Japan: "I start to get panicky and have to think over and over, be true to the poem be true to the poem."

507.10 *Tenjin*] Patron spirit, in Shintoism, of scholars and scholarship.

507.21 Aronowitz] Al Aronowitz (1928–2005), most often remembered as a pioneering rock journalist; in 1959 he wrote a series on the Beat poets for the *New York Post*.

507.25 *Claude Dalenberg*] See note 119.8.

509.1 Ohara] A rural village north of Kyoto.

510.14–15 Trading my mother tongue . . . stay here] Recalling his years in Japan in a 1977 interview, Snyder explained: "part-time I taught conversational English to the engineers of various electronics companies to make enough money to rent a little house, buy my food, ride a bicycle."

510.26 jackrolled] Robbed or pickpocketed, especially if one is drunk, drugged, or asleep.

511.16 bogies] Wheeled undercarriages of railroad cars.

511.21 furoshikis] Traditional square cloth wraps used to present gifts or transport goods.

512.22 Mt. Atago] At approximately 3,000 feet, the highest peak in the mountains surrounding Kyoto.

517.1 *Shasta Nation*] Snyder's reimagined name for northern California.

521.19 *kum*] Maidu: ceremonial roundhouse. Korean: a traditional, hollow-bodied musical instrument with six strings (also known as the geomungo or *kŏmungo*).

522.2 *Ed Schafer*] Edward H. Schafer (1913–1991) was a historian, translator, and longtime professor of Chinese at the University of California, Berkeley. Snyder contributed a foreword to his book *The Divine Woman: Dragon Ladies and Rain Maidens in T'ang Literature* (1973).

522.4–5 Mistress . . . Sagebrush] Artemis, goddess of wild animals in Greek myth, after whom the genus *Artemisia* (sagebrush) was named; see also note 164.17.

522.23 Bloody Run] See note 401.18.

523.15 *Alan Watts*] Watts (1915–1973), born in England, was a naturalized American author and lecturer who helped to popularize Asian theology and philosophy for Western audiences; his book *The Way of Zen* (1957) was particularly influential in the late 1950s and early 1960s.

524.16 Bundelkhand] See note 171.3.

524.17 Tārā] See note 271.7–8.

525.2   Shiva's dancing feet] The Hindu god Shiva is sometimes depicted as "Shiva Nataraja," Lord of the Dance; in dancing he creates and dissolves the universe.

527.23   the tallest tree of all] During the years when Snyder served on the California Arts Council, from 1974 to 1978, the world's tallest tree was believed to be the Libbey Tree, a 367-foot redwood (*Sequoia sempervirens*) located in Tall Trees Grove in Humboldt County, California.

528.15   Padma Sambhava] Also referred to as Guru Rinpoche, a semi-legendary Indian Buddhist mystic (c. eighth or ninth century CE) credited with introducing Tantric Buddhism to Tibet and with establishing the first Buddhist monastery there.

528.16   Lin-chi] Also known as Linji Yixuan (810–866), the founder of Chinese Ch'an Buddhism, from which Japanese Zen Buddhism evolved.

528.18   Ezra Pound] An expatriate American poet and critic, Pound (1885–1972) was a major figure among early modernist poets and an early influence on the poets of the Beat movement.

528.20   Lion roar] A Buddhist metaphor expressing the truth of Buddhist teaching, and unity of master and disciple.

529.27   *engawa*] In Japanese architecture, a transitional area between indoor and outdoor spaces, such as a porch or sunroom.

530.12   berberis] A large genus of flowering shrubs, commonly known as barberry.

532.3   *"Lassen's one big sweat lodge"*] Lassen Peak, in northern California, is an active volcano, surrounded by hot springs and steam vents.

532.4   the *Kukini* gamble] Among the Maidu of northern California and related tribes, *kukini* are guardian spirits inhabiting rocks, mountains, lakes, waterfalls, and sometimes animals. In his essay "Blue Mountains Constantly Walking," from *The Practice of the Wild* (1990), Snyder relates: "The Yana said that Mt. Lassen of northern California . . . is home to countless *kukini* who keep a fire going inside. (The smoke passes out through the smoke-hole.) They will enjoy their magical stick-game gambling until the time that human beings reform themselves and become 'real people' that spirits might want to associate with once again."

532.28   supers] Boxlike superstructures placed on top of the hive in beekeeping, for the storage of honey.

533.1   *Arktos*] Greek: bear. The word is part of the Ptolomaic name for the constellation Ursa Major (*Arktos megale*, the Great Bear); the star Arcturus means "guardian of the bear."

533.2   (*Pythagoras . . . Rhea*)] See the Phoenician philosopher Porphyry's *Vita Pythagorae* (*Life of Pythagoras*, c. 300 CE). Among the Greek Titans, Rhea was mother of the gods and a goddess of female fertility.

533.21 "The Great She Bear"] Ursa Major, translated from the Latin.

533.25 "Let the bastards . . . dark."] Slogan appearing on bumper stickers in oil-producing states during the early 1970s, in the context of increasing energy shortages and environmental concerns.

533.28 "Goat ropers need love too."] A bumper-sticker slogan quoted in the popular 1973 song "Up Against the Wall, Redneck Mother," written by Ray Wylie Hubbard (b. 1946) and recorded by Jerry Jeff Walker (1942–2020).

534.6 The Fox-girls] "Kitsune" is the Japanese word for "fox"; in several legends "Kitsune" have the ability to shapeshift into human form.

534.18 *Dan Ellsberg*] Snyder and Ellsberg (b. 1931) first met in Kyoto in 1960, when Ellsberg was a national security analyst for the RAND Corporation. He visited Snyder again at Kitkitdizze in 1970. Famous for his role in the 1971 release of the Pentagon Papers—a top-secret study of U.S. government decision-making during the Vietnam War—he devoted his subsequent career to antiwar activism.

535.6 *Chris Pearce*] Pearce (b. 1949), who grew up in Japan, cofounded the International Sake Association in Honolulu in 1987 and established World Sake Imports in 1998 for the purpose of bringing premium sakes to the United States.

535.28 nullipara] A woman (or female animal) who has never given birth.

536.24 Beale] Beale Air Force Base, about 40 miles north of Sacramento, California.

537.2 *Gary Holthaus*] Holthaus (b. 1932), a longtime resident of Alaska, is a poet, author, educator, and advocate for environmental and social justice causes.

538.1 "Deep tawnie cullour"] See *The Historie of Travaile into Virginia Britannia* by William Strachey (1572–1621), written in 1612: "They have a plomb which they call pessemmins, like to a medler, in England, but of a deeper tawnie cullour; they grow on a most high tree."

538.10 Tamopan] Japanese or Chinese persimmon, *Diospyros kaki.*

538.27 Genghis Khan's time] Genghis Khan (c. 1158–1227), the founder of the Mongol Empire, reigned from 1206 to 1227.

538.34 Mu Ch'i] Also spelled Muqi, Muxi, or Fachang (c. 1210–c. 1269), a Chinese Buddhist monk whose ink paintings—including *Six Persimmons*, now at the Daitoku-ji temple in Kyoto—were influential in Japanese art.

543.8 *Evolution Basin*] An area in Kings Canyon National Park, above the tree line.

544.1 *Custer's Battlefield*] Lt. Col. George Armstrong Custer (1839–1876) led troops of the U.S. Army's 7th Cavalry Regiment against Lakota, Northern Cheyenne, and Arapaho forces at the Battle of Little Bighorn, in southern

Montana, on June 25–26, 1876; he was killed during the battle and his troops were overwhelmingly defeated.

544.17 *Channeled Scablands*] See note 330.33–34.

545.11 *Home on the Range*] A popular cowboy song, its lyrics based on the 1873 poem "My Western Home," by Brewster M. Higley (1823–1911).

545.21 *Ananda*] The Ananda Meditation Retreat, a property adjacent to Snyder's home on the San Juan Ridge.

547.13 Dorjes] Five-pronged ritual objects used in Tibetan Buddhist ceremonies and said to cut through ignorance.

548.6 Sakura] Cherry blossom, the national flower of Japan.

548.16 *Gatha*] In Buddhist tradition, a verse recited aloud or in the mind along with the breath, as part of meditative practice.

554.14 *The Elusiad*] With a play on the word *elusive*, Snyder's mock-heroic title echoes that of Portugal's national epic, *The Luciad* (1572), by Luis de Camoëns (1524–1580).

554.16 HEROICKS] Heroic couplets, or rhyming pairs of lines in iambic pentameter.

554.17–18 *Clio . . . Erato*] Muses of history, eloquence, and lyric poetry.

554.25–29 *Lowie . . . Sapir*] Anthropologists Robert Harry Lowie (1883–1957), Ruth Benedict (1887–1948), and Edward Sapir (1884–1939).

556.1 *The Third Watch*] See Luke 12:38.

556.19 *Eorthan Modor's*] Eleventh-century Anglo-Saxon phrase meaning "Earth Mother."

556.23 *Kalpa*] A duration of time in Hinduism, spanning a complete cosmic cycle from the origination to the destruction of a world system.

557.9 Hermes] In Greek mythology, herald of the gods and a divine trickster.

557.15 Dewey] John Dewey (1859–1952), an American philosopher, psychologist, and educational reformer.

557.17 The Possum] T. S. Eliot (1888–1965) was nicknamed "Old Possum" by his fellow poet, Ezra Pound (1885–1972).

557.22 Kwakiutl] See note 77.16.

557.28 *Siva*] A variant spelling of *Shiva*, in Hinduism the creator, preserver, and destroyer of the universe.

558.2 Hoodlatch] See note 118.22.

559.15 *Ballad of Rolling Heads*] Including this poem in a letter to Allen Ginsberg from Kyoto, c. January 1957, Snyder commented: "The rolling heads song is NOT for publication but for amusement . . . Dig in title 'Ballad of Rolling Heads' the sly almost imperceptible allusion to 'Robespierre,' ho ho ho."

560.3   Cowley's last report] Malcolm Cowley (1898–1989), author of *Exile's Return* (1934) and other books, championed the publication of Kerouac's novel *On the Road* (1957) as an advisory editor for Viking Press, but had rejected some of his previous work, and often asked him to revise.

560.8   naked Peter] Peter Orlovsky (see note 169.2).

560.9   Neuri] Marilyn Arnold (see note 493.3).

560.10   Montgomery] John McVey Montgomery (1919–1992), one of Snyder's mountaineering friends; he appears in Kerouac's novel *The Dharma Bums* as Henry Morley.

560.11   Jinnie] Virginia Merrill Lehrman (1932–1998), an art student, model, and sometime girlfriend of Snyder's; she appears in *The Dharma Bums* as "Princess."

560.12   Du Peru] Peter S. Duperu (b. 1925), a friend of Allen Ginsberg in San Francisco around 1954; Ginsberg described him as "a mad Zen ex-amnesia shock patient."

560.16   La Vigne] Robert LaVigne (1928–2014), a San Francisco painter, illustrator, and set designer; Allen Ginsberg once described him as a "court painter" to the Beats.

560.19   poor Natalie] Natalie Jackson (1931–1955), an artist's model and store clerk who fell to her death, perhaps by suicide, in San Francisco. Fictionalized as Rosie Buchanan in Jack Kerouac's novel *The Dharma Bums*, she is described as "a real gone chick and friend of everybody of consequence."

560.21   the Bardo plane] See note 84.31.

560.24   Neal] Neal Cassady (1926–1968), a major personage of the 1950s Beat Generation and of the psychedelic and counterculture movements of the 1960s; he served as the model for the character Dean Moriarty in Jack Kerouac's *On the Road* (1957), and was one of the "Merry Pranksters" in Tom Wolfe's *The Electric Kool-Aid Acid Test* (1968).

561.5   Golden Boughs] See *The Golden Bough: A Study in Comparative Religion* (1890) by Sir James Gordon Frazer, and Book VI of Virgil's *Aeneid*, in which the myth of the golden bough is presented.

561.13–21   *After T'ao Ch'ien* . . . spring grass.] See the poem "New Corn" (as it has sometimes been translated) by Tao Yuanming (365–427), also known as T'ao Ch'ien.

562.4   *Anacreon*] Greek lyric poet (c. 582–c. 485 BCE) noted for his erotic poems and drinking songs.

563.37   *John Taylor's literal interlinear*] See Taylor's *The Odes of Anacreon, with a Literal Interlinear Translation, on the Plan Recommended by Mr. Locke* (1827).

564.21–29   *Joe Hill . . . died"* said he.] Hill (1879–1915), a Swedish American labor activist, songwriter, and member of the Industrial Workers of the World (the "Wobblies"), was executed for murder in November 1915 after a controversial trial; the quoted lines are from the poem "I Dreamed I Saw Joe Hill Last Night" by Alfred Hayes (1911–1985), set to music in 1936 by Earl Robinson (1910–1991).

564.28   Hungry Ghosts and Demons] In Buddhist tradition, Hungry Ghosts and Demons inhabit the lowest realms of suffering.

565.2   Justin Morgan] A Massachusetts horse breeder (1747–1798) and his famous stallion of the same name, who once pulled a heavy log to win "a gallon of rum," and who sired the Morgan horse breed.

566.4   *Cranium Press, & Clifford Burke*] Burke (b. 1942) published Snyder's *Spel Against Demons* (1970) at his Cranium Press, which he ran from 1962 to 1979.

566.18   Jack Wilson, Wovoka] Wovoka (c. 1856–1932), also known as Jack Wilson, was a Northern Paiute religious leader whose millenarian prophecies inspired the Ghost Dance movement of 1889–91.

569.32   *Burton Watson*] Watson (1925–2017) was an American sinologist and translator. In the mid-1950s, along with Snyder and others, he worked as a member of Ruth Sasaki's team in Kyoto translating Buddhist texts into English.

from NO NATURE

573.8–11   *Sierra Matterhorn . . . Thirty-one Years*] Matterhorn Peak, a 12,285-foot mountain in Yosemite National Park; Snyder climbed the mountain with Jack Kerouac in 1955, an ascent fictionalized in Kerouac's novel *The Dharma Bums* (1958).

573.25   Jeffrey Pine] See note 112.19.

574.14   *John and Jan Straley*] Both longtime residents of Sitka, Alaska, John Straley (b. 1953) now works as a criminal defense investigator and writes detective fiction, and his wife Jan Straley (b. 1953) is a marine biologist specializing in whale behavior.

576.18   the Chou dynasty . . . "Mu"] See note 78.30.

576.29   a Hall] In the summer of 1982, Snyder and others built a meditation hall—the Ring of Bone Zendo—in the field adjoining his house at Kitkitdizze, for the Buddhist community he helped to establish in 1974.

577.3   the year of the Persian Gulf] In 1991, the United States led an international invasion force against the Iraqi occupation of Kuwait, in what has since been called the First Iraq War.

578.2   *Carole*] Carole Lynn Koda (1947–2006), a 1968 Stanford psychology graduate, avid rock climber, and mother of two children, to whom Snyder was married in April 1991.

578.31–32   the *Dao De / Jing*] Also known as the *Tao Te Ching*, a classic Taoist work conventionally attributed to Lao Tzu (sixth century BCE).

579.2–5   Years after . . . building barricades] See *Building the Barricade* (*Budowałam barykadę*, 1979) by Polish poet Anna Świrszczyńska (1909–1984).

579.10   Robinson Jeffers] Jeffers (1887–1962) was an American poet and early icon of the environmental movement.

579.32   *panaka . . . chá*] Nisenan: woodpecker . . . oak tree.

580.3   Harriet Callicotte] Callicotte (1846–1888) was born in Green County, Kentucky, and buried in Carniero, Kansas; her daughter Lula Callicotte Wilkey (1870–1937) was Snyder's maternal grandmother.

580.16   *Tower Peak*] 11,755-foot mountain in the Sierra Nevada of California, at the northern boundary of Yosemite National Park.

583.20   channel-locks?] A brand of slip-joint pliers, designed to grip round objects, produced by Channellock since 1886.

583.29–30   This dolphin-drowned . . . sea.] See the final line of William Butler Yeats's "Byzantium," first collected in his *Words for Music Perhaps, and Other Poems* (1932).

584.1–2   *Samuel Palmer . . . Tate*] See *Moonlight, a Landscape with Sheep* (c. 1831–33) by British printmaker and landscape painter Samuel Palmer (1805–1881).

585.10   *Lew Welch*] See note 373.26.

MOUNTAINS AND RIVERS WITHOUT END

589.2–5   *Gen . . . Kyung-jin*] Snyder's sons with Masa Uehara, born in 1968 and 1969, and his adopted daughters, the children of Carole Koda, born in 1978 and 1983.

591.2   Milarepa] Jetsu Milarepa (c. 1052–c. 1135 CE), a semi-legendary Tibetan Buddhist disciple and poet.

591.17   Dōgen, "Painting of a Rice Cake"] A Japanese Zen master, poet, and philosopher, Dōgen Zenji (1200–1253) traveled to China as a young man and is credited with bringing the tradition of the Soto school to Japan on his return. His short essay "Painting of a Rice Cake" appears in his principal work, *Shōbō-genzō*.

595.2   *Ch'i Shan Wu Chin*] A twelfth-century Chinese hand scroll painted in ink and with slight coloration on silk, presently held in the Ingalls Library at the Cleveland Art Museum; its title translates as "Streams and Mountains Without End."

596.7 chinquapin] Common name applied to a variety of Chinese tree species in the genera *Castanopsis* and *Castanea*, and to several North American shrubs.

596.8 liquidambars] Trees in the genus *Liquidambar*, which includes species native to East Asia, North America, and Europe.

598.2 stamp the foot . . . turn] Movements characteristic of Japanese Noh drama.

599.12 *Highway 99*] See note 14.14.

599.26–27 Baxter . . . Raymond] See note 2.2–13.

600.2 Glacier and Marblemount] Locations in the North Cascades of Washington state, the latter the site of U.S. Forest Service district headquarters.

600.7 tin pants, snoose] Lumbermen commonly wear "tin pants," waterproofed by soaking them in paraffin; "snoose" is another name for snuff or finely powdered tobacco.

600.11 Dick Meigs] Richard L. Meigs (1924–2014), a fellow graduate of Reed College in the class of 1950, lived with his wife on a strawberry farm near Bellingham, Washington.

600.27 Mt. Vernon] County seat of Skagit County, Washington.

600.29 Kwakiutl] See note 77.16.

600.30 Burlington] City in Skagit County, Washington.

601.3 BC Riders] British Columbia motorcyclists.

601.6 Devil's Club] *Oplopanax horridus*, a shrub native to the Pacific Northwest; contact with its sharp, noxious spines can be extremely painful.

601.13 Salish] A Native American ethno-linguistic group of the Pacific Northwest.

601.16 Lake City] Snyder's boyhood hometown, now a section of Seattle, Washington.

601.23–24 "Forming the new . . . old"] See note 89.24–26.

601.27 Matsons] See note 103.1–2.

602.1–2 East Marginal Way . . . Duwamish slough] In the 1950s Boeing had extensive corporate and engineering facilities on East Marginal Way in south Seattle, alongside the Duwamish Waterway.

603.1 Centralia] Town in Lewis County, Washington, located between Seattle and Portland, Oregon.

603.14 Mary's Corner] Small town in Lewis County, Washington, south of Chehalis.

603.25 A.G.] Allen Ginsberg, who hitchhiked with Snyder through the Pacific Northwest in the winter of 1956.

603.28   Kelso] City near Mount St. Helens, in southwestern Washington.

604.12   Sokei-an] Also known as Shigetsu Sasaki (1882–1945), the first Zen master to settle permanently in the United States; in an attempt to understand the American character and its relationship to Zen, he wandered the American West, an original "Dharma bum."

604.24   Siuslaw] A river flowing from the mountains of Lane County, Oregon, to the Pacific, near Florence, Oregon.

604.27–28   Sujata . . . buttermilk] Believing that true knowledge might come from asceticism, Gautama and several companions undertook six years of physical hardships, including near starvation. When Gautama decided that extreme austerity was not necessary to achieve spiritual achievement, his first normal meal, said to be milk-rice, was offered to him by a milkmaid named Sujata.

605.6   the Siskiyou . . . Yreka] The Siskiyou Mountains extend from northwestern California to southwestern Oregon; Yreka is a small city in the Shasta Valley of northern California, south of the Siskiyou Mountains.

605.23   Carol & Billy's] Carol and Bill Baker (see note 473.1).

607.3   Six great highways] In Buddhist cosmology, within the endless cycle of birth, life, death, and rebirth known as saṃsāra there are six realms or paths, from the hellish *naraka* to the blissful *deva*.

608.14   Azalea, Myrtle Creek] Towns in Oregon, along present-day Interstate 5.

608.16   Project City] One of five communities built to support the construction of the Shasta Dam beginning in 1938, now part of the city of Shasta Lake, in Shasta County, California.

609.10   junction US 40   and highway 99] US 40, not to be confused with present-day Interstate 40, intersected with Highway 99 in Sacramento, California.

610.20   the Kalakala] A Puget Sound commuter ferry, in operation from 1935 to 1967.

610.34   cascara] See note 112.28.

611.3   Oregon grape and salal] Both evergreen natives with edible berries, Oregon grape may refer to a half dozen *Berberis* species; salal, *Gaulthiera shallon*, is in the heather family.

611.19   Get married in Vancouver] City in Washington state, north of Portland, where Snyder married Reed classmate Alison Gass in 1950.

612.35   Wu-t'ung trees] *Firmiana simplex* or Chinese parasol trees, often referred to or depicted in Chinese poetry and painting.

613.2   the Asp] The Anxious Asp, in San Francisco's North Beach neighborhood, was a popular Bohemian hangout from the late 1950s until 1967.

613.14   the Sunset] A neighborhood in San Francisco.

613.27   Stag, Argosy] Popular "men's adventure" magazines.

614.14   Paikaru and gyoza] A clear alcoholic beverage like the Chinese *baijiu*, fermented from sorghum and Japanese dumplings.

614.24–25   the Old Man] Oda Sessō Rōshi (1901–1966), Snyder's Zen teacher when he was studying at Daitoku-ji in Kyoto.

615.15   *The Elwha River*] Forty-five-mile long river on the Olympic Peninsula in Washington state.

616.16   *Bubbs Creek*] A tributary of the South Fork Kings River in the Sierra Nevada, flowing primarily within Kings Canyon National Park, California.

617.16   Locke] Locke McCorkle (see note 121.2).

617.19   Giant Orange] A chain of roadside juice stands founded in Tracy, California, in 1926.

617.34   tricouni] Brand name for a type of nail attached to the soles of mountain-climbing shoes.

617.36   Mark Tobey's scene] Tobey (1890–1976), who lived in and around Seattle for most of his life, was a painter associated with Abstract Expressionism, and a founding member of the Northwest School; like Snyder, he was a student of East Asian calligraphy.

617.38   Filson] C. C. Filson, founded in 1897 and now headquartered in Seattle, describes itself as "the premier outfitter for outdoorsmen . . . around the globe."

618.5–6   the green hat] In Jack Kerouac's novel *The Dharma Bums* (1958), Japhy Ryder—a character closely resembling Snyder—is said to possess "a funny green alpine cap that he wore when he got to the foot of a mountain . . . before starting to tromp up a few thousand feet."

618.13   Forester Pass] The highest point along the Pacific Crest Trail in the Sierra Nevada, on the boundary between Sequoia National Park and Kings Canyon National Park.

619.8   Parvati] Hindu goddess of fertility, beauty, harmony, and motherhood, the consort or wife of Shiva. Parvati (Sanskrit: daughter of the mountain) is the consort or wife of Shiva.

619.15   Shiva] See notes 224.19, 525.2.

619.16   Anahita] Persian goddess of fertility, water, healing, and wisdom.

619.17   Sarasvati] Along with Lakshmi and Parvati, Sarasvatī belongs to the Hindu *Tridevi*, the most important triad of great goddesses. Originally a river goddess, she is associated with knowledge and a love for harmony and rhythm as expressed in speech or music.

620.22   Whitney] Mt. Whitney in the Sierra Nevada, at over 14,500 feet the tallest mountain in the contiguous United States.

620.27   diamond drill] See note 77.20.

621.3   double mirror] See note 294.20.

621.9   sycamores of turquoise] In Egyptian mythology the sycamore tree stands at the eastern gate of heaven where the sun rises each morning out of darkness. Associated with the goddess Isis, it is known as the Tree of Life. Turquoise is prominent in the Egyptian death-and-resurrection story of Isis and Osiris (at times known, respectively, as "Lady of Turquoise" and "God of Turquoise").

621.12   Ras Tanura] A Saudi oil port.

621.17–19   boat of the sun . . . the waves before it] See the Egyptian *Book of the Dead* (c. 1550 BCE), as translated by E. A. Wallis Budge: "Rā sailed over the sky in two boats; the morning boat was called 'Mäntchet' . . . two fishes swam before the boat of Rā, and acted as pilots and warned him of coming danger."

621.25   Teilhard said . . . the planet"] See *The Phenomenon of Man* by French paleontologist and theologian Pierre Teilhard de Chardin (1881–1955), first published posthumously in 1955: "The dream upon which human research obscurely feeds is fundamentally that of mastering . . . the ultimate energy of which all other energies are merely servants; and thus, by grasping the very mainspring of evolution, seizing the tiller of the world."

622.8   AZURE RADIANCE TATHGATA] An epithet for the Buddha of Healing; the word *tathagata* indicates that the Buddha is beyond the world of transitory coming and going and therefore is "thus come."

622.15   Coyote old man] Discussing the Coyote figure in Native American myth and folklore in his essay "The Incredible Survival of Coyote," first published in *Western American Literature* in February 1975, Snyder comments: "Coyote Old Man. Not that he's 'old' now, in white-man times, but that he's always been old. Not the oldness of history, but the oldness of 'once upon a time'—outside history; in Dream Time, which surrounds us."

622.21   "Stewball"] English racehorse born in 1741 whose career, as an unlikely prospect who ultimately wins a race, became the subject of multiple folk ballads in Europe and America through the twentieth century.

622.24   Turquoise horse] In Navajo legend, the Sun-God, Johano-ai, rides a horse across the sky each day carrying the sun; when skies are blue, his horse is of turquoise.

623.6   svāhā] Used at the end of a mantra, a Sanskrit term roughly translatable as "amen" or "so be it."

623.25   Emperor Nimmyō] Nimmyō (810–850) reigned over Japan from 833 to 850, in the early Heian period.

623.26   Ono-no-Komachi] See note 160.15.

624.5–6   "Enchantment . . . up above"] From the song "San Antonio Rose," first recorded by Bob Wills and His Texas Playboys in 1938.

625.1   *Ramana Maharshi*] Sri Ramana Maharshi (1879–1950) was a Hindu saint who believed in self-realization as a means to enlightenment.

625.2   Ko-san] Sōkō Morinaga (see note 150.23).

625.15   *kam*] *kamp-, a Proto-Indo-European root, means "to bend, to curve."

625.18   Lazuli Bunting] *Passerina amoena*, a songbird with a bright blue head, named after the gemstone.

625.19   Kama, god of Love] In Hindu myth and iconography Kama or Kāmadeva carries a sugarcane bow and flower-tipped arrows to enhance desire.

625.20   Bhaishajyaguru . . . Yakushi] Sanskrit, Chinese, and Japanese names for the Buddha of Healing.

626.3–5   Glory of morning . . . "heavenly blue."] Ornamental cultivars of *Ipomoea tricolor*, commonly known as Mexican morning glory, the black seeds of which (*tlitliltzin*, in Nahuatl) contain LSD-like hallucinogenic compounds.

626.6   Amitabha] See note 29.7.

629.6–8   John Muir . . . Market] Muir (1838–1914), the Scottish American naturalist, managed his father-in-law's fruit ranch in Martinez, California, from 1881 to 1891, experimenting with high-value crops such as pears, and encouraging railroad expansion for agribusiness.

630.17   dongs and piastre] Vietnamese currency denominations.

630.31–32   Patna / long grain rice] A traditional rice variety, named after the capital of the Indian state of Bihar.

632.6   Varanasi] Also known as Benares, a city on the banks of the Ganges in Uttar Pradesh, India, and a major center for Hindu and Buddhist pilgrimage.

633.2   Genji] One of Snyder's cats when he lived in Kyoto, named after Prince Genji, whose exploits are narrated in Lady Murasaki's eleventh-century *Tale of Genji*. See also "The Genji Story" on page 480–81 of the present volume.

635.18   Lew] Lew Welch (see note 373.26).

637.1   *Mā*] According to Bob Steuding's *Gary Snyder* (1976), this poem reproduces the text of a letter Snyder found in an abandoned shack near his home at Kitkitdizze, written from mother to son. Mā, with the addition of a macron, is a Sanskrit word meaning both "mother" and "to form, make, build, construct."

638.2   Almanac] Most likely the western edition of *The Old Farmer's Almanac*, an American periodical published continuously since 1792, which includes information about the weather, astronomy, gardening, and planting, among other subjects.

641.26 *jinja*] A Shinto place of worship.

643.2–3 *When California . . . John Muir*] See Muir's essay "The Bee Pastures," collected in *The Mountains of California* (1894).

643.13 johnny-on-the-spots] Portable toilets.

643.15 floreals] Archaic: florals.

643.33 furz] A variant spelling of "furze," an evergreen shrub of the genus *Ulex*, with yellow flowers.

643.35 Blue Diamond Almonds] A brand name of Blue Diamond Growers, founded as the California Almond Grower's Exchange in 1910.

644.2–3 catfood . . . checkered sign] Ralston Purina, an animal-feed company founded in 1894, introduced its red and white "checkerboard" trademark in 1902.

644.15–24 *"The Great Central . . . might fly—"*] See note 643.2–3.

645.2 Fudo] The wrathful Buddhist deity Acala or Achala is known as Fudō Myō-ō in Japan, where he has been invoked as a defender of the nation; *yamabushi* mountain ascetics enshrine statues of him on peaks, in caves, and near waterfalls.

645.22–23 At Celilo . . . Warmspring] Celilo Falls, on the Columbia River at the border of Oregon and Washington state, was a longtime gathering place for various Native American tribes; the falls were submerged by the construction of the Dalles Dam in 1957.

647.8 Great Mind] See Dōgen Zenji's discussion of "the three minds" (*sanshin*) in his *Tenzo Kyokun* (*Instructions for the Chief Cook*, 1237); alongside "joyful mind" and "nurturing mind," the great or magnanimous mind "is like a mountain, stable and impartial. Exemplifying the ocean, it is tolerant and views everything from the broadest perspective."

649.24 *Bodhisattvas*] See note 16.15.

649.21–26 *"Why should we cherish . . . Avatamsaka Sūtra*] Known in English as the Flower Garland Sutra or Flower Ornament Sutra, the *Avatamsaka Sūtra* is a Mahayana Buddhist text anthologizing a variety of sutras written beginning around 100 CE; the epigraph is taken from a section of the sutra sometimes translated as "The Ten Vows of Samantabhadra Bodhisattva."

649.26 *Avatamsaka Sūtra*] Known in English as the Flower Garland Sutra or Flower Ornament Sutra, a Mahayana Buddhist text anthologizing a variety of sutras written beginning around 100 CE.

649.28–650.15 on the twenty-eighth day . . . before me."] A slightly altered version of the 1539 affidavit by which Francisco de Ulla took possession of Baja California for the Spanish.

650.16 SAN IGNACIO . . . REED CREEK] A town in northern Baja California Sur, Mexico, built on the Cochi settlement Kadakaamán ("Reed Creek.")

650.19 Casa Leree] A San Ignacio guesthouse, built in 1885.

650.25 Guerrero Negro] A salt-production center on the Baja California coast.

651.4 cardón] See note 327.8.

651.28–32 Charqui "jerky" . . . ch'arki] The English *jerky* comes from the American Spanish *charqui*, which in turn is from the Quechua *chárki*, meaning "dried flesh."

652.13 *Bos*] Genus containing the domestic cow, *Bos taurus*.

652.67 temedegua . . . Cochimi] The Temedegua—literally "valiant people"—were one of many Cochimi-speaking tribes inhabiting Baja California Sur.

653.4 Great Basin] A mostly arid region including parts of Nevada, Oregon, California, Utah, Idaho, Wyoming, and Baja California, lacking drainage to the sea.

653.14–16 the Pamir . . . Yamuna] Asian desert, mountain, and river regions through which Hsüan Tsang walked during his travels; a "doab" is a South Asian term for the land between two confluent rivers.

653.17–19 Sweetwater . . . San Juan] Rivers in North America and, in the case of the Amur, East Asia.

653.21 "emptiness"] *Śūnyatā*, often translated as "emptiness," is a Buddhist concept describing the interpenetrating, ever-flowing nature of all phenomena.

653.24 "mind only" / *vijñaptimātra*] Doctrine within the Yogācāra school of Buddhist philosophy, which teaches that objects lack reality except as part of consciousness or processes of knowing.

653.28 Canyon de Chelly] See note 258.29–259.2.

654.6 Nalanda] Site of an ancient university in what is now Bihar, India, after 400 CE a center of Mahāyāna Buddhist philosophy; see also note 169.12–30.

654.8 Diamond Seat . . . Vulture Peak] Thought to be the spot where the Buddha gained enlightenment, the Diamond Seat is an ancient stone slab located under the Bodhi tree, directly beside the Mahabodhi Temple at Bodh Gaya (Bihar, India). Vulture Peak, so named because it resembles a sitting vulture with its wings folded, is the mountainside in Rajgir, India, from which the Buddha delivered many central Mahāyāna sermons, such as the Heart Sutra and the Lotus Sutra.

654.13   Tārā, "Joy of Starlight"] See note 271.7–8.

654.15–19   Ghost bison . . . be gone.] Participants in the Ghost Dance move-
ment (see note 566.18) hoped, through dance, song, and prophecy, to bring
about an end to white expansion, reunite the living with the dead, and restore
traditional ways of life.

654.21   deep blue of Krishna] A major deity in Hinduism, Krishna is often
depicted as black- or blue-skinned.

655.6–7   Black Coyote . . . empty hat] According to an account reported
in James Mooney's *The Ghost-Dance Religion and the Sioux Outbreak of 1890*
(1896), when Wovoka—the spiritual leader of the Native American religious
movement known as the Ghost Dance (see note 566.18)—was asked for proof
that he was a legitimate prophet, he reached into his hat. Some witnesses saw
only "something black" emerge, but Southern Arapaho leader Black Coyote
(Watan-Gaa) looked into the hat and "saw the whole world."

655.19   the dragon in the spine] In Hinduism, *kundalini* ("coiled snake")
refers to a form of divine feminine energy residing at the base of the spine; this
energy may be awakened and channeled through meditation, breathing, or
chanting, leading to enlightenment.

658.5   Bristlecone Pine] The White Mountains of Inyo County, California,
sustain a grove of Great Basin bristlecone pines (*Pinus longaeva*), believed to
be the oldest non-clonal trees in the world, at 4,000 to 5,000 years old.

659.1–6   *The Circumambulation* . . . around Tam.] Snyder, Whalen, and
Ginsberg made this journey on October 22, 1965, chanting from Buddhist and
Hindu texts at points along their route.

659.11   Prajñāpāramitrā-hridaya-sūtra] Sanskrit title of the Heart Sutra (sev-
enth century CE), a central text of Mahāyāna Buddhism.

659.12   Dhāranī] In Buddhism, a ritual incantation or chant containing
esoteric words or syllables believed to convey protection or special powers on
utterance.

659.13   Four Vows] In Zen Buddhism there are four Bodhisattva vows: "Be-
ings are numberless, I vow to save them. Desires are inexhaustible, I vow to
end them. Dharma gates are boundless, I vow to enter them. Buddha's way is
unsurpassable, I vow to become it."

659.20   California laurel leaves] The leaves of the California bay tree, *Umbel-
lularia californica*, are highly aromatic.

659.27   chörten] A monument, often containing relics, constructed in mem-
ory of a Buddhist saint.

660.3   the Dipsea] Trail running from Mill Valley, California, to the Pacific.

660.6   Hari Om Namo Shiva] A Sanskrit mantra: "I bow to Lord Shiva."

660.16   saddhu] In Hinduism and Jainism, a religious ascetic.

660.21   gomoku-no-moto] Mixed vegetables, usually in soy sauce.

660.27   Om Shri Maitreya] A mantra in honor of Maitreya, the future Buddha who will teach enlightenment in the next age.

661.11   Mt. St. Helena] Mountain in Sonoma County, California (not to be confused with Mount St. Helens in Washington state).

662.5   Gopala Mantra] A mantra recited in honor of Krishna, who as a baby was called "Gopala" or "protector of cows."

662.16–17   shaking the staff / rings] The *shakujo*, a Buddhist monk's ceremonial staff with noise-making rings at its tip, is sometimes shaken during sutra recitation.

662.18   *The Canyon Wren*] Snyder published a slightly different version of this poem in *Axe Handles* (1983); see pages 447–49 in the present volume.

664.4   *Dibée*] Koyukon: sheep.

664.9   "by the midnight breezes strewn"] See "The Cloud," a poem by Percy Bysshe Shelley (1792–1822) first published in his collection *Prometheus Unbound* (1820).

664.25   Doonerak] Mountain in Alaska's central Brooks Range, now part of the Gates of the Arctic National Park.

665.15   Vajra] See note 77.20.

665.15   Koyukuk] A river in central Alaska, the Koyukuk is a tributary of the Yukon.

665.17   "The beat of her unseen feet"] See note 664.9.

665.28   Dall sheep horns] Mature males of the species *Ovis dalli*—a native sheep inhabiting subarctic mountain ranges in Alaska and western Canada—have thick, curved horns.

666.6   Midnight Mountain] A peak next to Mt. Doonerak in the Brooks Range.

666.26   to unbuild it again] Marpa the Translator (Marpa Lotsāwa, 1012–1097), a Tibetan Buddhist teacher, instructed his disciple Milarepa (see note 591.2) to build and unbuild multiple stone towers as an act of purification.

666.27–31   Koyukon riddle . . . who am I?"] See Richard Dauenhauer, "Koyukon Riddle-Poems," *Alcheringa 3* (1977); Dauenhauer's texts are reworkings of those published by Father Julius Jetté in "Riddles of the Ten'a Indians," *Anthropos*, January–February 1913.

667.13   *New York Bedrock*] The bedrock in which New York's skyscrapers are anchored, the Manhattan Schist, is exposed in some city parks.

668.13   prana-subtle] *Prana* is Sanskrit for "breath," "life force," or "soul."

669.5   "Claus the Wild Man"] Also known as Clause de Wilt or Claus the Indian Interpreter (fl. 1676–1701), a member of the Reckgawawanc tribe who acted as translator and political leader in the area around what is now Washington Heights, in upper Manhattan.

669.8   "Karacapacomont"] A "Squaw of the Weckquaesgeek" who, with her son Nemeran, sold the Reckgawawanc tribe's last landholdings on Manhattan Island to the Van Cortlandt family in 1701.

669.14   Couloir] A steep, narrow gully or crevasse in an otherwise solid mountain mass.

669.31   "the water lilies"] A series of impressionist paintings by Claude Monet (1840–1926), produced from 1896 to 1925.

671.9   arêtes] Edges formed by the meeting of two planes; in mountaineering, ridgelines formed by the meeting of two slopes.

672.5–6   *Haida Gwai . . . Hiellen River*] The Hiellen River meets the sea at Naikoon Beach, also known as Rose Point or Rose Spit, on Graham Island in the Haida Gwaii archipelago off mainland British Columbia, Canada; *Haida Gwaii* means "islands of the Haida people."

674.3–5   *Have you seen . . . this way?*] Snyder's adaptation of a traditional Ladakhi folk song.

674.6   Senge Chhu] "Lion River," Tibetan name for the Indus or its principal source.

674.8   Tethys Sea] During the Mesozoic Era, an ocean separating the supercontinents of Laurasia and Gondwana.

674.11   Sutlej] A tributary of the Indus, flowing through northern India and Pakistan.

674.14   Leh] Present-day capital of the Ladakh territory of India, and historical capital of the Himalayan Kingdom of Ladakh; Snyder attended the Ladakh Ecological Development Group conference in Leh in 1992.

674.28   "The long wide tongue of the Buddha"] In the Lotus Sutra, the Buddha is said to have a long broad tongue, an attribute conventionally interpreted as a sign of truth-telling. Song dynasty poet Su Shi (Su Dongpo, 1036–1101), in a verse presented to his Chan master Changzong, famously heard this "long broad tongue" in the sound of a stream beside Mt. Lu, an episode Snyder recounts in "We Wash Our Bowls in This Water" (see pages 697–99 in the present volume).

675.8   *gompa*] Tibetan Buddhist monastery or temple.

675.9   twa corbies] See note 260.24.

5 NOTES

675.23 *puja*] In Hinduism and Buddhism, an act or ceremony of worship or propitiation.

675.28–32 *In the lofty sky . . . remain unchanged.*] Snyder's adaptation of lines from a Ladakhi marriage song.

675.33 Angdu's] Snyder's guide when he explored Leh and its surroundings with his son Gen, in 1992.

676.18–19 Himalaya . . . Storehouse] The Sanskrit word *Himālaya* literally translates as "snow storehouse" or "snow dwelling."

676.24 naked Blue Samantabhadra] In Tibetan Nyingma tradition, Samantabhadra is the first or primordial Buddha, often depicted naked and blue in meditation.

676.25 Kalachakra] In Vajrayana Buddhism, Kalachakra means "wheel of time," but it is also the name of a series of Buddhist texts and a major practice lineage in Indo-Tibetan Buddhism.

676.25 Yamantaka] The "destroyer of death" deity of Vajrayana Buddhism.

677.6 "Black as bees . . . hair"] From a hymn to Tārā by Ngawang Lobsang Gyatso (1617–1682), the fifth Dalai Lama.

678.13 chang] Also spelled *chhaang*, a Tibetan and Nepalese alcoholic drink made of fermented barley, rice, or millet.

679.1 shawms] A European woodwind instrument, the *shawm* is similar to the Tibetan *gyaling* or "Chinese flute," used in religious observances.

679.18–23 *On the lofty mountain . . . unchanged.*] See note 675.28–32.

679.24 *The Bear Mother*] See note 288.4.

680.7 Nanren Lake] Lake in Kenting National Park in southern Taiwan; Snyder attended the Second International Conference on Literature and Religion at Fu Jen University in Taipei in September 1990.

685.5 Coyote and Earthmaker] See note 91.25–26.

687.4–6 *Raven's Beak River . . .* Alsek Lake] The Tatshenshini River (sometimes referred to as Raven's Beak River) flows into the Alsek River and Alsek Lake at the northern boundary of Glacier Bay National Park, in southeastern Alaska.

689.24–26 Hopi . . . Cahuilla] Native American tribes or northeastern Arizona and southern California, respectively.

690.6–7 "sagebrush of the glaciers . . . Rimbaud] In a letter of June 1872 to his friend Ernest Delahaye, French poet Arthur Rimbaud (1854–1891) describes absinthe as the "sauvage de glaciers."

690.10 Artemis] See note 94.6.

690.25–27   *Hail, Artemisia . . . other poems.*] Snyder's adaptation of lines from the Homeric "Second Hymn to Artemis."

691.1   *Cross-Legg'd*] Figuratively, this phrase may refer to a sitting position suitable for meditation, as well as to the Tantric practice known as "yab-yum," the primordial union of wisdom and compassion, depicted as a male deity in union with his female consort through interpenetration.

693.9   all this realm . . . ten miles long] Adams Inlet, in Alaska's Glacier Bay National Park.

694.7   Izanami] In Japanese mythology, Izanagi and his sister-wife Izanami are held to be the creators of the Japanese archipelago and the progenitors of many deities, including the sun goddess Amaterasu, the moon deity Tsuku-yomi, and the storm god Susanoo.

694.17   "Shining Heavens"] An epithet for Amaterasu, sun goddess in Japanese mythology.

694.18   her brother] Amaterasu's younger brother, Susanoo, is depicted as having contradictory qualities; as a storm god he acts impulsively at times yet in other stories he is a heroic figure.

694.23   Ame-no-uzume] In the Shinto religion, goddess of dawn, mirth, meditation, revelry, and the arts.

694.24   Mt. Kagu] Also known as Mount Amanokagu, one of the "three mountains of Yamato" (now Nara Prefecture) celebrated in Japanese poetry.

694.25   nishikigi] The winged spindle or Japanese brocade tree, *Euonymous alatus*.

695.8   *mai*] Traditional Japanese dance style associated with Noh drama.

696.2   *hi-kage* vine] *Hikage-no-kazura*, a clubmoss (*Lycopodium clavatum*) also known as ground pine.

696.3   *ma-saki* vine . . . sasa] *Trachelospermum asiaticum* or Asiatic jasmine, a vine with sweet-smelling white flowers, and Sasa, a bamboo genus.

696.17   omoshiri] interestingness.

698.24   Mt. Lu] Also known as Mount Lushan, a celebrated peak in Jiangxi province, China.

699.22   Payahu Nadu] The Owens Valley was called Payahu Nadu, the "Place of Flowing Water," by the ancient Numu people, ancestors of the Paiute.

699.27   the bristlecone pines] See note 658.5

700.10   Last Chance range] Mountain range in Inyo County, California, near the Nevada border.

701.7   the valleys "Salt" and "Death"] Saline Valley and Death Valley, both now located within Death Valley National Park, northeast of Los Angeles.

701.21–702.4 *"Bitter ghosts . . . all for?"*] Snyder's adaptation of lines from the Noh play *Yamamba*, attributed to Zeami Motokiyo (c. 1363–1443).

702.8–9 the Mountain Spirit . . . ragged hair?] Yamamba, a Japanese mythological figure featured in the Noh play of the same title, resembles this "Mountain Spirit."

703.34–35 *"When the axe-strokes . . . deeper*] Snyder's adaptation of lines from the Noh play *Yamamba*.

704.26 Vimalakilrti's . . . room] See note 492.23.

706.1 *Earth Verse*] This poem, Snyder noted in *A Sense of the Whole: Reading Gary Snyder's "Mountains and Rivers Without End"* (2015), "was written in the incredibly lonely Musgrave mountains of the central Australian desert."

706.11–12 a fierce gay poet . . . dangerous girl] Snyder traveled with Allen Ginsberg and Martine Algier (b. 1942) in September 1965.

706.16 Alvord desert] A dry lakebed located southeast of the Steens Mountains in southeastern Oregon.

706.18 Vya] A ghost town in northwestern Nevada.

707.15–18 carved stone inscriptions . . . DeWayne Williams] Folk artist De-Wayne "Doobie" Williams (1918–1995) created a series of rock sculptures and inscriptions in the Black Rock Desert near Gerlach, Nevada, from 1978 to 1992. Snyder published *Dooby Lane: A Testament Inscribed in Stone Tablets*, a book about the site, in 1996; an expanded edition appeared in 2016.

707.21 Lake Lahontan] A Pleistocene lake that once filled a large portion of the present-day Great Basin.

707.23 Columbian Mammoth] *Mammuthus columbi*, an extinct North American mammoth species.

708.22 King Lear] A summit in the Jackson Mountains of Humboldt County, Nevada, overlooking the Black Rock Desert to the west.

711.37–38 Hugo Munsterberg . . . landscape painting] See *The Landscape Painting of China and Japan* (1955); Munsterberg (1916–1995) was a founder of the art history department at SUNY New Paltz.

713.2 *hakama*] Traditional Japanese trouser- or skirt-like attire, worn over a kimono.

713.19 *kami*] In Shintoism, a local deity or genius loci.

714.3 Cid Corman] See note 129.22.

717.26 Paul Shepard] Shepard (1925–1996), an environmentalist and author, taught at Pitzer College and Claremont Graduate University.

719.20 Peter Coyote] An American actor, director, and author, born Robert Peter Cohon in 1941.

721.26 Sherman Paul] Paul (1920–1995), an English professor, was the author of many books including *In Search of the Primitive: Re-reading David Antin, Jerome Rothenberg, and Gary Snyder* (1986).

722.18 Ursula Le Guin] Le Guin (1929–2018) is most often remembered for her prize-winning works of speculative fiction.

DANGER ON PEAKS

725.4 Sahaptin] Language spoken by several Native American tribal groups in parts of Idaho, Oregon, and Washington, referred to by Native speakers as Ichishkin.

727.15 (back then) 9,677 feet] Mount St. Helens erupted on May 18, 1980, killing 57 people and losing approximately 1,300 feet in height.

728.4 Trapper Nelson packboards] Backpacks, based on an Inuit design, featuring a wooden frame and an easily detachable canvas bag; they were patented by Lloyd F. Nelson in 1924.

728.12 glissaded] Descended a snow-covered slope on one's feet or buttocks, controlling one's slide with one's feet or an ice axe.

728.21 schrund] From the German *bergschrund*, a crevasse formed when flowing glacier ice separates from immobile ice; often dangerous to mountaineers.

728.25 Mazama] Founded in 1894, the Mazamas are a Pacific Northwest mountaineering club with headquarters in Portland; Snyder earned membership in the club as a teenager.

728.28 alpenstock] A wooden staff capped at one end with an iron or steel spike, used in mountaineering.

729.6 Issa's] Known for his haiku poems and journals, Kobayashi Issa (1763–1828), better known simply as Issa (a pen name meaning "Cup-of-tea"), was a Japanese poet and lay Buddhist priest of the Pure Land sect.

729.16 five-colored banners] Tibetan prayer flags come in sets of five traditionally arranged from left to right in a specific order: blue (sky-space), white (air-wind), red (fire), green (water), and yellow (earth).

730.27 Robin] Robin Collins Coffee (see note 134.15).

732.7 tephra] Material ejected by an erupting volcano.

732.13 Fred Swanson] Frederick J. Swanson (b. 1943), an emeritus research geologist with the USDA Forest Service, specializes in the interrelations between geology and ecology in volcanic regions.

732.18 Dick Meigs] See note 600.11.

733.13 *lahar*] A violent slurry of pyroclastic material, rocky debris, and water flowing down from a volcano, typically along a river valley.

734.24   fireweed] *Chamaenerion angustifolium*, a wildflower able to spread rapidly in areas burned by fire.

735.7   Pele] Hawaiian goddess of volcanoes and fire.

735.8   Fudo] See note 645.2.

737.11   Han'-gul writing system] Alphabetic system used for writing the Korean language; it consists of 24 letters, including 14 consonants and 10 vowels.

737.31   chaco] An outdoor footwear brand originally specializing in sandals for river guides, founded in Chaco, Colorado, in 1989.

738.13   detritus-cycle] See note 349.33.

739.14   Loowit, lawilayt-lá, *Smoky Mâ*] Klickitat and Cowlitz names for Mount St. Helens, *lawilayt-lá* meaning "smoker" or "smoky"; the Sanskrit *mā* means both "mother" and "to form, make, build, construct."

739.15   gracias xiexie] "Thank you" in Spanish and Mandarin Chinese.

740.5   *wadis*] An Arabic term, dry riverbeds that contain water only when heavy rain occurs.

740.24   lake . . . *yin*] In Chinese cosmology, yin-yang describes interdependent complimentary forces; the lake is *yin*, the mountain *yang*.

743.2–3   PUTAH CREEK] Eighty-five-mile-long northern California creek running through Yolo, Solano, Napa, and Lake Counties; a creekside riparian reserve forms part of the campus of the University of California at Davis, where Snyder taught beginning in 1986.

743.16–17   *Eldridge Moores & Kim Stanley Robinson*] Moores (1938–2018) was a professor in the Earth and Planetary Sciences Department at the University of California at Davis. Robinson (b. 1952) is a writer of science fiction whose novels and stories often have ecological themes.

743.20   nomex] A flame-resistant synthetic fabric.

744.23   zendo] In the summer of 1892, Snyder and friends built "Ring of Bone," a zendo in the meadow behind his house at Kitkitdizze.

747.3   *Aravaipa Canyon*] The Aravaipa Canyon Wilderness, which includes the 11-mile-long Aravaipa Canyon, forms the northwest border of the Galiuro mountain range in Arizona.

747.4   MIMULUS] Monkeyflowers (genus *Mimulus*) are California native plants that offer bright, profusely blooming color.

747.12–16   TERCEL . . . the way they do.] The Tercel was a subcompact car model manufactured by Toyota from 1978 to 1999.

748.1   James Lee Jobe] Jobe (b. 1956) has served as poet laureate of Davis, California, since 2018.

748.14 redds] Spawning beds made by fish, especially salmon or trout, by clearing gravel from river bottoms.

748.14 Parks Bar] Gravel bar along the south fork of the Yuba River in Yuba County, California, the site of extensive gold-mining operations beginning in 1848.

748.21 *glacial erratic*] A non-local rock, deposited by a glacier.

749.22 Sierra Buttes] Sierra Buttes, a dominant peak in the northern Sierra Nevada, is the highest point in the Plumas National Forest, north of Snyder's home at Kitkitdizze.

751.7 KJ] Kyung-jin Robin (b. 1983), Carole Koda's adopted daughter and Snyder's stepdaughter.

751.13 Nanao] Nanao Sakaki (see note 141.11).

755.2 Laughlin's *Collected* . . . J] James Laughlin (1914–1997) founded New Directions, one of Snyder's publishers, in 1936; his *Collected Poems* appeared in 1994.

755.10 Pound at St. Elizabeth's?] Poet Ezra Pound (1885–1972) was confined at St. Elizabeth's, a Washington, D.C., psychiatric hospital, from 1945 to 1958.

755.27 Burt Watson's . . . Shu Shih] Watson's *Selected Poems of Su Tung-p'o*, gathering the works of the Song dynasty poet also known as Su Shih (1037–1101), was published in 1994.

755.30–31 Watershed Institute . . . B.L.M.] The Yuba Watershed Institute, formed in 1995 to protect biodiversity and promote sustainable use of natural resources within the Yuba River watershed, and the U.S. Bureau of Land Management, with which the institute has cooperative agreements.

756.16 Ko Un] Born in Japanese occupied Korea, Ko (b. 1933) is a novelist, poet, translator, and activist; Allen Ginsberg described him as "a magnificent poet, a combination of Buddhist cognoscente, passionate political libertarian, and naturalist historian."

756.22 Kevin Starr] Starr (1940–2017), at the time of his death a professor of history at the University of Southern California, served as California State Librarian from 1994 to 2004.

757.5 his strong wife Sang-wha] An emeritus professor in the English Department of Chung Ang University, Seoul, Lee Sang-Wha has published translations from Korean into English and vice versa, including two of Snyder's prose works.

757.13 Ok-ku] Born in Gwangju, South Korea, Ok-Koo Kang Grosjean (1940–2000) emigrated to the United States in 1963; she translated many works from Korean into English and vice versa, including Snyder's *No Nature* (1992), and published books of poetry, including *A Hummingbird's Dance* (1994).

757.17 *soju*] A clear, colorless, distilled alcoholic beverage of Korean origin (not to be confused with Japanese *shoyu*, soy sauce).

757.25–26 *the bay that now bears his name*] Drakes Bay, a feature of the Point Reyes National Seashore, is approximately 30 miles northwest of San Francisco.

757.32 Edo Woodcut] See note 207.14.

758.18 Charlie Johnson] No longer operational, Johnson's Oyster Company was founded by Charles Johnson in 1957 on the Drake Estero. His method for growing oysters used a technique developed by the Japanese of suspending the oysters on wires hung from racks.

758.33 sierra-cup of Gallo sherry] A "sierra-cup" is used for camping or backpacking; Gallo is a well-known winery and distributor headquartered in California.

759.1 a sip of Sack] A generic term, *sack* is an old synonym for *sherry* derived from the English usage referring to wine from Jerez, Spain, as "Sherris sack."

759.5 *Summer of '97*] Snyder's family and friends gathered in the summer of 1997 to assist in the renovation of his home at Kitkitdizze.

759.20 Bollingen for bucks] In 1997 Snyder won the $50,000 Bollingen Prize for Poetry, awarded by the Beinecke Library at Yale.

761.18–24 Cosumnes River . . . Lost Slough] Lost Slough, and the confluence of the Cosumnes and the Mokelumne, are just north of Mokelumne City in San Joaquin County, California.

761.28 Locke] An unincorporated town in Sacramento County, California, listed as a National Historic Landmark District in 1990 because of its history as a Chinese American rural community.

763.18 duff layers] Layers of decomposing organic matter on the forest floor, between mineral soil underneath and leaf litter above.

763.25 cambium layer] The growing part of the trunk of a tree, which annually produces new bark and new wood.

763.30 *Sarvamangalam*] A Sanskrit mantra meaning "May all be well" or "Good luck to all."

763.32 *Star Fire*] From August 25 to September 13, 2001, the Star Fire burned over 15,000 acres of the Eldorado National Forest, the Tahoe National Forest, and private land.

764.7 Stihl] German manufacturer of chainsaws and other handheld power equipment.

765.14 my craft friend Holly] Holly Tornheim (see note 395.17).

765.19–26 *Mariano Vallejo's . . . the Casa*] Vallejo (1807–1890), a Mexican military commander of Alta California and political leader in the new U.S. state of California from 1850 onwards, had Casa Grande constructed at Sonoma in 1836; it was mostly destroyed by fire in 1867. He expanded his library in 1831, when a collection of books forbidden by church authorities, the property of a German merchant, was discovered aboard the ship *Leonor*; he bought the books from the owner for 400 hides and 10 skins of tallow.

765.27   the old adobe] Vallejo ordered the construction of the Rancho Petaluma Adobe, a large ranch house, in 1836; it is now part of the Petaluma Adobe State Historic Park.

765.30   my sister's *Empty Shell* book] Thea Snyder Lowry published *Empty Shells: The Story of Petaluma, America's Chicken City* in 2000.

765.32–766.1   Charles Krug . . . Haraszthy] Krug (1825–1892) and Haraszthy (1812–1869) were pioneering California winemakers, the former founding the Charles King Winery in the Napa Valley in 1861 and the latter the Buena Vista Winery in Sonoma in 1857.

766.10–11   jimson weed . . . dark leaf] See notes 86.6 and 296.21.

767.9   the Bardo] See note 84.31.

771.7   *Claws / Cause*] Also published, in slightly different form, in *This Present Moment*; see page 842–43 in the present volume.

771.8   *Zenshin*] Zenshin Ryufu (see note 117.4).

771.23   corroboree] A term from an Australian aboriginal language for a ceremonial or celebratory meeting of peoples, usually including dance and music.

772.7   "Subaru"] Japanese name for the Pleiades star cluster.

773.9   *Maggie Brown Koller*] Brown (b. 1960?), the daughter of Bill and Zoe Brown, proprietors of Coyote Press, and later the wife of James Koller (1936–2014), editor of *Coyote's Journal*, had her ears pierced by Snyder when she was a girl in Bolinas.

774.12   Jean Koda] After internment during World War II, Yayeko Jean Koda (1919–2011) worked first with her husband and then with her brother-in-law to grow the family business, the Koda rice farm, in South Dos Palos, California.

775.9   *Sus*] The genus *Sus* includes domestic pigs (*Sus domesticus*) and their ancestor, the common Eurasian wild boar (*Sus scrofa*), along with other species.

776.1–3   Buttonwillow . . . Lake Tulare] A small community in Kern County, California, at the southern end of the San Joaquin Valley, where Lake Tulare extended over 500 square miles as recently as the mid-nineteenth century. Since that time, dams and canals for agricultural and municipal use have made Tulare a dry lake.

776.18   *Seamus Heaney*] Heaney (1939–2013), an Irish poet, playwright, and translator, was awarded the 1995 Nobel Prize in Literature.

777.12   *Philip Zenshin Whalen*] See note 117.4.

778.1 *Carole*] Carole Koda (see note 578.2).

778.23–24 *Slickhorn . . . San Juan River*] Containing multiple Ancestral Puebloan ruins and pictographs, Slickhorn Canyon sits at the southern edge of Cedar Mesa in Utah, eventually meeting the San Juan River within Glen Canyon National Recreation Area.

782.11 *Lost Slough, Cosumnes*] See note 761.18–24.

783.28 Jirka and Etsuko] Jirko Wein, a Czech-born maker of artisanal wood-stoves, and his wife Etsuko Seki, a weaver, live in the village of Inadani in the Japanese Alps.

783.30 Bobbu] Poet, musician, and peace activist Bob Uchida (b. 1952), a friend from Banyan Ashram.

784.10 My friend Deane] Deane Swickard, the head of the Folsom, California, office of the Bureau of Land Management.

785.20 Shandel] Sally ("Shandel") Parks (see note 193.11).

786.23 Toula Siete] Sieti (b. 1948), as her name is more often transliterated, is a former city planner who has translated Günter Grass, Thomas Mann, William Trevor, Joseph Roth, and others into Greek.

788.14 Shawna] Shawna Yang Ryan (b. 1976), author of the novel *Water Ghosts* (2009).

789.6 *kopje*] South African word for a small, isolated hill.

790.9 Mark Tobey] See note 617.36.

793.8 *grus canadensis*] The sandhill crane, now known as *Antigone canadensis.*

794.9 *The Heike Monogatari*] Also known as the Tale of the Heike, an epic account, compiled prior to 1330, of the struggle between the Taira and Mina-moto clans for control of Japan at the end of the twelfth century.

795.2 Bamiyan] The Buddhas of Bamiyan were two sixth-century monumen-tal statues of Vairocana Buddha and Gautama Buddha carved into the side of a cliff in the Bamiyan Valley of central Afghanistan; the statues were destroyed in March 2001 by the Taliban.

797.21–22 intra-samsaric] In Buddhist and Hindu cosmology, saṃsāra refers to the cycle of birth, existence, death, and rebirth that can only end when a person extinguishes desire and gains insight into impermanence and the reality of non-selfhood.

797.28 Issa's] See note 729.6.

798.6–14 A person who . . . simple realization."] See "Fallen Idols," an essay by Christopher Hitchens (1949–2011), an Anglo-American journalist and critic, published in *The Nation* on April 2, 2001.

799.13 Jeffers] Robinson Jeffers (see note 579.10).

800.23 Gold Dragon Mountain, Thunder Gate] Sensō-ji is also known in Japanese as Kin Ryu Zan, or Golden Dragon Mountain; the outer gate of the temple with red pillars is the Kaminarimon, or Thunder Gate.

800.26 Edo] Originally a fishing village, Edo grew to become the seat of the Tokugawa shogunate in 1603, and in 1868, following the end of the shogunate, the imperial capital, renamed "Tokyo."

800.30 Sumida River] River flowing through central Tokyo and into Tokyo Bay.

801.4–7 ("Form, sensation . . . no fear.")] From the seventh-century Heart Sutra.

801.24 *Mahāprajñāpāramitā*] A collection of sixteen Buddhist texts, including the Heart Sutra and the Diamond Sutra, known as "The Perfection of Wisdom"; the word *mahāprajñāpāramitā* is roughly translated in the penultimate line of Snyder's poem: "great wisdom of the path that goes beyond."

THIS PRESENT MOMENT

809.5 briggs & stratton] An American engine manufacturer, founded in 1908.

809.10 frass] Insect excrement and exuviae.

810.1 Tom] Tom Killion (b. 1953), an artist, printmaker, and historian, with whom Snyder has collaborated on illustrated books, including *The High Sierra of California* (2002), *Tamalpais Walking* (2009), and *California's Wild Edge: The Coast in Poetry, Painting, and History* (2016).

810.9 *Thornapple*] *Datura stramonium*, a flowering plant in the nightshade family sometimes used as a hallucinogen.

810.17 *The desert smells like rain*] See *The Desert Smells Like Rain: A Naturalist in Papago Indian Country* (1982) by nature writer and ethnobiologist Gary Paul Nabhan (b. 1952). Snyder sent Nabhan a copy of the poem in 2007.

810.20–21 two dams . . . came down] Removal work on the Glines Canyon Dam began September 15, 2011, and on the Elwha Dam on September 19, 2011.

811.16 puncheon] See note 53.22.

811.21 *Charles Freer*] Freer (1854–1919), an industrialist, left his large art collection to the Smithsonian Institution. The Freer Gallery of Art is located on the National Mall in Washington, D.C.

812.5–6 "Rivers and Mountains . . . Freer] *Mountains and Rivers Without End*, a Qing dynasty scroll painting in ink on paper at the Freer, attributed to Lu Yuan (fl. mid- to late seventeenth century), measures approximate 11 by 195 inches; it was previously believed to be the work of Xu Ben.

813.16 *Artemis and Pan*] Artemis, Greek goddess of the hunt, the wilderness, wild animals, the moon, and chastity; her symbols include a bow and arrow, a quiver, and hunting knives. Pan is the god of the wild, flocks, and forests; he has the hindquarters, legs, and horns of a goat, and is often affiliated with sexuality.

813.17–19 "The wildness . . . THOREAU] See Thoreau's essay "Walking," first published in *The Atlantic* in May 1862.

813.20–21 The "field" . . . *iworu*] "The original inhabitants of Japan, the Ainu," Snyder writes in his 1983 essay "Good, Wild, Sacred," "can see a whole system as in a very special sense sacred. Their term *iworu* means 'field' with implications of watershed, plant and animal life, and spirit force."

814.11 his wrath . . . Achilles] Achilles (in Homer's *Iliad*), enraged when his concubine and intended wife Briseis is taken from him by Agamemnon, king of Mycenae, withdraws from the battlefield, with tragic consequences for the Greeks.

815.1–9 *M.A.* . . . sister's name] Snyder visited Melissa Aston (b. 1973) and her family—Tim (1942–2008), Jean (b. 1948), Ramona (b. 1973), and Gabriel (b. 1971)—on Quadra Island, in British Columbia, around 1986; they had previously helped in the building of the Ring of Bone zendo at Kitkitdizze.

819.1 *Actaeon's Hounds*] See note 164.17.

820.2 the Palace of the Governors] A Spanish colonial administration building constructed in 1610, and the home since 1909 of the Museum of New Mexico.

821.4 *nag*-worship songsters] In Kerala, the *naagampatikal*, members of the *pulluran* caste, are the singers of snake songs on occasions set aside for snake-worship, such as Naga (or Nag) Panchami.

821.6 *marumakkathayam*] In Kerala, a system of matrilineal inheritance; the word literally means "inheritance by sisters' children."

824.13–15 affluent foreigners . . . write a book] Perhaps a reference to Frances Mayes's best-selling memoir *Under the Tuscan Sun: At Home in Italy* (1996), which includes recipes along with her narrative about the restoration of an abandoned villa in the Tuscan countryside.

824.28 Berry] Wendell Berry (see note 386.18–19).

825.16 *Michael des Tombe*] Born in The Hague, Netherlands, des Tombe (1941–2003)—an editor, writer, artist, and activist—came to live on San Juan Ridge in the 1970s and served as president of the South Yuba River Citizens League.

825.26 Tove . . . Za] Charlotte "Tove" Killgrew (b. 1939), Michael's wife, and her children.

827.4 *mala*] A string of prayer beads, commonly used in South Asian religions.

827.7 *Chiura Obata's Moon*] Obata (1885–1975), a Japanese American artist remembered for his landscapes in a variety of media, produced the color woodblock print *Evening Moon, Yosemite* as part of his 1930 "World Landscape Series"; see Snyder's recollection of him on page 711 of the present volume.

828.1–2 Jack and Nancy Todd . . . tilapia] In 1969, the Canadian marine biologist John Todd (b. 1939), his wife Nancy Jack Todd (b. 1938), and William McLarney (b. 1940), a freshwater fisheries biologist, founded the New Alchemy Institute on Cape Cod to develop technologies for sustainable living, including "solar ponds" stocked with tilapia, windmills, and organic sewage treatment systems.

829.4 crofters spade] Also known as a foot plough or *cas-chrom*, an implement traditionally used by Scottish tenant farmers for working difficult ground, with a heavy wooden handle bent near its lower end, and a sharpened piece of iron for a cutting edge.

830.7 let your people go] See Exodus 5:1.

831.16–18 Forest Hill . . . Sailor Meadow] Localities in Placer County, California, in the Sierra Nevada Mountains, west of Lake Tahoe.

831.28 *Barefoot Gen*] Japanese historical manga series by Keiji Nakazawa (1939–2012), first published in *Weekly Shōnen Jump* from 1973 to 1987 and inspired by Nakazawa's experiences as a survivor of Hiroshima.

833.4 the corral of Capella] Capella, from the Latin for "little goat," is the brightest apparent star in the constellation Auriga, the latter historically imagined to represent a goat herd. Modern astronomy has shown Capella to be a system of four stars.

842.10–11 *Claws / Cause*] Snyder also included this poem in *Danger on Peaks* (2004), in slightly different form; see page 771 in the present volume.

843.7–19 *Hai-en Temple . . . Triple Basket*] Haeinsa, a ninth-century Buddhist temple in the Gaya Mountains, west of Daegu, South Korea, houses over 80,000 thirteenth-century wooden printing blocks for the Korean *Tripitaka* or "triple basket," a collection of Buddhist texts noted for its completeness and accuracy.

844.16 *Mu Ch'i's Persimmons*] See note 538.34.

844.20 sumi painting] East Asian *sumi-e* or ink wash paintings are produced with brush and inkstick or *sumi*, made from soot and animal glue, on paper.

845.7 Benrido] A Kyoto printing establishment specializing in collotype fine-art reproductions.

845.12 Mike and Barbara's orchard] Mike Getz (b. 1939) and Barbara Getz (b. 1949) are long-term residents of the San Juan Ridge community.

845.20–21 *Dōgen . . . rice-cake.*"] See note 591.17.

845.22–846.9 *Bend in the Vlatava . . . Hrad*] The Vltava—the longest river in the Czech Republic, sometimes Anglicized as Vlatava—comes to a wide bend just east of Prague Castle, the Hrad.

846.23 *panaka*] Nisenan: woodpecker.

846.25   the *Daihishu*] Also known as the Dharani of Great Compassion, a chanted Buddhist sutra.

847.1   my poems for you] Probably Robin Collins (see note 134.15), for whom Snyder wrote "Four Poems for Robin" (on pages 134–36 of the present volume), "Robin" (on pages 156–57), and other poems.

848.10   *Otzi*] Also known as "The Iceman," the mummy of a man who lived from 3400 to 3100 BCE; his frozen body was discovered in September 1991 in the Otztal Alps, on the border between Austria and Italy, and is now displayed along with his belongings in the South Tyrol Museum of Archaeology in Bolzano, Italy.

848.18   Sella Pass] A mountain pass in the Dolomites, at over 7,000 feet, between the provinces of Trentino and South Tyrol.

854.17–21   *The Maremma . . . Pitigliano*] Traditionally populated by mounted cattle herders, the Maremma is a coastal area of western central Italy, including much of southwestern Tuscany and part of northern Lazio. Pitigliano is a Tuscan town about 50 miles southeast of the city of Grosseto.

855.15   duomo] Italian: cathedral.

855.17   *Alto Adige*] Also known as South Tyrol or the Province of Bolzano, a mountainous Italian province bordering Austria and Switzerland.

856.1   *Askesis, Praxis, Theôria*] *Askesis* is the exercise of rigorous self-discipline, especially mental, practiced as a means to spiritual growth. *Praxis* is the process by which a theory, lesson, or skill is enacted or realized. *Theôria* is an intellectual seeing, a contemplative knowledge of reality itself.

859.16–17   Her last / breath] Snyder's wife Carole Lynn Koda died in 2006.

859.22   Shakyamuni] See note 494.11.

859.25–26   "I met a walking . . . Thomas Quinn"] From "State of Arkansas," a traditional American ballad or "complaint song," first recorded in 1927 and performed by a variety of artists.

860.6   "Goodnight . . . time to go"] From the hit song "Goodnite, Sweetheart, Goodnite," written by Calvin Carter and James Hudson in 1951 and recorded by the McGuire Sisters in 1954.

860.15   Mumtaz Mahal] Mahal (1593–1631), the empress consort of Mughal emperor Shah Jahan (1592–1666), was laid to rest in the Taj Mahal in Agra, India, commissioned in 1632.

UNCOLLECTED POEMS, DRAFTS, FRAGMENTS, AND TRANSLATIONS

873.14   *Rhea*] In Greek mythology, the daughter of the earth goddess Gaia and the sky god Uranus.

873.15   the Bowman] Perhaps the god Apollo, often depicted with bow and arrow.

874.1–2   the lovely . . . Orpheus] In Book XI of Ovid's *Metamorphoses*, Orpheus, a renowned poet and musician, is torn to pieces by enraged women during their Bacchic orgies.

874.6   O daughters of Jerusalem] See Luke 23:28.

874.7–11   *Kasina* . . . red clay] In Theravada Buddhism, *kasinas* are objects (such as colored disks) or phenomena (such as air currents or flame) on which one focuses, as an aid to concentration in meditation; earth kasinas are preferably made with red clay.

874.16   *"Escaping Cambridge"*] Snyder published a revised version of this poem, "For George Leigh-Mallory," in *Left Out in the Rain*; see pages 461–62 in the present volume, and notes 461.22.

874.24   Kanchenjunga falls] A waterfall midway between the city of Darjeeling, in West Bengal, and the summit of Kanchenjunga, the third highest peak in the world, at 28,169 feet.

875.3   *Mr. President*] Lyndon Baines Johnson (1908–1973), president of the United States from November 1963 to January 1969.

875.15   bomb in Gilead] See Jeremiah 8:22.

876.2   Nihil C.] A punning reference to Neal Cassady (see note 560.24).

878.3   Chrysopylae] Greek for "golden gate," the name given to San Francisco's harbor on maps accompanying explorer John C. Frémont's *Geographical Memoir upon Upper California*, presented to the U.S. Senate in June 1848.

878.6–7   Devas of small merit . . . berries to eat] In his *Catena of Buddhist Scriptures from the Chinese* (1871), Samuel Beal writes: "There are also Dêvas of such scanty merit that they are sometimes seen in Jambudwipa plucking sour berries to eat. When men see their miserable appearance, and ask them who they are, they reply we are Asuras (fi-jin, not-men), Dêvas, alas! but of scanty merit! We have palaces and garments, but no food to eat." *Jambudvipa* is an ancient term for greater India, or for the human realm.

879.19   *The Elwha River*] First appearing in *Six Sections from Mountains and Rivers Without End* (1965), Snyder later published a revised version of the first section of this poem in *Mountains and Rivers Without End* (1996), and a revised version of its third section in *This Present Moment* (2015); see pages 615–16 and 810–11 in the present volume.

881.7   Theodora, Kitty-chan] One of a half dozen cats Snyder and his wife adopted while living in Kyoto.

883.14   OM A KA . . . SVĀHĀ] A Tantric Buddhist mantra for causing a city to tremble; also known as the spell of Aksobhya Tathagata.

883.28   Chief Joseph] See note 90.4.

884.1   Ishi] Ishi (c. 1861–1916) was the last surviving member of the Yahi people of the Sierra Nevada.

884.8   the Ghost Dance] See note 654.15–19.

884.14   HI'NISWA' VITA'KI'NI] "We are coming to life again" or "we shall live again"—a phrase from a Comanche Ghost Dance song first published in James Mooney's *The Ghost-Dance Religion and the Sioux Outbreak of 1890* (1896).

885.18   Mudra] In Buddhism and Hinduism, a symbolic pose or gesture, usually of the hands and fingers.

885.31   kali-yuga] Literally "age of strife," the fourth and worst of the four *yugas* or world ages that constitute a *yuga* cycle or epoch in Hindu cosmology; the present kali-yuga is said to have begun in 3102 BCE and will last 432,000 years.

886.12   Three Mysteries] In the practice of Tantric or Esoteric Meditation, body, speech, and mind are known as the "Three Mysteries"; they are to be engaged using mudras, mantras, and visualizations.

886.21–22   Namah samanta . . . ham nam] Sanskrit text of the *Mahāvairocana Tantra* or "Mantra of Compassionate Help," conventionally associated with the wrathful deity Acala (in Japan, Fudō Myō-ō); Snyder's idiosyncratic translation appears in the lines that follow.

887.6   vajra-shovel] See note 77.20.

887.21   *Kumarajiva's Mother*] Kumārajīva (344–413) was a Buddhist monk, scholar, translator, and philosopher from Kucha—an ancient Buddhist kingdom located in the vicinity of Kuqa, in what is now the Xinjiang Uyguy Autonomous Region of China—who settled in Chang'an. A founder of the Sanlun school of Mahayana Buddhism, he is remembered most for his translations of Buddhist texts from Sanskrit to Chinese. Little is known about his mother except that she was, as the poem states, a "princess of the royal line of Kucha" and that she influenced his early years, taking him with her as they traveled through Kucha, Kashmir, and Kashgar.

887.24–25   giva-giva/jiva-jiva] Kumarajiva's mother, Giva (or Jiva, or Jīvaka), was the sister of the king of Kucha. The word *jiva* itself, derived from the Sanskrit, refers to the "soul" or "the life force."

888.6   arhat] Buddhist term for an enlightened person (from the Sanskrit, "one who is worthy.")

891.8   *Swimming . . . Yuba River*] Composed in response to a Nevada City, California, ordinance against swimming naked.

892.19   sPhat!] A Sanskrit term meaning "to expand," "burst," or "blossom out."

892.21–22   ACHALA/"Immovable"] The wrathful deity Achala, from a Sanskrit term meaning "The Immovable," is called Fudō Myōō in Japan and Caṇḍamahāroṣaṇa in Tibet.

892.25   Sādhanas] In Hinduism and Buddhism, exercises or disciplines used to achieve spiritual aims.

892.28   Atasī flower] Common flax (*Linum usitatissimum*), a blue-flowered annual.

893.10   Benoytosh Bhattacharyya] Bhattacharyya (1897–1964) was a pioneer in the field of Tantric and Buddhist iconographical studies.

893.27   Kwannon] The Japanese counterpart of the Chinese Kuan Yin, or Guanyin ("One Who Hears the Sounds of the World"), Kannon (with an older spelling of Kwannon) is associated with compassion, a Goddess of Mercy, ultimately traced back to Avalokiteśvara, the bodhisattva who embodies the compassion of all Buddhas.

893.33   DAKINIS] See note 288.15.

894.1–2   YUBA, BEAR AND/FEATHER] Rivers near Snyder's home at Kitkitdizze, the Yuba and Bear tributaries of the Feather.

895.2–3   I saw the Mother . . . Pondicherry] In January 1962, Snyder and his wife Joanne Kyger visited the Sri Aurobindo Ashram in Pondicherry, India, founded by Mirra Alfassa (1878–1973), a French guru and occultist known to her followers as "The Mother."

895.3   darshan] In Hinduism, a time for direct visual contact with a deity, revered person, or sacred object.

895.25   Masa] Masa Uehara (see note 216.1).

895.32   *Tomorrow's Song*] See also "Tomorrow's Song" in *Turtle Island*, on pages 343–44 of the present volume.

896.10   *Gold, Green*] Written in commemoration of Arbor Day.

897.3–4   "You lead me . . . thistle"] See Psalms 23:2.

898.5   *Sarnath*] The Deer Park at Sarnath, in Uttar Pradesh, India, near Varanasi, is a Buddhist holy site, where Gautama Buddha first taught after his enlightenment.

899.7   rajagriha] Also known as Rajgir, an ancient city in Bihar, India, where the Buddha once taught; the ruins of Nalanda and present-day Nalanda University are nearby.

899.12   Amber] The capital of Rajasthan, near Jaipur.

899.15   Khajuraho] City in the Indian state of Madhya Pradesh, site of the Khajuraho monuments, famous for their erotic sculptures.

900.6   *Needles Country of the Canyonlands*] Canyonlands National Park is located in southeastern Utah near the town of Moab. Replete with canyons, mesas, and buttes, this high desert park is divided into four distinct districts: the Island in the Sky, the Needles, the Maze, and the combined rivers—the Green and Colorado—which carved two large canyons into the Colorado Plateau. The Needles District, which forms the southeastern portion of the park, is filled with colorful sandstone spires.

900.16–17   "woven/bamboo burden basket"] The Native American "burden basket" is a cone-shaped basket rimmed in buckskin with a flat or round bottom, cone jingles made of tin, and a carry strap used for collecting and carrying food; visitors are urged to place their burdens in such baskets before entering a home.

900.21   Wingate–Navajo–Chinle formations] Geological rock strata with different characteristics and appearances in Canyonlands include the Wingate and the Navajo formations (deposited in the Jurassic Period, 208 to 144 million years ago) and the (Triassic period, 245 to 208 million years ago).

900.28–29   Gaté gaté . . . svāhā] Buddhist mantra found at the end of the Heart Sutra, roughly translatable as "Gone, gone, gone over to the other shore, so be it."

901.2   Tom Dickman] Dickman is a member of the Wasatch Mountain Club in Salt Lake City, Utah.

901.5   Gale Dick] Dick (1926–2014), a fellow graduate of Reed College in the class of 1950, was a both a physicist and conservationist; in 1972 he cofounded "Save Our Canyons," an environmental group credited with the establishment of wilderness areas in the Wasatch Mountains of Utah.

901.32   summit cap] A technical term in mountaineering and rock-climbing, a "summit cap" is the harder or more resistant rock type overlying a weaker or less resistant rock type at the peak. The graphic that accompanies these lines is a sketch of Druid Arch that clearly shows the "summit cap" of the arch.

902.3–4   *Mahonia fremontii . . . Berberis*] A barberry species native to mountainous regions of the western United States, with pale yellow flowers, *Berberis fremontii* (as botanical authorities now refer to it), commonly known as Fremont's mahonia, was named in honor of John C. Frémont (1813–1890), who collected plant specimens in the 1840s during his five western exploring expeditions.

902.21   Diné/hogan ruin] The Navajo refer to themselves as Diné, meaning "The People" or "Children of the Holy People." A Diné hogan is a one-room structure; used as a dwelling or for ceremonial purposes, its entrance traditionally faces east.

906.14   Deaf Smith] Deaf Smith County, in Texas, was named for Erastus Smith (1787–1837), who was hard of hearing; due to the soil quality in Deaf Smith County it became an important center for organic farming, including organic wheat.

907.1–2   the *Sammamish . . . Skykomish*] The Puget Sound region of the Pacific Northwest has been called "Ish River country" because of the numerous river names ending in "ish," a suffix derived from Salishan languages meaning "the people of."

911.17   *Goosenecks of the San Juan*] A deep, winding meander in the San Juan River in San Juan County, Utah.

914.23–24   Fudo mantra . . . Yamabushi] See note 645.2.

914.24   gassho] A ritual Buddhist gesture used in greeting and meditation, both palms pressed together and held in front of one's face.

916.18–917.1   *Robert Duncan . . . Letters*] Duncan's *Letters*, a book of poetry, was first published by Jonathan Williams of Highlands, North Carolina, in 1958, in an edition of 450 signed and numbered copies. The Place, a bar on Grant Street in San Francisco, was a focal point of Beat culture from 1955 to 1959.

917.4–14   Neuri . . . a literary scholar] See note 493.3, and the poem "For a Far-Out Friend," on pages 11–12 of the present volume.

918.11   Nanda Devi] India's second highest mountain, at 25,643 feet.

918.16   Southern Cross] Also known as Crux, a constellation visible from the Southern Hemisphere.

918.19   Bodh Gaya] See note 187.16.

919.10   Suwa-no-se Island] See note 237.1.

923.5–6   the "Rainbow Skirt" . . . dances] These Tang dynasty songs and dances are said to have been choreographed by Yang Gui Fei from a dream of the emperor.

923.15   li] See note 27.18.

923.32   Omei Shan] Mount Emei, a 10,167-foot mountain in Sichuan province, considered a holy site by Chinese Buddhists.

924.20–21   Taiye Hibiscus,/Weiyang Willow.] Lake Taiya was an imperial lake in the Tang capital, Xi'an (Chang'an), and Weiyang Palace the principal Xi'an palace complex, sometimes claimed to be the largest palace ever constructed.

924.28   Wutong trees] See note 612.35.

925.17   the Hongdu school] A school of Daoism that attempts to summon the spirits of the dead.

925.29   Yellow Springs] See note 33.5.

926.39   Chang'an] Now Xi'an, capitan of Shaanxi province; during the Tang dynasty, an imperial capital and one of the most populous cities in the world.

928.6   Ch'en Shih-hsiang] See note 383.15–30.

928.9–10   the Han-shan poems . . . sixties.] See pages 25–41 in the present volume.

928.21   *Meng Hao-jan*] Also known as Meng Haoran (689/691–740), a major Tang dynasty poet and somewhat older contemporary of Wang Wei, Li Bai, and Du Fu; he was a major influence on other contemporary and subsequent poets of the High Tang era because of his focus on the natural world.

929.2   *Wang Wei*] Wang Wei (699–759), one of the most famous men of arts and letters of his time, was a Tang dynasty poet, musician, painter, and politician.

930.3   Tu Mu] Also known as Du Mu (803–852), a late Tang dynasty poet best known for his lyrical and romantic quatrains.

930.15   Yuan Chen] Also known as Yüan Chen (779–831), a Chinese novelist, poet, and politician of the middle Tang dynasty, and a member of Bai Juyi's literary circle.

930.21   Po Chü-i] Also known as Bai Juyi (see pages 920–21 in the present volume).

931.2   *Tu Fu*] See note 490.1.

931.12   *Ling Ch'e*] A Buddhist monk or pilgrim.

931.13   Liu Ch'ang-ch'ing] Also known as Liu Changqing (709–785) or Wen-fang, a Tang dynasty poet and politician.

931.23   Wang Chih-huan] Also known as Wang Zhihuan (688–742), a Tang dynasty poet most often remembered for the present poem; Crane Tower (or Stork Tower) is located in Yongji, Shanxi province.

932.2   Lo Tsung-yuan] Also known as Liu Zongyuan (773–819), a Tang dynasty poet, prose writer, and politician; although approximately 180 of his poems have survived, he is better known as one of the "Eight Great Prose Masters of the Tang and Song."

932.8   Wang Ch'ang-ling] A major Tang dynasty poet and politician, Wang Ch'ang-ling (698–756) is best known for his poems describing fictional battles in the frontier regions of western China. He was executed during the An Lushan Rebellion.

932.13   Lo-yang] Situated on the central plain of China, Luoyang (Lo-yang) is among the oldest cities in China and one of the cradles of Chinese civilization.

932.17–18   Maple Bridge Near Su-chou] Hanshan (or Cold Mountain) Temple was built to the west of Suzhou (Su-chou) where three canals intersect; there is a classical Chinese bridge over the Grand Canal called the Maple Bridge, which dates back at least to the Tang dynasty. On Chinese New Year's Eve, people gather at the bridge to hear the bells of the temple, as described in the poem.

932.20   Chang Chi] Also known as Zhang Ji (c. 712–779), a Tang dynasty poet from Huzībei; his "Maple Bridge Night Mooring," included in the classic anthology *Three Hundred Tang Poems*, has made the ringing of the bells in Hanshan Temple famous.

Index of Titles and First Lines

*This book is set in 10 point ITC Galliard, a face designed
for digital composition by Matthew Carter and based
on the sixteenth-century face Granjon. The paper is acid-free
lightweight opaque that will not turn yellow or brittle with age.
The binding is sewn, which allows the book to open easily and lie flat.
The binding board is covered in Brillianta, a woven rayon cloth
made by Van Heek–Scholco Textielfabrieken, Holland.
Composition by Gopa & Ted2, Inc.
Printing by Sheridan Grand Rapids, Grand Rapids MI.
Binding by Dekker Bookbinding, Wyoming MI.
Designed by Bruce Campbell.*

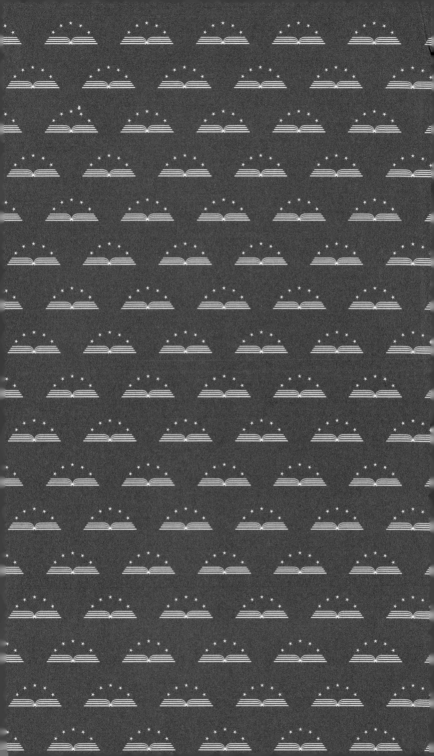